Lecture Notes
in Business Information Processing   **363**

Series Editors

Wil van der Aalst
  RWTH Aachen University, Aachen, Germany
John Mylopoulos
  University of Trento, Trento, Italy
Michael Rosemann
  Queensland University of Technology, Brisbane, QLD, Australia
Michael J. Shaw
  University of Illinois, Urbana-Champaign, IL, USA
Clemens Szyperski
  Microsoft Research, Redmond, WA, USA

More information about this series at http://www.springer.com/series/7911

Slimane Hammoudi · Michał Śmiałek ·
Olivier Camp · Joaquim Filipe (Eds.)

Enterprise Information Systems

20th International Conference, ICEIS 2018
Funchal, Madeira, Portugal, March 21–24, 2018
Revised Selected Papers

 Springer

Editors
Slimane Hammoudi
MODESTE/ESEO
Angers, France

Olivier Camp
MODESTE/ESEO
Angers, France

Michał Śmiałek
Warsaw University of Technology
Warsaw, Poland

Joaquim Filipe
INSTICC and
Polytechnic Institute of Setúbal
Setúbal, Portugal

ISSN 1865-1348   ISSN 1865-1356   (electronic)
Lecture Notes in Business Information Processing
ISBN 978-3-030-26168-9   ISBN 978-3-030-26169-6   (eBook)
https://doi.org/10.1007/978-3-030-26169-6

This Springer imprint is published by the registered company Springer Nature Switzerland AG
The registered company address is: Gewerbestrasse 11, 6330 Cham, Switzerland

Preface

The present book includes extended and revised versions of a set of selected papers from the 20th International Conference on Enterprise Information Systems (ICEIS 2018), held in Funchal-Madeira, Portugal, during March 21–24, 2018.

ICEIS 2018 received 242 paper submissions from 46 countries, of which 8% are included in this book. The papers were selected by the event chairs and their selection is based on a number of criteria that include classifications and comments provided by the Program Committee members, the session chairs' assessment, and also the program chairs' global view of all the papers included in the technical program. The authors of selected papers were then invited to submit revised and extended versions of their papers having at least 30% innovative material.

The purpose of the 20th International Conference on Enterprise Information Systems (ICEIS) was to bring together researchers, engineers, and practitioners interested in advances and business applications of information systems. Six simultaneous tracks were held, covering different aspects of enterprise information systems applications, including enterprise database technology, systems integration, artificial intelligence, decision support systems, information systems analysis and specification, internet computing, electronic commerce, human factors, and enterprise architecture.

We are confident that the papers included in this book will strongly contribute to the understanding of some current research trends in enterprise information systems. Such systems require diverse approaches to answer challenges of contemporary enterprises. Thus, this book covers such diverse but complementary areas as: data science and databases, ontologies, social networks, knowledge management, software development, human–computer interaction, and multimedia.

We would like to thank all the authors for their contributions and the reviewers for their hard work, which helped ensure the quality of this publication.

March 2018

Slimane Hammoudi
Michał Śmiałek
Olivier Camp
Joaquim Filipe

Organization

Conference Co-chairs

Olivier Camp	MODESTE/ESEO, France
Joaquim Filipe	INSTICC and Polytechnic Institute of Setúbal, Portugal

Program Co-chairs

Slimane Hammoudi	ESEO, MODESTE, France
Michal Smialek	Warsaw University of Technology, Poland

Program Committee

Evgeniy Abakumov	All-Russia Research Institute of Automatics, Russian Federation
Amna Abidi	LIAS LAB (ENSMA, FRANCE), LARODEC LAB (ISG, Tunisia), France
Manuel E. Acacio	Universidad de Murcia, Spain
Adeel Ahmad	Laboratoire d'Informatique Signal et Image de la Côte d'Opale, France
Patrick Albers	ESEO, École Supérieure d'Électronique de l'Ouest, France
Eduardo Alchieri	Universidade de Brasilia, Brazil
Mohammad Al-Shamri	Ibb University, Yemen
Luis Álvarez Sabucedo	University of Vigo, Spain
Omar Alvarez-Xochihua	Universidad Autónoma de Baja California, Mexico
Rachid Anane	Coventry University, UK
Andreas Andreou	Cyprus University of Technology, Cyprus
Plamen Angelov	Lancaster University, UK
Leandro Antonelli	LIFIA, Universidad Nacional de La Plata, Argentina
Josephina Antoniou	Uclan Cyprus, Cyprus
Agnese Augello	Istituto di Calcolo e Reti ad Alte Prestazioni, Consiglio Nazionale delle Ricerche, Italy
Lerina Aversano	University of Sannio, Italy
Ramazan Aygun	University of Alabama in Huntsville, USA
Mirjana Bach	University of Zagreb, Croatia
Youcef Baghdadi	Sultan Qaboos University, Oman
José Banares Bañares	Universidad de Zaragoza, Spain
Veena Bansal	Indian Institute of Technology Kanpur, India
Cecilia Baranauskas	State University of Campinas - Unicamp, Brazil
Ken Barker	University of Calgary, Canada
Jean-Paul Barthes	Université de Technologie de Compiègne, France

Bernhard Bauer — University of Augsburg, Germany
Imen Ben Fradj — Research Laboratory in Technologies of Information and Communication and Electrical, Tunisia
Domenico Beneventano — Università di Modena e Reggio Emilia, Italy
François Bergeron — TELUQ-Université du Québec, Canada
Jorge Bernardino — Polytechnic Institute of Coimbra, ISEC, Portugal
Edward Bernroider — Vienna University of Economics and Business, Austria
Ana Bertoletti De Marchi — Universidade de Passo Fundo, Brazil
Ilia Bider — DSV, Stockholm University, Sweden
Sandro Bimonte — IRSTEA, France
Zita Bošnjak — University of Novi Sad, Serbia
Jean-Louis Boulanger — CERTIFER, France
Andrés Boza — Universitat Politècnica de València, Spain
Alexander Brodsky — George Mason University, USA
Rebecca Bulander — Pforzheim University of Applied Science, Germany
David Cabrero Souto — University of A Coruña, Spain
Coral Calero — University of Castilla La Mancha, Spain
Daniel Callegari — PUCRS Pontificia Universidade Catolica do Rio Grande do Sul, Brazil
Manuel Capel-Tuñón — University of Granada, Spain
João Luís Cardoso de Moraes — Federal University of São Carlos, Brazil
Glauco Carneiro — Universidade Salvador (UNIFACS), Brazil
Angélica Caro — University of Bio-Bio, Chile
Diego Carvalho — Federal Centre of Engineering Studies and Technological Education, Brazil
Fernando Carvalho — Universidade Federal Do Ceará, Brazil
Laura M. Castro — Universidade da Coruña, Spain
Luca Cernuzzi — Universidad Católica Nuestra Señora de la Asunción, Paraguay
Max Chevalier — Institut de Recherche en Informatique de Toulouse UMR 5505, France
Nan-Hsing Chiu — Chien Hsin University of Science and Technology, Taiwan
Witold Chmielarz — Warsaw University, Poland
Betim Cico — Epoka University, Albania
Elder Cirilo — Federal University of São João del-Rei, Brazil
Daniela Claro — Universidade Federal da Bahia (UFBA), Brazil
Pedro Coelho — State University of Rio de Janeiro, Brazil
Isabelle Comyn-Wattiau — Cnam & Essec, France
Antonio Corral — University of Almeria, Spain
Jean-Valère Cossu — My Local Influence - MyLI, France
Henrique Cota de Freitas — Pontifícia Universidade Católica de Minas Gerais, Brazil
Broderick Crawford — Pontificia Universidad Catolica de Valparaiso, Chile
Beata Czarnacka-Chrobot — Warsaw School of Economics, Poland

Carlos León de Mora	University of Seville, Spain
Da-Yin Liao	Straight & Up Intelligent Innovations Group Co., USA
Panagiotis Linos	Butler University, USA
Kecheng Liu	University of Reading, UK
Wendy Lucas	Bentley University, USA
André Ludwig	Kühne Logistics University, Germany
Mark Lycett	Royal Holloway, University of London, UK
Yongsheng Ma	University of Alberta, Canada
Cristiano Maciel	Universidade Federal de Mato Grosso, Brazil
Rita Maciel	Federal University of Bahia, Brazil
S. Makki	Lamar University, USA
Tiziana Margaria	University of Limerick and Lero, Ireland
Krassimir Markov	Institute of Information Theories and Applications, Bulgaria
Antonio Martí Campoy	Universitat Politècnica de València, Spain
David Martins de Matos	L2F/INESC-ID Lisboa/Instituto Superior Técnico, Universidade de Lisboa, Portugal
Riccardo Martoglia	University of Modena and Reggio Emilia, Italy
Katsuhisa Maruyama	Ritsumeikan University, Japan
Wolfgang Mayer	University of South Australia, Australia
Rafael Mayo-García	CIEMAT, Spain
Marcin Michalak	Silesian University of Technology, Poland
Jerzy Michnik	University of Economics in Katowice, Poland
Harekrishna Misra	Institute of Rural Management, India
Michele Missikoff	ISTC-CNR, Italy
Lars Mönch	FernUniversität in Hagen, Germany
Valérie Monfort	LAMIH Valenciennes UMR CNRS 8201, France
Fernando Moreira	Universidade Portucalense, Portugal
Nathalie Moreno	University of Malaga, Spain
Joice Mota	Instituto Federal Catarinense, Brazil
Javier Muguerza	University of the Basque Country UPV/EHU, Spain
Andrés Muñoz Ortega	Catholic University of Murcia (UCAM), Spain
Pietro Murano	Oslo Metropolitan University, Norway
Tomoharu Nakashima	Osaka Prefecture University, Japan
Omnia Neffati	King Khaled University (Saudi Arabia) and RIADI LAB (Tunisia), Saudi Arabia
Leandro Neves	Ibilce/São Paulo State University (Unesp), Brazil
Vincent Ng	The Hong Kong Polytechnic University, SAR China
Ovidiu Noran	Griffith University, Australia
Joshua Nwokeji	Gannon University, USA
Edson Oliveira Jr	Universidade Estadual de Maringá, Brazil
Ermelinda Oro	National Research Council (CNR), Italy
Wendy Osborn	University of Lethbridge, Canada
Carla Osthoff	Laboratorio Nacional de Computação Cientifica, Brazil
Mieczyslaw Owoc	Wroclaw University of Economics, Poland
Malgorzata Pankowska	University of Economics in Katowice, Poland
Pance Panov	Jožef Stefan Institute, Slovenia

Luis Enrique Sánchez	Universidad de Castilla-la Mancha, Spain
Jurek Sasiadek	Carleton University, Canada
Sissel Schär	University of Bern, Switzerland
Jeanne Schreurs	Universiteit Hasselt, Belgium
Isabel Seruca	Universidade Portucalense, Portugal
Lisa Seymour	University of Cape Town, South Africa
Ahm Shamsuzzoha	University of Vaasa, Finland
Jianhua Shao	Cardiff University, UK
Ali Shareef	The Maldives National University, Maldives
Bernadette Sharp	Staffordshire University, UK
Markus Siepermann	TU Dortmund, Germany
Sean Siqueira	Federal University of the State of Rio de Janeiro (UNIRIO), Brazil
Seppo Sirkemaa	University of Turku, Finland
Michal Smialek	Warsaw University of Technology, Poland
Michel Soares	Federal University of Sergipe, Brazil
Damires Souza	Federal Institute of Education, Science and Technology of Paraiba, Brazil
Marco Spohn	Federal University of Fronteira Sul, Brazil
Clare Stanier	Staffordshire University, UK
Chris Stary	Johannes Kepler University of Linz, Austria
Hans-Peter Steinbacher	University of Applied Science Kufstein, Austria
Hiroki Suguri	Miyagi University, Japan
Sagar Sunkle	Tata Consultancy Services, India
Marcos Sunye	Federal University of Parana, Brazil
Reima Suomi	University of Turku, Finland
Nestori Syynimaa	University of Jyväskylä, Finland
Zoltán Szabó	Corvinus University of Budapest, Hungary
Ryszard Tadeusiewicz	AGH University of Science and Technology, Poland
Efthimios Tambouris	University of Macedonia, Greece
Mohan Tanniru	Oakland University, USA
Sotirios Terzis	University of Strathclyde, UK
Lucinéia Thom	Universidade Federal do Rio Grande do Sul, Brazil
Claudio Toledo	São Paulo University, Brazil
Leandro Tortosa	Universidad de Alicante, Spain
Dimitar Trajanov	Cyril and Methodius University, Skopje, Macedonia, The Former Yugoslav Republic of
Joseph Trienekens	Open University Heerlen, Netherlands
Carolina Tripp	Universidad Autónoma de Sinaloa, Mexico
Theodoros Tzouramanis	University of the Aegean, Greece
Mario Vacca	Italian Ministry of Education, Italy
Athina Vakali	Aristotle University, Greece
Carlos Valêncio	UNESP, Brazil
Michael Vassilakopoulos	University of Thessaly, Greece
Dessislava Vassileva	Sofia University St. Kliment Ohridski, Bulgaria
Jose Vazquez-Poletti	Universidad Complutense de Madrid, Spain

Aldo Vecchietti	Instituto de Desarrollo y Diseño, INGAR CONICET-UTN, Argentina
Gizelle Vianna	UFRRJ, Brazil
Melina Vidoni	Institute of Development and Design, INGAR CONICET-UTN, Argentina
Gualtiero Volpe	Università degli Studi di Genova, Italy
Vasiliki Vrana	Technological Educational Institute of Central Macedonia, Greece
Boris Vrdoljak	University of Zagreb, Croatia
Hans Weghorn	BW Cooperative State University Stuttgart, Germany
Janusz Wielki	Opole University of Technology, Poland
Adam Wojtowicz	Poznan University of Economics, Poland
Stanislaw Wrycza	University of Gdansk, Poland
Shuxiang Xu	University of Tasmania, Australia
Rossitsa Yalamova	University of Lethbridge, Canada
Hongji Yang	Leicester University, UK
Qishan Yang	Dublin City University, Ireland
Ping Yu	University of Wollongong, Australia
Geraldo Zafalon	São Paulo State University, Brazil
Luciana Zaina	UFSCar, Brazil
Brahmi Zaki	RIADI, Tunisia
Ewa Ziemba	Economic University in Katowice, Poland
Eugenio Zimeo	University of Sannio, Italy
Hans-Dieter Zimmermann	FHS St. Gallen University of Applied Sciences, Switzerland

Additional Reviewers

Luisa Carpente	University of A Coruña, Spain
Zineb El Akkaoui	The National Institute of Posts and Telecommunications, Morocco
Ricardo Geraldi	State University of Maringá, Brazil
Nathan Henderson	University of Alabama in Huntsville, USA
Enrico Mensa	Università Degli Studi di Torino, Italy
Len Noriega	University of Manchester, UK
Maryam Radgui	INSEA, Laboratoire Systèmes d'Information, Systèmes Intelligents et Modélisation Mathématique, Morocco
Truong Tran	Data Media Lab, USA

Invited Speakers

Alexander Brodsky	George Mason University, USA
Plamen Angelov	Lancaster University, UK
Salvatore Distefano	Università degli Studi di Messina, Italy
David Aveiro	University of Madeira/Madeira-ITI, Portugal

Contents

A Computer-Based Framework Supporting Education in STEM Subjects

Georg Peters[1,2], Tom Rückert[1], and Jan Seruga[2(✉)]

[1] Department of Computer Science and Mathematics,
Munich University of Applied Sciences, Lothstrasse 34, 80335 Munich, Germany
{georg.peters,tom.rueckert}@hm.edu
[2] Faculty of Education and Arts, Australian Catholic University, 25A Barker Road,
Strathfield, NSW 2135, Australia
jan.seruga@acu.edu

Abstract. Education is considered as a key factor for competitiveness on micro- as well as on macro-economic levels, i.e., for a single person, a company, or a country. Several industries have been identified with significant current and/or future workforce shortages. They include diverse areas, such as the health and the technology sectors. As a result, initiatives to foster STEM (science, technology, engineering and mathematics) have emerged in many countries. In this paper, we report on a project of Australian Catholic University and Munich University of Applied Sciences. These universities have developed a framework to support STEM education. The framework is based on R-Project, a leading free software environment that has gained increasing attention particularly in the field of data analysis (statistics, machine learning etc.) in the past decade. The framework is intended to address the following three main challenges in STEM education: mathematics and, in the field of technology, algorithmic programming and dynamic webpage development.

Keywords: Education · STEM subjects · R-Project

1 Introduction

We are currently experiencing a significant transformation of economic structures worldwide, due to information technology. The digital revolution is considered as a disruptive innovation which impacts the daily life of humans, companies, and countries. The extent of this transformation can be demonstrated by the fact that most of the six most valuable enterprises in the technology sector today (Apple, Amazon, Alphabet, Microsoft, Facebook and Alibaba) [17] did not even exist twenty years ago. However, even though virtually everybody is aware of the significant impact of information technology, there seems to have been little action to address these challenges in education. Let us briefly discuss two paradoxes in this context:

© Springer Nature Switzerland AG 2019
S. Hammoudi et al. (Eds.): ICEIS 2018, LNBIP 363, pp. 1–21, 2019.
https://doi.org/10.1007/978-3-030-26169-6_1

- Since the industrial revolution started approximately 250 years ago, technology has influenced almost everybody's life. The digital revolution is another phase in this revolution which has significant impact on our daily life. However, this seems not to be correlated with an interest in the underlying technology. Many students seems to be more interested in using technology than in developing or even understanding it.
- Education in STEM subjects has been identified as of strategic importance for the competitiveness of employees, companies and countries, but it seems that many countries offer only halfhearted support for STEM education. An indicator of such half-heartedness is the often discussed discrepancy between verbal and financial support for (STEM) education.

To help address these challenges in STEM education Australian Catholic University and Munich University of Applied Sciences joined forces and set up a project to develop a computer-based framework supporting education in STEM subjects. In particular, the framework focuses on mathematics, algorithmic programming and dynamic webpage development. The objective of this article is to introduce this framework. It continues our work started in [29,30] and is an extended and developed version of those papers. In the following section, we identify and examine the needs, challenges and stakeholders in STEM education. Then, in Sect. 3 we define our requirements for an optimal computer-based framework supporting STEM education. Based on these requirements we also analyze possible technologies (programming languages and numerical/scientific platforms) for such a framework and select the most appropriate. In the subsequent section, we describe our framework and discuss its properties. The paper ends with a conclusion in Sect. 6.

2   STEM Education: Needs, Challenges, and Stakeholders

While the need for STEM education and the needs of stakeholders [5] in STEM education overlap, we have separated needs and stakeholders in the following sections. In Sect. 2.1 we describe the general need for STEM education as often addressed in public, which leads to our definition of a triangle of challenges in Sect. 2.2. In Sect. 2.3 we identify the stakeholders and discuss them in more detail.

2.1   The Need for STEM Education

The need to promote training in STEM subjects has been stressed by companies and governments for many years. Mathematics is often considered to be of special importance because of its catholicity and precision. In science, technology and engineering, mathematics is equally important. Thus, engineering and technology companies actively promote mathematics.

Dieter Zetscher, chairman of Daimler AG, for example, regards mathematics as the royal discipline (cited at Neunzert and Prätzel-Wolters [23]): "As does no other science, mathematics helps us in our branch to solve the most varied sorts of problems – and it is exactly this universal applicability that makes it the royal discipline." And Peter Löscher, chairman of Siemens from 2007–2013, describes the role of mathematics as follows (cited at Neunzert and Prätzel-Wolters [23]): "Mathematics – this is the language of science and technology. This makes it a driving force behind all high technologies and, thus, a key discipline for industrial nations. Without mathematics, there is no progress and technical innovation." But it is not only classic engineering companies, like Daimler and Siemens, that rely on mathematics. Data and the analysis of data is considered as one of the key competitive factors in virtually every industry. Today these activities are often subsumed under the term data science [7].

Software programming, to a certain extent, is another context-free universally applicable method. Programming skills are considered as important not only for professional software developers but also for everybody else independently of the profession. For example, Apple's CEO Tom Cook told students (cited at Clifford [4]): "If I were a French student and I were 10 years old, I think it would be more important for me to learn coding than English. I'm not telling people not to learn English in some form – but I think you understand what I am saying is that this is a language that you can [use to] express yourself to 7 billion people in the world. [...] I think that coding should be required in every public school in the world." And German chancellor Angela Merkel pointed out in a panel discussion (translated from Merkel [19]): "I am convinced [...] that the ability to program, the easy ways of programming, that children should learn to do this. Because they will then have a basic understanding of how a robot works, how certain things work, how an app is created."

Although there is an obvious need for STEM subjects and STEM subjects are promoted by leading companies and many governments there is still a gap between demand and supply for experts in this field. It is a challenge to motivate a sufficient number of young people to study these subjects at school and universities. In countries, like Germany, that are poor in natural resources, expertise in STEM subjects is essential for a prosperous economy. However, mathematics students in many of these countries performed at only an average level in the recent PISA study of OECD countries. German school students, for example performed only slightly above average in the PISA study [25]. This is in line with many other European countries. Most countries on the American continent performed under average, with the exception of Canada. According to a study by Neuhauser and Cook the interest in STEM subjects generally improved except in mathematics [22]: "The 2016 U.S. News/Raytheon STEM Index recorded a slight rise in hiring, education and general interest in technology and engineering over last year, while math education and general interest in science declined." The PISA study identifies students from eastern Asian countries like China, South Korea and Singapore as top performers in mathematics (see Fig. 1).

Despite excellent job prospects, it is still a challenge to motivate a sufficient number of students, particularly in so called western countries, to step into these fields and secure a sound education in mathematics, computer science and information systems at schools and universities. This challenge is already addressed in research, see, e.g., Ruthven and Hennessy [32] who proposed a technology model to support mathematics education.

2.2 Triangle of Challenges

Since both mathematics and software programming are universally applicable methods, they play pivotal roles within the STEM subjects. Therefore, we address mathematics and software programming in our framework. In the field of software programming we focus primarily on algorithmic programming, but we also cover dynamic webpage development. We regard dynamic webpage development as a beneficial side effect of the framework: it helps us generate web-based tutorials; pedagogically, it supplements mathematics and algorithmic programming; and it leads to illustrative results and, therefore, motivates students.

Fig. 1. PISA - performance in mathematics in selected countries in 2015 [26].

We summarize the subgroup within our framework (mathematics, algorithmic programming and webpage development within the STEM subjects) as a triangle of challenges as depicted in Fig. 2.

2.3   Stakeholders in STEM Education

Stakeholders are entities who have some kind of (economic) interest in a subject. When there is a scarcity of some kind there is competition for these scarce resources. In our context, it could be competition between companies for customers, or competition between graduates for a job. To discuss the implications on this competitiveness we recall Friedman's phases of globalization [6]:

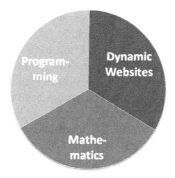

Fig. 2. Triangle of challenges.

– Globalization 1.0 (from large to medium): In the first phase of globalization, countries globalized. Friedman associates this with the so called discovery of America by Christopher Columbus and assigns Globalization 1.0 a time frame from 1492 to 1820.
– Globalization 2.0 (from medium to small): Globalization 2.0 is linked to the globalization of companies in the beginning of the nineteenth century. This is also associated with the emerging industrial revolution in the nineteenth century and runs from 1820 to 2000.
– Globalization 3.0 (from small to tiny): In globalization 3.0, individuals are globalized. The beginning of globalization 3.0 is related to the dot.com bubble [16] around the year 2000 which marks the beginning of the breakthrough of Internet technologies.

These phases of globalization are closely related to competition. In contrast to globalization 1.0 when countries started to compete and globalization 2.0 when companies started to compete internationally, in globalization 3.0 individuals are also competing with each other globally. This means that, for example, an American graduate not only competes with another American graduate for a job but also with graduates from other countries. While the first two levels of globalization are well-known, globalization 3.0 might still be not as obvious but has a significant impact on students and employees in a wider context. It is no longer sufficient to rely on, or hide behind, a country's (strong) economy or its (highly) competitive industries. In globalization 3.0, individuals compete directly with each other worldwide.

This leads to our first three stakeholders: countries, companies and students (or more generally employees). As a fourth group of stakeholders we add teachers and lecturers at schools and universities. This group might not have direct economic interests from their professional point of view but, in their teaching role, they are one of the main stakeholders in education. We briefly discuss the stakeholders thus:

- Countries. We use the term country as synonymous with government and society. The objectives of a country include fostering a competitive economy, providing job opportunities and generating high tax revenues. Governments support structural change. As governments administer taxes on a fiduciary basis their objective is also to spend revenues economically and responsibly.
- Companies. To remain competitive companies need a highly-skilled workforce, particularly in areas which show promise.
- Students. Education is a key asset. To maximize their ability to negotiate their position in the labor market, students should strive for the best education in areas where shortages are present or forecasted.
- Teachers. In contrast to countries, companies and students, teachers do not have a direct economic interest. Their interests are more content-related, e.g., they find it rewarding to receive positive feedback and recognition for their teaching. However, they need to be supported and prepared to teach STEM subjects with technology [24].

Based on the stakeholders' needs, we define the requirements for a computer-based framework supporting STEM education and select an appropriate platform for the framework.

3   Requirements for and Selection of a Computer-Based Framework Supporting STEM Education

3.1   Requirements for a Computer-Based Framework

The requirements for a computer-based framework supporting STEM education are derived from the needs of the stakeholders. We think it is essential to address these needs if the framework is to be successful; the needs are summarized below and are discussed in the subsequent paragraphs [29]:

- Cost efficiency
- Platform independence
- Size of the platform network
- Comprehensiveness of the mathematical implementations
- Support for possible levels of user experience.

Criterion: Cost Efficiency. Education is strategically important for countries since it helps to strengthen economies in a globalized world. It is a key factor in a prosperous economy. Education is also an important strategy to diminish poverty and inequality. However, in striking contrast to these benefits, educational sectors seem to be subject to funding restrictions and cutbacks virtually worldwide (see, for example [2, 10, 12]). One reason might be that the results of education are often not directly attributed to education; another might be that the benefits of education are often long term. Both these reasons make investment in education less than appealing to government facing short term election cycles.

Funding is a challenge for many educational institutions in mature economies and in developing countries it may face even bigger obstacles. Further, for many students it is a challenge to purchase necessary teaching materials, including books. Therefore, a core criterion for our framework is that it should be cost efficient. Excluding hardware, this means that the framework should be easily available and free.

Criterion: Platform Independence. In the discussion on the cost efficiency criterion we excluded hardware since we do not think that free hardware is a realistic goal. However, in our second criterion we require the framework to be as platform-independent as possible. This would maximize the accessibility of the framework. We identified two kinds of platform-independencies that are partly overlapping:

- Independence from device platforms. The framework should run on a diverse range of devices like personal computers and tablets but also on smartphones. This would diminish the hardware requirements, particularly for students when they want to run the framework on their private devices.
- Independence from operating systems. The arguments for independence from a particular operating system are similar to our discussion on the need for independence from device platforms. The framework should run on all major operation systems for smartphones, tablets and personal computers.

This criterion of independence of devices and operating systems requires a browser-based solution.

Criterion: Size of the Platform Network. Often the number of adopters of a product increases its utility for a single user. Arthur [1] discussed this phenomenon in the context of increasing returns to adoption. For example, positive effects on learning can be observed since the support (blogs, books etc.) for a popular product is normally better than support for a niche product. Today, network effects are discussed with respect to the leading Internet companies. This discussion is backed by the theory of network externalities [11]. For example, the de facto standards of office document formats virtually force the user to use certain office software to avoid compatibility issues when exchanging the documents with colleagues.

Obviously, a platform for STEM education is a product whose utility increases when the number of users also increases. Therefore, we consider the size of the supporting network behind the framework as an important criterion for our platform.

Criterion: Comprehensiveness of the Mathematical Implementations. Ideally, the platform should comprehensively cover the fields of mathematics that are defined in the respective curricula of schools and universities. This would lead to seamless and integrated learning experience for the students.

This prevents set-up times that would occur if the working environment, i.e., the platform, were to be changed. Thus, comprehensive coverage of relevant mathematical methods by the platform contributes to the optimal long-term learning outcome of the students.

The comprehensiveness of the mathematical implementations can be considered as a horizontal criterion as it defines the range of different mathematical methods. The criterion that we discuss in the next paragraph, "Criterion: Possible Levels of User Experience", describes the depth of student understanding in a particular area and it can be considered as a vertical criterion.

Criterion: Possible Levels of User Experience. Ideally, an educational framework should address absolute beginners as well as advanced experts. This means that a student can continue using the educational framework during the whole "lifecycle" of learning. Hence, students can concentrate on content and do not need to spend setup time when the learning environment needs to be changed, e.g., when the students want to move forward to the next level of learning. This would minimize a possible break point where a student may consider withdrawing from STEM subjects. Further, an integrated framework provides a spirited and motivating environment where beginners can be supported by experts and experts may learn from questions asked by beginners.

3.2   Evaluation of Possible Platforms for a Computer-Based Framework

The framework supporting STEM education can be realized in different ways. For example, it could be implemented from scratch in a multi-purpose programming environment like C/C++ or Java. Another possibility would be to use apps and webpages dedicated to mathematics teaching like MATH 42 or MalMath. Alternatively one could leverage off a numerical computing environment like Mathematica or MATLAB. We distinguish between these three alternatives in our evaluation for the best platform for our framework:

- Multi-purpose programming languages
- Apps and webpages dedicated to mathematics teaching
- Numerical computing environments

Multi-purpose Programming Languages. Multi-purpose programming languages like C/C++ and its derivatives or Java, are excellent platforms for the development of a wide range of applications. Furthermore, many of the programming languages are free and run on many operating systems.

For our purpose C/C++ is of special interest. Due to its efficiency, C/C++ has been a leading programming environment for mathematical/numerical tasks in industry and academia. This has led to many corresponding libraries which support the programming of mathematical/numerical tasks. However, we would consider C/C++ as too challenging for newcomers to mathematics and programming. This would possibly lead to frustration among the students and would, therefore, be counterproductive to our objectives. In addition, most of the other programming languages have their strength and main areas of applications in fields other than mathematics. Therefore, they are not ideally suitable for our purpose to teach mathematics.

The programming language Python has also attracted attention in the field of data analysis over the past decade. One of Python's objectives is that it should be easy to learn and implement. In the field of data analysis, this has led to many supportive libraries. Further, according to the TIOBE index of July 2018 that ranks the popularity of programming languages [34], Python is one of the most popular at rank #4 with a strong growth rate of 2.81% in comparison to the previous month. Regarding job postings, it is second just behind Java [20]. Python, therefore would be an excellent platform for our framework. As discussed above, we consider the other programming environments are not optimal for our framework.

Apps and Webpages Dedicated to Mathmatics Teaching. Over the past decade, several excellent apps and webpages supporting mathematical education have been developed. They include, Mathway (https://www.mathway.com), MATH 42 (http://math-42.com), MalMath (http://www.malmath.com) and Wolfram Alpha (http://www.wolframalpha.com).

Math 42 reports on its webpage that it is attracting more than 2 million students worldwide. Wolfram Alpha (from the vendor Wolfram of the numerical computing environment Mathematica) offers an impressive array of mathematical methods. Beyond mathematics Wolfram Alpha is also a search engine that provides preprocessed and structured information in many subject fields, including, e.g., country information and information on celebrities.

These apps and webpages focus on mathematics and provide exercises and related explanations on mathematical theory and background. They do not address (algorithmic) software programming that might be of interest for advanced students whose goal is to develop their own programs addressing particular problems.

As already discussed, our framework should holistically address mathematics, including (algorithmic) programming. These apps and webpages dedicated to mathematics teaching do not meet this objective.

Numerical Computing Environments. Numerical computing tools provide specialized environments for development and application in data analysis. Their functionalities include an integrated development environment, a specialized programming language, and extensive support for graphics. A basic numerical computing environment can also be extended by several software libraries addressing special fields in numerical computing.

The core features of these numerical computing environments include integrated development environments, purpose-built programming languages, graphing utilities and substantial libraries. Numerical computing environments, therefore, generally address our criterion about possible levels of user experience. All these environments are excellent bases for the framework.

Interest in these numerical computing environments has increased in the past decade due to the increasing needs and interest in data science. Lists of statistical software packages for numerical computing environments can be found at Wikipedia (https://www.wikipedia.org) under the keywords "list of statistical packages" and "comparison of numerical analysis software".

Leading commercial tools are, e.g., MATLAB (https://www.mathworks.com) and Mathematica (http://www.wolfram.com/mathematica). MATLAB is a leading numerical computing environment, particularly in natural science, engineering and technology. It can be expanded by many libraries that address special subjects in natural science, engineering and technology. Particular areas that are mentioned on the webpage of MATLAB include deep learning, computer vision, signal processing, quantitative finance and risk management, robotic and control engineering.

Mathematica can also be applied in a wide range of areas and is frequently used in industry. It also integrates mathematical symbolic computation functionality, i.e., it can be used to symbolically integrate or differentiate many other symbolic computation functionalities. Its mathematical symbolic computation functionality makes Mathematica a leading tool in the educational sector. So, with regard to their functionality and quality, both leading commercial environments would be very well suited as a platform for our framework. However, our criterion of cost efficiency requires that the framework should be easily accessible and free of charge. As discussed above, we consider this criterion as essential. Therefore, we need to exclude these commercial numerical computing environments as possible bases for our framework.

Popular free numerical computing environments include GNU Octave (https://www.gnu.org/software/octave), R-Project (https://www.r-project.org), and Scilab (http://www.scilab.org).

GNU Octave and Scilab position themselves as free alternatives to MATLAB as they are more or less compatible (GNU Octave more so than Scilab). According to the TIOBE index [34] the MATLAB programming language ranks #15 and is, therefore, one of the leading special purpose languages in the field of data analysis and mathematics. Hence, both GNU Octave and Scilab would be very suitable platforms for our framework.

A further alternative is R-Project. R emerged as a free alternative to the statistical programming language S [9] and has gained increasing attention in academia as well as in industry [35]. In July 2018, TIOBE [34] ranks R as fourteenth most popular programming language and, therefore, as the most popular special purpose programming language in the field of numerical computing. Misirlakis [20] puts it into the group of "up and comers" in a survey and Heller [8] describes R as "heating up". At the time of writing it is at #11 in the ranking of the most in-demand programming languages. Furthermore, it is the most liked programming language in a recent survey [13]. Hence, regarding the current momentum behind the free numerical computing environment, we regard R as stronger as GNU Octave and Scilab.

3.3   Summary and Selection of the Platform

We consider classic general purpose programming languages like C/C++ or Java as too complex for beginners and not focused enough on mathematics. In comparison, Python is easy to use and supports data analysis. Many of the apps and webpages providing teaching support in mathematics are excellent but they lack functionalities to support advanced students who are looking for programming options. All the discussed numerical computing environments are suitable as platforms for our framework. From its functionalities we consider Mathematica as the optimal platform. However, since we think that it is essential that the framework is free of (software) cost, we need to exclude commercial platforms like Mathematica and MATLAB. The free numerical computing environments are suitable as platforms for our framework. Beyond them, we favor R over GNU Octave and Scilab since it seems to be the most popular.

Python and R, therefore, emerge as the most suitable platforms for the framework. In the data analysis community the pros and cons of Python and R are intensively discussed. Basically, Python was designed as a "real" programming language that has been recently adopted in the data analysis community and seems to have a higher computational performance than R.

R, however, originated from the statistical community which puts it closer to mathematics. We regard this as an advantage in the context of our project. Therefore, we decided to use R, rather than Python, as the platform for our framework.

Table 1 summarized the evaluation of possible platforms. The circled plus ($\oplus$) indicated that a criterion is matched by the platform, while the circled dot ($\odot$) shows that the criterion match is acceptable. The circled minus ($\ominus$) leads to exclusion of the platform; rendering further evaluation of the remaining criteria unnecessary.

In the following section, we discuss important properties of R that are relevant in the context of our framework.

Table 1. Summary of the evaluation of possible platforms.

	Cost efficiency	Platform ind.	Size of network	Math. impl.	Math. Levels
General purpose programming languages					
C, Java ...					⊖
Python	⊕	⊕	⊕	⊙	⊕
Mathematics apps and webpages					
MATH 42 ...					⊖
Numerical computing environments					
Mathematica	⊖				
MATLAB	⊖				
GNU Octave	⊕	⊕	⊙	⊙	⊙
R-Project	⊕	⊕	⊕	⊙	⊕
Scilab	⊕	⊕	⊙	⊙	⊙

Legend: ⊕ matched, ⊙ acceptable, ⊖ leads to exclusion.

4   Basic Properties of R-Project

4.1   Adoption of R in Academia and Industry

The R project was launched by the University of Auckland as an alternative to S [9]. Initially, its main focus was on statistical methods. In the meantime it covers a diverse range of mathematical methods and several areas of data analysis. A reason for its rich portfolio of methods is that everybody can contribute packages to R, e.g., in academia, many researchers not only use R for data analysis but also contribute packages to R. Many R packages are written by the researchers who actually developed the algorithms.

In recent years, R has gained momentum not only in academia but also in industry [35]. Major information technology companies, like Microsoft or Oracle, support R. Microsoft bought the R specialist Revolution Analytics in 2015 and has enriched its product portfolio by Microsoft R Server. R can be used in Microsoft's Azure [27]. Further, Oracle [28] supports R through its Oracle R Enterprise solution. Many other companies also support and or use R.

4.2   Basic Structure of R

R (https://www.r-project.org) is platform independent, i.e., it runs on Linux, macOS and Windows. It is accessible by an integrated console or several integrated development environments, with RStudio (https://www.rstudio.com) probably the most popular (see Fig. 3 for a screenshot).

This allows a console based programming style as well as the opportunity to develop programs and packages. Extensive support is available for R:. online tutorials and blogs are available and several books have been published, e.g.,

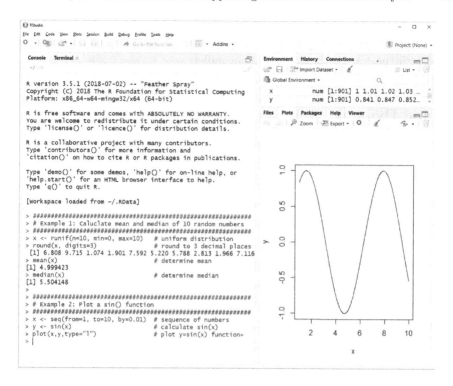

Fig. 3. An example for RStudio IDE.

by Matloff [18] or Teetor [33]. There is also a fairly comprehensive introduction available on R websites [36].

Besides it algorithmic core, it also provides extensive support for graphics [21] and exporting/reporting functions. For instance Leisch developed the package Sweave [14,15] that generates LaTeX files. The Markdown package (see [31] and the webpage https://rmarkdown.rstudio.com) helps to generate R reports formatted as Word, HMTL or LaTeX/PDF documents. Its basic workflow is shown in Fig. 4.

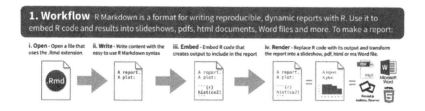

Fig. 4. R's Markdown package workflow [31].

R also has a package, the Shiny package [3], that backs the development of dynamic webpages. Impressive examples for such dynamic webpages can be found at https://www.shiny.rstudio.com/gallery.

5   A Framework Supporting Mathematics, Programming and Dynamic Webpage Development

In this section, we show how our framework supports different level of mathematics education and also provides insights into programming and dynamic webpage development. In mathematics education we distinguish between exercise-based mathematics (see Sect. 5.1) and mathematics and programming tasks as we discuss in Sect. 5.2. Finally, in Sect. 5.3 we show how dynamic webpage development can be integrated into our curriculum.

5.1   Exercise-Based Mathematics

By exercise-based mathematics we mean tasks that are designed to apply mathematics. Examples are:

- Solve the following rule of three ...
- Determine in curve sketching the y-intercepts of the function ...

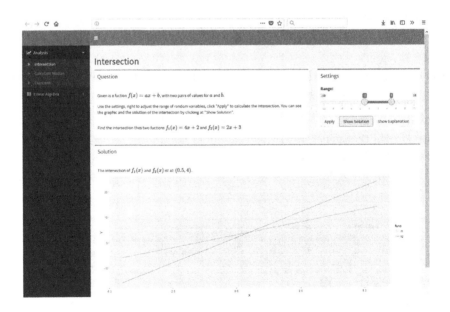

Fig. 5. Example for a mathematics task on a personal computer.

This approach is similar to the app- and web-based tools like MATH 42 and MalMath. In R, we use the Shiny package to develop such corresponding

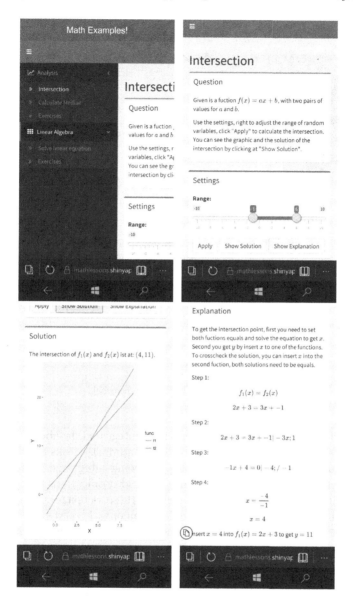

Fig. 6. Example for a mathematics task on a smartphone.

webpages. As they are HTML-based, they can be accessed universally, independent of a particular operating system and a particular class of device (personal computer, tablet or smartphone).

An example for a mathematical task on a personal computer is shown in Fig. 5 while an example for an exercise accessed from a smartphone is depicted in Fig. 6.

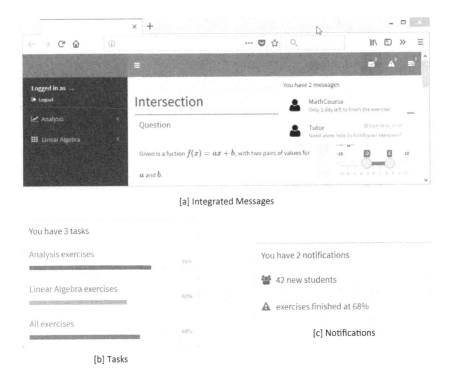

Fig. 7. Dashboard of the framework.

We intend to enrich our framework with an integrated dashboard with functionalities like the progress/completion rate of a student's tasks and basic social media functions. See Fig. 7 for screenshots showing integrated messages (sub-figure [a]) and boards for tasks (sub-figure [b]) and notifications (sub-figure [c]).

As we will discuss later, the development of these webpages is an integrated part of our challenge "dynamic webpage development". It serves two objectives, the extension of the portfolio of mathematics tasks and training in dynamic webpage development.

5.2 Programming Tasks in Mathematics

In contrast to exercise-based mathematics, programming tasks in mathematics addresses two of our challenges, i.e.:

- Mathematics
- (Algorithmic) programming

We can cover the range from the application of mathematics to, let us call it, algorithmic mathematics. As we need to develop programs, we use the console of R or an IDE like RStudio.

With respect to the state of knowledge of the students we can use different levels of programming to formulate a mathematical problem, stretching from the use of basic mathematical functions implemented in R to a more algorithmic programming style.

Using Basic Mathematical Functions. As R has a rich portfolio of mathematical functions, these functions can be directly used to solve a mathematical problem. E.g., when the mean of the numbers 3, 4, 8, 9, 2 is to be determined we simply have to enter:

```
x <- c(3, 4, 8, 9, 2)
mean(x)
```

or even just

```
mean(c(3, 4, 8, 9, 2))
```

This programming style would also be the preferred "R style" since it uses the same features and functions that R offers.

Intermediate Mathematics and Programming. An intermediate approach would be to resolve the `mean()` function by the sum divided by the number of objects:

```
x <- c(3, 4, 8, 9, 2)
sum(x)/length(x)
```

Advanced Education in Algorithmic Programming. An advanced representation for calculating a mean would be the sum further resolved and programmed using the R's `for{}` command:

```
x <- c(3, 4, 8, 9, 2)
sumVector <- 0
lengthVector <- length(x)
for(i in 1:lengthVector){
    sumData <- sumData + x[i]
}
sumData
```

Note, that the programs presented in the paragraphs "Intermediate Mathematics and Programming" and "Advanced Education in Algorithmic Programming" would not be considered a good R programming style since they neglect convenient R functions. However, our objective here is to show the mathematical background of the means and use algorithmic programming.

5.3   Education in Dynamic Webpage Development

Finally, as discussed in Sect. 5.1 we can use the need to develop a portfolio of web-based exercises in mathematics to offer training in the development of dynamic webpages. This is a win-win situation since it addresses two of our challenges.

```
90      #Intersection Plot
91 ▾    output$intersec.distPlot <- renderPlot({
92
93          #returns if button "Show Solution" is not pressed
94          if (intersec.status$doPlot == FALSE) return()
95
96          ds <- intersec.data$data
97
98          ggplot(ds$data, aes(x=x, y=y, color=func)) + geom_line() + labs(x = "X", y = "Y")
99
100     })
101
102     #Intersection answer
103 ▾   output$intersec.answer <- renderUI({
104         if (intersec.status$doPlot == FALSE) return()
105
106         ds <- intersec.data$data
107
108         #' Using MathJax for formulas in LaTeX http://shiny.leg.ufpr.br/daniel/019-mathjax/
109         withMathJax(
110             sprintf(
111             "The intersection of \\(f_1(x)\\) and \\(f_2(x)\\) ist at: \\((%s, %s)\\).",
112             ds$x.PoI,ds$y.PoI
113             )
114         )
115     })
```

Fig. 8. Example for Shiny code.

As can be seen in the small example depicted in Fig. 8, Shiny code is intuitive and easy to understand. Although the Shiny package is a highly specialized environment, it provides a good starting point for the introduction of dynamic webpage development.

6   Conclusion

In this paper, we presented a framework that supports selected facets of STEM education, namely mathematics, software programming and dynamic webpage development. After identifying the stakeholders and analyzing the requirements for such a platform, we evaluated possible platforms for the framework and selected R-Project as the most suitable. Then we introduced the framework.

The framework provides good support for STEM education and enriches teaching in these fields. As the platform R is free, it provides unrestricted access to educational institutions and students. Furthermore, the framework is open in a sense that everybody can use, modify or extend it and, therefore, adapt it to their personal needs. It covers the whole lifecycle of education, from web-based simple mathematics tasks for beginners to sophisticated applications within the R environment, a platform that is also used by professionals and senior academics. We consider the framework as a very useful tool within STEM education and hope that it addresses users' needs.

Trademarks

References

1. Arthur, W.B.: Competing technologies, increasing returns, and lock-in by historical events. Econ. J. **99**(394), 116–131 (1989)
2. Bagshaw, E.: University funding legislation set to be rushed through to parliament. Sydney Morning Herald, Fairfax Media, September 2017. http://www.smh.com.au/federal-politics/political-news/university-funding-legislation-set-to-be-rushed-through-to-parliament-20170906-gyc6zs.html
3. Chang, W.: Package 'shiny' (2017). https://cran.r-project.org/web/packages/shiny/shiny.pdf
4. Clifford, C.: Apple CEO Tim Cook: learn to code, it's more important than English as a second language. CNBC MAKE IT, October 2017. https://www.cnbc.com/2017/10/12/apple-ceo-tim-cook-learning-to-code-is-so-important.html
5. Freeman, R.E., Reed, D.L.: Stockholders and stakeholders: a new perspective on corporate governance. Calif. Manage. Rev. **25**(3), 88–106 (1983)
6. Friedman, T.L.: The world is flat. Guest Lecture at Massachusetts Institute of Technology, May 2005. https://archive.org/details/20050516Mit-ThomasLFriedman-WorldFlat
7. Hayashi, C.: What is data science? Fundamental concepts and a heuristic example. In: Hayashi, C., Yajima, K., Bock, H.H., Ohsumi, N., Tanaka, Y., Baba, Y. (eds.) Data Science, Classification, and Related Methods. STUDIES CLASS, pp. 40–51. Springer, Tokyo (1998). https://doi.org/10.1007/978-4-431-65950-1_3
8. Heller, M.: Hot data analytics trends - and 5 going cold. CIO, October 2017. http://www.cio.com/article/3213189/analytics/10-hot-data-analytics-trends-and-5-going-cold.html
9. Ihaka, R.: Past and future history. Technical report, Statistics Department, University of Auckland (1998). https://www.stat.auckland.ac.nz/~ihaka/downloads/Interface98.pdf
10. Karp, P.: Simon Birmingham says universities will have to learn to live with cuts and fee increases. The Guardian - Australian Edition, Guardian Media Group, Sydney, Australia, August 2017. https://www.theguardian.com/australia-news/2017/aug/30/simon-birmingham-says-universities-will-have-to-learn-to-live-with-cuts-and-fee-increases
11. Katz, M.L., Shapiro, C.: Network externalities, competition, and compatibility. Am. Econ. Rev. **75**(3), 424–440 (1985)
12. Kaufmann, M.: Bundesländervergleich: Studienplätze sind immer schlechter finanziert. Spiegel Online, SPIEGELnet GmbH, Hamburg, Germany, December 2016. http://www.spiegel.de/lebenundlernen/uni/studienplaetze-sind-immer-schlechter-finanziert-a-1123944.html

13. Krill, P.: Stack overflow reveals the most-disliked programming languages, November 2017. https://www.infoworld.com/article/3235651/application-development/stack-overflow-reveals-the-most-disliked-programming-languages.html
14. Leisch, F., R-core: Sweave user manual. Technical report, ETH Zuerich (2006)
15. Leisch, F.: Sweave: dynamic generation of statistical reports using literate data analysis. In: Härdle, W., Rönz, B. (eds.) Compstat, pp. 575–580. Physica, Heidelberg, Germany (2002). https://doi.org/10.1007/978-3-642-57489-4_89
16. Ljungqvist, A., Wilhelm, W.J.: IPO pricing in the dot-com bubble. J. Financ. **58**(2), 723–752 (2003)
17. Mateu, K.: Digital giants overtake industry - US Internet companies are the World's most valuable enterprises. Press Release of Ernst & Young Global Limited, July 2018. https://www.ey.com/ch/en/newsroom/news-releases/news-release-ey-digital-giants-overtake-industry
18. Matloff, N.: The Art of R Programming: A Tour of Statistical Software Design. No Starch Press, San Francisco (2011)
19. Merkel, A.: StZ im Gespräch / treffpunkt foyer - Dr. Angela Merkel. Stuttgarter Zeitung & Stuttgarter Nachrichten, September 2007. https://youtu.be/h2ifRKQqTus
20. Misirlakis, S.: The 7 most in-demand programming languages of 2018. Codingdojo Blog, December 2017. https://www.codingdojo.com/blog/7-most-in-demand-programming-languages-of-2018/
21. Murrell, P.: R Graphics, 2nd edn. CRC Press, Taylor & Francis Group, Boca Raton (2011)
22. Neuhauser, A., Cook, L.: 2016 U.S. News/Raytheon STEM index shows uptick in hiring, education. U.S. News & World Report (2016). https://www.usnews.com/news/articles/2016-05-17/the-new-stem-index-2016
23. Prätzel-Wolters, D., Neunzert, H.: Problems trump methods: a somewhat different mathematics from a somewhat different institute. In: Neunzert, H., Prätzel-Wolters, D. (eds.) Currents in Industrial Mathematics, pp. 3–30. Springer, Heidelberg (2015). https://doi.org/10.1007/978-3-662-48258-2_1
24. Niess, M.J.: Preparing teachers to teach science and mathematics with technology: developing a technology pedagogical content knowledge. Teach. Teach. Educ. **21**(5), 509–523 (2005)
25. OECD: Germany: Country note - results from PISA 2015 (2016). https://www.oecd.org/pisa/PISA-2015-Germany.pdf
26. OECD: PISA: Programme for international student assessment (2016). https://www.oecd.org/pisa, accessed
27. Olavsrud, T.: Microsoft closes acquisition of R software and servicesprovider. CIO (2015). http://www.cio.com/article/2906456/data-analytics/microsoft-closes-acquisition-of-r-software-and-services-provider.html
28. Oracle Inc.: Oracle R Enterprise. http://www.oracle.com/technetwork/database/database-technologies/r/r-enterprise/overview/index.htm
29. Tou, J.T.: Information systems. In: von Brauer, W. (ed.) GI 1973. LNCS, vol. 1, pp. 489–507. Springer, Heidelberg (1973). https://doi.org/10.1007/3-540-06473-7_52
30. Peters, G., Rückert, T., Seruga, J.: Some potentials of the R-Project environment for teachers' and students' education in mathematics, algorithms' programming and dynamic website development. In: Langran, E., Borup, J. (eds.) Society for Information Technology & Teacher Education International Conference (SITE), pp. 1816–1821. Association for the Advancement of Computing in Education (AACE), Washington, DC, March 2018. http://www.learntechlib.org/p/182774/

31. RStudio Inc.: R Markdown cheat sheet (2014). https://www.rstudio.com/wp-content/uploads/2015/02/rmarkdown-cheatsheet.pdf
32. Ruthven, K., Hennessy, S.: A practitioner model of the use of computer-based tools and resources to support mathematics teaching and learning. Educ. Stud. Math. **49**(1), 47–88 (2002)
33. Teetor, P.: R Cookbook. O'Reilly Media, Sebastopol (2011)
34. TIOBE software BV: TIOBE index for July 2018, Jul 2018. https://www.tiobe.com/tiobe-index/
35. Vance, A.: Data analysts captivated by R's power. New York Times (2009). http://www.nytimes.com/2009/01/07/technology/business-computing/07program.html
36. Venables, W.N., Smith, D.M.: An introduction to R. 3.5.1 edn. (2018). https://cran.r-project.org/doc/manuals/R-intro.pdf

Online Content's Popularity Metrics: RDF-Based Normalization

Hiba Sebei[(✉)], Mohamed Ali Hadj Taib,
and Mohamed Ben Aouicha

Multimedia, InfoRmation Systems and Advanced Computing Laboratory,
Sfax, Tunisia
hiba.enis@gmail.com, mohamedali.hadjtaieb@gmail.com,
mohamed.benaouicha@fss.usf.tn

Abstract. Social network websites are mainly constructed around the notion of user identities, as set up on the bases of their profiles, and online generated contents such as texts, videos, photos. Still, while some profiles gain an important position in the network, others do not. Similarly, some online generated contents appear to gain a great deal of attention from the part of users, whereas others are completely ignored. In this context, the notion of profile and online content related popularity has come to the forefront. Additionally, several studies turn out to be focused on the area of popularity associated analysis and prediction. Noteworthy, however, is that the popularity evaluative metrics prove to vary from a social network to another. In this respect, the present work is conceived to deal with such challenges through an advanced proposal whereby a unified presentation of popularity metrics related to each social entity, across several social networks, is put forward. Accordingly, a hierarchical structure of popularity metrics, as enhanced with a particular RDF presentation, is suggested, along with a brief summary of wide range of methods used to analyze such entities related popularities.

Keywords: Popularity · Social networks · Social entity · Social features ·
SPI · RDF

1 Introduction

The present work is an extension of the previously established study [21] in the 20th International Conference on Enterprise Information Systems. It proposes a new presentation of social entities related metrics based on an RDF presentation along with summary of the methods used for popularity quantification.

Over the last decade, online social media websites have noticed an exponential growth in the number of active users, as no less than 313 million monthly users have been recorded to be active[1] on Twitter, over 1 billion users[2] on YouTube and about

---

[1] https://www.statista.com/statistics/282087/number-of-monthly-active-twitter-users/.

[2] https://www.youtube.com/intl/fr/yt/about/press/.

S. Hammoudi et al. (Eds.): ICEIS 2018, LNBIP 363, pp. 22–41, 2019.
https://doi.org/10.1007/978-3-030-26169-6_2

2.23 billion monthly active users[3] con Facebook. These facts support well the explosion of the amount of user-generated data on such websites. In fact, the relevant statistics appear to reveal that about 95 million photos[4] are shared every day on Instagram, billion hours of videos watched every day[5] on YouTube, and about 500 million tweets sent every day (See footnote 4) on Twitter.

This flux of data has not always acquired the same rate of attention from the part of users, as mentioned by Lerman and Hogg [14], stating that among 1600 new stories submitted on Digg, only a handful of them turn out to gather thousands of votes, while others are completely ignored by users. It is actually such findings which helped enhance the emergence of the popularity notion related to each social media content entity such as videos, photos, and texts. In this regard, popularity represents the corresponding amount of attention as directed from users to the content [9, 20].

Studying the popularity of social entities is a beneficial task for both social media data consumers and producers. Most efforts made on the popularity of social entities focus on the analysis of popularity evolution and the prediction of popularity likely to help avoid information overload. This could be achieved through providing users with the most popular content and companies with the opportunity to boost their business strategy. Through the study of social entities' popularity, researchers try to find satisfactory responses to such questions as: how the social items' popularity could be boosted? Would the studied items be popular or not? If, yes, to what extent would they be popular in both of the short and long terms? Can an item's popularity be quantified prior to its creation?

For a social entity's popularity to be thoroughly investigated, researchers have identified three shared requirements: popularity measures, popularity features and methods. However, for a specific type of social entity to be studied, the popularity metrics appear to vary from an online social media website to another, particularly corresponding to likes on Facebook, diggs on Digg, and views on YouTube. Even within the same website, popularity can be measured in different ways, mainly through the number of views or a combination of both of the views and comments corresponding number. The previously established study [21] that is conceived to advance a proposed hierarchical structure of the metrics. Additionally, a service provided interface (SPI) is also put forward. The conceived SPI is intended to define services liable to implementation via the social networks associated APIs, with the aim of gathering the existing features, whereby the popularity degree could be quantified independently of the social media websites. However, the present work is intended to provide a new normalized view of popularity metrics, likely to help in handling the new social networks' sourced metrics. Therefore a simple presentation of an RDF-based normalization scheme is proposed for the normalization. An illustration of the study associated problem and purposes is depicted in Fig. 1, below.

The remainder of this work is structured as follows. In a first place, the paper applied terminology is thoroughly highlighted. In a second place, a review of the works

---

[3] https://newsroom.fb.com/company-info/.

[4] https://www.socialpilot.co/blog/social-media-statistics.

[5] https://www.youtube.com/intl/fr/yt/about/press/.

dealing with the notion of popularity is exposed, whereby a summary of the popularity metrics related to each social entity is established. A discussion of the wide range of popularity metrics available makes subject of Sect. 3. As for Sect. 4, it involves a depiction of a hierarchical representation for the popularity metrics along with a proposed RDF presentation of popularity across social networks. This section also introduces a materialization attempt of the proposed normalization framework as administered under an implemented Service Provider Interface (SPI). Concerning Sect. 5, a summary of the popularity prediction methods relevant classification is introduced. In a last stage, new research potential directions and perspective lines are suggested.

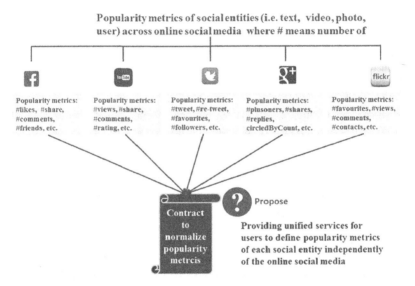

Fig. 1. Illustration of the problematic corresponding to the variety of social entities' popularity metrics across different online social media websites and the necessity of popularity metrics normalization [21]

2   Related Works: Social Media Popularity

This section is devoted to outline the notion of popularity and its relevant terminology, as associated with social entities enabling to structure the content, as generated across online social media websites.

2.1   Popularity Notion

In the relevant literature, several efforts have been focused on studying popularity as closely associated with social entities. Some of them, mainly [5, 8, 15], are motivated by the information overload as stemming from online social media data, attempting to predict the social entities attached popularity in a bid to help users receive the most critical events and digital contents. While others, such as [3, 9, 10], are motivated by the acts discovered to be popular on social media with a tendency of becoming essential for companies and even for people. As such, they try to understand and figure out the social items relating properties making an item stand as more popular than another, with the intention of helping people boost the popularity of their content even more. Other studies, such as [17], appear to concentrate on improving the marketing strategies and developing the diffusion strategies by undertaking to predict the outcomes that some real-world cases are likely to bring about. As it is the case, for instance, with a movie revenue estimation [9], or predicting popular items, a useful undertaking for websites owners, as stated by Quan et al. [20], for distinguishing the most accurate of resources, as popular content leads to a remarkable increase in traffic requiring early handling to prevent any possible technical problem from taking place. In this regard, several studies appear to be focused on the popularity aspect of social entities. Accordingly, Li et al. [15] have proposed to categorize such studies into two major classes: the first includes those focusing on popularity prediction in microblogs such as Twitter, while the second is devoted to predicting popularity in media-sharing websites, such as YouTube. Concerning the first category, popularity is related to textual entities, such as a tweet on Twitter, as for the second category, popularity is relative to such media content as videos and photos.

With respect to the state-of-the-art research proves to reveal that the works related to the social media content popularity appear to cover several social entities such as textual content, as in [6, 8, 13, 17], videos, as in [3, 9], photos as it is the case with [10, 19], as well as the users' popularity in their social media websites as discussed in few relevant works [4, 9]. As already stated, popularity identifies the amount of attention paid by the user to the content. Hence, for an effective analysis and prediction of each social media entity relating popularity, among the already cited ones (i.e., texts, videos, photos, and users), it is necessary to identify the metrics of popularity, the features and establishing a link binding such metrics by means of some quantification maintaining algorithms and relevant methods.

2.2   Terminology

Popularity Measures: are popularity defining metrics that vary from a study to another [10].

Popularity Features: represent different factors related to the target social entity, likely to affect its popularity [8, 10]. In effect, measuring the social entities' popularity constitutes a difficult task owing mainly to the existence of a wide range of factors likely to influence the quantification of popularity [2].

Methods: are processes used to figure out the correlation between popularity measures and features, as factors influencing the social media entities' popularity.

2.3   Social Entities

During the first age of social media, the users' generated content appear to focus on the texts themselves (blogs). Then, by integrating the web 2.0 technology, as a social media website-constructing platform, the user-generated contents turn out to take extra forms such as videos, photos and audios, with each form being considered a social entity in itself. Besides, the user is attributed a profile, considered as a social entity. As several researchers consider to focus on studying popularity relative to each type of user-generated data, we propose, in the next section, to classify the related works with respect to the social entities studied (i.e., texts, videos, photos and users).

3   Social Entities: Popularity Quantification

The state of the art reveals that identifying a specific social entity's relevant popularity measures and features are discovered to vary within the same online social media websites, in as much as they vary across different websites. These issues are presented and discussed with regard to each social entity in the following sections.

3.1   Text

Among the relevant studies, several works appear to focus on treating the Twitter messages attached popularity, considering them as textual entities. In this regard, Hong et al. [8] propose to define the popularity measure as the number of textual entity related re-tweets, while accounting for message content, temporal information features, metadata of messages and users, as well as the structural properties of the users' social graph as influential features of the Twitter figuring messages' popularity. Other studies, however, prove to focus on specific textual entities as a hashtag on twitter messages. In this respect, Ma et al. [17] suggest predicting the hashtag relating popularity by presenting the number of users who post at least one tweet containing the hashtag within the given time period as a popularity measure. They, then, specify two major categories of popularity features: content features and contextual features. Accordingly, content features refer to lexical data derived from the hashtag and the tweet containing it (e.g., the number of segment words in a hashtag). Concerning the contextual features, they are related to data derived from the social graphs as formulated by Twitter users (e.g., the number of tweets containing the hashtag). On analyzing news as a textual entity, Lerman and Hogg [14] try to predict the popularity degree of news through the Digg website. They assess the news' popularity in the form of the number of votes a story accumulates on Digg. As for Wu and Shen [25], they use the number of re-tweets that the news tweet gathers from the users on Twitter.

3.2   Image

On investigating the popularity of images on Flickr, McParlane et al. [19] define several popularity measures as being the number of image related views. He considers three main features associated with the image context (e.g., time, day, size, flash, and orientation), visual appearance related to the image pixel extracted information (e.g. color, faces, etc.) and user context (e.g. gender, account, contacts, etc.). Concerning Khosla et al. [10], they undertake to study the photos relating popularity on Flickr by considering the number of associated views as a measure of popularity. They combine both of the image content features (e.g. color, number of objects described, vision, etc.), and social-context features (e.g., the user's contact, users' groups, mean view, title, description, etc.) as features useful for studying image popularity. In turn, Gelli et al. [7] propose to study the popularity prediction of images, as based on Flickr photos, by considering the number of views expressed on Flickr as a popularity metric including three main features: user related features (i.e. metadata related to the author of the image), visual features (e.g. color), and context features (i.e. the image related tags and description).

3.3 Video

Several related studies appear to concentrate on examining the YouTube figuring videos' popularity range. Worth citing among them are Chatzopoulou et al. [3], who propose to define popularity on the basis of the number of views. They also consider the number of comments, ratings and favorites as features whereby the evolution of the YouTube appearing video sequences' popularity could be recognized. Similarly, Figueiredo [5] considers the number of views as a popularity measure. He classifies the features into three main classes, the first of these classes deals with the video content (e.g. video category, upload date, etc.). The second class refers to the link associated features (e.g., the referrer first date and referrer number of views). As for the third class, it concerns the popularity features as measured throughout a well-defined time period (e.g., number of views, number of comments, number of favorites, etc.). In this regard, Jiang et al. [9] also exploit not only the number of views as a measure of popularity, but also define different popularity features to study viral YouTube videos. More particularly, they account for such factors as the video metadata, (e.g. id, title, text description, category, number of raters, number of likes, number of dislikes), the video uploading user relevant metadata, (e.g. user ID, name, profile view count, etc.), the view associated historic, (e.g. comments, likes and dislikes), the number of in-links in other social media, along with the video related comments. With respect to Trzcinski and Rokita [24] conducted study, it is axed on investigating the videos related popularity prediction, following the examination of two datasets: a YouTube based set and a Facebook based one. Regarding the YouTube video sequences, popularity metrics are expressed via the number of views, comments, favorites and ratings, while the Facebook videos' popularity metrics correspond to the number of shares, likes and comments.

3.4 User

On studying the popularity evolution of the online social media user as figuring in MySpace, considered as a popular online social medium, Couronné et al. [4] identify two popularity measures, namely, the contents' audience and the user's authority. While the former is devoted to identifying the number of visits to the artist's page, the latter serves to determine the number of people recommending the artist by establishing links with him/her. The authors take into account two main features: the music attached features (e.g. the number of visits to the profile, number of comments the visitors have left on the profile, etc.), and the search variables that determine the number of Twitter posts bearing the artist's name issued during the last month, as well as the number of the Yahoo! search engine scored results when searching the artist's name. Zafarani and Liu [27] discuss the variation marking the users' popularity across sites, as the individual joins multiple sites and quantifies the user's popularity based on the number of friends.

Table 1 categorizes the popularity factor related works as scored with respect to each type of social entity. It also depicts the features and metrics as used in each study's relevant context.

Table 1. Categorization of popularity related works based on the type of social media entities [21]

Social entity	Reference	Measures	Features
Text	[8]	The number of re-tweets	Message content, temporal information features, metadata of messages and users, structural properties of the users' social graph
	[17]	The number of users who post at least one tweet containing the hashtag	The number of users who post at least one tweet containing the hashtag
	[14]	The number of votes	Story metadata, historic of votes, the list of friends of the top-ranked users
	[25]	The number of re-tweets	Metrics related to the topology of the re-tweet propagation (e.g. date of creation, number of direct followers receiving update, number of followers viewed the news, etc.)
	[19]	The number of views and number of comments	Image's context (e.g. time, day, size, flash, orientation), Visual appearance (e.g. color, faces, etc.) and user context (e.g. gender, account, contacts, etc.)
Image	[10]	The number of views	Image content features (e.g. color, objects in the image, vision, etc.), Social context features (e.g. user's contact, users' groups, mean view, title, description, etc.)
	[7]	The number of views	User features (i.e. metadata related to the author of the image) and visual features and Context features (i.e. tags and description related to the image)
	[3]	The number of views	The number of comments, ratings and favorites
Video	[5]	The number of views	Video content (e.g. video category, upload date, etc.), Link features (e.g. referrer first date and referrer number of views) and Popularity features (e.g.

(continued)

Table 1. (*continued*)

Social entity	Reference	Measures	Features
			number of views, number of comments, number of favorites, etc.)
	[9]	The number of views	Video metadata (e.g. id, title, text description, category, number of raters, etc.), user metadata (e.g. user ID, name, profile views count, etc.), historic of view (e.g. Comments, likes and dislikes), the number of in-links and the video comments
	[24]	YouTube: the number of views, comments, favorites and ratings Facebook: the number of shares, likes and comments	Visual features (e.g. Video characteristics, color, etc.), Temporal features: refer to the number of views and number of social interactions (e.g. number of shares, likes and comments)
User	[4]	The audience of the contents: number of visits of the artist's page User's Authority: number of people recommending the artist by linking to him	Music variables (e.g. the number the visits of the profile, the number of comments visitors have left on the profile) Search variables the number of the Twitter post containing the artist name in the last month, the number of results of the Yahoo! search engine when searching the artist's name

3.5 Discussion

The present study has brought about two major outcomes. In a first place, it highlights well the lack of specifically reliable metrics whereby the popularity factor could be overly expressed. In a second place, the popularity metrics turn out to be expressed differently from a social medium to another.

Lack of Specific Metrics to Express Popularity Metrics. For a specific social entity (i.e. text, video, photo, and user) to be effectively studied, a variety of metrics are used by the researcher to express popularity. The variety of such metrics within the same social entity type is reflected in the same online social media website. In the case of studying the popularity of an image on Flickr, for instance, McParlane et al. [19] define three main sets of image context related features, visual features and user context features. As for Khosla et al. [10], they define other feature sets, namely, the image content and social context features. It is worth mentioning, also, that despite the apparent difference noticeable in the metric sets nomenclature as applied in both works, some kind of overlap appears to persist between these sets. Indeed, as the user context set considered by McParlane et al. [19] involves user metadata, the social context features' set, as considered by Khosla et al. [10], also account for such a dimension.

A Variety of Popularity Metrics across Different Online Social Media Websites. In this respect, Hong et al. [8] undertake to consider a textual entity application case. In effect, the popularity of a Twitter figuring message as a textual entity is expressed on the basis of the number of re-tweets, while the authors in [13] prove to measure the popularity relative to a post made by a brand page on the basis of comments number as gathered by the target post. Besides, Trzcinski and Rokita [24] consider measuring the popularity of a YouTube displayed video by considering the number of views, comments, favorites and ratings. As for Facebook, they count the number of shares, likes and comments as popularity measures. In turn, Khosla et al. [10] highlight the variety of popularity metrics, citing that for a certain image, popularity can correspond to "the number of likes on Facebook, the number of pins on Pinterest or the number of diggs on Digg". Two main questions arise as to the variety of parameters used to analyze a particular social entity's relative popularity. The first question is that of how to evaluate the popularity distinguishing parameters' subjectivity, as advanced by Cappallo et al. [2]. As for the second question, it relates to how to break away with the specific parameters, associated with each social media website, to be able to express the popularity range.

In this paper, we are mainly interested in answering the second question by proposing a factorization of the different popularity metrics relative to each type of online social entity, independently of the social media website source. This factorization process will be expressed via a Service Provider Interface (SPI) as derived from the conclusive services provided by the study, with respect to the already discussed social entities: texts, videos, images and users.

4 Normalized Popularity Metrics and the Proposed Service Provider Interface

In this section, a normalization of the different social entities' popularity metrics is put forward, as based on the previous section described state of the art, as well as the various popularity metrics, as extracted from a number of online social media websites (e.g. Twitter, Facebook, YouTube, Google+ and Flickr), relative to each social entity.

4.1 Normalization of Popularity Metrics Across Online Social Media Websites

Based on the studies already cited in the previous section, we consider the popularity related to the social entities: text, video, photo and user. We also consider distinguishing between the two main entity categories: user entity and media entity.

User: the variety of purposes lying behind using social network websites reveals an identification of a wide range of self-presentations prevailing on those websites. Social networks are used by simple individuals to establish social or business relationships, as well as by organizations and companies to promote a marketing purpose, or by a community of individuals to a group people with common social or professional interests or by non-physical individuals such as the presentation of an event or a channel. Hence, different entities persist, enabling to identify a large array of users across the network ranging from profiles, groups, pages and events. It is also worth distinguishing between a popular type of user and a user of an influence type. A popular user does not necessarily imply that he/she is influential. The difference between popularity and influence is discussed in [12], where the authors adapt the number of followers related to a Twitter user to stand as a popularity measure, while proving its inefficiency regarding the quantification of the user's influence.

Describing the user associated popularity is treated through three main categories of metrics: user profile metadata, referring to metadata created during the profile's creation, (e.g. name, gender, age, member duration, etc.), user activities metadata, which reflect the extent to which the user is active in his network (e.g. number of posts, number of posted media), and the profile's connectivity metadata, which reflects the user's relationships as established within the network (e.g. number of contacts, number of friends, number of followers, etc.).

Media. This term refers to the different types of online social media user-generated contents: texts, videos and photos.

Presentation: refers to image, video and textual entities. It is worth mentioning, in this respect, is that the textual entity can refer to a tweet on Twitter, a Facebook post or an activity posted on Google plus. Actually, a textual entity could well embed media entities.

Normalization: based on the related works, it is clear that each social entity popularity corresponding metrics help define two major categories of metrics: metrics related to the target entity's content, along with the target entity context related metrics.

The content metrics: correspond to parameters extracted from the target entities' contents (i.e., videos, images, texts). These metrics are obtained based on such advanced techniques as sentiment analysis, clustering and natural language processing [10] applied to textual entities as devised by Ma et al. [17], to derive lexical parameters from hashtag as content features. The task becomes even harder when the content feature turns out to be derived from media objects [2, 10], case in which advanced techniques, such as computer vision and machine learning, as implemented by Khosla et al. [10], appear to be imposed for content features to be extracted from a particular image. The media items relating content features (i.e. images and videos) correspond to visual features, such as colors, objects in images (e.g. people faces) [10, 19], as well as to visual sentiment features as set by Gelli et al. [7].

The contextual metrics: refer to the target social entity related parameters that do not entail the application of complex algorithms and techniques to be reached. Actually, these metrics could be directly extracted from any online social networks, as a category of social media (e.g. Facebook, Twitter, Google+, etc.), using the application provided interface (API), as offered by such websites. These metrics vary from a social network to another. Thus, the parameters associated with popularity metrics, as relating to different social entities (e.g. textual entity from Twitter and Google plus, using the Twitter Search API and Google plus REST API respectively, etc.), could be extracted.

The relevant results are depicted on Table 2, illustrating some social-entity instances as derived from different social media websites and outlining the related popularity metrics. We focus on the contextual metrics in a bid to normalize them independently of the online social media websites. Accordingly, we distinguish between two main categories of contextual metrics: media contextual metrics and media-author contextual metrics.

Media Contextual Metrics. Refer to the target media relating metadata, as divided into media metadata and user feedback metadata. To note, media metadata refer to two sets of data. A first set that describes the end users' metadata as generated during the media entity upload and devoted to describing the relevant entity (e.g., a video description, tags, date of the upload, etc.). As for the second set of metadata, it is generated following the media upload (e.g., accumulated comments, related media, etc.). Then, the user relating feedback metadata refer to the user activities resulting metrics as associated with the media. These metadata can either express a simple feedback from the user's part (i.e., do not require any explicit activity from the user), as the number of views is counted as soon as the user visits the media, or it can refer to an explicit feedback accumulated, following an explicit activity from the user's part (sharing media, rating a video, like or dislike a post etc.). Upon execution of such activities, a number of popularity metrics can be generated (e.g., number of likes, favorites, ratings, etc.). Noteworthy, also, is that the user generated feedback metrics are characterized with their closely associated dynamics as they evolve through time.

Media Author Metrics. Several researchers, mainly [10, 20, 22], discuss the impact of user connectivity who uploads the target entity relevant popularity, using the metadata related to the media entity-formulating author. The author associated contextual metrics are those which help define the user relevant popularity, as discussed in the paragraph above, and refer to the user's profile metadata, e.g., the user's gender, that can be directly extracted using the social network API, or on the basis of their names as figuring on the target social network, as stated in [19]. They also include both of the user relating activities metadata and connectivity metadata.

Figure 2 defines the media entity popularity metrics, presented in a hierarchical manner, highlighting the different factorization levels. It also illustrates the user entity associated popularity as depicted via the media author popularity (the red framed part).

Table 2. Social entities instance and its related popularity metrics across different social media websites [21]

Social entity	Social entity instance	Social Media	Measures	Features
Text	Tweet	Twitter	FavoriteCount, HashtagEntities, id, retweetCount, text, user, CreatedAt, etc.	Twitter Search API[a]
	Activity	Google Plus	Id, Activity author, Activity publishedAT, Activity Title, Activity URL, Activity content, Activity replies, etc.	Google+ API[b]

(continued)

Table 2. (*continued*)

Social entity	Social entity instance	Social Media	Measures	Features
	Comment	YouTube	AuthorChannelUrl, AuthorName, ViewerRating, LikeCount, Text, publishedAt	YouTube API[c]
	Post	Facebook	Id, shares, admin_creator, created_time, description, link, message, place, picture, source, etc.	Facebook Graph API[d]
Video	Video	YouTube	ChannelId, description, PublishedAt, title, Url, ViewCount, CommentCount, DislikeCount, FavoriteCount, etc.	YouTube API
	Embedded video	Twitter	URL, id, sizes (e.g large, medium, etc.), duration_millis, Video formats, video aspect ratios, updated_at, title, etc.	Twitter Search API
	Video	Facebook	ad_breaks, backdated_time, created_time, id, description, from, length, place, source, title	Facebook Graph API
Photo	Photo	Flickr	Owner (id, name, etc.), title, description, number of comments, tags, URL, number of favorites	Flickr API[e]
	Embedded photo	Twitter	URL, id, sizes (e.g large, medium, etc.)	Twitter Search API
	Photo	Facebook	Id, album, backdated_time, created_time, from, icon, height, link, name, place, etc.	Facebook Graph API
User	Page	Facebook	About, created time, number of likes, number of fans, name, picture, id, and category	Facebook Graph API
	Profile	Twitter	Id, Name, Screenname, createdAT, StatusesCount, Description FavoritesCount FollowersCount, FriendsCount, User Tweets: list of tweets	Twitter Search API

[a]https://developer.twitter.com/en/docs
[b]https://developers.google.com/+/web/api/rest/
[c]https://developers.google.com/youtube/v3/docs
[d]https://developers.facebook.com/docs/graph-api
[e]https://www.flickr.com/services/api/misc.overview.html

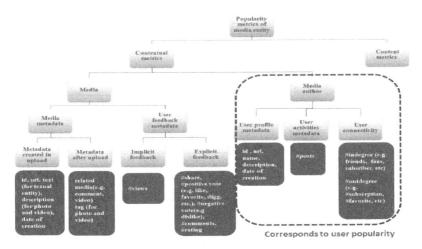

Fig. 2. Hierarchical presentation of the media entity popularity metrics with common metrics across online social media websites [21]

This hierarchy is materialized through implementation of an extensible application that provides its users with a set of unified services allowing to determine the popularity instances related to social entities, independently of online social media websites.

4.2 RDF-Based Normalization

The major requirement necessary to fulfill for the normalization of popularity metrics to take place can be summed up into two major points:

- Extensibility: deals with the support of popularity metrics as stemming from new online social networks.
- Variety: refers to the variety of popularity metrics' structure (e.g. likes on Facebook and digs on Digg).

Hence, for the above requirements to be maintained, an appeal is made to the Resource Description Framework RDF, as a data representation scheme on the web. The RDF enables the encoding, exchange and reuse of structured metadata [1]. Additionally, it provides a platform for publishing both human-readable and machine-treatable-vocabularies, designed to enhance the reuse and extension of metadata semantics among disparate information communities [18]. To note, an RDF based expression rests on a collection of triples. Each triple designs a subject, object and predicate, and a set of such triples is dubbed an RDF graph. This structure mode is applied for the purpose of modeling the popularity metrics across social networks. An excerpt of the result is illustrated on Fig. 3, with 15 classes being set up to design the subjects, objects and predicates under the headings "has data type" and "subClassOf", to designate the relationship binding the different classes.

```
<?xml version="1.0"?>
<rdf:RDF xmlns="http://www.semanticweb.org/user/ontologies/2018/7/popularity#"
    xml:base="http://www.semanticweb.org/user/ontologies/2018/7/popularity"
    xmlns:rdf="http://www.w3.org/1999/02/22-rdf-syntax-ns#"
    xmlns:owl="http://www.w3.org/2002/07/owl#"
    xmlns:xml="http://www.w3.org/XML/1998/namespace"
    xmlns:xsd="http://www.w3.org/2001/XMLSchema#"
    xmlns:rdfs="http://www.w3.org/2000/01/rdf-schema#">
    <owl:Ontology rdf:about="http://www.semanticweb.org/user/ontologies/2018/7/popularity"/>

    <!-- http://www.semanticweb.org/user/ontologies/2018/7/popularity#has -->

    <owl:ObjectProperty rdf:about="http://www.semanticweb.org/user/ontologies/2018/7/popularity#has">
        <rdfs:domain rdf:resource="http://www.semanticweb.org/user/ontologies/2018/7/popularity#Author_Activities_Metadata"/>
        <rdfs:domain rdf:resource="http://www.semanticweb.org/user/ontologies/2018/7/popularity#Author_Connectivity"/>
        <rdfs:domain rdf:resource="http://www.semanticweb.org/user/ontologies/2018/7/popularity#Author_Profile_Metadata"/>
        <rdfs:domain rdf:resource="http://www.semanticweb.org/user/ontologies/2018/7/popularity#ExplicitFeedBack"/>
        <rdfs:domain rdf:resource="http://www.semanticweb.org/user/ontologies/2018/7/popularity#ImplicitFeedBack"/>
        <rdfs:domain rdf:resource="http://www.semanticweb.org/user/ontologies/2018/7/popularity#MetaData_During_Upload"/>
        <rdfs:domain rdf:resource="http://www.semanticweb.org/user/ontologies/2018/7/popularity#Metadata_After_Upload"/>
        <rdfs:range rdf:resource="http://www.semanticweb.org/user/ontologies/2018/7/popularity#Data_Type"/>
    </owl:ObjectProperty>
```

Fig. 3. Popularity metrics based an excerpt RDF presentation

4.3   Proposed Service Provider Interface

Based on the previous sections cited studies, we aim to implement the proposed normalization of popularity metrics relevant to each social entity, independently of online social media websites.

In this context, we put forward a normalization procedure in the form a Service Provider Interface (SPI). The SPI is considered as a contractual charter binding users, for a unified definition (kind of standardization, or normalization) of the popularity metrics, corresponding to the different social entities (i.e., texts, videos, photos and users), to take place independently of the online social media they belong to. In addition, the SPI allows users to create extensible applications, through determining a set of public interfaces and abstract classes that a service defines.

These interfaces are implemented to allow the creation of extensible applications, as based on the social media entities' popularity. By means of example, one could well cite the prediction and detection of online trending topic that helps define the most trending topic across the online community independently of the social network, the detection of most popular brand sales in online communities and the identification of the most popular users on their corresponding networks. The whole of these applications requires identifying the most popular social items across several social media. Thus, to avoid the heterogeneity of metrics across social networks, the SPI helps provide the end-users with the opportunity to define the popularity metrics of each social entity by simply implementing the abstract provided method. The creation of the contract of the social entities' popularity normalization is achieved through implementation of an SPI composed of two main interfaces: the media popularity interface and the user popularity interface.

- Media popularity interface: helps define the SPI specification of the media popularity service. It includes methods that define the media entity metadata, the media's author metadata and the user feedback metrics, as based on the social entity relevant URL.

- User popularity interface: refers to the user popularity service associated SPI. It provides methods whereby the user' metadata, activities and connectivity, as used to study popularity, could be determined.

Moreover, the proposed normalization solution helps offer a set of service provider classes that display the implementation of services offered by the media and user popularity interfaces. These services offer to store the social entities corresponding URLs and their related popularity information. It is also worth citing that the proposed solution implements a service loader class, as introduced by the class *Popularity ServiceLoader* that follows the Singleton design pattern and works as a template for the relationships and interactions among classes and ensures that only a single class instance is ever created.

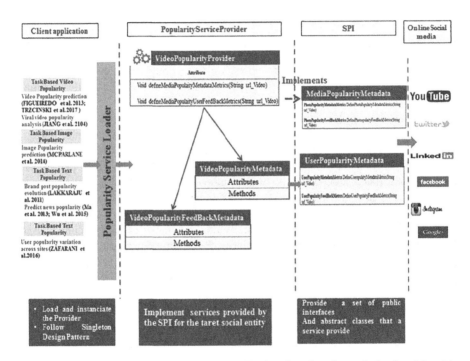

Fig. 4. Integration of the proposed SPI in the applications based on the analysis of social entities popularity [21]

Figure 4 presents an excerpt from the whole implemented model. It focuses on the case of video entity, but it is worth stating that the definition of other media entities popularity (i.e., text and photo) implements a user popularity interface, as already introduced. The SPI consumer extends the popularity interfaces and implements its services to instantiate his/her own popularity according to the application needs and data availability. The architecture of the SPI consumption is described in Fig. 4. The Client application identifies a task related to a specific social entity (e.g. predict video popularity). He identifies the target social media websites from which he could define his/her popularity metrics (e.g. YouTube videos and Facebook videos). The client implements the services relative to the target entity popularity. Hence, the invocation of the specific services (e.g. in video popularity interface) and the instantiation of popularity is based on the metrics extracted from the target social media. The developed SPI is available on GitHub under the link https://github.com/SebeiHiba/SocEntPopularitySPI. The details that do not figure clear in Fig. 4 can be viewed within the previous link figuring code.

5 Popularity Prediction Methods

Following the normalization based RDF, users can tackle one of the various approaches used to measure the social entities relevant popularity. In fact, several popularity-predicting methods are proposed to detect online content, with respect to its impact on wide range of areas, such as economic trends, recommendation systems, brand advertising, etc. In this respect, the popularity predicting methods have been widely evolved, moving from methods that focus just focus on textual contents, such as tweets, to those predicting multi-media online content popularity, such as online videos [16] and images [7, 10], along with those relevant to predicting the user's popularity [27]. Several classifications of prediction methods are also proposed. In this regard, Li et al. [15] propose to categorize these approaches into three major groups: regression-based approaches, classification-based approaches and the model-based ones. In turn, Kong et al. [11] classify these methods into two main categories, specifically, the feature-based discriminative methods and the generative model based ones. Another classification mode is based on the type and granularity of metrics as used for prediction purposes, as proposed mainly by Tatar et al. [23]. It consists in considering methods belonging to a single domain category and methods that belong to a cross-domain category. Table 3 provides a summary of the proposed classification of popularity prediction methods according to the previously cited works.

Table 3. Popularity prediction method categorizations

Reference	Categories	Definition	Methods
[15]	Regression based approach	Defines methods that are based on the exploitation of the historical popularity of the target entity	State/patterns, SVR [10], Multivariate
	Classification-based approach	Considers the popularity prediction process as a classification task	Logistic regression [9], Linguistic classifier, Trend discovery [5], Concept drift-based popularity [15]

(*continued*)

Table 3. (*continued*)

Reference	Categories		Definition	Methods
	Model-based approach		Defines methods that are based on the designs of models (e.g. survival analysis, content propagation, hidden Markov model, etc.)	Modified hidden Markov model (HMM) [10]
[11]	Feature-based discriminative methods		Defines methods that are based on classification and regression algorithms after an identification of popularity related features	Classification and regression algorithms
	Generative model based methods		Designs popularity prediction methods based on the description of generative process of the dynamic popularity evolution	Stochastic models of user behavior [14]
[23]	Single domain category	Before publication	Methods based on the exploitation of the information about the item metadata and the connection of user who published this item. The considered information belong to the website in which the item is published	Support Vector Machine [24], Naive Bayes [26], Decision Trees, Random Forests
		After publication	Defines methods that are based on information about the attention paid to the target item and belongs to one target web site	Log-linear, Linear regression, Multivariate linear regression, logistic regression [9]
	Cross domain category		Defines methods that use information about the target entity across web sites	Linear regression, logistic regression [27]

6 Conclusion and Potential Research Trends

The present work is designed to investigate the popularity metrics as related to classifying and categorizing the online flowing social contents, namely, texts, images, videos and users, across the social network sites. Based on the reached results, the paper ends up with reaching some significantly noticeable conclusions, drawn on the basis of major state of the art schemes. In the first place, the study of social items popularity requires the presence of three main components: the features, measures, and methods. In a second place, popularity metrics turn out to vary across social networks, and even within the same social network, for a specified target type of social items. In a third place, the related works dealing with popularity appear to converge as to the popularity prediction process. In this respect, the present work is intended to tackle the problem of the of popularity metrics variety as predominant across social networks, through advancing a unified presentation of the popularity metrics by relying on the RDF scheme. The proposed presentation is founded after metrics available in the state of the art frameworks, along with those extracted from the social networks APIs. In addition, the paper presents a peculiar SPI likely to serve as a unified contract or charter among the concerned users, whereby the social entities' attached popularity could be overly expressed independently of the other different online social media. Made available to researchers, the SPI scheme is intended to provide a platform of basic services, liable to extension, through which social entities popularity could be well defined.

Noteworthy, also, is that the present research draws on a global view about the methods used for popularity prediction. As a future research line, field specialists could well lay greater focus on injecting the RDF presentation as a layer in the proposed SPI framework for an easier, and rather effective, access and extension of popularity metrics to take place.

References

1. Candan, K.S., Liu, H., Suvarna, R.: Resource description framework: metadata and its applications. ACM SIGKDD Explor. Newsl. **3**(1), 6–19 (2001)
2. Cappallo, S., Mensink, T., Snoek, C.G.M.: Latent factors of visual popularity prediction. In: Hauptmann, A.G., et al. (eds.) ICMR, pp. 195–202. ACM (2015)
3. Chatzopoulou, G., Sheng, C., Faloutsos, M.: A first step towards understanding popularity in YouTube. In: INFOCOM IEEE Conference on Computer Communications Workshops, pp. 1–6. IEEE (2010)
4. Couronné, T., Stoica, A., Beuscart, J.-S.: Online social network popularity evolution: an additive mixture model. In: Memon, N., Alhajj, R. (eds.) ASONAM, pp. 346–350. IEEE Computer Society (2010)
5. Figueiredo, F.: On the prediction of popularity of trends and hits for user generated videos. In: Leonardi, S., Panconesi, A., Ferragina, P., Gionis, A. (eds.) WSDM, pp. 741–746. ACM (2013)

6. Gao, S., Ma, J., Chen, Z.: Popularity prediction in microblogging network. In: Chen, L., Jia, Y., Sellis, T., Liu, G. (eds.) APWeb 2014. LNCS, vol. 8709, pp. 379–390. Springer, Cham (2014). https://doi.org/10.1007/978-3-319-11116-2_33

7. Gelli, F., Uricchio, T., Bertini, M., Bimbo, A.D., Chang, S.-F.: Image popularity prediction in social media using sentiment and context features. In: Zhou, X., et al. (eds.) ACM Multimedia, pp. 907–910. ACM (2015)

8. Hong, L., Dan, O., Davison, B.D.: Predicting popular messages in Twitter. In: Srinivasan, S., Ramamritham, K., Kumar, A., Ravindra, M.P., Bertino, E., Kumar, R. (eds.) WWW (Companion Volume), pp. 57–58. ACM (2011)

9. Jiang, L., Miao, Y., Yang, Y., Lan, Z., Hauptmann, A.G.: Viral video style: a closer look at viral videos on YouTube. In: Proceedings of International Conference on Multimedia Retrieval (ICMR 2014), pp. 193, 8 p. ACM, New York (2014)

10. Khosla, A., Das Sarma, A., Hamid, R.: What makes an image popular? In: Proceedings of the 23rd International Conference on World Wide Web, International World Wide Web Conferences Steering Committee, pp. 867–876 (2014)

11. Kong, Q., Mao, W., Liu, C.: Popularity prediction based on interactions of online contents. In: CCIS, pp. 1–5. IEEE (2016)

12. Kwak, H., Lee, C., Park, H., Moon, S.: What is Twitter, a social network or a news media? In: Proceedings of the 19th International Conference on World Wide Beb (WWW 2010), pp. 591–600. ACM, New York (2010)

13. Lakkaraju, H., Ajmera, J.: Attention prediction on social media brand pages. In: Macdonald, C., et al. (eds.) CIKM, pp. 2157–2160. ACM (2011)

14. Lerman, K., Hogg, T.: Using a model of social dynamics to predict popularity of news. In: Rappa, M., et al. (eds.) WWW, pp. 621–630. ACM (2010)

15. Li, C.-T., Shan, M.-K., Jheng, S.-H., Chou, K.-C.: Exploiting concept drift to predict popularity of social multimedia in microblogs. Inf. Sci. **339**, 310–331 (2016)

16. Li, H., Ma, X., Wang, F., Liu, J., Xu, K.: On popularity prediction of videos shared in online social networks. In: He, Q., Iyengar, A., Nejdl, W., Pei, J., Rastogi, R. (eds.) CIKM, pp. 169–178. ACM (2013)

17. Ma, Z., Sun, A., Cong, G.: On predicting the popularity of newly emerging hashtags in Twitter. JASIST **64**, 1399–1410 (2013)

18. Miller, E.: An introduction to the resource description framework. D-Lib Magaz. **25**, 15–19 (1998)

19. McParlane, P.J., Moshfeghi, Y., Jose, J.M.: "Nobody comes here anymore, it's too crowded"; predicting image popularity on Flickr. In: Kankanhalli, M.S., Rueger, S., Manmatha, R., Jose, J.M., van Rijsbergen, K. (eds.) ICMR, p. 385. ACM (2014)

20. Quan, H., Milicic, A., Vucetic, S., Wu, J.: A connectivity-based popularity prediction approach for social networks. In: ICC, pp. 2098–2102. IEEE (2012)

21. Sebei, H., Hadj Taieb, M.A., Ben Aouicha, M.: Popularity metrics' normalization for social media entities. In: Hammoudi, S., Smialek, M., Camp, O., Filipe, J. (eds.) ICEIS, vol. 1, pp. 525–535. SciTePress (2018)

22. Szabó, G., Huberman, B.A.: Predicting the popularity of online content. Commun. ACM **53**, 80–88 (2010)

23. Tatar, A.-F., de Amorim, M.D., Fdida, S., Antoniadis, P.: A survey on predicting the popularity of web content. J. Internet Serv. Appl. **5**, 8:1–8:20 (2014)

24. Trzcinski, T., Rokita, P.: Predicting popularity of online videos using support vector regression. IEEE Trans. Multimed. **19**, 2561–2570 (2017)

25. Wu, B., Shen, H.: Analyzing and predicting news popularity on Twitter. Int. J. Inf. Manage. **35**, 702–711 (2015)
26. Yu, B., Chen, M., Kwok, L.: Toward predicting popularity of social marketing messages. In: Salerno, J., Yang, S.J., Nau, D., Chai, S.-K. (eds.) SBP 2011. LNCS, vol. 6589, pp. 317–324. Springer, Heidelberg (2011). https://doi.org/10.1007/978-3-642-19656-0_44
27. Zafarani, R., Liu, H.: Users joining multiple sites: friendship and popularity variations across sites. Inf. Fus. **28**, 83–89 (2016)

Supporting Gamified Experiences for Informal Collaborative Groups

Samuel Timbó, Juliana de Melo Bezerra[✉],
and Celso Massaki Hirata

ITA, São José dos Campos, Brazil
samuelmtimbo@gmail.com, {juliana,hirata}@ita.br

Abstract. Gamification is the application of game-design elements and game principles in non-game contexts. Gamification is being successfully applied in a diverse set of areas such as Education, Business, Human Resources, Health, and Entertainment. In general, gamified systems are designed and implemented for specific contexts. There is not a multipurpose approach that can be applied to many contexts. Informal groups are composed of members who come together online to perform work or social activities, fostering engagement, commitment and participation. We propose a framework to support the design of gamified experiences in general scenarios for collaborative informal groups. We built a context agnostic tool, called *Gamefy*, to evaluate the framework. We then evaluated motivation and flexibility enabled by the tool. We also employed the framework to assess the perceived usefulness of gamification features in two particular contexts. We then were able to identify key features to gamified experiences, and the possibility of differences in features' importance depending on context.

Keywords: Gamification · Collaboration · Framework · Technology · Gamified experience

1 Introduction

There is a need for motivational tools for many challenges found in society. Gamification is the application of game-design elements and game principles in non-game contexts. It uses games' elements to produce engagement and increase productivity in contexts where human motivation plays an important role. The technique is based on the motivational incentives to tasks that are aligned with the group's goal. It aims to encourage people to overcome obstacles towards the desired behavior [9, 12].

Gamification has proved its efficacy throughout several cases and studies. Gamification is being applied in a diverse set of areas such as Education, Business, Human Resources, Health, and Entertainment. The increasing use of gamification can be associated with both the success of games in engagement and the technology advancements, especially those connected to the software development. The advent of better development and design tools enables the creation of gamified platforms that seek to increase engagement by leveraging the social interaction between their users.

© Springer Nature Switzerland AG 2019
S. Hammoudi et al. (Eds.): ICEIS 2018, LNBIP 363, pp. 42–57, 2019.
https://doi.org/10.1007/978-3-030-26169-6_3

In the design, rewards are used for players who accomplish desired tasks (or challenges) and competition is applied to engage players. Types of rewards include points, achievement badges or levels, the filling of a progress bar, or providing the user with virtual currency. Making the rewards for accomplishing tasks visible to other players or providing leader boards are ways of encouraging players to compete. In general, gamified systems are designed and implemented for specific scenarios; they are not flexible enough to support general scenarios.

Informal groups are composed of members who come together online to perform work or social activities, fostering engagement, commitment and participation [7, 10, 23]. Informal groups are self-organized, in a way that they require no external coordination to fluidly engage in the gamified experience. In such groups, users are responsible for deciding what is important for the group, following their own rules. For instance, users have the power to define a set of activities to be accomplished by the group, either in an individual or in a collective level. These groups are usually built on top of the trust relationship between their members; so they are expected to be small. We consider that the members of the informal groups interact in a collaborative way.

Motivated by the nonexistence of a simple and multipurpose approach that can be applied to many contexts; we propose a framework to support the design of gamified experiences in general scenarios for collaborative informal groups. The framework has seven main guidelines to aid the definition and development of gamified experiences. The framework indicates directives about how to setup the group; how to promote creation, rating and achievement of challenges; how to provide visibility of the gamified experience and to stimulate it; and how to monitor users' experience aiming to keep it operational and successful.

In order to evaluate the framework, we build a context agnostic tool, called *Gamefy*, and experiment it. The tool provides a set of features, driven from the framework, for creating gamified experiences in diverse environments. It is based on a simplified process and an easy to use platform that makes available a set of predefined game elements, giving the users the ability to create their own gamified experiences from scratch. We apply the framework, together with Technology Acceptance Model (TAM) [8], to evaluate perceived usefulness of gamification features in two particular contexts. The objective is to be able to identify functionalities and their relative importance in a way to develop a more customized system later.

The paper is organized as follows. Section 2 presents the background of our work. Section 3 describes the proposed framework to support the design of gamified experiences. Section 4 details the tool, whose implementation is driven from the proposed framework. Section 5 presents the use of the framework to identify features to a gamified experience considering perceived usefulness of participants. Finally, conclusions and future work are presented in Sect. 6.

2 Background

There has still been a lot of debate on the exact definition of gamification [9]. As indicated above, here, we consider gamification as the use of game elements and game design techniques in non-game contexts. Successful applications of gamification can be attributed to the careful choice of game elements and game design techniques, taking into consideration the peculiarities of each context. Game elements are the set of tangible artifacts usually found inside games. They represent the toolbox one has to work with in order to build a gamified experience. Between the most common game elements, we can list score, badges, rewards, resources, powers, items, leaderboard, quests, levels, progression, and avatars.

Game design techniques comprise heuristics and principles that a game designer has accumulated through experience that are used to address design problems found in the development of a game. This knowledge is deeply related to a broad range of areas such as Engineering, Design, and Psychology. The game design techniques can also be seen as general guidelines on how game elements should be used to produce a desired behavior inside the game. Some game design techniques are balance, competition, community, challenge, chance, choices, feedback, fun, learning, and fairness. By non-game contexts, we mean real-life scenarios that are not intrinsically related to games such as Business, Education, Health, and Entertainment. Gamification is related to non-game contexts as the users who engage on a gamified system are not doing so by the sole purpose of having fun, but rather to contribute with a goal they have in that given context such as learning, social impact, personal improvement, and sales increasing [5, 16, 18].

Gamification has been used in distinct contexts. In the context of organizations, applications of gamification are outlined in [3, 6, 14] and [22]. For instance, Aziz and Mushtaq [3] use gamification to enhance productivity and motivation of employees, and to promote engagement in new initiatives of the company. Gamification has been applied in the context of smart environments [15, 16, 20, 24]. For example, Syah [24] focus on making employees contribute to energy saving using mobile applications; while Kazhamiakin et al. [15] aim to facilitate and foster positive voluntary attitudes of citizens.

In the education context, gamification is in general used to provide fun and challenging atmosphere to students [4, 13, 15, 19, 21]. In the area of Health, gamification is used to make rehabilitation or reeducation process more effective and motivating for patients [1, 2, 26]. For example, Alimanova et al. [2] focus on hand rehabilitation, while Adaji and Vassileva [1] treat obesity. Most applications of gamification are commonly systems specialized in a given goal or area. Therefore, those systems are hardly replicable in other areas. Kazhamiakin et al. [15] deal with the possibility of replication by proposing a way to design gamification in smart cities. García et al. [11] provides a solution for applying gamification but it is specific to Software Engineering development. There is a lack of a multipurpose framework for aiding the design of gamified experiences in distinct contexts.

In a previous work [25], we proposed a system for gamified experiences in multipurpose contexts. We extend this work by structuring a framework. The framework is composed of seven guidelines. For each guideline, we add directives to make it more objective and detail how it can be accomplished. We also discuss how to use the framework to identify key features in gamified experiences for given contexts using perceived usefulness. In the next section, we present our proposal.

3   A Framework to Support the Design of Gamified Experiences

We structure a framework with seven guidelines. We structure the guidelines in three main groups, according to Fig. 1: initialization, core and supporting. The initialization is mainly regarding the creation of the gamified experience. The core guidelines include the creation, rating and achievement of challenges, which are the essence of a gamified experience. The supporting guidelines include visibility and stimulation of the experience, as well as the monitoring the experience evolution. Below we detail each guideline by providing directives about how it can be accomplished.

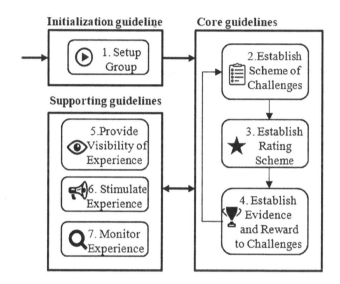

Fig. 1. Framework guidelines.

3.1   Guideline G1: Setup the Group

Any individual can create a gamified experience by describing its name and its purpose according to its context. For instance, the group can be called "Fit in" with the objective of collaboratively help each other to have a healthier life. The way the group is defined should be an agreement among its users. The group creator assumes the administrator role, having as main responsibility the maintenance of a flourishing experience. The group creator then invites individuals to participate of the group. Individuals who accept the invitation become group's members. Any member can at any time invite new members to the group.

In case of informal collaborative teams, it is expected that all members have the same permissions to participate in the gamified experience, since the essence is aligned to allow all users to contribute in the same way. An additional feature can be considered to large teams with the need to have two kinds of roles: general members and administrator members. General members only participate in the gamified experience.

Administrator members also have the responsibility to configure the experience, for instance by performing activities as inviting members, creating and rating challenges. The best configuration for each group depends on the group's setup. In case of "Fit In" group, it can be defined as a completely collaborative group, where every user has the full access to content creation, being able to create challenges, rating and assigning trophies on free will.

3.2 Guideline G2: Establish the Scheme of Challenges

A challenge is a task that if accomplished helps the group to fulfill the group goal. Challenges are the core game element of the system mechanics. They represent tasks designed to help the user to do his/her part on the group's goal. The goal of a challenge creation is to define it in a way it motivates the users (or a set of target users) to perform the underlying task. An example of challenge in the "Fit in" group could be "No chocolate: Resisting chocolate for two months".

An important directive to define a challenge is that it should not be a regular and trivial activity of the group. It should be an activity that addresses strategy and motivation, enabling members to contribute to the group goal. In an informal collaborative group, it is recommended that any member can create a challenge. One member can perform a given challenge only once; in order to keep the motivating factor associated to the challenge. Challenge should be opened to all members, so anyone is able to take it.

In the challenge creation, the number of times that the challenge can be performed by distinct members can be defined, in a way to stimulate members to take the challenge promptly. There can be two types of challenges: challenges to be performed individually, and challenges to be performed in team. The idea of a team challenge is to stimulate collaboration and team support when developing tasks. In case of team challenge, mechanisms should be created to support the invitation of members to compound a specific team. Different types of requirements can be set to complete a team challenge, for instance it could suffice that only one member of the team completes the challenge. Another type is that all members in team must complete the challenge so that the challenge is considered achieved.

3.3 Guideline G3: Establish the Rating Scheme

Rating represents the action of giving an evaluation to a challenge. It is a way to indicate the importance of the challenge. Rating should be a compromise between the perceived difficulty of a challenge and its importance for the group goal. Members can be moved to take challenges with high rates in a way to contribute more to the group and to conquer more relevant challenges. So rating is also associated to members' motivation.

Different schemes can be established to rate challenges in informal collaborative groups, but they need to be an agreement between the members. Experience can only ask the challenge creator to indicate a rating value. The experience can allow any member to contribute with a rating value to existent challenges. Experience can also require a rating value to members who desire to perform a given challenge. Finally, the experience should provide a final rating value associated with the challenge. The final rating can be, for instance, the mean of received ratings or the maximum among them.

3.4   Guideline G4: Establish Evidence and Reward to Challenges

Members can freely choose challenges to perform. Members can provide evidences about the accomplishment of a given challenge, for instance a photo or a document that exemplifies the achievement. The main idea is to promote involvement of members, making the gamified experience more social and involving to the group. Other important aspect of evidence is to allow members to remember and revive his/her experience.

A member that reaches a challenge collects a trophy associated to that challenge. Trophies are the representation of achievement inside the system's gamified experience. They are tokens intended to be collected by the group's players. Once a user performs the task proposed on a challenge, he is able to "win" the respective trophy, adding the correspondent rating value to his/her own total score.

Therefore, the administrator members have to define how to provide evidence of challenges completed and how to reward them.

3.5   Guideline G5: Provide Visibility of the Gamified Experience

Any member should be informed about news and changes in the experience. For instance, when a challenge is created, or when a challenge reaches the maximum rate. Therefore, the member knows that there is room to contribute. A general concern about notifications is the possible overloads of messages to members, which in turn can negatively affect their motivation. A way to deal with this problem is to allow members to configure notifications that they desire to receive. A communication channel can be established for a specific purpose, for example, to support members to debate regarding a specific challenge. Groups use communication technologies generally available in social media. The idea is to integrate the gamified experience with existent social media.

Any member should be able to check his/her achievements, by accessing the list of conquered challenges and associated trophies. A member can also visualize achievements of other members, aiming to verify others' performance and compare with his/her own. Additional features can be created to provide access to results of teams, in case of existence of team challenges. To have a leaderboard is other interesting directive. Leaderboard is basically an area that presents members' scores in an ordered list, aiming to provide recognition of engaged member and to create an environment of competition inside the group.

3.6   Guideline G6: Stimulate the Gamified Experience

In order to promote the gamified experience, it is important to stimulate members to participate and contribute. The goal is to provide awareness of the gamified experience. A directive is to have an invitation mechanism for taking actions, for instance to a member invite other to propose a challenge, or to take an existent challenge. A feature can use statistical information about the gamified experience to inform members where they can contribute, for instance challenges that members can take, challenges still without any accomplishments, or challenges without rating values. Additional scores can be attributed to members that perform such specific actions. Experience can also allow creating challenges related to the promotion of the gamified experience itself. Examples of these challenges are "Create two challenges" or "Promote a face-to-face meeting of the group". One possible concern with the strategies chosen to stimulate the gamified experience is not to disrupt the group's main objective by focusing solely on fun of the games.

3.7 Guideline G7: Monitor the Gamified Experience

Monitoring the gamified experience is especially important to group creator and other members concerned about the evolution of the gamified experience. A directive is to have a timeline to show actions of each member, including for instance the created and conquered challenges. Other directive is a dashboard with metrics and indicators about the usage of the gamified experience, for example the quantity of created challenges, and the quantity of members participating recently. Therefore, it can be possible to keep up with the members' behavior and later identify actions to improve the gamified experience.

4 Developing a Tool to Gamified Experience in Distinct Contexts

We developed a web application named *Gamefy* to provide the infrastructure for users to create collaborative gamified experiences. The focus is on initialization and core guidelines of the proposed framework. The following features were implemented: create a group; edit a group; leave a group; add members; change members' privileges; remove members; add a challenge; view a challenge; edit a challenge; rate a challenge; remove a challenge; add a trophy (win a challenge); remove a trophy; check challenges tab; check trophies tab; and check leaderboard tab.

Figure 2 shows the main interface of the tool. On the left, there is the list of groups to which the user belongs. There are three tabs: challenges, trophies and leaderboard. The challenge tab is in evidence with the challenges of group "Top Coders", whose goal is to enhance programming abilities. Each challenge has a name, an icon and a number (points to conquer if the user "wins" the challenge). Figure 3 shows a specific challenge called "Give it a chance!", whose purpose is to "Learn the basics of PHP".

Fig. 2. Challenges tab of the tool [25].

The stars represent the assessment of the challenge by the user. If the user accomplishes such challenge, he clicks on "Win" and receives a trophy associated to it. All trophies are accessed in the respective task. The points associated to the challenge are added in the user score, which can be accessed in the leaderboard tab in Fig. 2.

Fig. 3. Visualization of a challenge in the tool [25].

We design an experiment to assess two main aspects of the tool: motivation and flexibility. By motivation, we mean the tool features are seen as motivating aspects. By flexibility, we mean the possibility to use the tool in different contexts. In the experiment, we had fourteen voluntary participants, who were undergraduate students in an engineering program. Participants had to perform a set of tasks and later to respond an evaluation. Participants should perform core tasks in the system: create a new group based on a chosen context and goal; add challenges; rate challenges they created based on their difficulty; and be rewarded of challenges completed. During the operation of the gamified experience, members win (add it to their trophies) one of the available challenges; check up their trophies; and check up the leaderboard.

Later, participants evaluated sentences with respect to motivation and flexibility enabled by the tool features, using a five-point Likert scale (from 1 - strongly disagree, 2 - disagree, 3 - neutral, 4 - agree, and 5 - strongly agree). The sentences are: motivation to create new groups (M1), motivation to add new challenges (M2), motivation to rate the challenges (M3), motivation to see trophies (M4), motivation to see the leaderboard (M5), motivation to have in the experience challenges created of other members (M6), and motivation to check trophies acquired by other members (M7). The participants also evaluated these aspects related to tool flexibility: the tool ability to cope with the given group (Fx1), the tool ability to increase engagement of members with group goal (Fx2), and the possibility of application of the tool to other groups (Fx3). Results are shown in Fig. 4.

Regarding motivation, we observed that the main stimulating features for the contexts used in the experiment were trophies (M4) and leaderboard (M5). It was interesting to confirm that in gamified experiences, users are stimulated by conquering challenges and the associated points. Such achievements are important for personal

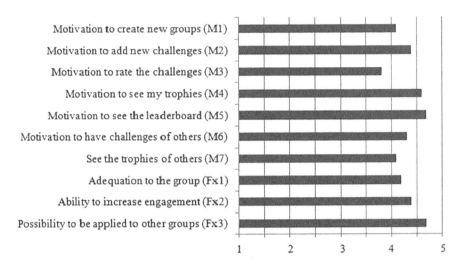

Motivation to create new groups (M1)
Motivation to add new challenges (M2)
Motivation to rate the challenges (M3)
Motivation to see my trophies (M4)
Motivation to see the leaderboard (M5)
Motivation to have challenges of others (M6)
See the trophies of others (M7)
Adequation to the group (Fx1)
Ability to increase engagement (Fx2)
Possibility to be applied to other groups (Fx3)

Fig. 4. Tool evaluation.

pleasure (by acquiring trophies) or for comparison with other users (by checking status in leaderboard). Other well-evaluated aspects are the possibility to create challenges (M2) and to accept challenges created by others (M6). It in turn indicates the essential aspect of the gamification in informal groups, where users are up to develop content in a self-organizing structure. The creation of groups (M1) was well evaluated, but it is important to mention that it is a single step moved by the need in a given context. A not so well evaluated aspect was to see trophies of others (M7), which is interesting because users are interested in their ranking but not in the others' achievements in detail. The lowest evaluation was assigned to rating challenges (M3), maybe because, in the current tool, all users were obliged to evaluate challenges that intend to conquer. In term of flexibility, the tool was considered flexible in supporting distinct contexts in the experiment, since it was adequate to groups (Fx1) and it has a potential in increasing engagement (Fx2). Moreover, participants acknowledge that it can be employed to other groups (Fx3).

5   Identifying Key Features to Gamified Experiences in Specific Contexts

The Technology Acceptance Model (TAM) [8] is a theoretical model of the effect of system characteristics on user acceptance of computer-based information systems. According to TAM, the user's attitude towards using a system is a major determinant of whether he/she actually uses it. In turn, the attitude towards using a system depends on both 'perceived usefulness' and 'perceived ease of use'. 'Perceived usefulness' is defined as "the degree to which an individual believes that using a particular system would enhance his/her job performance". 'Perceived ease of use' refers to "the degree to which a person believes that using a particular system would be free from effort" [8].

One application of such model is to enable system designers to evaluate proposed new systems before their implementation [17].

We focus on 'perceived usefulness' to identify important features of a given gamified experience. We worked with two contexts in parallel. The first context considers a group of engineering students with a learning goal. The second context considers a group of female undergrad students that work in the 'Women in STEM2D' program, whose goal is to attract and develop women in STEM2D (Science, Technology, Engineering, Mathematics, Manufacturing, and Design) areas. The creation of a gamified experience in the educational group intends to promote learning and involvement. The STEM2D context can benefit from the gamified experience by stimulating participants to take more effective and extended actions to meet group goal. Here we call the first context as "Education", and the second context as "STEM2D".

We developed a questionnaire to assess the perceived usefulness of features related to a gamified experience in both contexts. Features were driven from guidelines of the proposed framework. Table 1 presents features and their relation with guidelines. For evaluating features, participants use the following scale: 'very important', 'important', 'less important' and 'not important'. In the beginning of the questionnaire, participants should inform their previous knowledge about gamification (using the scale: 'none', 'poor', 'good', 'very good' and 'excellent'). A brief introduction about gamification was provided for participants, presenting definition, advantages and examples. At the end, participants should also inform if they believe it is interesting to create the gamified experience in that context (using the scale: 'strongly agree', 'agree', 'disagree' and 'strongly disagree').

There were five respondents in the Education context, and eight respondents in STEM2D context. In the Education context, four participants declared to have 'none' previous knowledge about gamification, followed by one participants with 'good' knowledge. In the STEM2D context, seven had 'none' and one has 'good' knowledge about gamification. In Education context, two participants strongly agree and four participants agree to apply gamification in their contexts. In STEM2D context, five participants strongly agree, two participants agree, and one disagrees that gamification can be applied in their contexts.

Table 1. Features driven from framework guidelines.

Guideline Id	Feature Id	Feature description
G1	F1	Any member can invite new members to the group
G2	F2	Any member can create a challenge
G2	F3	Any member can perform any challenge
G2	F4	There can be defined the number of times a challenge can be performed by distinct members
G2	F5	A challenge can also be performed in teams
G3	F6	A challenge should have an associated rating value to indicate its importance

(continued)

Table 1. (*continued*)

Guideline Id	Feature Id	Feature description
G3	F7	The challenge creator should indicate a rating value
G3	F8	A member can rate any challenge
G3	F9	A member, who performs a challenge, should assign a rating value to it
G4	F10	Members can freely choose challenges to perform
G4	F11	Members can provide evidences about the accomplishment of a given challenge
G4	F12	A member, who reaches a challenge, collects a trophy associated to that challenge
G4	F13	A member, who reaches a challenge, adds its rating value to his/her own total score
G5	F14	It must have mechanisms to provide visibility of the gamified experience
G5	F15	Any member should be informed about news and changes in the gamified experience
G5	F16	Any member should be able to check his/her achievements, by accessing the list of conquered challenges and associated trophies
G5	F17	A member can visualize achievements of other members
G5	F18	A member can visualize achievements of teams
G5	F19	It must have a communication channel. E.g. for discussing about a given challenge
G5	F20	It must have a leaderboard with a list of members and scores
G6	F21	It must have mechanisms to stimulate the gamified experience. E.g. to make members contribute more
G6	F22	It must have a mechanism for inviting members to take actions
G6	F23	It must have a mechanism for informing members of possible actions
G6	F24	It must be allowed to create challenges to promote the gamified experience itself
G7	F25	It must have mechanisms to monitor the gamified experience. E.g. to see its usage in time
G7	F26	It must have a timeline to show actions of a member during the time
G7	F27	It must have a dashboard with metrics and indicators about the usage of the gamified experience

Figure 5 presents the evaluation of gamification features regarding their usefulness in the Education context. Interesting results can be observed regarding the importance of features related to each framework guideline. Regarding guideline G1 (Setup the Group), the possibility of members invite others was not well evaluated, probably because the fix and pre-defined number of students in the course. Considering guideline G2 (Establish the Scheme of Challenges), more important features were considered to allow members to perform any challenge and to have team challenges.

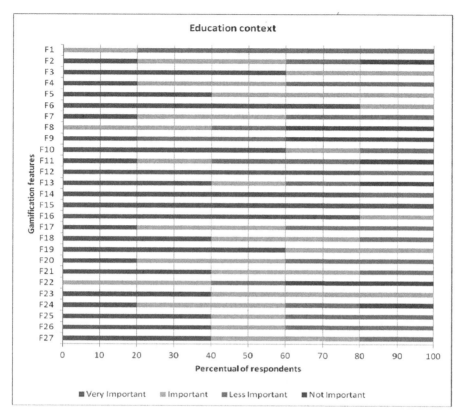

Fig. 5. Perceived usefulness of gamification features in the Education context.

Towards guideline G3 (Establish the Rating Scheme), respondents agree with the relevance of rating challenges, and indicate a preference for the challenge creator to rate the challenge. With respect to guideline G4 (Establish Evidence and Reward to Challenges), it was considered important the collection of trophies and their related scores. Concerning to guideline G5 (Provide Visibility of the Gamified Experience), respondents indicate the relevance of having members informed about the gamified experience, providing visibility of members' achievements and establishing a communication channel. In relation to guideline 6 (Stimulate the Gamified Experience), to inform members about possible actions was better evaluated that to have a mechanism for inviting members to take actions. Towards guideline 7 (Monitor the Gamified Experience), a dashboard can be more effective than timelines with members' actions.

Figure 6 presents the evaluation of gamification features regarding their usefulness in the STEM2D context. Regarding guideline G1 (Setup the Group), the invitation of new members by others was indicated as relevant. Considering guideline G2 (Establish the Scheme of Challenges), the freedom to perform any challenge was even more important than the freedom to create challenges. The existence of team challenges was also well evaluated. Towards guideline G3 (Establish the Rating Scheme), results had the same trend as in the Education context, by showing that rating is important and better defined by challenge creator. With respect to guideline G4 (Establish Evidence and Reward to Challenges), evidences of conquered challenges were considered critical, followed by challenges scores and later by trophies. It is interesting to note that evidences were not a key feature in the Education context. Concerning to guideline G5 (Provide Visibility of the Gamified Experience), to check teams' achievements was more desirable than individuals' achievements. It is also indicates the relevance of a communication channel and a leaderboard. In relation to guideline G6 (Stimulate the Gamified Experience), results were again similar to Education context regarding the preference for informing possible actions instead of having invitations by others. Towards guideline 7 (Monitor the Gamified Experience), timeline and dashboard were considered good mechanisms to monitor the gamified experience.

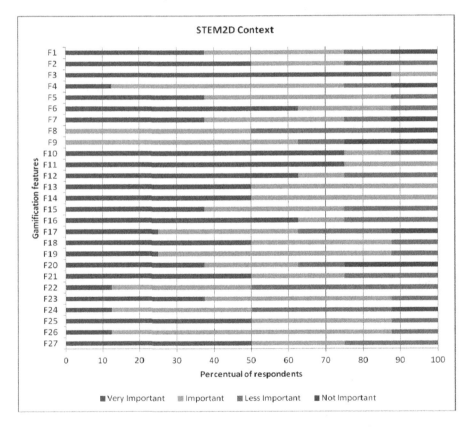

Fig. 6. Perceived usefulness of gamification features in the STEM2D context.

In Fig. 7, we compare the percentages of respondents that considered each gamification feature as 'very important' and 'important'. Some features were considered critical for both contexts, with at least 80% of approval by respondents, for instance F3

(Any member can perform any challenge), F5 (A challenge can also be performed in teams), F6 (A challenge should have an associated rating value to indicate its importance), F10 (Members can freely choose challenges to perform), F14 (It must have mechanisms to provide visibility of the gamified experience), F18 (A member can visualize achievements of teams), F19 (It must have a communication channel), and F23 (It must have a mechanism for informing members possible actions). Other features had similar importance in both contexts, for example F17 (A member can visualize achievements of other members). Other features had a distinct degree of importance depending on the context, for instance F11 (Members can provide evidences about the accomplishment of a given challenge) and F25 (It must have mechanisms to monitor the gamified experience) were more important to STEM2D context.

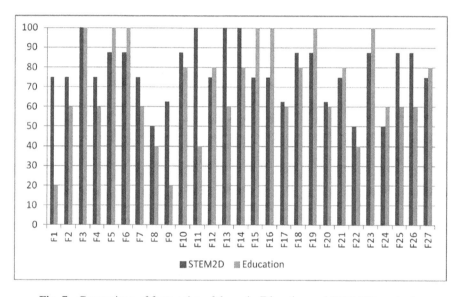

Fig. 7. Comparison of features' usefulness in Education and STEM2D contexts.

6 Conclusions

Gamification aims to increase group productivity in a given context based on the games' effectiveness to produce engagement. We propose a framework that provides guidelines for creating gamified experiences in distinct contexts for informal collaborative groups. We created the *Gamefy* tool that is context agnostic, but focusing on the initialization and core guidelines of the proposed framework. It has predefined game elements that enable groups to define their own gamified experiences. Therefore, gamification becomes an easier technique to apply because the tool can be used straight on. We conducted an experiment that confirmed positive aspects of the tool regarding its motivating potential and its flexibility to cope with distinct contexts. The tool can be improved and expanded in many ways. The addition of new game elements available for the creation of groups is likely to represent an effective approach to increase the system's overall usage. There is also the potential to implement features related to supporting guidelines, in a way to stimulate the experience even more.

Through the framework guidelines, we identified features that can be implemented in gamified experiences. We evaluated the importance of such features in two contexts, considering their perceived usefulness by participants. We observed that there are critical features for both contexts, such as the freedom to create challenges and choose those to reach, the need to inform challenges' importance using rating values, and the existence of challenges to be performed in groups. Other important features were related to both visibility and stimulation of the experience. In the experiment, we also noted a preference of some features in detriment of others depending on the context. For example, the need of evidences for completed challenges and the existence of mechanisms to monitor the gamified experience. The evaluation aids the identification of features for a context and then supports the development of a dedicated gamified experience. Results can also be used to improve the *Gamefy* tool in a way to provide key features and a configuration mechanism to allow groups customize their gamified experience according to their preferences. We argue that the framework makes it easy to adopt gamification as an accessible technique in a broad range of scenarios.

Acknowledgements. A special thanks to Johnson&Johnson company for funding the "Women in STEM2D" program. The work of the third author was supported by the CNPq (*Conselho Nacional de Desenvolvimento Científico e Tecnológico*) under grant number Universal 01/2016 403921/2016-3.

References

1. Adaji, I., Vassileva, J.: A gamified system for influencing healthy e-commerce shopping habits. In: Proceedings of the Conference on User Modeling, Adaptation and Personalization - UMAP (2017)
2. Alimanova, M., et al.: Gamification of hand rehabilitation process using virtual reality tools. In: Proceedings of the IEEE International Conference on Robotic Computing (2017)
3. Aziz, A., Mushtaq, A.: Usage of gamification in enterprise: a review. In: Proceedings of the International Conference on Communication, Computing and Digital Systems - C-CODE (2017)
4. Azmi, S., et al.: Attracting students' engagement in programming courses with gamification. In: Proceedings of the IEEE Conference on e-Learning, e-Management and e-Services - IC3e (2016)
5. Cechetti, N.P., et al.: Gamification strategies for mobile device applications: a systematic review. In: Proceedings of the Iberian Conference on Information Systems and Technologies - CISTI (2017)
6. Chow, S., Chapman, D.: Gamifying the employee recruitment process. In: Proceedings of the International Conference on Gameful Design, Research, and Applications (2013)
7. Counts, S.: Group-based mobile messaging in support of the social side of leisure. In: Proceedings of the Computer Supported Cooperative Work - CSCW, vol. 16, no. 1, pp. 75–97 (2007)

8. Davis, F.D.: A technology acceptance model for empirically testing new end-user information systems: theory and results. Ph.D. Thesis. Massachusetts Institute of Technology (1985)
9. Deterding, S., Dixon, D., Khaled, R., Nacke, L.E.: From game design elements to gamefulness: defining gamification. In: Proceedings of the MindTrek 2011, pp. 9–15. ACM Press (2011)
10. Ferreira, L.M., Bezerra, J.M., Hirata, C.M.: An approach to collaborative management of informal projects. In: Proceedings of the International Conference on Enterprise Information Systems - ICEIS (2017)
11. García, F., Pedreira, O., Piattini, M., Cerdeira-Pena, A., Penabad, M.: A framework for gamification in software engineering. J. Syst. Softw. **132**, 21–40 (2017)
12. Hanraths, O., et al.: Questlab: a web-framework for gamification of seminars. In: Proceedings of the Hawaii International Conference on System Sciences (2016)
13. Heryadi, Y., Muliamin, K.: Gamification of M-learning Mandarin as second language. In: Proceedings of the International Conference on Game, Game Art, and Gamification - ICGGAG (2016)
14. Herzig, P., Ameling, M., Schill, A.: A generic platform for enterprise gamification. In: Proceedings of the 2012 Joint Working Conference on Software Architecture & 6th European Conference on Software Architecture (2012)
15. Kazhamiakin, R., et al.: A gamification framework for the long-term engagement of smart citizens. In: Proceedings of the IEEE International Smart Cities Conference - ISC2 (2016)
16. Liu, Y., et al.: Gamifying intelligent environments. In: Proceedings of the International ACM Workshop on Ubiquitous Meta User Interfaces - Ubi-MUI (2011)
17. Madson, D.S.: Framework for evaluating user acceptance of individual system functionalities: a case study on the editor role for the PUMA glossary. M.Sc. thesis. University of Tampere (2017)
18. Marczewski, A.: Even Ninja Monkeys Like to Play: Gamification, Game Thinking and Motivational Design. Gamified UK (2015)
19. Morey, J., et al.: Gamifying foundational STEM skills. In: Proceedings of the Asia-Pacific World Congress on Computer Science and Engineering (2016)
20. Papaioannou, T.G., et al.: IoT-enabled gamification for energy conservation in public buildings. In: Proceedings of the Global Internet of Things Summit - GIoTS (2017)
21. Schäfer, U.: Training scrum with gamification. In: Proceedings of the IEEE Global Engineering Education Conference (2017)
22. Schuldt, J., Friedemann, S.: The challenges of gamification in the age of Industry 4.0. In: Proceedings of the Global Engineering Education Conference - EDUCON (2017)
23. Schuler, R.P., et al.: The doing of doing stuff: understanding the coordination of social group-activities. In: Proceedings of the ACM Conference on Human Factors in Computing Systems. ACM (2014)
24. Syah, R.A.: IoT/Smart building as employee gamification engine for measurable ROI. In: Proceedings of the International Electronics Symposium - IES (2016)
25. Timbo, S.M., Bezerra, J.M., Hirata, C.M.: A multipurpose system for gamified experiences. In: Proceedings of the International Conference on Enterprise Information Systems - ICEIS (2018)
26. Wen, M.H.: Applying gamification and social network techniques to promote health activities. In: Proceedings of the International Conference on Applied System Innovation - ICASI (2017)

Payment Authorization in Smart Environments: Security-Convenience Balance

Adam Wójtowicz[(✉)] and Jacek Chmielewski

Department of Information Technology,
Poznań University of Economics and Business,
al. Niepodległości 10, 61-875 Poznań, Poland
{awojtow,chmielewski}@kti.ue.poznan.pl
http://www.kti.ue.poznan.pl/en/adam_wojtowicz.html
http://www.kti.ue.poznan.pl/en/jacek_chmielewski.html

Abstract. One of the major roadblocks to mass adoption of smart environments and IoT services (and IoE in future) is the lack of ubiquitous solutions for passive and at the same time secure payment authorization at physical locations where services are provided. The main research goal of this work is to comprehensively evaluate such system proposed by the authors. When customers approach a point of sale it identifies them using face biometrics. After the order is completed, the system takes advantage of multimodal context-aware payment authorization to make a multi-criteria selection of the authorization method, optimally to make the whole process fully passive. All this enables a controlled balance between payment security and convenience for the client and for the seller. Empirical tests at an existing point of sale have been performed, the usage data have been collected, statistically analyzed and confronted with formulated research hypotheses.

Keywords: Context-aware authorization · Payment authorization · Passive identification · Multimodal authorization · Face recognition

1 Introduction

Online payment solutions used by e-commerce and m-commerce systems influence also traditional brick-and-mortar stores. A number of physical stores use online payment solutions similar to the ones used on the Internet. Their online nature increases security of a physical checkout process, but does little to increase convenience of the process. A customer still has to put down her merchandise, find a credit card or a smartphone, swipe it or hand it over to the cashier, and finally confirm the purchase, for example with a pin code. The sequence of actions is similar to paying with cash or even longer. We claim that with a proper system within smart environment, it is possible to do it in a way that is more convenient and as secure as necessary in a given context. Usually, security

S. Hammoudi et al. (Eds.): ICEIS 2018, LNBIP 363, pp. 58–81, 2019.
https://doi.org/10.1007/978-3-030-26169-6_4

and convenience are presented as opposite extremes of the same scale, but our research aims to enhance both security and convenience of the payment process, at the same time.

The non-cash, online-enabled, physical payment process needs to check whether the customer is capable of settling the bill. To this end, it requires a dependable customer identification solution and a trusted source of billing information. The first point is currently covered by a smart card (in plastic or digital form) and the second point is covered by a trusted hardware terminal connecting securely to a trusted third-party (e.g. a bank). It is possible to make the whole physical payment process much more convenient by exploiting the fact of physical presence of a customer, which is neglected or not fully exploited by existing payment solutions. Taking it into account, it is possible to base the customer identification not on what the customer has or knows, but on who the customer is, making the identification passive and relieving the customer. We focus especially on routine, recurring transactions that constitute patterns of payments for transaction history of almost all users of smart environment.

In the presented approach the customer service process is changed, from a traditional sequence: order (O_1) followed by a payment (P_1), into a sequence: passive identification (I_2), order (O_2), payment authorization (P_2) (cf. Fig. 1). It is assumed that during I_2 face-based passive customer identification takes place, and during P_2 multiple devices (mobile or stationary, client's or seller's) can be used contextually to simplify the payment authorization process as much as possible, optimally to make it fully passive, while maintaining the necessary security level. The system takes advantage of the ability to recognize the context in which users perform various transactions, which is unique to smart environments. In order to dynamically determine the optimal trade-off between security and convenience, context-based risk and trust assessment model has been developed. The simplification of the payment process concerns reducing the execution time of the process and minimizing the number of operations required to be performed by the client.

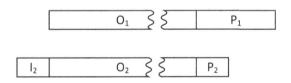

Fig. 1. Stages of customer service sequence.

The significant element of this work is the evaluation of the proposed approach with empirical tests in a real environment. The evaluation is based on a system for which technical feasibility is discussed in [1]. Evaluation scenario employs the system servicing regular transactions at PoS of existing retailer. In the data analysis activities, usage data are confronted with four research hypotheses related to security and convenience attributes of the approach.

H_1: Automatic transactions provide users with higher convenience level and similar duration as compared to traditional transactions.

Contactless card payment (estimated approx. $5\,s$ long) has been assumed as a reference traditional transaction. Assuming stages O_1 and O_2 are comparable in terms of execution time (cf. Fig. 1), the goal is to get the total duration of I_2 and P_2 equal or less than the duration of P_1. Please note that this assumption is pessimistic since in the evaluated system I_2 of a new customer can take place during a previous customer service, and therefore duration of I_2 may not impact the total duration of the customer service.

H_2: Automatic payments reduce the number of user actions undertaken for transaction authorization down to zero.

H_3: In the real-world environment using the prototype system will result in more than 80% successful face identification attempts. In the group of successful face identification attempts, more than 80% is not preceded by earlier misidentification.

H_4: Applying context-based authorization method selection based on trust, risk and convenience criteria results in gradually decreasing transaction duration.

This work is an extended version of the conference paper [2]. It is composed of six main sections. Section 1 is an introduction to the research problem and the proposed solution along with posed hypotheses. Section 2 provides background information on existing payment solutions and on user identification based on face biometrics. Section 3 summarizes functionalities arising from the adopted business scenario, that guide the design of the proposed solution. Section 4 delivers details on the system evaluation and experiment design. Section 5 contains comprehensive evaluation results. The final Sect. 6 concludes the evaluation and the whole article.

2   Background

2.1   Payment Authorization in Smart Environments

Making user environment smart implies that it becomes aware of when and how its services are used. This enables supporting the users with automation of routine tasks and procedures. For example the smart city infrastructure can be used to identify citizen intentions and run operations such as user authentication in the background, even without explicit actions performed by the citizen. The presented research is focused on a particular type of background operations – automatic payments, which are a crucial feature of smart environments. This feature will be increasingly used for billing users for the use of city infrastructure, goods or services. This includes services such as "smart parking", bridge toll collection, or public transport.

First "smart parking" systems were composed of parking stations broadcasting wireless signals to specialized transponders installed in cars [3]. The transponder had to be activated manually to start periodically deducting an amount specified by the parking station. It was not fully passive for a driver, however more convenient than cash payments at a parking station. With the growth of smart city infrastructure (e.g. an optical wireless sensor network [4] or RFID-based solutions [5]) it is possible to automatically detect when a car stops at a particular parking spot and when it leaves, thus enabling full automation of parking payments.

Similar technologies are used for road toll collection. In such a case there is a need to identify a vehicle crossing a specific point. This identification can be done automatically with the use of RF identifiers installed in vehicles [6] or by optical recognition of car plates [7]. From the point of view of the driver, she simply drives through the toll collection point and her account is debited automatically. Such systems can be further enhanced with sensor fusion, for example to collect toll based on the number of occupants in the vehicle [8] or to become multi-purpose traffic management solutions [9].

The problem of enabling automatic payments becomes more complex, when there is a need to identify humans, not just objects such as car. An example of such case is public transport, where each passenger should be ticketed according to her travel. Many existing solutions require the use of contactless chip cards or smartphone applications – both of which require active participation of the passenger in the ticketing process [8]. A fully passive ticketing solutions, so called implicit ticketing, is possible with BLE (Bluetooth Low Energy) technology, where the passenger only needs to carry a special BLE token or a capable smartphone and the payment is performed in the background [10, 11].

The concept of passive transactions can be exploited also in the context of citizens using city services not related directly to the city infrastructure, for example: ordering services or documents at a municipal office or buying products or services at a local retail store. One of notable examples of automatic payment systems in the retail domain is Google Hands Free [12] proposed by Google. The Hands Free application uses Bluetooth Low Energy, WiFi, location services, and other sensors on the user's device to detect user presence near PoS. This enables the user to pay hands-free, without getting out the smartphone or opening the application. During the transaction, verbal declaration of participation is required from the user (the system is not fully passive), and identity verification with initials and profile photo from the cashier. Google is also running early experiments using automated facial identification to further simplify the checkout process with in-store camera.

The payment system that is based on facial recognition to a larger extent, called Zero-Effort Payments (ZEP), has been proposed in [13], where the authors interestingly discuss system evaluation results. The face identification results are promising, but the recognition is human assisted, i.e. a ranking of 5 most probable identities is presented to the human operator who manually chooses the right one. The recognition process demands a heavy computational load since a number of faces are tracked at given moment. Also the authors point out the low face recognition accuracy without supporting localization device. In their system BLE localization devices are used to significantly reduce the face recognition error rate. Therefore, it must be noted that both ZEP and Google

Hands Free are not deviceless systems, i.e. although a user does not need to manipulate with her device during the payment process, she needs to carry a switched on device during customer identification and service.

Also Uniqul system [14] has been deployed to provide fully deviceless payments authorized with user face image. However, it requires the user to type a PIN number when face identification has a low confidence level or tap the confirmation button on the in-shop tablet in the opposite case. Therefore, it cannot be considered as fully passive approach from the end-user perspective.

There are also payment systems based on face recognition that utilize end-user smartphone camera. MasterCard has proposed a simple to use mobile solution [15] that allows customers to authenticate their online purchases using their own face images. It refers to the selfie phenomenon, which is natural for a number of end-users. The application verifies image authenticity by detecting eyes blinking during image acquisition. MasterCard's approach is designed for online shopping, not brick-and-mortar trade. Contrarily, Lucova, using BLE technology proposes a system called FreshX [16] that also is based on selfie face image authorization, however it is dedicated for brick-and-mortar cafeterias. Such approaches, although natural, are neither deviceless nor passive, and security concerns can be serious.

There is a number of research and industry effort related to seamless payments focused on other biometrics than face, e.g. fingerprints, or palm recognition. For instance Liquid Pay [17] identifies customers by their fingerprints and, for extra security, by veins and electrical signals emitted by the human body. It has been installed in restaurants, fitness clubs and theme parks. Payment systems based on the Fujitsu PalmSecure technology [18] recognizing vein patterns in whole palm are being tested by [19] or [20] in many cafeterias. However, those technologies, although deviceless, stable and relatively mature, cannot be perceived as passive.

Also, there are significant advancements in the field of NFC-based contactless payments for EMV smart cards that have become de facto standard [21] for low-risk transaction authorization in brick-and-mortar retail trade. Nowadays, this technology migrates from smartcard to mobile device as a carrier. Mobile services and application such as Apple Pay [22], Samsung Pay [23] or Android Pay [24] have been proposed to allow smartphone users for transaction authorization with their devices. However, these solutions mimic traditional card-based payments and are neither deviceless nor passive.

As a result of the research reported in [1,2], a transaction system that is fully hands-free and does not require explicit user actions for routine payments has been proposed. Similarly to automatic toll collection where one just drives through a tunnel and her account is debited in the background one just places the order and leaves with the merchandise and the payment is performed in the background. All this in a passive manner: without requiring any additional actions, based on the optical recognition of customers using face biometrics. The goal of this work is to present the results of the quantitative evaluation of the proposed approach.

2.2   Identification with Face Biometrics

Face biometrics gains popularity due to availability of high resolution cameras, increasing computational power of image processing devices and development of pattern recognition and machine learning algorithms. Because of its naturality face biometrics is more acceptable for end-users than many other biometric methods, but, on the other hand, the ability to collect face images without user acceptance may raise privacy concerns [25].

Generally, face recognition, as in the case of other biometric systems, consists of three main steps: acquisition of biometric data with a sensor, converting the data into a digital template, and comparison of the template with a reference template. In various approaches recognition can be based on a single image, image sequence, 3D image, or near-infrared/thermogram image.

Usually, face recognition is preceded by face detection and image segmentation, which are aimed at cropping face image from a larger image. Image segmentation can be performed automatically: either based on knowledge about specific image features that are common for human faces, or, in case of image sequences, based on human body movement features, that allow for detection of so called skeleton and face localization relative to the skeleton.

After segmentation, the face is recognized by comparison against an image base. Applying face recognition to user identification requires using less accurate one-to-many comparison model, as opposed to one-to-one model useful for user verification. In various approaches to face recognition, algorithms are based either on vectors describing whole face images or face geometry. In the former algorithm group, the reduction of face image representation to vectors is performed in order to preserve the information reflecting specific face features and to reject the noise resulting from e.g. variable lighting. Consequently, a face image is represented as a linear combination of simplified base images, namely Eigenfaces. These methods can be either global (indivisible face), or local (distinct representation for different face regions). In turn, the geometry-based algorithms from the latter group are able to represent geometrical relations between selected details (e.g. eyes and mouth) and to mutually compare whole details sets. Hybrid approaches combining both face features and face geometry are also developed.

There are three main groups of research challenges related to face recognition [26], i.e. variation of face shape, variation of face acquisition geometry and variation of face acquisition conditions. Variation of face shape includes short-term variations related to speaking process or emotion expression, as well as long term variations related to ageing, putting on weight, injuries, make-up, facial hair, haircut and using wearables (glasses, hats). Variation of acquisition geometry results from variable distance (scale) and orientation of the face relative to the camera. Variation of face acquisition conditions is related to variable camera parameters (e.g. white balance, noise reduction, etc.) and also to variable environment conditions (variable or uneven lighting, occlusions).

3   Evaluated Approach

3.1   Passive User Identification

To enable full payment automation it is necessary to use passive customer identification based on detection of the presence of a particular person at a particular location. Detection of the presence of a person may rely on what the person has (an object), or who she is (biometrics). The third option, based on what the person knows (the knowledge), is not applicable here, because it requires an active participation of the identified person. The passive identification based on objects can be performed, for example, by the use of radio identifiers (Bluetooth beacon technology). However, this approach assumes that the person identified will always have to carry a relevant object. Passive method of identification, which seems to be the best to use in the scenario under consideration, is therefore biometrics. Face recognition is the biometric method that can be utilized effectively without the active participation of the identified person. A method of this type does not require any specific action on the part of the customer. Just her mere presence in a particular place, in this case – on the seller premises, is sufficient. It is necessary, however, to equip the seller location with appropriate infrastructure and to register customer face images in a database. The assumed approach is to maintain the database on the payment operator (PO) side which is less burdensome for the customer. It requires only a one-time registration of face biometric controlled by the PO, which could offer the appropriate customer identification service for a number of vendors, e.g. city-wide smart environment. At the same time, it appears that this variant is easier to implement in practice because of the higher level of trust that customers have in POs. Moreover, PO acts as a "trusted third-party" in the customer–seller relation.

For passive identification, face recognition based on a single image has a number of drawbacks. Apart from the risk of false matchings that would not be corrected automatically, such approach would require an additional effort from the seller side ("taking a photo") and would require active unnatural face presentation from the user. However, it can be assumed that there is short but continuous time period in which a user prepares to the transaction (e.g. walks over, looks through the offer). This few second period can produce several dozen of face images and this is the proposed timespan for the initial identification. As an element of the proposed system, rule-based heuristic algorithm has been developed in which final identification decision is a result of a number of face matchings calculated within given time period. Therefore, a low number of false matchings does not impact the final identification decision. If the data stream introduces a significant portion of new face matchings, the final identification is gradually improved and seamlessly updated on the seller device.

For a single-frame matchings standard Eigenfaces algorithm is used, cf. Sect. 2.2. If a positive matching takes place, the identifier of the recognized user is returned along with recognition coefficient X. Since, as it has been mentioned, single recognitions can be erroneous, the heuristic algorithm has been introduced into the decision process and it is responsible for the final identification decision.

It collects a number of faces N recently detected (not: recognized or matched to a template) with their X coefficients. The approach based on moving frame has been applied, i.e. in each iteration N last images are analyzed, even if in previous iteration some of them have already been analyzed. The size of the frame is limited not only by a number of images, but also by time period, i.e. images are excluded from the frame if they are too distant in time to be possibly related to the recognized user (e.g. one minute old).

Such sets of values describing detected/recognized faces are checked for compliance with three conditions:

1. $L_A > P_1 * N$ (correct recognitions number)
2. $L_A > P_2 * L_{NonA}$ (advantage of correct recognitions over misrecognitions)
3. $L_A^X > P_3 * L_A$ (correct recognitions quality)

Where:

L_A – number of images in the image sequence of N images, in which a user A has been recognized with the best coefficient;

L_{NonA} – number of images in the image sequence of N images, in which users that are not a user A have been recognized with the best coefficient; it does not include images in which no user has been recognized;

L_A^X – number of images in the image sequence of N images, in which a user A has been recognized with the best coefficient if the coefficient is less than or equal to X.

For user A in order to be recognized all three conditions must be fulfilled. Values of heuristic algorithm's parameters: N, P_1, P_2, P_3 and X have been calculated experimentally (40, 0.2, 1.0, 0.5 and 3700) – the single conditions are rather loose because of the conjunction logic of the approach.

Instead of Eigenfaces any other algorithm could operate underneath the proposed heuristic algorithm. Eigenfaces algorithm has been chosen to show that even for relatively simple single-frame recognition algorithm, the proposed approach allows for fairly robust user identifications in practice. The key element is taking advantage of a long stream of individual recognitions, even if they can be ambiguous, in the manner described above in this section.

It is worth noting that as additional criteria improving the recognition accuracy, information obtained at the client side from sensor about face distance (too distant faces are uncertain), user attention (rotated faces are uncertain), or user mimics (images too different from neutral-mimics templates) can be taken into account. Improved recognition accuracy would reduce time delays related to unsuccessful data processing. Also scalability of the solution would be improved due to reduction of computational power requirements (lower number of recognitions) and of communication effort. Similar benefits could be obtained by using pre-recognizers trained to recognized user height or sex, and thus pre-segmenting the template database before actual matching.

3.2 Payment Authorization

The postulated payment automation is used for routine payments, i.e. recurring payments that meet certain patterns and seller-client trust requirements. In practice, the scope and characteristics of applicable patterns and requirements is different for different POs, depending on their expectations and the data they process. There is no way to permanently define the thresholds for such requirements, because in practice they are different for each customer-seller pair and also they may change over time. Therefore, it is assumed that values of parameters describing a payment, which include: level of seller's trust to the client, level of client's trust to the seller, and transaction risk level, are provided by external systems of the PO (fraud detection system, client profiling systems, etc.). Consequently, it is necessary to use a mechanism that will dynamically evaluate the parameters for a particular payment, and based on an extensible set of rules will determine whether the payment can be classified as routine or not, and if not, which authorization methods should be allowed to make sure the required security level is maintained. The mechanism takes into account various trust/risk requirements for biometric-based, possession-based and knowledge-based authorization methods, for active and passive methods, for methods based on client and seller infrastructure, and various convenience levels of the particular authorization methods. The details of this model are elaborated in [1].

3.3 System Architecture

In the proposed approach, a distributed architecture with components localized both at the client side and at the PO side, and to some extent also at the seller side, is assumed. On the client side BYOD model is assumed, so on this side only software that integrates with client devices is required. At the seller side hardware-software solution has been designed enabling the identification of clients and the use of a universal API for integration with sales/loyalty system of the seller. At the PO side there is a set of software modules that represent the main elements of the system logic. It is assumed that the software is running on infrastructure of the PO and is available remotely through a secured communication channel. Low-level description of components and technical feasibility of a system being an implementation of the presented approach, is elaborated in the work [1].

Client Side. The software running on client devices (*App*) is a mobile application that integrates with a client device and carries out the following functions:

- registering the client device in the system of the PO, along with information about authorization methods supported by the device, e.g., geolocation, entering a code on the keyboard, performing a gesture on the touch screen, executing a gesture in space, scanning a fingerprint, recording a voice;
- receiving and presenting notifications about the need to authorize a non-routine payment or about the status of completion of the payment processing, e.g., payment failure due to lack of funds;

– supporting payment authorization methods and transferring the credentials of the selected authorization method to the PO.

The *App* component is a mobile application which can be built in native or hybrid technology that allows to handle system notifications and to use hardware features of mobile devices, such as fingerprint reader. In the prototype it has been implemented as standalone native application for the Android mobile operating system supporting three authorization methods: acceptance, PIN, and fingerprint. In practice, this element of the system can be easily integrated with a pre-existing mobile application of the PO.

Seller Side. At the seller side there is a software-hardware component responsible for the registration of client's face images at the PoS (*Cam*). In the prototype the *Cam* component has been developed on the basis of a dedicated software (.NET Framework) running on a mobile PC that uses the depth-aware camera sensor, which facilitates the process of capturing face images. These images are streamed to the PO side, to the component responsible for customer identification based on biometric features of the face (*Ident*). Also, at the seller side seller's sales/loyalty software (*Sell*) operates, which receives customer identification and payment status notifications, and communicates with remote components localized at the operator side, using defined API calls. It is assumed that the seller sales/loyalty software (*Sell*) is a third-party software and as such is not a part of the system – the system design includes only the API. However, since the research evaluation requires a custom implementation of this component, the prototype of the external sales/loyalty system has been prepared as a native application for the Android operating system. The prototype implementation of the *Sell* component supports the seller-side authorization method, namely the client's PIN on the seller's device, and an ability to identify customers with an RFID tag.

PO Side. At the PO side there are components implementing all key functions of the system. The *Ident* component is a client identification subsystem, which is using client face images sent from the PoS and patterns previously registered in the biometric database of the PO. It operates according to a procedure described in detail in Sect. 3.1. The *ID*, *Devs*, and *Auth* components are repositories storing client identifiers, information about authorization methods supported by client's devices, and patterns of correct authorization results, respectively. All these three components provide an API for communication with other components and implement logic necessary for their operations. The *Proc* component is a payment risk processor, which is responsible for classifying the payment as routine/non-routine and making the selection of possible sets of authorization methods required for a specific non-routine payment, cf. Sect. 3.2. This processor communicates with other components of the PO system to obtain the information necessary to classify a payment or calculate the risk of a non-routine payment, e.g., the history of previous transactions between the client and the seller, fraud detection systems. The *Proc* also uses the data for formal verification of payment feasibility, e.g. the balance of the account, the client consent to automate payments. The main operator-side component is the *Trans* component, which is the payment processor responsible for carrying out the process of customer identification and authorization of payment. It also provides APIs for the seller *Sell* system. The *Trans* controls the information (i.e. payment authorization requests and payment status notifications) being transferred to the *App* component and to the seller *Sell* system, that is necessary to carry out the entire process.

Individual components operating on the PO side can be tightly integrated or they can work independently while maintaining proper communication between them. For the purpose of the evaluation all operator-side components apart from *Ident* have been implemented on Java platform and operate within a Restlet server, which provides HTTP-based REST API for selected components. The notifications sent to *App* and *Sell* components are realized on the basis of an external communication service, namely Google Cloud Messaging. Additionally, to enable full system evaluation the *Trans* component deployed in the prototype implements functions of an electronic wallet and client (and seller) transaction history analyzer. To mimic real fraud detection and client profiling systems the values of the parameters required by the *Proc* to evaluate transactions have been calculated taking into account data such as: total number of transactions of the client and the seller, number of transactions between the client and the seller, typical amount of transaction between the client and the seller, and transaction amount. This way, the prototype simulates the use of external systems of the PO, making it independent of the availability of these systems. Also, it can be used for experiments involving the functionality currently not shared by external systems of POs.

3.4 Data Flow

The communication sequence (Fig. 2) implemented in the system begins with a set of messages that initiate the process and then forks into two sequences: the first one for routine payments and the second one for non-routine payments. The sequence is as follows:

1. An instance of the *Cam* component operating at a particular *PoS* sends a registered client facial image (*face*) to the *Ident* component. Along with the image of the face, *Ident* also receives information about the seller (S) and about the specific *PoS*.
2. *Ident* uses the database of biometric face templates to find the client ID *Kf*. Next, the *Ident* passes information to the *Trans* that a *PoS* of seller S should receive information about the client (Kf).
3. *Trans* uses client ID provided by *Ident* (Kf) and the repository *ID* to find the client identifier attributed to her by the seller S (Ks). If the client has not registered her identifier given to her by the seller S, the *ID* returns the PO client identifier K. *Trans* sends a notification to the *Sell* system of the seller S at the *PoS* that the client (Ks or K) has been identified.

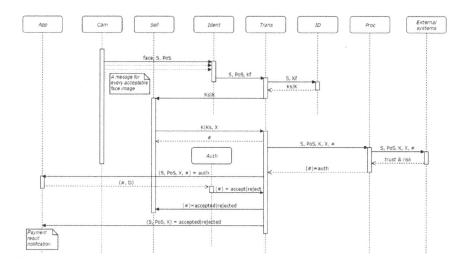

Fig. 2. Communication sequence for non-routine payment.

4. The *Sell* system of the seller S at the *PoS* displays client identification information along with a photo allowing the salesman to confirm or reject the identification. If the identification is accepted, the procedure continues with step 5. In the case of rejection the procedure restarts from step 1.
5. The *Sell* system of seller S, using defined API, provides *Trans* with a debit request for client $Ks \mid K$ and amount X.
6. *Trans* confirms the request responding with a unique payment identifier #, locks funds on the account of client K and requests payment classification from the *Proc* component.

Routine Payment

7. *Proc* retrieves the necessary data from external systems of the PO, classifies the payment as routine, positively verifies formal conditions for the payment, and in response informs *Trans* about the option for completing the payment in automatic mode (*auto*).
8. *Trans* charges the customer's account and transmits notification about the successful completion of the payment to the *Sell* system of seller S at the *PoS* and to all instances of the *App* component of the customer K. *Trans* pulls information about instances of the *App* component, which should be notified, from the *Devs*.

Non-routine Payment

7. *Proc* retrieves the necessary data from external systems of the PO, classifies the payment as non-routine, positively verifies formal conditions for the payment, and in response sends information about the need to authorize transaction along with a list of possible sets of authentication methods (*auth*) to *Trans*.

8. *Trans* sends a notification about the need for payment authorization together with an indication of what authorization methods can be used on a particular device, to instances of the *App* component of the client *K*, indicated by *Proc* in the *auth* set.

9. An instance of the *App* component used by the client *K* to input the authorization data transmits the data (*D*) to the *Auth* component using defined API.

10. *Auth* verifies the correctness of the authorization data and transmits information on the acceptance or rejection of the authorization to the *Trans*.

11. In the case of acceptance, *Trans* charges the customer's account and transmits notification about the successful completion of the payment to the *Sell* system of seller *S* at the *PoS* and to all instances of the *App* component of the customer *K*.

    In the case of rejection, *Trans* decides to recommence the payment evaluation (step 7) or to terminate the payment processing with appropriate notification transmitted to the *Sell* system of seller *S* at the *PoS* and to all instances of the *App* component of the customer *K*.

    Trans pulls information about instances of the *App* component which should be notified from the *Devs*.

4 Experiment Design

4.1 Setup

The evaluation requires conducting empirical tests of the system in conditions as close to regular as it is possible. Evaluation scenario assumes that after prototype system is designed and implemented, it is deployed in real PoS that in future could be a cooperator of the metropolitan smart environment, and its usage data are collected and analyzed. During the analysis the data are confronted with research hypotheses related to system usability formulated in Sect. 1.

In the experiment an existing PoS (local bar "The End Cafe") with a group of its regular customers who usually conduct a typical (routine) transactions has set a research environment. It has allowed for collecting results reflecting requirements of intelligent PoS while maintaining reasonable experiment time and number of participants.

The system has been used by 22 users (14 women, 8 men), for the period of 16 days (7th to 22nd). The participants were selected from existing clients of the bar that visited it at least 2–3 times per week, are familiar with internet banking and utilize contactless payment cards at least once a week. The age of participants was in the range of 20 to 30. The bar staff has been informed about the system setup and trained to use it for customer service properly. The prototype system has been parametrized to classify a payment as a routine after two or three similar payments. In order to allow participants to make a number of payments, each has been provided with 150 PLN worth electronic wallet. During the experiment participants have spent totally 2837 PLN and have performed 251 payments, which is more than 10 payments per person.

The participants have made transactions according to their will and have not been steered nor pushed in any way neither by staff nor by researchers. At the same time, logging subcomponents of the system's components have been used to log every significant system event. The events have been defined to build complete and detailed descriptions of every possible customer service path. During the experiment neither technical nor organizational difficulties that could have impact on the results have been reported.

4.2   User Registration

After the participants recruitment, each participant has been equipped with RFID marker in the form of a card, sticker or fob, and the application instances have been installed on participants' smartphones. In the PO-side component responsible for user identification there have been stored sets of face image patterns, which have been registered with a seller-side component responsible for tracking, acquiring, segmenting, filtering, and streaming user face images at the PoS, according to the strict procedure. Ten different (mimics, angles, distances) images of each face have been collected. It has introduced desired diversity of the training set, also because of different face lighting on the images of different kind, with different face rotation or distance. It has to be noted that the sensor has not been installed in this same horizontal axis as typical location of user face, but slightly above and rotated. This also has had impact on requirements regarding diversified orientation of the faces in the training set (both "ahead" and "slightly upwards, towards camera"). During initial tests it has been confirmed that three-quarter views decrease recognition accuracy and therefore they have been excluded from training process. Detected faces have been visually outlined, which facilitates choosing optimal acquisition moments, so that operator has a control over the training set quality (framing, distance, sharpness, angle, lost tracking). Face registration has been performed at the PoS, which has two main advantages. First, it facilitates registration by not requiring any additional client's visits in the operator's location. Second, the registration environment conditions are similar to recognition environment conditions which improves recognition accuracy.

Name, ID photo, face and RFID identifiers, as well as user identifiers in the seller and operator systems have been stored in the dedicated component at the PO side. In another PO-side component, device vendor, model and OS version, as well as device token (for PUSH communication within Google Cloud Messaging) and list of supported authorization methods have been stored. In the authorization component, patterns for authorization method, PIN and optionally fingerprint hash have been stored.

Before the user registration procedure each participant underwent an individual in-depth interview and was briefly informed about the system operation. Additionally, a web page explaining the idea of automatic payments and system operation was published and presented to all participants.

4.3 Data Collection

During the experiments a number of event classes has been registered in components' logs. In the process of user identification the following event classes are registered: face detection event, recognition event, confirmation event, "reject and change the method" event, "reject and try again" event, and transaction abort event. In the process of transaction authorization the following event classes are registered: transaction start, acceptance, transaction decline, and sending authorization request to client/seller.

For those events, apart from exact timestamp, the following identifiers are registered: identification method identifier, client identifier, transaction identifier, identifiers of available authorization methods, identifiers of used authorization methods, transaction status (e.g. button code, reason for the rejection), as well as many parameters related to face identification, such as: number of detected faces, correct recognitions number, advantage of correct recognitions over misrecognitions, correct recognitions quality, average and median of recognitions and misrecognitions quality, and identifiers of the decision rules that are fulfilled.

Apart from data collected by the system itself, all participants were invited for a second round of in-depth interviews where they could express their opinion about the system operation.

5 Evaluation Results

The results described in the first subsection contain an overview of users opinions gathered during and after the experiment. The results presented in next two sections have been obtained as an effect of data mining and statistical analysis of three distinct log sets, generated by four components of the system. The results from the second subsection are related to user identification phase, and the results from the third subsection are related to subsequent phase, i.e. transaction authorization phase.

5.1 Users Opinions

During the experiment randomly selected transactions were followed by a request to fill in a short questionnaire regarding the subjective quality of user experience. The questionnaires were provided via regular payment mobile application immediately after the transaction. In 83 responses collected from these questionnaires the majority of respondents indicated that in their opinion the automatic payment procedure is more convenient (61.4%) and more secure (52%) than a traditional contactless payment. They also responded that the whole process was faster (50%) than a traditional contactless payment.

During the second round of in-depth interviews all participants were encouraged to present their own opinions about the system. The opinions include both positive and negative statements. Positive statements can be summarized by the following keywords: convenience, speed, innovation. Negative statements were focused mostly on inconveniently long identification time. It is also worth to notice that some participants felt uncomfortable when their personal data (photo and name) intended for the sales clerk could be visible to other clients in the queue, which pinpoints that the seller-side of the system should protect privacy of clients data.

5.2   User Identification

Totally, there were 282 successful user identifications performed by the system. This value does not indicate the number of performed transactions, since there are cases where for a single identification a sequence of transactions is conducted, and there are cases where successful identification does not precede successful transaction authorization.

Identification Methods. From among successful identifications, as much as 72% have been conducted with face biometrics, and only 28% with RFID card, despite the fact, that every user has been equipped with such card and could freely use it. A number of successful identifications in the respective experiment weeks for different identification methods is presented in Fig. 3.

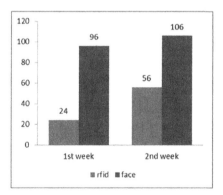

Fig. 3. Number of successful identifications for different identification methods in respective weeks [2].

Accuracy of Identification with Face Biometrics. Out of all attempts to identification with face, i.e. cases where a new client has appeared at PoS willing to identify himself or herself with a face, 202 have been successful and 43 have failed, which gives about 82.45% accuracy. In the group of successful face-based identification attempts, 173 have not been preceded by any earlier unsuccessful attempts (named as "seamless identifications"), and 29 have been preceded by unsuccessful attempts (named as "difficult identification") within time period of

30 s. Seamless identifications percentage for the first week of the experiment is
81.25% and for the second week of the experiment is 89.62%.

High percentage of successful identifications has persisted in the consecutive
days of the experiment and it has never dropped below 72%, which is presented
in Fig. 4. The labels on horizontal axis denote days of December, two weeks from
December 7th to December 18th. Weekends and pre-Christmas days (December
21st and 22nd) are excluded because of very low number of clients at the campus
bar in those days producing non-representative results.

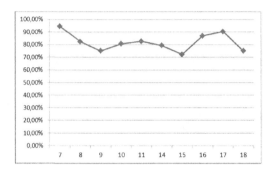

Fig. 4. Percentage of successful face identifications in the consecutive days [2].

Duration of the Identification with Face Image. Duration of the face
identification has been measured from the moment of the first face recognition
of the user (even if the recognition does not fulfill the heuristic criteria of the
final identification, even if the face image appears once, and even if it belongs to
the "misrecognitions" set), to the moment of receiving the identification message
at the seller's device. The median of identification duration is 34 s.

Independently, the durations of the seller confirmations have been measured,
i.e. time between the moment of receiving the identification message at the
seller's device and the moment of seller's manual approval with the button.
The median of confirmation time is 3 s.

5.3   Payment Authorization

During the evaluation, 225 transactions have been successfully conducted, 92%
of them required single authorization attempt, and 8% required repeated authorization.

Authorization Duration. Average duration of the transaction authorization
for transactions that require single attempt is 10,5 s and median of this duration
is below 1 s (because of the relatively high number of automatic authorizations).
In the rare cases when repeated authorization has been required (e.g. a user
inputs wrong PIN), the duration has been much longer (Fig. 5). Authorization

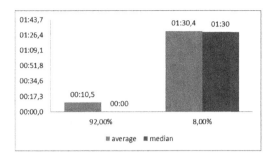

Fig. 5. Average and median authorization durations in case of single and repeated authorization [2].

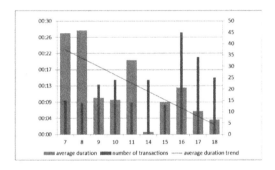

Fig. 6. Average authorization durations for respective days [2] (Color figure online).

duration is measured from the moment when the order is already put together, through transaction authorization process, to the payment settlement done.

In Fig. 6 median durations of authorizations (blue bars) for respective days are depicted. Evident decrease of the transaction duration is observed, which is a consequence of familiarizing users with the system as well as of constantly increasing fraction of automatic authorizations during the evaluation (because of building a history of transactions that increases trust). Downward trend (trend line) is strengthened by the fact that in the last three days (16–18) in which the durations have been short, the highest number of transactions have been conducted (red bars).

User Faults During Payment Authorization. Percentage of transactions requiring repeated authorization in the respective days is presented in Fig. 7. Clear downward trend can be observed. As in the case of transaction duration, it is a consequence of familiarizing users with the system as well as of constantly increasing fraction of automatic authorization method which eliminates user faults.

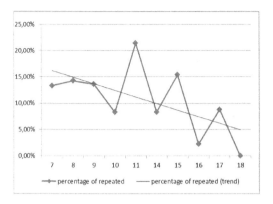

Fig. 7. Percentage of transactions requiring repeated authorization in the respective days [2].

Context-Based Authorization Method Choice. In Fig. 8 a number of successful authorizations in the respective days for different authorization methods is visualized. Increasing usage of automatic method is visible. It is a consequence of users' building a history of transaction that increases level of trust, which is one of the conditions for choosing this method by the system. It confirms that system works according to expectations.

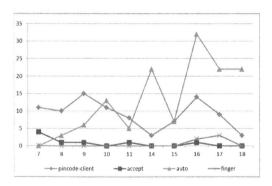

Fig. 8. Number of successful authorizations in the respective days for different authorization methods [2].

The above-mentioned tendency is visible better if data are expressed relatively, which is presented in Fig. 9.

In Fig. 10 medians of transaction durations for different authorization methods for respective weeks are presented. It can be observed that durations of manual accept authorization (with a smartphone) in the second week are lower than in the first week. The main reason for this advantageous trend is gaining experience by users with the new notification and confirmation interface. The

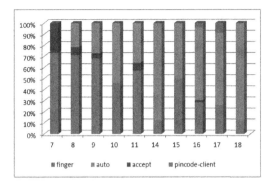

Fig. 9. Distribution of different authorization methods in the respective days [2].

PIN-based authorization duration is constant since this method is already known for users and since PIN always requires few seconds to be typed, regardless of user experience. Authorizations with fingerprint have been performed only few times (since only few users have used devices with a fingerprint scanner) and only in the second week, thus their durations cannot be considered as representative.

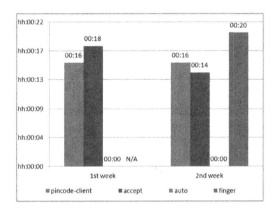

Fig. 10. Medians of authorization durations for different authorization methods in respective weeks [2].

5.4   Results Analysis

Obtained results allow for verifying particular research hypotheses defined in the Sect. 1. The hypothesis H_1 has not been confirmed during the evaluation. Although median of authorization durations is far below 5 s limit, the second component of the total duration, i.e. identification, takes much longer time (cf. Sect. 5.2). It results in conclusion that the applied approach to face recognition needs further optimization. The long recognition time is not caused by computation complexity nor performance issues, but by too frequent inaccurate (conflicting) recognitions in the image sequence which delay obtaining consistent result for a given user. This difficulty can be overcome by employing additional filters that can detect and eliminate error-prone frames from the video stream and by optimizing parameters of heuristic for the final identification.

The hypothesis H_2 has been confirmed. In cases when passive identification and authorization have been conducted, all the users had to do was to verbalize the order and pick up the products. One aspect of the identification process has been shifted to the seller (manual confirmation of a single identification result), but practically it had no significant influence on the duration of the whole process (cf. Sect. 5.2).

The collected data confirm the hypothesis H_3. The percentage of the successful identifications based on face biometrics is 82.45%, and the percentage of the "seamless" face identifications within the group of successful identification is 85.64%.

Also the hypothesis H_4 has been confirmed. Data presented in Sect. 5.3 show that payment authorization duration is gradually decreasing as users build a history of transaction that increases level of trust, which is a one of the conditions for choosing more convenient and fast authorization methods.

To sum up, analysis of the collected quantitative data allows for confirming three of four research hypotheses. In case of rejected hypothesis, the element that needs further optimization can be easily identified. Generally, the evaluation has confirmed that the approach proposed for passive transaction authorization is achievable despite the difficulties introduced by variable real-world conditions at PoS.

As a future work it is planned to analyze additional factors extracted from the video signal and depth data (e.g. user height, mimics, pose, age, sex) and non-video features (behavioral patterns for time, place, amount, type of good) that can be used to improve the recognition quality, speed, and security of the system.

Before order completion face-based user identification is confirmed by the cashier. This input combined with image data and non-image data can constitute a data source for supervised machine learning deployed at system runtime. With this technique an adaptive user identification could be developed. It would further improve the system accuracy since conditions at a PoS change over time and vary at different PoS and since users change their look. Moreover, a knowledge obtained from machine learning module deployed at runtime would improve context modelling capabilities that impact trust assessment and the authorization method choice.

6   Conclusions

The results of the evaluation confirm that the proposed modus operandi for the automatic authorization as well as its goals and benefits are achievable under the constraints of a real-world PoS. Prototype system build based on proposed architecture and algorithms indeed has allowed evaluation participants to authorize routine payments in passive mode. The seller just confirms the single identity recognized by the system with one tap, and does not need to choose between possible matchings losing his time and focus like it is required by systems reported in the related works. The main advantage of the proposed approach comes from its context-awareness and dynamic authorization method selection, which allows for gradually achieving the trust level required for passiveness. The right balance between convenience and security, which are always at odds, is constantly provided.

The system introduces added value for all actors of the process: payment operator, seller (service provider), and the end-user. By providing end-users and sellers with trusted and effective payment service, the PO reduces security concerns from all sides and can attract newcomers. The tool for dynamic assessment of the type of payment (routine/non-routine) goes beyond the model adopted for contactless payment cards (hard limit quota). By using the transaction context and dynamically assessing payment risk level and trustworthiness of the participants, the system dynamically selects the most appropriate authorization methods of the payment. Rules for dynamic selection take into account the various authorization methods supported by client devices, as well as methods supported by other devices in the end-user environment, e.g. passive face recognition at a seller's location. It is possible to use multiple authorization methods simultaneously, which, if necessary, allows for greater authorization robustness. All this enables a controlled balance between security and convenience of payment for the client and the seller. On the other hand, contrary to proprietary approaches, the assumption of the openness is not violated in the proposed approach. The functionalities of sellers' and PO's services are not coupled together, thus competition between different sellers is possible which can leverage quality of services within the whole PO network.

From the point of view of the seller, the key advantage is the fact that the customer has to be identified for the purpose of payment at the beginning of the transaction. This information may be used to introduce improvements in the customer service process. By moving the moment of identification to the beginning of the service process and by providing the seller's sales/loyalty system with information about customer identification, it becomes possible to use a wide range of tools to support personalized service regardless of the knowledge and memory of individual employees serving clients.

Most of all, introducing the presented approach is beneficial for the end customer. She gains on every functional element of the system. Starting with fast and convenient realization of routine payments and the ability to use convenient authorization methods for non-routine payments, to full personalization of service and automation of loyalty procedures. In the routine payment scenario, the client orders products, receives the merchandise and leaves without having to search for any attribute necessary to authorize the payment.

Acknowledgements. The research was supported by Santander Universidades. We thank our colleagues from Bank Zachodni WBK and Symetria who provided insight and expertise that greatly assisted the research.

References

1. Wójtowicz, A., Chmielewski, J.: Technical feasibility of context-aware passive payment authorization for physical points of sale. Pers. Ubiquitous Comput. **21**, 1113–1125 (2017)
2. Wójtowicz, A., Chmielewski, J.: Face-based passive customer identification combined with multimodal context-aware payment authorization: evaluation at point of sale. In: Proceedings of the 20th International Conference on Enterprise Information Systems, ICEIS 2018, vol. 1, pp. 555–566 (2018)
3. Hassett, J.: Automatic debiting parking meter system. US Patent 5,351,187 (1994). https://www.google.com/patents/US5351187
4. Chinrungrueng, J., Sunantachaikul, U., Triamlumlerd, S.: Smart parking: an application of optical wireless sensor network. In: 2007 International Symposium on Applications and the Internet Workshops, p. 66 (2007)
5. Mainetti, L., Patrono, L., Stefanizzi, M.L., Vergallo, R.: A smart parking system based on IoT protocols and emerging enabling technologies. In: 2015 IEEE 2nd World Forum on Internet of Things (WF-IoT), pp. 764–769 (2015)
6. Al-Ghawi, S.S., Hussain, S.A., Rahbi, M.A.A., Hussain, S.Z.: Automatic toll e-ticketing system for transportation systems. In: 2016 3rd MEC International Conference on Big Data and Smart City (ICBDSC), pp. 1–5 (2016)
7. Ta, T.D., et al.: Automatic number plate recognition on electronic toll collection systems for Vietnamese conditions. In: Proceedings of the 9th International Conference on Ubiquitous Information Management and Communication, IMCOM 2015, pp. 29:1–29:5. ACM, New York (2015)
8. Nakagawa, A.: Method of automatically adjusting toll collection information based on a number of occupants in a vehicle. US Patent App. 14/316,488 (2015). https://www.google.com/patents/US20150379782
9. He, W., Li, Q., Hua Sun, W.: Discussion on multi-sensor detector fusion of Internet of Things in vehicle management (2015)
10. Narzt, W., Mayerhofer, S., Weichselbaum, O., Haselböck, S., Höfler, N.: Be-in/be-out with bluetooth low energy: implicit ticketing for public transportation systems. In: 2015 IEEE 18th International Conference on Intelligent Transportation Systems, pp. 1551–1556 (2015)
11. Narzt, W., Mayerhofer, S., Weichselbaum, O., Haselböck, S., Höfler, N.: Bluetooth low energy as enabling technology for be-in/be-out systems. In: 2016 13th IEEE Annual Consumer Communications Networking Conference (CCNC), pp. 423–428 (2016)
12. Google: Google hands free (2015). https://get.google.com/handsfree/
13. Smowton, C., Lorch, J.R., Molnar, D., Saroiu, S., Wolman, A.: Zero-effort payments: design, deployment, and lessons. In: Proceedings of the 2014 ACM International Joint Conference on Pervasive and Ubiquitous Computing, UbiComp 2014, pp. 763–774. ACM, New York (2014)
14. Anh Tran, Q., et al.: Finnish grocery retailing market assessment for the deployment of payment innovation: case: uniqul face recognition payment application (2016)
15. Bowyer, K.W.: Selfies to emerge as both payment, anti-fraud solution. Biometric Research, Virtual Special Issue (2015)
16. Lucnova: Freshx (2015). https://www.freshxapp.com/
17. LiquidPay: Liquid pay (2015). http://www.liquidpay.com/

18. Fujitsu: Palmsecure pay (2011). http://www.fujitsu.com/us/solutions/business-technology/security/palmsecure/
19. Biyo: Biyo wallet (2014). http://biyowallet.com/
20. Lee, J.: JCB piloting Fujitsu palm vein authentication technology for payments (2015). http://www.biometricupdate.com/201510/jcb-piloting-fujitsu-palm-vein-authentication-technology-for-payments
21. Alliance, S.C.: EMV and NFC: complementary technologies that deliver secure payments and value-added functionality (2012). http://www.smartcardalliance.org/resources/pdf/EMV_and_NFC_WP_102212.pdf
22. Apple: Apple pay (2014). http://www.apple.com/apple-pay/
23. Samsung: Samsung pay. http://www.samsung.com/us/samsung-pay/ (2015)
24. Google: Android pay. https://www.android.com/pay/ (2015)
25. Wójtowicz, A., Cellary, W.: New Challenges for User Privacy in Cyberspace. CRC Press, Boca Raton (2018)
26. Bolle, R.M., Connell, J.H., Pankanti, S., Ratha, N.K., Senior, A.W.: Guide to Biometrics. Springer, New York (2013)

An Intelligent and Data-Driven Decision Support Solution for the Online Surgery Scheduling Problem

Norman Spangenberg[1($\boxtimes$)], Christoph Augenstein[1], Moritz Wilke[1],
and Bogdan Franczyk[2]

[1] University of Leipzig, Information Systems Institute, Leipzig, Germany
{spangenberg,augenstein}@wifa.uni-leipzig.de
[2] Wroclaw University of Economics, Wroclaw, Poland
franczyk@wifa.uni-leipzig.de

Abstract. In operational business situations it is necessary to be aware of and to understand what happens around you and what probably will happen in the near future to make optimal decisions. For example, Online Surgery Scheduling is the planning and control task of Operating Room Management and includes decisions that are difficult to deal with due to high cognitive and communicational efforts to gather the needed information. In addition, several uncertainties like complications, cancellations and emergencies as well as the need to monitor and control the interventions during execution distinguish the operational decision tasks in surgery scheduling from the tactical and strategical planning decisions. However, the emerging trend of connecting devices and intelligent methods in analytics, facilitate innovative approaches for decision support in this area. With the utilization of these concepts, we propose a data-driven approach for a Decisions Support System including components for monitoring, prediction and optimization in Online Surgery Scheduling.

Keywords: Decision Support System · Online Surgery Scheduling ·
Surgical phase recognition · Machine Learning · Optimization

1 Introduction

Healthcare in general is a high public expenditure and especially hospitals hold a large share of its costs. Inside hospitals, the intensive care unit and the operating room (OR) area are the facilities with cost rates up to 3000€ per hourroom [1]. OR management deals with the organization and coordination of all tasks concerning surgical interventions in order to minimize costs as well as to increase degree of utilization of each room. A special role, the so called OR manager, is responsible for operational planning in the OR area, in particular for the supervision of all surgery-related resources and for complying with a created surgery schedule according to diverse performance indicators. So, for OR managers there is an ongoing pressure to optimize operational processes, e.g. increase resource utilization or reduce OR downtime.

© Springer Nature Switzerland AG 2019
S. Hammoudi et al. (Eds.): ICEIS 2018, LNBIP 363, pp. 82–103, 2019.
https://doi.org/10.1007/978-3-030-26169-6_5

In OR area optimizing operational processes is heavily correlated with assessing actual length of interventions in order to preserve the surgery schedule. Currently, this schedule is based on a fixed timetable created a day before. Any changes, e.g. due to urgent interventions, to delays in surgery but also due to late arrival of patients in the OR area, have to be incorporated into the schedule manually by the OR manager. As a result the schedule is often outdated within a few minutes and needs to be modified on-the-fly as the associated uncertainties and dynamics occur. Most challenging for an OR manager in this case is to predict the remaining time for each intervention but is also heavily dependent on the manager's experience. Moreover, he has to facilitate this task by continually visiting all the rooms and asking for the actual state of each intervention. Upon his experience, the OR manager is then capable of estimating the remaining time and thus knows when to call for the next patient. Resulting changes to the schedule are updated manually, mostly on sheets of paper. If we could instead provide a system, which allows for an accurate prediction based on surgical phases, we would be able to relieve the OR managers and also we would be able to reduce requirements on the job significantly which in turn could relieve skilled personal. For OR managers to accomplish these goals they have to be capable of monitoring all relevant resources and objects of the environment. Certainly, the automated monitoring of surgeries has gained momentum with the help of cameras and the analysis of the resulting videos [2,3] but have their main drawback in restrictive privacy policies i.e patients are not allowed to be somehow identified (e.g. by their faces or even by individual tattoo's or scars). Instead, we propose to make use of smart healthcare products to monitor surgeries. For instance, devices from the field of laparoscopic surgery are able to communicate their actual conditions and parameter sets (cf. Fig. 1). Even though laparoscopic surgeries also involve the use of cameras, these videos are not necessarily able to help identifying persons and aside from that there are also different kinds of laparoscopic devices which only provide some kind of sensor data.

Having the ability to monitor whats going on in each OR, we can tackle the OR manager's problems to preserve the schedule and to adapt quickly to changes. In healthcare the online surgery scheduling (OSS) may lead to a solution in that it is understood as an contemporaneous job with a very short-term perspective that includes the execution, monitoring and control of schedules that were constructed the day before [4]. It thus covers significant parts of the problems, e.g. the management of the everyday operations like reducing OR downtime and increasing the efficiency in a very short-term perspective [5]. According to [6] OSS addresses the monitoring and control of the processes during execution, and encompasses for example reacting to unforeseen events. However, there are few systems so far that tackle intra-day surgery scheduling and allow OR managers to get necessary information and support the decisions based on this information.

In response to these problems, we propose a novel approach for a Decision Support System (DSS), that provides OR managers in the OSS tasks with real-time information and updated surgery schedules. This approach utilizes intelligent Data Analytics methods like data stream analysis, Machine Learning and Optimization. Within this context, we present a solution (cf. Sect. 4) for

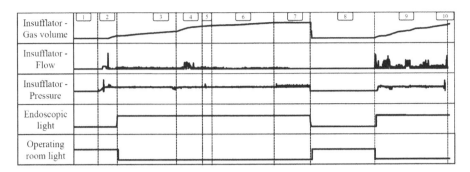

Fig. 1. Parameter values of monitored surgical devices.

real-time monitoring of OR's (cf. Sect. 4.1), predicting the remaining time of each intervention (cf. Sect. 4.2) and to build an initial schedule as well adapt it to changes during the day (cf. Sect. 4.3). In order to demonstrate the benefits of such a system we also provide information on how we evaluated it with the help of a prototype (cf. Sect. 5). Prior to this, we give an introduction to the OSS problem formulation (cf. Sect. 2) and present the related work (cf. Sect. 3) relevant to our approach.

2   Problem Formulation

Similar to other planning and control processes, OR management can be hierarchically separated into a strategical, tactical and operational level, concerned with different planning horizons. Strategical OR management deals with sizing core resources like staff and room, over a planning horizon of a year or more. Tactical OR management has a midterm planning horizon for the rough planning of a Master Surgery Schedule. Finally, the operational level of OR management is divided into offline and online OR management, considering the substantiation of tactical OR plans for a one-week planning horizon before schedule execution (offline) and the control and rescheduling of an intra-day planning horizon during schedule execution (online). The main task of operational OR management is Online Surgery Scheduling (OSS), ensuring the execution of the surgery schedule, completing all planned and unplanned surgeries this day [7]. From now on, all unexpected changes and events require immediate decisions, making OSS the most challenging and time-sensitive task in OR management. Accurate surgery scheduling is a necessity for efficient and frictionless operations in the OR area. Is this not the case, ambiguities and delays occur in the operations that further lead to interruptions, unused resources and dissatisfied staff or patients. Several subtasks can be deduced from these characteristics, which all are accompanied with challenges for gathering necessary information.

Monitoring of the OR Area. This implies the collection of necessary information to be aware of the current situation or unforeseen events in the OR area [8]. This information might come from computerized information systems, like the hospital information system or by the interaction with surgical staff. However, there is still much communicational efforts with surgeons needed to collect timely information and real-time updates of current status and surgical phases, delays or critical events [4]. In addition, several uncertainties and frequent changes characterize the monitoring of the OR area, that arise from varying surgery durations and resource availability as well as stochastically occurring patient no-shows or arrivals of emergency patients [9]. Therefore, OR monitoring often is associated with a lack of knowledge that has to be completed with the experience of the OR manager, that make delays and cancellations often seem intrinsic for processes in the OR area [10].

Estimating Remaining Surgery Durations. Based on the observation of the current situation and conditions, the prediction of upcoming events and outcomes of surgery-related processes is another important task in OSS. The most significant process parameter for predicting future outcomes is the remaining time to the end of the surgery, meaning the time elapsed between the moment the patient is introduced to the OR and leaves the OR [11].

Reliable predictions of surgery durations are needed to make optimal decisions in OR scheduling, e.g. for calling the next elective patient to minimize patient waiting times or reduce OR idle times, if a surgery was shorter than predicted. Further, when surgeries are longer than predicted, subsequent ones need to be postponed or canceled [12]. Both cases lead to inefficiencies in the use of the ORs, recurring communications between staff, patients and OR managers, and an overload of the preoperative holding area [13].

Remaining intervention times are difficult to predict due to several factors. Often the scope of an intervention is not known in advance and becomes apparent not before the surgery is already in progress [14]. For running cases, the current status and recent events during the intervention are influencing parameters. Since current conditions, recent progress and states are not easily recognizable, OR managers need substantial experience knowledge and external information to make reliable predictions. Hence, personnel requests and inspections in the OR are necessary to complete the comprehension of the current situation in the OR area as well as obtain real-time information, e.g. for contemporaneous assignment and scheduling of emergent procedures. The absence of objective and reliable predictions adds complexity to OSS, since the OR manager is forced to interpret various situations to adapt the surgery schedule [13].

Rescheduling of Surgeries. Initial surgery schedules created in the offline planning phase are often obsolete right after the beginning of the surgery day [4], due to unexpected events like delays, cancellations or urgent add-on cases require the modification of the current surgery schedule. The rescheduling of a surgery is challenging in terms of necessary experience knowledge and cognitive efforts for weighing planning alternatives, due to the uncertainties and dynamics in OR operations. The possible actions for OSS include the assignment and

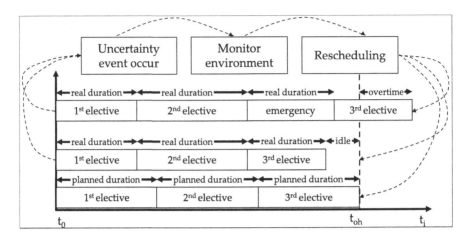

Fig. 2. OSS problem for a single OR including the challenges due to changing intervention durations and introducing emergent cases [17].

scheduling of emergency procedures, the cancellation of cases, as well as the reassignment of ORs and start times for already planned interventions [4]. Then, a reevaluation and rescheduling of the current surgery schedule is performed and, depending on its value of improvement, the plan is modified or remains unchanged. The main objectives and measurements for determining the value of a plan are for example resource overtime, hospitalization costs, intervention costs, OR utilization, waiting times, and patient or personnel preferences [9].

Compared to other scheduling problems in manufacturing or production environments, surgical interventions cannot be suspended and later continued at the same point. Thus, the OSS problem is treated as a predictive-reactive scheduling problem where upcoming events have to be predicted and unforeseen events have reacted to. This means, OSS is represented as a two-stage process, consisting of an initial predictive schedule that models the desired behavior of the OR area. Then, in the reactive part, this schedule is modified in response to certain events during execution [4,15,16]. In this work, we assume that a valid initial schedule exists and focus in the this section on the reactive task of OSS. This is based on a mixed integer linear programming (MILP) approach to model the OSS problem already described in [17]. Since it is a dynamic scheduling problem, it implies updating the schedule defined the previous day in reaction to external effects like incoming emergencies or internal changes like deviations (see Fig. 2). According to the rescheduling framework of [15], the OSS problem described in this work can be seen as a dynamic scheduling problem with variable arrivals of patients. The OSS problem consists of a number of characteristics, assumptions, resources and constraints. The model includes a set of indices for capacities and resource requirements of interventions, surgeons, ORs and their available time slots. Further, several parameters describe properties of the resources and entities like estimated durations, states about availability, urgency and modifiability. The model has two planning variables to optimize the schedule which are the assigned OR and the starting time of an intervention.

The number of surgeries to be scheduled on the tagged day is not known in advance, since it is likely that emergencies occur. A surgical intervention i is characterized by its surgeon s_i, the estimated duration d_i before or during the intervention and its urgency u_i according to the scale elective, urgent and emergent. Further, a modification parameter is introduced to block interventions in a specific OR at a specific time manually or after start. For each surgeon indexed s, I_s denotes the set of jobs that are performed by that surgeon.

The objective is to find an assignment σ of interventions to available OR time slots and surgeons depending on the intervention duration, considering several optimization criteria and goals. The most important criteria for the OR manager – besides treatment quality – is maximizing OR utilization of each OR $\omega_u(o_\sigma)$, according to the method of Hans and Verbeekel [6], including the duration of all interventions per day and the available OR working hours.

$$Max\ \omega_u(o_\sigma) = \sum_{i=1}^{I} \frac{d_i}{l} \tag{1}$$

The objective of minimizing waiting time $\omega_w(\sigma)$ should lead to the fast scheduling of non-electives by introducing the urgency factor u and the penalty costs for the waiting time of an intervention c^w.

$$Min\ \omega_w(\sigma) = \sum_{i=1}^{I} uc^w \tag{2}$$

Further, all types of surgeries are assigned as early as possible, thus the solver minimizes overtimes $\omega_o(\sigma)$. Adding penalty costs β_u for each canceled or reassigned intervention should lead to the effect that valid schedules with fewer reassignments/cancellations are preferred (3).

$$Min\ \omega_o(\sigma) = \sum_{i=1}^{I} \beta_u i_{canc} \tag{3}$$

3 Related Work

3.1 Surgical Phase Detection

With the increasing digitization and process-orientation in hospitals, surgical phase detection became a very popular field of research in recent years. Especially, the integration of systems for data collection purposes evolved within each OR and in the entire OR area. Starting with the acquisition of video and image signals, standardization approaches (e.g. IEC 80001-1) and new technologies led to the integration of medical devices in clinical networks [18]. Several research projects and vendors of medical devices advance the development of fully integrated ORs, allowing to automatically collect and process data representing intra-operative surgical activities and phases. However, current approaches in this field differ in their data sources and statistical methods for information generation.

A method that produces high-quality data – but very time consuming – is the surgical phase detection by human observations. This observations are valuable for training models but hardly applicable in daily operations in the OR area. For instance, Franke et al. [19] use observations from inside the OR to create surgical process models and time predictions. Ahmadi et al. [20] enrich retrospectively video data with annotations about surgical phases and performed activities. Other contribution solely use image- or video-based data, e.g. collected by endoscopic or microscope cameras [2,21]. Such approaches annotate the raw image data with additional information by linguistic concepts. Electronic signals of surgical devices are used by Padoy et al. and Malpani et al. [22,23]. In addition Meissner et al. [24] used radio frequency identification (RFID) sensors for instrument recognition and accelerometers to infer the performed surgical action. In these approaches only the usage of an instrument is employed for surgical phase detection, they do not consider advanced manifestations of device parameter, which would probably increase detection accuracy. Dergachyova et al. [25] use a mixed approach by combining data of endoscopic videos and instrument usage data [25]. They also utilize surgical process models for future and advanced information generation but lack with details about event pattern modeling and implementation in an application system.

3.2   Remaining Intervention Time Prediction

Research in remaining intervention time prediction can be distinguished into online and offline methods [26]. The focus of this work is on online approaches which make intra-operative predictions in the course of ongoing surgeries. Franke et al. [19] present an approach for the prediction of remaining intervention times based on generalized surgical process models and a simulation-based prediction algorithm. However their approach relies on manually collected data of surgical low-level tasks, implying that human support for data gathering within the OR is needed. Hence the approach is not applicable in fully-automatized and integrated information systems. Furthermore the feature set for simulation is quite small because only the current surgical phase and their average time are used for time prediction. Guedon et al. [13] also propose a real-time and online prediction system for remaining surgery times based on the data of surgical devices. They employ a Support Vector Machine algorithm for the classification of surgeries into remaining time intervals based on their former device usage pattern. Their prediction model only rests upon one parameter of the electrosurgical device that is generally modified in the middle of a surgery. This means that only few surgical activities are recognized and the predictions are only made in intermediate phases of a surgery. Time series analysis and signal processing on surgical workflow data is performed by Maktabi et al. [26] to predict intervention time. They state, that using time periodicity instead of average time-dependent parameters make predictions more accurate. Again this approach uses just one feature for time prediction and further only represents three surgical phases. Further, the described intraoperative online processing pipeline is lacking in technical and implementation details.

3.3   Online Surgery Scheduling

Lots of research has been published discussing the improvement of efficiency in surgery department and OR management. Surgery scheduling in general is one of the highly adapted problems of operations research and scheduling research community. Although many approaches propose that future research has to be conducted in utilizing new data and information sources, few approaches were published that make use of it. Demeulemeester et al. [5] as well as Erdogan et al. [27] state that operational support for real-time scheduling is not researched well in contrast to other domains where real-time approaches can be found. Atkin et al. [28] developed an approach for operational support for online scheduling of airport runways with a deterministic scheduling algorithm. [29] describe an approach to compose primitive context information of location sensors to support real-time accident handling in fleet management use case. As well, the problem of monitoring and scheduling multiple production plants is tackled by an information system including an algorithmic pipeline [30].

Since the OSS problem differentiates in aspects of uncertainty and unpredictability to the characteristics of these domains, the approaches cannot be replicated to the OR area. E.g. in manufacturing use cases the production process can be paused and proceeded within the same state of the item, which is not possible within a surgery [4]. Nevertheless, in surgery scheduling literature several research paper address the OSS problem and suggest approaches for supporting decision makers. Several comprehensive reviews of existing literature were conducted, that cover the various levels of the surgery scheduling problem [4,5,8,27]. Dios et al. [31] provide a DSS for OR managers to plan different decision tasks like medium-term and short-term schedules. Further, it is focused on handling elective patients so it lacks in supporting very short-term planning tasks like handling deviations in intervention times or emergency patients. Erdogan et al. [32] describe a stochastic integer programming model for dynamic sequencing and scheduling of appointments in hospitals with the goal to minimize the weighted sum of direct waiting time and waiting time until appointment for patients. Though, they include different kinds of uncertainties like process durations or number of customers, the model isn't directly portable to OSS since it doesn't involve important surgical characteristics like urgency. Riise et al. [9] propose an approach for a generalized operational surgery scheduling problem that is able to support decision making on different planning levels and with different characteristics. Hence, it helps planning elective patients as well as rescheduling by integrating urgent and emergent patients. Since, they argue that it is also applicable for intra-day rescheduling, the evaluation only focuses on scheduling on a weekly or daily level. Samudra et al. [11] used a discrete event simulation model for the patient scheduling model considering uncertainties like varying estimations and arrivals of unplanned surgeries to avoid excessive overtimes in the OR area. They handle rescheduling of elective patients as well as including non-electives in the current surgery schedule since it represents the hospitals reality. They also use a estimated surgery duration model based on mean values of similar OR sessions but without feature-based machine learning model.

Van Essen et al. [33] developed a DSS that is providing the three best adjusted OR schedules according to variability in surgery duration and emergencies. This system is based on a linear integer programming model with the goal to accomplish the preferences of all stakeholders and departments as good as possible. Further, the objective function includes penalties for canceling surgeries or overtime minimization. It doesn't include the reassignment of surgeries to different ORs which leads to a reduced flexibility in scheduling and hence reduced efficiency. The previously presented approaches treat the OSS problem on an algorithmic level, but don't take into account that information collection and DSS architecture considerations could also show improvements.

4   Solution Approach

Our solution reflects the partitioning of the problem into unique subtasks. Thus, we built an solution with the help of three subsystems: The situation subsystem Sect. 4.1, responsible for gathering necessary information about surgeries, the prediction subsystem Sect. 4.2, responsible for predicting the remaining time for each surgery and finally the rescheduling subsystem Sect. 4.3, responsible for rescheduling surgeries and incorporating urgent interventions. The architecture depicted in Fig. 4 shows the proposed solution approach with its subsystems and relations.

4.1   Situation Detection Subsystem (SDS)

We assume that surgeries are sequences of phases, where each phase is a set or sequence of activities executed by a surgeon. By detecting intra-surgical phases within a surgery the added value is mainly created for real-time monitoring of running surgeries. Necessary data came from the KARL STORZ OR1^{TM} integrated OR system. Data are produced by several devices, namely the insufflator, high frequency coagulation and cutting device, as well as endoscopic and OR light sources. The respective data sources provide real-time information composed of properties, configuration settings and physical quantities of device parameters. Overall 157 different parameters were collected, but not all are suitable for detecting surgical activities. Some of the parameters have binary values, mostly representing the current usage of a device. Others describe physical values like volume and pressure of the carbon dioxide. For our use case we only use parameters which are changing during a surgery. Figure 1 shows in extracts the most expressive features of an example data set. These data depict current and recent states of, for example of OR equipment (e.g. lights) and surgical devices (e.g. electro-surgical devices).

We defined rules and patterns and used a pattern recognition engine that is capable of handling low-level data streams and that provides information about surgical phases as a result. These data streams were partitioned into time-windows and monitored for patterns, thresholds and average values of parameters. The SDS takes data from medical devices and administrative data to build a context and provides an integrated view on the ongoing situation and supports the OR managers' perception in terms of awareness of a given situation. With this, we can significantly reduce efforts for managing the OR area. In order to be able to provide intra-surgical phases the SDS was realized as follows:

Although each intervention of the same surgery type is similar in its activities, the shape of data is never identical. Thus, we needed to analyze data visually as well as with the help of descriptive statistics. This step aimed at finding generally valid characteristics in the given data. For instance, the parameter of the electro-surgical device potentially denotes a specific part of a surgery because it is only used in a particular temporal range. As a result, we had a set of common features, delimitation and temporal relationships of potential surgical phases across several instantiations for a specific surgical type. The following Fig. 3 shows an illustrative example of the pattern "Placing trocars". It shows data of three devices and five parameters for this surgical phase. On the lowest level, e.g. the insufflator parameters *flow*, *pressure* and *gas volume* are monitored separately and represent atomic events. In order to create more complex events a combination of atomic events is defined. In this example we define a specific state change for instance an increasing and decreasing flow. Such complex events can then be combined again and so on. To complete the example, we combine all insufflator events to a complex event, which in combination with events from other devices form the complex event of "placing trocars".

Consequently, we used the detected phases two-fold: We visualized progress of a surgery by reporting detected phase events in data graphs and thus supported information gathering. Further, information about surgical phases depicted main input for predicting the remaining time of surgeries. A more detailed description can be found in [34].

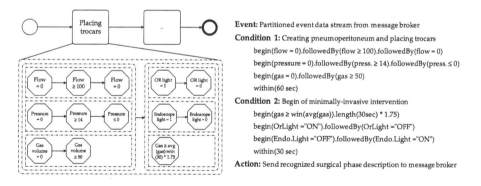

Fig. 3. Event pattern and pseudo code representation of the phase "Placing trocars".

4.2   Prediction Subsystem (PS)

The projection of environmental future states is based on the understanding of a situation and needs lots of domain knowledge and experience. Only these abilities allow quick responses on events, as well as proactive decisions for deterministic behavior in certain, already known situations. In our approach we address these challenges by realizing a subsystem for remaining intervention time estimation. The PS utilizes the concept of the Lambda architecture (cf. Fig. 4), which combines batch and stream data processing [35]. Applications using this concept benefit of the in-depth analytics possible with batch layer and low-latency of the streaming layer. The batch layer is used to process historic data of the recognized surgical phases and to train a regression model that computes a value for the remaining intervention time. We choose a regression algorithm approach for remaining time predictions, since classification algorithms output is less expressive and usable then the continuous outcome variables of regression. In Spangenberg et al. [36] we considered the algorithms of Linear Regression, Decision Tree Regression, Random Forest Regression as well as Multilayer Perceptron Regression, leading to the result that Random Forest Regression achieved the best results regarding to prediction accuracy. The underlying model is build with a regression algorithm based on five features provided by the SDS and additional data from resource databases like the Hospital Information System:

Event Name: The name of the recognized current surgical phase. Some phases are unique to a specific surgery type, while others can be found among multiple surgeries. Each surgery begins with a phase called START and ends with a phase called END.

OPS Code: The OPS code is the official German classification of medical procedures [37]. It holds different granularity of information about the given surgery and is used extract three features. E.g. the OPS Code of a sigmaresection is transformed to the OPS category 5-45, subcategory 5-455 and procedure (5-455.75).

Time Stamp: The time stamp gives information about the starting time of the current phase (or the end of the surgery in case of phase END). It is used to determine the features TIME_PASSED, the time since start of the surgery – and TIME_UNTIL_END – time until the end of surgery. The latter is the target variable that we aim to predict from the other features.

Operating Room: The room in which the surgery takes place. Master et al. [38] claim that the location of a surgery contains basic information about its complexity. Additionally different equipped OR rooms may haven an influence on the procedure.

Phase History: A vector containing information about recent surgical phases. Accurate predictions need the comprehension and involvement of the surgical workflow. Since phases in some cases appear more than once in a surgery the previous phase can give important indications for the current progress.

The current phase as well as an event history based on previously detected phases are factored into the model. As well, the OR and the OPS code have huge influence on the model. These are the input for the regression model to calculate an estimated value for the respective surgery based on the described features. The resulting models are stored in a model database and read by the online prediction component, which represents the speed layer of the Lambda architecture. The online prediction component again is interrelated with the SDS, meaning that a new recognized surgical phase triggers the recomputation of the remaining time. It loads the model and aligns detected phases in running surgeries with the model to update the estimated intervention time. Lastly, this starts triggering the upcoming rescheduling subsystem.

4.3   Rescheduling Subsystem (RS)

After collecting information of the PS, the RS starts to adapt the current schedule to events and changes in surgeries. The RS is responsible for the generation of valid surgery schedules based on the resources and constraints described in Sect. 2. Rescheduling is triggered by several factors, for example changes in remaining durations of running interventions based on the machine learning model. Further, adding emergent or urgent patients to the set of interventions leads to the execution of the rescheduling procedure.

We use a metaheuristics approach for solving the optimization problem of the rescheduling task. Metaheuristics are not supposed to guarantee finding an optimal solution for the optimization problem, but finding an appropriate solution in a given amount of time, which is necessary for our goal to give real-time

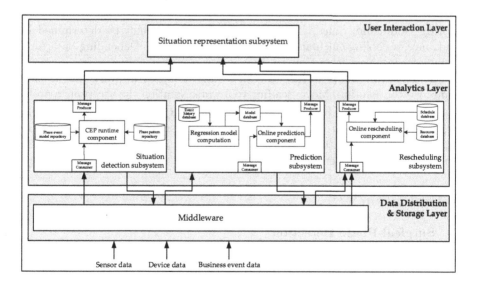

Fig. 4. Architecture model of the subsystems and relations.

decision support. To be more precise, we use the Simulated Annealing algorithm, described in more detail by [39] because it has been successfully used in dynamic scheduling domain before, it is scalable and finds near optimal solutions as well [40]. The search space is defined by two vectors: One for the OR assignments of each surgery and second a vector for non-overlapping time-slots including surgeons, surgical team and ORs. Hence, the planning variables are OR and the combination of starting time slot and the intervention duration and the solver optimizes the rescheduling result according to the goals defined in (1)–(3) in Sect. 2. The cost function incorporates all cost factors of the constraints described in Sect. 2. Violations of the hard constraints, e.g. two surgeries at the same time in the same OR, are not allowed. The quality of a valid schedule is determined by the minimization of the soft constraints. Our metaheuristic consists of the following computational steps, based on the principle of local search:

Initial Solution: To get a satisfying, but non-optimal and mostly not feasible solution, initial solution of a schedule that afterward could be optimized, we use the First Fit Approximation algorithm. The algorithm assigns the interventions to a available planning value (in our case ORs and available time slots) and further takes the already initialized interventions into account. Since, First Fit doesn't change an planning entity after assigning, it terminates after initializing all interventions.

Move Selection: Moves are chosen indiscriminately as it is common for Simulated Annealing algorithm. A move is selected if it is equal or greater than the best move. Furthermore, non-improving moves are also picked with a certain probability according to its score and the time gradient. In the early phase of the calculation process the probability of selecting sub-optimal moves is higher than in later phases.

Cooling Schedule: Since, an ideal cooling method cannot be determined in advance, a cooling calculation for temperature is used. Depending on a time gradient decreases from time to time by a constant quantity.

Acceptance and Stop Criterion: Moves are accepted in every case if they improve the solution. Moves leading to a worse solution the acceptance probability is determined by $e^{\frac{-f}{temp}}$, where f describes the cost function and $temp$ the current temperature. The whole procedure stops when the calculation gains a final temperature T_{min} or exceeds a given amount of time due to the near real-time requirement of the system.

5   Evaluation

5.1   Surgical Phase Detection

To evaluate the suitability of the SDS, the derived and implemented recognition rules were evaluated with data sets of surgical interventions recorded in the Department of Surgery at Heidelberg university hospital. Due to many existing data sources as well as emergent technologies, which could extend our approach in future, we use the stream data processing framework Esper CEP. Table 1 shows the effectiveness of the SDS. The overall accuracy of our approach for the recognition of surgical phases in sigmaresection interventions is about 83%. The phases with the highest prediction rates are the placing trocars phase, the begin and end of the non-minimally invasive tasks and the retracting of the trocars. This is because of very expressive parameter pattern in the data of the medical devices. For placing and retracting trocars these are the insufflator parameters of pressure, flow and gas volume (see Fig. 3) which depict the drop and rise of the parameters at the creation of the pneumoperitoneum and the insertion of the trocars in the abdominal cavity. The non-minimally invasive tasks have high prediction rates as well, due to the opposite usage of the OR lights and the endoscope lights. The phases of preparation and dividing rectum are not as good recognizable. One reason for unrecognized or incorrect classified phases may appear due to erratic parameter characteristics.

For more comprehensive evaluation we applied the generated rules on a set of laparoscopic proctocolectomy interventions, to enlarge the number of data sets for evaluation purposes. Due to the similarity of some of the surgical activities across different surgical types in laparoscopy, we used these data sets to evaluate common phases. The results are also shown in Table 1. Finally we have an overall prediction rate of 76% for common phases in other surgical types. This value could be increased by dropping the data sets which don't have a non-minimally invasive phase. We keep this data sets to simulate a reasonable environment with different surgery types and methods.

5.2   Prediction Subsystem

A leave-one-out cross validation was performed on the level of surgeries, so 14 surgeries were used to train the model and one was taken out of the genuine data set to validate the resulting model. This process was repeated for each surgery. To find the best possible prediction approach we evaluated the performance of

Table 1. Evaluation of surgical phase recognition for laparoscopic surgeries (n = 15).

Surgical phase	sigmaresection	proctocolectomy
Placing trocars	100.0%	88.8%
Preparation	66.7%	44.4%
Venting Fume	66.7%	88.8%
Dividing rectum	66.7%	–
Extracting rectosigmoid	83.3%	–
Preparing extra-abdominally	83.3%	77.7%
Preparing intra-abdominally	83.3%	77.7%
Retracting trocars	100.0%	100.0%
Overall	83.3%	76.4%

Table 2. Comparison of approaches for remaining intervention time prediction. The mean absolute error is defined as: $\text{MAE} = \frac{1}{n}\sum |y_i - f_i|$. n is the number of samples, f_i is the predicted value of the i-th sample and y_i its real value. The MAE/MSD ratio describes the proportion of the prediction deviation and the length of the surgery, since long surgeries are presumably more difficult to predict, thus having a higher MAE.

Authors	Procedure type	MSD	MAE	$\frac{\text{MAE}}{\text{MSD}}$
Franke et al. 2013 [19]	neurosurg. discectomy	75	13.4	0.18
Franke et al. 2013 [19]	brain tumor removal	241	29.3	0.12
Guedon et al. 2016 [13]	lap. cholecystectomy	-	14	-
Li et al. 2017 [41]	trauma resuscitation	46.6	6.5	0.14
Maktabi et al. 2017 [26]	lumbar discectomy	54	21.45	0.39
Twinanda et al. 2018 [42]	lap. cholecystectomy	38.1	4.2	0.11
This work	lap. sigmaresection & proctocolectomy	183.3	16.44	0.089

our approach with several algorithms (for more details see [36]). The Random forest regression algorithm performs better than the other algorithms on the data set. It is important to consider the different mean surgery lengths and standard deviations in the data set. The surgery data used in our evaluation has a mean length of 183.8 min (std 50 min). Since the accuracy of remaining time predictions is most important for the timing of the scheduling and preparation of the next surgery, it is not relevant at the very beginning of the procedure. Hence, an increased accuracy at the end of a surgery is crucial for the usability of the system. Some of the discussed related papers also present prediction errors in minutes that are comparable to our results. They are shown along with the used surgical procedure and their mean time in Table 2. Our systems results are comparable and in some cases better than the current approaches. It has to be taken into account that all systems are evaluated on different data and different kinds of surgeries which are of different length and complexity. Therefore, the comparison can not be used to determine one of the prediction engines clearly outperforming the others. This could only be achieved by a benchmark that uses unified input data. We can draw the conclusion that the prediction error of our system ranges in the same magnitude as current systems. However, we have to acknowledge that the underlying data base is quite small since it is hard to get appropriate data sets and necessary validation information.

5.3   OSS

To evaluate the RS, we used a data set of 15 surgeries with real-world data that produced a low-level event stream to simulate a surgery day and feed the SDS. The detected intra-surgical phases trigger the calculation of remaining intervention times and use this information afterward to start rescheduling. With this data, we simulated an OR area environment, representing 10 ORs each with

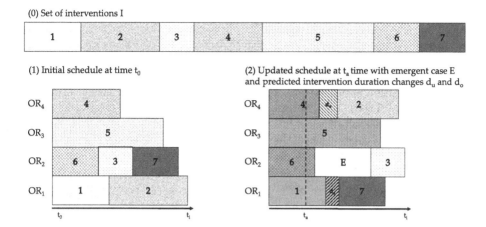

Fig. 5. Performance of the Rescheduling Subsystem for OSS [17].

10 hours of operation/day and 4 starting time slots/hour. In this stage the interventions can have five different states:

- Planned: Intervention is introduced to the system, but OR or time slot are not assigned already.
- Scheduled: OR or time slots are assigned, but intervention didn't start yet.
- In progress: Intervention is running and changes in running intervention time are likely but OR isn't moveable.
- Reassigned: Scheduled intervention is reassigned to other OR or time slot.
- Canceled: Are delayed with higher priority for next day.

Observations showed that each running intervention updates its predicted remaining time on an average of 20 times so the rescheduling is triggered the same number. Further, the observations indicate that the metaheuristic provides good solutions according to tardiness and schedule stability. Few reassignments or cancellations are done by the algorithm and non-elective interventions, that are fed into system as well, are assigned fast (see Fig. 5).

First implication of the proposed system for productive operations is, that the notable number of updates to the surgery schedule will increase. This is due to the fact that domain knowledge of the OR manager, e.g. for remaining intervention times, is now modeled and leads to a higher degree of transparency, since less information and thus decisions are based on experience-based knowledge and human estimations. For the OR manager two major improvements can be noted. First, the whole process for information collection in the OR area is simplified. Second, the cognitive efforts for combining current states, estimations, available resources and potential emergencies to an updated surgery schedule, what is done without software support so far, is reduced significantly.

5.4   Prototypical Evaluation

We also instantiated the presented architecture model of Fig. 4, resting upon state-of-the-art technologies and deployed it in a Hadoop-based four-node cluster. According to the evaluation framework FEDS this means a formative and artificial evaluation approach [43]. The formative aspects of the evaluation focus on the outcome of the artifact for the described problem since we want to improve results of the decision processes in OR area. Namely, the *Technical Risk & Efficacy* evaluation strategy was conducted due to the high costs and risks for evaluation in the OR environment. By using a set of real-world data streams of surgeries, including medical and surgical device data as well as historical data of surgical phase events and the possibility to add emergent patients, a synthetic, but realistic scenario of a day in OR area was created.

Currently, surgical devices and OR equipment produce 65,000 events per hour in a single intervention. Hence, we choose a scalable approach for data processing and storage, since it is conceivable that in a production environment several ORs run in parallel. Further, the amounts of data of available sensors or smart devices soon will exceed the processing capacities of a single-node architectures. The data ingestion and distribution layer was realized with the Apache Kafka message broker, due to its prevalence in Big Data use cases backed up in its scalability and reliability. The various data structures are stored in a plain Hadoop distributed file system (HDFS). Since each piece of information has different requirements, the usage of more efficient storage layers on top, e.g. Apache Accumulo, has to be considered in the design concept for future improvements. To implement the SDS we used the Complex Event Processing method for the conceptual foundation. The resulting rules and patterns were realized with the Esper CEP engine [44] since its strong expressiveness and good scalability. To implement the PS we borrowed the concept of a Machine Learning model described in [36] and implemented it with scalable Big Data frameworks to be conscious for increasing amounts of data and complexity. In the back-end, a batch processing component based on Apache Spark [45] generates and updates periodically Random Forest models. Further, alignments of newly recognized surgical phases are performed with an online method implemented in Apache Kafka Streams [46]. The resulting remaining time prediction of an intervention is presented in the front-end, in a dashboard view, as shown in Fig. 6. In case of delays the attention of the user is gained with salient colored frames. Finally, for the OSS problem, we modeled and implemented the RS, consisting of a domain model of OR area resources and several planning constraints, e.g. to prioritize emergent patients, prevent double occupancy or minimize reassignments. To solve the optimization problem of finding a feasible and efficient solution for assigning all interventions to an OR and a corresponding time slot, the OptaPlanner [48] constraint solver is utilized. This rescheduling process is triggered by detected surgical phase events, which lead coincidentally to an updated predicted intervention time. With this solution approach we provide near real-time responses to detected surgical phases in the ORs. A screenshot of this visualization component can be seen in Fig. 7. The underlying data of OR resources are connected

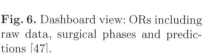

Fig. 6. Dashboard view: ORs including raw data, surgical phases and predictions [47].

Fig. 7. Surgery scheduling view: initial schedule and after rescheduling due to emergency (of a simulated OR plan) [47].

to OptaPlanner via RESTful interfaces and the resulting updated schedules are visualized with the timetable.js framework [49].

We demonstrated this prototype and the scenario to a group of domain experts to rate criteria for evaluating Information System artifacts [17]. Operational feasibility as well as usefulness were rated high since the majority of the experts see the potential of the prototype for daily business and are sure that the artifact will reduce communication and cognitive efforts of the users.

6 Conclusion

In this paper we presented a novel solution approach for supporting the OSS problem by a real-time DSS that allows situation awareness for the OR manager by better information representation and prevention of information overload. The proposed approach denotes an innovative solution since most of the current approaches operate on the tactical and strategical planning and scheduling with longer time horizons. Real-time data of surgical and OR devices were utilized to monitor current states of each surgery. Predictive Analytics methods and an online optimization technique were employed to provide the decision-maker with additional information about remaining intervention times and suggestions for rescheduling in case of uncertainties and emergencies.

This work is the first that provides an integrated architecture and the necessary processing and analytics components for data-driven DSS that provides real-time information to support OSS. The approach allows the automated detection of surgical phases to monitor the states of laparoscopic surgeries, which has short time delays due to the use of real-time data. Based on this information about current surgical phases, a Predictive Analytics component for remaining intervention times is presented. This is integrated in the lambda architecture concept, consisting of a batch layer for model computation and an streaming layer for online predictions in response to the detection of a surgical phase. Consequently, an online optimization technique was employed that utilizes the prior information and a metaheuristics approach to provide the decision-maker with additional information about remaining intervention times and suggestions for rescheduling in case of uncertainties and emergencies.

From a research point-of-view, the presented approach and its description in an architecture model represent artifacts that can utilized by other hospitals to transfer our approach to their environment. In addition, the prototypical implementation provides a proof-of-concept for an approach that allows real-time decision support for OSS. Hence, the application presented in this paper is an innovative artifact for researchers as well as for practitioners since - according to Demeulemeester [5] - few of the presented scientific approaches for supporting OR managers and improving OSS were implemented respectively largely focus on daily or weekly planning horizons.

However, there are several limitations of our research that must be addressed in future work: In this work we focused on the utilization of data of surgical devices and OR equipment related to laparoscopic surgeries. Future studies should integrate data sources that are available in other surgical methods, e.g. using image- and video-data of minimally-invasive surgeries [2], identify instrument usage in open surgical procedures [50] or location sensor data [51]. The SDS was realized with a rule-based approach and the Complex Event Processing technology, that needs a prior knowledge-intensive process [34]. The usage of Time Series Analysis as well as artificial neural networks methods [3] seam to have the potential to reduce this modeling efforts and allow automated approaches. The Predictions Subsystem utilizes the feature set provided by the SDS as well as resource and surgery information contained in the surgery schedule. The accuracy of the prediction model could be improved by the integration of patient-specific information like age, gender, medical history, among others. The Rescheduling Subsystem so far uses information of the current surgery schedule about necessary staff and resources. Modeling more resources and constraints would lead to a more realistic model of the OR environment. The evaluation of the architecture was done with the prototypical implementation and means a proof-of-concept. Future investigations should focus on an exhaustive and more naturalistic system evaluation has to be done to measure the artifacts performance in a real hospital setting.

Acknowledgments. This paper was funded by the German Federal Ministry of Education and Research under the project Competence Center for Scalable Data Services and Solutions Dresden/Leipzig (BMBF 01IS14014B) and by the German Federal Ministry of Economic Affairs and Energy under the project InnOPlan (BMWI 01MD15002E).

References

1. Macario, A.: What does one minute of operating room time cost? J. Clin. Anesth. **22**, 233–236 (2010)
2. Katić, D., et al.: Bridging the gap between formal and experience-based knowledge for context-aware laparoscopy. Int. J. Comput. Assist. Radiol. Surg. **11**, 881–888 (2016)

3. Twinanda, A.P., Shehata, S., Mutter, D., Marescaux, J., de Mathelin, M., Padoy, N.: EndoNet: a deep architecture for recognition tasks on laparoscopic videos. IEEE Trans. Med. Imaging **36**, 86–97 (2017)
4. May, J.H., Spangler, W.E., Strum, D.P., Vargas, L.G.: The surgical scheduling problem: current research and future opportunities. Prod. Oper. Manag. **20**, 392–405 (2011)
5. Demeulemeester, E., Belién, J., Cardoen, B., Samudra, M.: Operating room planning & scheduling. In: Handbook of Healthcare Operations Management: Methods and Applications, pp. 121–152 (2013)
6. Hans, E.W., Vanberkel, P.T.: Operating theatre planning and scheduling. In: Hall, R. (ed.) Handbook of Healthcare System Scheduling. International Series in Operations Research & Management Science, vol. 168, pp. 105–130. Springer, Boston (2012). https://doi.org/10.1007/978-1-4614-1734-7_5
7. Dexter, F., Epstein, R.H., Traub, R.D., Xiao, Y.: Making management decisions on the day of surgery based on operating room efficiency and patient waiting times. Anesthesiology **101**, 1444–1453 (2004)
8. Guerriero, F., Guido, R.: Operational research in the management of the operating theatre: a survey. Health Care Manag. Sci. **14**, 89–114 (2011)
9. Riise, A., Mannino, C., Burke, E.K.: Modelling and solving generalised operational surgery scheduling problems. Comput. Oper. Res. **66**, 1–11 (2016)
10. Guido, R., Conforti, D.: A hybrid genetic approach for solving an integrated multi-objective operating room planning and scheduling problem. Comput. Oper. Res. **87**, 270–282 (2017)
11. Samudra, M., Demeulemeester, E., Cardoen, B., Vansteenkiste, N., Rademakers, F.E.: Due time driven surgery scheduling. Health Care Manag. Sci. **20**, 326–352 (2017)
12. Eijkemans, M.J.C., van Houdenhoven, M., Nguyen, T., Boersma, E., Steyerberg, E.W., Kazemier, G.: Predicting the unpredictablea new prediction model for operating room times using individual characteristics and the surgeon's estimate. J. Am. Soc. Anesth. **112**, 41–49 (2010)
13. Guédon, A., et al.: 'It is time to prepare the next patient' real-time prediction of procedure duration in laparoscopic cholecystectomies. J. Med. Syst. **40**, 271–277 (2016)
14. Samudra, M., van Riet, C., Demeulemeester, E., Cardoen, B., Vansteenkiste, N., Rademakers, F.E.: Scheduling operating rooms: achievements, challenges and pitfalls. J. Sched. **19**, 493–525 (2016)
15. Vieira, G., Herrmann, J., Lin, E.: Rescheduling manufacturing systems: a framework of strategies, policies, and methods. J. Sched. **6**, 39–62 (2003)
16. Aytug, H., Lawley, M.A., McKay, K., Mohan, S., Uzsoy, R.: Executing production schedules in the face of uncertainties: a review and some future directions. Eur. J. Oper. Res. **161**, 86–110 (2005)
17. Spangenberg, N., Wilke, M., Augenstein, C., Franczyk, B.: Online surgery rescheduling - a data-driven approach for real-time decision support. In: Proceedings of the 20th International Conference on Enterprise Information Systems, ICEIS 2018, Funchal, Madeira, Portugal, 21–24 March 2018, vol. 1, pp. 336–343 (2018)
18. Niederlag, W., Lemke, H.U., Strauß, G., Feußner, H. (eds.): Der digitale Operationssaal. Health Academy, vol. 2. De Gruyter, Berlin (2014)
19. Franke, S., Meixensberger, J., Neumuth, T.: Intervention time prediction from surgical low-level tasks. J. Bio. Inf. **46**, 152–159 (2013)

20. Ahmadi, S.-A., Sielhorst, T., Stauder, R., Horn, M., Feussner, H., Navab, N.: Recovery of surgical workflow without explicit models. In: Larsen, R., Nielsen, M., Sporring, J. (eds.) MICCAI 2006, Part I. LNCS, vol. 4190, pp. 420–428. Springer, Heidelberg (2006). https://doi.org/10.1007/11866565_52

21. Lalys, F., Bouget, D., Riffaud, L., Jannin, P.: Automatic knowledge-based recognition of low-level tasks in ophthalmological procedures. Int. J. Comput. Assist. Radiol. Surg. **8**, 39–49 (2013)

22. Padoy, N., Blum, T., Ahmadi, S.A., Feussner, H., Berger, M.O., Navab, N.: Statistical modeling and recognition of surgical workflow. Med. Image Anal. **16**, 632–641 (2012)

23. Malpani, A., Lea, C., Chen, C.C.G., Hager, G.D.: System events: readily accessible features for surgical phase detection. Int. J. Comput. Assist. Radiol. Surg. **11**, 1201–1209 (2016)

24. Meissner, C., Meixensberger, J., Pretschner, A., Neumuth, T.: Sensor-based surgical activity recognition in unconstrained environments. Minim. Invasive Ther. Allied Technol. MITAT Off. J. Soc. Minim. Invasive Ther. **23**, 198–205 (2014)

25. Dergachyova, O., Bouget, D., Huaulme, A., Morandi, X., Jannin, P.: Automatic data-driven real-time segmentation and recognition of surgical workflow. Int. J. Comput. Assist. Radiol. Surg. **11**, 1081–1089 (2016)

26. Maktabi, M., Neumuth, T.: Online time and resource management based on surgical workflow time series analysis. Int. J. Comput. Assist. Radiol. Surg. **12**, 325–338 (2017)

27. Erdogan, S.A., et al.: Surgery planning and scheduling. In: Wiley Encyclopedia of Operations Research and Management Science. Wiley Online Library (2010)

28. Atkin, J.A.D., Burke, E.K., Greenwood, J.S., Reeson, D.: On-line decision support for take-off runway scheduling with uncertain taxi times at London heathrow airport. J. Sched. **11**, 323–346 (2008)

29. Ngai, E., Leung, T., Wong, Y.H., Lee, M., Chai, P., Choi, Y.S.: Design and development of a context-aware decision support system for real-time accident handling in logistics. Decis. Support Syst. **52**, 816–827 (2012)

30. Guo, Z.X., Ngai, E., Yang, C., Liang, X.: An RFID-based intelligent decision support system architecture for production monitoring and scheduling in a distributed manufacturing environment. Int. J. Prod. Econ. **159**, 16–28 (2015)

31. Dios, M., Molina-Pariente, J.M., Fernandez-Viagas, V., Andrade-Pineda, J.L., Framinan, J.M.: A decision support system for operating room scheduling. Comput. Ind. Eng. **88**, 430–443 (2015)

32. Erdogan, S.A., Gose, A., Denton, B.T.: Online appointment sequencing and scheduling. IIE Trans. **47**, 1267–1286 (2015)

33. van Essen, J.T., Hurink, J.L., Hartholt, W., van den Akker, B.J.: Decision support system for the operating room rescheduling problem. Health Care Manag. Sci. **15**, 355–372 (2012)

34. Spangenberg, N., Augenstein, C., Franczyk, B., Wagner, M., Apitz, M., Kenngott, H.: Method for intra-surgical phase detection by using real-time medical device data. In: 30th IEEE International Symposium on Computer-Based Medical Systems, pp. 1–8 (2017)

35. Marz, N., Warren, J.: Big Data: Principles and Best Practices of Scalable Realtime Data Systems. Manning Publications Co., Greenwich (2015)

36. Spangenberg, N., Wilke, M., Franczyk, B.: A big data architecture for intra-surgical remaining time predictions. Procedia Comput. Sci. **113**, 310–317 (2017)

37. Graubner, B.: OPS Systematisches Verzeichnis 2014: Operationen-und Prozeduren-schlüssel-Internationale Klassifikation der Prozeduren in der Medizin Version 2014. Deutscher Ärzteverlag (2013)
38. Master, N., Scheinker, D., Bambos, N.: Predicting pediatric surgical durations (2016). arXiv preprint: arXiv:1605.04574
39. Kirkpatrick, S., Gelatt, C.D., Vecchi, M.P.: Optimization by simulated annealing. Science **220**, 671–680 (1983)
40. Ceschia, S., Schaerf, A.: Dynamic patient admission scheduling with operating room constraints, flexible horizons, and patient delays. J. Sched. **19**, 377–389 (2016)
41. Li, X., et al.: Progress estimation and phase detection for sequential processes. Proc. ACM Interact. Mob. Wearable Ubiquitous Technol. **1**, 1–20 (2017)
42. Twinanda, A.P., Yengera, G., Mutter, D., Marescaux, J., Padoy, N.: RSDNet: learning to predict remaining surgery duration from laparoscopic videos without manual annotations (2018). arXiv preprint: arXiv:1802.03243
43. Venable, J., Pries-Heje, J., Baskerville, R.: FEDS: a framework for evaluation in design science research. Eur. J. Inf. Syst. **25**, 77–89 (2016)
44. EsperTech Inc.: Esper (2018)
45. Apache Software Foundation: Apache spark - lightning-fast cluster computing (2018)
46. Apache Software Foundation: Kafka streams - the easiest way to write mission-critical real-time applications & microservices (2018)
47. Spangenberg, N., Augenstein, C., Franczyk, B., Wilke, M.: Implementation of a situation aware and real-time approach for decision support in online surgery scheduling. In: 31st IEEE International Symposium on Computer-Based Medical Systems, CBMS 2018, Karlstad, Sweden, 18–21 June 2018, pp. 417–421 (2018)
48. Red Hat Inc.: Optaplanner - constraint satisfaction solver (2018)
49. TimeTable.js: A javascript plugin for beautiful responsive timetables (2018)
50. Glaser, B., Dänzer, S., Neumuth, T.: Intra-operative surgical instrument usage detection on a multi-sensor table. Int. J. Comput. Assist. Radiol. Surg. **10**, 351–362 (2015)
51. Nara, A., Allen, C., Izumi, K.: Surgical phase recognition using movement data from video imagery and location sensor data. In: Griffith, D.A., Chun, Y., Dean, D.J. (eds.) Advances in Geocomputation. AGIS, pp. 229–237. Springer, Cham (2017). https://doi.org/10.1007/978-3-319-22786-3_21

A Fuzzy Reasoning Process for Conversational Agents in Cognitive Cities

Sara D'Onofrio[1](✉), Stefan Markus Müller[2], and Edy Portmann[1]

[1] Human-IST Institute, University of Fribourg, Fribourg, Switzerland
{sara.donofrio,edy.portmann}@unifr.ch
[2] APP Unternehmensberatung AG, Bern, Switzerland
stefan.mueller@app.com

Abstract. Facing the challenges in a city that is to be understood as a complex construct, this article presents a solution approach for the further development of existing conversational agents, which should be used particularly in cities, for instance, as a source of information. The proposed framework consists of a fuzzy analogical reasoning process (based on structure-mapping theory) and a network-like memory (i.e., fuzzy cognitive maps stored in graph databases) as additions to the general architecture of a chatbot. Thus, it represents a concept of a global fuzzy reasoning process, which allows conversational agents to emulate human information processing by using cognitive computing (consisting of soft computing methods and cognition and learning theories). The framework is already in the third iteration of its development. Three experiments were conducted to examine the stability of the theoretical foundation as well as the potential of the framework.

Keywords: Cognitive city · Cognitive computing · Conversational agent · Design science research · Fuzzy Analogical Reasoning · Fuzzy reasoning · Human smart city · Smart city · Soft computing · Transdisciplinary research

1 Introduction

The ever-increasing urbanization requires cities to deal with emerging challenges (e.g., energy consumption, dwindling living space, human well-being). As citizens produce an enormous amount of data every day, it poses an additional challenge to fetch these large amounts and the variety of urban data to use them. The processing of vast amounts of data and the inclusion of semi- or unstructured data as well as heterogeneous data types and sources require advanced analysis tools and mechanisms. Moreover, the increasing fuzziness in information, for instance, what it means to consume *low* energy or how a *family-friendly* neighborhood should look like, also requires new technological solutions to receive such perceptions of citizens. Therefore, the increased use of information and communication technologies in cities must be accelerated.

A city that invests in advanced information and communication technologies to optimize existing urban processes is referred to as a smart city [42]. These technologies can include anything such as sensor-based systems to collect data, online platforms for the information exchange among citizens or mobile applications to retrieve helpful

© Springer Nature Switzerland AG 2019
S. Hammoudi et al. (Eds.): ICEIS 2018, LNBIP 363, pp. 104–129, 2019.
https://doi.org/10.1007/978-3-030-26169-6_6

urban information (e.g., traffic news). Although a smart city aims to comprise not only technological fields, it rather represents a technocratic concept (i.e., a concept based on scientific and technical knowledge). This is particularly useful regarding an increase in efficiency across combined urban systems. However, it is not only efficiency that needs to be addressed in a city but also sustainability and resilience to prepare the city and its citizens for the emergent urban challenges mentioned above [16].

Speaking of citizens: To design and ultimately implement urban services based on their needs, citizens must be involved into urban development. This participation can take different forms, depending on individual involvement and commitment. However, through the use of urban services, each individual citizen gets involved substantially in driving the city forward by providing data and by sharing their needs using advanced information and communication technologies. Hence, citizens turn into the *drivers of change* in the development of urban systems, which can lead to new forms of participatory governance [39]. To further improve the human-centered model of a city, the use of technologies can again be exploited. Cognitive computing represents such a technological approach that could help to manage the huge amount of data and to foster self-contained communication among citizens as well as between citizens and those responsible for a city [27].

Cognitive systems do not only recognize the meaning of the information being processed but also create cognitive links between different chunks of information. The aim is to develop computer systems that can mimic the cognitive abilities of a human (e.g., learning, reasoning) and thus process the produced data of a city in a human-like way. Cognitive computing therefore enables supplementing computer systems with cognitive processes and accelerating urban development to foster cognitive cities [14]. A cognitive city refers to a concept of a city based on the investments of a smart city that complements existing urban information and communication technologies with technologically feasible cognitive (human-like) processes.

One possibility to use advanced information and communication technologies for public benefit in a city is the use of conversational agents (e.g., chatbots, virtual assistants). These agents represent a dialogue system, which is accessible through an interface (e.g., Web page, mobile application) and able to conduct a conversation and/or to execute transactions [47]. However, the capabilities of such dialogue systems are still very limited. In this context, it is not expedient to consider what a computer system might be capable of but rather to consider how humans process information and then to inflict this ability to the computer system. Humans perceive and process information in different ways, depending on existing knowledge, experience, education, attitudes and faith [48]. But there are ways of information processing that all individuals commonly use, such as analogical reasoning.

This article focuses on structure-mapping theory, a framework from cognitive science that gradually explains how humans create analogies [18]. Based on this, a conceptual framework has been designed to allow a dialogue system to create analogies during an interaction with a human. Because of the variety of dialogue systems, the authors concentrate on text-based chatbots.

This article represents an extension of the article "Fuzzy Analogical Reasoning in Cognitive Cities – A Conceptual Framework for Urban Dialogue Systems", written by Müller et al. [37], which has been published in the proceedings of the 20th International

Conference on Enterprise Systems (ICEIS 2018) as well as of the article "Fuzzy Reasoning Process in Cognitive Cities – An Exploratory Work on Fuzzy Analogical Reasoning Using Fuzzy Cognitive Maps", written by D'Onofrio et al., which has been published in the proceedings of the IEEE International Conference on Fuzzy Systems (FUZZ-IEEE 2018). The authors herewith present a new conceptual framework – fuzzy analogical reasoning – for text-based chatbots, a main component of a fuzzy reasoning process to be developed, to emulate human analogical reasoning based on soft computing techniques. The extension mainly consists of a more intense analysis in the area of conversational agents.

This article is an outline of a work-in-progress. The authors pursue an approach derived from design science research [26] that is advanced by transdisciplinary research [51] and follows the law of parsimony [31]. Section 2 presents the theoretical background; the approach itself is outlined in Sect. 3 and evaluated in Sect. 4; Sect. 5 concludes the article with a discussion.

2   Theoretical Background

Starting with the demonstration of how a city can be transformed into a cognitive city and followed by the explanation of cognitive computing, the components of the latter, namely soft computing as well as cognitive and learning theories, are highlighted. This way, the bridge to analogical reasoning, focusing on structure-mapping theory, will be built. Finally, conversational agents are introduced, capable of supporting the development of cognitive cities based on cognitive computing approaches.

2.1   The Vision of a Cognitive City

Cities are difficult to manage because they represent a combination of complex, interdependent and non-linear systems that need to collaborate with each other (i.e., a system of systems) [27]. Due to this complexity, it is essential to discuss the concept of a city and to consider strategies for an enhanced urban living standard. A concept, which promises to improve urban life, is smart city.

The term smart city is often used but there is still no definition that is academically or industrially accepted but some attempts at defining it [10]. According to Giffinger et al. [23], a smart city is a city that operates in a forward-looking manner in economic, social and environmental fields. It seeks efficient and effective solutions for the respective area to improve the quality of services for citizens. Caragliu et al. [8] support this description but specify it with regard to the solution approaches required. In their opinion, a smart city is a city that makes investments in human and social capital as well as in information and communication technologies to drive sustainable economic growth and a high quality of life with efficient use of natural resources. Portmann and Finger [42] describe a smart city as a network of citizens and advanced information and communication technologies, which require a well-functioning communication infrastructure. This description supports the statement of Harrison et al. [25], who express that a city, which combines the various urban infrastructures (e.g., physical, information technology, social and business) to leverage the collective intelligence, might be a smart city. It is evident that a smart city impacts not only urban governance in the narrower sense but also numerous other fields of action.

Another key feature of a smart city is the collection and analysis of urban data and their preparation into information [24]. By using ubiquitous sensors, personal devices, social networks and other data-acquisition systems, a city can capture and synthesize data comprehensively from different urban systems [10]. Urban data (e.g., human's behavior in public places, traffic flows, visitor rates at specific events) allow for understanding how urban processes work and how they are perceived by the city's stakeholders [39]. Building upon advanced information and communication technologies, smart urban systems, such as dialogue systems, represent potential starting points for enriching civic interaction, supporting collaboration and empowering citizens with new abilities to source information and to actively propose new ideas [41]. This provides information about the stakeholders' needs, which are an integral part of urban development, and gives cities an integrated view on issues (e.g., urban living space, healthcare, mobility).

Thereof, citizen-centric and participatory models of urban governance can be established, allowing for the development of human smart cities by putting citizens in the foreground. Thereby, it is essential to balance the technical proficiency of information and communication technologies with softer features such as social engagement, citizen empowerment and civic interaction in physical and virtual settings [39, 41]. Virtual settings demand stakeholders' acceptance of new technologies. Hence, it is required to evaluate how technological components will be affecting not only technological and economic but also ecological and social urban processes.

To encourage the acceptance of new technologies, existing urban computer systems can be supplemented by cognitive computing. Cognitive computing comprises, among other things, the ability to process natural language in a human-like way as well as to acquire cognitive abilities, such as remembering, learning and reasoning [13]. The development of cognitive systems enables cities learn based on incoming data and to react to changes in their environments (based on past experiences) [27]. Thus, systems become increasingly capable of dealing with a human living environment that is constantly changing and getting more complex [36]. Addressing urban resilience is where cognitive cities' leading edge is most significant: They fully understand themselves as socio-technical systems that need to withstand external shocks (e.g., heat waves, water shortages, riots) [16]. Through the mutual communication, systems as well as citizens learn from each other and build together a collective knowledge base [34, 46]. This leads to a closer relationship between a city's responsible and its citizens, making urban processes not only more efficient and effective, but also establishing the city more attractive as an urban living space.

In the end, by building upon information and communication technologies, shared infrastructures, citizens' social networks and collective intelligence, coupled with innovative service provision and (participatory) governance structures, cities can cope with complex challenges, such as big data, urbanization and digitalization and can thus become efficient, sustainable and resilient [42].

2.2   The Emergent Era of Cognitive Computing

From the authors' perspective, the essential components of cognitive computing are the interaction as well as the mutual complementation of soft computing and cognitive and learning theories. These components are introduced more detailed below.

2.2.1   Soft Computing: Techniques Based on Fuzzy Logic

Fuzzy logic represents an extension of traditional logic where p can be true or false or have an intermediate truth value. Such an intermediate truth value is an element of a finite or infinite set T of potential truth values (i.e., fuzzy characterization of a numerical truth value) [55], ranging over a finite or infinite number of fuzzy subsets that lie within T (e.g., true, more or less true, neither true nor false, more or less false, false) [54].

This allows a generalization of conventional set theory, namely fuzzy set theory, where an element x of a finite or infinite set X is no longer either contained or not in a crisp subset A in X. It can be contained in a fuzzy subset $\tilde{A}$ in X to a certain degree instead. Hence, it is possible to define a membership function $\mu_{\tilde{A}}(x)$, which shows to what degree (i.e., from no membership to full membership) that an element x is contained in a fuzzy subset $\tilde{A}$ in X [53]:

$$\mu_{\tilde{A}}(x) \to [0, 1] \tag{1}$$

To build fuzzy sets, it is required that humans decompose information from its wholeness into indistinguishable, similar and functional clumps (i.e., information granules) [57]. By breaking down information into various levels of abstraction and classifying information in different levels of granularity (e.g., general words represent high levels of granularity, specific words express low levels of granularity) [52], fuzzy granulation helps to wrap up data and reduce the complexity of the existing data set.

To represent the fuzzy information granules (considered as knowledge) in an understandable way, fuzzy cognitive maps (as a possible network-like memory) can be used to structure and model them, as proposed by D'Onofrio et al. [13]. Fuzzy cognitive maps are uncertainty-extended enlargements of conventional cognitive maps, which allow for representing a network-like fuzzy graphs structure to enable causal reasoning. They consist of concepts C_i (i.e., nodes), containing values A_i (i.e., quantity of its corresponding physical value), and linkages between them m_i (i.e., edges). Enriched by fuzzy logic, nodes C_i and edges m_i can take fuzzy states (e.g., "little", "strong" instead of [0, 1]) and show to which degree one concept affects another (i.e., causal relationships). A causal relationship is expressed by the weight of its edge that typically takes a value between $[-1, 1]$. By means of an adjacency matrix M, a fuzzy cognitive map and its causal conceptual centrality can be replicated, as shown in Fig. 1 [30].

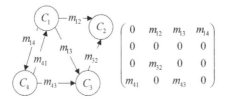

Fig. 1. Example of a fuzzy cognitive map with its adjacency matrix M [13].

For instance, the adjacency matrix M illustrated above contains amongst other an edge from node C_1 to node C_3. Its weight is expressed by m_{13} and indicates how C_1 causally influences C_3: If $m_{13} > 0$, C_1 increases C_3; if $m_{13} < 0$, C_1 decreases C_3; and if $m_{13} = 0$, C_1 has no influence on C_3 [30]. Causal relationships between nodes C_i can also be described by linguistic values (e.g., words) complementing weight of edges.

Furthermore, fuzzy information granules provide the basis for using computing with words, allowing to describe human-like reasoning based on fuzzy logic. Computing with words uses linguistic instead of numerical or symbolical variables and values. A basic application of this technique are fuzzy IF-THEN rules. Assumed that a linguistic variable U with a value u is related to another linguistic variable W with a value w – by a membership function as per fuzzy set theory – such that it is $f(U) \rightarrow W$, where $u \in U$ and $w \in W$, the following fuzzy IF-THEN rules can potentially be applied to trigger decisions derived from fuzzy information [56]:

$$f : \text{if } u \text{ is cheap then } w \text{ is small}$$
$$f : \text{if } u \text{ is expensive then } w \text{ is large} \tag{2}$$

Besides fuzzy IF-THEN rules, there are more applications of computing with words that build upon the concept of a generalized constraint. Since most real-world constraints are tolerant to fuzziness, this concept strives to define degrees of fuzziness based on computing with words. As the following formula shows, the generalized constraint has a basic form that is adjustable to a variety of real-world modalities [58]:

$$GC : X \text{ is } r \; R \tag{3}$$

Thereby, X is a constrained variable and R a fuzzy constraining relation. The modularity (i.e., linguistic meaning) of R is identified by r, an indexing variable that is adjustable (e.g., equal "=", possibilistic "blank", probabilistic "r") [58]. By adjusting, for instance, the fuzzy constraining relation R to possibilistic semantics, r is abbreviated to a blank space and the generalized constraint is modified as follows [56]:

$$GC : X \text{ is } R \tag{4}$$

With possibilistic semantics, a fuzzy relation R constrains a variable X by playing the role of the possibility distribution of X. If u is a generic value of X, and μ_R is a membership function in R, the semantics of R can be defined as follows [56]:

$$\text{Poss}\{X = u\} = \mu_R(u) \tag{5}$$

Soft computing methods foster human-like reasoning and facilitate the application of cognition and learning theories, such as analogical reasoning.

2.2.2 Analogical Reasoning: Structure-Mapping Theory

The construction of synthetic cognition is currently amongst other one of the most stimulating research fields. One way to design synthetic cognition or at least move into this direction is to apply analogical reasoning to computer systems. An analogy represents an abstraction of higher-order human cognition, also referred to as symbolic information processing. Symbolic information processing describes a complex form of referential association that typically involves humans mapping one situation onto another to acquire new information, to reason and to learn new knowledge. Thereby, humans mainly focus on relational similarity between two situations, which is based on labeled relations [5]. Derived from this, an analogy is apparent if a relation between a pair of data elements d and e is structurally similar to a relation between another pair of data elements g and h (e.g., *district is to city as chapter is to book*) [3].

One approach for analogy and, in general, similarity is the theoretical framework of structure-mapping theory. It explains gradually how humans map data elements of a familiar situation (i.e., base) onto data elements of an unfamiliar situation (i.e., target) to understand and draw new inferences about the latter [18]. Analogies and similarities can basically be characterized by a set of three sub-processes: retrieval, mapping and evaluation [19].

Given that humans encounter a situation where they are first required to process unknown data elements, attributes (i.e., features) of the data elements and relationships (i.e., structures) between them must be encoded by human working memory [5]. This triggers a reminder of similar data elements in the long-term memory (i.e., processed data elements from previous situations) so that either objective or relational similarities can be found. Objective similarities are recognized more often than relational similarities since they are easier to remember due to superficialities [19, 22]. Based on Gentner and Markman [20], Fig. 2 shows the distinction between objective similarity and relational similarity and is further explained below.

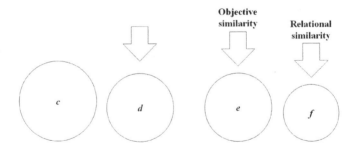

Fig. 2. Distinction between objective similarity and relational similarity.

After the retrieval of unknown data, the mapping process starts. This central sub-process requires that two similar situations exist and are disclosed to each other. First, the alignment takes place, in which two situations are aligned due to their similarity, to draw new inferences from the base to the target. Humans create mappings from one situation onto the other, where each mapping contains a series of correspondences either between attributes of data elements or relationships among each other [19, 22]. As shown in Fig. 2, the circle size as an attribute of the data elements can emerge in a feature-based correspondence (i.e., objective similarity) between the data elements d and e, since they have the same circle size (i.e., $d = e$). Regarding a monotonous increase in size (i.e., $c > d$, $e > f$), they have the same structural relationship, which in turn can be described in a structure-based correspondence (i.e., relational similarity) between a pair of data elements c and d and another pair of data elements e and f. In contrast to retrieval, it is more likely to map structure-based correspondence when two similar situations are simultaneously presented during mapping [20].

Secondly during the mapping process, the inference of candidates is carried out. Based on common patterns of entities (i.e., attributes, relations), which have emerged from the alignment of two situations, humans make new presumptions (i.e., candidate inferences) about the target. Pursuing structural consistency and systematicity, humans complete these patterns and familiarize with unknown data elements. Different types of similarity (e.g., literal similarity, surface similarity, analogy) may present the outcome of the mapping of two situations, depending on whether correspondences between single data elements emphasize their attributes or their relationships among one another. Thereby, an analogy occurs if and only if humans familiarize with a target by drawing inferences based on relational pattern completion [18].

Finally, candidate inferences need to be evaluate. Three classes of criteria exist to do this, namely factual correctness and adaptability, goal relevance and new knowledge gain. The first refers to evaluating how true a candidate inference is. If inferences relate to the future and cannot be verified immediately, they might get revised after some time, depending on an inference's adaptability (i.e., how easy it is to modify its entities of the base to fit the target). The second evaluates how a candidate inference supports the current goals of the reasoning person. The last one measures to which extent a candidate inference adds new knowledge to a person's knowledge base. These three criteria are mostly independent of one another. Moreover, the evaluation can take part on the level of single candidate inferences or on that of the created similarity or analogy as a whole [19, 22].

2.3   Conversational Agents: Chatbots

Conversational agents are computer systems designed for responding to users in natural language, thereby imitating human conversation. Based on technical advances in natural language processing, conversational agents are today used in various application areas such as customer services [44]. This has made conversation a key element to human-machine interaction and conversational agents to human-machine interfaces [33]. Since natural language is the connecting component between the human and the computer system, it is important that the conversational agent can imitate a certain degree of human language mastery.

There are various types of conversational agents. Some of them use speech or text and others are embodied and make use of body movements with facial features and also speech to interact with the user. This article focuses on text-based conversational agents, where different kinds of agents exist, such as chatbots or virtual assistants. According to Stucki et al. [47], the two terms are similar, but not synonymous. A chatbot is a system that is able to enter into a dialogue with a human user and perform certain tasks independently (e.g., retrieving information or filling out a form automatically). The chatbot can be activated by the user via natural language commands. The desired information can also be provided by the chatbot in natural language. Hence, the essential aspect of a chatbot is the natural language dialogue. The virtual assistant, by contrast, focuses on automating or simplifying a digital process for a user. This means that virtual assistants must first and foremost support the completion of tasks in real time (e.g., switching off lights, creating music lists), while chatbots can be used just for conversation without necessarily having carried out a task [47]. The focus of this article is put on chatbots.

The architecture of a chatbot can vary and ranges from strictly controlled dialogue systems (e.g., input via clickable selection list) to fully functional natural language dialogue systems that offer more freedom to the user (e.g., text input in natural language). The dialogue between user and chatbot usually starts with a user input (e.g., question) entered through the interface (e.g., chat window). First, the system tries to understand this input and filter out what the user wants. Natural language processing methods, more concretely, syntactic and semantic operations, can be applied for this purpose. Syntactic operations (e.g., tokenization, lemmatization) concentrate on structures of the sentence and on functions of individual elements therein (e.g., components, morpheme), while semantic operations (e.g., named entity recognition, bag-of-words representation) focus on the meaning of elements [4]. How these methods are selected and combined for preprocessing (or normalizing) the data depends on the problem, the available data and its quality as well as the trained model of the chatbot (static vs. dynamic). After normalizing the input, essential keywords for the user's possible intent can be extracted and classified (i.e., intent matching). Various methods can be used for this step – from simple pattern matching to multi-layer neural networks [28]. As soon as the chatbot has recognized the user's intent, it must procure necessary resources via so-called backend calls (e.g., knowledge databases or transaction systems) to generate the best possible response. If no intent is found, an answer is generated anyway (e.g., saying no information is found). The answer can be created either by a rule-based approach, such as IF-THEN rules, or by a machine learning approach, such as a neural network with learning algorithms [47]. Advanced chatbots usually use machine learning to adapt to new information or requirements emerging from the environment. It is useful to log incoming inputs and store them in an existing knowledge base to improve intent matching continuously. A possible architecture is shown in Fig. 3, which reflects essential aspects of a chatbot.

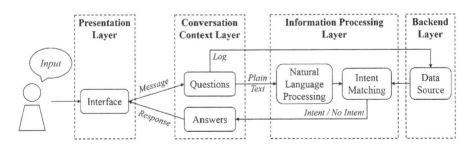

Fig. 3. Architecture of a chatbot.

To generate right answers, the chatbot must be able to put the user's intent into the right context. Hence, potential contexts must be stored in the chatbot. The vocabulary of a chatbot can vary depending on the domain. In most cases, chatbots are used in specific and isolated domains, which reduce the complexity of potential user requests and require the vocabulary that only covers essential terms and contexts. Even if the number of user requests is limited, requests may also come from outside the domain, as users tend to explore how human the conversational agent behaves [47]. In addition, spelling mistakes, ambiguous utterances or unknown words can make the input processing more difficult and thus endanger the interaction between humans and computer systems. For this reason, this article deals with the processing of contextless words in relation to human-machine interaction via the interface of a text-based chatbot.

Conversational agents may be used to replace existing job roles (or persons) or to support people in their activities, such as smart home bots are doing today. The authors focus on conversational agents that can complement and support humans [44]. The aim is to achieve a human-machine symbiosis [11], because there will be tasks that humans will not be able to master due to their limited attention span or limited time and therefore other instances, such as conversational agents, will be needed to help humans in their tasks.

3 Conceptual Framework: Fuzzy Reasoning

In this section, related work is briefly outlined first, followed by the presentation of the concept and the step-by-step specification of the proposed fuzzy analogical reasoning process as well as the suggestion of an additive, network-like memory.

3.1 Related Work

In cognitive science, research aims not only to understand how people create and use analogies to expand their knowledge, but also how computer systems can mimic human analogical reasoning. In relation to structure-mapping theory, several computational models cover different sub-processes of analogical reasoning (e.g., MAC/FAC for retrieval [17], SME for mapping [15]). Artificial intelligence architectures, consisting of varied combinations of these models, have proven to be useful for analogical reasoning to solve numerous problems, such as clustering of hand-drawn sketches [9]. In addition, attempts to enable analogical reasoning have already been made with methods of natural language processing (e.g., denominal verb interpretation [35], word sense disambiguation [2]). However, since natural language processing is mainly based on statistical methods and none of these artificial intelligence systems mentioned above link analogical reasoning to the understanding of cognitive systems as proposed in this article, they have no tolerance for the uncertainty (in terms of perceptions) that is central to biological systems. Thus, previous efforts in imitating human cognition approximately have not succeeded [45].

It seems obvious to use methods that can address and process the uncertainty of the environment. Since natural language consists of linguistic variables (e.g., words), the inclusion of soft computing techniques can improve dialogue systems [59]. Although there are first attempts in this field, such as a system based on computing with words [29] or a perception-based system [1], these developments rarely foster reasoning and dialogue in the way that people process information [59], for example through the creation of analogies. Since it is proposed that cognitive systems use soft computing techniques to understand and extract heterogeneously structured information from natural language [58], their ability to create analogies should also take into account in the processing of vague information. The approach of fuzzy analogical reasoning presented below could therefore be a suitable basis for the further development of the global reasoning process based on cognitive computing.

3.2   Concept

Based on the previous work of Bouchon-Meunier and colleagues [6, 7], the proposed framework builds upon an analogical scheme for approximate reasoning that allows computer systems to interact with users in natural language. This analogical scheme is needed for approximate reasoning that describes a kind of reasoning that is neither entirely precise nor completely imprecise [7, 54]. From a series of imprecise premises an approximate conclusion is deduced [49] that represents human's ability to take rational decisions in complex and uncertain environments [7]. This approach enables systems to approach to human cognition and thus to do justice to the essential component of biological systems (i.e., uncertainty in terms of perceptions).

Approximate reasoning is an application of the compositional rule of inference, a basic rule of inference proposed by fuzzy logic that extends the familiar rule of inference (i.e., generalized modus ponens), stating *if X is true and implies Y, then Y is true* [49]. The compositional rule of inference can be used to solve a simultaneous system of relational assignment equations where linguistic variables (e.g., sentences, words) are assigned to fuzzy constraints [54]. Assumed that A, B and C are fuzzy sets with respective membership functions μ_A, μ_B and μ_C, the compositional rule of inference can be applied to a linguistic variable Y with a value y based on another linguistic variable X with a value x [58]:

$$\mu_C(y) = \max_\mu(\mu_A(x) \wedge \mu_B(x, y)) \tag{6}$$

Thereby, $\wedge$ denotes the conjunct that indicates the intersection of membership functions μ_A and μ_B. This represents a linguistic approximation to the solution of the simultaneous equations:

$$\frac{\begin{array}{c} X \text{ is } A \\ (X, Y) \text{ is } B \end{array}}{Y \text{ is } C} \tag{7}$$

Building upon the compositional rule of inference based on fuzzy logic and relational similarity proposed by structure-mapping theory, it is possible to link analogical concepts to soft computing by drawing the analogical scheme that is illustrated in Fig. 4 [21, 55].

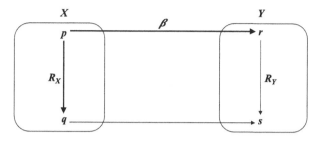

Fig. 4. Analogical scheme [7].

The analogical scheme assumes two linguistic variables X and Y that can originate from the same domain (i.e., universe) or not. Furthermore, p and q are values that X can take whereas r and s are possible values for Y. Thereby, p and r are known to be linked by β. Since the relation R_X between q and p is also known, it is possible to find s that is to r through the relation R_Y as q is to p through R_X [7]. Therefore, R_X and R_Y are part of a structure-based correspondence that is based on β. In addition to that, $F(X)$ and $F(Y)$ denote respective sets of fuzzy (sub-)sets of X and Y (i.e., $[0, 1]^X$, $[0, 1]^Y$). Hence, for given relations $\beta \subset [0, 1]^X \times [0, 1]^Y$, $R_X \subset [0, 1]^X \times [0, 1]^X$ and $R_Y \subset [0, 1]^Y \times [0, 1]^Y$, a mapping $R_{\beta RXRY}$ that provides a linguistic value s is defined as follows [6]:

$$R_{\beta RXRY} : [0, 1]^X \times [0, 1]^Y \times [0, 1]^X \rightarrow [0, 1]^Y,$$
$$\text{satisfying } \forall x \in F(X) \text{ and } \forall y \in F(Y) \text{ such that } x\beta y,$$
$$\text{and } \forall x' \in [0, 1]^X \text{ such that } xR_X x', \qquad (8)$$
$$\text{and } y = R_{\beta RXRY}(x, y, x),$$
$$\text{and } y' = R_{\beta RXRY}(x, y, x') \text{ such that } x'\beta y' \text{ and } yR_Y y'$$

The analogical scheme and its ability to compute linguistic variables and thus familiarize unknown data elements by mapping relational similarity might help cognitive systems to further approach human cognition [6, 7]. This conceptual framework would extend the general chatbot architecture, as shown in Fig. 5:

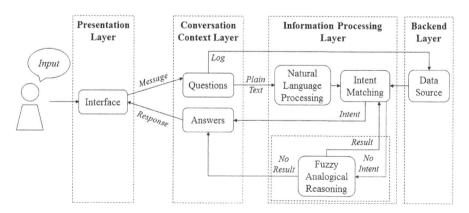

Fig. 5. Chatbot architecture including fuzzy analogical reasoning.

3.3   Use Case Specification

The proposed fuzzy analogical reasoning process presents an essential component of the global fuzzy reasoning process to be developed. Therefore, the pseudocode (see Table 1) is presented first, which describes roughly the essential steps of the fuzzy reasoning process. An example is then used to go through the process, whereby the primary focus is on fuzzy analogical reasoning.

Table 1. Pseudocode.

Fuzzy reasoning process
Input: Question posed in natural language
Output: Answer described in natural language
1 Pose a question in natural language (user)
2 Preprocess the question using natural language processing methods (system)
3 Classify these data elements (system) 　**a** If data element is *unknown*, continue with 4 　**b** If data element is *known*, continue with 6
4 Create analogy (system) 　**a** Apply generalized constraint: Y *is* R_Y 　**b** Apply compositional rule of inference: 　　*If X is R_X and implies (X,Y) is $\beta R_X R_Y$, then Y is R_Y* 　**c** Apply analogical scheme and project mapping 　　**c1** If data element is *known*, continue with 3b 　　**c2** If data element is *unknown,* continue with 5
5 Search a dialogue with the user (system) 　**a** If user responds, continue with 2 　**b** If user does not respond, the process ends here
6 Match the intent of the question with existing answer candidates (system)
7 Retrieve the resource required (system)
8 Generate answer (system)

1 The reasoning process is triggered by a user's question posed in natural language. The question could be, for example, "*What kind of flat in Zurich do I get by paying a little extra?*".

2 The system uses the concept of fuzzy granulation and divides the formulated sequence into data elements (i.e., words or groups of words). This function is similar to the syntactic method called tokenization (i.e., splitting up tokens resp. words) from natural language processing. From the question posed above, the corresponding words might be: *what, kind of, flat, in Zurich, do, I, get, by paying, a little extra*. To simplify the processing, lemmatization is applied to convert all words back into their lexicon base form, in: *what, kind of, flat, in Zurich, do, I, get, by pay, a little extra*. To exclude general words without meaning (e.g., articles, preposition) to avoid distorting the context, a stopword-list can be used. Thus, the list may consist now of *what, flat, Zurich, get, pay, a little extra*.

3 By completing the fuzzy granulation process (cf. [57]), the system needs to clarify through alignment with existing stored knowledge whether it understands single data elements. Therefore, fuzzy sets are formed based on information granules to give meaning. In this example, the following classification is possible: *what* belongs to certain degrees to the fuzzy set *factoid question*, *Zurich* to the fuzzy set *city*, *get* and *pay* to the fuzzy set *infinitive*, and *flat* and *a little extra* remain unknown.

4 As *flat* and *a little extra* remain unknown, it is required to find a relation between existing stored knowledge and unknown data elements [40] (i.e., creating analogies by applying the analogical scheme). Before that, however, the system applied computing with words by forming a generalized constraint for data elements that are unknown [56]. Two linguistic variables X and Y are assumed for the unknown information: X represents a domain with possible values p (e.g., *house*) and q (e.g., *flat*), and Y another domain that can take values r (e.g., *expensive*) and s (e.g., *a little extra*). Assuming furthermore possibilistic semantics of a fuzzy constraining relation R_Y, the system can formulate a GC for Y [56]:

$$GC : Y \text{ is } R_Y,$$
$$\text{where } Poss\{Y = r\} = \mu_{RY}(r) \tag{9}$$
$$\text{and } Poss\{Y = s\} = \mu_{RY}(s)$$

Next, the system may use resemblance relations (cf. [7]) to gain a somewhat known value for q (*flat*) based on a known relation R_X between the unknown data element q (*flat*) and a known data element p (*house*). Having retrieved a relation R_X between linguistic values p (*house*) and q (*flat*), the system becomes capable of drawing the analogical scheme to gain a known value for an unknown data element s (*a little extra*) [6], as shown in Fig. 6:

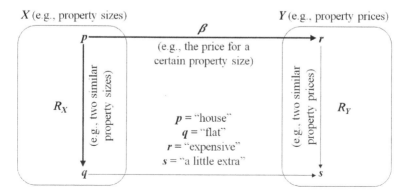

Fig. 6. Analogical scheme with example.

Therefore, the system can use a fuzzy-based application of the compositional rule of inference (i.e., approximate reasoning), as stated in Eq. (6). To exemplify the compositional rule of inference with a notional example about *price-performance ratio*, it is recollected that citizens rating a rental apartment as *rather expensive* perceive the rental apartment mostly as a *poor price-performance ratio*. This is because the index category *rather expensive* has a quite high membership degree in fuzzy subset *poor price-performance ratio*. Hence, it can be stated that *a rather expensive rental apartment has a poor price-performance ratio*. Thus, the linguistic value *poor price-performance ratio* is assigned to the fuzzy restriction on *rather expensive*. Furthermore, if it can be stated that *rather expensive* and the next higher, adjoining index category *expensive* are *approximately equal* (i.e., fuzzy restriction on both index categories), it may be concluded that *an expensive rental apartment has a more or less poor price-performance ratio*.

Based on resemblance relations (i.e., p and q are apparently known to be related by R_X), *house* and *flat* are approximately equal and, thus, *flat* is more or less *expensive*. Since the linkage β between p and r is also known (i.e., *house* belongs to the fuzzy set *expensive* to a not negligible degree), it is possible to gain a known value for s, which is to q as r is to p, drawing an inference R_Y between data elements r and s [7]. In terms of structure-mapping theory, a structure-based correspondence is projected based on β [18]. Therefore, the system can project a mapping $R_{\beta RXRY}$, which provides it with a linguistic value for s based on relations β, R_X, R_Y, expressed by their membership grades in respective sets of fuzzy (sub-)sets of X and Y (i.e., μ_{RX}, μ_{RY}) [6]:

$$
\begin{aligned}
R_{\beta RXRY} : \mu_{RX}(p) &\times \mu_{RY}(r) \times \mu_{RX}(q) \to \mu_{RY}(s), \\
\text{where } \beta &\subset \mu_{RX}(p) \times \mu_{RY}(r) \\
\text{and } R_X &\subset \mu_{RX}(p) \times \mu_{RX}(q) \\
\text{and } R_Y &\subset \mu_{RY}(r) \times \mu_{RY}(s)
\end{aligned}
\tag{10}
$$

Assuming that *a little extra* is to *flat* as *flat* is to *house*, the system creates a mapping to understand *a little extra* in relation to *flat*. Therefore, *a little extra* belongs to the linguistic variable of *property prices* and *flat* belongs to the linguistic variable of *property sizes*. The system ends the analogical reasoning process by classifying all data elements as known.

5 Since all data elements are known, no consultation with the user is needed.

6 By defragmenting all data elements, the intent matching can begin by extracting the intent out of keywords of which a question consists. The keywords of the intent in this example would be "*what, flat, Zurich, get, pay, a little extra*".

7 Based on the intent, the best possible answer is retrieved through the knowledge base. In this case, it could be a website about selected apartments that match the condition required or a contact list of real estate agents for receiving more information.

8 The system generates an answer in natural language for the processing, such as "*You'll find on the website* www.xy.ch *real estate agents who would like to give you information about flats for rent in Zurich.*".

For reasons of understanding, the single steps were explained only roughly without going into too much detail. Currently, the reasoning process is set at a simple level to draw first learnings. Further work will be needed to make the reasoning process as human-like as possible. For a start, the authors agree with a simple text-based question-answering system, which can be accessed via a chatbot interface.

3.4   Add-On: Network-like Memory

The fuzzy reasoning process can only work if it can access a knowledge base that does not necessarily need structured data but is able to put available data (whether unstructured, semi-structured or structured) into context. D'Onofrio et al. [13] have already addressed this aspect and suggested using fuzzy cognitive maps (stored in graph databases). With the ability to aggregate concepts and their respective relationships to a graph-like structure as well as to allow for (modifiable) feedback displayed by fuzzy-weighted digraphs [30], fuzzy cognitive maps further facilitate the process of fuzzy analogical reasoning [13]. In particular, the possibility of demonstrating causal relationships and connecting various networks (i.e., different knowledge structures) simplifies analogy creation. Since fuzzy cognitive maps are only for modeling data and as such not able to execute the common functions of a database (such as making queries), it is necessary to store fuzzy cognitive maps in a way to be able to retrieve them at any point in time. Due to the increasing fuzziness in data, NoSQL databases, which have a tolerance for less or not structured data, are especially suitable. Thereby, graph databases seem to be most suitable for storing fuzzy cognitive maps, as they both have a similar underlying structure, for instance, similar graph-like networks with nodes and edges [43]. Applied in areas with highly connected data, such as social media, graph databases may provide a possible solution to the digital embedding of huge amounts of data, modelled by fuzzy cognitive maps [13].

Assuming that graph databases are suitable and serve as a storage location, fuzzy cognitive maps need to be created. Thereby, data collection and aggregation are the steps required to build a knowledge base. Having gathered information, there exist different approaches to build knowledge bases using fuzzy cognitive maps, for instance, self-organizing maps [50] or the application of ontology matching and semantic similarity [32]. Therefore, if the system needs to retrieve information to create an analogy, it can use partial match retrieval operations (e.g., resemble relations) to get data from the knowledge base (i.e., fuzzy cognitive maps stored in graph databases). Consisting of similarities, differences and indices (modelled by nodes and edges), fuzzy cognitive maps show causal relationships between memorized fuzzy clusters and their (sub-)sets to enable the matching between unknown and known data elements. As such relations are expressed by their membership grades in respective sets of fuzzy (sub-)sets, they allow for a combination of the analogical scheme, resemble relations and fuzzy cognitive maps [13].

As illustrated in Fig. 7, the authors therefore do not only suggest a new concept of fuzzy reasoning but also recommend building a network-like knowledge base as an add-on to optimally support information retrieval, a crucial part for the fuzzy analogical reasoning process. This composition was evaluated by experiments and interviews as described in the next chapter.

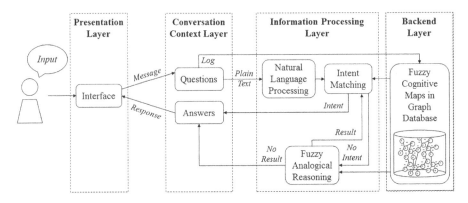

Fig. 7. Chatbot architecture including network-like memory.

4 Evaluation

Following a transdisciplinary approach, the authors conducted three evaluations: A workshop with a random group of participants, a laboratory experiment with selected participants and finally expert interviews with researchers with a respective scientific background. The procedure and results of the evaluation are described below.

4.1 Workshop-Based Experiment: Questions and Answers

In May 2017, the authors conducted a workshop with the name "Designing Cognitive Systems" in Bern, Switzerland. One of the authors led the experiment and accompanied the participants through the whole workshop. Three goals were pursued:

(1) to become more familiar with citizens' requirements for new (smart) systems,
(2) to reinforce theories about the relation between questions and answers, and
(3) to get insights about the human reasoning process.

Nine males and two females, all between 20 and 50 years old and with various professional backgrounds (e.g., computer science, geography, economics), participated in the workshop. It lasted two hours in total, whereby the experiment took half an hour.

In the workshop, the focus was set on cognitive computing. Therefore, an introduction about cognitive computing was given, supported with illustrative examples (e.g., video sequence of IBM Watson in the game show Jeopardy![1]), to build a theoretical foundation for the experiment. Afterwards, a discussion about the term human-machine interaction (an essential component of intelligent systems) began, exchanging opportunities and threats of computer systems that are able to compute and communicate in natural language. The following insights have emerged from the discussion: Most participants were sceptical about (smart) systems, such as IBM Watson[2] or

---

[1] cf. https://www.youtube.com/watch?v=WFR3lOm_xhE&list=RDYgYSv2KSyWg&index=4.

[2] cf. https://www.ibm.com/watson.

autonomous vehicles by Google[3], which are able to autonomously make decisions. However, some participants stated that they are curious to test such systems. Hence, even if there is a certain scepticism, the curiosity to try out new things tends to prevail. The participants even considered using such systems in the future if they would turn out to be advantageous for them.

Afterwards, the main experiment was conducted to address the second and third goal. Questions and answers, especially the ability to respond as best as possible, are important components of a conversational agent. There is a distinction between different kinds of questions: yes/no questions, "W"-questions (e.g., *who is Alan Turing?*), indirect requests (e.g., *I would like to know more about Alan Turing*), and commands (e.g., *name all places where Alan Turing had been working*) [38]. Dialogue systems heavily use "W"-question words as they clearly indicate the type of answer, such as *when* (i.e., date), *who* (i.e., person) and *where* (i.e., location) [12]. To check if "W"-questions effectively affect their respective answers, five "W"-questions (i.e., *who, where, when, how long, how*) stated in German were asked in the first part of the workshop. The results showed that almost every participant answered in the same way, even if the answers were not identically (e.g., *whole name* vs. *last name*). For illustration, some questions are presented with the answers received: To the question "*Who leads the experiment?*", everyone answered with a name, obviously with the one of the moderating author. Asking "*Where does the experiment take place*", all participants stated a location. Their responses were only differing in their granularity (e.g., *Bern* vs. *Impact Hub Bern*). For the question "*What is the name of the workshop*" the answers varied a little bit, as some of the participants could not remember the title. Therefore, many different names, such as "*Cognitive Computing*", "*Workshop*", "*Design and Cognition*" and others, were said but the essence of the mentioned names was coincided with the workshop's actual name "*Designing Cognitive Systems*". Considering the semantics of all answers, it is apparent that the same thing can be meant, but it is expressed in different ways. Therefore, it is necessary that the system understands how to interpret the input and what meaning is probable.

The second part of the workshop consisted of responding to three questions that were impossible to answer because of their semantics. The questions were "*How quickly does darkness spread?*", "*Is abbreviation a long word?*" and "*Where do lucky devils grow?*". Even if the "W"-word provided hints on how to answer the questions, no meaningful linking with existing knowledge was possible. Therefore, the participants tried to create analogies using familiar situations and thus responded with information that most likely matched themselves individually. Although the questions were obviously not meant seriously, responses such as "*haunted forest*", "*land of milk and honey*" and "*wonderland*" were given to the question about "*lucky devils*". No one considered the possibility of stating that there is no answer at all (even though that would have been the correct answer). Hence, the second part of this experiment underlined the complexity of finding an answer and demonstrated how important reference models are to create possible analogies in human memory.

---

[3] cf. https://www.google.com/selfdrivingcar.

4.2   Laboratory Experiment: Structure-Mapping Theory

To decide on whether the fuzzy analogical process has a stable theoretical foundation (i.e., structure-mapping theory), a laboratory experiment was conducted in May 2017 to examine how structure-mapping theory effectively reflects human analogical reasoning. Its purpose was to document how far subjects would follow theoretical predictions of structure-mapping theory if they created analogies to find relations between their existing knowledge and unknown concepts.

Seven males and three females, all between 25 and 30 years old, of Swiss nationality and with academical background (e.g., business administrations, linguistics), participated in the experiment. The participants have been requested individually to participate and this without any compensation in prospect. The paper-pencil experiment was led by one of the authors (i.e., experimenter) and lasted 20 min. To ensure that subjects are not only anonymous towards other subjects but also the experimenter (i.e., double-blind anonymity), another author of this article was responsible for the random assignment of subjects to the two treatments that this experiment comprised, pursuing a 1×2 between-subject design. The two treatments were split into an experimental treatment and a control treatment (both consisted of five questions) and were completed by five subjects each. The language of this experiment was German.

Structure-mapping theory predicts that objective similarity (i.e., similarities represented by superficialities) is more likely to be retrieved by humans than relational similarity [19]. Therefore, this laboratory experiment aimed to test the following hypotheses:

H1: If humans need to retrieve a familiar situation (i.e., base) by their own memory to understand and draw new inferences about an unfamiliar situation (i.e., target), they tend to encode objective similarity (i.e., surface similarity) rather than relational similarity (i.e., analogy).

H2: If an unfamiliar situation (i.e., target) immediately comes with a familiar situation (i.e., base), which can be used to understand and draw new inferences about the former (e.g., analogical argumentation in a discussion), humans tend to encode relational similarity (i.e., analogy) rather than objective similarity (i.e., surface similarity).

The treatment variable in this experiment described whether subjects needed to retrieve a familiar situation by their own memory to map any form of similarity onto an unfamiliar situation. It was nominally scaled (i.e., 0 = control treatment; 1 = experimental treatment). Therefore, subjects in the experimental treatment were called upon to retrieve a base by themselves, whereas subjects in the control treatment are given both target and base simultaneously. Figure 8 illustrates the two variants of such familiar or unfamiliar situations.

For both treatments it was measured afterwards which form of similarity that subjects had tended to encode either through their choices (i.e., control treatment) or their own drawings (i.e., experimental treatment). The dependent variable here was nominally scaled as well and took the values 0 (i.e., relational similarity) or 1 (i.e., objective similarity). These measurements served to investigate the statistical correlations and conditional probability distributions between the two elicited variables. Since the sample of this experiment comprises ten subjects only and does not follow any

Fig. 8. Comparative example of a task in the questionnaire for the control treatment (left) and that for the experimental treatment (right).

sampling plan to achieve a somewhat random sample, this section is limited to a descriptive statistical analysis. The authors have received the following results:

H1: The descriptive univariate analysis indicated that subjects in the experimental treatment encoded relational and objective similarity equally. Although they needed to retrieve a base by their own memory, subjects did not tend to draw graphical representations that primarily shared an objective similarity with the target.

H2: Conditional probability distributions of the control treatment suggested that subjects clearly tended to encode relational similarity rather than objective similarity, as they were given both target and base simultaneously.

To conclude the testing of both hypotheses, a bivariate data analysis was conducted. A moderate correlation was received between the form of similarity, which subjects tended to encode, and whether they needed to retrieve a familiar situation by themselves to map this similarity onto an unfamiliar situation.

4.3   Expert Interviews

Based on the findings to date, the authors decided to ask experts from various disciplines, such as computer science, mathematics, linguistics, to review the framework of fuzzy analogical reasoning, including the extension of network-like memory. Moreover, the authors asked for constructive inputs regarding how the framework can be improved, and also to answer some questions to assess the potential of such a concept.

Eight experts agreed to participate, without any compensation in prospect. Small bugs were found, suggestions for improvements by means of the use of other formulas were made and other ideas were expressed regarding how the framework could be further developed. The authors evaluated the inputs and integrated them into the previous version [13] such that the version of this article is the most current version (i.e., with integrated feedbacks from two experiments and various expert interviews).

In addition, two questions were asked to obtain their opinion on this solution approach. The first question was about whether the experts had already heard of the term *fuzzy analogical reasoning* and could conceive of anything by it. The authors wanted to clarify if this concept is known. Experts, who responded with a positive answer, were also asked if they know systems of today that use such a reasoning process or something similar. Three of eight had already heard of this term, but none of them could name an existing system that makes use of its potential. The answers to the first few questions showed that the concept introduced by Bouchon-Meunier and

Valverde [7] several years ago still has innovation potential and it is therefore important to keep working on it.

The second question was to assess the future potential of this framework. The experts were asked whether they could think of possible applications of such a framework and whether this would optimize existing systems (in terms of an improved dialogue management). All experts responded positively. They are convinced that, especially in relation to cognitive cities, enhanced dialogue systems are required and therefore approaches such as fuzzy analogical reasoning are of high relevance for the urban future.

However, one of the experts was critical and explained that the idea of making computer systems more human-like would be good and necessary, but the question remains if soft computing or similar methods effectively help to achieve this goal. He proposed to evaluate the applied methods regarding their usefulness and effectiveness to determine if they prove themselves as expedient. In contrast, one of the experts supported the application of fuzzy methods (e.g., fuzzy similarity, resemblance and equivalence relations), as they could help to retrieve partial information from a knowledge base to represent uncertainty. Another expert highlighted human-centered design by emphasizing again that human features in a system allow for accelerating customer acceptance.

The authors got critical but, in general, positive feedback and were encouraged to continue investigating this research area and to further develop the framework.

5 Discussion

With the growing diversity of information (text, images, sound, etc.) from heterogeneous sources (social networks, e-mails, books, and more), it is becoming increasingly difficult for users to find the information that satisfy their needs, particularly in highly connected areas, such as cities. Since the development of modern technologies, thereof especially dialogue systems endowed with human-like behaviour (e.g., Siri[4] from Apple or Alexa[5] from Amazon), more and more proprietary conversational agents have been embedded in personal technologies and devices (e.g., smartphones and tablets) [33]. To enhance the performance of today's conversational agents based on, among other things, machine learning, the authors propose a fuzzy analogical reasoning framework based on soft computing and cognition and learning theories to approach human information processing.

Soft computing is an umbrella term for various methods, with which the processing of imprecise, uncertain and vague information by computer systems is considered. The ability to process linguistic variables in the form of words is essential, as the core of interaction between cities and citizens and among citizens is natural language [13]. However, the ability to process natural language is not yet sufficient. Insights into humans' cognition and behavioral patterns are necessary to process information in a

---

[4] cf. https://www.apple.com/ios/siri.

[5] cf. https://developer.amazon.com/alexa.

human-like way and to prepare it appropriately for stakeholders. The approach of connected learning through cognition and learning theories allows for developing computer systems with human abilities (e.g., learning, reasoning). By making systems with such abilities natural to stakeholders, it might be possible to achieve a human-machine symbiosis. This refers to a supportive cooperation between human and machine, where both parties learn from each other and create a larger knowledge base collectively rather than individually (i.e., collective intelligence [34]) [11, 13].

Therefore, this article presents a global fuzzy reasoning process by first presenting its core framework of fuzzy analogical reasoning, which is based on fuzzy methods as well as on structure-mapping theory. By applying an analogical scheme to allow approximate reasoning, dialogue systems might be able to create analogies and thus better respond to input, especially in cases when words are ambiguous. With this ability, systems become capable of responding more adequately to the needs of citizens and thus to support them in the complex environments of a city.

However, not only information processing is an essential part of an intelligent system but also the knowledge database, from which it extracts information to provide adequate answers. Like humans, systems need a memory. Therefore, the authors additionally present an add-on in the form of a graph database, in which knowledge is modeled by means of fuzzy cognitive maps. With the basic structure of graphs, fuzzy cognitive maps allow for forming connections across different knowledge structures and thus to illustrate the context of information more naturally than simple relational storage methods.

Three iterations in the form of conception, prototyping and evaluation have shown that the theoretical foundations cover an essential part of human information processing. Furthermore, experts confirmed that such an approach has the potential to be particularly useful in cities. As more and more dialogue systems, such as conversational agents, are in demand, information processing approaches that do justice to human cognition most probably will be required in the future.

6 Limitations and Outlook

This article is a work-in-progress and presents the current state of a major project. Therefore, some limitations have to be considered, which should be addressed in prospective work.

The first limitation relates to the fact that the transformation of a city into a smart respectively cognitive city is so far viewed from a rather technocratic perspective, without taking into account other aspects, such as social commitment and sustainability. Such topics might be advanced with technology but are not inherently linked to it. Nonetheless, this framework represents a way to improve communication within a city among citizens as well as between its authorities and citizens by making information (e.g., regarding governance topics) transparent and easier to access.

Second, the framework is currently in a conceptual phase. A fully comprehensive proof-of-concept has not yet been developed. First attempts were made to find out how a chatbot works (incl. natural language processing, intent-matching and information retrieval), but the additional modules – fuzzy analogical reasoning and network-like memory – have not yet been implemented. Their development is in progress, however.

Third, the three evaluations took place with small test groups. The number of test subjects should be larger for reasons of significance. Nevertheless, the results provide information on whether the authors tend to be on the right track. Larger test groups are planned for the first proof-of-concept.

Acknowledgements. The authors would like to thank the participants and volunteers of both experiments as well as the experts for their valuable input.

References

1. Ahmad, R., Rahimi, S.: A perception based, domain specific expert system for question-answering support. In: IEEE/WIC/ACM International Conference on Web Intelligence, Hong Kong, pp. 893–896. IEEE/WIC/ACM (2006)
2. Barbella, D., Forbus, K.D.: Analogical word sense disambiguation. Adv. Cogn. Syst. **2**(1), 297–315 (2013)
3. Barr, N., Pennycook, G., Stolz, J.A., Fugelsang, J.A.: Reasoned connections: a dual-process perspective on creative thought. Think. Reason. **21**(1), 61–75 (2015)
4. Barrière, C.: Natural Language Understanding in a Semantic Web Context. Springer, Cham (2016). https://doi.org/10.1007/978-3-319-41337-2
5. Boteanu, A., Chernova, S.: Solving and explaining analogy questions using semantic networks. In: Proceedings of the Twenty-Ninth AAAI Conference on Artificial Intelligence, Austin, pp. 1460–1466. AAAI (2015)
6. Bouchon-Meunier, B., Mesiar, R., Rifqi, M.: Compositional rule of inference as an analogical scheme. Fuzzy Sets Syst. **138**(1), 53–65 (2003)
7. Bouchon-Meunier, B., Valverde, L.: A fuzzy approach to analogical reasoning. Soft. Comput. **3**(1), 141–147 (1999)
8. Caragliu, A., Del Bo, C., Nijkamp, P.: Smart cities in Europe. In: 3rd Central European Conference in Regional Science (CERS 2009), pp. 45–59 (2009)
9. Chang, M.D., Forbus, K.D.: Using analogy to cluster hand-drawn sketch-based educational software. AI Mag. **35**(1), 76–84 (2014)
10. Chourabi, H., et al.: Understanding smart cities: an integrative framework. In: Hawaii International Conference on System Sciences, Maui, pp. 2289–2297 (2012)
11. Cooley, M.: On human-machine symbiosis. In: Gill, K.S. (ed.) Human Machine Symbiosis: The Foundations of Human-Centered Systems Design, pp. 69–100. Springer, London (2012). https://doi.org/10.1007/978-1-4471-3247-9_2
12. Cooper, R.J., Rüger, S.M.: A simple question answering system. In: Proceedings of TREC-9 (2000)
13. D'Onofrio, S., Müller, S.M., Papageorgiou, E.I., Portmann, E.: Fuzzy reasoning in cognitive cities – an exploratory work on fuzzy analogical reasoning using fuzzy cognitive maps. In: 2018 IEEE International Conference on Fuzzy Systems (FUZZ-IEEE 2018), Rio de Janeiro, Brazil (2018)
14. D'Onofrio, S., Portmann, E.: Cognitive computing in smart cities. Inform. Spektrum **40**(1), 46–57 (2017)
15. Falkenhainer, B., Forbus, K.D., Gentner, D.: The structure-mapping engine: algorithm and examples. Artif. Intell. **41**(1), 1–63 (1989)

16. Finger, M., Portmann, E.: What are cognitive cities? In: Portmann, E., Finger, M. (eds.) Towards Cognitive Cities. SSDC, vol. 63, pp. 1–11. Springer, Cham (2016). https://doi.org/10.1007/978-3-319-33798-2_1

17. Forbus, K.D., Gentner, D., Law, K.: MAC/FAC: a model of similarity-based retrieval. Cogn. Sci. **19**(2), 141–205 (1995)

18. Gentner, D.: Structure-mapping: a theoretical framework for analogy. Cogn. Sci. **7**(1), 155–170 (1983)

19. Gentner, D., Forbus, K.D.: Computational models of analogy. Cogn. Sci. **2**(3), 266–276 (2011)

20. Gentner, D., Markman, A.B.: Analogy – watershed or Waterloo? Structural alignment and the development of connectionist models of cognition. In: Conference on Neural Information Processing Systems, San Francisco, pp. 855–862 (1992)

21. Gentner, D., Rattermann, M.J., Forbus, K.D.: The roles of similarity in transfer: separating retrievability from inferential soundness. Cogn. Psychol. **25**(4), 524–575 (1993)

22. Gentner, D., Smith, L.: Analogical reasoning. In: Ramachandran, V.S. (ed.) Encyclopedia of Human Behavior, pp. 130–136. Elsevier, Oxford (2012)

23. Giffinger, R., Fertner, C., Kramar, H., Kalasek, R., Pichler-Milanovic, N., Meihers, E.: Smart Cities: Ranking of European Medium-sized Cities. Centre of Regional Science, Vienna (2007)

24. Habenstein, A., D'Onofrio, S., Portmann, E., Stürmer, M., Myrach, T.: Open smart city: good governance für smarte städte. In: Meier, A., Portmann, E. (eds.) Smart City: Strategie, Governance und Projekte, pp. 47–71. Springer, Wiesbaden (2016). https://doi.org/10.1007/978-3-658-15617-6_3

25. Harrison, C., et al.: Foundations for smarter cities. IBM J. Res. Dev. **54**(4), 1–16 (2010)

26. Hevner, A., Chatterjee, S.: Design science research in information systems. In: Hevner, A., Chatterjee, S. (eds.) Design Research in Information Systems. Integrated Series in Information Systems, vol. 22, pp. 9–22. Springer, Boston (2010). https://doi.org/10.1007/978-1-4419-5653-8_2

27. Hurwitz, J., Kaufman, M., Bowles, A.: Cognitive Computing and Big Data Analytics, 1st edn. Wiley, Indianapolis (2015)

28. Kassibgi, G.: Soul of the machine: how chatbots work. Medium. https://medium.com/@gk_/how-chat-bots-work-dfff656a35e2. Accessed 30 Aug 2018

29. Khorasani, E.S., Rahimi, S., Gupta, B.: A reasoning methodology for CW-based question answering systems. In: Di Gesù, V., Pal, S.K., Petrosino, A. (eds.) WILF 2009. LNCS (LNAI), vol. 5571, pp. 328–335. Springer, Heidelberg (2009). https://doi.org/10.1007/978-3-642-02282-1_41

30. Kosko, B.: Fuzzy cognitive maps. Int. J. Man Mach. Stud. **24**(1), 65–75 (1986)

31. Laird, J.: The law of Parsimony. Monist **29**(3), 321–344 (1919)

32. Lee, D.H., Lee, H.: Construction of holistic fuzzy cognitive maps using ontology matching method. Expert Syst. Appl. **42**, 5954–5962 (2015)

33. Luger, E., Sellen, A.: "Like Having a Really Bad PA": the Gulf between user expectation and experience of conversational agents. In: Proceedings of the Conference on Human Factors in Computing Systems (CHI 2016), New York, California, pp. 5286–5297 (2016)

34. Malone, T.W., Bernstein, M.S.: Handbook of Collective Intelligence, 1st edn. MIT Press, Cambridge (2015)

35. McFate, C., Forbus, K.D.: Analogical generalization and retrieval for denominal verb interpretation. In: Conference of the Cognitive Science Society, pp. 1277–1282. Cognitive Science Society, Austin (2016)

36. Mostashari, A., Arnold, F., Mansouri, M., Finger, M.: Cognitive cities and intelligent urban governance. Netw. Ind. Q. **13**(3), 4–7 (2011)
37. Müller, S.M., D'Onofrio, S., Portmann, E.: Fuzzy analogical reasoning in cognitive cities: a conceptual framework for urban dialogue systems. In: Proceedings of the 20th International Conference on Enterprise Information Systems (ICEIS 2018), Funchal, Madeira (2018)
38. Nalawade, S., Kumar, S., Tiwari, D.: Question answering system. Int. J. Sci. Res. **3**(5), 439–444 (2014)
39. Oliveira, A., Campolargo, M.: From smart cities to human smart cities. In: 48th Hawaii International Conference on System Sciences, HICSS, Kauai, pp. 2336–2344 (2015)
40. Pedrycz, A., Hirota, K., Pedrycz, W., Dong, F.: Granular representation and granular computing with fuzzy sets. Fuzzy Sets Syst. **203**(1), 17–32 (2012)
41. Planum: The Human Smart Cities Cookbook. J. Urban. **28**(1) (2014)
42. Portmann, E., Finger, M.: Smart Cities! Ein Überblick. HMD Praxis Wirtsch. **52**(4), 470–481 (2015)
43. Robinson, I., Webber, J., Eifrem, E.: Graph Databases. O'Reilly, Beijing (2013)
44. Seeger, A.M., Pfeiffer, J., Heinzl, A.: When do we need a human? Anthropomorphic design and trustworthiness of conversational agents. In: Proceedings of the Sixteenth Annual Pre-ICIS Workshop on HCI Research in MIS, Seoul, Korea (2017)
45. Seising, R., Sanz, V.: From hard science and computing to soft science and computing – an introductory survey. In: Seising, R., Sanz, V. (eds.) Soft Computing in Humanities and Social Sciences. Studies in Fuzziness and Soft Computing, vol. 273, pp. 3–36. Springer, Heidelberg (2012). https://doi.org/10.1007/978-3-642-24672-2_1
46. Siemens, G.: Connectivism: a learning theory for the digital age. Int. J. Instr. Technol. Distance Learn. **2**(1), 3–10 (2005)
47. Stucki, T., D'Onofrio, S., Portmann, E.: Chatbot- Der digitale Helfer im Unternehmen: Praxisbeispiele der Schweizerischen post. In: Reinheimer, S. (ed.) Wertbeitrag Wissen. HMD Praxis der Wirtschaftsinformatik, pp. 725–747. Springer Fachmedien, Wiesbaden (2018)
48. Tschudi, F., D'Onofrio, S.: Wie wir durch unsere Denk- und Handlungsmuster beeinflusst werden. In: Meier, A., Seising, R. (eds.) Vague Information Processing. HMD Praxis der Wirtschaftsinformatik, pp. 467–471. Springer Fachmedien Wiesbaden, Wiesbaden (2018)
49. Turksen, I.B., Zhong, Z.: An approximate analogical reasoning approach based on similarity measures. IEE Trans. Syst. Man Cybern. **18**(6), 1049–1056 (1988)
50. Wehrle, M., Portmann, E., Denzler, A., Meier, A.: Developing initial state fuzzy cognitive maps with self-organizing maps. In: International Workshop on Artificial Intelligence and Cognition, Turin, Italy (2015)
51. Wickson, F., Carew, A.L., Russell, A.W.: Transdisciplinary research: characteristics, quandaries and quality. Futures **38**(9), 1046–1059 (2006)
52. Yao, Y.Y.: Three perspectives of granular computing. J. Nanchang Inst. Technol. **25**(2), 16–21 (2006)
53. Zadeh, L.A.: Fuzzy sets. Inf. Control **8**(1), 338–353 (1965)
54. Zadeh, L.A.: The concept of a linguistic variable and its applications to approximate reasoning. Inf. Sci. **8**, 199–249 (1975)
55. Zadeh, L.A.: Fuzzy logic. IEEE Comput. **21**(4), 83–93 (1988)
56. Zadeh, L.A.: Fuzzy logic = computing with words. IEEE Trans. Fuzzy Syst. **4**(2), 103–111 (1996)
57. Zadeh, L.A.: Toward a theory of fuzzy information granulation and its centrality in human reasoning and fuzzy logic. Fuzzy Sets Syst. **90**(2), 111–127 (1997)

58. Zadeh, L.A.: Toward a generalized theory of uncertainty (GTU) – an outline. Inf. Sci. **172** (1), 1–40 (2005)
59. Zadeh, L.A.: From search engines to question answering systems – the problems of world knowledge, relevance, deduction and precisiation. In: Sanchez, E. (ed.) Fuzzy Logic and the Semantic Web, 1st edn., pp. 163–210. Elsevier, Amsterdam (2006)

A Resource-Aware Model-Based Framework for Load Testing of WS-BPEL Compositions

Moez Krichen[1,2](✉), Afef Jmal Maâlej[2], Mariam Lahami[2],
and Mohamed Jmaiel[2,3]

[1] Faculty of Computer Science and Information Technology, Al-Baha University,
Al Bahah, Kingdom of Saudi Arabia
[2] ReDCAD Research Laboratory, National School of Engineering of Sfax,
University of Sfax, B.P. 1173, Sfax, Tunisia
{moez.krichen,afef.jmal,mariam.lahami}@redcad.org
[3] Research Center for Computer Science,
Multimedia and Digital Data Processing of Sfax,
B.P. 275, Sakiet Ezzit, 3021 Sfax, Tunisia
mohamed.jmaiel@enis.rnu.tn

Abstract. Nowadays, Web services compositions are playing a major role in the implementation of different types of distributed architectures. Such applications usually provide services to hundreds of users simultaneously. Load Testing is considered as an important type of testing for Web services compositions, as such applications require concurrent access by many users simultaneously. In this context, load testing for these types of applications seems an important task in order to discover problems under high loads. For this goal, we propose a model-based resource aware test architecture aiming to study the behavior of WS-BPEL compositions taking into account load conditions. The main contribution of this work consists of (a) adopting the timed automata formalism to model the system under test and to generate digital-clock test suites (b) identifying the best node for hosting each tester instance, then (c) running load tests and recording performance data and finally (d) analyzing the obtained logs in order to detect problems under load. Our approach is illustrated by means of a case study from the healthcare domain.

Keywords: Web services composition · Distributed load testing ·
Timed automata · Test generation · Distributed log analysis ·
Performance monitoring · Resource awareness ·
Distributed execution environment · Tester instance placement

1 Introduction

Web services compositions (particularly BPEL [3] compositions) offer different utilities to a huge number of users simultaneously. Load testing [4] is an important

This article is an extended version of our paper [19] presented in ICEIS 2018.

challenge of testing these applications, which is frequently performed in order to ensure that a system satisfies a particular performance requirement under a heavy load. In our context, load refers to the rate of incoming requests to a given system during a period of time.

In this context, load testing is an important activity that permits to detect programming errors, which would not be discovered if the composition is executed for a short time or with a small workload. These errors only appear when the system under test is executed during a long period of time or under a high load. Moreover, a given system may be correctly implemented but fails under some special load conditions due to external causes (e.g., hardware failures, misconfiguration, buggy load generator, etc.) [13]. Thus, it is important to detect and solve these different problems.

To deal with the various challenges related to load testing, we proposed in a previous work [18] a methodology which combines functional and load testing for BPEL compositions. Indeed, our study is based on conformance testing concept which verifies that a system implementation performs according to its specified requirements. For more details, monitoring BPEL compositions behaviors during load testing was proposed in order to perform later an advanced analysis of test results. This step aims to identify both causes and natures of detected problems. For that, the execution context of the application under test is considered while periodically capturing, under load, some performance metrics of the system such as CPU usage, memory usage, etc. Recognizing problems under load is however a challenging and time-consuming activity due to the large amount of generated data and the long running time of load tests. During this process, several risks may happen and undermine the System Under Test (SUT) quality and may even cause software and hardware failures such as SUT delays, memory, CPU overload, node crash, etc. Such risks may also impact the tester itself, which can produce faulty test results.

To overcome such problems, we extend our previous approach dealing with functional and load testing of BPEL compositions by distribution and resource awareness capabilities. Indeed, supporting test distribution over the network may alleviate considerably the test workload at runtime, especially when the SUT is running on a cluster of BPEL servers. Moreover, it is highly demanded to provide a resource-aware test system, that meets resource availability and fits connectivity constraints in order to have a high confidence in the validity of test results, as well as to reduce their associated burden and cost on the SUT. To show the feasibility of the proposed approach, a case study in the health care domain is introduced, its BPEL process is outlined and it is applied to the context of resource aware load testing.

The remainder of this paper is organized as follows. In Sect. 2, we present some BPEL concepts. Our formal test generation framework is presented in Sect. 3. Section 4 is dedicated to describe our proposed testing approach for the study of BPEL compositions under load conditions. Then, we describe in Sect. 5 our resource-aware tester deployment solution. In Sect. 6, we illustrate our test solution by means of a case study in the healthcare domain. Section 7 contains discussions about some works addressing load testing issue, test distribution and test resource awareness. Then Sect. 8 presents some advantages and limitations of our proposed solution. Finally, Sect. 9 provides a conclusion that summarizes the paper and discusses items for future work.

2   BPEL Concepts

Our approach is applicable whatever the used orchestration language is, in particular for BPEL based orchestration processes. According to OASIS[1] [3], a BPEL specification is a model and a grammar for describing the behavior of a business process based on interactions between the process and its partners. It is XML based and it allows sharing distributed data, even through multiple organizations, by employing a combination of Web services.

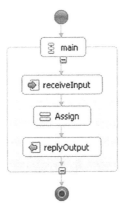

Fig. 1. A Hello World BPEL process

BPEL syntax consists of a set of activities which can be classified into two categories: basic activities and structured activities. Basic activities allow to invoke an operation of a partner Web service (*invoke* activity), to present the composition like a new Web service with the *receive* activity for describing the reception of a request and the *reply* activity to generate an answer. There are other activities such as *assign, wait, link,* etc. Structured activities use the basic activities to describe sequential execution (*sequence*) and parallel executions (*flow*), connections (*switch, if*), loops (*forEach, repeateUntil, while*), and finally alternate ways (*pick*).

The syntax of BPEL makes it possible also to declare variables, with the *variable* beacon, and to define partner Web services, with *partnerLink*. The latter can be defined as a link generated between a Web service and the process during the invocation of a Web service or, also, as a link created between the BPEL process

---

[1] Organization for the Advancement of Structured Information Standards.

and the client which calls it. Besides, this language integrates a mechanism of exception management (*throw, catch*), as well as a mechanism of compensation (*compensate*) which makes it possible to cancel an entire transaction in case of service failure for example.

Figure 1 depicts a simple Hello World BPEL process which receives an input string from a client and responses it exactly that input. Therefore, an activity which assigns the received input to the output is added within the BPEL flow.

3   Formal Test Generation Framework

3.1   Timed Automata

Let R be the set of non-negative reals. Given a finite set of *actions* Act, the set $(\mathsf{Act} \cup \mathsf{R})^*$ of all finite-length *real-time sequences* over Act will be denoted $\mathsf{RT}(\mathsf{Act})$. $\epsilon \in \mathsf{RT}(\mathsf{Act})$ is the empty sequence. Given $\mathsf{Act}' \subseteq \mathsf{Act}$ and $\rho \in \mathsf{RT}(\mathsf{Act})$, $\mathsf{P}_{\mathsf{Act}'}(\rho)$ denotes the *projection* of ρ to $\mathsf{Act}' \cup \mathsf{R}$, obtained by "erasing" from ρ all actions not in $\mathsf{Act}' \cup \mathsf{R}$. Similarly, $\mathsf{DP}_{\mathsf{Act}'}(\rho)$ denotes the (discrete) projection of ρ to Act'. For example, if $\mathsf{Act} = \{a, b\}$, $\mathsf{Act}' = \{a\}$ and $\rho = a\,1\,b\,2\,a\,3$, then $\mathsf{P}_{\mathsf{Act}'}(\rho) = a\,3\,a\,3$ and $\mathsf{DP}_{\mathsf{Act}'}(\rho) = a\,a$. The time spent in a sequence ρ, denoted $\mathrm{time}(\rho)$ is the sum of all delays in ρ.

We assume given a set of actions Act, partitioned in two disjoint sets: a set of *input actions* $\mathsf{Act}_{\mathsf{in}}$ and a set of *output actions* $\mathsf{Act}_{\mathsf{out}}$.

A *timed labeled transition system* (TLTS) over Act is a tuple $(S, s_0, \mathsf{Act}, T_d, T_t)$, where:

- S is a set of *states*;
- s_0 is the initial state;
- T_d is a set of *discrete transitions* of the form (s, a, s') where $s, s' \in S$ and $a \in \mathsf{Act}$;
- T_t is a set of *timed transitions* of the form (s, t, s') where $s, s' \in S$ and $t \in \mathsf{R}$.

We use standard notation concerning TLTS. For $s, s', s_i \in S$, $\mu, \mu_i \in \mathsf{Act} \cup \mathsf{R}$ and $\rho \in \mathsf{RT}(\mathsf{Act})$, we have:

- $s \xrightarrow{\mu} s' \stackrel{Def}{=} (s, \mu, s') \in T_d \cup T_t$;
- $s \xrightarrow{\mu} \stackrel{Def}{=} \exists s' : s \xrightarrow{\mu} s'$;
- $s \not\xrightarrow{\mu} \stackrel{Def}{=} \not\exists s' : s \xrightarrow{\mu} s'$;
- $s \xrightarrow{\mu_1 \cdots \mu_n} s' \stackrel{Def}{=} \exists s_1, \cdots, s_n : s = s_1 \xrightarrow{\mu_1} s_2 \xrightarrow{\mu_2} \cdots \xrightarrow{\mu_n} s_n = s'$;
- $s \xrightarrow{\rho} \stackrel{Def}{=} \exists s' : s \xrightarrow{\rho} s'$;
- $s \not\xrightarrow{\rho} \stackrel{Def}{=} \not\exists s' : s \xrightarrow{\rho} s'$.

We use timed automata [1] with deadlines to model urgency [6,25]. A *timed automaton over* Act is a tuple $A = (Q, q_0, X, \mathsf{Act}, \mathsf{E})$, where:

- Q is a finite set of *locations*;
- $q_0 \in Q$ is the initial location;

- X is a finite set of *clocks*;
- E is a finite set of *edges*.

Each edge is a tuple (q, q', ψ, r, d, a), where:

- $q, q' \in Q$ are the source and destination locations;
- ψ is the *guard*, a conjunction of constraints of the form $x \# c$, where $x \in X$, c is an integer constant and $\# \in \{<, \le, =, \ge, >\}$;
- $r \subseteq X$ is a set of clocks to *reset* to zero;
- $d \in \{\mathsf{lazy}, \mathsf{delayable}, \mathsf{eager}\}$ is the *deadline*;
- $a \in \mathsf{Act}$ is the action.

A timed automaton A defines an infinite TLTS which is denoted L_A:

- Its states are pairs $s = (q, v)$, where $q \in Q$ and $v : X \to \mathsf{R}$ is a clock *valuation*.
- $\mathbf{0}$ is the valuation assigning 0 to every clock of A.
- S_A is the set of all states and $s_0^A = (q_0, \mathbf{0})$ is the initial state.
- Discrete transitions are of the form $(q, v) \xrightarrow{a} (q', v')$, where $a \in \mathsf{Act}$ and there is an edge (q, q', ψ, r, d, a), such that:
  - v satisfies ψ;
  - and v' is obtained by resetting to zero all clocks in r and leaving the others unchanged.
- Timed transitions are of the form $(q, v) \xrightarrow{t} (q, v + t)$, where $t \in \mathsf{R}, t > 0$ and there is no edge (q, q'', ψ, r, d, a), such that:
  - either $d = \mathsf{delayable}$ and there exist $0 \le t_1 < t_2 \le t$ such that $v + t_1 \models \psi$ and $v + t_2 \not\models \psi$;
  - or $d = \mathsf{eager}$ and $v \models \psi$.
- A state $s \in S_A$ is *reachable* if there exists $\rho \in \mathsf{RT}(\mathsf{Act})$ such that $s_0^A \xrightarrow{\rho} s$.
- The set of reachable states of A is denoted $\mathsf{Reach}(A)$.

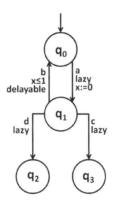

Fig. 2. An example of a timed automaton.

An example of an extended timed automaton $A = (Q, q_0, X, \mathsf{Act}, \mathsf{E})$ over the set of actions $\mathsf{Act} = \{a, b, c, d\}$ is given in Fig. 2 where:

- $Q = \{q_0, q_1, q_2, q_3\}$ is the set of locations;
- q_0 is the initial location;
- $X = \{x\}$ is the finite set of clocks;
- E is the set of edges drawn in the Figure.

3.2   Digital-Clock Tests

Let A_S be a new specification over Act and let tick a new output action, not in Act. We define a digital-clock test (DC-test) for the specification A_S as a total function

$$D : (\mathsf{Act} \cup \{\mathsf{tick}\})^* \rightarrow \mathsf{Act_{in}} \cup \{\mathsf{Wait}, \mathsf{Pass}, \mathsf{Fail}\}. \tag{1}$$

The DC-test can observe all input and output actions, plus the action tick which is assumed to be the output of the tester's digital clock. We assume that the tester's digital clock is modeled as a *tick-automaton*, which is a special TAIO with a single output action tick. Two examples of (periodic) tick-automata are shown in Fig. 3.

The execution of a DC-test is obtained by constructing the parallel product of three TIOLTSs, namely, the test D, the implementation A_I, and the tick-automaton Tick.

Formally, we say that A_I *passes* the DC-test D with respect to digital clock Tick, denoted A_I passes (D, Tick), if state Fail is not reachable in the product $A_I \| \mathsf{Tick} \| D$. In the same manner we have A_I fails (D, Tick) if Fail is reachable in $A_I \| \mathsf{Tick} \| D$.

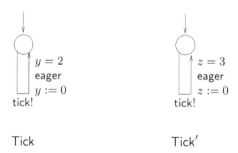

Fig. 3. Two examples of tick-automata.

3.3   Test Generation

We adapt the test generation algorithm of [27]. In a nutshell, the algorithm constructs a test in the form of a tree. Any node of the tree corresponds to a set of states S of the specification which represents the current "knowledge" of the tester about the test state. The test is extended by adding successors to a

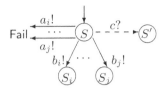

Fig. 4. Generic test-generation scheme [15].

leaf node, as shown in Fig. 4. For all *illegal* outputs a_i (the outputs that cannot take place from any state in S) the test leads to Fail. For every legal output b_i, the test moves to node S_i, which is the set of states the specification can be in after generating b_i. If there exists an input c which can be accepted by the specification at some state in S, then the test may decide to produce this input (dashed arrow from S to S'). At any node, the algorithm may decide to stop the test and label this node as Pass.

We first compute the product $A_S^{\mathsf{Tick}} = A_S \| \mathsf{Tick}$. This produces a new TAIO which has as inputs the inputs of A_S and as outputs the outputs of A_S plus the new output tick of Tick.

For $a \in \mathsf{Act}$ and $t \in \mathsf{R}$, we define the following operators on A_S^{Tick}:

$$\mathsf{dsucc}(S, a) = \{s' \mid \exists s \in S \ : \ s \xrightarrow{a} s'\} \tag{2}$$

$$\mathsf{tsucc}(S, t) = \{s' \mid \exists s \in S \ : \ s \xrightarrow{t} s'\} \tag{3}$$

$$\mathsf{usucc}(S) = \{s' \mid \exists s \in S \, . \, \exists t' \in \mathsf{R} \ : \ s \xrightarrow{t'} s'\}. \tag{4}$$

$\mathsf{dsucc}(S, a)$ contains all states which can be reached by some state in S after executing action a. $\mathsf{tsucc}(S, t)$ contains all states which can be reached by some state in S via a sequence ρ which contains no observable actions and takes exactly t time units. The two operators can be implemented using standard data structures for symbolic representation of the state space and simple modifications of reachability algorithms for timed automata [28]. $\mathsf{usucc}(S)$ contains all states which can be reached by some state in S via a sequence ρ which contains no observable actions. Notice that, by construction of A_S^{Tick}, the duration of ρ is bounded: since tick is observable and has to occur after a bounded duration.

Finally, we apply the generic test-generation scheme presented above. The root of the test tree is defined to be $S_0 = \{s_0^{A_S^{\mathsf{Tick}}}\}$. Successors of a node S are computed as follows. For each $a \in \mathsf{Act_{out}} \cup \{\mathsf{tick}\}$, there is an edge $S \xrightarrow{a} S'$ with $S' = \mathsf{dsucc}(\mathsf{usucc}(S), a)$, provided $S' \neq \emptyset$, otherwise there is an edge $S \xrightarrow{a} \mathsf{Fail}$. For this first possible choice, the node S is said to be an *output node*. If there exists $b \in \mathsf{Act_{in}}$ such that $S'' = \mathsf{dsucc}(\mathsf{tsucc}(S, 0), b) \neq \emptyset$, then the test generation algorithm may decide to emit b at S, adding an edge $S \xrightarrow{b} S''$. For this second choice, S is said to be an *input node*.

```
1    S ← {s_0^{A_S^{Tick}}};
2    D ← the one-node tree with root S;
3    while(true)
4       foreach(leaf S of D distinct from Pass and Fail)
5          if(valid_inputs(S) ≠ ∅)
6             i ← pick({0, 1, 2});
7          else i ← pick({1, 2});
8          endif;
9          case(i = 0) :
10            b ← pick(valid_inputs(S));
11            S' ← dsucc(tsucc(S, 0), b);
12            append edge S --b--> S' to D;
13         case(i = 1) :
14            foreach(a ∈ Act_out ∪ {tick})
15               S' ← dsucc(usucc(S), a);
16               if(S' ≠ ∅)
17                  append edge S --a--> S' to D;
18               else append edge S --a--> Fail to D;
19               endif;
20            endforeach;
21         case(i = 2) : replace S with Pass in D;
22      endforeach;
23   endwhile;
```

Fig. 5. Off-line DC-test generation [15].

Off-line DC-test generation is performed by the algorithm shown in Fig. 5. The algorithm uses the following notation:

- Given a nonempty set X, pick(X) chooses randomly an element in X.
- Given a set of states S, valid_inputs(S) is defined as the set of valid inputs at S, that is: $\{a \in \text{Act}_{in} | \text{dsucc}(\text{tsucc}(S, 0), a) \neq \emptyset\}$.
- D denotes the DC-test the algorithm generates (An example of a simple DC-test is shown in Fig. 6).

3.4 Coverage

The proposed generation algorithm is only partially specified. It has to be completed by specifying a strategy for marking nodes as input or output, for choosing which of the possible outputs to emit and for choosing when to arrest the test.

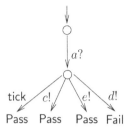

Fig. 6. An example of a DC-test.

One possible way is to resolve these choices randomly. This may not be satisfactory when some completeness guarantees are required or when repetitions must be avoided as much as possible. Another option is to generate an *exhaustive* test suite up to a depth k specified by the user. This approach has a major limitation which corresponds to the so-called *explosion* problem, since the number of tests is generally exponential in k.

To alleviate the above mentioned problems, several approaches have been proposed for producing test suites with respect to some *coverage criteria*. Different criteria have been proposed for software, such as statement coverage, branch coverage, and so on [23]. For the TA case existing techniques attempt to cover either a time-abstracting quotient graph [24]) or abstractions of the space of states (e.g., the region graph [26] or structural elements of the specification such as locations or edges [9]. In [5], a technique for generating test suites from coverage criteria is introduced. The coverage criteria are modeled as *observer automata*.

Here, we use a technique [15] for covering locations, states or edges of the specification. Our solution relies on the concept of *observable graph* [15]. The observable graph OG of the composed automaton A_S^{Tick} is computed as follows:

- The initial node of the graph is $S_0 = \text{usucc}(\{s_0^{A_S^{\text{Tick}}}\})$.
- For each generated node S and each $a \in \text{Act} \cup \{\text{tick}\}$, a successor node S' is generated and an edge $S \xrightarrow{a} S'$ is added to the graph.

Extrapolation techniques are used to ensure that the graph remains finite.

4   Study of WS-BPEL Compositions Under Load

Our proposed approach is based on gray box testing, which is a strategy for software debugging where the tester has limited knowledge of the internal details of the program. Indeed, we simulate in our case the different partner services of the composition under test as we suppose that only the interactions between this latter and its partners are known. Furthermore, we rely on the online testing mode considering the fact that test cases are generated and executed simultaneously [21]. Moreover, we choose to distribute the testing architecture components on different nodes in order to realistically run an important number of multiple virtual clients.

4.1   Load Distribution Principle

When testing the performance of an application, it can be beneficial to perform the tests under a typical load. This can be difficult if we are running our application in a development environment. One way to emulate an application running under load is through the use of load generator scripts. For more details, distributed testing is to be used when we reach the limits of a machine in terms of CPU[2], memory or network. In fact, it can be used within one machine (many VMs[3] on one machine). If we reach the limits of one reasonable VM in terms of CPU and memory, load distribution can be used across many machines (1 or many VMs on 1 or many machines). In order to realize remote load test distribution, a test manager is responsible to monitor the test execution and distribute the required load between the different load generators. These latters invoke concurrently the system under test as imposed by the test manager.

4.2   Load Testing Architecture

In this section, we describe a proposed distributed framework for behavior study of BPEL compositions under load conditions [18]. For simplicity reasons, we consider that our load testing architecture is composed, besides the SUT and the tester, of two load generators[4], as depicted in Fig. 7.

As shown in Fig. 7, the main components of our proposed architecture are:

- *The System under test (SUT)*: a new BPEL instance is created for each call of the composition under test. A BPEL instance is defined by a unique identifier. Each created instance invokes its own partner services instances by communicating while exchanging messages.
- *The tester (Tester)*: it represents the system under test environment and consists of:
  - *The Web services (WS1, ..., WSm)*: these services correspond to simulated partners of the composition under test. For each call of the composition during load testing, new instances of partner services are created.
  - *The Queues (Queue WS1, ..., Queue WSm)*: these entities are simple text files through which partner services and the Tester Core exchange messages.
  - *The Loader*: it loads the SUT specification described in Timed Automata, besides the WSDL files of the composition under test and the WSDL files of each partner service. Moreover, it defines the types of input/output variables of the considered composition as well as of its partner services.
  - *The Tester Core*: it generates random input messages of the BPEL process under test. It communicates with the different partner services of the composition by sending them the types of input and output messages.

---

[2] Central Processing Unit.

[3] Virtual Machines.

[4] More machines may be considered as load generators in order to distribute the load more efficiently.

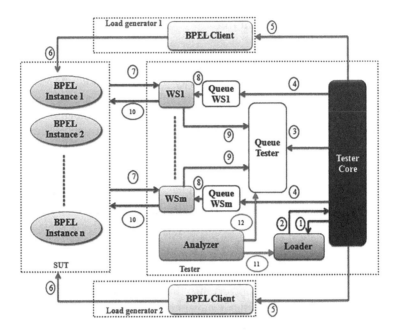

Fig. 7. Load testing architecture [19].

In case of partner services which are involved in synchronous communications, the Tester Core sends information about their response times to the composed service. Finally, it distributes the load between the two generators. It orders each one to perform (more or less) half of concurrent calls to the composition under test, and passes in parameters the time between each two successive invocations besides the input variable(s) of the system.

- *The test log (QueueTester)*: it stores the general information of the test (number of calls of the composition under test, the delay between the invocation of BPEL instances, etc.). Also it saves the identifiers of created instances, the invoked services, the received messages from the SUT, the time of their invocations and the verdict corresponding to checking of partner input messages types. This log will be consulted by the Analyzer to verify the functioning of the different BPEL instances and to diagnose the nature and cause of the detected problems.
- *The test analyzer (Analyzer)*: this component is responsible for offline analysis of the test log QueueTester. It generates a final test report and identifies, as far as possible, the limitations of the tested composition under load conditions.
- *The load generators (BPEL Client)*: these entities meet the order of the Tester Core by performing concurrent invocations of the composed service. For that, they receive from the tester as test parameters the input(s) of the composition

under test, the number of required process calls and the delay between each two successive invocations.

Besides, we highlight that load testing of BPEL compositions in our approach is accompanied by a module for the monitoring of the execution environment performances, aiming to supervise the whole system infrastructure during the test. Particularly, this module permits the selection, before starting test, of the interesting metrics to monitor, and then to display their evolution in real-time. In addition, the monitoring feature helps in establishing the correlation between performance problems and the detected errors by our solution.

4.3   Automation of Load Test Analysis

Current industrial practices for checking the results of a load test mainly persist ad-hoc, including high-level checks. In addition, looking for functional problems in a load testing is a time-consuming and difficult task, due to the challenges such as no documented system behavior, monitoring overhead, time pressure and large volume of data. In particular, the ad-hoc logging mechanism is the most commonly used, as developers insert output statements (e.g. printf or System.out) into the source code for debugging reasons [10]. Then most practitioners look for the functional problems under load using manual searches for specific keywords like *failure*, or *error* [12]. After that, load testing practitioners analyze the context of the matched log lines to determine whether they indicate functional problems or not. Depending on the length of a load test and the volume of generated data, it takes load testing practitioners several hours to perform these checks.

However, few research efforts are dedicated to the automated analysis of load testing results, usually due to the limited access to large scale systems for use as case studies. Automated and systematic load testing analysis becomes much needed, as many services have been offered online to an increasing number of users. Motivated by the importance and challenges of the load testing analysis, an automated approach was proposed in [18] to detect functional and performance problems in a load test by analyzing the recorded execution logs and performance metrics. In fact, performed operations during load testing of BPEL compositions are stored in QueueTester. In order to recognize each BPEL instance which is responsible for a given action, each one starts with the identifier of its corresponding BPEL instance (BPEL-ID). At the end of test running, the Analyzer consults QueueTester.

Hence, our automated log analysis technique takes as input the stored log file (QueueTester) during load testing, and goes through three steps as shown in Fig. 8:

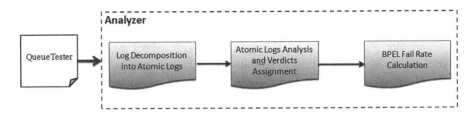

Fig. 8. Automated log analysis technique [19].

- *Decomposition of QueueTester*: based on BPEL-ID, the Analyzer decomposes information into atomic test reports. Each report is named BPEL-ID and contains information about the instance which identifier is BPEL-ID.
- *Analysis of atomic logs*: the Analyzer consults the generated atomic test reports of the different BPEL instances. It verifies the observed executed actions of each instance by referring to the specified requirements in the model (Timed Automata). Finally, the Analyzer assigns corresponding verdicts to each instance and identifies detected problems.
- *Generation of final test report*: this step consists in producing a final test report recapitulating test results relatively to all instances and also describing both nature and cause of each observed FAIL verdict.

It is true that our load test analysis is automated. Yet, the analysis of the atomic logs is performed sequentially for each BPEL instance, which may be costly especially in term of time execution. Another limitation consists in using only one instance of tester and thus one analyzer for each test case. To solve this issue, we propose to use more than one instance of the tester which are deployed in distributed nodes and connected to the BPEL process under test. Each tester instance studies the behavior of the composition considering different load conditions (SUT inputs, number of required process calls, delay between each two successive invocations, etc.).

5   Constrained Tester Deployment

In this section, we deal with the assignment of tester instances to test nodes while fitting some resource and connectivity constraints. The main goal of this step is to distribute efficiently the load across virtual machines, computers, or even the cloud. This is crucial for the test system performance and for gaining confidence in test results.

Figure 9 illustrates the distributed load testing architecture in which several tester instances are created and connected to the BPEL process under test. These instances run in parallel in order to perform efficiently load testing.

It is worthy to note that each tester instance includes an analyzer component that takes as input the generated atomic test reports of the different BPEL instances, and generates as output a Local Verdict (LV). As depicted in Fig. 10, we define a new component called Test System Coordinator which is mainly charged with collecting the local verdicts generated from the analyzer instances

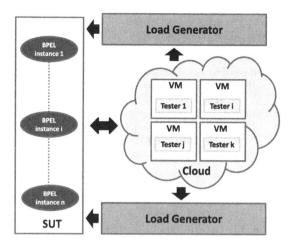

Fig. 9. Distributed load testing architecture [19].

and producing the Global Verdict (GV). As shown in Fig. 11, if all local verdicts are PASS, the global verdict will be PASS. If at least one local verdict is FAIL (respectively INCONCLUSIVE), the global verdict will be FAIL (respectively INCONCLUSIVE).

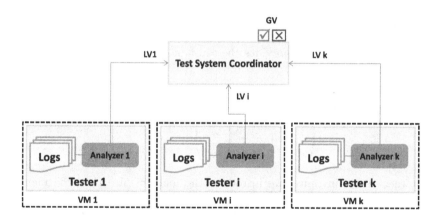

Fig. 10. Distributed load test analysis architecture [19].

Once the distributed load testing architecture is elaborated, we have to assign efficiently its components (i.e., its tester instances) to the execution nodes. To do so, we have defined two kinds of constraints that have to be respected in this stage: resources and connectivity constraints. They are detailed in the following subsections.

```
Input: The array LocalVerdicts.
Output: The global verdict.

1: BEGIN
2: for i = 0 to LocalVerdicts.size − 1 do
3:    if (LocalVerdicts[i]==FAIL) then
4:        return FAIL
5:    end if
6:    if (LocalVerdicts[i]==INCONCLUSIVE) then
7:        return INCONCLUSIVE
8:    end if
9: end for
10: return PASS
11: END
```

Fig. 11. Generation of the global verdict [19].

5.1 Resource Constraints Formalization

In general, load testing is considered a resource consuming activity. As a consequence, it is essential to apply resource allocation during test distribution in order to decrease test overhead and raise confidence in test results.

For each component in the test environment, three resources have to be monitored: the current CPU load, the available memory and the energy level. The state of each resource can be directly measured on each component by means of internal monitors.

Formally, these resources are represented through three vectors: C that contains the CPU load, R that provides the available RAM and E that introduces the energy level.

$$
C = \begin{pmatrix} c_1 \\ c_2 \\ \vdots \\ c_m \end{pmatrix} \quad R = \begin{pmatrix} r_1 \\ r_2 \\ \vdots \\ r_m \end{pmatrix} \quad E = \begin{pmatrix} e_1 \\ e_2 \\ \vdots \\ e_m \end{pmatrix}
$$

For each tester instance, we introduce the memory size (i.e., the memory occupation needed by a tester during its execution), the CPU load and the energy consumption properties. We suppose that these values are provided by the test manager or computed after a preliminary test run. Similarly, they are formalized over three vectors: D_c that contains the required CPU, D_r that introduces the required RAM and D_e that contains the required energy by each tester.

$$
D_c = \begin{pmatrix} dc_1 \\ dc_2 \\ \vdots \\ dc_n \end{pmatrix} \quad D_r = \begin{pmatrix} dr_1 \\ dr_2 \\ \vdots \\ dr_n \end{pmatrix} \quad D_e = \begin{pmatrix} de_1 \\ de_2 \\ \vdots \\ de_n \end{pmatrix}
$$

As the proposed approach is resource aware, checking resource availability during test distribution is usually performed before starting the load testing process. Thus, the overall required resources by n tester instances must not exceed the available resources in m nodes. This rule is formalized through three constraints to fit as outlined by (1) where the two dimensional variable x_{ij} can be equal to 1 if the tester instance i is assigned to the node j, 0 otherwise.

$$\begin{cases} \sum_{i=1}^{n} x_{ij}dc_i \le c_j & \forall j \in \{1, \cdots, m\} \\ \sum_{i=1}^{n} x_{ij}dr_i \le r_j & \forall j \in \{1, \cdots, m\} \\ \sum_{i=1}^{n} x_{ij}de_i \le e_j & \forall j \in \{1, \cdots, m\} \end{cases} \tag{5}$$

5.2   Connectivity Constraints Formalization

Dynamic environments are characterized by unpredictable and frequent changes in connectivity caused by firewalls, non-routing networks, node mobility, etc. For this reason, we have to pay attention when assigning a tester instance to a host computer by finding at least one path in the network to communicate with the component under test.

More generally, we pinpoint, for each test component, a set of forbidden nodes to discard during the constrained test component placement step. From a technical perspective, either Depth-First Search or Breadth-First Search algorithms can be used to firstly identify connected execution nodes in the network and secondly to compute a set of forbidden nodes for each test component involved in the test process. This connectivity constraint is denoted as follows:

$$x_{ij} = 0 \quad \forall j \in forbiddenNode(i) \tag{6}$$

where $forbiddenNode(i)$ is a function which returns the set of forbidden nodes for a test component i.

Finding a satisfying test placement solution is merely achieved by fitting the former constraints (5) and (6).

5.3   Tester Instance Placement Optimization

Looking for an optimal test placement solution consists in identifying the best node to host the concerned tester in response with two criteria: its distance from the node under test and its link bandwidth capacity. For this aim, we are asked to attribute a profit value p_{ij} for assigning the tester i to a node j. For this aim, a matrix $\mathcal{P}_{n \times m}$ is computed as follows:

$$p_{ij} = \begin{cases} 0 & \text{if} \quad j \in forbiddenNode(i) \\ maxP - k \times step_p & \text{otherwise} \end{cases} \tag{7}$$

where $maxP$ is constant, $step_p = \frac{maxP}{m}$, k corresponds to the index of a node j in a *Rank Vector* that is computed for each node under test. This vector corresponds to a classification of the connected nodes according to both criteria: their distance far from the node under test and their link bandwidth capacities.

Consequently, the constrained tester instance approach generates the best deployment host for each tester instance involved in the load testing process by maximizing the total profit value while satisfying the former resource and connectivity constraints. Thus, it is formalized as a variant of the Knapsack Problem, called *Multiple Multidimensional Knapsack Problem* (MMKP) [11].

$$MMKP = \begin{cases} maximize \quad \mathcal{Z} = \sum_{i=1}^{n} \sum_{j=1}^{m} p_{ij} x_{ij} & (8) \\ subject \quad to \quad (5) \quad and \quad (6) \\ \sum_{j=1}^{m} x_{ij} = 1 \quad \forall i \in \{1, \cdots, n\} & (9) \\ x_{ij} \in \{0, 1\} \quad \forall i \in \{1, \cdots, n\} \\ and \quad \forall j \in \{1, \cdots, m\} \end{cases}$$

Constraint (8) corresponds to the objective function that maximizes tester instance profits while fitting resource (1) and connectivity (2) constraints. Constraint (9) indicates that each tester instance has to be assigned to at most one node.

Figure 12 displays the main instructions to solve this MMKP problem. First of all, resource constraints have to be defined (see lines 2–4). Second, forbidden nodes for each test component are identified and then connectivity constraints are deduced (see lines 5–7). Then, an objective function is calculated (see line 8) and then maximized (see line 9) to obtain an optimal solution.

Input: $\mathcal{P}_{n \times m}$: profit matrix
$\quad\quad\quad$ R,C,E: provided resources by m nodes
$\quad\quad\quad$ D_r,D_c,D_e: required resources by n tests
Output: x (the two dimensional variable)

1: **BEGIN**
2: Constraint ram[]=defineResourceConstraint(x,R,D_r)
3: Constraint cpu[]=defineResourceConstraint(x,C,D_c)
4: Constraint en[]=defineResourceConstraint(x,E,D_e)
5: **for** $i = 1$ to n **do**
6: $\quad$ $con.add(ConnectConstraint(x, forbiddenNode(i)))$
7: **end for**
8: **if** a feasible solution is required **then**
9: $\quad$ $x = solve(ram, cpu, en, con)$
10: **else**
11: $\quad$ $\mathcal{Z} = defineObjectiveFunction(x, \mathcal{P})$
12: $\quad$ $x = maximize(\mathcal{Z}, ram, cpu, en, con)$
13: **end if**
14: **return** x
15: **END**

Fig. 12. Resolution of MMKP problem.

5.4   Implementation of Tester Instance Placement

In this section, we show the use of a well-known solver in the constraint programming area, namely Choco [14], to compute either an optimal or a satisfying solution of the MMKP problem [17]. Among several existing solvers like

```
 1   //Model declaration
 2   CPModel model = new CPModel();
 3   // Variables declaration
 4   IntegerVariable [][]  X = new IntegerVariable[n][m];
 5   for (int  i = 0; i < n; i++) {
 6   for (int  j = 0; j < m; j++) {
 7                   X[i][j] = Choco.makeIntVar("X" + i+j, 0, 1);}}
 8   //Objective variable declaration
 9   IntegerVariable Z = Choco.makeIntVar("P", 1, n*maxp,Options.V_OBJECTIVE);
10   //Modelling knapsack constraints
11   IntegerVariable [][] XDual = new IntegerVariable[m][n];
12   for (int  i = 0; i < m; i++) {
13        for (int  j = 0; j < n; j++) {
14              XDual[i][j] = X[j][i];}}
15   Constraint [] cols_ram = new Constraint[m];
16   Constraint [] cols_cpu = new Constraint[m];
17   Constraint [] cols_en = new Constraint[m];
18   for (int  j = 0; j < m; j++) {
19        cols_ram[j] = Choco.leq(Choco.scalar(Dr,XDual[j]),R[j]);
20        cols_cpu[j] = Choco.leq(Choco.scalar(Dc,XDual[j]),C[j]);
21        cols_en [j] = Choco.leq(Choco.scalar(De,XDual[j]),E[j]);}
22   model.addConstraints(cols_ram);
23   model.addConstraints(cols_cpu);
24   model.addConstraints(cols_en);
25   //adding a constraint for each forbidden node
26   Constraint [] forbiden_nodes = new Constraint[l]; int k=0;
27   for (int  i = 0; i < n; i++)
28        for (int  j = 0; j < m; j++) {
29             if(P[i][j]==0){
30                  forbiden_nodes[k] = Choco.eq(X[i][j],0); k++;}
31             }
32   model.addConstraints(forbiden_nodes);
33   //Objective function
34   IntegerExpressionVariable [] exp1=new IntegerExpressionVariable [n];
35   for (int  i = 0; i < n; i++)
36        exp1[i]=Choco.scalar(P[i], X[i]);
37   model.addConstraint(Choco.eq(Choco.sum(exp1),Z));
38   //Create the solver
39   Solver s = new CPSolver();
40   s.read(model);
41   //Solve the problem
42   s.maximize(s.getVar(Z), false);
```

Fig. 13. Mapping of the MMKP formulation to the Choco-based code.

GeCoDe[5] and CPLEX[6], Choco is selected because it is one of the most popular within the research community. Also, it offers a reliable and stable open source Java library widely used in the literature to solve combinatorial optimization problems.

Due to all these features, Choco is retained in this paper to model and to solve the test placement problem while fitting several resource and connectivity constraints. First, we make use of the Choco Java library to translate the mathematical representation of the test placement problem into the Choco-based code. Second, we use it to solve this problem in both modes: in a satisfaction mode by computing a feasible solution or in an optimization mode by looking for the optimal solution.

As shown in Fig. 13, we create a *Constraint Programming Model*(CPModel) instance which is one of the basic elements in a Choco program (see line 2). Then, we declare the variables of the problem, generally unknown. Lines 4–7 show the declaration of the x_{ij} variable and its domain. Moreover, we display in line 9 the declaration of the objective function that maximizes the profit of test components placement.

Recall that for each assignment of a tester instance i to a node j a profit value p_{ij} is computed according to two criteria :ink bandwidth capacities. In lines 15–24, the resource constraints to be satisfied are expressed and added to the model. For each forbidden node, the constraint $x_{ij} = 0$ is also defined (see lines 25–31). Once, the model is designed, we aim next to solve it by building a solver object as outlined in line 39.

6   TRMCS Case Study

To demonstrate the applicability of our approach, we propose a case study from the healthcare field highlighted in the subsection below.

6.1   Case Study Description

The Teleservices and Remote Medical Care System (TRMCS) provides monitoring and assistance to patients who suffer from chronic health problems. Due to the modern needs of medicine, the proposed care system can be enhanced with more sophisticated services like the acquisition, the storage and the analysis of biomedical data.

We adopt the BPEL process shown in Fig. 14. We assume that it is composed of several Web services namely:

- The Storage Service (SS);
- The Analysis Service (AnS);
- The Alerting Service (AlS)
- The Maintenance Service (MS).

---

[5] http://www.gecode.org.
[6] http://www-03.ibm.com/software/products/fr/ibmilogcpleoptistud.

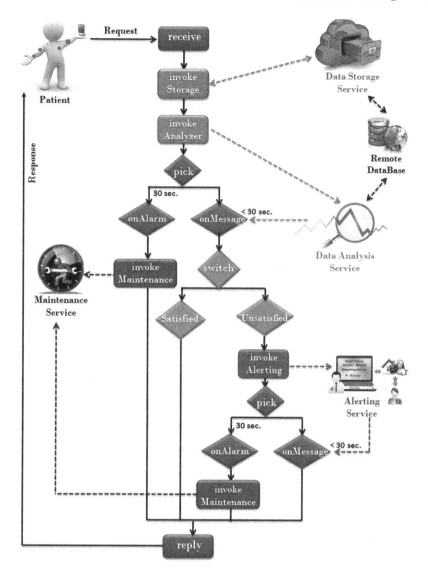

Fig. 14. The TRMCS process [19].

For a given patient suffering from chronic high blood pressure, measures like the arterial blood pressure and the heart-rate beats per minute are gathered periodically (for instance three times everyday). For the collected measures, a request is sent to the TRMCS process. First, the *Storage Service* is called to save periodic reports in the medical database. Then, the *Analyzer Service* is requested to analyze the gathered data in order to check whether some thresholds are exceeded or not. This analysis is conditioned by a timed constraint.

In fact, the process should receive a response from the AnS before reaching 30 s. Otherwise, the process sends a connection problem report to the Maintenance Service. If the analysis response is received before reaching 30 s, two scenarios are studied. If thresholds are satisfied, a detailed reply is sent to the corresponding patient. Otherwise, the Alerting Service is invoked in order to send urgent notification to the medical staff (such as doctors, nurses, etc.).

Similar to the Analysis Service, the Alerting Service is conditioned by a waiting time. If the medical staff is notified before reaching 30 s, the final reply is sent to the corresponding patient. Otherwise, the Maintenance Service is called.

We suppose that the TRMCS application can be installed in different cities within the same country. Thus, we suppose that several BPEL servers are used to handle multiple concurrent patient requests. From a technical point of view, we adopt Oracle BPEL Process Manager[7] as a solution for designing, deploying and managing the TRMCS BPEL process. We also opt for Oracle BPEL server. The main question to tackle here is how to apply our methodology of load testing for BPEL composition without introducing side effects and in a cost effective manner?

6.2   Resource Aware Load Testing for TRMCS

In order to check the satisfaction of performance requirements under a heavy load of patients requests, we apply our resource aware load testing approach. For simplicity, we concentrate at this stage on studying the load testing of a single BEPL server while the load is handled by several testers simulating concurrent patient requests. For this goal, we consider a test environment composed of four nodes: a server node ($N1$) and three test nodes ($N2$, $N3$ and $N4$). As shown in Fig. 15, we suppose that this environment has some connectivity problems. In fact, the node $N4$ is forbidden to host tester instances because no route is available to communicate with the BPEL instance under test.

To accomplish distributed load tests efficiently and without influencing test results, tester instances Ti have to be deployed in the execution environment while fitting connectivity and resources constraints (e.g., energy and memory consumption, link bandwidth, etc.).

Thus, we need to compute a best placement solution of a given tester Ti. First of all, the node $N4$ is discarded from the tester placement process because the link with the BPEL server is broken. Consequently, the variable x_{i4} equals zero. Second, we compute the *Rank Vector* for the rest of connected test nodes and we deduce the profit matrix. We notice here that the profit p_{ij} is maximal if the tester Ti is assigned to the server node $N1$ because assigning a tester to its corresponding node under test and performing local tests reduces the network communication cost. This profit decreases with respect to the node index in the *Rank Vector*. For instance, $N3$ is considered a better target for the tester Ti than the node $N2$ even though they are located at the same distance from the

---

[7] http://www.oracle.com/technetwork/middleware/bpel/.

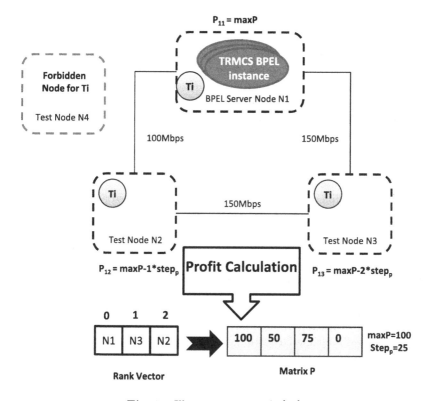

Fig. 15. Illustrative example [19].

server node because the link bandwidth between the two nodes $N3$ and $N1$ is greater than the one between $N2$ and $N1$.

For instance, in the case of four nodes and a given tester Ti (Fig. 15), the optimal solution of placement can be the test node $N1$. Thus, the computed variable x_i is as follows:

$$x_i = \big(1, 0, 0, 0\big)$$

7   Related Works

In the following, we discuss some existing works addressing load testing in general, test distribution and test resource awareness.

7.1   Existing Works on Load Testing

Load testing and performance monitoring become facilitated thanks to existing tools. In fact, load testing tools are used for software performance testing in order to create a workload on the system under test, and measure response times under this load. These tools are available from large commercial vendors such as Borland, HP Software, IBM Rational and Web Performance Suite, as well as Open source projects. Web sites. Krizanic et al. [16] analyzed and compared several existing tools which facilitate load testing and performance monitoring, in order to find the most appropriate tools by criteria such as ease of use, supported features, and license. Selected tools were put in action in real environments, through several Web applications.

Despite the fact that commercial tools offer richer set of features and are in general easier to use, available open source tools proved to be quite sufficient to successfully perform given tasks. Their usage requires higher level of technical expertise but they are a lot more flexible and extendable.

There are also different research works dealing with load and stress testing in various contexts. Firstly, Yang and Pollock [29] proposed a technique to identify the load sensitive parts in sequential programs based on a static analysis of the code. They also illustrated some load sensitive programming errors, which may have no damaging effect under small loads or short executions, but cause a program to fail when it is executed under a heavy load or over a long period of time. In addition, Zhang and Cheung [30] described a procedure for automating stress test case generation in multimedia systems. For that, they identify test cases that can lead to the saturation of one kind of resource, namely CPU usage of a node in the distributed multimedia system. Furthermore, Grosso et al. [8] proposed to combine static analysis and program slicing with evolutionary testing, in order to detect buffer overflow threats. For that purpose, the authors used of Genetic Algorithms in order to generate test cases. Garousi et al. [7] presented a stress test methodology that aims at increasing chances of discovering faults related to distributed traffic in distributed systems. The technique uses as input a specified UML 2.0 model of a system, extended with timing information. Moreover, Jiang et al. [13] and Jiang [12] presented an approach that accesses the execution logs of an application to uncover its dominant behavior and signals deviations from the application basic behavior.

Comparing the previous works, we notice that load testing concerns various fields such as multimedia systems [30], network applications [8], etc. Furthermore, all these solutions focus on the automatic generation of load test suites. Besides, most of the existing works aim to detect anomalies which are related to resource saturation or to performance issues as throughput, response time, etc. Besides, few research efforts, such as Jiang et al. [13] and Jiang [12], are devoted to the automated analysis of load testing results in order to uncover potential problems. Indeed, it is hard to detect problems in a load test due to the large amount of data which must be analyzed. We also notice that the identification of problem cause(s) (application, network or other) is not the main goal behind load testing, rather than studying performance of the application under test, this fact explains why few works address this issue. However, in our work, we are able to recognize if the detected problem under load is caused by implementation anomalies, network or other causes. Indeed, we defined and validated our approach based on interception of exchanged messages between the composition under test and its partner services.

Thus it would be possible to monitor exchanged messages instantaneously, and to recognize what is the cause behind their loss or probably their reception delay, etc. Studying the existing works on load testing, we remark that the authors make use of one instance tester for both the generation and execution of load test cases. To the best of our knowledge, there is no related work that proposes to use multiple testers at the same time on the same SUT. Thus we do not evoke neither testers placement in different nodes nor their management.

7.2 Existing Works on Test Distribution

The test distribution over the network has been rarely addressed by load testing approaches. We have identified only two approaches that shed light on this issue.

In the first study [2], the authors introduce a light-weight framework for adaptive testing called *Multi Agent-based Service Testing* in which runtime tests are executed in a coordinated and distributed environment. This framework encompasses the main test activities including test generation, test planning and test execution. Notably, the last step defines a coordination architecture that facilitates mainly test agent deployment and distribution over the execution nodes and test case assignment to the adequate agents.

In the second study [22], a distributed in vivo testing approach is introduced. This proposal defines the notion of *Perpetual Testing* which suggests the proceeding of software analysis and testing throughout the entire lifetime of an application: from the design phase until the in-service phase. The main contribution of this work consists in distributing the test load in order to attenuate the workload and improve the SUT performance by decreasing the number of tests to run.

Unlike these approaches, our work aims at defining a distributed test architecture that optimizes the current resources by instantiating testers in execution nodes while meeting resource availability and fitting connectivity constraints. This has an important impact on reducing load testing costs and avoiding overheads and burdens.

7.3 Existing Works on Test Resource Awareness

As discussed before, load testing is a resource-consuming activity. In fact, computational resources are used for generating tests if needed, instantiating tester instances charged with test execution and finally starting them and analyzing the obtained results. Notably, the bigger the number of test cases is, the more resources such as CPU load, memory consumption are used. Hence, we note that the intensive use of these computational resources during the test execution has an impact not only on the SUT but also on the test system itself. When such a situation is encountered, the test results can be wrong and can lead to an erroneous evaluation of the SUT responses.

To the best of our knowledge, this problem has been studied only by Merdes work [20]. Aiming at adapting the testing behavior to the given resource situation, it provides a resource-aware infrastructure that keeps track of the current resource states. To do this, a set of resource monitors are implemented to observe the respective values for processor load, main memory, battery charge, network bandwidth, etc. According to resource availability, the proposed framework is able to balance in an intelligent manner between testing and the core functionalities of the components. It provides in a novel way a number of test strategies for resource aware test management. Among these strategies, we can mention, for example, *Threshold Strategy* under which tests are performed only if the amount of used resources does not exceed thresholds. Contrary to our distributed load testing architecture, this work supports a centralized test architecture.

8   Advantages and Limitations

Related to our previous work [18] in which the test system is centralized on a single node, several problems may occur while dealing with load testing. In fact, we have noticed that not only the SUT, which is made up of several BPEL instances, can be affected by this heavy load but also the relevance of the obtained test results. In order to increase the performance of such test system and get confidence in its test results, testers and analyzers are distributed over several nodes. In this case, load testing process is performed in parallel.

Moreover, our proposal takes into consideration the connectivity to the SUT and also the availability of computing resources during load testing. Thus, our work provides a cost effective distribution strategy of testers, that improves the quality of testing process by scaling the performance through load distribution, and also by moving testers to better nodes offering sufficient resources required for the test execution.

Recall that the deployment of our distributed and resource aware test system besides BPEL instances is done on the cloud platform. It is worthy to note that public cloud providers like Amazon Web Services and Google Cloud Platform offer a cloud infrastructure made up essentially of availability zones and regions. A region is a specific geographical location in which public cloud service providers'data centers reside. Each region is further subdivided into availability zones. Several resources can live in a zone, such as instances or persistent disks. Therefore, we have to choose the VM instances in the same region to host the testers, the analyzers and the SUT. This is required in order to avoid the significant overhead that can be introduced when the SUT and the test system components are deployed in different regions on the cloud.

9   Conclusion and Future Work

In this paper, we proposed a distributed and resource-Aware model-based framework for load testing of WS-BPEL compositions. The proposed framework is based on the model of timed automata which allows to describe the behaviour of the system under test in a formal manner. The considered model is then used to generate test sequences automatically. The generated tests are digital-clock tests in the sense that time is observed in a digital fashion which is realistic assumption in practice since time cannot be measured with an infinite precision. For that purpose we need to propose a particular timed automaton which models the behaviour of the considered digital-clock. Then we compute the parallel product of the specification and the digital-clock timed automata before applying the test generation algorithm.

During the test execution phase, the test sequences are attributed to testers which are in charge of executing them. These testers need to be placed in a smart way taking into account the available resources of the components of the system and the connectivity constraints of the between the different nodes. For that goal, we proposed a formalization of the different constraints to consider during testers placement. As a result we obtained an instance of a classical optimization problem which can be solved using existing techniques from the operational research field and the constraint programming area. More precisely, the obtained problem is called Multiple Multidimensional Knapsack Problem (MMKP). Existing tools in the literature can be used to solve this problem. For instance, we may use the Choco tool used to compute either an optimal or a satisfying solution of the problem in hands.

Many extensions for our work are possible. A first future direction consists in implementing the proposed approach in order to validate it at an experimental level. We may also look for suitable heuristics for solving the optimization problem we have in hands in order to accelerate the resolution of the placement problem. An other direction for future work is to enrich the set of constraints and equations to solve with more parameters and details of the system under test to make our optimization problem more realistic and more precise. Moreover it may be useful to consider an incremental way to solve the optimization task. That is after a dynamic change of the system under test occurs we may think about finding a way to build the new placement strategy by updating the old one in order to make that task less time and resource consuming. Finally for the case of large systems it may be useful to divide these systems into smaller subsystems and to apply the tester distribution task on each of them separately.

References

1. Alur, R., Dill, D.: A theory of timed automata. Theor. Comput. Sci. **126**, 183–235 (1994)
2. Bai, X., Dai, G., Xu, D., Tsai, W.: A multi-agent based framework for collaborative testing on web services. In: Proceedings of the 4th IEEE Workshop on Software Technologies for Future Embedded and Ubiquitous Systems, and the 2nd International Workshop on Collaborative Computing, Integration, and Assurance (SEUS-WCCIA 2006), pp. 205–210 (2006)
3. Barreto, C., et al.: Web Services Business Process Execution Language Version 2.0 Primer. OASIS, May 2007
4. Beizer, B.: Software Testing Techniques, 2nd edn. Van Nostrand Reinhold Co., New York (1990)

5. Blom, J., Hessel, A., Jonsson, B., Pettersson, P.: Specifying and generating test cases using observer automata. In: Grabowski, J., Nielsen, B. (eds.) FATES 2004. LNCS, vol. 3395, pp. 125–139. Springer, Heidelberg (2005). https://doi.org/10.1007/978-3-540-31848-4_9

6. Bornot, S., Sifakis, J., Tripakis, S.: Modeling urgency in timed systems. In: de Roever, W.-P., Langmaack, H., Pnueli, A. (eds.) COMPOS 1997. LNCS, vol. 1536, pp. 103–129. Springer, Heidelberg (1998). https://doi.org/10.1007/3-540-49213-5_5

7. Garousi, V., Briand, L.C., Labiche, Y.: Traffic-aware stress testing of distributed systems based on UML models. In: Proceedings of ICSE 2006, Shanghai, China, 20–28 May 2006, pp. 391–400. ACM (2006)

8. Grosso, C.D., Antoniol, G., Penta, M.D., Galinier, P., Merlo, E.: Improving network applications security: a new heuristic to generate stress testing data. In: Proceedings of GECCO 2005, Washington DC, USA, 25–29 June 2005, pp. 1037–1043. ACM (2005)

9. Hessel, A., Larsen, K.G., Nielsen, B., Pettersson, P., Skou, A.: Time-optimal real-time test case generation using UPPAAL. In: Petrenko, A., Ulrich, A. (eds.) FATES 2003. LNCS, vol. 2931, pp. 114–130. Springer, Heidelberg (2004). https://doi.org/10.1007/978-3-540-24617-6_9

10. James, H.H., Douglas, C.S., James, R.E., Aniruddha, S.G.: Tools for continuously evaluating distributed system qualities. IEEE Softw. **27**(4), 65–71 (2010)

11. Jansen, K.: Parametrized approximation scheme for the multiple knapsack problem. In: Proceedings of the 20th Annual ACM-SIAM Symposium on Discrete Algorithms (SODA 2009), pp. 665–674 (2009)

12. Jiang, Z.M.: Automated analysis of load testing results. In: Proceedings of ISSTA 2010, Trento, Italy, 12–16 July 2010, pp. 143–146. ACM (2010)

13. Jiang, Z.M., Hassan, A.E., Hamann, G., Flora, P.: Automatic identification of load testing problems. In: Proceedings of ICSM 2008, Beijing, China, 28 September–4 October 2008, pp. 307–316. IEEE (2008)

14. Jussien, N., Rochart, G., Lorca, X.: Choco: an open source Java constraint programming library. In: Proceeding of the Workshop on Open-Source Software for Integer and Contraint Programming (OSSICP 2008), pp. 1–10 (2008)

15. Krichen, M., Tripakis, S.: Conformance testing for real-time systems. Form. Methods Syst. Des. **34**(3), 238–304 (2009)

16. Krizanic, J., Grguric, A., Mosmondor, M., Lazarevski, P.: Load testing and performance monitoring tools in use with ajax based web applications. In: 33rd International Convention on Information and Communication Technology, Electronics and Microelectronics, Opatija, Croatia, 24–28 May 2010, pp. 428–434. IEEE (2010)

17. Lahami, M., Krichen, M., Bouchakwa, M., Jmaiel, M.: Using knapsack problem model to design a resource aware test architecture for adaptable and distributed systems. In: Nielsen, B., Weise, C. (eds.) ICTSS 2012. LNCS, vol. 7641, pp. 103–118. Springer, Heidelberg (2012). https://doi.org/10.1007/978-3-642-34691-0_9

18. Maâlej, A.J., Krichen, M.: Study on the limitations of WS-BPEL compositions under load conditions. Comput. J. **58**(3), 385–402 (2015). https://doi.org/10.1093/comjnl/bxu140

19. Maâlej, A.J., Lahami, M., Krichen, M., Jmaïel, M.: Distributed and resource-aware load testing of WS-BPEL compositions. In: Proceedings of the 20th International Conference on Enterprise Information Systems, ICEIS 2018, Funchal, Madeira, Portugal, 21–24 March 2018, vol. 2, pp. 29–38 (2018). https://doi.org/10.5220/0006693400290038

20. Merdes, M., Malaka, R., Suliman, D., Paech, B., Brenner, D., Atkinson, C.: Ubiquitous RATs: how resource-aware run-time tests can improve ubiquitous software systems. In: Proceedings of the 6th International Workshop on Software Engineering and Middleware (SEM 2006), pp. 55–62 (2006)
21. Mikucionis, M., Larsen, K.G., Nielsen, B.: T-UPPAAL: online model-based testing of real-time systems. In: Proceedings of ASE 2004, Linz, Austria, 20–25 September 2004, pp. 396–397. IEEE Computer Society (2004)
22. Murphy, C., Kaiser, G., Vo, I., Chu, M.: Quality assurance of software applications using the in vivo testing approach. In: Proceedings of the 2nd International Conference on Software Testing Verification and Validation (ICST 2009), pp. 111–120 (2009)
23. Myers, G.: The Art of Software Testing. Wiley, Hoboken (1979)
24. Nielsen, B., Skou, A.: Automated test generation from timed automata. In: Margaria, T., Yi, W. (eds.) TACAS 2001. LNCS, vol. 2031, pp. 343–357. Springer, Heidelberg (2001). https://doi.org/10.1007/3-540-45319-9_24
25. Sifakis, J., Yovine, S.: Compositional specification of timed systems. In: Puech, C., Reischuk, R. (eds.) STACS 1996. LNCS, vol. 1046, pp. 345–359. Springer, Heidelberg (1996). https://doi.org/10.1007/3-540-60922-9_29
26. Springintveld, J., Vaandrager, F., D'Argenio, P.: Testing timed automata. Theor. Comput. Sci. **254**, 225–257 (2001)
27. Tretmans, J.: Testing concurrent systems: a formal approach. In: Baeten, J.C.M., Mauw, S. (eds.) CONCUR 1999. LNCS, vol. 1664, pp. 46–65. Springer, Heidelberg (1999). https://doi.org/10.1007/3-540-48320-9_6
28. Tripakis, S.: Fault diagnosis for timed automata. In: Damm, W., Olderog, E.-R. (eds.) FTRTFT 2002. LNCS, vol. 2469, pp. 205–221. Springer, Heidelberg (2002). https://doi.org/10.1007/3-540-45739-9_14
29. Yang, C.D., Pollock, L.L.: Towards a structural load testing tool. SIGSOFT Softw. Eng. Notes **21**(3), 201–208 (1996). https://doi.org/10.1145/226295.226318
30. Zhang, J., Cheung, S.C.: Automated test case generation for the stress testing of multimedia systems. Softw. Pract. Exper. **32**(15), 1411–1435 (2002)

Collectively Constructing the Business Ecosystem: Towards Crowd-Based Modeling for Platforms and Infrastructures

Anne Faber[1(✉)], Sven-Volker Rehm[2], Adrian Hernandez-Mendez[1], and Florian Matthes[1]

[1] Technical University of Munich,
Boltzmannstrasse 3, 85748 Garching, Germany
{anne.faber,adrian.hernandez,matthes}@tum.de
[2] WHU - Otto Beisheim School of Management,
Burgplatz 2, 56179 Vallendar, Germany
sven.rehm@whu.edu

Abstract. In this conceptual article, we highlight group modeling and crowd-based modeling as an approach for collectively constructing business ecosystem models. Based on case study examples, we showcase how engaging in the collective activity of crowd-based modeling supports the creation of value propositions in business ecosystems. Such collective activity creates shared, IS-embedded resources on the network level that align the diverse set of ecosystem stakeholders such as firms, public actors, citizens, and other types of organizations. Based on extant research, we describe the roles involved in building ecosystem models that inform and reconfigure shared infrastructures and platforms.

Keywords: Business ecosystem · Collaborative modeling · Group modeling · Crowd-based modeling · Digital platform · Digital infrastructure · Data governance

1 Introduction

Business ecosystems have gained interest from researchers and practitioners as companies as well as public organizations increasingly recognize the relevance of their complex business environment. This environment consists of all value creation activities related to development, production and distribution of services and products and comprises suppliers, manufacturers, customers, and entrepreneurs. Coping with the challenges and opening up the opportunities that arise in these business ecosystems is a reality for most companies nowadays [1]. The growing relevance of business ecosystems substantiates through the perceived *shift of the competitive environment from single companies and their supply chains towards ecosystems competing against each other* [2].

We define *business ecosystems as the holistic environment of an organization covering current and potential future business partners, such as customers, suppliers, competitors, regulatory institutions and innovative start-ups.* As such entities

© Springer Nature Switzerland AG 2019
S. Hammoudi et al. (Eds.): ICEIS 2018, LNBIP 363, pp. 158–172, 2019.
https://doi.org/10.1007/978-3-030-26169-6_8

continuously enter and leave the ecosystem, or change their role within the ecosystem, ecosystems exhibit high dynamics. Peltoniemi and Vuori [1] provide a comprehensive definition of business ecosystems that emphasizes this adaptive characteristic. Moore [3] uses the metaphor of biological ecosystems as a basis for his initial definition of business ecosystems. Metaphorically, as in natural ecosystems, the economic success of an enterprise can therefore depend on the individual 'health' and capability to evolve with their business ecosystem. In the ecosystem, the participating companies as individuals adopt varying levels of influence on the overall health of the ecosystem, taking up roles as keystone or niche player [4].

The types of business ecosystems described in extant literature vary between ecosystems around one focal firm, such as Wal-Mart or Microsoft [4], ecosystems of a specific market exploiting specific digital technologies, such as application programming interfaces (API) [5] or mobile phones and platforms [6] or ecosystems established around a singular technology platform, such as Google and Apple [7].

Thus, because ecosystems potentially influence the economic success of businesses, enterprises increasingly realize the need to *analyze their business ecosystem*. Through continuous monitoring, changes within an enterprises' ecosystem might be identified and addressed through dedicated strategies or adaptations [8]. Enterprises aim to "learn what makes the environment tick" [9] and improve or adapt one's own business activities accordingly.

However, analyzing business ecosystems is principally impossible for one single stakeholder to achieve because of the abundancy and complexity of processes and data that would need to be observed, recorded, documented or otherwise be made visible. This is why in this conceptual paper we acclaim for an approach to use crowdsourcing of ecosystem-related data in order to create ecosystem models that can be exploited to learn about the ecosystem and to predict future developments [10] and that inform and configure shared platforms and infrastructures and as such become valuable for the entire ecosystem [11]. As case studies from our previous research suggest, such ecosystem models can be considered as IS-embedded network resources [12], i.e., network-level, shared resources that support the creation of value propositions for all involved stakeholders as users of the ecosystem model.

However, crowdsourcing approaches to model business ecosystems so far have not been implemented or observed in practice. This is why in this article we discuss the boundary conditions for such an approach and its principle benefits.

2 Related Work

2.1 Business Ecosystem Modeling and Ecosystem Data

Business ecosystems have early been defined as collection of interacting firms [3]. Until today, research on this concept has been extensive [13]. Sako [7] defined three meta-characteristics of business ecosystems—sustainability, self-governance, and evolution —to contribute to a better distinction of the ecosystem concept from clusters or networks. Thereby, he focuses on "value-creating process (…) rather than… industrial sector". Basole et al. [14] characterized business ecosystems as an interconnected, complex, global network of relationships between companies, which can take on different *roles*, such as suppliers, distributors, outsourcing firms, makers of related products or services, technology providers, and a host of other organizations [4]. The boundaries, characteristics and the evolving, dynamic structure [1] of a business ecosystem are not only affected by these different roles, but by the fact that firms continuously enter and leave the ecosystem [15]. Recently, researchers have focused their efforts on the *challenges for ecosystem formation* that derive from various contexts, such as technology, e.g., the Internet of Things (IoT) [15], or policy, e.g., emerging smart cities [16]. This led to emergence of a discourse about identifying appropriate ways to model business ecosystems [17], such as *frameworks* to grasp the scope of ecosystem complexity [16, 18] or *visualizations*, which are developed to aid at understanding the topology of such an ecosystem, as well as emerging structures and patterns [18, 19].

Ensuing previous research, *our conceptualization of business ecosystem models* takes into account both, the static network of entities, i.e., firms, technologies, and the dynamic network characteristics, i.e., the relationships between entities and activities, all changing over time. Entities include companies of every size as well as corporations, public sector organizations, universities and research facilities, and other parties that influence the ecosystem [1], all linked via different kinds of relationships. All these elements need to be incorporated into the business ecosystem model. Which *entities* and *relationship types* need to be modeled depends decidedly on the requirements put forward by the (business) stakeholders using the business ecosystem model for their ecosystem-related decisions. Their needs and demands that define which (visual) views are relevant, and which insights are vital for generating and adapting the model.

Past research has shown that *visualizations of business ecosystems* on basis of such models indeed support decision-makers in their ecosystem-related tasks and decisions [5, 8, 20]. In order to spot anomalies, identify keystone and niche players of the ecosystem, or recognize change patterns and trends, visualizing data can help to derive value from ecosystem data [21].

'*Ecosystem data*' as the basis for modeling is diverse and ranges from technology-related information about applied standards and platforms to market information and legal regulations. Basole et al. [14] characterized it to be 'large and heterogeneous'. Relevant for the business aspect of an enterprise's business ecosystem as we have observed in our case studies, is information about business partners, competitors, partnerships and offered solutions, cooperative initiatives, as well as start-ups and their strategies [22]. This information can be obtained from a wide range of sources, such as publicly accessible databases, enterprise or institutional presences and publications, or blogs and news articles. Successfully collecting ecosystem data sets distinct limits concerning the value and usefulness of visualizations in the ecosystem analysis or business development [12]. However, no solution has been determined so far that might resolve the issue of *how comprehensive amounts of ecosystem data can be obtained and validated* for their usefulness and efficacy towards ecosystem-related tasks and decisions [18, 23].

In addition, to include a broad perspective and involve diverse aspects of the ecosystem, not only various data sources but also various types of *stakeholder groups* need to be taken into account. These groups provide for both, diverse ways to access ecosystem data, and own interests to use the ecosystem model. Depending on the ecosystem in focus, these groups can range from company representatives in case of a company-internal business ecosystem modeling approach, to boards, associations' interest group, or online communities. Including these stakeholder groups into joint model creation and model evaluation is generally discussed under the header of *collaborative modeling*. As related literature has vividly discussed, collaborative modeling processes enhance the quality and scope of achievable results through iterative interactions and collaborative knowledge exchanges [24].

2.2 Business Ecosystem Visualization in Visual Analytic Systems (VAS)

Park et al. [25] presented a Visual Analytic System (VAS) to nurture the perception of business ecosystems. It addresses three salient design requirements related to distinct complications in the context of supply chain ecosystems. After extensive research on modeling and visualizing ecosystems, and analyzing different types of business ecosystems [1, 5, 8, 15, 16, 18] the VAS empowers its users to interactively explore the supply network by offering multiple views within an integrated interface as well as data-driven analytic features. The authors suggest and test five visualization types (*layouts*) to visualize the dynamic networked structures of their problem context.

These layouts include Force-directed Layout (FDL), Tree Map Layout (TML), Matrix Layout (MXL), Radial Network/ Chord Diagram (RCD), and Modified Ego-Network Layout (MEL). Interactive features, such as clicking, dragging, hovering, and filtering, are essential parts of the visualizations. These layouts are used by us as the baseline for the design of our own VAS in our problem context. Nonetheless, further designs exist, such as bi-centric diagrams that visualize the relative positioning of two focal firms [8, 15] or cumulative network visualization [5].

Current research on ecosystems at large uses data-driven approaches, i.e., sets of data are collected from commercial databases on business and economic data, or drawn from social or business media [5, 15]. Implications of this approach are, first, the VAS users need to understand the relevance and quality of sources that can provide data for the ecosystem model, and second, the guiding questions and rules for the visualizations are clear. When both the model and the visualizations can be adapted to host diverse business perspectives and intentions, it is possible that different VAS users can create their own VAS instances in order to facilitate setting the focus on distinct data sources and structures.

3 Agile Modeling Framework for Business Ecosystem Modeling

3.1 Business Ecosystem Explorer (BEEx): Visual Analytic System (VAS) Implementation

In order to engage with business ecosystem modeling, we propose an *agile modeling framework*, which *technically* resides upon the 'Hybrid Wiki' approach suggested by Reschenhofer et al. [26], and which from a *use perspective* allows to follow an agile modeling process (see Sect. 5). This framework addresses the dynamic structure of business ecosystems as it supports the *evolution of the model as well as its instances at runtime* by stakeholders and ecosystem experts, i.e., users without programming knowledge or skills. We have implemented the framework as *Business Ecosystem Explorer (BEEx)* on basis of an existing integrated, adaptive collaborative Hybrid Wiki system. The latter system not only serves as a Knowledge Management System application development platform, including features necessary for collaboration, data management, and decision support, but which also implements other features such as tracing back changes to the responsible user, including the time and date the change was made. In our case studies, we have used its underlying Hybrid Wiki metamodel to create business ecosystem models.

The *Hybrid Wiki metamodel* comprises the following model building blocks: Workspace, Entity, EntityType, Attribute, and AttributeDefinition. These concepts structure the model inside a *Workspace* and capture its current snapshot in a data-driven process (i.e., as a bottom-up process). An *Entity* consists of *Attributes*, which have a name, can be of different data types (i.e., strings, numbers, references on other *Entities*), and are stored as key-value pairs. *Attributes* can be instantiated at runtime, and this helps to seize structured information about an *Entity*. The *EntityType* facilitates grouping related *Entities*, such as organizations or persons. It consists of several *AttributeDefinitions*, which can define validators for the *Attributes* of the corresponding *Entities*, like multiplicity or link value validators, which in turn leads to increased cohesion among the *Attribute* values.

3.2 Business Ecosystem Explorer Model

Our agile framework relies on two models that each provide features for creation and adaption, first, the *ecosystem data model*, and second, the ecosystem view model. Both models are encoded using the Hybrid Wiki metamodel.

The *ecosystem data model* contains the EntityTypes of relevance for the business ecosystem in focus. The *ecosystem view model* is encoded as one EntityType called *visualizations*. Each visualization has two elements: the first element is the *link* between the data model and the visualizations. The second element is the *specification* of the visualizations using a declarative language. Five main building blocks enable static and dynamic visualization features; these are (a) *data*, including data but also all data transformations; (b) *marks*, covering the basic description of the visualized symbols, e.g., shape and size of a node; (c) *scales*, containing visual variables, such as the color coding; (d) *signals*, including the different interaction options, e.g., dragging and dropping of entities; and in some instances (e) *legends*.

This approach allows making changes to the models at runtime, thus updating the visualizations instantly when the data model is changed by, e.g., adding new categories or changing or deleting categories. Figure 1 gives an example of categories of organizations and their types, which both can be adapted at runtime.

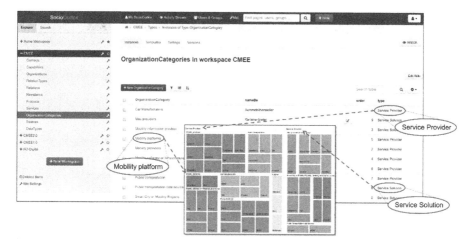

Fig. 1. List of categories and types in BEEx and conversion to Tree Map Layout (TML) [22].

3.3 Business Ecosystem Explorer Views

Currently, the framework comprises six different views: a landing page, a list of all entities, a relation view, a detail view with entity information, a visualization overview, and several visualizations. All views include a menu bar at the top of the page, which provide links to the other views, as illustrated in Fig. 2.

4 Case Studies Informing Our Concept of Crowdsourcing

The design-oriented research results presented here are based on our insights on own software engineering design work, a field test of the developed system and two case studies we conducted in close collaboration with industry partners.

The research was initiated within a smart city initiative pursued by a European city with a population of more than 2.5 m in its urban area and more than 5.5 m in its metropolitan region. The business ecosystem of focus is mobility ecosystem is antic-ipated to embrace more than 3.000 firms in the automotive, traffic and logistics sectors residing in the urban area and more than 18.000 firms in these sectors in the metropolitan region.

Within this initiative, the agile modeling framework was used to model the mobility business ecosystem relevant for the initiative. As a first evaluation, we conducted two rounds of interviews. Within the first round, we conducted nine interviews in semi-structured form with nine different companies within two months presenting a pre-defined business ecosystem model using a force-directed layout. All interviewees stated that the business ecosystem model supported them in understanding the relations within the presented business ecosystem and that their knowledge of this ecosystem was increased. We used the interview results to update the existing prototype.

In the second interview round, we conducted three in-depth interviews with three additional companies. To obtain a wider range of opinions, we selected three

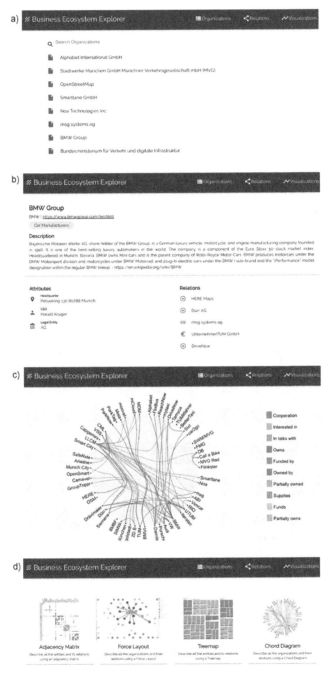

Fig. 2. Business Ecosystem Explorer views: (a) Searchable list view of all entities, (b) Detail view of one entity providing additional information which are stored as Attributes, (c) Chord Diagram, (d) Overview of additional existing visualizations besides the Chord Diagram: Adjacency Matrix, Force Layout, and Treemap [22].

companies from different fields of activity. Namely, an automotive OEM, a publicly funded non-research institution and a software company whose main business area addresses the connected mobility ecosystem. The prototype as visualized in Fig. 2 was used in this interview round. All companies agreed that the prototype fosters the understanding of the presented ecosystem and two emphasized that it would be interesting to use such a tool within their enterprise to collaboratively manage the business ecosystem evolution.

This initial evaluation was followed by two case studies conducted with two industry partners targeting different business ecosystems. One an automotive company, the other a publishing company, both headquartered in Europe with a high interest in modeling and visualizing business ecosystems of their specific focus but no modeling activities in place before the studies. With both organizations, several workshops were conducted in the period from December 2017 to June 2018. All involved stakeholders from both companies had access to the provided BEEx framework (see Sect. 3) and had used it to instantiate and model their business ecosystem of focus. After performing the agile collaborative modeling process as presented in Sect. 5, for each study, the existing prototype was adapted comprising two tailored visualizations of the business ecosystem.

5   Agile Collaborative Modeling of Business Ecosystems

5.1   Agile Modeling Process

Based on insights and experience from our case studies, we propose the generic, *agile modeling process* depicted in Fig. 3 to model business ecosystems in a collaborative process. The process consists of five steps overall. Three teams are involved in the process, the *Ecosystem Editorial Team*, the *Modeler Team*, and a team of *Management Stakeholders*.

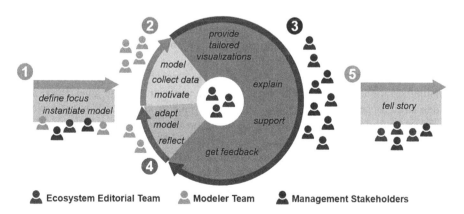

Fig. 3. Agile modeling process to collaboratively instantiate, manage and adapt the business ecosystem model (adapted from [22]).

In a first phase (process step no. 1 in Fig. 3), the focus of the business ecosystem is defined, e.g., an ecosystem established around a technology platform, an ecosystem of a specific market exploiting specific digital technologies [7] or ecosystems around one focal firm, and the model instantiated, for which both the data model and the view model are set up. When the data model is instantiated, the relevant entities of the ecosystem are defined, along with corresponding attributes. Additionally, the preliminary relation types between the entities need to be identified and set. When the view model is set up, the type of visualization including the specifications for this visualization are established, guided by the Ecosystem Editorial and Modeler Team. Further, all stakeholders with various roles should be included into the requirements elicitation of the models to ensure tailored visualizations in the upcoming phases of the process.

The next phase of the process is threefold and repeated iteratively. It consists of gathering the data about the ecosystem according to the data model (process step 2), the provision of tailored visualization according to the view model (process step 3) and the adaption steps in which both models are modified using feedback collected from involved stakeholders (process step 4). This step finishes as soon as the stakeholders' requirements and needs are satisfied.

In the final process step, the created visualizations are used to extract knowledge about the ecosystem, which contributes to a better understanding of the ecosystem in focus.

5.2 Agility Through Collaborative and Group Modeling

Agility particularly becomes evident in short-term iterative cycles of process steps 2 to 4, by *collaboratively* prototyping and consolidating tailored visualizations. Insights achieved about the ecosystem inform conceptualization of adapted business strategies, thus creating new questions towards the ecosystem and motivating formulation of modified decisions or amended tasks, which in turn create new impetus to change the model, collect data, and improve or alter visualizations.

The concept of *collaborative modeling* arose in the 70's and since gained increased popularity together with the increased need for collaboration among experts [27, 28]. However, collaborative processes for business ecosystem modeling and instantiation of such models have not been discussed in existing literature, but in various other fields, such as group decision support system modeling [29], business process modeling [24], and enterprise architecture modeling [30].

According to Richardson and Andersen [31], essential roles for collaborative modeling are the facilitator, the process coach, the recorder, and the gatekeeper. They are described as follows: (a) *facilitator*, monitoring the group process and stimulating the model building effort; (b) *modeler*, focusing on the model out-come; (c) *process coach*, observing the process and the dynamics of the participants; (d) *recorder*, documenting the modeling process; and (e) *gatekeeper*, responsible for the process and major decision maker. These roles may be associated to different persons, but one person might also incorporate several roles at once [27].

In the following sections, we detail the activities of each of the three teams involved in our agile modeling process with regard to the roles in collaborative modeling as described in extant literature.

5.3   Ecosystem Editorial Team

The Ecosystem Editorial Team is present and active in all process steps and contributes highly to the outcome of the modeling initiative and the overall perceived success. This group integrates several roles for collaborative modeling in addition to roles specific for the software development. We map the generic roles to business ecosystem specific activities of the Ecosystem Editorial Team in Table 1.

Table 1. Roles of the Ecosystem Editorial Team in a collaborative business ecosystem (BE) modeling process.

Role name	Description	Activities within BE modeling
Process coach	"A person who focuses not at all on content but rather on the dynamics of individuals and subgroups within the group." [31]	Guides the entire process of modeling and visualizing the ecosystem in focus. Is aware of the ecosystem-specific challenges in each process step and can intervene
(View) design expert	Responsible for capturing the requirements and challenges for creating visualizations. The designer suggests multiple visual alternatives to address the data visualization needs and demands, prioritizes them, and evaluates which alternative best addresses the identified requirements. Finally, she selects specific visualizations for the implementation. The (View) Design Expert therefore creates visualization mock-ups that capture the business data, user interface (styles and template), and configurable options and interactive features	Selects recent business ecosystem specific visualizations from research and practice to use for visualization mock ups fitting to the created model. Expert of the declarative visual language in use, which she can apply to create interactive and tailored business ecosystem visualizations
Recorder	"Strives to write down or sketch the important parts of the group proceedings. Together with the notes of the modeler/reflector and the transparencies or notes of the facilitator, the text and drawings made by the recorder should allow a reconstruction of the thinking of the group. This person must be experienced enough as a modeler to know what to record and what to ignore." [31]	Documenting the business ecosystem focus, the decisions made by the entire team regarding chosen entities to model, information sources used and visualizations selected. Also documenting the knowledge extracted within each story telling process step

5.4   Modeler Team

The members of the Modeler Team contribute their knowledge about the ecosystem in focus and are vital for creating and continuous updating the model. The facilitator, acting as a bridge between the management stakeholders, the Ecosystem Editorial Team and the modelers. Group members acting as modelers identify suitable data sources to use, both company internal and external, relevant entities, attributes and relations for the data model. With the usage of a declarative visual language, the modelers are also enabled to adapt the view model.

We mapped these two generic roles to business ecosystem specific activities of the Modeler Team in Table 2.

Table 2. Roles of the Modeler Team in a collaborative business ecosystem (BE) modeling process.

Role name	Description	Activities within BE modeling
Facilitator	"Functions as group facilitator and knowledge elicitor. This person pays constant attention to group process, the roles of individuals in the group, and the business of drawing out knowledge and insights from the group. This role is the most visible of the five roles, constantly working with the group to further the model building effort." [31]	Participates in all five process steps. Close exchange with the management stakeholders. Contributes to the decision of the business ecosystem focus and acts as link between the modeler team, the Ecosystem Editorial Team and the management stakeholder
Modeler	"Focuses not at all on group process but rather on the model that is being explicitly (and sometimes implicitly) formulated by the facilitator and the group. The modeler/reflector serves both the facilitator and the group. This person thinks and sketches on his or her own, reflects information back to the group, restructures formulations, exposes unstated assumptions that need to be explicit, and, in general, serves to crystallize important aspects of structure and behavior." [31]	Identifies leader and relevant entities of the ecosystem and creates the ecosystem data model. Can also be involved in the view model creation process using the declarative visual language

5.5   Management Stakeholders

The Management Stakeholders are those using the business ecosystem model created in the process for their business decisions. Thus, they receive the tailored visualizations and provide feedback on how to adapt these for future use. This group is mainly responsible for the business ecosystem focus set in the beginning. They provide resources for the business ecosystem modeling process.

We mapped the generic roles to business ecosystem specific activities of the Management Stakeholders in Table 3.

Table 3. Roles of Management Stakeholders in a collaborative business ecosystem (BE) modeling process.

Role name	Description	Activities within BE modeling
Gatekeeper	"A person within, or related to, the client group who carries internal responsibility for the project, usually initiates it, helps frame the problem, identifies the appropriate participants, works with the modeling support team to structure the sessions, and participates as a member of the group. The gatekeeper is an advocate in two directions: within the client organization he or she speaks for the modeling process, and with the modeling support team he or she speaks for the client group and the problem. The locus of the gatekeeper in the client organization will significantly influence the process and the impact of the results." [31]	Decision maker responsible for the business ecosystem focus and the outcome of the modeling process. Communicates the tailored visualizations to the higher management and stakeholder. Uses the story told and the knowledge gained to advertise the initiative
Stakeholders	Top management and department heads with significant responsibility, business decision maker	Receives the provided interactive visualizations. Contributes to the process by providing feedback how both models should be adapted for specific management decisions in context of the business ecosystem in focus

6   The Idea of Crow-Based Modeling of Business Ecosystems

As from our case study experience, the insights that can be gained from an agile modeling process – apart from the quality of visualizations – significantly depend on the availability of ecosystem data and stakeholder feedback. Hence, the data available during step 2 (data gathering) of our generic agile modeling process (see Fig. 3) delimits the reliability and efficacy of visualizations. Similarly, the feedback obtainable during step 4 (feedback collection) defines which novel insights or stimuli potentially originate, motivating to refine the model focus and broaden the support to ecosystem-related tasks and decisions.

In our case studies, we have also observed that a significant number of today's ecosystem-related tasks and decisions—that affect multiple levels or stages of value creation across larger areas—cannot be accomplished on basis of existing corporate information repositories or limited data sources. *Crowd-based modeling* provides an approach to integrate diverse views and create more realistic models including more relevant factors.

This is why we claim for extending the base of involved modelers to a crowd-based approach. Our case studies have pointed us towards thinking about the 'crowd' as to overcome the difficulty of collecting substantially meaningful and comprehensive amounts of data. What the 'crowd' is depends on the usage of visualizations in the respective ecosystem use case. In corporate settings, these uses might lie in defining corporate strategies in face of competitor movements. In smart city contexts, as we have witnessed in one of our case studies, the 'crowd' was established through public authorities as well as corporate firms and citizens (see also the discussion on crowd energy in [32]). Looking at the heterogeneity of business ecosystems and related strategic and entrepreneurial challenges, it seems plausible to engage in a more intensive involvement of the diverse set of stakeholders to business ecosystem modeling. Depending on the context, citizens, corporate employees, protagonists of start-up communities, local authorities, but also IoT providers, social network service providers, and others, could all benefit from contributing to building open, shared ecosystem models and visualizations.

In this respect, the question of whether actors are motivated to contribute freely, i.e., without direct remuneration, to building shared, and eventually publically available resources, must be further investigated. Earlier research has extensively studied and theoretically framed the boundary conditions and quality of outcomes in cooperating on shared resources [33–35]. We believe that a viable approach might lie in the provision of visualization services to core ecosystem stakeholders that deliver a helpful tool for ecosystem-related tasks in addition to freely available visualizations, in order to achieve reciprocity in contributing and profiting from ecosystem models [36]. Such visualization services could take over the task to moderate between the roles we have identified from previous literature and instantiated in our agile modeling process. Contributing stakeholders might assume several different roles during the interaction with a visualization service—a practice we have observed and exercised in our case studies.

A future advancement will lie in the *automated* inclusion of data into modeling and visualizing. The—ethically responsible—evaluation of social network data or of IoT data for instance might hold unseen value propositions for understanding such contexts as traffic organization in metropolitan areas to adapt mobility services, or as start-up communities to stimulate innovation by explicating relationship patterns that arise from the plethora of interactions at the individual entrepreneurs' level.

Overall, from a modeling perspective, tackling business ecosystem related challenges will see a shift from enterprise-level IS, or 'enterprise systems' to network-level IS-embedded resources. Such network-level resources will require to obtain buy-in from diverse stakeholder groups of an ecosystem as a smart city or a local start-up community or others. Then the 'critical mass' to obtain reliable and effective ecosystem data might be met, being more comprehensive than currently existing corporate or consulting agencies' information repositories.

Lastly, in all use cases for ecosystem models and visualizations, ecosystem data governance becomes a vital challenge—even more so than in the current debate on user data in social networks and the like. We believe that cooperative societies founded by ecosystem members or local citizens might be a way to moderate in these issues as the provision of data for modeling will encompass purposeful individual action and willful sharing of knowledge for the common good.

References

1. Peltoniemi, M., Vuori, E.: Business ecosystem as the new approach to complex adaptive business environments. In: Proceedings of eBusiness Research Forum, pp. 267–281 (2004)
2. Bosch, J.: Speed, data and ecosystems: the future of software engineering. IEEE Softw. **33** (1), 82–88 (2016)
3. Moore, J.: The Death of Competition: Leadership and Strategy in the Age of Business Ecosystems. HarperBusiness, New York (1997)
4. Iansiti, M., Levien, R.: Strategy as ecology. Harv. Bus. Rev. **82**(3), 68–81 (2004)
5. Evans, P.C., Basole, R.C.: Revealing the API ecosystem and enterprise strategy via visual analytics. Commun. ACM **59**(2), 26–28 (2016)
6. Sørensen, C., De Reuver, M., Basole, R.C.: Mobile platforms and ecosystems. J. Inf. Technol. **30**(3), 195–197 (2015)
7. Sako, M.: Business ecosystems: how do they matter for innovation? Commun. ACM **61**(4), 20–22 (2018)
8. Basole, R.C., Huhtamäki, J., Still, K., Russell, M.G.: Visual decision support for business ecosystem analysis. Expert Syst. Appl. **65**, 271–282 (2016)
9. Porter, M.: How competitive forces shape strategy. Harv. Bus. Rev. 102–117 (1979)
10. Morecroft, J.D.W., Sterman, J.D. (eds.): Modeling for Learning Organizations. Productivity Press, Portland (1994)
11. Constantinides, P., Henfridsson, O., Parker, G.G.: Introduction – platforms and infrastructures in the digital age. Inf. Syst. Res. (2018)
12. Rehm, S.-V., Faber, A., Goel, L.: Visualizing platform hubs of smart city mobility business ecosystems. In: 38th International Conference on Information Systems, pp. 1–10 (2017)
13. Guittard, C., Schenk, E., Burger-Helmchen, T.: Crowdsourcing and the evolution of a business ecosystem. In: Garrigos-Simon, F.J., Gil-Pechuán, I., Estelles-Miguel, S. (eds.) Advances in Crowdsourcing, pp. 49–62. Springer, Cham (2015). https://doi.org/10.1007/978-3-319-18341-1_4
14. Basole, R.C., Russell, M.G., Huhtamäki, J., Still, K., Park, H.: Understanding business ecosystem dynamics: a data-driven approach. ACM Trans. Manag. Inf. Syst. **6**(2), 1–32 (2015)
15. Park, H., Basole, R.C.: Bicentric diagrams: design and applications of a graph-based relational set visualization technique. Decis. Support Syst. **84**(April), 64–77 (2016)
16. Visnjic, I., Neely, A., Cennamo, C., Visnjic, N.: Governing the city. Calif. Manag. Rev. **59** (1), 109–140 (2016)
17. Uchihira, N., Ishimatsu, H., Inoue, K.: IoT service business ecosystem design in a global, competitive, and collaborative environment. In: Portland International Conference on Management of Engineering and Technology (PICMET), pp. 1195–1201 (2016)
18. Iyer, B.R., Basole, R.C.: Visualization to understand ecosystems. Commun. ACM **59**(11), 27–30 (2016)

19. Leonardi, P.M.: When flexible routines meet flexible technologies: affordance, constraint, and the imbrication of human and material agencies. MIS Q. **35**(1), 147–167 (2011)
20. Huhtamaki, J., Rubens, N.: Exploring innovation ecosystems as networks: four European cases. In: Proceedings of the Annual Hawaii International Conference on System Sciences, pp. 4505–4514 (2016)
21. Vartak, M., Huang, S., Siddiqui, T., Madden, S., Parameswaran, A.: Towards visualization recommendation systems. ACM SIGMOD Rec. **45**(4), 34–39 (2017)
22. Faber, A., Hernandez-Mendez, A., Rehm, S.-V., Matthes, M.: An agile framework for modeling smart city business ecosystems. In: Proceedings of the 20th International Conference on Enterprise Information Systems, pp. 39–50 (2018)
23. Hao, J., Zhu, J., Zhong, R.: The rise of big data on urban studies and planning practices in China: review and open research issues. J. Urban Manag. **4**(2), 92–124 (2015)
24. Dollmann, T., Houy, C., Fettke, P., Loos, P.: Collaborative business process modeling with CoMoMod: a toolkit for model integration in distributed cooperation environments. In Proceedings of the 20th IEEE International Workshops on Enabling Technologies: Infrastructure for Collaborative Enterprises, pp. 217–222 (2011)
25. Park, H., Bellamy, M.A., Basole, R.C.: Visual analytics for supply network management: system design and evaluation. Decis. Support Syst. **91**, 89–102 (2016)
26. Reschenhofer, T., Bhat, M., Hernandez-Mendez, A., Matthes, F.: Lessons learned in aligning data and model evolution in collaborative information systems. In: Proceedings of the 38th International Conference on Software Engineering Companion, pp. 132–141 (2016)
27. Renger, M., Kolfschoten, Gwendolyn L., de Vreede, G.-J.: Challenges in collaborative modeling: a literature review. In: Dietz, J.L.G., Albani, A., Barjis, J. (eds.) CIAO!/EOMAS - 2008. LNBIP, vol. 10, pp. 61–77. Springer, Heidelberg (2008). https://doi.org/10.1007/978-3-540-68644-6_5
28. Vennix, J.A.M., Andersen, D.F., Richardson, G.P., Rohrbaugh, J.: Model building for group decision support: issues and alternatives in knowledge elicitation. In: Morecroft, J.D.W., Sterman, J.D. (eds.) Modeling for Learning Organizations. Productivity Press, Portland, pp. 29–49 (1994)
29. Liu, F., Zhang, C.: Role-based collaborative model of group decision support system. In: 7th International Conference on Fuzzy Systems and Knowledge Discovery, pp. 1039–1043 (2010)
30. Roth, S., Hauder, M., Matthes, F.: Collaborative evolution of enterprise architecture models. In: CEUR Workshop Proceedings, vol. 1079, pp. 1–12 (2013)
31. Richardson, G.P., Andersen, D.F.: Teamwork in group model building. Syst. Dyn. Rev. **11** (2), 113–137 (1995)
32. Gstrein, M., Hertig, Y., Teufel, B., Teufel, S.: Crowd energy – das kooperationskonzept für smart cities. In: Meier, A., Portmann, E. (eds.) Smart City. EH, pp. 277–303. Springer, Wiesbaden (2016). https://doi.org/10.1007/978-3-658-15617-6_14
33. Ostrom, E.: Governing the Commons: The Evolution of Institutions for Collective Action. Cambridge University Press, Cambridge (1990)
34. Ostrom, E.: Collective action and the evolution of social norms. J. Econ. Perspect. **14**(3), 137–158 (2000)
35. Olson, M.: The Logic of Collective Action: Public Goods and the Theory of Groups. Harvard University Press, Cambridge (1965)
36. Fehr, E., Gächter, S.: Fairness and retaliation: the economics of reciprocity. J. Econ. Perspect. **14**(3), 159–181 (2000)

Survey of Vehicular Network Simulators: A Temporal Approach

Mauricio J. Silva[1]([⊠])(ID), Genilson I. Silva[2], Celio M. S. Ferreira[1], Fernando A. Teixeira[3], and Ricardo A. Oliveira[1](ID)

[1] Universidade Federal de Ouro Preto, Ouro Preto, MG, Brazil
`badriciobq@gmail.com`, `celio@linuxplace.com.br`, `rrabelo@gmail.com`
[2] Instituto Federal Sudeste Minas Gerais, Barbacena, MG, Brazil
`genilsonisrael@gmail.com`
[3] Universidade Federal de Sao Joao Del Rei, Sao Joao Del Rei, MG, Brazil
`teixeira@ufsj.edu.br`

Abstract. Evaluating protocols and applications for Intelligent Transportation Systems is the first step before deploying them in the real world. Simulations provide scalable evaluations with low costs. However, to produce reliable results, the simulators should implement models that represent as closely as possible real situations. In this survey, we provide a study of the main simulators focused on Intelligent Transport Systems assessment. Additionally, we examine the temporal evolution of these simulators giving information that leads to an overview understanding of how long the scientific community takes to absorb a new simulator proposal. The conclusions presented in this survey provide valuable insights that help researchers make better choices when selecting the appropriate simulator to evaluate new proposals.

Keywords: Vehicular Network Simulators · Traffic Simulators · Mobility models

1 Introduction

The performance evaluation of algorithms and protocols for vehicular networks has been a constant topic of research [57]. Given the unique characteristics of vehicular networks, recent works have pointed towards the emergence of new traffic models and the impact analysis of these models on the behavior of proposed protocols and algorithms [6,65]. Recent work in this area has pointed towards the emergence of new models of traffic and the analysis of impact of these models in the behavior of protocols and algorithms of vehicular networks. Research in this area should be continuous and it must also support the development of

This study was financed in part by the Coordenação de Aperfeiçoamento de Pessoal de Nvel Superior - Brasil (CAPES) - Finance Code 001, Brazilian research agency (CNPq), the Research Foundation of the State of Minas Gerais (FAPEMIG) and the Federal University of Ouro Preto (UFOP).

© Springer Nature Switzerland AG 2019
S. Hammoudi et al. (Eds.): ICEIS 2018, LNBIP 363, pp. 173–192, 2019.
https://doi.org/10.1007/978-3-030-26169-6_9

testbeds so that applications can be evaluated. These models must be fed by data collected in current networks so that it is possible to make a reasonably accurate estimate of performance of new applications. Such an assessment is a challenge, and can usually be done using three different methods, which are mathematical analysis, Field Operational Tests (FOTs) and simulations [6,22,40,65]. Each of these methods has its advantages and disadvantages, and the method to be used should be chosen cautiously as it directly influences the results.

Mathematical Analysis allows an analytical study of the problem, and can provide valuable information, allowing a better understanding of the designed system. Statistical distributions are used to generate the models that are necessary for the simulation. However, this method tends to simplify certain simulation parameters such as the mobility models. Such simplifications can lead to inaccurate results. Field Operational Tests (FOTs) allow a better evaluation of applications and protocols for vehicular networks. In this type of analysis, the devices are exposed to real environments, which can lead to unpredicted situations. The disadvantages related to this type of test usually involve high costs in terms of time and money as well as the difficulty to perform large-scale tests. Simulations make it possible to assess the new proposals on a large scale and at low cost. However, similarly to what happens in the mathematical analysis, complex models need to be simplified so that they can be simulated. Again, this simplification must be done cautiously, as they may make the results inaccurate.

Researchers prefer to evaluate their proposals through the simulation method, which demands simulators that produce results increasingly closer to reality [23]. At first, Researchers used to believe that Vehicular Networks were a specific application of Mobile Networks, and for that reason, random models have been applied to simulate the vehicles' mobility. It was not long ago that they realized that vehicular networks had their own characteristics, so specific mobility models should be proposed to represent them. The vehicular mobility models evolved from random models, where the mobility of all nodes was generated in a single file that was used as input to a Network Simulator (called Offline), to the behavior-based models, where Network and Traffic Simulators interact to represent the behavior of the driver (called Online).

The state of the art on vehicle network simulations is the combination of network simulators (developed by computer scientists) with road traffic simulators (developed by traffic engineers). Thus, vehicular mobility is handled by experts in traffic, and communication is handled by experts in computing. Although the data flow between both simulators, allowing decisions to be made during the simulation, these decisions are still modeled mathematically. Humans are complex beings, whose decisions can be influenced by several factors (such as humor, sex, maturity, etc.). Applying a statistical model to describe this behavior can lead to inaccurate and unwanted results.

Unfortunately, the more realistic a simulator is, the harder it is to use it. Because of this, one of the biggest difficulties in simulating a Vehicular Network is to ensure that the mobility patterns of a real environment are reproduced. According to [51] and [37], existing simulators that use models that are able to generate scenarios closer to the real ones, are often complex to use. As a result, many of the new proposed protocols and algorithms are evaluated using customized simulators, which introduce bias and compromise the reproducibility of these algorithms by other members of the scientific community [39].

In this paper, we survey the main simulators for Vehicular Networks describing the models implemented in each one, the main features, and the applicability. Then, we provide an overview of the Vehicular Network Simulators evolution allowing the understanding of how the Vehicular Network Simulators evolved from the beginning until now. The reader will comprise how long the scientific community need to absorb a new approach for a Vehicular Network Simulator and if we have a pragmatic solution for Vehicular Network Simulators. Additionally, we will provide valuable insights to help researchers make better choices when selecting the appropriate simulator to evaluate their proposals. We extend Silva *et al.* [49] providing a complete vehicular simulators assessment and pointing out the new directions of the vehicular simulator research presenting the new paradigms that have gained the attention of the scientific community.

The rest of this article is organized as follows: Sect. 2 presents the necessary requirements to obtain better results in Specific-Domain Simulators. In Sect. 4 we survey the most used simulators to assess algorithms and protocols for Vehicular Networks, describing their features and drawbacks. Sect. 5 discusses the temporal evolution and the future challenges related to Vehicular Simulations. Finally, we conclude the paper in Sect. 6.

2   Background of Vehicular Network Simulators

Over the years the research community, industry and government have focused more and more attention to the Vehicular Networks. They have interested in propose not only applications focused on traffic safety but also applications to improve the quality of services provided to the drivers. However, such applications should be tested, evaluated and validated in a controlled environment before being deployed in the real world.

Despite mathematical analyses and FOTS provide valuable insights about the vehicular behavior in a general way, simulation is, by far, the preferred method by the research community to evaluate new proposals of protocols and algorithms for vehicular networks. Simulations allow us to take scalable evaluations, with low cost and an acceptable degree of realism. Scalability and low cost are well-defined requirements in a simulation. However, vehicular networks have their mobility requirements, and for a simulation to have an acceptable degree of realism, it is necessary that the mobility models comply with such requirements. To deal with this, Zemouri *et al.* [65] classified the Network Simulators in three classes, according to the way that the simulator is built, called: **Offline**, **Embedded** and **Online**. We will use the same classification because we believe that in addition to being simple, it encompasses all existing proposals unambiguously. Following we will provide details about each simulator category.

2.1 Categories of Vehicular Simulators

In the **Offline** approach (Fig. 1), trace files are extracted from onboard devices in the vehicles, usually navigation systems like GPS, to get the real movement of vehicles. There are lots of trace data sets publicly available to be used [59], but, typically, these data sets are collected from specific vehicles, as examples, fleets of taxis or buses or even a restrict group of vehicles and does not represent traffic behavior as a whole. Additionally, using these data sets only ensures that the newly evaluated applications work well on the same vehicle class as the dataset. Another way to get trace files is using a traffic simulator. Thus, it is possible to generate the total traffic of a city.

This approach allows the nodes in the network simulator to move in accordance with the data read from the trace files. It is called offline because the trace file is not modified after it has been generated. This implies that there is no interaction between the mobility and network simulators. Some simulators that are in this category are BonnMotion [7], MOVE [27] and VanetMobiSim [24].

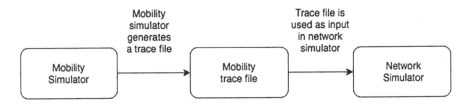

Fig. 1. Vehicular simulators: **Offline** approach.

In the **Embedded** approach (Fig. 2) the traffic and Network Simulators are natively coupled to form a single simulator. In fact, most of the platforms of this category were either designed for traffic simulations or for Network Simulations, not both. Some modules that would allow such platforms to be used in Vehicular Networks were later implemented, for instance, VISSIM that has MOVE [27], the NCTUns [63] and VCOM [28] as embedded modules.

The **Online** approach (Fig. 3) was introduced to address the limitations of the previous two approaches. It provides a bidirectional communication between Network Simulators (developed by computer scientists) and Traffic Simulators (developed by traffic engineers). Thus, vehicular mobility is handled by experts in traffic, and communication is handled by experts in computing. In the online approach the Network Simulator controls the traffic simulator by sending commands that modify the behavior of the nodes. The Traffic Simulator responds to the Network Simulator with the position of the affected node. This approach is considered, thus far, the best solution for simulations in Vehicular Networks, for it allows a high degree of realism.

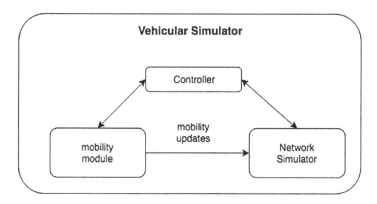

Fig. 2. Vehicular simulators: **Embedded** approach.

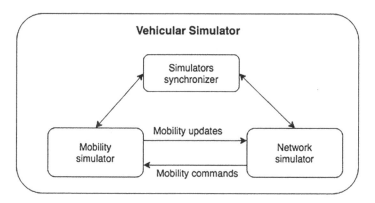

Fig. 3. Vehicular simulators: **Online** approach.

3   Simulators

Vehicular Networks Simulators face many challenges. Some of them are related to the communication, more specifically, physical layer, link layer, and, in some cases, transport layer. The other challenges are related to the mobility, which is one of the main factors that affect the assessment of protocols and applications for vehicular networks. Communication challenges are dealt with by the Network Simulator, which must implement all models needed to represent a real vehicle-to-vehicle communication. Mobility challenges are dealt with by the mobility simulator, which is responsible for all models needed to represent a real vehicle mobility, including change lane models, driver behavior models, traffic sign models, etc. In the following subsections, we present the main simulators used by the scientific community in each specific-domain (network and mobility), and also show how these simulators were combined to achieve better results.

3.1   Network Simulators

Simulations based on discrete events have become the main method used by simulators. In this type of simulator, simulation behavior is not based on continuous equations, but rather in discrete events distributed in time. To this end, the simulation creates an event queue ordered by the time when the event should occur, and maintain an instantaneous clock that, at the end of an event, moves to the beginning of the next one. As a result, the simulation can run faster or slower, depending on the number of events that are in the queue. The simulation ends when the event queue is empty or the time previously established for the simulation ends. The most used simulators for Vehicle Networks are based on discrete events and will be discussed in greater detail below.

OMNeT++: It is a Discrete Event Simulator [60] that allows communication modeling in networks, parallel systems and distributed systems. Available since 1997 under the GPL, it has become one of the most used simulators by the scientific community. The OMNeT++ was designed from the beginning to support large-scale simulations. For this reason, it was built completely modular, enabling better reuse of code and facilitating the implementation of new libraries that extend its functionality. As an example, we can mention the INET, which is an open-source framework that has the models to simulate mobile, wired and wireless networks. The OMNeT++ modular feature, allows each model to be implemented separately and then combined to form a protocol stack similar to the real one. INET has models of the physical layer (PPP, Ethernet and 802.11), various communication protocols (IPV4, IPV6, TCP, SCTP, UDP) and various application models.

ns-2: This simulator [2] is one of the most popular and it is widely used by the academic community. Its first version was launched in 1996, and derived from its ns-1 predecessor. It includes detailed models of a great number of TCP variations and many applications (such as HTTP traffic). It also supports wired and wireless networks modeling. In the wireless networks field, there are models for routing algorithms such as AODV and DSR, as well as models for the MAC protocol of the 802.11b protocol specification.

GloMoSim: It is a modular library for parallel simulation of wireless networks. This library was developed to be extended and combined and it has an API defined to each layer of the communication protocol stack. The GloMoSim [66] has implemented: MAC layer of 802.11b protocol in detail; routing algorithms to wireless networks (AODV, DSR, and some others); transport layer protocol TCP; some application in the application layer level. Moreover, new protocols can be developed to extend GloMoSim capabilities. Executing a parallel model in GloMoSim is often transparent to the user. An interface can be used to set up the simulation parameters and also to designate a mapping strategy for running a parallel simulation.

GTNetS: It is a network simulator that had its development focused on parallelism. For this reason, it has shown a good performance as well as good scalability, even considering networks with millions of elements. The GTNetS [43] was implemented in C++ using the object-oriented paradigm, which allows an easy extension of existing protocols. The GTNetS implements the following models: on the physical layer, it has implemented the 802.11, for wireless simulations, and the 802.3, for wired simulations. On the network layer, it has implemented the routing protocols AODV and DSR for wireless and the BGP and IEGRP for wired simulations. On the transport layer, it has implemented the TCP and UDP protocols. Finally, the application layer includes implementations for FTP, P2P, and client-server applications. The community has not provided support for GTNetS since 2008.

SWANS: *Scalable Wireless Ad hoc Network Simulator* [9] is a Wireless Network Simulator that can be used for sensor networks. It was built on top of the *Java in Simulation Time* (JIST) simulation platform. The JIST is general purpose *engine* simulation based on discrete events, which was developed in the JAVA language. This simulator is focused on high performance and efficiency, and it simulates networks with four times higher performances than the ns-2 networks, with the same system requirements and level of detail [26]. Jist/Swans was developed to meet the needs related to simulations of wireless networks and sensor networks. One of the main advantages of Jist/Swans is that it allows simulation of networks that require large-scale tests.

Although all Networks Simulators mentioned above have mobility models for Mobile Network Simulations, they should not be used to simulate a vehicular network. The most used simulators for Vehicle Networks are based on discrete events and will be discussed in greater detail below. That is because the Network Simulators implement random models, and as we have seen before, these models do not represent real mobility. A good alternative is to delegate the vehicular mobility to a Traffic Simulator.

3.2   Traffic Simulators

When Vehicular Networks emerged, researchers believed that it was a specific application of Mobile Networks. It means that at the beginning, Vehicular Network Protocols were evaluated using random models. Such models worked perfectly for Mobile Networks, because generally it was about networks that simulated human behavior in an open field, such as a university campus or a conference. But it soon became clear that the random models did not represent the vehicular mobility, which produced undesirable results when evaluating new protocols.

Since then the study of vehicular mobility has become an open topic of constant research. This researches resulted in an evolution from random models, where the direction, speed and origin and destination points were chosen completely randomly, to models that extract information from actual maps and aim to generate vehicular mobility that are closer and closer to reality.

Thus far, several proposals of models and tools that simulate vehicular mobility have emerged. Some of them are based on mathematical models that simulate the streets as well as the driver's behavior. Others use maps to extract all kinds of information possible, for instance, the limits of the streets, the number of lanes, the direction of the tracks, the speed limits of each vehicle category, etc. Some of the main Traffic Simulators will be mentioned below.

VISSIM: It was proposed by [18] in 1994, is a stochastic simulator of microscopic vehicular mobility, meaning that it simulates the behavior of each car individually. The quality of a traffic simulator is highly dependent on the quality of the traffic flow model. For this reason, the cars in queue and the lane change models are both part of VISSIM kernel. The model of cars in queue describes the behavior of a vehicle with respect to the vehicle that is in front of it, and may include overtaking models when there is a lane change model. Instead of using a deterministic cars in queue model, VISSIM uses a model based on a psychological study created in 1974 [20].

To simulate the traffic model, VISSIM takes into account the following parameters: Technical data of the vehicle (vehicle size, maximum speed, maximum acceleration, maximum deceleration and vehicle position), driver behavior (desired speed, acceleration versus desired speed, driver is desired security) and interactions between various drivers (vehicles limits, tracks limits, next traffic light).

VISSIM has standardized and well-defined interfaces that allow C-based programs to be implemented and integrated to it. This allowed the first Bidirectionally Coupled Simulators to emerge [21,35]. Bidirectionally Coupled Simulators are formed by the combination of a Traffic Simulator with a Network Simulator.

SUMO: Another Traffic Simulator widely used by the academic community is the *SUMO* [31]. SUMO is the acronym for *Simulation of Urban Mobility*, and it is a platform for Microscopic Traffic Simulation, intermodal and multimodal, of continuous space and discrete events. The development of SUMO started in 2001, but it was only in 2002 that it was released under the GPL [32].

SUMO is not only a Traffic Simulator, but rather a set of applications that help perform and prepare traffic simulations. To allow greater flexibility, various configuration file formats are supported. These files can be imported from other tools or generated by SUMO itself. As previously mentioned, simulations representing the real world need high quality mobility models. For this reason, the SUMO has tools to generate the Network Topology, the vehicles and the traffic demand.

In SUMO, the real-world networks are represented as graphs, where nodes are the intersections and streets are represented by edges. The intersections consist of their own position, plus information about their shape and right-of-way rules. The edges are one-way connections between two nodes, and they have geometry information, the permitted classes of vehicles and the maximum speed allowed. Two tools can be used to generate the network topology, which are the *"netconverter"* and *"netgenerate"*. The *"netconverter"* allows the topology to be imported from other tools, such as VISSIM, OpenStreetMaps, etc. The *"netgenerate"* allows the generation of three different types of networks, which are manhatam grid, circular spider network and random network, as shown in Fig. 4.

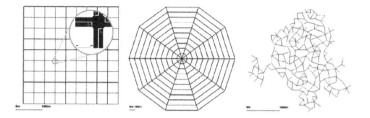

Fig. 4. Examples of networks generated by *"netgenerate"*, from left to right, manhatam grid, circular spider network and random network (figure extracted from [31]).

SUMO is a purely Microscopic Traffic Simulator. Because it is multimodal, it allows not only car traffic modeling, but also the modeling of public transport systems, rail systems and any other system that may influence or participate in the simulation.

STRAW: Acronym of STreet RAndom Waypoint, [11] was developed in 2005 and is publicly available[1] for download. It was implemented as an extension of SWANS (Scalable Wireless Ad Hoc Network Simulator) [8], a Java-based, publicly available, and scalable Wireless Network Simulator. The STRAW extract topology information, like road names, location, and shapes of roads, from a TIGER data set to create the topology of the network.

According to [45], the car-following model is used to control the nodes movement and intersection management. As a drawback, the STRAW does not support lane changing and not consider a vehicle's current lane when it attempts to make a turn.

VanetMobiSim: The *VanetMobiSim* [24] is an extension of CanuMobiSim [55], a general purpose User Mobility Simulator. Coded in Java, both are platform independent and produce traces that can be used by different Network Simulators such as ns-2 [2], QualNet [3] and GloMoSim [66]. CanuMobiSim provides an easily extensible architecture for mobility. However, the fact that it is designed for multiple purposes causes the level of detail in specific scenarios to be reduced. The VanetMobiSim therefore is a dedicated extension for Vehicle Networks.

As we have seen, a critical aspect for Vehicle Networks is the need for a simulation to reflect, as closely as possible, the actual behavior of vehicular traffic. When dealing with vehicular mobility models, we can separate the scenarios in a macro and a micro views.

In the macro view, both the network topology and its structure (number of lanes and direction) must be taken into account. Other factors that are relevant are the characteristics of the traffic (speed limits and vehicle restrictions by class), the presence of traffic restrictions (traffic signs and traffic lights) and finally the effects caused by points of interest (path between home and job).

VanetMobiSim allows the network topology to be formed using 4 classes [19], which are: *user-defined graph, GDF map, TIGER map* and *Clustered Voronoi*

---

[1] http://www.aqualab.cs.northwestern.edu/projects/111-c3-car-to-car-cooperation-for-vehicular-ad-hoc-networks.

Graph. In all cases, the network topology is implemented as a graph where the edges limit the movement of vehicles. To generate real mobility, VanetMobiSim allows the specification of parameters to generate routes and to calculate the path between the points of origin and destination. In the routes generation, the points of interest can either be randomly generated or selected by the user. As for generating the path between the two points, the following three techniques are allowed: shortest path, lowest cost (takes traffic jam into account) or a combination of both.

Micro mobility refers to the behavior of each driver individually when interacting with other drivers or the road infrastructure. Examples of parameters that need to be informed to the models of micro mobility are: Travel speed in different traffic conditions, deceleration and overtaking criteria, driver behavior in the presence of intersections and traffic lights and general attitudes of the driver (which are usually related to age, sex, maturity, etc.). To model micro mobility parameters the VanetMobSim implemented two models that are familiar to researchers in the field, which are the Fluid Traffic Model (FTM) [48] and the Intelligent Driver Model (IDM) [58].

MOVE: It was implemented in Java and run in the top of SUMO. MOVE [27] consists of two main components: the Map Editor and the Vehicle Movement Editor. To build the road topology, the Map Editor allows three possibilities, which are: (i) the user can create the map manually, (ii) The map can be generate automatically and; (iii) the map can be imported from existing real maps, such as TIGER database. The Vehicle Movement Editor allows the user to specify the trip and the route that vehicles should take. Then, the data is fed into SUMO to generate a mobility trace, which can be used by network simulators such as ns-2 and QualNet to simulate a realistic vehicle movement. One of the main strengths of MOVE is the fact that it was implemented to allow users to rapidly generate realistic mobility models for Vehicular Networks.

In the previous sections, we presented the main simulators for a specific-domains which are relevant to Vehicular Networks. In the next section we will help the reader understand how the Vehicular Network researchers combined traffic simulators with Network Simulators to get a reliable analysis of protocols and applications on vehicular environments.

4   Vehicular Network Simulators

It is clear to Vehicular Networks researchers that neither Traffic Simulators or Network Simulators meet all the requirements for a simulation. An alternative to solve this problem would be to record the mobility generated by a Traffic Simulator in a trace file and then use this file on the Network Simulator to update the position of the nodes. However, this approach does not allow mobility to be influenced by the network simulator, and therefore, does not reflect the topology changes. The current state of the art is the bidirectional coupling between Traffic and Network Simulators. To make it possible, both simulators run the same simulation and exchange information on the status of each node. Although this approach enables high degree of realism, it requires the exchanging of a lot of messages between the simulators, which results in high computational cost when it is used in large scenarios. Characteristics and restrictions of bidirectionally coupled simulators are discussed below.

MSIECV: The *MSIECV*, also called *VISSIM/NS-2*, [35] is the first simulator to propose the bidirectionally coupling between traffic and network simulators. The MSIECV architecture (Fig. 5) combines the ns-2 Network Simulator, VISSIM Traffic Simulator, and the Matlab/Simulink Applications Simulator. A simulation controller was implemented to manage the interaction between all simulators. A sync class was implemented to ensure that Traffic and Network Simulators are synchronized in time during their execution.

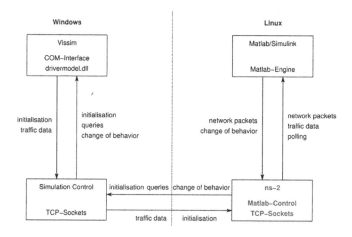

Fig. 5. Architecture of MSIECV simulator (figure extracted from [35]).

CORSIM: Wu *et al.* [64] proposed a simulator that combines CORSIM to control the mobility of vehicles and the QualNet to model the communication between them. These two simulators were combined using a distributed simulation software package called the Federal Simulations Development Kit (FDK) [38]. The FDK implements services defined in the Interface Specification of High-level Architecture [46]. Also, a Communication Layer was developed to define interactions between CORSIM and QualNet.

GrooveNet: *GrooveNet* [36], for Linux, was developed in 2006, and it was implemented in C++ and Qt. All types of vehicles communications are supported, that is, vehicle-to-vehicle, and vehicle-to-infrastructure through DSRC and 802.11. For vehicular mobility, the GooveNet includes the models for car-following, traffic light, lane changing and simulated GPS. Despite the authors say that the models were validated, they did not provide any information about its implementation. The main characteristic highlighted by the authors, is the ability of GrooveNet to make hybrid simulations, including real and simulated vehicles.

VanetSim: *VanetSim* [56] had its first version developed in 2008, but it was only in 2014 that its stable version was made available. Developed in Java, it is open source (GNU GPLv3) and can be downloaded in http://www.vanet-simulator. org/. The VanetSim was specifically designed to analyze attacks on privacy and security. To ensure a approximated real-world simulation providing realistic results, the VanetSim implements the state-of-the-art micro-mobility model [33] and allows the importing of the network topology from OpenStreetMap[2].

VCOM: *VCOM* [28] is a hybrid library which combines the micro traffic simulator VISSIM with a discrete event based inter-Vehicle Communication Simulator. The VCOM takes advantage from mathematical modeling to reduce the number of events generated by the communication. According to the authors, this approach can overcome ns-2 by a considerable speed-up. Also, an application module that contains all application logic provides a well-defined interface to simplify the implementation and evaluation of new applications.

NCTUns: *NCTUns* [62] and MoVES [10] are Embedded Simulators developed respectively in 2007 and 2008, which implement their own network and traffic models. The difference between them is that MoVES was developed to be a Parallel and Distributed simulator. Another simulator that was proposed in the same year as NCTUns is the AutoMesh [61]. The AutoMesh implements a Custom Mobility Simulator, but uses ns-2 as network simulator.

ExNS3: The *ExNS3* [5] is extended from the ns-3 and implements custom traffic models to be applied in Vehicular Network Simulations. Unlike ExNS3, the *TraNS* [42] uses ns-2 for network simulation and SUMO for traffic simulation. A TraCI interface is used to allow data exchange between the Network and Traffic Simulators.

OVNIS: The OVNIS [41], proposed in 2010, is one of the bidirectionally coupled simulator that uses SUMO as Traffic Simulator and ns-3 as Network Simulator. Another simulator that uses SUMO and ns-3 is the HINTS [65], proposed in 2012. HINTS differs from previously mentioned simulators by using a hybrid approach to generate vehicular mobility. It manages to bring together the best of both worlds, that is, the flexibility of the online approach and low computational cost of the offline approach. The authors mention that the new approach advances the state of the art in terms of performance by using resources more efficiently, thereby reducing the simulation time and the computational cost.

Veins: It is a simulation framework that provides coupling of the OMNET++ Network Simulator with the SUMO Traffic Simulator. It was initially proposed in 2008 by [51], after the authors discuss the development of simulators for Vehicular Networks. But it was only in [50], in 2011, that it gained greater visibility in the academic community. The coupling between the OMNeT++

---

[2] http://www.openstreetmap.org.

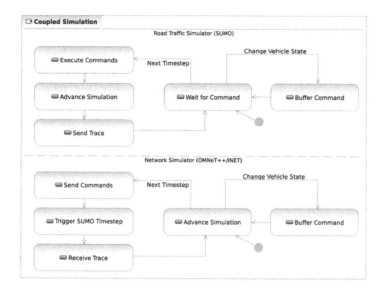

Fig. 6. Overview of the coupled simulation framework (figure extracted from [50]).

and SUMO happens through dedicated communication modules that have been implemented for both. During the simulation, these communication modules exchange information over TCP. Figure 6 shows details about the state machines of road traffic and network simulator communication modules.

VSimRTI: Unlike the other bidirectionally coupled simulators, the VSim-RTI [47] is a runtime simulation infrastructure that enables integration between any pair of simulators. Its goal is to make it as easy as possible for the user to prepare and implement a simulation. To achieve this, it uses a high-level architecture (HLA) simulation and modeling standard defined by the IEEE [1] (Fig. 7). For immediate use, a set of simulators is already coupled to VSimRTI, such as the Traffic Simulators VISSIM and SUMO, the Network Simulators JIST/SWANS and OMNeT++ and the Application Simulator VSimRTI_APP as well as various data analysis tools.

iTETRIS: The iTETRIS [44] is a simulation platform developed in 2013, which is freely available to members of the iTETRIS community. It integrates and extends the SUMO and ns-3, which are two open source platforms widely used for traffic and network simulations. The iTETRIS is an open source platform, and its architecture is completely modular, which facilitates for the community to expand it in the future. It was designed to be aligned with international standards, more specifically, to be compatible with the ETSI architecture for intelligent transport systems, and it allows simulations to use either the 802.11p [53] or the ETSI ITS G5 standards.

SimITS: The SimITS [25] was proposed in 2010. It is a bidirectional simulator that couples the SUMO and ns-3. The authors had implemented a class to

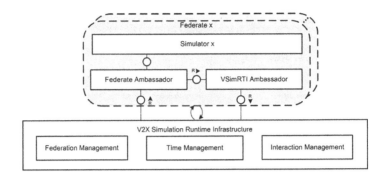

Fig. 7. Architecture of VSimRTI simulator (figure extracted from [47]).

synchronize SUMO and ns-3 and an ITS communication protocol stack that provides a safety application, a transport protocol, a network beaconing protocol, and a geoRouting protocol.

Webots/ns-3: Llatser *et al.* [34] proposed in 2017 a framework that combines the Webots submicroscopic simulator with the ns-3 network simulator. Webots is a powerful submicroscopic simulator and that it is based on the Open Dynamic Engine (ODE) library. It was, at first, proposed to be applied on mobile robotics, latter, it was extended to support simulation on ITS. A previous effort bringing OMNeT++ with Webots has been presented in [12] in 2008.

Although the Bidirectionally Coupled Simulators allow simulations to be performed with a high degree of realism, some issues that are not treated by them need to be considered. As an example, we can mention the traffic demand, in which unrealistic traffic can be generated if random origin and destination points are chosen. Or, the poor quality of the maps, where the absence or incompleteness of information can influence network topology. Another factor that should be taken into consideration is the presence of different elements in the network. In the case of Vehicular Networks, future efforts should be applied to the insertion of elements in the simulation such as *Unmanned Aerial Vehicles* (UAVs), people walking and autonomous cars.

5 Discussions

To understand the current state and future challenges in Vehicular Network Simulators it is necessary to know how the evolution happened from the beginning. As we can see on Fig. 8, until 2005 the applications and protocols proposed for Vehicular Networks had to be evaluated using random models. That is because all existing simulators until then had others purposes, more specifically, the Traffic Simulators were developed and used exclusively by traffic engineers, and Network Simulators were proposed to be applied in other types of networks, typically, sensor networks.

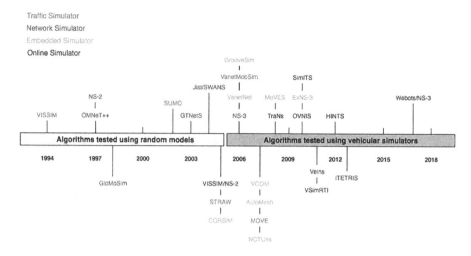

Fig. 8. Evolution timeline of Vehicular Network simulators (figure best viewed in colors). (Color figure online)

This scenario changes when, in 2005, [35] proposed the MSIECV, which combines VISSIM (a micro-traffic simulator) with ns-2 (a network simulator) to generate scenarios that are closer to real ones. It is important to highlight that the technique proposed by [35] comprises the current state-of-the-art. Although MSIECV was the first Vehicular Network Simulator to combine Traffic and Network Simulators (Online Simulators), it was only with Veins that this approach gained prominence in the scientific community. The Veins Simulator was published three years latter by [51] and took more three years to be consolidated [50].

We believe that one of the reasons for the lack of attention of the scientific community with the MSIECV, is the fact that VISSIM is a commercial tool that is not freely available. On the other hand, the Veins uses two freely and well-established tools that have a bigger support of the community, which are OMNeT++ and SUMO.

The Fig. 8 also shows that most of the existing Vehicular Network Simulators were proposed over a period of 3 years after the first one was proposed, in 2005. During this period, the computer scientists used to believe that implementing mathematical models to represent vehicular mobility was the better solution (Embedded Simulators). In 2008, [50] turned the bidirectionally coupling between Traffic and Network Simulators more popular, thus gaining attention of the researchers. It is important to notice, that the scientific community took five year to absorb the concept of Online Simulators, and three year more to start to use them.

As far as we know, after 2013 to date, there has been no significant effort to propose new Vehicular Network Simulators. We believe that this is due to the fact that the scientific community changed focus and concentrated their efforts on implementing new models and improving the existing ones. Some examples of these models are: 802.11p [16], DSRC/WAVE [15], Obstacle Shadowing [52] and Antenna Patterns [14].

However, we noticed that recent research points to two new directions: (i) the use of machine learning to improve the vehicular simulator models, and (ii) the integration between the simulation world and the real world. As we can see in [29], the authors integrated the SUMO traffic simulator with OMNeT++ network simulator and applied machine learning techniques to improve the canal capability to communicate considering realistic Ray-tracing simulation. Additionally, many works have been using machine learning to improve the vehicular simulators aimed to produce realistic results, for example, Fan *et al.* [17] used machine learning to predict travel time based on historical data collected from tolls, Dogru *et al.* [13] and Tomas *et al.* [54] used forest classifiers to detect traffic accident, and Abdoos *et al.* [4] used multiagent Q-learning to control traffic lights.

The other approach that has gained attention from the research community recently is the integration between the simulation environment and the real world. In this approach real vehicles are equipped with devices that are able to send data to a system integrated with a simulator. Thus, the simulation reproduces the real behavior collected from these devices integrated with simulated vehicles ensuring scalability and realism. The first simulator observed by us that uses this approach is the GrooveNet [36]. The GrooveNet is an embedded simulator that have implemented all communication and mobility models. This simulator allows real vehicles to send data to a simulator environment but not allows that the simulator to send data to the real vehicles. Recently, Klingler *et al.* [30] have been proposed a more complete and flexible framework to integrate the simulation environment and the real world. This framework uses the well established Vehicular simulator Veins and allows communication in both directions, that is, from the simulator to the real vehicles and from the real vehicles to the simulator.

6   Conclusions

Evaluate new proposals of applications and protocols for Vehicular Networks is crucial before deploying them in the real world. Simulation is the preferred method by the community to conduct this evaluation because it provides scalability at low costs.

This survey presents the main simulators available to the research community conduct the assessment of their applications, and we showed the features of each simulator. Thus, we presented a temporal evolution of vehicular applications assessment from random models until the current state-of-the-art of vehicular network simulators. We discussed how random models produce unfeasible results and how vehicular simulators have emerged and evolved from embedded simulators to bidirectionally coupling of traffic and network simulators aimed to solve the problems related to the random models.

In addition, we point out the new directions of the vehicular simulator research presenting the new paradigms that have gained the attention of the scientific community. We conclude the paper showing that the scientific community took more than five years to consolidate and use a new simulator paradigm.

References

1. IEEE Standard for Modeling and Simulation (M&S) High Level Architecture (HLA) - Framework and Rules. IEEE Standard 1516–2000, pp. 1–22 (2000)
2. ns-2. http://www.isi.edu/nsnam/ns/ (2017). Accessed 29 Sept 2017
3. QualNet. http://web.scalable-networks.com/content/qualnet (2017). Accessed 30 Sept 2017
4. Abdoos, M., Mozayani, N., Bazzan, A.L.C.: Traffic light control in non-stationary environments based on multi agent q-learning. In: 2011 14th International IEEE Conference on Intelligent Transportation Systems (2011)
5. Arbabi, H., Weigle, M.C.: Highway mobility and vehicular ad-hoc networks in ns-3. In: Proceedings of the Winter Simulation Conference (2010)
6. Arellano, W., Mahgoub, I.: TrafficModeler extensions: a case for rapid VANET simulation using, OMNE, SUMO, and VEINS. In: 10th High Capacity Optical Networks and Emerging/Enabling Technologies (2013)
7. Aschenbruck, N., Ernst, R., Gerhards-Padilla, E., Schwamborn, M.: BonnMotion: a mobility scenario generation and analysis tool. In: Proceedings of the 3rd International ICST Conference on Simulation Tools and Techniques (2010)
8. Barr, R.: An efficient, unifying approach to simulation using virtual machines. Ph.D. thesis (2004)
9. Barr, R., Haas, Z.J., Van Renesse, R.: Scalable wireless ad hoc network simulation. In: Handbook on Theoretical and Algorithmic Aspects of Sensor, Ad hoc Wireless, and Peer-to-Peer Networks, pp. 297–311 (2005)
10. Bononi, L., Felice, M.D., D'Angelo, G., Bracuto, M., Donatiello, L.: MoVES: a framework for parallel and distributed simulation of wireless vehicular ad hoc networks. Comput. Netw. **52**, 155–179 (2008)
11. Choffnes, D.R., Bustamante, F.E.: An integrated mobility and traffic model for vehicular wireless networks. In: Proceedings of the 2nd ACM International Workshop on Vehicular Ad Hoc Networks (2005)
12. Cianci, C.M., Pugh, J., Martinoli, A.: Exploration of an incremental suite of microscopic models for acoustic event monitoring using a robotic sensor network. In: 2008 IEEE International Conference on Robotics and Automation, ICRA 2008 (2008)
13. Dogru, N., Subasi, A.: Traffic accident detection using random forest classifier. In: 15th Learning and Technology Conference (2018)
14. Eckhoff, D., Brummer, A., Sommer, C.: On the impact of antenna patterns on VANET simulation. In: 8th IEEE Vehicular Networking Conference (2016)
15. Eckhoff, D., Sommer, C.: A multi-channel IEEE 1609.4 and 802.11p EDCA model for the veins framework. In: 5th ACM/ICST International Conference on Simulation Tools and Techniques for Communications, Networks and Systems (2012)
16. Eckhoff, D., Sommer, C., Dressler, F.: On the necessity of accurate IEEE 802.11p models for IVC protocol simulation. In: 75th IEEE Vehicular Technology Conference, pp. 1–5 (2012)
17. Fan, S.K.S., Su, C.J., Nien, H.T., Tsai, P.F., Cheng, C.Y.: Using machine learning and big data approaches to predict travel time based on historical and real-time data from taiwan electronic toll collection. Soft. Comput. **22**(17), 5707–5718 (2018)

18. Fellendorf, M.: VISSIM: a microscopic simulation tool to evaluate actuated signal control including bus priority. In: 64th Institute of Transportation Engineers Annual Meeting (1994)
19. Fiore, M., Harri, J., Filali, F., Bonnet, C.: Vehicular mobility simulation for VANETs. In: 40th Annual Simulation Symposium (2007)
20. Fritzsche, H.T., Ag, D.B.: Amodel for traffic simulation. Traffic Eng. Control **35**, 317–321 (1994)
21. Gorgorin, C., Gradinescu, V., Diaconescu, R., Cristea, V., Ifode, L.: An integrated vehicular and network simulator for vehicular ad-hoc networks. In: Proceedings of the European Simulation and Modelling Conference (2006)
22. Guan, S., Grande, R.E.D., Boukerche, A.: Real-time 3D visualization for distributed simulations of VANets. In: IEEE/ACM 18th International Symposium on Distributed Simulation and Real Time Applications (2014)
23. Harri, J., Filali, F., Bonnet, C.: Mobility models for vehicular ad hoc networks: a survey and taxonomy. IEEE Commun. Surv. Tutor. **11**(4), 19–41 (2009)
24. Härri, J., Filali, F., Bonnet, C., Fiore, M.: VanetMobiSim: generating realistic mobility patterns for VANETs. In: Proceedings of the 3rd International Workshop on Vehicular Ad Hoc Networks (2006)
25. Hrizi, F., Filali, F.: simITS: an integrated and realistic simulation platform for vehicular networks. In: Proceedings of the 6th International Wireless Communications and Mobile Computing Conference (2010)
26. Kargl, F., Schoch, E.: Simulation of MANETs: a qualitative comparison between JiST/SWANS and ns-2. In: Proceedings of the 1st International Workshop on System Evaluation for Mobile Platforms (2007)
27. Karnadi, F.K., Mo, Z.H., Lan, K.: Rapid generation of realistic mobility models for VANET. In: 2007 IEEE Wireless Communications and Networking Conference (2007)
28. Killat, M., et al.: Enabling efficient and accurate large-scale simulations of VANETs for vehicular traffic management. In: Proceedings of the 4th ACM International Workshop on Vehicular Ad Hoc Networks (2007)
29. Klautau, A., Batista, P., Prelcic, N., Wang, Y., Heath, R.: 5G MIMO data for machine learning: application to beam-selection using deep learning. In: Proceedings on Information Theory and Applications Workshop, pp. 1–6 (2016)
30. Klingler, F., Pannu, G.S., Sommer, C., Dressler, F.: Poster: connecting simulation and real world: IEEE 802.11p in the loop. In: Proceedings of the 23rd Annual International Conference on Mobile Computing and Networking (2017)
31. Krajzewicz, D., Erdmann, J., Behrisch, M., Bieker, L.: Recent development and applications of SUMO - Simulation of Urban MObility. Int. J. Adv. Syst. Meas. **5**, 128–138 (2012)
32. Krajzewicz, D., Hertkorn, G., Rössel, C., Wagner, P.: SUMO (Simulation of Urban MObility)-an open-source traffic simulation. In: Proceedings of the 4th Middle East Symposium on Simulation and Modelling (2002)
33. Krauß, S.: Microscopic modeling of traffic flow: investigation of collision free vehicle dynamics. Ph.D. thesis (1998)
34. Llatser, I., Jornod, G.S., Festag, A., Mansolino, D., Navarro Oiza, I., Martinoli, A.: Simulation of cooperative automated driving by bidirectional coupling of vehicle and network simulators. In: IEEE Intelligent Vehicles Symposium (IV) (2017)
35. Lochert, C., Barthels, A., Cervantes, A., Mauve, M., Caliskan, M.: Multiple simulator interlinking environment for IVC. In: Proceedings of the 2nd ACM International Workshop on Vehicular Ad Hoc Networks (2005)

36. Mangharam, R., Weller, D., Rajkumar, R., Mudalige, P., Bai, F.: GrooveNet: a hybrid simulator for vehicle-to-vehicle networks. In: 3rd Annual International Conference on Mobile and Ubiquitous Systems - Workshops (2006)
37. Marfia, G., Pau, G., De Sena, E., Giordano, E., Gerla, M.: Evaluating vehicle network strategies for downtown portland: opportunistic infrastructure and the importance of realistic mobility models. In: Proceedings of the 1st International MobiSys Workshop on Mobile Opportunistic Networking (2007)
38. McLean, T., Fujimoto, R., Fitzgibbons, B.: Next generation real-time RTI software. In: 5th IEEE International Workshop on Distributed Simulation and Real-Time Applications (2001)
39. Mota, V.F., Cunha, F.D., Macedo, D.F., Nogueira, J.M., Loureiro, A.A.: Protocols, mobility models and tools in opportunistic networks: a survey. Comput. Commun. **48**, 5–19 (2014)
40. Nimje, T.G., Dorle, S.: A survey on various mobility models to improve realistic simulation and accuracy of IVC protocols. In: International Conference on Emerging Trends in Computing, Communication and Nanotechnology (ICE-CCN) (2013)
41. Pigné, Y., Danoy, G., Bouvry, P.: A platform for realistic online vehicular network management. In: IEEE Globecom Workshops (2010)
42. Piórkowski, M., Raya, M., Lugo, A.L., Papadimitratos, P., Grossglauser, M., Hubaux, J.P.: TraNS: realistic joint traffic and network simulator for VANETs. SIGMOBILE Mob. Comput. Commun. Rev. **12**, 31–33 (2008)
43. Riley, G.F.: Large-scale network simulations with GTNetS. In: Proceedings of the 2003 Winter Simulation Conference (2003)
44. Rondinone, M., et al.: iTETRIS: a modular simulation platform for the large scale evaluation of cooperative ITS applications. Simul. Model. Pract. Theory **34**, 99–125 (2013)
45. Rothery, R.W.: Car following models. In: Traffic Flow Theory (1992)
46. Russo, K.L., Shuette, L.C., Smith, J.E., McGuire, M.E.: Effectiveness of various new bandwidth reduction techniques in ModSAF. In: Proceedings of the 13th Workshop on Standards for the Interoperability of Distributed Simulations (1995)
47. Schünemann, B.: V2X simulation runtime infrastructure VSimRTI: an assessment tool to design smart traffic management systems. Comput. Netw. **55**, 3189–3198 (2011)
48. Seskar, I., Maric, S.V., Holtzman, J., Wasserman, J.: Rate of location area updates in cellular systems. In: IEEE 42nd Vehicular Technology Conference (1992)
49. Silva, M.J., Silva, G.I., Teixeira, F.A., Oliveira, R.A.: Temporal evolution of vehicular network simulators: challenges and perspectives. In: Proceedings of the 20th International Conference on Enterprise Information Systems (2018)
50. Sommer, C., German, R., Dressler, F.: Bidirectionally coupled network and road traffic simulation for improved IVC analysis. IEEE Trans. Mob. Comput. **10**, 3–15 (2011)
51. Sommer, C., Dressler, F.: Progressing toward realistic mobility models in VANET simulations. IEEE Commun. Mag. **46**(11), 132–137 (2008)
52. Sommer, C., Eckhoff, D., Dressler, F.: IVC in cities: signal attenuation by buildings and how parked cars can improve the situation. IEEE Trans. Mob. Comput. **13**(8), 1733–1745 (2014)
53. Teixeira, F.A., e Silva, V.F., Leoni, J.L., Macedo, D.F., Nogueira, J.M.S.: Vehicular networks using the IEEE 802.11p standard: an experimental analysis. Veh. Commun. **1**, 91–96 (2014)

54. Thomas, R.W., Vidal, J.M.: Toward detecting accidents with already available passive traffic information. In: 2017 IEEE 7th Annual Computing and Communication Workshop and Conference (2017)
55. Tian, J., Hahner, J., Becker, C., Stepanov, I., Rothermel, K.: Graph-based mobility model for mobile ad hoc network simulation. In: 2002 Proceedings of 35th Annual Simulation Symposium (2002)
56. Tomandl, A., Herrmann, D., Fuchs, K.P., Federrath, H., Scheuer, F.: VANETsim: an open source simulator for security and privacy concepts in VANETs. In: 12th International Conference on High Performance Computing Simulation (HPCS) (2014)
57. Tornell, S.M., Calafate, C.T., Cano, J.C., Manzoni, P.: DTN protocols for vehicular networks: an application oriented overview. IEEE Commun. Surv. Tutor. **17**, 868–887 (2015)
58. Treiber, M., Hennecke, A., Helbing, D.: Congested traffic states in empirical observations and microscopic simulations. Phys. Rev. E **62**, 1805–1824 (2000)
59. Uppoor, S., Trullols-Cruces, O., Fiore, M., Barcelo-Ordinas, J.M.: Generation and analysis of a large-scale urban vehicular mobility dataset. IEEE Trans. Mob. Comput. **13**(5), 1061–1075 (2014)
60. Varga, A.: OMNeT++. In: Wehrle, K., Güneş, M., Gross, J. (eds.) Modeling and Tools for Network Simulation, pp. 35–59. Springer, Heidelberg (2010). https://doi.org/10.1007/978-3-642-12331-3_3
61. Vuyyuru, R., Oguchi, K.: Vehicle-to-vehicle ad hoc communication protocol evaluation using realistic simulation framework. In: 2007 Fourth Annual Conference on Wireless on Demand Network Systems and Services (2007)
62. Wang, S.Y., et al.: NCTUns 4.0: an integrated simulation platform for vehicular traffic, communication, and network researches. In: IEEE 66th Vehicular Technology Conference (2007)
63. Wang, S., Chou, C.: NCTUns tool for wireless vehicular communication network researches. Simul. Model. Pract. Theory **17**(7), 1211–1226 (2009)
64. Wu, H., Lee, J., Hunter, M., Fujimoto, R., Guensler, R., Ko, J.: Efficiency of simulated vehicle-to-vehicle message propagation in Atlanta, Georgia, I-75 corridor. Transp. Res. Rec.: J. Transp. Res. Board **1910**, 82–89 (2005)
65. Zemouri, S., Mehar, S., Senouci, S.M.: HINTS: a novel approach for realistic simulations of vehicular communications. In: Proceedings of the 4th Global Information Infrastructure and Networking Symposium (2012)
66. Zeng, X., Bagrodia, R., Gerla, M.: GloMoSim: a library for parallel simulation of large-scale wireless networks. In: Proceedings 12th Workshop on Parallel and Distributed Simulation (1998)

Graph Modeling for Topological Data Analysis

Silas P. Lima Filho(✉), Maria Claudia Cavalcanti(✉),
and Claudia Marcela Justel(✉)

Military Institute of Engineering, Rio de Janeiro, RJ, Brazil
silaslfilho@gmail.com, {yoko,cjustel}@ime.eb.br

Abstract. The importance of bringing the relational data to other models and technologies has been widely debated. In special, Graph Database Management Systems (DBMS) have gained attention from industry and academia for their analytic potential. One of its advantages is to incorporate facilities to perform topological analysis, such as link prediction, centrality measures analysis, and recommendations. There are already initiatives to map from a relational database to graph representation. However, they do not take into account the different ways to generate such graphs. This work discusses how graph modeling alternatives from data stored in relational datasets may lead to useful results. The main contribution of this paper is towards managing such alternatives, taking into account that the graph model choice and the topological analysis to be used by the user. Experiments are reported and show interesting results, including modeling heuristics to guide the user on the graph model choice.

Keywords: Data modeling · Centrality measures · Link prediction · Heuristics

1 Introduction

Nowadays, Relational Database Management Systems (DBMS) are still the most commonly used technology to store information. This technology has shown advantages, even though there are some performance and representation issues. These issues have motivated new proposals and paradigms in order to improve how the data is represented, stored and retrieved. Graph DBMS is one of these alternative approaches.

The lack or loss of information should be one of the main concerns with respect to reality modeling. While designing a database, specifically in the modeling stage, the designer is interested in representing some real phenomena. Usually, this process involves two steps: the conceptual and the logical modeling steps. The first one consists in representing concepts and their relationships, without the commitment to a specific DBMS. The second one, consists in mapping the entities and concepts designed in the preceding step, as elements of a DBMS.

In the case of a Relational DBMS, those entities are usually mapped into tables, while relationships are either mapped into tables or attributes. In Graph

© Springer Nature Switzerland AG 2019
S. Hammoudi et al. (Eds.): ICEIS 2018, LNBIP 363, pp. 193–214, 2019.
https://doi.org/10.1007/978-3-030-26169-6_10

DBMS, entities are usually represented as nodes, and their relationships are usually represented as edges. Differently from Relational databases, the relationships are explicitly represented. Moreover, graphs have been largely used for applications such as recommendation systems, social networks analysis, tracing routes and so on. This analytic potential has motivated many approaches to support the mapping of data stored in relational systems into graphs [2,15,16].

However, mapping data into graph is not an easy task. This paper aims to explore alternative modelings in order to provide richer analysis and inferences. The key idea consists on assisting the user on the task of graph modeling, based on the analysis of a conceptual schema, derived from a relational schema of a database. The main contribution is the identification of a set of heuristics, which take into account the intended topological analysis and guide the user on choosing the modelings that may be useful. These heuristics were identified based on the results of some experiments, which applied topological analysis (centrality measures and link prediction) over two datasets, using different modeling choices.

This work is organized as follows: Sect. 2 presents some basic concepts used throughout the paper. Section 3 describes the related works on graph database modeling and on mapping the relational data to graph structures. Section 4 presents the motivation for deriving heuristics and describes how the experiments were conducted. Section 5 presents the experiments, as well as their results, and the heuristics that emerged based on them. Finally, the last section concludes the work, pointing to some future directions.

2   Basic Foundations

This section presents basic concepts about social network analysis, graph modeling and relational database modeling.

2.1   Social Networks Analysis

In recent years, social networks have been widely discussed. This research area has received great attention not only from researchers and scientists, but also from the industry. Social networks concepts can be applied in different scenarios and domains. Easley and Kleinberg [5] show a list of distinct scenarios such as friendship, influence and collaboration networks for relationship examples among people. Biological networks, electric distribution networks, pages and web links computer networks are examples of connections between objects and concepts.

Several social network analysis techniques and metrics were developed over recent years. Some of these have addressed graph topology. The focus of this work is to use the graph model, in order to represent a network and subsequently obtain the inherent information from their entities i.e. nodes and edges.

A first intuitive analysis can be done by counting the quantity of relationships in the graph i.e. edges, a node is part. With this information at hands, another type of analysis can employ the graph topology to find the best routes through the nodes. For instance, if a hypothetical message were sent between every pair of nodes, it can be determined the more common node in all the paths used to send the message. Some metrics widely used in this context are called **Centrality Measures**, such as Degree, Closeness, Betweenness, Authority and Hub centralities. In our experiments, four metrics from Nowell and Kleinberg [10] have been used for centrality measures. Those four centrality measures will be formally defined below. Let $G = (V(G), E(G))$ be a graph.

- **Degree Centrality**: is the simplest centrality measure defined as the quantity of edges connected to a node in a graph G. It is denoted by

$$C_d(x) = |\Gamma(x)|.$$

- **Closeness Centrality**: relies on the distance from a node to all other nodes in the graph, and it is the sum of inverse of each smaller distance between that pairs of nodes. The higher node closeness coefficient, the shorter the distance between that node and the remaining graph, it is denoted by

$$C_c(x) = \sum_{s \in V(G), s \neq x} \frac{1}{d(x, s)}$$

where $d(x, s)$ is the distance between nodes x and s in G.

- **Betweenness** measures the amount of times that a node is present in the shortest path between two other nodes. Nodes with high betweenness value are the most prominent to control graph information flow. We denote betweenness centrality by

$$C_b(x) = \sum_{s \neq t \neq x \in V(G)} \frac{n_{s,t}^x}{g_{s,t}}$$

where $n_{s,t}^x$ is the number of shortest paths between nodes s and t that contain the node x; and $g_{s,t}$ is the total number of shortest paths between nodes s and t, $\forall s \neq t \in V(G)$.

- **Authority** and **Hub**: we describe these two metrics together because are strong correlated and used in directed networks. Newman [11] states that high central nodes are those which are pointed by others with high central value. However, it is possible for a node to have high centrality if it points to a central node. We can distinguish the nodes which point to important nodes, **Hub**, from those which are pointed several times and thus are prominent, **Authority**. Those two concepts have been created to identify the page relevancy on the web and are based on the idea of acknowledging high connected pages highly connected through links to other pages.

Another important point to be considered is how the social networks can evolve over the time. In other words, with the progress of the time, the entities of some network will still be the same? Can nodes disappear in some environment? Will the number of edges/connections increase or decrease? In both cases, what the reason of such behaviour? In this work we are interested in predict future relations between entities, knowing that they are not related in the current state of the graph. This problem is known as **Link Prediction** [1].

In our experiments, three metrics from Nowell and Kleinberg [10] have been used for link prediction. Those metrics can be classified in two types: one based in common neighbors and other based in path assembling. All the considered metrics produce a coefficient for a pair of nodes x, y non connected by an edge in the graph. Common neighbors metrics analyze in different ways the number of common neighbors of x and y. Path assembling metrics measures in some sense the paths between a pair of nodes in the graphs. Jaccard and Adamic/Adar coefficients are classified as common neighbors metrics, meanwhile Katz coefficient as path assembling metric. Next, the three metrics will be formally defined.

- **Jaccard** coefficient is stated by

$$score(x; y) = \frac{|\Gamma(x) \cap \Gamma(y)|}{|\Gamma(x) \cup \Gamma(y)|}$$

- **Adamic/Adar** coefficient is defined by

$$score(x; y) = \sum_{z \in \Gamma(x) \cap \Gamma(y)} \frac{1}{\log(|\Gamma(z)|)}$$

- **Katz** coefficient is defined by

$$score(x, y) = \sum_{l=1}^{\infty} \beta^l |paths_{x,y}^l|$$

where $paths_{x,y}^l$ is the set with all the paths with length l between nodes x, y, and β is an arbitrary value. In our experiments, we defined $\beta = \frac{1}{\lambda_1}$, and λ_1 is the greatest eigenvalue of the adjacency matrix of the graph.

2.2   Relational and Graph Modeling

As mentioned before, there is no doubt about the importance of modeling a database. Heuser [8] states that a data model must be expressive enough to create database schemas. Put differently, it must be sufficiently expressive for modeling reality into schemas. Designing a database schema is a task which ordinarily goes through two steps with different levels of abstraction: conceptual and logical modeling. These two steps are needed due to the complexity of the reality that the designer intends to model. The main idea is to conduct the modeler from the reality level into some logical data structure that may represent real objects. The ER model [3] is frequently employed to design conceptual schemas, where objects and relationships of the real world are represented as entities (classes of objects) and their relationship types (see Fig. 1), respectively. In the second step, these entities and relationships are then mapped into a logical schema. The Relational Model [4] is extensively used to create logical schemas, where tables are defined as the structures that will actually store the data. For instance, if the domain involves actors and movies, these can be modeled as entities 1 and 2. The actor's participation on a movie can be modeled as a relationship between those two entities.

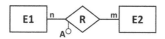

Fig. 1. Suggested model for an general situation. Figure from [6].

Different from database modeling, that aims at the storage and management of data, graph modeling aims at data analysis, such as social network analysis or, in particular link prediction. The need to address both goals has led to the rise of graph oriented DBMS (GDBMS). These systems use a graph structure to store data. Neo4J[1] is one of the most used GDBMS.

Rodriguez [12] points to several different graph structures. For example, some graph structures are able to represent different features for each vertex or edge, such as labels, attributes, weight, etc. In his article, he presents a hierarchic classification, where graph structures are organized according to their expressivity (number of features allowed). The structure known as *property graph*, is the most commonly used by graph manipulation tools (e.g. Neo4J), due to its expressiveness.

Graphs may be modeled based on data items that come from databases. In order to map data items from a relational database to a graph structure, it is necessary to count on both conceptual and logical schemas. The modeler can use them to identify which data items will be represented as vertices, and which references can become edges in the graph database. However, this is not an easy task, specially when there is a variety of analysis that can be performed.

The following section presents some initiatives in this direction. However, to the best of our knowledge, there are no methods or guidelines to assist the graph modeler in doing such task, taking into account the analysis to be performed.

3   Related Work

Some works have already approached the task of graph modeling based on data from the relational model databases. Even if some of them face the same problem, they have different modeling motivations. We highlight three of them as follows.

Firstly, De Virgilio et al. published two papers about modeling. In the first one, [14], the authors have developed an analysis over the relational schema. In the second one, [15], the authors highlight that a thoughtful conceptual analysis, based on the conceptual schema (ER), is needed to perform the graph modeling. The authors suggest a "template" graph where some entities and relationships

---

[1] http://neo4j.com/developer/example-data/.

are grouped in one single node depending of defined requirements. Consequently, the number of entities in the schema will be reduced. With this, the authors optimize the query processing.

Another interesting article was published by Wardani and Küng's [16]. In this work, a graph similar to relational database conceptual schema is build, avoiding semantic losses. The authors use both, relational and conceptual schemas, to create specific mapping rules, such as to use foreign key attributes to map a(n) relationship/edge between two nodes.

While the previous mentioned articles propose the creation of property graphs, Bordoloi et al. [2] presents a hypergraph construction method from a relational schema. Initially, star and dependence graphs are built, evidencing the dependence relations between table attributes. Next, these graphs are merged in a single hypergraph. It represents the database schema, where the nodes represent relations' attributes and the edges are attributes' (functional and referential) dependencies. Based on that hypergraph, a new one is generated from the initial data, where each attribute value from the relation tuples turns into a node, and the dependence relations are instantiated as well. However, this is a complex graph with too many nodes. To simplify this graph and avoid node redundancy, a suggested method includes an analysis of common domains between attributes. Therefore, another schema hypergraph is built taking that analysis into account, where attributes from the same domain, which are in different tables, are represented just once. Finally, a data hypergraph is built based on the schema hypergraph, where a single node represents a value from a specific domain. Although, in this approach, all attribute values are available for analysis, a hypergraph is not easy to analyze, since most algorithms and tools are not able to deal with hypergraphs.

Other authors propose some systems/frameworks to deal with graph analysis. Some of them provide graph analytical facilities, while others provide support for data mapping from relational databases in to graph representation. Next, we briefly describe three of those works.

Vertexica [9] is a relational database system that provides a vertex-centric interface which helps the user/programmer to analyze data contained in a relational database, using graph-based queries. The authors affirm that Vertexica allows easy-to-use, efficient and rich analysis on top of a relational engine.

"Aster 6", from Teradata [13], is similar to Vertexica. It enables the user to combine different analysis techniques, such as embedding graph functions within SQL queries. This solution is an extended multi-engine processing architecture, able to handle large-scale graph analytics.

Xirogiannopoulos [17,18] presents a graph analysis framework called Graph-Gen. This framework converts relational data into a graph data model. And also allows the user to perform graph analysis tasks or execute some algorithms over the obtained graph. DSL language - which is based on Datalog - is used to perform extractions from the relational database. To the best of our knowledge, this is the only work that discusses the relevance of obtaining different feasible graph models from the same dataset. However, it does not guide the user on the graph modeling choices.

It is worth to say that none of these works take into account the topological analysis while choosing a graph modeling alternative.

4   Managing Graph Alternatives Approach

Figure 2 summarizes the proposed approach. First, we assume that it is possible to get an ER schema from a relational logical schema (**LS**) using some reverse engineer technique [8]. Sometimes it is difficult to get some automatic support for this action. However, it is important to produce the ER schema, due to its semantic richness and expressiveness in representing the reality. To do this, it may be necessary to count on the domain specialists.

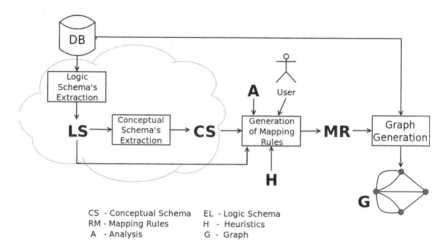

Fig. 2. Flow chart for the proposed approach. Figure from [7].

Then, taking the ER schema (**CS**), we analyze each pair of entities (E_1, E_2) for which there is a relationship (R), as the example in Fig. 1. At this point, the designer may consider different graph modeling alternatives. The idea is to stimulate a deeper exploration of the schema to obtain different graphs. However, this is not an easy task, since there are many different analysis, and besides, there are some (more than one) graph modeling alternatives that can be explored. Therefore, the main goal of this work is to come up with some user support. We assume that given a set of analysis algorithms (**A**) and a set of heuristics (**H**), it is possible to lead the user on choosing a useful graph modeling. Finally, based on the user choice, a set of mapping rules (**MR**) will transform data into the desired graph (**G**).

To identify such heuristics, some experiments were performed with focus on link prediction algorithms. The next section describes them, as well as their results and the extracted heuristics.

5   Experiments, Results and Heuristics

In this section, we present the experiments which helped us to come up with the heuristics for choosing a graph modeling that would fit the desired analysis demand. The experiments were performed over well-known and open datasets. Thus, it was possible to easily explore the results, their impact on models and identify some kind of pattern which helped in the creation of the heuristics.

The experiments were organized according to the dataset used and the type of applied analysis. This section presents three experiments. The first two are related to centrality measures and the last one focuses on link prediction analysis. All three experiments generate heuristics, which are presented after the discussion of the results.

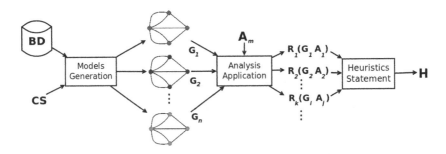

Fig. 3. Flow chart for the heuristic construction. Figure from [7].

Figure 3 shows the flow chart for the heuristic construction. Given a dataset (DB) and a conceptual schema (CS), different graph modelings $(G_1, G_2, \cdots, G_n)$ are generated. And for all these options, a pre-selected analysis set $(A_1, A_2, \cdots, A_m)$ is applied. Results have been generated from each pair graph-analysis $R_k(G_i, A_j)$, such that $(1 \leq k \leq n \times m)$, and from such results, heuristics (H) were created.

Although there are different kinds of graphs, for this work we used the property graph, presented in Sect. 2.2. Our choice is laid on its wide use in the literature.

5.1   Zachary's Karate Experiment - Centrality Measure Analysis

For this experiment, we have considered an ordinary and usual conceptual modeling situation: a pair of entities (E_1, E_2) connected by two distinct relationships (R_1, R_2). Even though it is a simple example, exploring an ordinary case like that, allows us to apply and compare different analysis and metrics results.

The used dataset is based on a well-known social network named Zachary [19]. It consists of 34 members of a karate club and their friendship relations. The dataset created had just one entity to represent the club members, and two optional and semantically different relationships between them: *"friend of"* and *"played with"*. Figure 4 shows the ER schema for this database. Since friendship relations were already known, we included some extra data (randomly generated) to populate the new relationship *"played with"* between club members. The idea of the first experiment was to investigate how centrality measures can be affected by considering two semantically different relationships as edges in the graph.

This experiment was performed in two stages. Both analyzed the following centrality measures: betweenness, closeness and degree.

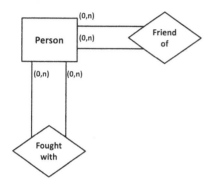

Fig. 4. Database Conceptual Schema which represents and entity with two different self-relationship. Figure from [6].

Fig. 5. Zachary Network with the two types of relationships. Figure from [6].

On the first stage of investigation the analyzed graph (Model 1) which is shown on Fig. 5 was generated with nodes representing persons and the edges representing both types of relationships. On the second experiment stage the analyzed graph (Model 2) was similar to the first one. However, on the second model, relationships of type *"Fought with"* were not considered. Therefore the original network of friendship was maintained.

Table 1 shows the analysis results produced in this experiment. The data was stored on Neo4j which is a NoSQL database management system. While for the centrality measures it was used the Gephi software, which is normally used for graph manipulation and visualization.

Table 1. Centrality measure results for both models on Zachary Experiment. Table from [6].

Node	Model 1			Model 2		
	Betweenness	Closeness	Degree	Betweenness	Closeness	Degree
1	152,19	1,6	16	231,0	1,758	16
34	102,99	1,66	17	160,5	1,81	17
4	12,5	2	7	6,2	2,15	6
22	24	1,9	6	0	2,6	2
24	14,6	2,0	8	9,3	2,5	5
30	9,7	1,9	7	1,5	2,6	4

Result Analysis. The results from Table 1 can help us to understand better the modeling's influence over the results obtained for the centrality measures. It shows that depending on the modeling choice, model 1 or model 2, the analysis results may be significantly affected.

Analyzing Model 2 results, which represented only friendship relationships, nodes 1 and 34 had the highest values for betweenness centrality. Now, analyzing Model 1 results, with both relationships, nodes 1 and 34 were also the most central ones. However, there was a significant increase on centrality values for nodes 4, 22, 24 and 30. These results can be interpreted as follows: those nodes represent fighters who had participated on many tournaments and championships, like node 22, for which betweenness and degree values had the most significant increase.

Thus, the question is: what should be taken into consideration to measure the popularity within the academy? Maybe to measure popularity means to analyze social visibility. In this case it seems to be interesting to analyze friendship relationships and also fight events. On the other hand, if the idea is to analyze only emotional bonds, then it would be enough to analyze only friendship relationships.

As more types of relationships are taken into account, more edges will appear on the graph, and naturally, the centrality measures will be affected. Thus, if the aim is to find the most central nodes, e.g. with the highest betweenness value, then there must be a modeling decision on which types of relationships are important for the centrality analysis. There is a semantic difference between the relationships on the Zachary example and this justifies the reason why these relationships are represented distinctly in the database. But if the aim is to do network analysis, and both relations are semantically relevant to the analysis, then both must be represented on the graph.

Though just one entity has been used in this experiment's database, in a general sense, the same observation must be used in a case where there are two distinct entities that have more than one type of relationship between them. Therefore, from Zachary's experiment conclusions, a heuristic was derived as follows. It formalizes how to map data into a graph, when the conceptual schema presents a similar case.

Heuristic I: Assuming that there are two entities E_1 and E_2, not necessarily distinct, from conceptual schema CS, and that there are distinct relationships between them $R_1, R_2, ..., R_n$, if the desired analysis "focuses on" a specific relationship R_i modeled on the graph, and there is $j \neq i$, such that R_j has the same semantic relevance than R_i, then R_j has to be modeled on graph. More formally as follows.

Let be:

- $G = (V, A)$; graph
- $CS = (E, R)$; conceptual schema
- $E = \{E_1, E_2, ..., E_p\}$; set of entities from schema CS
- $R = \{R_1, R_2, ..., R_q\}$; set of relationships from schema CS

- $E_i = \{e_i^1, e_i^2, ...\}$; set of instances from entity E_i
- $R_k = \{r_k^1, r_k^2, ...\}$; set of instances from relationship R_k
- $r_k^z = (e_i^x, e_j^y)$; one instance from R connects a pair of entity instances from E

Since:

- $E_1, E_2 \in E; e_1^x \in E_1; e_2^y \in E_2$;
- $R_1 \in R$;
- $r_1^z \in R_1; r_1^z = (e_1^x, e_2^y)$;

Mapping for the graph G we have:

- $\forall e_1^x \in E_1, e_1^x \in V$;
- $\forall e_2^y \in E_2, e_2^y \in V$;
- $\forall r_1^z \in R_1, r_1^z \in A$;
- If $\exists j \neq 1 \mid r_j^c = (e_1^a, e_2^b)$ and $R_j \approx R_1$ so $\forall r_j^c \in R_j; r_j^c \in A$

Figure 6 illustrates the choice of relationships $R_i, ...R_j$ between the entities E_1 and E_2 from conceptual schema that will be used to construct a graph where each node represents an entity and each edge represents one of the chosen relationships.

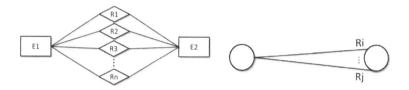

Fig. 6. Representation of the heuristic obtained on Zachary Experiment. Figure from [6].

5.2 SMDB Experiment - Centrality Measure Analysis

This experiment uses a different conceptual schema usual construction, where there is **a pair of entities** (E_1, E_2), which are connected by only one **binary relationship** with a multivalued attribute A (see Fig. 1). This schema construction also appears recurrently in database modeling projects.

The dataset used in this experiment, named SMDB, has more instances of nodes and edges than the one used in the first experiment. SMDB is available together with the Neo4J tool. It contains data about *persons* (125 instances) and *movies* (38 instances), and the relationships *"acted in"* and *"directed"* between them. In this dataset, the "acted in" relationship fits the conceptual schema case under study, as shown in Fig. 7. From this conceptual schema case it was possible to explore three graph model variations. The relationship *"acted in"* relationship has an attribute to represent the *"role"* that some person plays in that movie. It is a multivalued attribute meaning that the same person may play more than one role in the same movie.

The idea of the second experiment was to investigate how topological measures can be affected by varying the representation of a relationship. First as an edge, then as a node, and finally as multiple nodes. Figures 8, 9, 10 show the graph examples of the variations of graph modeling for this experiment.

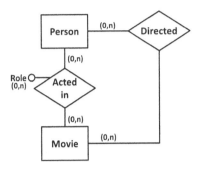

Fig. 7. ER schema for the Experiments datasets. Figure from [6].

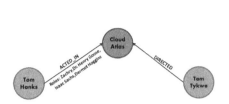

Fig. 8. Graph example generated from SMDB - Model 3. Figure from [6].

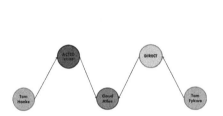

Fig. 9. Graph example generated from SMDB - Model 4. Figure from [6].

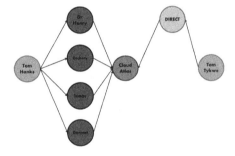

Fig. 10. Graph example generated from SMDB - Model 5. Figure from [6].

This experiment was divided into three stages. Each stage considered a specific variation of the graph model. All the stages analyze the topological measures, betweenness and closeness. In addition, hub and authority, which are centrality measures for directed graphs, were also computed for each node. The results were achieved by the use of two tools, Gephi, to compute the centrality measures, and Neo4j, to store the data.

Conceptual schema entities (*Person* and *Movie*) are represented as nodes in the first stage of this experiment. Relationships are represented as edges in the graph and there are two types of them: *Acted* and *Directed*. Figure 8 shows an example of the graph at this stage. The relationship *Acted* in the conceptual schema has the attribute *Role*. This information is not shown in that figure, but it is kept in the graph as an edge attribute.

The second stage differs from the first one because relationships are mapped as nodes. Therefore, in this stage the graph has four types of nodes, as shown in Fig. 9. Edges in this graph have no attributes or labels. There are edges between nodes *Person* and *Acted*, *Acted* and *Movie*, *Movie* and *Directed*, and finally between *Directed* and *Movie*.

In the third stage, the *Acted* node type is substituted by a new node type, called *Role*. The *Role* node represents each role that a person had played in a movie. New kinds of edges are also added to the graph, between nodes *Actor* and *Role*, and between nodes *Role* and *Movie*. Figure 10 shows the graph example generated for the third stage of the experiment.

Results Analysis. Tables 2, 3 and 4 show some results for centrality measures: closeness, betweenness, authority and hub for SMDB experiment. Only some of the nodes with the highest values for each centrality metric are listed. It was considered directed and not-directed edges.

Table 2. Centrality measures results for model 3 on SMDB Experiment. Table from [6].

Model 3			
Non directed		Directed	
Closeness	Betweenness	Authority	Hub
Clint Eastwood	Tom Hanks	A few good men	Aaron Sorkin
Richard Harris	A few good men	Jerry Macguire	Al Pacino
Chris Columbus	Cloud Atlas	Speed Racer	Andy Wach.
Dina Meyer	Keanu Reeves	The Green Mile	Annabella Sci.
Ice-T	Jack Nicholson	Stand By Me	-

Table 3. Centrality measures results for model 4 on SMDB Experiment. Table from [6].

Model 4			
Non directed		Directed	
Closeness	Betweenness	Authority	Hub
Richard Harris	Tom Hanks	A Few Good Men	Aaron Sorkin
Clint Eastwood	A few good men	Jerry Macguire	Al Pacino
Chris Columbus	Cloud Atlas	Speed Racer	Andy Wach.
ACTED_IN	ACTED_IN	The Green Mile	-
ACTED_IN	Keanu Reeves	Stand By Me	-
DIRECTED	Jack Nicholson	A League Their Own	-
Dina Meyer	The Green Mile	Cloud Atlas	-

The results showed that the same three nodes had the highest values for Closeness and Betweenness centrality measures. On models 3 and 4 it is possible to note a change between the second and third places. On model 5, the node that represents the *Cloud Atlas* movie takes the second place on the ranking of betweenness values. This place is filled by node *a Few Good Men* on model 4. This situation is due to the fact that *Cloud Atlas* movie node has a lot of roles represented by a few actors. Note also, that this *Movie* node has the highest Authority value on model 5, i.e., many other nodes point to it.

Another interesting observation is the *Hugo Weaving Person* node. It does not appear at high positions on the Betweenness ranking for models 3 and 4. This particular actor has a lot of roles connected to the *Cloud Atlas Movie* node, and is connected also to other *Movie* nodes in the graph. Thus *Hugo Weaving* node has a bigger probability to be in the path of distinct pairs of nodes, and because of that it has the highest betweenness value for model 5.

Table 4. Centrality measures results for model 5 on SMDB Experiment. Table from [6].

Model 5			
Directed		Directed	
Closeness	Betweenness	Authority	Hub
Richard Harris	Tom Hanks	Cloud Atlas	Aaron Sorkin
Clint Eastwood	Cloud Atlas	A few good men	Al Pacino
Chris Columbus	A few good men	Jerry Macguire	Andy Wach
English Bob	Keanu Reeves	Speed Racer	-
Bill Munny	The Green Mile	The green mile	-
DIRECTED	Jack Nicholson	Stand By Me	-
Dina Meyer	Hugo Weaving	A League Their Own	-
Ice-T	"Paul Edgecomb"	Sleepless in Seattle	-

In general, it is understood that nodes with high betweenness values affect neighbor nodes betweenness values. Thus, we can conclude that when considering a relationship as a graph node, it may reduce the neighborhood impact. This is verified when comparing models 3 (relationship modeled as an edge) and 4 (relationship modeled as a node) results.

However, when a relationship multivalued attribute between two entities is represented as a node, this makes the related entities corresponding nodes increase their values in terms of betweenness and authority centrality measures. It means that if a node already has high centrality values for model 4, it has a good chance to increase these values for model 5, taking a higher position in the ranking.

In other words, representing relationship attributes in the conceptual schema as nodes in the graph, can increase entities importance on the analysis. Therefore it is important to evaluate if they should be represented like nodes or edges in the graph. According to the observations of this experiment, it was obtained the following heuristic.

Heuristic II. Assuming an R relationship $(n : m)$ between two entities E_1 and E_2, if an attribute P associated to R is relevant to the analysis, then P must be modeled as a node on the graph, connected to the nodes which represent entities E_1 and E_2 by two edges R' and R''. More formally as follows:

Given:

- $G = (V, E)$; graph
- $CS = (E, R, Pe, Pr)$; conceptual schema
- $E = \{E_1, E_2, ...\}$; set of entities from schema CS
- $R = \{R_1, R_2, ...\}$; set of relationships from schema CS
- $E_i = \{e_i^1, e_i^2, ...\}$; set of instances of entity E_i
- $R_k = \{r_k^1, r_k^2, ...\}$; set of instances from relationship R_k
- $r_k^z = (e_i^x, e_j^y)$; one instance of R_k connects to a entity' pair of instances E
- $Pe = \{Pe_1, Pe_2, ...\}$; set of properties (attributes) from Entities of schema CS
- $Pr = \{Pr_1, Pr_2, ...\}$; set of properties (attributes) from Relationships of schema CS
- $Pr_k = \{Pr_k^1, Pr_k^2, ...\}$; set of properties (attributes) from a R_k of a set R of schema CS
- $pr_k^{w,z} = (v_1, v_2, ...)$; set of attribute values Pr_k^w from relationship R_k associated to a relationship instance r_k^z.

Since:

- $E_1, E_2 \in E; e_1^x \in E_1; e_2^y \in E_2$;
- $R_1 \in R$;
- $r_1^z \in R_1; r_1^z = (e_1^x, e_2^y)$;
- $Pr_1^1 \in Pr_1$;
- $pr_1^{1,z} = (v_1, v_2, ..)$;

On mapping to graph G we have:

- $\forall e_1^x \in E_1, e_1^x \in V$;
- $\forall e_2^y \in E_2, e_2^y \in V$;
- If Pr_1^1 is important to R_1 relationship and Pr_1^1 is multivalued, then $\forall r_1^z$ and $\forall v_s \in pr_1^{1,z}: v_s \in V$ and $(e_1^x, v_s), (v_s, e_2^y) \in A$.

5.3 SMDB Experiment - Link Prediction Analysis

In this experiment, link predictions metrics were used in the context of movies dataset SMBD. A first version of the results obtained was presented in [7]. In order to predict connection between contemporary people in the dataset, only information about movies in a restricted time window are considered. The time window chosen correspond to years 1992–2012.

Data about name and birthday of people; movie title, releasing data and tagline; relationships about acting have been maintained. To store the dataset as a graph the **Neo4j** was considered and to analyze and visualize graphs, the **igraph (R)** package module was used.

This experiment can be divided in three stages. Each stage corresponds to a variation in graph model representation. The goal of the first two stages is to evaluate the impact of topological changes in the link prediction results.

In the first stage, the graph model keeps two types of nodes and one type of relationship between them. Nodes can be of *Person* or *Movie* type. The *Person* type nodes have one attribute called *Name*. *Movie* type nodes have three attributes: *Title*, *Releasing* and *Tagline*. The edges have just one type, *Acted_in*, and only one attribute, *Role*. Actors can have more than one role in their attribute. Figure 11 shows a graph cut-off obtained in this stage.

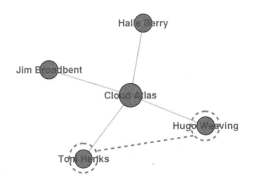

Fig. 11. SMDB graph cut-off for model 1. Figure from [7]. (Color figure online)

The second stage keeps the same information about the graph of the first stage. However, in the this stage there are three types of nodes: *Person, Movie* and *Acting*. The edges of *Acted_in* type of the first stage (connecting *Person* or *Movie* nodes) are now represented as *Acting* type nodes. Moreover, *Acting* nodes have an attribute called *Role*. In the graph of the second stage, nodes are connected by edges with no label and no attributes. Figure 12 shows a graph cut-off for this stage.

The graph model of the third stage have a small difference when compared with the second one. Nodes and edges are of the same type and have the same attributes in both models. But, in the new graph model, *Acting* nodes are split

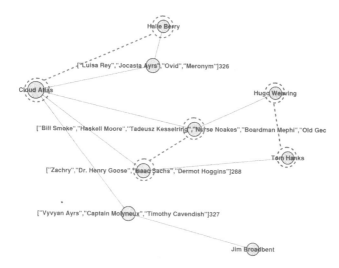

Fig. 12. SMDB graph cut-off for model 2. Figure from [7]. (Color figure online)

in as many *Role* type nodes as there are distinct role values for the *Role* attribute of the second stage. For instance, if some actor has two or more roles in a movie, the *Acting* node of graph model 2 will be split into two or more different *Role* nodes, each one representing a single role of the actor in that movie. Figure 13 shows a cut-off of the graph for the third stage.

Results Analysis. Using the corresponding metrics, it was possible to extract predicted edges. Some of the results were easy to understand and give a suggested edge between two nodes not connected before.

For instance, Katz coefficient was computed for every pair of nodes in the three stages of the experiment. Table 5 shows for four pairs of nodes the Katz coefficient obtained in each graph model. The analyzed pairs are *Person x Person* and *Movie x Movie*, the type of nodes present in the all graph models. On the other hand, there are some pairs of nodes that can not be analyzed in all the three graph models. For instance, common neighbor metrics as Jaccard and Adamic/Adar can not be computed for pairs of type *Person x Person* or *Movie x Movie* in graph models of stages 2 and 3.

Comparing the three Figs. 11, 12 and 13, we can observe the different conditions to compute common neighbor coefficient value for each type of pairs of nodes in the three graph models. For a specific pair of nodes, *Hugo Weaving* and *Tom Hanks* (highlighted in blue), the Jaccard and Adamic/Adar coefficients can be computed in first model, because in the corresponding graph they share the same neighbor, *Cloud Atlas* (Fig. 11). In the second model, it is not possible to compute the common neighbor metrics for this specific pair of nodes, because they do not share common neighbors (Fig. 12). However, in model 2 it is possible to compute those coefficients for the corresponding *Acting* nodes (highlighted in

Table 5. Katz coefficients for suggested pairs for 3 models in SMDB dataset (enclosed in brackets the ranking of each pair *Person x Person* and *Movie x Movie*). Table from [7].

	Model 1	Model 2	Model 3
Tom Hanks x Meg Ryan	0.188 - [363]	0.006 - [4239]	0.023 - [4629]
Tom Hanks x Bill Paxton	0.196 - [360]	0.006 - [4247]	0.022 - [4635]
The Matrix x The Matrix Reloaded	0.295 - [110]	0.009 - [4030]	0.010 - [6766]
Apollo 13 x The Polar Express	0.089 - [543]	0.002 - [5246]	0.075 - [2524]

blue). In model 3, it is not possible to compute the Jaccard and Adamic/Adar coefficients for the mentioned pair, for the same reasons mentioned in model 2 (Fig. 12).

Another example appears in model 1. It is not possible to compute Jaccard and Adamic/Adar coefficients for the pairs of nodes *Person x Movie*, because these types of nodes are adjacent in the corresponding graph, so they do not have common neighbors. However, it is possible to compute those coefficients in models 2 and 3 for that type of pair. The same occurs for pairs of type *Person x Person* and *Movie x Movie*. As said before, some pairs of nodes can be used to predict links by common neighbor based coefficients or not, depending on the chosen model.

Heuristics III-VIII. The following heuristics were identified based on an ordinary conceptual schema situation, frequently found in any domain, where a pair of entities are connected by one binary relationship, with a multivalued attribute, as explained previously.

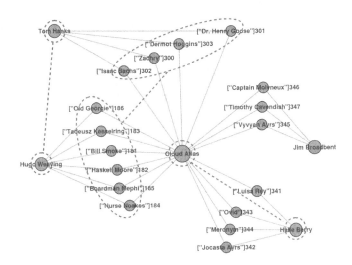

Fig. 13. SMDB graph cut-off for model 3. Figure from [7]. (Color figure online)

With respect to link prediction analysis, different graph modelings allow different interpretations and predictions. In other words, the choice of the graph modeling and the analysis to be used on it, depends on what it is intended to predict. The following heuristics addresses this issue.

Given the conceptual schema situation represented by Fig. 1, the first task is to decide the type of relations desired to predict. The different type of relations are: $E_{1i} \times E_{1j}$, $E_{2i} \times E_{2j}$, $E_{1i} \times E_{2j}$, $R_i \times R_j$, $A_i \times A_j$, $E_i \times R_j$ e $E_i \times A_j$. Once the type of relation to be predicted is defined, then just some of the following graph modelings possibilities will attend the needs. Consider the following alternatives:

Model 1: Instances of entities E_1 and E_2 as nodes, instances of relationship R as edges with labels;

Model 2: Instances of entities E_1 and E_2, and instances of relationship R are nodes connected by edges without labels;

Model 3: Instances of entities E_1 and E_2, and values of attributes A from R are nodes, which are connected by edges without labels.

Table 6 shows the correspondence between these three possible graph modeling, and five types of relation (pairs) predictions, identifying which model for each type of pairs of entities supports the metrics (Jaccard, Adamic/Adar, Katz) used for prediction.

Table 6. Suggested pairs of nodes for all metrics and models. Table from [7].

	$E_{1i} \times E_{1j}$	$E_{2i} \times E_{2j}$	$E_{1i} \times E_{2j}$	$R_i \times R_j$	$A_i \times A_j$	$E_i \times R_j$	$E_i \times A_j$
Model 1	Jaccard, Katz, Adamic/Adar	Jaccard, Katz, Adamic/Adar	Katz	-	-	-	-
Model 2	Katz	Katz	Jaccard, Katz, Adamic/Adar	Jaccard, Katz, Adamic/Adar	-	Katz	-
Model 3	Katz	Katz	Jaccard, Katz, Adamic/Adar	-	Jaccard, Katz, Adamic/Adar	-	Katz

For instance, for the first graph modeling possibility (model 1), if the user intends to predict pairs of nodes of the same entity, $E_{1i} \times E_{1j}$ or $E_{2i} \times E_{2j}$, then, all metrics (Jaccard, Adamic/Adar and Katz) are applicable. On the other hand, if the user intends to predict relations between different entities, $E_{1i} \times E_{2j}$, only path assembling predictions, such as Katz, are applicable. Based on Table 6, a set of heuristics can be formulated as follows:

Heuristic III: For predictions $E_{1i} \times E_{1j}$ or $E_{2i} \times E_{2j}$: Model 1 may be used for Jaccard, Katz and Adamic/Adar analysis; Models 2 and 3 may be used only for Katz analysis.

Heuristic IV: For predictions $E_{1i} \times E_{2j}$: Model 1 may be used only for Katz analysis; Models 2 and 3 may be used for Katz, Adamic/Adar and Jaccard analysis.

Heuristic V: For predictions $R_i \times R_j$: Model 2 may be used for Katz, Adamic/Adar and Jaccard analysis.

Heuristic VI: For predictions $A_i \times A_j$: Model 3 may be used for Katz, Adamic/Adar and Jaccard analysis.

Heuristic VII: For predictions $E_i \times R_j$: only Model 2 may be used for Katz analysis.

Heuristic VIII: For predictions $E_i \times A_j$: only Model 3 may be used for Katz analysis.

In the experiment described before, only three modeling alternatives and three prediction metrics were used. Other modeling alternatives and prediction metrics can be addressed in order to obtain more heuristics.

6   Conclusion and Future Works

In this work we discussed the benefits of graph modeling alternatives to represent data from relational databases. By means of experiments, we show that these alternatives can lead to different results. In addition, we also realized that it is important to guide the user on the choice of the graph model. In order to facilitate the user, we propose that the modeling choice should take into account the topological analysis to be applied on the data.

Three experiments were performed, using two different datasets and considering two type of analysis: centrality measures and link prediction. For centrality, closeness, betweenness, authority, hub and degree measures were applied on Zachary's Karate Club and SMDB datasets. For link prediction, the chosen metrics were Jaccard, Adamic/Adar and Katz, and those metrics. Those metrics were applied on SMDB dataset. Based on the experiments results, a set of heuristics were identified for the centrality measures analysis and link prediction. In the case of link prediction, a complementary experiment can be found in a previous work [7]. In that experiment, TMDB dataset was used to validate the heuristics presented in Sect. 5.3. The results obtained emphasize that both, conceptual and logical modeling are important for the task of mapping from a relational database into a graph representation.

The main contribution of this work is the set of heuristics to support graph modeling from relational database. Intended users are now capable to properly deal with modeling choices, relying on these heuristics.

Future works include additional experiments, using datasets from different domains, and a larger set of analytical coefficients, in order to validate or, maybe extend these heuristics. Moreover, as the reported experiments focus on binary relationships of the conceptual model, we plan to use other modeling constructs, such as n-ary relationships, specialization/generalization, and aggregation.

Acknowledgments. This work was developed by the first author as part of the requirement for his Master's Degree. The authors would like to thank CAPES, the Brazilian Governmental Agency, for the scholarship granted to the post-graduate student.

References

1. Aggarwal, C.C.: Social Network Data Analytics, 1st edn. Springer, Boston (2011). https://doi.org/10.1007/978-1-4419-8462-3
2. Bordoloi, S., Kalita, B.: Designing graph database models from existing relational databases. Int. J. Comput. Appl. **74**(1), 25–31 (2013)
3. Chen, P.P.S.: The entity-relationship model; toward a unified view of data. ACM Trans. Database Syst. **1**(1), 9–36 (1976)
4. Codd, E.F.: A relational model of data for large shared data banks. Commun. ACM **13**(6), 377–387 (1970)
5. Easley, D., Kleinberg, J.: Networks, Crowds, and Markets: Reasoning About a Highly Connected World. Cambridge University Press, New York (2010)
6. Filho, S.P.L., Cavalcanti, M.C., Justel, C.M.: Graph modeling from relational databases - (Portuguese). In: 2017 XLIII Latin American Computer Conference, CLEI 2017, Córdoba, Argentina, 4–8 September 2017, pp. 1–10 (2017). https://doi.org/10.1109/CLEI.2017.8226384
7. Filho, S.P.L., Cavalcanti, M.C., Justel, C.M.: Managing graph modeling alternatives for link prediction. In: Proceedings of the 20th International Conference on Enterprise Information Systems, ICEIS 2018, Funchal, Madeira, Portugal, 21–24 March 2018, vol. 2, pp. 71–80. SciTePress (2018)
8. Heuser, C.: Projeto de Banco de Dados: Volume 4 da Série Livros didáticos informática UFRGS - (Portuguese). Bookman (2009)
9. Jindal, A., Rawlani, P., Wu, E., Madden, S., Deshpande, A., Stonebraker, M.: Vertexica: your relational friend for graph analytics!. Proc. VLDB Endow. **7**(13), 1669–1672 (2014). https://doi.org/10.14778/2733004.2733057. http://dx.doi-org.ez29.capes.proxy.ufrj.br/10.14778/2733004.2733057
10. Liben-Nowell, D., Kleinberg, J.: The link-prediction problem for social networks. J. Am. Soc. Inf. Sci. Tech. **58**(7), 1019–1031 (2007)
11. Newman, M.: Networks: An Introduction. Oxford University Press Inc., New York (2010)
12. Rodriguez, M.A., Neubauer, P.: Constructions from dots and lines. Bull. Am. Soc. Inf. Sci. Technol. **36**(6), 35–41 (2010)
13. Simmen, D., et al.: Large-scale graph analytics in aster 6: bringing context to big data discovery. Proc. VLDB Endow. **7**(13), 1405–1416 (2014). https://doi.org/10.14778/2733004.2733013
14. Virgilio, R.D., Maccioni, A., Torlone, R.: Converting relational to graph databases. In: First International Workshop on Graph Data Management Experiences and Systems (2014)
15. De Virgilio, R., Maccioni, A., Torlone, R.: Model-driven design of graph databases. In: Yu, E., Dobbie, G., Jarke, M., Purao, S. (eds.) ER 2014. LNCS, vol. 8824, pp. 172–185. Springer, Cham (2014). https://doi.org/10.1007/978-3-319-12206-9_14
16. Wardani, D.W., Küng, J.: Semantic mapping relational to graph model. In: 2014 Computer, Control, Informatics and Its Applications, pp. 160–165 (2014)
17. Xirogiannopoulos, K., Khurana, U., Deshpande, A.: GraphGen: exploring interesting graphs in relational data. PVLDB **8**(12), 2032–2043 (2015)

18. Xirogiannopoulos, K., Srinivas, V., Deshpande, A.: GraphGen: adaptive graph processing using relational databases. In: Proceedings of the Fifth International Workshop on Graph Data-management Experiences & Systems, GRADES 2017, pp. 9:1–9:7. ACM, New York (2017). https://doi.org/10.1145/3078447.3078456. http://doi-acm-org.ez29.capes.proxy.ufrj.br/10.1145/3078447.3078456
19. Zachary, W.W.: An information flow model for conflict and fission in small groups. J. Anthropol. Res. **33**, 452–473 (1977)

Automatic Mapping of Business Process Models for Ontologies with an Associated Query System

Lukas Riehl Figueiredo[(✉)] and Hilda Carvalho de Oliveira[(✉)]

Institute of Geosciences and Exact Sciences (IGCE),
São Paulo State University (Unesp), Rio Claro, Brazil
lukas.riehl@unesp.br, hildaz@rc.unesp.br

Abstract. Business process models are employed in organizational environments to improve the understanding in the interactions between different sectors. They also help to better visualize the interdependencies from the processes that compose these environments. However, the understanding of these models is often limited to the visual representation of their elements. In addition, as the business process models become more complex, their readability and navigability are affected. It is difficult to represent and properly understand the implicit knowledge and the interdependencies of these models. The use of ontologies as a representation of business process models opens a complementary perspective to provide semantics to business processes. Ontologies conceptualize and organize the information that is embedded and unstructured in the business processes and that must be explored. They structure the implicit knowledge that is present in the business processes, enabling the understanding of this knowledge by machine. They also facilitate the sharing and reuse of knowledge by various agents, human or artificial. In this context, this work presents a systematic process to automatically map a business process model in BPMN v2.0 to an ontology, allowing to consult information about the model. To automate this systematic process, the PM2ONTO tool was developed, aiming to generate the ontology in OWL automatically, and made available predefined queries, elaborated with SPARQL, for querying information about the business process models.

Keywords: Business process model ·
Documentation of business process model · BPMN · XPDL ·
Ontology · OWL · SPARQL

1 Introduction

Business process models have been increasingly used as strategic tools by different enterprise organizations in different business areas, aiming to ease adaptations to internal and market changes. These models help business professionals in the understanding of the interactions between various sectors, as well as the interdependencies between the processes that compose an organizational environment. Despite of their

© Springer Nature Switzerland AG 2019
S. Hammoudi et al. (Eds.): ICEIS 2018, LNBIP 363, pp. 215–238, 2019.
https://doi.org/10.1007/978-3-030-26169-6_11

importance, the business processes are not always present in an organization knowledge base, being their manipulation and visualization limited to the modeling tools [1].

The understanding of the business domain is also essential for professionals in the area of Information Technology (IT), since they develop software solutions, which requirements must be adherent to the business environment. Business process models can assist these professionals in software development and also in automating the organization's process flows. However, the great difficulty faced by IT professionals in the understanding of the business domain is due to the distance between the vision/language of these professionals and those belonging to the business area. The notations used in these areas differ from each other, which causes a lack of communication between professionals of both areas. This involves the Requirements Engineering process, as observed by Przybylek [2].

The BPMN notation (Business Process Model Notation), a standard of the OMG (Object Management Group), presents a wide variety of graphical resources for the visual representation of a business process model elements. BPMN is a flexible, adaptable, comprehensive and easy-to-use notation by business professionals who can present different levels of knowledge [3]. On the other hand, although increasingly used worldwide, the BPMN notation presents a relatively complex specification for process modelers. The specification also does not rely on a standard documentation of business process models.

Problems with readability and navigation over the elements of a business process model can arise as these models become extensive. Often, the reading of these models is limited to the understanding of the graphic elements that compose the models and their relations. Moreover, the representation of the implicit knowledge of the elements from the models is complex, as well as the interdependencies that are not always clear in these models [4].

Some works, such as Gómez-Pérez [5], propose an ontological approach to business processes. In this approach, the processes are annotated semantically through ontologies, which makes them readable by a machine. Although they follow the ontological perspective, these works do not present an automated process that performs the mapping of a business process model to an ontology.

The representation of business process models through ontologies brings innumerable benefits to the understanding of these models. Ontologies contribute to the conceptualization and organization of knowledge that is implicit and unstructured in a business process. This knowledge can't be obtained from the visualization of business process models. It is also possible to understand this knowledge by a machine, since the ontologies can be expressed computationally.

In this way, this paper aims to present a systematic process for the automated mapping of business process models in BPMN v2.0 to ontologies described in the OWL (Web Ontology Language) language. With the representation through ontologies, it is possible to better evidence the relationships and interdependencies between the elements of a business process model. It is possible to consult these models using software systems, since they are represented by computational structures.

The input element for the systematic process is a business process model exported previously to one or more files in the language XPDL (XML Process Definition Language) v2.2 language. This language is specified by the WfMC (Workflow Management

Coalition) organization and provides an XML-structured file, which contains the process definitions. Before being exported, the model that will be used in the systematic process must satisfy some criteria, based on good modeling practices, besides presenting documentation of its elements.

The expected result with the application of the systematic process is a mapping of BPMN graphic elements, as well as the documentation in each of them, to the classes of a process ontology, evidencing the relationships and interdependencies among these elements.

In order to automate the systematic process presented, the tool PM2ONTO (Process Model to Ontology) was developed, which generates an ontology and allows predefined queries on the generated ontologies. This tool uses as input the XPDL files corresponding to the business process model that will be mapped to the generated ontology at the end of the systematic process. To perform queries about the generated ontologies, there were encoded instructions in the SPARQL (SPARQL Protocol and RDF Query Language) language. The Protégé system was used for the visualization and validation of the generated ontologies.

For a better understanding of the context of this work, Sect. 2 presents some related works that follow an ontological approach for the business process models, basically involving the generation of ontologies from these models. The objective is to show other important directions and differences in relation to the goal of this work. Section 3 presents the steps of the systematic process for automated mapping of business process models to ontologies. In Sect. 4 is presented an overview of PM2ONTO tool, as well as the process of mapping the XPDL elements considered in this work to the classes of the ontology, which uses as a basis a previously defined metamodel. Section 5 presents the application of the systematic process in a real business process model, as well as an evaluation of the results obtained. The final considerations and the future works are presented in Sect. 6.

2 Related Work

Some papers deal with the generation of ontologies from business process models. Among them, we stand out: [1, 6–8] and [9].

Although some present similar points to this work, none of them propose a systematic process for automated mapping of business process models to ontologies. The following five works presented differ basically in the following points: XPDL version used, mode of mapping the elements of BPMN to classes of an ontology, quantity of relationships and interdependencies considered, besides the use of different ontologies types.

Among the selected papers, only Haller et al. [6] and Missikoff et al. [7] export the models to the XPDL language. However, both works use versions prior to XPDL v2.2. In addition, BPMN elements are not considered individually in mapping to the ontology, as in this work. On the other hand, Guido, Pandurino and Paiano [1] define only basic relations between the elements of BPMN, not deeply exploring interdependencies. Nevertheless, in this work, all the possible relations that can be extracted from the context where each element is at the model are defined. The explored inter-dependencies evidence the relationship between two or more elements from the model.

The work of Guido, Pandurino and Paiano [1] defines a metamodel for BPMN notation v2.0. This metamodel is formed by classes and properties to compose an ontology, like this work. The metamodel also encompasses the same BPMN elements with the following main classes: graphical_element (subclasses swimlane, flow_object, connecting_object, artifact and date), lane, pool, and supporting_element (subclasses event_detail and participant). The definition of disjunction constraint classes is done as instances and object properties. However, the relations defined for the BPMN elements are limited and not self-explanatory. This makes difficult the understanding of inter-dependencies that exist in business process models. In addition, this form of treatment also makes it difficult to define ontology queries, since these queries often require interdependencies for meaningful responses. In this work, these types of problems were mitigated, since the metamodel contemplates both the direct relationships existing in the business process model and the interdependencies and elements involved in them.

Haller et al. [6] define a process ontology, called oXPDL, which is based on a file defined in the XPDL v2.0 language. The authors aim to apply ontology concepts to XPDL process models, so that semantic value is added to the elements of them. To achieve this goal, the authors present a tool that automatically performs the conversion of process instances to the oXPDL ontology. This ontology is described through five aspects: functional, control, informational, organizational and operational.

Missikoff et al. [7] seek to add semantics to the business process schemas with the use of formalisms and rules. For this, the authors propose the creation of a framework based on the BPAL (Business Process Abstract Language) language. This language is used in conjunction with domain ontologies to capture the knowledge of business processes. The capture results in an enterprise knowledge base. It is important to observe that, in this work, the construction of the knowledge base does not use logical formalisms, but rather a direct mapping of the BPMN elements to an ontology in OWL.

Fanesi, Cacciagrano and Hinkelmann [8] use the definition of a unified ontology (composed of several layers) based on the OWL-FA language (an extension of OWL-DL), with the objective of adding greater semantic value to the business process models. This ontology is composed by three layers: the first layer of the ontology is formed by metamodels composed by ontology classes; the second layer consists in instances of the classes present in the first layer; and the instances from this second layer compose the third layer. The authors use the multilayer ontology with the intention of allowing queries for the ontology on several aspects of a business process model. The ontology defined by the authors must categorize each class corresponding to an element of BPMN, as well as its instance, in a layer. In the explored approach by the authors, concepts can be classified as classes, instances or even as classes and instances at the same time. Following a different direction from the work of Fanesi, Cacciagrano, and Hinkelmann [8], in this work, all the elements of a model are defined as classes. This definition benefits the categorization of these elements from the ontology, as well as the definition of relations and interdependencies between them. The definition by means of classes also facilitates the definition of SPARQL queries for the ontologies.

Among the selected papers, only Fanesi, Cacciagrano and Hinkelmann [8] define queries for the generated ontologies. These queries serve as examples to explore the ontology classes and their relations. The authors also base themselves on these queries to raise some problems of representing the business process models in ontologies. Both the defined queries and the surveys carried out by the authors helped to define the systematic process presented in this paper.

Ternai, Török and Varga [9], like this work and Guido, Pandurino and Paiano [1], define a metamodel for the mapping of a business process model to an ontology. These models must first be exported to a well-structured and standardized XML file using the BOC ADONIS modeling platform [10]. The metamodel defined by the authors for the generation of the ontology is composed of the following classes: Actor, IT_System, Data_Object, Process_Step and Decision_Point. A script in the XSLT (Extensible Stylesheet Language for Transformation) language is used to generate the ontology from the business process model. If the script does not follow a predefined structure, not all template elements will be mapped to the ontology. The mapping present in the systematic process of this work uses, instead of a structured script, a metamodel that can be applied in any XPDL file to obtain the classes that will compose the ontology, because it is in conformity with the existing definitions in the XPDL files.

Although these authors define a metamodel, Ternai, Török and Varga [9] did not exploit all the elements of a business process model and their relations. For example, for the activities succeeded by a gateway, only the "Followed by" relation is considered in the metamodel, indicating the sequence of those elements in the model. On the other hand, this work explores all the relations between an activity and a gateway that are present in the XPDL files used as input to the systematic process. The context in which the element is found in the model is considered for the definition of relations and interdependencies. In this way, the metamodel defined in this work considers relations beyond those visible from the graphical representation of the elements in a business process model.

3   A Systematic Process for Automatic Generation of the Ontology

In this section is presented the systematization of the steps for the automatic generation of an ontology described in OWL from a business process model in BPMN v2.0. The expected objective is the correct mapping of the BPMN graphic elements, as well as the documentation associated with these elements, for the ontology classes. This ontology should emphasize the relationships and interdependencies among the elements of the business process model.

In this direction, Sect. 3.1 presents twelve criteria necessary for the mapping to the ontology to be successful. Section 3.2, presents the steps of the process to generate in an automated manner an ontology that represents the business process model selected for the generation.

3.1　Criteria to Business Process Models

In this work, the following BPMN elements are considered in the business process models: activities, sub-process, events, gateways (exclusives, inclusives and parallels), artifacts (groups and annotations), data objects, data stores, extended attributes, pools, lanes, sequence flows and message flows [4]. These elements are among the 20% most used in business process models, according to Borger [11].

The graphic elements from the model must be associated with textual documentation. Since there is no standardized way to structure this textual documentation of the BPMN elements, its format may follow the format of the used BPMN modeling system.

Before being applied to the systematic process, business process models must satisfy the following criteria, which are based on good modeling practices [4]:

- C1: every process must have a unique event, start event and at least one end, with names "Start" and "End" respectively;
- C2: a process must contain at least one participant;
- C3: the textual documentation of each BPMN element must contain at least one of its descriptive properties: name, description or documentation;
- C4: the name of an activity must use a verb in the infinitive;
- C5: the type of activities must always be defined;
- C6: elements of the same type must not have the same name;
- C7: an activity must be performed by at least one actor;
- C8: activity actions must not be assigned as gateway names (gateways represent the routing logic after a decision making);
- C9: sequence flows of an exclusive gateway must be named, except in the case that there are only two flows representing "Yes" or "No". In this case, only one of the names can be explicit and the other can be deduced;
- C10: sequence flows of an inclusive gateway must be named;
- C11: activities that are preceded by a parallel gateway must be connected at the end by another parallel type gateway;
- C12: activities that are preceded by an inclusive gateway must be connected at the end by another gateway of the inclusive type.

Some of these criteria are based on some of the business heuristics defined by Nogueira and Oliveira [12]. The heuristics defined by the authors are classified into four groups, with the BH (Business Heuristic) representation: business heuristics to document events (BHe), activities (BHa), decision flows (BHg), and artifacts and data stores (BHd). Table 1 presents the business heuristics considered in this work, which were used both for the definition of some criteria and for the verification of some relations between the elements of business process models. Among the criteria that were based on business heuristics are the C6 and C7. The C6 criteria were defined based on the heuristic BHa3, with the objective of avoiding the generation of an ontology containing concepts referring to the elements of the activity type of a model of processes with repeated names. Criteria C7, in turn, was defined based on the heuristic BHa1, to enable the mapping of the relation between an activity and the actor responsible for its execution. This relation is expressed in the ontology by means of the property "isPerformedBy" (Sect. 4.1).

Table 1. Business heuristics considered in this work [12].

Heuristic	Type	Description
BHa1	Heuristic for activities (*Who* item)	Each activity must contain the information of its executor
BHa3	Heuristic for activities (*What* item)	Activity name must be unique in model
BHe5	Heuristic for events (*When* item)	The information about the start of the event must be validated
BHd2	Heuristics for artifacts and data stores (*Who* item)	The data stores and artifacts must be related to the activities that manipulate their information
BHd7	Heuristics for artifacts and data stores (*When* item)	The data stores and artifacts must be related to the activities that manipulate their information

3.2 Ontology's Generation

The process for the generation of the ontology is composed by three steps, being the latter optional. These steps should be performed sequentially in the order defined below for a business process model, which must be in conformity with the criteria presented in Sect. 3.1 [4]:

- **Step 1:** the business process model in BPMN notation v2.0 must be exported to the XPDL v2.2 language through a system for business process modeling. Considering that the model has n subprocesses, this export will generate n + 1 XPDL files. This occurs when the subprocesses are defined as processes invoked by the main process (they are treated as a sub-process from the main process);
- **Step 2:** the PM2ONTO ("Process Model to Ontology") tool should be used to generate the ontology automatically, using the XPDL files generated in the previous step as input. The result will be an ontology defined in the OWL language that represents the original business process model. The PM2ONTO tool executes the following steps in this order, as illustrated in Fig. 1:

    2.1. Reading and mapping the XPDL elements for the classes defined from Meta2Onto metamodel (Sect. 4.1), which contemplate the BPMN elements considered in this work. It is important to highlight that the existing relationships for the XPDL elements that represent external organizations (pools) to the main process from the model are not considered for the generated ontology;

    2.2. Generation of the process ontology, which is composed by the concepts and the relation properties based on the classes generated in step 2.1;

    2.3. Storage of the generated process ontology in a database and provision of this ontology OWL file for download.

- **Step 3 (optional):** the Protégé tool (v5.0.0 or higher) can be used to validate and visualize the generated ontology. It is also possible with the use of this tool to apply one of the Reasoners existing in it. These structures have resources for inference. The inferences are made on the basis of the existing axioms for the generated ontology. Thus, the inferred form of this ontology is generated. This step is optional and it is recommended that it be executed when there is a need to verify the relations generated after the inference.

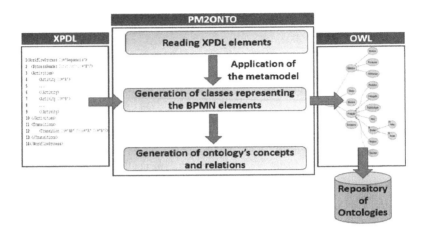

Fig. 1. Overview of the PM2ONTO tool [4].

The Reasoner, present in Step 3, is an inference mechanism, defined as a structure capable of making logical inferences from a set of semantic facts or existing axioms in an ontology [13]. They also rely on descriptive logic to verify the consistency of the ontology and to automatically compute the hierarchy class.

4   PM2ONTO Tool

The PM2ONTO tool was developed in Java v1.8 language and can be used from a Web browser for the generation of ontologies (source code: https://github.com/lukasriehl/pm2onto). PM2ONTO also allows queries about these generated ontologies (Fig. 2). Queries are defined in the SPARQL language and are used to extract basic information from the elements as well as their relations within a business process model [4]. The objective of the tool development was to automate the systematic process presented in this work.

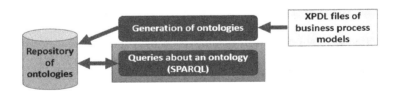

Fig. 2. Functionalities of the PM2ONTO tool [4].

For the generation of ontologies, creation and manipulation of the queries the Apache JENA freeware framework was used. The Hibernate framework (an implementation of the Java Persistence API) was used for object-relational persistence and mapping of the database; this allowed the storage of the generated ontologies in a database. The database system used was MySQL v. 5.7. The Protégé tool (v. 5.0.0 or higher) can be used to visualize and validate the generated ontologies [4].

Section 4.1 presents the process for the automatic mapping of elements of the XPDL files to the classes of the generated ontology. A short explanation of the choice for certain elements of XPDL is also presented. On the other hand, Sect. 4.2 presents the predefined queries in the current version of the PM2ONTO tool, as well as a short description of each of those queries.

4.1   Mapping Metamodel's Classes to Ontology's Classes

In order to enable the mapping of the BPMN elements to the concepts of the ontology, a metamodel was defined in UML (Unified Modeling Language) for this work, called Meta2Onto. Figure 3 shows a part of this metamodel in UML. Table 2, shows the relations present between the classes of the metamodel.

As can be seen in Fig. 3, all Meta2Onto metamodel classes, with the exception of the "Actor" class, have at least the following basic textual attributes: identifier, name, description, and documentation. They also present the type attribute, which makes possible the categorization in the generated ontology. The "Actor" class does not contain the type attribute, but contains the other basic textual attributes mentioned The Meta2Onto metamodel is composed by 21 classes, divided into 3 categories:

- Main classes, which are composed by the following elements of BPMN: "Process", "Pool", "Activity", "SubProcess", "Event", "Gateway", "Actor" and "Artifact";
- Auxiliary or enumerated classes, which define the types and other specificities of BPMN elements: "SubProcessType", "ActivityType", "GatewayType", "Event-Type", "ArtifactType", "GatewayDirection", "GatewayOutputs" and "EventTrigger";
- Relation classes, which define the relation between two and more elements of BPMN: "isSuccededBy", "UsesInput", "ProducesOutput", "ExchangesMes-sageWith" and "ExecutedBy".

Table 2. Present relations in Meta2Onto metamodel [4].

Relation	Source element	Target element
Is succeeded by	SubProcess, Activity, Event, Gateway	SubProcess, Activity, Event, Gateway
Is executed by	Activity	Actor
Exchanges message with	SubProcess, Activity, Event, Gateway, Actor and Pool	SubProcess, Activity, Event, Gateway, Actor and Pool
Uses input	Activity	Artifact
Produces output	Activity, Event	Artifact

The information defined in the XPDL file about the relative (coordinated) positioning of the elements in the business process model was not considered in this work. The information considered relevant to this work in the XPDL files refers to the following elements: processes, pools, lanes, subprocesses, activities, gateways and events.

The relations among these elements, defined as transitions, associations, executors (of activities), among others, were also considered from the XPDL files.

After being inserted the XPDL files related to a process model as input in the PM2ONTO tool, the elements of each XPDL file are analyzed for the Meta2Onto metamodel application and generation of the ontology. For this, Table 3 shows how the matches between the XPDL elements and the metamodel classes were made.

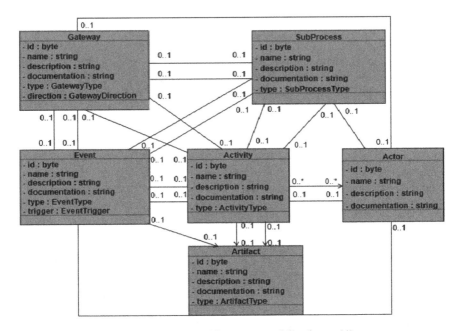

Fig. 3. Part of Meta2Onto metamodel's classes [4].

Table 3. Correspondence between XPDL elements and Meta2Onto metamodel's classes [4].

XPDL element	Metamodel's class
WorkflowProcess	Process
Pool	Pool
Performer	Actor
Activity (with element Task defined)	Activity
Activity (with element Event defined)	Event
Activity (with element Route defined)	Gateway
ActivitySet	SubProcess
DataStore	Artifact
DataObject	Artifact
Artifact	Artifact
Artifact (with ArtifactType defined as Annotation)	Annotation

(continued)

Table 3. (*continued*)

XPDL element	Metamodel's class
Artifact (with ArtifactType defined as Group)	Group
ExtendedAttribute	ExtendedAttribute
Transition	SucceededBy
MessageFlow	ExchangesMessageWith
Activity (with element Performer defined)	ExecutedBy
Data Association	UsesInput/ProducesOutput
Data Store Reference	UsesInput/ProducesOutput

The other elements of the XPDL files were not considered for class mapping in this work. The selected XPDL elements are considered basic in business process modeling because they appear in almost all models. The relations and interdependencies of these elements have also been included in the metamodel, as well as the common textual attributes of the elements: identifier, name, description, documentation and type. Among the attributes that were not considered in the metamodel version in this work, we highlight: details of the implementation of the activities of a business process and attributes that refer to graphic information of the elements of the models.

The elements identified as "Performer" have been mapped to the "Actor" class of the metamodel. The elements "DataStore", "DataObject" and "Artifact" have been mapped to the "Artifact" class of the metamodel. The "Activity" elements present in each of the process flows can define one of the following metamodel classes: "Activity", "Event" or "Gateway".

The actors were associated with the activities they perform from the mapping of the "Performer" elements when found within the "Activity" element. In this case, the relations between the actors and their activities were mapped to the "ExecutedBy" class of the metamodel.

The relations between the data objects and/or data stores with the activities or events defined in the XPDL files through the "DataAssociation" and "DataStoreReference" associations were mapped to the "UsesInput" and "ProducesOutput" classes.

When the "Activity", "Event" and "Gateway" classes present extended attributes associated with them, then those attributes must be mapped to the "ExtendedAttribute" class. In this work, the extended attributes bring important value to the ontology. These attributes are not always available in all BPMN modeling systems but are very useful and their use is encouraged. The extended attributes aid in the documentation of the business process model and in the identification of some software elements for this work. Figure 4 shows an example of an extended attribute defined for an activity ("Validate Invoice").

The categorization of these attributes in the ontology was performed based on some of the requirements heuristics (Table 4) defined by Nogueira and Oliveira [12].

The application of these heuristics allowed to identify if an extended attribute was a business rule, functional requirement or non-functional requirement. This identification was made through the names of the attributes. Attributes with the name "BR", "RN" or "RULE" are classified as business rules. Attributes with the name "FR" or "RF" are classified as functional requirements. Finally, attributes with the name "NFR" or "RNF" are classified as non-functional requirements.

In the mapping present in this work, after the identification of software requirements (business rules, functional and non-functional requirements), the "ActivitySet" elements were analyzed and mapped as subprocesses. For each occurrence of an "ActivitySet", the previous steps of mapping BPMN elements to the classes were repeated, aiming to define all the elements belonging to the subprocesses.

The XPDL elements that represent transitions (identified by "Transition") were mapped to the "SucceededBy" class of the metamodel. This class is composed of two attributes: source element and destination element. The message flows ("MessageFlow" element) have been mapped to the "ExchangesMessageWith" class, which is also formed by the "source element" and "target element" attributes.

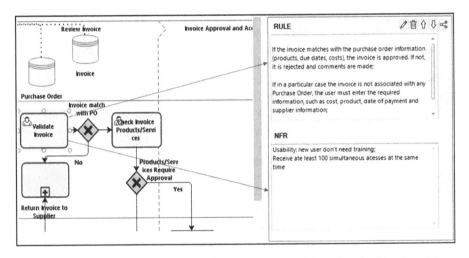

Fig. 4. Example of an extended attribute defined for an activity using the Bizagi modeler.

Table 4. Requirements heuristics considered in this work [12].

Heuristic	Type	Description
RH4	Heuristic of non-functional requirements	– The activities must have their type selected: "User", "Service" ou "Script" – Identify in the activities the extended attributes of the type "RNF"
RH5	Heuristic of business rules for decision flows	– Identify the decision flows – Identify business rules from the documentation of these flows
RH6	Heuristic of business rules for activities	– Identify the activities of type "User", "Service" or "Script" – Identify business rules from the extended attributes of type "RULE"
RH8	Heuristics for functional requirements	– Identify the activities of type "User", "Service" or "Script" – Identify functional requirements from the textual documentation of the activities

The Meta2Onto metamodel was created to define the possible classes and relations from the generated ontology by the systematic process. The ontology classes are categorized into levels according to the BPMN elements to which they refer. This categorization can be observed in Fig. 5. Each existing class in the metamodel is analyzed and then included as a new class in ontology, according to the defined categorization. The first level classes are:

- "AuxiliaryElements": this class is composed by the following subclasses: "EventTriggers", "GatewayDirections" and "GatewaysOutputs". The "EventTriggers" class defines the possible triggers for the event triggering. The "GatewayDirections" class, in turn, defines the possible directions of a gateway (divergent or convergent). The "GatewaysResponses" class defines the possible gateway return types;
- "Model": a class that contains the main information of the original business process model;
- "ModelElements": is covered by the classes of the business processes themselves (subclasses of "Process") and its elements (subclasses of "ProcessElements"). This class is composed by the classes of all the elements of a model. It relates to the "Model" class through the "isComposedBy" object property, indicating that a business process model is formed by a set of BPMN elements.

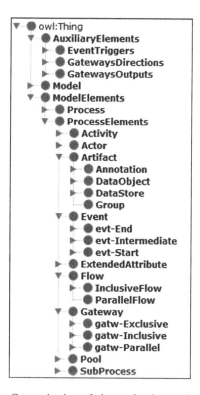

Fig. 5. Categorization of classes for the ontology [4].

The class "ProcessElements", present in the second level of the ontology, contains the subclasses: "Activity", "Actor", "Artifact", "Event", "ExtendedAttribute", "Flow", "Gateway" and "SubProcess". It is important to mention that the "Activity", "Event", "Flow", "Gateway" and "SubProcess" classes are categorized according to the type to which they belong. The Gateway class, for example, is categorized as "Exclusive," "Parallel," and "Inclusive," because only the exclusive, parallel, and inclusive gateways are considered in this work.

In order to better describe the "Model", "ModelElements" classes, besides the classes belonging to the second level of the ontology, the following data properties were defined, indicating the textual attributes of the elements of a business process model: "id", "name", "description" and "documentation". For the definition of software requirements, the boolean properties "isBusinessRule", "isFunctionalRequirement" and "isNonFunctionalRequirement" were created. The existence of the "true" value for these Boolean properties indicates that the class containing this property is identified as a business rule, functional requirement, or non-functional requirement, i.e., an element that is a software requirement.

The ontology classes are related through object properties. In this work, these properties relate two or more classes from the ontology and are divided into two groups:

– Basic properties: define the direct relations that can be assumed by the BPMN elements (Table 5). They are formed from the transitions, message flows, and associations present in XPDL files. Inverse properties have been defined for some basic object properties, such as "isPerformedBy", whose inverse property is "isExecutorOfActivity";

Table 5. Basic object properties defined for the ontology [4].

Property	Domain	Range
isComposedBy	Model	ModelElements
isPartOfProcess	Pool, SubProcess, Activity, Event, Gateway, Actor, Artifact	Process
isPartOfSubProcess	Activity, Event, Gateway, Actor, Artifact	SuProcess
isPartOfGroup	SubProcess, Activity, Event, Gateway, Actor, Artifact	Group
isSucceededBy	SubProcess, Activity, Event, Gateway	SubProcess, Activity, Event, Gateway
isPrecededBy	SubProcess, Activity, Event, Gateway	SubProcess, Activity, Event, Gateway
isPerformedBy	Activity	Actor
isExecutorOfActivity	Actor	Activity
usesInput	Activity	DataStore, DataObject
producesOutput	Activity, Event	DataStore, DataObject
hasExtendedAttribute	Activity, Gateway, Event	ExtendedAttribute
isAnnotatedBy	SubProcess, Activity, Event, Gateway	Annotation
communicatesWith	Pool, SubProcess, Activity, Event, Gateway	Pool, SubProcess, Activity, Event, Gateway

– Advanced properties: these properties aim to provide a better understanding of the interdependencies of the subprocesses, activities, gateways and events present in a business process model. Table 6 shows the four advanced properties defined, which are explained below.

Table 6. Advanced object properties defined for the ontology [4].

Property	Domain	Range
isActivateWhenEventIsTriggered	SubProcess, Activity, Event, Gateway	Event
isExecutedWhen [Name of the activity before the gateway] OutputIs	SubProcess, Activity	GatewaysOutputs
isExecutedAfterParalelExecutionOf	SubProcess, Activity	ParallelFlow
isExecutedAfterInclusiveExecutionOf	SubProcess, Activity	InclusiveFlow

The object property "isExecutedAfterParallelExecutionOf" defines the relation between a subprocess, activity, event, or gateway with the parallel flow that precedes it, if this occurs. It is important to enhance that this property is related to criteria C11, presented in Sect. 3.1, which indicates that all elements between two parallel gateways define parallel flows. All parallel flows that must be run before an activity are included as a subclass of the "ParallelFlow" class and associated with the "isExecutedAfterParallelExecutionOf" property.

The object property "isExecutedAfterInclusiveExecutionOf" is formed basically by almost the same characteristics as the "isExecutedAfterParallelExecutionOf" property. The only difference is in its usage restriction, where all elements between two inclusive gateways define an inclusive flow. All inclusive flows that must be performed before an activity are included as subclass of the "InclusiveFlow" class and associated with the "isExecutedAfterInclusiveExecutionOf" property.

4.2   Queries About the Generated Ontology

The implicit relations and interdependencies present in a business process model indicate the existence of knowledge that cannot be obtained simply by the observation of the model through modeling tools. In an extensive and highly complex model, the readability of its elements and relations is affected. Current business process modeling tools also do not provide resources for defining and executing queries about the business process models.

On the other hand, the representation through an ontology allows queries about the business process models, aiming to explore the classes and relations existing in the ontology. In addition, ontology representation enables the use of inferences, which can also be obtained through the execution of defined queries in the SPARQL language.

Thus, the PM2ONTO tool includes a set of pre-defined and structured queries in the SPARQL v1.1 language, so that users can obtain relevant information about the ontology.

Queries are classified into two groups, according to the type of information they return: Basic and Advanced.

Basic queries provide information about BPMN elements that have been mapped as classes to the ontology, regardless of the relation defined for those classes. These queries can use the following data properties defined for classes as filters: identifier, name, description, and documentation. It is also possible to filter by "type" the classes "SubProcess", "Activity", "Event", "Gateway" and "Artifact". The expected outputs for basic queries are the main information about one or more BPMN elements, i.e., identifier, name, type, description, and documentation. The possible filters for these queries are related to the values of the data properties from the ontology classes that will be exploited through the executed queries.

The Advanced Queries were inspired by the work of Fanesi, Cacciagrano and Hinkelmann [8]. The authors defined queries with the objective of helping to understand the necessary elements, as well as their relationships, in a business process model. However, most of these queries are done only about the relation between the activities and the performers of them from the model. Other elements, such as gateways and events, are not considered for the definition of queries. In contrast to Fanesi, Cacciagrano and Hinkelmann [8], in this work, were defined queries that relate, in addition to activities and their executors, the following BPMN elements: pools, gateways, events, sequence and message flows. In addition, the extended attributes of the elements of a business process model are also explored.

The eleven Advanced Queries defined in this work provide information about the relations and interdependencies between the classes generated for the BPMN elements. These queries were defined based on the existing object properties to relate two or more classes of an ontology and are listed below:

1. Activities performed by a specific actor;
2. Predecessor/successor element of a filtered element in the query;
3. Elements that perform messages exchanges;
4. Elements identified as functional requirements;
5. Elements identified as non-functional requirements;
6. Elements identified as business rules;
7. Elements that use an artifact as input;
8. Activities that produce an artifact as output (Fig. 6);
9. Activities preceded by an exclusive gateway;
10. Activities preceded by an inclusive gateway;
11. Activities preceded by a parallel gateway.

The Advanced queries were created aiming to explore the following relations and interdependencies between the elements of a business process model, considered relevant to this work: (1) relations of activities with their executors and the decision flow to which they are related; (2) activities or events that use some artifact as input to their processing; (3) activities that produce output artifacts after their processing; (4) elements from different pools that are interconnected through message exchanges; (5) predecessors and successors of the elements in the business process model.

In addition to improving the visualization of relations and interdependencies, advanced queries can also help identify software requirements by identifying functional and non-functional requirements as well as business rules (queries n° 4, 5 and 6, respectively). It is important to observe that the generated ontologies, when used in conjunction with the presented queries, can help to elicit and specify the requirements of a software solution.

Table 7 presents a summary of these eleven advanced queries defined for the PM2ONTO tool, in order to explore the relations and interdependencies in the business process models:

```
PREFIX rdf: <http://www.w3.org/1999/02/22-rdf-syntax-ns#>
PREFIX owl: <http://www.w3.org/2002/07/owl#>
PREFIX xsd: <http://www.w3.org/2001/XMLSchema#>
PREFIX rdfs: <http://www.w3.org/2000/01/rdf-schema#>
PREFIX j.0: <http://www.semanticweb.org/ontology/exampleOntology#>
PREFIX j.1: <http://www.semanticweb.org/ontology/exampleOntology#producesOutput#>

SELECT DISTINCT  ?id ?name ?description ?documentation
WHERE
  { ?x    rdfs:subClassOf    j.0:Activity ;
  |       j.0:id             ?id .
          j.0:name           ?name .
          j.0:description    ?description .
          j.0:documentation  ?documentation .
    ?activity rdfs:subClassOf ?activity_produces_output_restriction .
    ?activity_produces_output_restriction
          owl:onProperty j.1:
  }
```

Fig. 6. SPARQL code for advanced query number 8 [4].

Table 7. Summary of advanced queries defined in the PM2ONTO v1.0 system.

Query number	Description
1	Identifies which activities are under the responsibility of a participant in the process
2	Identifies the context which each element is embedded in a process, based on its predecessor and successor
3	Explain the interaction between two elements of different pools in a process. The interaction in this case is represented by the exchange of messages
4, 5 and 6	Identifies the elements of a business process model that represent software requirements, thus supporting the specification of software requirements
7	Identifies the elements that need resources for their proper functioning in the context in which they are present in the process
8	Identifies the activities that generate resources after their execution in the context in which they are present in the process
9, 10 and 11	Identifies the activities of a process that are performed after a decision taking or routing of the actions taken in the process

5   Example of Application of the Proposed Process

In order to show how to apply the systematic process presented in Sect. 3, the business process model in BPMN v2.0 "Accounts Payable" of the repository was selected: http://www.bizagi.com/en/community/process-xchange. This model basically consists of document validation activities (e.g. Invoices) sent by suppliers, so that the payment will be released later.

This model counts with four lanes: the accounting sector, areas of the administrative manager, financial assistant and of reception. Figure 7 shows the "Accounts Payable" model, which also includes the "Return Invoice to Supplier" subprocess.

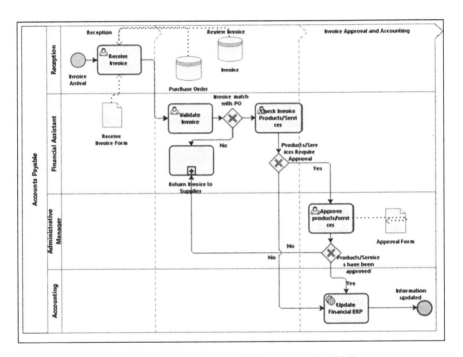

Fig. 7. Business process model "Accounts Payable".

In all, the "Accounts Payable" model counts with the following elements:

- 1 pool;
- 4 participants;
- 8 activities (5 of the "User" type, 1 of "Script" type, 1 of "Manual" and 1 of "Service" type);
- 5 events (2 of the "Start" type and 3 of the "End" type);
- 4 *gateways* (4 of the "Exclusive" type);
- 4 data objects;
- 2 data stores;

- no annotation;
- 4 extended attributes.

In relation to the adjustments required after the twelve criteria were verified (Sect. 3.1), the "Accounts Payable" model required few modifications to be stay in conformity with those criteria. In this model, were necessary the following adjustments in relation to the indicated criteria:

- C2: it was necessary to define the participants of the process "Accounts Payable";
- C3: some elements, such as the "end events" of the main process and subprocess, have been adjusted with definition of name and documentation;
- C5: the activities "Receive Invoice" and "Justify the rejection" were adjusted with the definition of the types in each one of them;
- C7: all the activities were associated with a particular actor for the execution of these activities.

After the necessary adjustments, the model in question was exported to XPDL v2.2 through the Bizagi modeling system (v3.1.0.01). A directory containing the XPDL file was generated. This file has been selected as input to the tool PM2ONTO, in order to apply Step 2 of the systematic. Steps 2.1 to 2.3 were then executed by the tool, generating the Accounts Payable Model ontology. A part of the generated ontology is shown in Fig. 8:

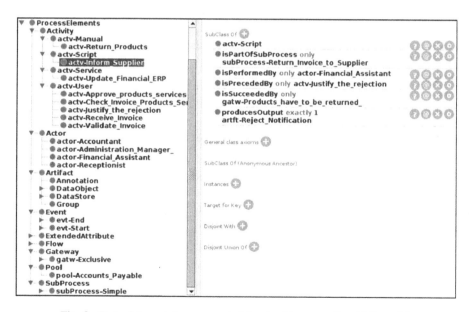

Fig. 8. Part of the ontology generated for the "Accounts Payable" model.

The generated ontology presented the following elements:

- 38 classes;
- 245 axioms;
- 3 business rules;
- 7 functional requirements;
- 4 non-functional requirements.

It is important to mention that all the BPMN elements and the associated documentation to them were mapped to the ontology as well as the relations between the elements. The ontology generated from the model allowed to better identify the interdependencies of this model. Example: the relation between two activities that are between a gateway, indicating that the routing of this flow of decision, after the execution of the activity that precedes it, invoked a certain activity. This interdependence is observed in the ontology by means of the axioms defined from the object property "isExecutedWhen [Activity Name] OutputIs".

Table 8 presents a comparison between the number of the flow's objects in "Accounts Payable" model and the number of classes of the generated ontology. In Table 9, the comparison is made between the number of connection objects of the model and the number of axioms generated by the object properties from the ontology. Table 10 presents the possible results after the execution of the eleven queries, based on the specified filters:

Table 8. "Accounts payable" model: number of flows versus classes generated.

BPMN element (flow object)	Quantity in model	Ontology class	Mapped quantity for the ontology
Process	1	Process	1
Pool	1	Pool	1
Participant	4	Actor	4
Subprocess	1	SubProcess	1
Activity	8	Activity	8
Event	5	Event	5
Gateway	4	Gateway	4
Data store	2	DataStore	2
Data object	4	DataObject	4
Annotation	0	Annotation	0
Extended attribute	4	ExtendedAttribute	4

Table 9. "Accounts Payable" model: connection elements versus generated axioms.

BPMN element (connection objects)	Quantity in the model	Object property from the ontology	Quantity of axioms with the property
Common sequence flow	10	isSucceededBy isPrecededBy	28
Message flow	0	communicatesWith	0
Flow sequence after exclusive gateway	8	isExecutedWhen[Name of the Activity]OutputIs	4
Flow sequence after parallel gateway	0	isExecutedAfterParallelExecutionOf	0
Flow sequence after inclusive gateway	0	isExecutedAfterInclusiveExecutionOf	0
Flow sequence after an event	0	isActivatedWhenEventIsTriggered	2
Association between an artifact and an activity, subprocess, event or gateway	6	– usesInput – producesInput – isAnnotatedBy	6
Performances (activity association with participant)	9	– isPerformedBy – isExecutorOfActivity	18

Table 10. Examples of results for the predefined queries.

N°	Filters	Results
1	Actor Name = 'Recepcionist'	Activity Name = 'Receive Invoice'
2	Activity Name = 'Validate Invoice'	Predecessor Name = 'Receive Invoice', Successor Name = 'Invoice match with PO'
3	Activity Name = 'Validate Invoice'	No results
4	Extended Attribute Name = 'FR'	Extended Attribute Name = 'FR'
5	Extended Attribute Name = 'RULE'	Extended Attribute Name = 'RULE'
6	Extended Attribute Name = 'NFR'	Extended Attribute Name = 'NFR'
7	Activity Name = 'Receive Invoice'	Data Object Name = 'Receive Invoice Form'
8	Activity Name = 'Inform Supplier'	Data Object Name = 'Reject Notification'
9	Gateway Name = 'Invoice match with PO'	Activity Name = 'Validate Invoice'
10	Gateway Name = 'Invoice match with PO'	No results
11	Gateway Name = 'Invoice match with PO'	No results

6   Conclusion

The goal of this paper was to present a systematic process, formed by three steps, for the automated mapping of business process models in BPMN v2.0 for ontologies in OWL. Some papers in this direction have been found in the literature, as presented in Sect. 2. However, these works do not exploit a considerable amount of BPMN elements, as well as the relations and interdependencies existing in a business process model. It is also important to highlight that some of these works do not propose an automated solution for the ontologies generation.

Many benefits can be gained with the representation of a business process model through an ontology. Ontologies improve both the visualization of the elements and the documentation of the model, as well as become clearer the interdependencies contained in these models. Representation by ontologies allows for inferences and queries about business process models. In addition, the readability of complex models (including subprocesses and documentation) is benefited, since ontologies present their classes categorized, which does not affect their readability as they become more extensive, in contrast to the models of business processes. This categorization of classes belonging to ontologies improves the organization, form of identification and navigability between these concepts.

Ontologies also make possible business process models to be used by different software systems, since they are machine-readable structures.

The navigation in a business process model through an ontology facilitates the understanding of the activities and the resources that exists in this model. It is possible to insert knowledge in the ontologies and to share it among the business teams and other teams of an organization, including the Information Technology (IT) team. Thus, the views of business and IT teams can be more aligned to the domain of interest, which also facilitates communication between them.

For the generation of more complete ontologies after the application of the systematic process, it is necessary that the business process models satisfy twelve criteria (C1 to C12) defined in Sect. 3.1, which are based on good modeling practices.

To automate the systematic process presented in this paper, the P2MONTO (Process Model to Ontology) tool was developed, which receives as input one or more XPDL files referring to a business process model. After that, a representative ontology from the model, described in the OWL language, is generated.

It is important to mention that ontologies enable comprehensive queries about business process models that are relevant to business and IT teams and that could not often be answered only by model representation in BPMN. Also, the business process modeling tools alone do not present resources for queries involving elements and interdependencies from the model; with tools for ontologies this is possible.

As future work to improve the process for the generation of ontologies, it is possible to verify the viability for using classes available by the "Schema.org" community, at the following address: http://schema.org/docs/full.html. These classes serve to describe concepts from different areas. They are structured hierarchically, being formed by super classes, describing generic concepts, and subclasses, describing more specific concepts of an area of interest.

The query system in the PM2ONTO tool can also be improved using the Apache Jena Fuseki. This is a feature present in the Apache JENA framework that provides an HTTP (Hypertext Transfer Protocol) protocol, allowing the execution of SPARQL queries for ontology data. In this way, the user could create their queries as needed, not being limited to the predefined queries of this work. In addition, there would have no longer the necessity to store the ontologies in a database, since the generated ontologies would be applied directly to Apache Jena Fuseki.

In order to improve the validation process from the generated ontologies and to evaluate their usability, the methodology proposed by Pizzoleto and Oliveira [14] can be used in the future. These authors define a systematic that is based on software usability testing techniques for evaluating enterprise ontologies. The objective is to verify, through human interaction, the navigability, facility/flexibility of use and apprehensibility of the ontologies, as well as to detect possible inconsistencies.

In this way, the ontologies could be adjusted according to the results of the tests. Usability tests could also be applied to the PM2ONTO tool to evaluate the interaction with potential users of the system. These tests could be based on heuristics or with the participation of users.

References

1. Guido, A.L., Pandurino, A., Paiano, R.: An ontological meta-model for business process model and notation. Int. J. Bus. Res. Manage. (IJBRM) **7**, 1–13 (2016)
2. Przybylek, A.: A business-oriented approach to requirements elicitation. In: Proceedings of the 9th International Conference on Evaluation of Novel Approaches to Software Engineering, Lisbon, pp. 1–12 (2014)
3. Correia, A., Abreu, F.B.: Enhancing the correctness of BPMN models. In: Varajão, J.E., Cruz-Cunha, M.M., Martinho, R. (eds.) Improving Organizational Effectiveness with Enterprise Information Systems, pp. 241–261. IGI Global, Hershey (2015)
4. Figueiredo, R.L., Oliveira, H.C.: Automatic generation of ontologies from business process models. In: Proceedings of 20th International Conference on Enterprise Information Systems (ICEIS), Funchal, pp. 81–91. SciTePress (2018)
5. Gómez-Pérez, J.M.: Studies on Semantic Web: Acquisition and Understanding of Process Knowledge Using Problem Solving Methods. IOS Press, Amsterdam (2010)
6. Haller, A., Marmolowski, M., Oren, E., Gaaloul, W.: oXPDL: a process model exchange ontology. DERI - Digital Enterprise Research Institute, 1–14 (2007)
7. Missikoff, M., Proietti, M., Smith, F.: Linking ontologies to business process schemas. IASI-CNR Tech (20), 1–20 (2010)
8. Fanesi, D., Cacciagrano, D.R., Hinkelmann, K.: Semantic business process representation to enhance the degree of BPM mechanization - an ontology. In: Proceedings of IEEE International Conference on Enterprise Systems, Basel, pp. 21–32 (2015)
9. Ternai, K., Török, M., Varga, K.: Corporate semantic business process management. In: Gábor, A., Kő, A. (eds.) Corporate Knowledge Discovery and Organizational Learning. KMOL, vol. 2, pp. 33–57. Springer, Cham (2016). https://doi.org/10.1007/978-3-319-28917-5_2
10. BOC Group Homepage. https://uk.boc-group.com/adonis. Accessed 19 Oct 2017
11. Borger, E.: Approaches to modeling business processes: a critical analysis of BPMN, workflow patterns and YAWL. Softw. Syst. Model. **3**, 305–318 (2012)
12. Nogueira, F.A., Oliveira, H.C.: Application of heuristics in business process models to support software requirements specification. In: Proceedings of 19th International Conference on Enterprise Information Systems, Funchal, pp. 1–12 (2017)

13. Kim, T., Park, I., Hyun, S.J., Lee, D.: MiREOWL: Mobile Rule Engine for OWL. In: Proceedings of 34th IEEE Computer Software and Applications Conference Workshops (COMPSACW), Seoul, pp. 317–322 (2010)
14. Pizzoleto, A.V., Oliveira, H.C.: A systematic approach to evaluate enterprise ontologies using testing techniques of software usability. In: Proceedings of the 14th International Conference on Software Engineering Research and Practice, Las Vegas, pp. 125–131 (2016)

DaVe: A Semantic Data Value Vocabulary to Enable Data Value Characterisation

Judie Attard[(✉)] and Rob Brennan

KDEG, ADAPT Centre, School of Computer Science and Statistics, O'Reilly Institute,
Trinity College Dublin, Dublin 2, Ireland
{attardj,rob.brennan}@cs.tcd.ie

Abstract. While data value and value creation are highly relevant in today's society, there is as yet no consensus data value models, dynamics, measurement techniques or even methods of categorising and comparing them. In this paper we analyse and categorise existing aspects of data that are used in literature to characterise and/or quantify data value. Based on these data value dimensions, as well as a number of value assessment use cases, we also define the Data Value Vocabulary (DaVe) that allows for the comprehensive representation of data value. This vocabulary can be extended to allow for the representation of data value dimensions as required in the context at hand. This vocabulary will allow users to monitor and asses data value throughout any value creating or data exploitation efforts, therefore laying the basis for effective management of value and efficient value exploitation. It also allows for the integration of diverse metrics that span many data value dimensions and which most likely pertain to a range of different tools in different formats. DaVe is evaluated using Gruber's ontology design criteria, and by instantiating it in a deployment case study. This paper is an extension of Attard and Brennan (2018) [3].

Keywords: Data value · Data value chains · Ontology · Linked Data ·
Data governance · Data management · Data value dimensions

1 Introduction

In recent years, it has become popular to refer to data as the new oil. This probably stems from the value that data is capable of providing through its exploitation. All data has social and commercial value [4], based on the impact of its use in different dimensions, including commercial, technical, societal, financial, and political. In fact, data has become an essential part of products and services throughout all sectors of society. Despite the growing appreciation of data as a valuable asset, there is little work on how to directly assess or quantify the value of specific datasets held or used by an organisation within an information system. For example, existing literature on data value chains, such as [8,26], simply describe processes that create value on a data product, however they do not actually discuss how to measure or quantify the value of data. Such data value assessment requires the monitoring of the dimensions that characterise data value within a data value chain, including data quality, usage of data, and cost. In real-world information systems this involves integration of metrics and measures

© Springer Nature Switzerland AG 2019
S. Hammoudi et al. (Eds.): ICEIS 2018, LNBIP 363, pp. 239–261, 2019.
https://doi.org/10.1007/978-3-030-26169-6_12

from many sources, for example; log analysis, data quality management systems, and business functions such as accounting. Without assessment, effective management of value and hence efficient exploitation is highly unlikely [5].

Amongst a number of challenges that hinder the quantification and assessment of data value, the lack of consensus on the definition of data value is an evident challenge that requires attention. Part of this challenge is due to the complex, multi-dimensional nature of value, as well as the importance of the context of use when estimating value. This indicates the need for terminological unification and building a common understanding of the domain, both for practitioners and for integrating the results of value assessment tools. The interdisciplinary nature of this field also resulted in a variety of term definitions. Moreover, current data value models, dynamics, and methods of categorisation or comparison, are also highly heterogeneous. These differences can be attributed to the different domains of study, as well as the various motivations for measuring the value of data (i.e. information valuation). Examples of these purposes include; ranking of results for question answering systems [2], information life cycle management [7,20], security risk assessment [36], and problem-list maintenance [22].

The aim of this paper is to answer the following two research questions:

RQ1: *What are existing dimensions that characterise data value?*

RQ2: *To what extent can data value dimensions be modelled as an ontology?*

By studying these questions we aim to gain insight into data value dimensions and the relevant data value metrics that are used to quantify data value, in order to provide a comprehensive model for exchange of data value metadata, and enable the creation of data value assessment frameworks or toolchains built on many individual tools that assess specific value dimensions.

In this extended paper we therefore contribute to the field by exploring the various data value dimensions identified in literature, as well as the data value definitions and models that they are based on. With the aim of providing terminological unification, we categorise the identified dimensions, and also provide brief definitions. Thereafter we define the Data Value Vocabulary (DaVe); a vocabulary that enables the comprehensive representation of data value in an information system, and the measurement techniques used to derive it. The Data Value Vocabulary is expressed as Linked Data so that tools or dataset owners can easily publish and exchange data value metadata describing their dataset assets. In order to ensure interoperability of the vocabulary, we reuse concepts from existing W3C standard vocabularies (DCAT [28] and DataCube [9]). Moreover, in order to cater for this rapidly evolving research area, and also for the extensive variety of possible contexts for information valuation, we designed DaVe to allow users to extend the vocabulary as required. This will allow users to include metrics and data value dimensions as needed, whilst also keeping the defined structure. In this paper we also gather together a set of data value assessment use cases derived from literature, and provide evaluation of the model through a structured evaluation of the ontology under Gruber's ontology design criteria, as well as through an example instantiation of the data value model in a deployment case study.

The rest of this paper is structured as follows: In Sect. 2 we define a number of keywords to set a common ground for the terminology used in this paper, Sect. 3 discusses related work with respect to data value definitions, dimensions, and models, Sect. 4

provides further insight into data value dimensions, Sect. 5 describes a set of use cases for data value assessment metadata, Sect. 6 derives common requirements from the use cases, Sect. 7 presents the Data Value Vocabulary (DaVe) and documents our design process, Sect. 8 evaluates the vocabulary with respect to objective criteria for knowledge sharing and through a case study, and finally Sect. 9 presents our conclusions.

2 Terminology

Due to the interdisciplinary nature of this topic, many relevant terms integral to the topic of data value are used in different contexts. In this section we therefore define such terms in the way we will use them throughout this paper.

Data - The Oxford dictionary defines data to be *"Facts and statistics collected together for reference or analysis"*[1]. Data can be gathered from sensors such as weather data, from surveys such as a census, or otherwise collected as a byproduct of a process or service, such as data about orders from an online retailer. Data can exist either in a digital manner or in a physical document. Moreover data can be represented in different formats, including text, images, and numbers.

In literature there are some distinctions made between data, information, and knowledge, where the latter two are usually defined to be data with the addition of 'interpretation' and experience respectively. In this paper we use 'data' in the generic sense in order to also include information and knowledge, since data certainly does not need to be in a "raw" state in order to have value. We here therefore treat the three terms as synonyms.

Value - In the generic sense of the term, Oxford dictionary defines value to be *"The regard that something is held to deserve; the importance, worth, or usefulness of something"*[2]. While this applies in most, if not all, contexts, different disciplines would have more specific definitions. For example, in economics, the definition and measurement of value would be in terms of currency. Other definitions, such as sentimental value, would be in terms of personal or emotional associations rather than material worth. It is quite evident that these varying definitions are tied to the subjective and contextual nature of value. With the aim of characterising the latter concept, we define value to be a number of different dimensions that in an aggregate manner represent the worth return of the thing in question.

Data Value - There are various definitions, interpretations, and aspects of data value in literature, however there is no agreed-upon standard. Based on the definition of value we provide above, in terms of data value is characterised by a number of dimensions such as quality, cost, volume, and content amongst others, that can provide us with the actual or potential benefit resulting from exploiting this data through its usage, selling, etc. This benefit, or worth return, can be financial profit or cost reduction, more efficiency or efficacy in executing a process, gaining insight/knowledge, more informed decision making, etc.

---

[1] https://en.oxforddictionaries.com/definition/data (Accessed 24th August 2018).

[2] https://en.oxforddictionaries.com/definition/value (Accessed 24th August 2018).

Data Value Model - In relevant literature, authors define data value models as a representation of the value of data. These representations include aspects that characterise data and its value.

Dimensions - In the context of (data) value, we define dimensions to be aspects that characterise the data. Due to the subjective and contextual nature of value, some dimensions may be considered to be more characteristic of value than others in a specific context. For example, the timeliness of weather sensor data might be considered to be more valuable than the accuracy of the data for weather forecasting.

Metrics - Metrics are used to measure dimensions. In the context of data value, metrics can be subjective or objective and qualitative or quantitative, depending on the dimension in question.

3   Related Work

Data value is recognised as a "key issue in information systems management" [40]. Data value is not a new concept; it has been extensively explored in the context of data value chains [4, 8, 25, 26, 30, 34]. The rationale of these data value chains is to extract the value from data by modifying, processing, and re-using it. Yet, to date, the literature on data value chains only provides varying sequences and/or descriptions of the processes required to create value on a data product, as opposed to directly exploring data value and its quantification. This makes it challenging for stakeholders to easily identify what **characterises** data value. Hence methods and metrics to measure it are still immature [38]. We here explore existing definitions and models that aim to define data value, as well as dimensions that are identified as aspects that characterise data value.

3.1   Data Value Definitions

The multi-dimensional nature of value, as well as the relevant role that context plays in the quantification of data value, both complicate the task of defining data value. In fact, there is as yet no agreed upon definition of data value, and the existing literature offers varying definitions. For example, Jin et al. define the value of data as a commodity to be determined by its use-value [20]. Maina similarly considers the perceived value by the users of the data [29], whilst Turczyk et al. express value to be the probability of further use [39]. Wijnhoven et al. consider data value to be subjectively determined by a number of characteristics, including size, date of modification, and number of accesses [41]. Al-Saffar and Heileman define information value to be a function of trust in the source, and the impact of a specific piece of information on its recipient [2], whilst Castelfranchi identifies the value of knowledge to be derived from its use and utility, and also from its necessity and reliability [6]. Sajko et al. on the other hand establish data value to be characterised by meaning to business, cost, and time [36].

3.2   Data Value Dimensions

Data value in literature is also depicted through different dimensions, matching the definition of data value that is being followed. These dimensions indicate that the value of data can very in different contexts, such as different points in time, and when being used by different consumers. For example, Chen considers usage over time to be the dimension that quantifies data value [7]. Higson and Waltho similarly consider the number of users to indicate the value of data, where the more people who use this data within an enterprise, then the greater the value of the data [19]. Moody also considers usage to be a dimension that characterises data value [31]. In fact, he also points out that unused data is actually a liability due to the costs of storage and maintenance, and yet no value is extracted from it. Wijnhoven et al., amongst other dimensions, also consider usage (through the number of accesses) as an indicator of data value [41].

Many of the data value dimensions covered in literature also overlap with data quality dimensions that are very much in line with recent research on data quality dimensions [42]. For example, Otto considers the quality of the data, which fluctuates during the data life cycle, to influence the value of data [33]. Viscusi and Batini concur, whilst specifically mentioning accuracy, completeness, accessibility, relevance, and timeliness to indicate data value [40]. Whilst pointing out its context dependence, Moody also indicates data accuracy to impact the value of data [31]. Apart from generic data quality, Higson and Waltho also discuss timeliness as a dimension that indicates data value [19]. Similarly, Ahituv suggests timeliness and format to be data value dimensions [1]. Even and Shankaranarayanan follow a similar reasoning where they focus on the intrinsic value of data and consider data quality dimensions that are both context independent and context dependent [14].

Utility, or the relevance of data to a business, is also a popular data value dimension in existing literature. Sajko et al. consider utility as a dimension of data value [36]. They define utility to be the ability of information to provide the required results. Viscusi and Batini also identify utility as a characterisation of data value, and they break it down into financial value, pertinence, and transaction costs [40]. Wijnhoven et al. also use utility, along with a number of other file attributes, to define data value [41]. Moody also discusses utility as a measure for the value of data, however he also points out that this approach of quantifying the value of data is challenging due to the difficulty and subjectivity of determining the specific future cash flows related to the data as an asset [31].

Examining existing literature that tackles the definition of data value resulted in a plethora of different dimensions along to the popular ones mentioned above. For instance, along with utility, Sajko et al. also identify meaning to business and cost as data value dimensions [36]. In a similar manner, Ahituv considers cost, along with data contents, to be data value dimensions [1]. Laney, on the other hand, explores the applicability to the business and the availability to competitors [24]. Higson and Waltho also consider the uniqueness of data (i.e. the unavailability of the same data to other competitors) to add to the data's value [19]. These authors also point out that the business user satisfaction is an indicator of data value. Al-Saffar and Heileman veer towards a more context-dependent dimension: the impact that specific data can have on the existing knowledge base [2]. They suggest using impact, as well as trust, to subjectively measure information value. Cost is also considered as a relevant dimension of data value. For instance, Chen uses the cost of information production, reproduction, and acquisition as indicators of data value [7]. Moody also discusses cost in context of data valuation paradigms [31].

3.3   Data Value Models

Despite the lack of consensus on the definition or characterisation of data value, formal methods for establishing the value of data or information have been studied at least since the 1950s in the field of information economics (or infonomics). Yet, the large variety of data value dimensions results in an equally large number of domain-specific models that singularly are not adequate to provide a domain-independent, comprehensive, and versatile view of data value. To date, there has been no attempt to specify a formal data value knowledge model. Moreover, existing models cannot be considered for providing complete answers to the queries and scenarios as identified in the use cases in Sect. 5. However one advantage of adopting a Linked Data approach is that our model can be interlinked with existing W3C standard models of usage, quality and dataset descriptions to form a complete solution for use cases like data governance driven by data value.

Moody and Walsh define seven "laws" of information that explain its unique behaviour and relation to business value [31]. They highlight the importance of metadata, saying that *"[f]or decision-making purposes just knowing the accuracy of information is just as important as the information being accurate"*. They also identify three methods of data valuation: utility, market price, and cost (of collection), and conclude that utility is in theory the best option, but yet impractical, and thus cost-based estimation is the most effective method. Sajko et al. differentiate between two methods for data valuation, namely a qualitative approach that is based on the relevance of data for the business, and a quantitative approach that is based on cost variables [36].

Other existing models, while representing a valid data value dimension, do not (yet) adequately model all aspects. For instance, the Dataset Usage Vocabulary (DUV) [27] fails to model usage statistics, such as number of users, frequency of use, etc. The W3C Dataset Quality Vocabulary (daQ) [11] is relevant but is specialised for capturing data quality metrics rather than data value metrics. Since these may overlap it sets an important requirement for the data value vocabulary that its metric definitions are compatible with those of the data quality vocabulary. In fact, Otto has also recently argued that research efforts should be directed towards determining the functional relationship between the quality and the value of data [33].

4   Categorising Data Value Dimensions

In the literature covered in Sect. 3 we identified a plethora of dimensions used to characterise data value. This variety emphasises the obvious lack of an existing standard for identifying the value of data. It also emphasises that context is a data value dimension that is quite relevant in any data value definition or quantification effort; which most authors in literature seem to agree with [13]. An important thing to note here is that from the literature we explored, we termed any data value aspect mentioned as a 'dimension' of data value. Yet, some of these dimensions are better termed as data value metrics. Our reason behind using 'dimensions' as a blanket term is to avoid being too specific at this stage, and risk discarding relevant data value aspects that are mentioned in literature. We clarify this aspect further in Sect. 7.

Table 1. Overview of dimensions identified in literature and their categorisation.

Categorisation	Intrinsic	Extrinsic	Data value dimensions in literature
Usage		✓	Usage, No. of users, No. of accesses
Cost		✓	Cost, production cost, reproduction cost, acquisition cost
Quality	✓		Quality, timeliness, accuracy, completeness, accessibility, relevance
Applicability to business		✓	Meaning to business, applicability to business
Utility		✓	Utility
Uniqueness		✓	Uniqueness, availability
Impact		✓	Impact, customer satisfaction, new knowledge/contents
Trust	✓		Trust, believability
File attributes	✓		File attributes, contents, format

Table 1 provides an overview of the dimensions mentioned in the literature covered in Sect. 3. Whilst not comprehensive, the table indicates the complexity of characterising data value. This table also clearly indicates the need for terminological unification, as many dimensions identified in literature are termed differently, but essentially mean the same thing. In an attempt to provide a generic characterisation of data value, we therefore categorise the various similar dimensions using a single term. We also indicate the nature of the dimension; intrinsic to refer to dimensions that are relevant to aspects of the data itself, and extrinsic to refer to dimensions that are more related to

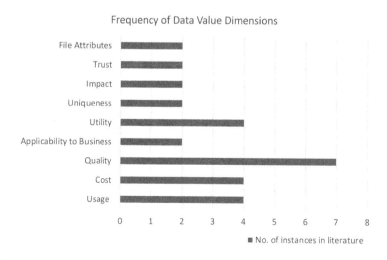

Fig. 1. Frequency of data value dimensions as mentioned in the analysed literature.

the context of use. In Fig. 1 we also show the frequency with which each dimension was mentioned in the literature we analysed. It is quite evident that the Quality data value dimension has the highest frequency. This might be an indication that data quality is regarded as a dimension that highly impacts data value.

4.1 Data Value Dimensions Definitions

We here provide a brief description of each of the categorising dimensions we identify in Table 1.

Usage - Authors such as Moody argue that data has no intrinsic value, yet it only becomes valuable when people use it [31]. Therefore, the more the data is used, the more valuable it becomes [20]. On this note, the usage of data is a domain frequently used to identify the value of data. Usage can include multiple aspects, including usage count, usage time, the source of usage, and the purpose of usage [7]. Usage can also be estimated (through usage patterns) for a future point in time, to provide a "value forecast" for data.

Cost - Similar to any other asset, data has a cost. This can be cost of capturing, producing or acquiring information, cost of selling, cost of storing, cost of maintaining, and cost of replacing or reconstruction costs [7,31,36,40].

Quality - This dimension is related to a number of aspects of the data that indicate its fitness for use [21]. These aspects can include the completeness, accuracy, timeliness, clarity, and accessibility.

Applicability to Business - Data is applicable to a business if it is relevant to one or more processes within the context of data exploitation.

Utility - Utility characterises data value in terms of use (value in use) and the benefits that can be derived from it [29,31,40].

Uniqueness - Data that is more unique and specific to the context in question will have more value potential than data that is easily obtainable. The more scarce data is, the more competitive advantage it will provide to its owner [23].

Impact - This dimension portrays the degree of change that the information will generate with its use [2]. For example, this can be quantified through data similarity; where if new data is very similar to existing data, then the impact will be much lower than if the new data provides new insight, or through customer satisfaction.

Trust - Data is considered to be more valuable when it is deemed credible and trustworthy by the entities using it [23].

File Attributes - These are aspects that are usually intrinsic to the data itself. These aspects or attributes may include the actual contents of the data, the size, the date of modification, and the format and structure in which the data is represented.

5 Use Cases

This section has the purpose of illustrating scenarios where a data value vocabulary can be applied. We here analyse a set of use cases that will provide us with the relevant information to then identify requirements for the vocabulary. We provide a description for each use case and then we proceed to demonstrate some of the main challenges to be addressed by the data value model. Based on these challenges, a set of requirements for a data value vocabulary are abstracted, usually as competency questions [35].

5.1   Data Value Monitoring

Data monitoring focuses on assessing and reporting data value throughout the value chain by gathering metrics on datasets, the data infrastructure, data users, costs and operational processes. In Brennan et al. we identified the data value monitoring capability as a fundamental part of any control mechanism in an organisation or information system that seeks to maximise data value, and hence data-driven innovation [5]. Data value monitoring provides us with a number of challenges that include the following:

- Integration of diverse metrics that cover various data value dimensions and which most likely pertain to a range of different tools, and therefore also exist in different formats. The goal here is to be able to build unified views of value from many data sources.
- Intelligent identification of the appropriate metrics that can be implemented on a given data asset. This could be supported by a knowledge model of the available metrics, the tools available to collect them, and how metrics are related to differing data value dimensions.
- Providing explanations about the context and measurement of a metric when reporting on data value assessment results, for example in data governance applications.
- Accommodating new metrics in order to cater for the evolving nature of data value and the relevant tools and metrics.

The use of a common vocabulary for data value metric metadata can mitigate the above challenges. This can be done through the annotation of the results of different tools, therefore supporting data integration. If the vocabulary is capable of identifying links between metrics and tools, it would be possible to query a knowledge base using the data value vocabulary in order to select appropriate tools. It would also be possible to support users in interpreting metric measurements of data value by encoding the context and metric definitions. For example, a user would be able to more easily understand a "Usage" metric if the definition of the metric is included, such as "This metric measures the number of times this dataset was accessed since its creation". The context would then provide further details on how the metric was used, such as the date it was executed, or the user who was running the metric.

5.2   Curating Data

Data curation is an intensive process that often requires human input from expensive and time-poor domain experts [16]. In Attard et al. we identify curation as a role that stakeholders can undertake whilst participating within a data value network [4]. The optimisation of the data curation process is therefore a possible application area, where data value estimates can be used to direct human effort. This has the following challenges:

- Monitoring data value in a curation environment (see above use case).
- Using data value estimates to identify which data value dimensions of a dataset are both scoring poorly and are suitable for remediation through data curation processes, e.g. increasing data quality.

- Enabling a data curator to identify which value dimensions for a dataset are relevant to a specific data value chain, and to incorporate them in a dataset description. This is to support targeting the most significant data value dimensions during the curating process and throughout the value chain.

5.3 Data Management Automation

Data value metrics have already been applied to drive automated data management processes, however most of such initiatives represent distinct value-driven systems that use data value metrics and estimates for a single application or purpose. Examples include file migration [39], data quality assessment [15], and information lifecycle management [7]. Ideally, data value-driven automation would be more generalised, whereby integrated tool-chains of applications would enable the results or output of one tool to be consumed by other tools in order to execute subsequent activities or tasks, such as dataset repair after value assessment. This use case has the following challenges:

- Enabling the coherent view of relevant dimensions and value calculations originating from diverse tools. This challenge is especially relevant due to the diverse value metrics and lack of common representation semantics in existing tools.
- No common format to express data value metric thresholding or targets.
- Capturing of the relationships between data value, data assets, dataset metadata, data quality metrics, and data quality engineering methods, tools and processes. This would enable the application of probabilistic or semantic reasoning to be applied to goal-setting, monitoring, and control of the automated data management control loop.

5.4 Data Governance Based on Data Value

According to Tallon, data governance must become a facilitator of value creation as well as managing risk [38]. However, organisations are still not fully capable of understanding how big data can create value [12]. The governance of Big Data could drive business model innovation [10], i.e. the appropriate deployment of data to develop new products and services based on the data, or the exploitation of data to transform how key organisational functions operate. Essentially, the most direct way to map between corporate strategy and data operations is to create links between data assets and organisational value as a basis for data governance. The challenges of this use case are as follows:

- Flexibly representing data value so that it can be related to other business domain models such as data assets, business goals, key employees, and organisational knowledge.
- Optimal execution of data value chains. Existing data value chains are not optimally executed, in part due to a lack of data value estimates.
- Supporting operational decision making processes by informing them of high relevance and high value data assets and organisational information channels or processes.

- Identification of value faults or issues within data value chains over time in order to initiate mitigating actions.
- Estimating data value for data acquisition decisions to ensure its utility and "worth" in a specific context.

6   Requirements for a Data Value Vocabulary

Based on the data value dimensions that are discussed in existing literature, as well as through the use cases and challenges described above, we have established the following requirements for the data value vocabulary. Each requirement has been validated according to three criteria: (1) Is the requirement specifically relevant to data value representation and reasoning? (2) Does the requirement encourage reuse or publication of data value meta data as (enterprise) linked data? (3) Is the requirement testable? Only requirements meeting those three criteria have been included.

1. The vocabulary should be able to represent data value comprehensively through a common representation.
2. It must be possible to extend the vocabulary with new metrics and assign them to specific data quality dimensions;
3. Data value metrics should enable the association to a set of measurements that are distributed over time;
4. It should be possible to associate a data asset (dataset) to a set of documented, and, if available, standardised value metrics;
5. It must be possible to associate a metric with a specific tool or toolset that supports generation of that metric; and
6. It must be possible to define the meaning of data value in the context of a specific data asset in terms of a number of dimensions, metrics and metric groups.

In addition we adopt the general requirements for data vocabularies from the W3C Data on the Web Best Practices Use Cases and Requirements working group note[3] to guide us on vocabulary engineering requirements:

- Vocabularies should be clearly documented;
- Vocabularies should be shared in an open way;
- Existing reference vocabularies should be reused where possible; and
- Vocabularies should include versioning information.

7   Data Value Vocabulary - DaVe

In this section we use ontology engineering techniques and standard vocabularies in order to define a vocabulary that enables the comprehensive representation of data value. This vocabulary will enable the quantification of data value in a concrete and standardised manner. The Data Value Vocabulary[4] (DaVe) is a light-weight core vocabulary for enabling the representation of data value quantification results as linked data. This will allow stakeholders to easily re-use and manipulate data value metadata, whilst also representing information on the dataset in question in other suitable vocabularies such as the W3C DCAT vocabulary for metadata describing datasets.

---

[3] https://www.w3.org/TR/dwbp-ucr/.

[4] http://theme-e.adaptcentre.ie/dave/.

7.1 Vocabulary Design

Data value is both subjective and context dependent. This particular characteristic of data value makes the definition of a generic data value vocabulary quite challenging. In fact, varying contexts of use will require the quantification of different value dimensions, and therefore the use of the relevant metrics. In Fig. 2, we present DaVe, an abstract metadata model that, through extending the vocabulary, enables a comprehensive representation of Data Value. This representation will also be fluid in that it will allow the use of custom data value dimensions that are relevant to the context in question, whilst also maintaining interoperability. For DaVe we follow the Architectural Ontology Design Pattern[5] which affects the overall shape of the ontology and aims to constrain how the ontology should look like. This pattern is shared with the Dataset Quality Vocabulary (daQ) for its structure, and thus increases interoperability between the vocabularies and easily allows reuse of data quality metrics as metrics for data value dimensions when deemed appropriate.

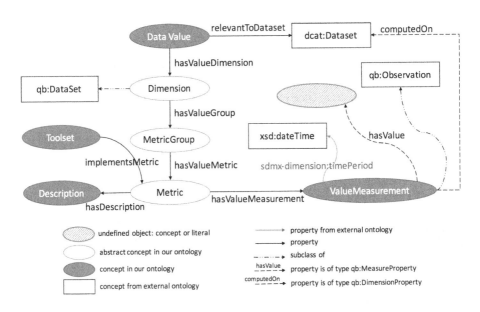

Fig. 2. The Data Value Vocabulary - DaVe [3].

All data value metadata will be contained in the *DataValue* concept, which is essentially the central concept within DaVe. As shown in Fig. 2, in DaVe, we distinguish between three layers of abstraction. A DataValue concept consists of a number of different *Dimensions*, which in turn contain a number of *MetricGroups*. Each Metric Group then has one or more *Metrics* that quantify the Dimension that is being assessed. This relationship is formalised as follows:

---

[5] http://ontologydesignpatterns.org/wiki/Category:ArchitecturalOP.

Definition 1

$$V \subseteq D,$$
$$D \subseteq G,$$
$$G \subseteq M;$$

where V is the DataValue concept (dave:DataValue), $D = \{d_1, d_2, ..., d_x\}$ is the set of all possible data value dimensions (dave:Dimension), $G = \{g_1, g_2, ..., g_y\}$ is the set of all possible data value metric groups (dave:MetricGroup), $M = \{m_1, m_2, ..., m_z\}$ is the set of all possible data value metrics (dave:Metric), and $x, y, z \in \mathbb{N}$ [3].

These three abstract classes are not intended to be used directly in a DataValue instance. Rather, they should be used as parent classes to define a more specific data value characterisation. We describe the abstract classes as follows:

- **dave:Dimension** - This represents the highest level of the characterisation of data value. A Dimension contains a number of data value Metric Groups. It is a subclass of qb:DataSet; the W3C Data Cube DataSet. This enables rich metadata to be attached describing both the structure of the data collected in this dimension, and conceptual descriptions of the dimensions through W3C Simple Knowledge Organisation System (SKOS) models[6].
- **dave:MetricGroup** - A metric group is the second level of characterisation of data value, and represents a group of metrics that are related to each other, e.g. by being a recognised set of independent proxies for a given data value dimension.
- **dave:Metric** - This is the smallest unit of characterisation of data value. This concept represents metrics that are heuristics designed to fit a specific assessment situation. The dave:ValueMeasurement class is used to represent an instance of an actual measurement of a data value analysis.

The RDF Data Cube Vocabulary [9] and the Data Catalog Vocabulary (DCAT) [28] W3C standard vocabularies are both used in DaVe. The DCAT Vocabulary, through dcat:Dataset, has the purpose of identifying and describing the dataset that is analysed with the intention of measuring its value. On the other hand, the Data Cube Vocabulary enables the representation of data value metadata of a dataset as a collection of readings. This is essential to provide for the requirements as identified in Sect. 6. Therefore, through the use of the Data Cube Vocabulary, users of DaVe will be able to:

- view all the metrics and their respective value measurements, grouped by dimension;
- view the various available value measurements for a specific metric (typically collected at different points in time as the dataset evolves);

We describe the remaining concepts within DaVe as follows:

- **dave:ValueMeasurement** - As a subclass of qb:Observation, this concept enables the representation of multiple readings of a single metric, as they occur, for

---

[6] https://www.w3.org/2004/02/skos/.

example, on different points in time, or otherwise for different revisions of the same dataset. `dave:ValueMeasurement` also provides links to the dataset that the metric was computed on through the `dave:computedOn` property, a timestamp when the metric was computed through the `sdmx-dimension:timePeriod` property, and the resulting value of the metric through the `dave:hasValue` property. The latter value is multi-typed since results might vary amongst different types, including boolean, floating point numbers, integers, etc.

- **`dave:Toolset`** - This concept provides a link to a toolset or framework that provides functionality for a specific metric, therefore enabling users to easily identify the toolsets supporting the value metrics they require.
- **`dave:Description`** - This concept provides an overview of the metric and the context in which it is used.

7.2 Extending and Instantiating the Ontology

In order to comprehensively model data value, a user will need to extend the DaVe vocabulary with new data value measures that inherit the defined abstract concepts `dave:Dimension`, `dave:MetricGroup`, and `dave:Metric`. This will enable a user to represent data value in the specific domain at hand. Figure 3 portrays how DaVe can be extended with specific data value measures (T-Box). These measures can then be used to represent actual data value metadata (A-Box). In Fig. 3 we extend DaVe with Cost as an example of the `dave:Dimension` concept, Economic Value as an example of `dave:MetricGroup`, and PurchaseCost as an example `dave:Metric`. According to LOD best practices, such extensions should not be included in DaVe's own namespace. For this reason we recommend users to extend DaVe in their own namespaces. In future work we plan to provide sample dimension and metric specifications using DaVe that will be refined via community feedback and serve as a catalog of examples that DaVe users can reuse directly or draw upon to build their own specifications.

8 Evaluating DaVe

In this section we provide preliminary evaluation of the DaVe vocabulary in two ways; by leading out a structured analysis on the features of the ontology, and by applying the vocabulary to a use case in order to validate its usability and capability of modelling data value in context.

8.1 Design-Oriented Evaluation

In Table 2 we present the evaluation of the DaVe vocabulary in accordance to the desired qualities expected from a well designed ontology. We here implement a methodology that follows the structured analysis approach laid out in [37]. We therefore define a number of generic and specific criteria, and evaluate our ontology according to how it fares with regard to these criteria.

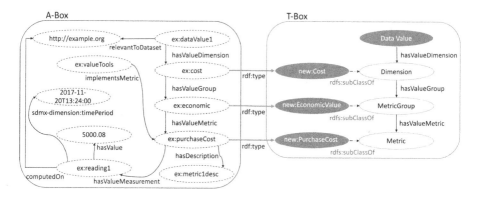

Fig. 3. Extending DaVe - A-Box and T-Box [3].

We have also evaluated the ontology in accordance to one of the most widely adapted, objective criteria for the design of ontologies for knowledge sharing; the principles proposed by Gruber [18].

- **Clarity** - DaVe meets two of Gruber's three criteria for clarity in ontological definitions as follows:
  1. Conceptualisation in DaVe focuses solely on modelling the requirements for recording data value metric measurements and their grouping into data value dimensions, irrespective of the computational framework in which these will be implemented (Gruber's "independence from social and computational contexts");
  2. Definitions in DaVe (such as the definition of `dave:Metric`) have not been asserted in every case using necessary and sufficient conditions, due to the additional complexity this definition style places on the interpretation of the vocabulary (Gruber's recommendation of providing logical axioms); and
  3. Finally, DaVe has been very well documented with labels and comments (Gruber's requirement for natural language documentation).

- **Coherence** - There are two aspects to coherence according to Gruber:
  1. Definitions in an ontology must be logically consistent with the inferences that can be derived from it; and
  2. The logical axioms of the ontology and its natural language documentation should be consistent.

DaVe has been checked using popular reasoners for logical consistency, although further work will have to be done on applications and field trials to explore the range of the inferences possible and to validate them. DaVe has been extensively documented using inline comments, labels and metadata using the LODE[7] documentation generation framework. This process ensures that ontology engineers working on DaVe can easily update the documentation when updating the vocabulary and

---

[7] http://www.essepuntato.it/lode.

Table 2. Evaluating the DaVe vocabulary [3].

Generic criteria	Evaluation
Value addition	(1) The vocabulary adds data value specific metadata to the processes of data management/data governance/data value chain management, and enriches information about datasets to include data value metrics and their collection context. Tools can then use this context dependent information for automation and automatic generation purposes.
	(2) DaVe is used to provide details about the data value assessment process outcomes.
	(3) It links together related concepts in data value, data quality, data usage and data catalogs.
	(4) DaVe can also help inform governance decision-making or reasoning about data value dimensions, metrics, and tools in a governance knowledge base, for example to enable metric selection or combination.
Reuse	(1) Potential reuse across a wider community of data producers, data value chain managers, dataset managers, ontology engineers of new or related vocabularies.
	(2) Potential users and uses of DaVe include developers of data profiling/assessment tools, data governance platforms, decision support systems, and business intelligence systems.
	(3) The vocabulary is easy to reuse and published on the Web together with detailed documentation. It defines a general abstraction of value dimensions and metrics that can be extended for specific use cases or domains. Furthermore, the models are extendable and can be inherited by specialised domain ontologies for specific data governance platforms.
Design and technical quality	(1) All ontologies have been designed as OWL DL ontologies, in accordance to ontology engineering principles [32].
	(2) Axiomatisations in the ontologies have been defined based on the competency questions identified during requirements scoping.
	(3) The vocabulary has been validated by the OOPs! ontology pitfall scanner (http://oops.linkeddata.es/).
	(4) The ontology contains descriptive, licensing, and versioning metadata.
Availability	The ontology has been made publicly available at http://theme-e. adaptcentre.ie/dave. Furthermore, it has been given persistent w3id URIs, deployed on public facing servers, and is content negotiable. The vocabulary is licensed under a Creative Commons Attribution License. DaVe has also been registered in LOV (http://lov.okfn.org/dataset/lov/vocabs/dave).
Sustainability	The ontology is deployed on a public Github repository. It is supported by the ADAPT Centre, a long-running Irish government funded research centre. Long term sustainability has been assured by the ontology engineers involved in the design.

Table 2. (*continued*)

Specific criteria	Evaluation
Design suitability	The vocabulary has been developed in close association with the requirements emerging from potentially exploiting applications, as presented in the use cases section of this paper. Thus they closely conform to the suitability of the tasks for which they have been designed.
Design elegance and quality	Axiomatisation in the ontologies have been developed following Gruber's principles of clarity, coherence, extendability, minimum encoding bias, and minimum ontological commitment [18]. These ontologies are based on the ADAPT Centre's past history of vocabulary standards development with the W3C.
Logical correctness	The ontologies have been verified using DL reasoners for satisfiability, incoherency and inconsistencies. The OOPs! model checker has been deployed to validate the ontologies.
External resources reuse	Concepts from external ontologies such as W3C's Data Cube and the DCAT vocabulary have been used in DaVe. Moreover, other ontologies such as the Data Quality Ontology daQ and the Dataset Usage Vocabulary DUV can be used in instances of the ontology as required by the user and the context of data use.
Documentation	The vocabulary have been well documented using rdfs:label, rdfs:comment and author metadata. HTML documentation via the LODE service (http://www.essepuntato.it/lode) has also been enabled. All ontologies have been graphically illustrated. This paper also documents the vocabulary, its use cases and provides example instances.

that documentation generation is automatic and nearly instantaneous, which facilities validation and consistency checking.

- **Extendibility** - Gruber states that to ensure extendibility, a vocabulary should allow for monotonic extensions of the ontology. For DaVe we have reused the structural pattern of the Data Quality ontology (DaQ), where we define an abstract metric framework designed to be extended with new data value concepts as required, whilst still maintaining the defined structure and existing definitions.
- **Minimal encoding bias** - For wider adoption of the ontology, Gruber states that the ontology should use a conceptualisation mechanism that minimises the dependencies on encoding formats. DaVe has been formalised in OWL 2, which is a W3C standard for representing ontologies on the Web. It has its foundations in Description Logics. Multiple serialisation formats are available for the ontology. The axiomatisation in DaVe is therefore accessible to all tools and frameworks that support these serialisations. There are limits to the expressivity of OWL [17] and it has modelling quirks that impact on any conceptualisations it captures, but nonetheless it has been designed specifically for knowledge capture and to minimise the impact on models.
- **Minimum ontological commitment** - Gruber's final test requires that an ontology should only make assertions that require only a minimum commitment from

implementing agents, providing them the flexibility to extend and enrich the ontology, albeit in a monotonic way. DaVe meets this criteria in at least two ways:

1. It minimises the number of imported ontologies. Each imported ontology or referenced term has been assessed for the impact it has on the overall model and incomplete, inconsistent, or overly wide ontologies have not been included.
2. Rather than providing a static model of the data value domain based on our current understanding, DaVe provides a framework of value dimensions, metrics, and measurements with their relationships which is designed to be extended to incorporate new metrics, dimensions, and tools.

8.2 Use Case Driven Evaluation

In this section we describe a deployment scenario for DaVe in MyVolts Ltd.[8]; an Irish data-driven online retailer, that wishes to assess data value to drive internal business process optimisation.

MyVolts is a successful SME with a 15 year track record that develops and operates a highly automated internet retail and business intelligence system. They are a significant source for consumer device power supplies in the markets where they operate. They have served over 1 million customers in the USA, Ireland, the UK, France, and Germany. Aside from importing and designing standard power supplies, MyVolts also produce their own power products. This SME collects, manages and analyses data on their customers, the evolving market of power supply device specifications, and the power supply needs of all consumer electronics. They gather this data through monitoring social media, web sales data such as Amazon top seller lists, customer queries and complaints, and device manufacturer homepages. Through this process they discover new consumer electronic devices, which then need to be categorised, profiled for potential sales value, and have their power supply technical specifications (voltage, polarity, tip type, and dimensions) mined from open web data. There are an estimated 5.5 million consumer electronics devices on sale today and the number of powered devices is growing rapidly. A major challenge that MyVolts encounter is the lack of standardised machine-readable repositories. This means that PDF is the dominant data publication format that MyVolts have to deal with. The integration of this data while maintaining strict quality control is a major issue for MyVolts' semi-automated data collection system (which may be modelled as a data value chain).

Our aim here is to identify how to model data value in this context in order to optimise this data value chain. This requires five specific steps:

1. Identify data value as it occurs within the value chain (data value creation/consumption);
2. Identify the data value dimensions that are relevant in this context;
3. Model data value using DaVe;
4. Implement model and metrics to quantify data value; and
5. Adapt data value chain accordingly.

---

[8] http://myvolts.com/.

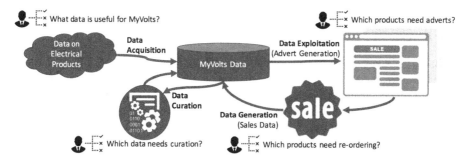

Fig. 4. MyVolts data value chain example [3].

In Fig. 4 we portray an example of a data value chain within MyVolts that shows various value creating processes as well as decision-making processes. Through this figure we can identify the following as relevant data value dimensions (not exhaustive):

- Quality - Data must be accurate, timely, accessible, complete, etc.
- Cost - Data must have manageable costs, including production, maintenance, or purchasing costs.

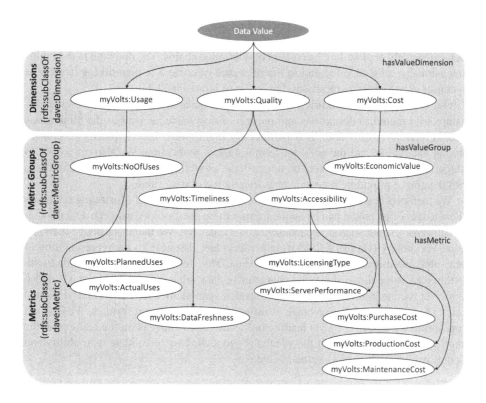

Fig. 5. MyVolts data value model based on DaVe [3].

– Usage - Data with more uses (actual or planned) will be more valuable to MyVolts, as it will have more impacts on the data value chain.

Based on the above data value dimensions, in Fig. 5 we provide a T-Box example using DaVe for the MyVolts data value chain scenario. Once this model is applied and the data value is quantified using the relevant metrics, a stakeholder from MyVolts can then analyse how to exploit this data value monitoring information in order to optimise their data value chain. For example, the optimisation of the data acquisition process can be achieved by first analysing the quality of the data to be acquired, and also its purchasing cost. This will ensure that an optimal decision is made when acquiring the data, and that the data will provide maximal benefits for its intended use. It also demonstrates the ease of definition of a consistent schema for all assessment tools to have their data uplifted. For example, the R2RML mapping language can be used to map usage data stored in a relational database into a semantic format using DaVe's structure, which will allow for easy integration and unified querying.

Through this use case driven evaluation we have a preliminary validation of the DaVe vocabulary. We demonstrate its flexibility in enabling the comprehensive modelling of data value, as well as its potential impact on data exploitation.

9   Conclusion

Data is increasingly being considered as an asset with social and commercial value. The exploitation of data is ongoing in many dimensions of society, and data value has been extensively explored in the context of data value chains. Yet, due both to the multi-dimensionality of data value and to the relevance of context in quantifying it, there is no consensus of what characterises data value or how to model it.

Our first contribution in this paper is therefore the analysis of existing relevant literature with regard to definitions and models of data value, as well as the dimensions used to quantify data value. This particularly highlighted the complexity of characterising data value, and the need for terminological unification. We also proceeded to categorising the existing data value dimensions, as well as providing their definitions, with the aim of providing a generic characterisation of data value.

We then proceed to identify a set of use cases with the aim of illustrating scenarios where a data value model can be applied. From these use cases we also extract a number of requirements that such a vocabulary should cater for. We therefore define the Data Value Vocabulary (DaVe); a light-weight vocabulary that enables the representation of data value quantification results as linked data. This vocabulary can be extended with custom data value dimensions that characterise data value in a specific context. It also allows for the integration of diverse metrics that span many data value dimensions and which most likely pertain to a range of different tools in different formats. We lead out a preliminary evaluation by (1) leading out a structured analysis on the features of the ontology, and (2) by applying the vocabulary to a use case to validate its usability and capability of modelling data value in context.

By enabling the comprehensive representation of data value, DaVe allows users to monitor and assess the value of data as it occurs within any data value chain, as data is being exploited. This will in turn enable the effective management of value, and hence efficient exploitation of data.

Acknowledgements. This research has received funding from the ADAPT Centre for Digital Content Technology, funded under the SFI Research Centres Programme (Grant 13/RC/2106), co-funded by the European Regional Development Fund and the European Union's Horizon 2020 research and innovation programme under the Marie Sklodowska-Curie grant agreement No. 713567.

References

1. Ahituv, N.: A systematic approach toward assessing the value of an information system. MIS Q. **4**(4), 61 (1980). https://doi.org/10.2307/248961
2. Al-Saffar, S., Heileman, G.L.: Semantic impact graphs for information valuation. In: Proceedings of the Eighth ACM Symposium on Document Engineering, DocEng 2008, pp. 209–212. ACM, New York (2008). https://doi.org/10.1145/1410140.1410181
3. Attard, J., Brennan, R.: A semantic data value vocabulary supporting data value assessment and measurement integration. In: ICEIS 2018 - Proceedings of the 20th International Conference on Enterprise Information Systems, vol. 2 (2018)
4. Attard, J., Orlandi, F., Auer, S.: Exploiting the value of data through data value networks. In: Proceedings of the 10th International Conference on Theory and Practice of Electronic Governance, ICEGOV 2017, pp. 475–484 (2017). https://doi.org/10.1145/3047273.3047299
5. Brennan, R., Attard, J., Helfert, M.: Management of data value chains, a value monitoring capability maturity model. In: Proceedings of 20th International Conference on Enterprise Information Systems (ICEIS 2018) (2018, to appear)
6. Castelfranchi, C.: In search of a principled theory of the 'value' of knowledge. SpringerPlus **5**(1), 1617 (2016). https://doi.org/10.1186/s40064-016-3205-2
7. Chen, Y.: Information valuation for information lifecycle management. In: Second International Conference on Autonomic Computing (ICAC 2005), pp. 135–146. IEEE, June 2005. https://doi.org/10.1109/ICAC.2005.35
8. Crié, D., Micheaux, A.: From customer data to value: what is lacking in the information chain? J. Database Mark. Cust. Strategy Manage. **13**(4), 282–299 (2006). https://doi.org/10.1057/palgrave.dbm.3240306
9. Cyganiak, R., Reynolds, D., Tennison, J.: The RDF data cube vocabulary. W3C recommendation, World Wide Web Consortium (W3C) (2014)
10. Davenport, T.H.: How strategists use "big data" to support internal business decisions, discovery and production. Strategy Leadersh. **42**(4), 45–50 (2014). https://doi.org/10.1108/SL-05-2014-0034
11. Debattista, J., Lange, C., Auer, S.: Representing dataset quality metadata using multidimensional views. In: Proceedings of the 10th International Conference on Semantic Systems - SEM 2014, pp. 92–99. ACM Press, New York, September 2014. https://doi.org/10.1145/2660517.2660525
12. Demirkan, H., Delen, D.: Leveraging the capabilities of service-oriented decision support systems: putting analytics and big data in cloud. Decis. Support Syst. **55**(1), 412–421 (2013). https://doi.org/10.1016/j.dss.2012.05.048
13. Engelsman, W.: Information assets and their value, pp. 1–10 (2007)

14. Even, A., Shankaranarayanan, G.: Value-driven data quality assessment. In: Proceedings of the 2005 International Conference on Information Quality (MIT IQ Conference) (2005)
15. Even, A., Shankaranarayanan, G., Berger, P.D.: Evaluating a model for cost-effective data quality management in a real-world CRM setting. Decis. Support Syst. **50**(1), 152–163 (2010). https://doi.org/10.1016/j.dss.2010.07.011
16. Francois, P., et al.: A macroscope for global history. Seshat Global History Databank: a methodological overview. Dig. Humanit. Q. **10**(4) (2016)
17. Grau, B.C., Horrocks, I., Motik, B., Parsia, B., Patel-Schneider, P., Sattler, U.: OWL 2: the next step for OWL. Web Semant. **6**(4), 309–322 (2008). https://doi.org/10.1016/j.websem. 2008.05.001
18. Gruber, T.R.: Toward principles for the design of ontologies used for knowledge sharing. Int. J. Hum.-Comput. Stud. **43**(5–6), 907–928 (1995). https://doi.org/10.1006/ijhc.1995.1081
19. Higson, C., Waltho, D.: Valuing information as an asset. SAS the Power To Know, pp. 1–17, November 2010
20. Jin, H., Xiong, M., Wu, S.: Information value evaluation model for ILM. In: 2008 Ninth ACIS International Conference on Software Engineering, Artificial Intelligence, Networking, and Parallel/Distributed Computing, pp. 543–548. IEEE (2008). https://doi.org/10.1109/SNPD.2008.112
21. Juran, J.M.: Juran's Quality Control Handbook, 4th edn. McGraw-Hill, New York (1974)
22. Klann, J.G., Schadow, G.: Modeling the information-value decay of medical problems for problem list maintenance. In: Proceedings of the 1st ACM International Health Informatics Symposium, IHI 2010, pp. 371–375. ACM, New York (2010). https://doi.org/10.1145/1882992.1883045
23. Laney, D.: Infonomics: the economics of information and principles of information asset management (2011)
24. Laney, D.: Gartner analytic ascendancy model (2012)
25. Latif, A., Us Saeed, A., Hoefler, P., Stocker, A., Wagner, C.: The linked data value chain: a lightweight model for business engineers. In: Proceedings of International Conference on Semantic Systems, pp. 568–576 (2009)
26. Lee, C.C., Yang, J.: Knowledge value chain. J. Manage. Dev. **19**(9), 783–794 (2000)
27. Lóscio, B.F., Stephan, E.G., Purohit, S.: Data usage vocabulary (DUV). Technical report, World Wide Web Consortium (2016). http://www.w3.org/TR/vocab-duv/
28. Maali, F., Erickson, J., Archer, P.: Data catalog vocabulary (DCAT). W3C recommendation, World Wide Web Consortium (2014). http://www.w3.org/TR/vocab-dcat/
29. Maina, C.: Just-in-case or just-in-time library services: the option and usage valuation of libraries and information services (2004)
30. Miller, H.G., Mork, P.: From data to decisions: a value chain for big data. IT Prof. **15**(1), 57–59 (2013). https://doi.org/10.1109/MITP.2013.11
31. Moody, D., Walsh, P.: Measuring the value of information: an asset valuation approach. In: Seventh European Conference on Information Systems (ECIS 1999), pp. 1–17 (1999). https://doi.org/citeulike:9316228
32. Noy, N.F., Mcguinness, D.L.: Ontology development 101: a guide to creating your first ontology. Technical report (2001)
33. Otto, B.: Quality and value of the data resource in large enterprises. Inf. Syst. Manage. **32**(3), 234–251 (2015). https://doi.org/10.1080/10580530.2015.1044344
34. Peppard, J., Rylander, A.: From value chain to value network:: insights for mobile operators. Eur. Manage. J. **24**(2–3), 128–141 (2006). https://doi.org/10.1016/j.emj.2006.03.003
35. Ren, Y., Parvizi, A., Mellish, C., Pan, J.Z., van Deemter, K., Stevens, R.: Towards competency question-driven ontology authoring. In: Presutti, V., d'Amato, C., Gandon, F., d'Aquin, M., Staab, S., Tordai, A. (eds.) ESWC 2014. LNCS, vol. 8465, pp. 752–767. Springer, Cham (2014). https://doi.org/10.1007/978-3-319-07443-6_50

36. Sajko, M., Rabuzin, K., Bača, M.: How to calculate information value for effective security risk assessment. J. Inf. Organ. Sci. **30**(2), 263–278 (2006)
37. Solanki, M., Božić, B., Freudenberg, M., Kontokostas, D., Dirschl, C., Brennan, R.: Enabling combined software and data engineering at Web-scale: the ALIGNED suite of ontologies. In: Groth, P., et al. (eds.) ISWC 2016. LNCS, vol. 9982, pp. 195–203. Springer, Cham (2016). https://doi.org/10.1007/978-3-319-46547-0_21
38. Tallon, P.P.: Corporate governance of big data: perspectives on value, risk, and cost. Computer **46**(6), 32–38 (2013). https://doi.org/10.1109/MC.2013.155
39. Turczyk, L.A., Heckmann, O., Steinmetz, R.: File valuation in information lifecycle management. In: Proceedings of the Thirteenth Americas Conference on Information Systems, Keystone, Colorado (2007)
40. Viscusi, G., Batini, C.: Digital information asset evaluation: characteristics and dimensions. In: Caporarello, L., Di Martino, B., Martinez, M. (eds.) Smart Organizations and Smart Artifacts. LNISO, vol. 7, pp. 77–86. Springer, Cham (2014). https://doi.org/10.1007/978-3-319-07040-7_9
41. Wijnhoven, F., Amrit, C., Dietz, P.: Value-based file retention. J. Data Inf. Qual. **4**(4), 1–17 (2014). https://doi.org/10.1145/2567656
42. Zaveri, A., Rula, A., Maurino, A., Pietrobon, R., Lehmann, J., Auer, S.: Quality assessment for linked data: a survey. Semant. Web J. **7**, 63–93 (2015)

Multi-view Navigation in a Personalized Scientometric Retrieval System

Nedra Ibrahim[✉], Anja Habacha Chaibi, and Henda Ben Ghézala

RIADI Laboratory/ENSI, University of Manouba, 2010 Manouba, Tunisia
Nedra.ibrahim@ensi-uma.tn,
{anja.habacha,henda.benghezala}@ensi.rnu.tn

Abstract. Given the large number of scientific productions, it becomes difficult to select those that meet the needs of researchers in scientific information and from certain sources of trust. One of the challenges facing researchers is finding quality scientific information that meets their research needs. In order to guarantee a quality result, a research method based on scientific quality is required. The quality of scientific information is measured by scientometrics based on a set of metrics and measures called scientometric indicators. In this paper we propose a new personalized information retrieval approach taking into account the researcher quality requirements. The proposed approach includes a scientometric document annotator, a scientometric user model, a scientometric ranking approach and different results visualization methods. We discuss the feasibility of this approach by performing different experimentations on its different parts. The incorporation of scientometric indicators into the different parts of our approach has significantly improved retrieval performance which is rated for 41.66% in terms of F-measure. An important implication of this finding is the existence of correlation between research paper quality and paper relevance. The revelation of this correlation implies better retrieval performance.

Keywords: Qualitative search · Scientometrics · Document annotation · Re-ranking · User profile · Visualization · Cartography

1 Introduction

Given the large number of scientific productions, it becomes difficult to select those that meet the needs of researchers in scientific information. One of the challenges facing researchers is finding qualitative scientific information that meets their research needs. The quality of scientific research is perceived as a criterion for the validation of research work. In order to guarantee a qualitative result, an information retrieval system based on scientific quality is required.

The two main issues affecting researchers' search for information are the information overload and heterogeneity of information sources [1]. In return, the researcher's scientific production should respond to his institution's qualitative requirements and have some quality indicator. Thus, a potential solution to help the researcher is to rely on his scientific quality requirements to improve retrieval results. This paper is an extension of our previously publisher work [2]. This paper discusses how a researcher creates his

S. Hammoudi et al. (Eds.): ICEIS 2018, LNBIP 363, pp. 262–282, 2019.
https://doi.org/10.1007/978-3-030-26169-6_13

definition of quality that can be used to drive a specific information search. However, several practical questions arise when dealing with research paper retrieval: How to integrate the scientific quality into the personalized information retrieval (IR) process? Which quality elements should be integrated? At which level the quality should be integrated? What will be the contribution of quality integration? To answer all these questions, we proposed a personalized retrieval system based on scientometric evaluation. To improve our work [2], we propose a multi-view results visualization method given the special needs of researchers. This visualization method provides to the researchers the possibility of analyzing and interpreting search results.

The remainder of the paper is organized as follows: Sect. 2 describes the existing approaches on personalized research papers' retrieval. Being the focus of our approach, Sect. 3 is dedicated to the study of researcher's needs when searching for scientific information. Section 4 is devoted to present the proposed approach and the three basic modules of the system. The fourth module of search results visualization and analysis will be detailed in Sect. 5. In Sect. 6, the results of our experimentation will be discussed. Finally, Sect. 7 concludes with a summary.

2 Personalized Research Paper Retrieval

The web has greatly improved the access to scientific literature. The progress of science has often been hampered by the inefficiency of traditional methods of disseminating scientific information. We reviewed some personalized research paper's retrieving systems. We classified them into two categories: personalization of ranking and recommendation.

Singh et al. [3] proposed to rank research-papers based on citation network using a modified version of the PageRank algorithm [4]. Tang et al. [5] ranked authors based on h-index and conferences' impact.

In research-paper recommendation, the Content-Based Filtering (CBF) was the predominant recommendation class. The majority utilized plain terms contained in the documents [6], others used n-grams, or topics based on Latent Dirichlet Allocation (LDA) [7]. DLib9 (Machine Readable Digital Library) [8] is a web-service that generates recommendations based on a single document. Moreover, it offers different recommendation approaches, such as stereotype-based and content based algorithms with additional re-ranking using bibliometric data. Few approaches also utilized non textual features, such as citations or authors. The CORE recommender [9] uses collaborative filtering and content-based filtering. Another approach used co-citations to calculate document relatedness [10]. CiteSeer has a user profiling system which tracks the interests of users and recommends new citations and documents when they appear [11]. It used citations instead of words to find similar scientific articles. Some recommendation approaches built graphs to generate recommendations. Such graphs typically included papers that were connected via citations. Some graphs included authors, users and publishing years of the papers [12].

However, in the previous studies little attention has been given to the user. In [3], research-paper ranking approach didn't take into account the user preferences. In [5], the authors focused on ranking authors or conferences according to one of the impact criteria, which cannot match all users' preferences. The majority of research paper recommendation approaches was a content based [6, 8, 9]. In which, the authors focused on extracting text from the title, abstract, introduction, keywords, bibliography, body text and social tags. Some other approaches used different information such as citation or authors [10–12]. The problem with these approaches is in that they did not allow users to define their preferences. In fact, they did not take into account that researcher satisfaction might depend not only on accuracy or citations but on the information quality.

3 Study of the Researcher's Needs

The researcher tries to produce a scientific qualitative production according to the strategy of his research institution. To validate its scientific production, the researcher must meet a set of qualitative criteria such as:

- Having publications in impacted journals and/or classified conferences.
- Having publications with a specific number of citations.
- Having a certain number of publications.
- Citing qualitative references.
- Citing trusted authors (belonging to well-known affiliations with a certain number of publications and citations).

Thus, the researcher needs to initiate a qualitative research according to his qualitative preferences after choosing his own definition of quality. When using the online bibliographic databases, the researcher finds some difficulties such as:

- Which conference ranking system to choose?
- Which impact indicator to consider?
- Which bibliographic database to choose?
- How to manage differences between the different bibliographic databases?
- How to validate his choice?

A scientific paper is considered to be an indicator of researchers' scientific production. The assessment of research papers can be performed by a set of measures which are the scientometric indicators [13]. In this context, scientometrics is defined as all quantitative aspects of the science of science, communication science and science policy [14]. Ibrahim et al. [15] studied all the elements affecting the research paper quality. Amongst the large set of scientometric indicators existing in the literature, Ibrahim et al. [15] selected the better ones reflecting the real paper impact. They showed that we can assess paper quality by combining a set of scientometric indicators which include: publications number, citations number, h-index [16], journal impact factor [17] and conference ranking.

The scientometric indicators have been used by bibliographic databases, such as Science Citation Index (SCI) [18], Google Scholar [19], CiteSeer [20] and Microsoft Academic Search [21]. Also, we note the existing of several ranking systems providing scientific journal ranking and conference ranking according to their impact. Thomson ISI annually publishes the Journal Citation Report[1] (JCR) which includes a number of indicators among which the Journal Impact Factor (JIF) [17]. The portal of the Association Core[2] provides access to the logs of journal and conference classification. The SCImago Journal & Country Ranking portal[3] (SJR) provides a set of journal classification metrics and quality evaluation.

4 Proposed Scientometric Approach for Personalized Research Paper Retrieval

The quality of the information source is very important for institution quality improvement and literature review validation [22]. The proposed system should be a solution to the researchers' problematic when searching for relevant information. We propose a personalized IR system dedicated to researchers to automate and facilitate the selection of qualitative research papers [2]. We integrated scientific quality in the process of retrieval and personalization of the system.

Figure 1 presents an extension of the proposed system model presented in [2]. The proposed system is composed of four basic modules: a scientometric retrieval system, a user profile management module, a user profile exploitation module and results visualization module. The first module is the scientometric retrieval system which is based on a scientometric annotator. The second module is the user profile management module. We enriched the user profile model by scientometric indicators to build the scientometric profile ontology. The third module is the user profile exploitation for which we propose a scientometric approach for re-ranking research papers. The fourth module is a new method for results visualization and analysis proposed as an extension of the global system. We propose different approaches of results visualization: cartographic view, list view and analytic view. In the following, we detail each of the four modules.

The challenges of the proposed system are:

- Collecting researcher's preferences.
- Synchronizing between different online bibliographic databases to extract quality indicators.
- Selecting the most significant quality indicators.
- Extracting good quality indicators.
- Updating the various indicators.

---

[1] https://clarivate.com/products/journal-citation-reports/.

[2] http://portal.core.edu.au/conf-ranks/.

[3] https://www.scimagojr.com/journalrank.php.

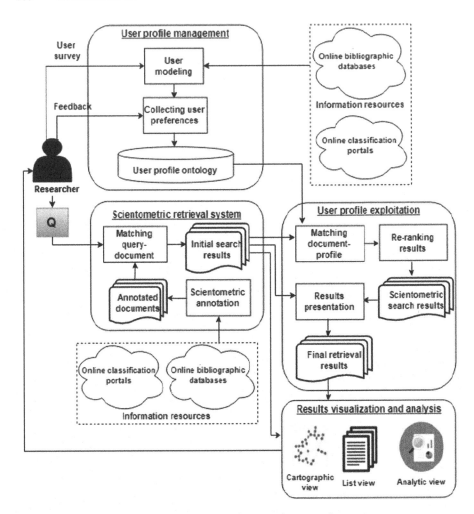

Fig. 1. Proposed scientometric approach.

4.1 Scientometric Retrieval System

To improve search results, we propose the application of scientometrics in the IR process. In this section, we specify how to integrate scientometrics at the indexing level.

We propose a scientometric annotator which is an automatic process. It allows the extraction of relevant indicators to each document from the online bibliographic databases. A document can be a conference or a journal paper, thesis or master report. Amongst the large set of scientometric indicators existing in the literature, we selected the most ones reflecting the real paper impact. We used the selected indicators to annotate research papers. Scientometric annotation is author centered, document-centered, and venue-centered. It consists on representing and using a set of sciento-metric indicators:

- The impact of the author as an indicator of the researcher quality.
- The impact of the journal/conference as an indicator of the container quality.
- The impact of the research group as an indicator of the search environment quality.
- The impact of the paper as an indicator of the content quality.

The scientometric annotation is carried out on different parts of the document structure: front, body and back. The body is the content of the document. The front contains the title, the authors, the conference/journal and the affiliation. The back contains the references. We annotate research papers from online databases.

The annotation process consists of three data processing steps. The first step is the pre-treatment. It consisted on the construction of descriptive annotation from an online paper. The second step is the indicators' extraction. It consists on the extraction of the scientometric indicators corresponding to each document from the online database. The third step is the enrichment and the reconstruction of the Extensible Markup Language (XML) annotation file. It consists on the enrichment with the scientometric annotation and the reconstruction of the XML annotation file. The annotation file included the descriptive and scientometric annotations. Figure 2 gives an example of the produced XML annotation file.

```xml
<Publication id="55">
  <DescriptiveAnnotation>
    <Title>Semantic similarity between search engine queries using temporal correlation</Title>
    <Author Affiliation="Microsoft" Name="Steve Chien"/>
    <ArticleContainer Name="World Wide Web Conference Series - WWW" Info=", pp. 2-11, 2005" Type="Conference"/>
    <Abstract>...investigate the idea of finding semantically related search engine queries based on their ; in other w(
      popularities...discover a wide range of semantically similar queries. finally, we develop a method of efficientl(
      query using far less space and time...</Abstract>
  </DescriptiveAnnotation>
  <scientometricAnnotation>
    <bodyLevel>
      <docCitationNumber> 73</docCitationNumber>
      <coAuthorNumber>2</coAuthorNumber>
    </bodyLevel>
    <authorLevel>
      <authorName>Steve Chien</authorName>
      <authorPosition>1</authorPosition>
      <authorPublications> 68 </authorPublications>
      <authorCitations> 697 </authorCitations>
      <authorhindex>22</authorhindex>
    </authorLevel>
    <confLevel>
      <confPublicationNumber> 2,920</confPublicationNumber>
      <confCitationNumber> 60,820</confCitationNumber>
      <confSelfCitationNumber> 2,435</confSelfCitationNumber>
      <confRank>A</confRank>
    </confLevel>
    <affiliationLevel>
      <affiliationHindex>Microsoft</affiliationHindex>
      <groupCitations> 1,643,352 </groupCitations>
      <groupPublications> 110,583</groupPublications>
    </affiliationLevel>
  </scientometricAnnotation>
</Publication>
```

Fig. 2. Example of XML annotation file.

The main limitations of the annotation process are:

- The diversity of information resources: we note the existence of several online bibliographic databases providing a large number of papers. In order to solve this problem, we have chosen the bibliographic database which provides the widest range of scientometric indicators.
- Updating scientometric indicators: after the annotation of the document, we must start a continuous updating process.
- The diversity of scientometric indicators: a single paper may have different values representing the same scientometric indicator in different bibliographic databases. To solve this problem, we propose a synchronization module. The synchronization consists on choosing the most recent value.

4.2   User Profile Management

Personalization aims to facilitate the expression of user needs and enables him/her to obtain relevant information. The user profile management module consists on the definition of a scientometric user model. Based on this model, we collect the user preferences to construct the user profile ontology.

We proposed a scientometric user profile model in which we integrated the dimension: "scientometric preferences". This dimension represents the researchers' needs by incorporating different scientometric indicators to the user profile. The profile model is an instantiation of the generic model described in the work of Ibrahim et al. [23].

We performed a user study to select the indicators that interest the researchers. The selected indicators were incorporated into the user profile model. It stores the necessary information describing the quality of a research paper according to the researcher's needs. These preferences are organized into five SubDimensions which are the different entities affecting the paper's quality. The quality of each entity is measured by a set of scientometric indicators which represent the attributes of each SubDimension:

- Author quality: is measured by the mean of four attributes (h-index, citations number, publications number and author position).
- Content quality: is measured by the mean of the paper citations number and the co-authors number.
- Journal or conference quality: scientific journals or conferences are containers of research papers. A good quality of the journal promotes the selection of the document. The quality of the paper container is evaluated by its ranking, number of citations, number of publications and number of self-citations.
- Affiliation quality: we consider the quality of author's affiliation measured by the group h-index, the number of publications, the number of citations and the number of self-citations.

On the other hand, each SubDimension is extended on ExtSubDimension by moving to a higher level of abstraction. Each ExtSubDimension will be organized into attributes which represent the scientometric indicators measuring its quality:

- Career quality: We associate the quality of career to the author quality as an extension. The quality of author career is measured by the number of years spent by the author on research in a specific discipline, and his current title.
- Source quality: We designate by the source of scientific documents the bibliographic databases such as: Google Scholar, DBLP and MS Academic Search. The quality of information source is measured by the number of publications, the interval of time and the number of domains covered by the source.
- Publisher quality: the quality of the container can be extended to the evaluation of publisher quality which can affect the quality of papers. This latter is measured by the number of specialties, the number of published journals or conferences.
- Organization quality: we extended the affiliation quality to the organization quality measured by the Shanghai ranking (in the case of academic organizations), the number of publications and the number of citations.
- Association quality: For each conference, we join his association (e.g. IEEE). The quality of conference association is measured by the number of specialties covered by the association and the number of conferences organized by the association.

The proposed user profile is based on implicit and explicit interaction with the user. Collecting user preferences is based on the user navigation to measure his interest to a given entity. We collect user preferences from the number of pages the user reads, user's interaction with the papers (downloads, edits, views) and citations. Otherwise, the interactions are explicit because we ask the unknown user to define his quality preferences according to a set of scientometric preferences.

Based on the user preferences, we construct the user profile ontology. The profiles are containers of knowledge about the user. We opted for ontology to represent the scientometric preferences of the user. The ontology domain covers the scientometric domain (assessment tools, measures and indicators) conducted for a scientific research evaluation.

4.3 User Profile Exploitation

The proposed personalization approach is based on the exploitation of the user profile to re-rank documents according to the user preferences. We proposed a scientometric re-ranking approach based on users' quality preferences [24]. We define a scientometric score based on scientometric indicators deriving from user profile. This score is used to re-rank search results and to deliver qualitative information at the top ranks.

For each of the returned results (A_i), we calculate its similarity to the user profile. Then, we re-rank the search results according to the similarity score. We propose a scientometric score as a combination of the scientometric indicators of the user model.

We calculate the scientometric score which we note as Q. This scientometric score was the result of the application of an adapted mathematical model of weighted sums considering the scientometric preferences of the user. The equation that describes the proposed scientometric score [24] is as follows:

$$Q(A_i) = \sum_{j=1}^{n} W_{SUB} * Q_{SUB}(A_i) + \sum_{j=1}^{n} (W_{SUB} + W_{EXT}) * Q_{EXT}(A_i), \forall i \in [1, m] \quad (1)$$

Q_{SUB} and Q_{EXT} represent respectively the quality of each SubDimension and ExtSubDimension. W_{SUB} and W_{EXT} are the importance weights attributed by the user to each SubDimension and ExtSubDimension.

We calculate the scientometric rank based on the scientometric score. Then, we determine the final rank based on the initial rank and the scientometric rank. Equation (2) represents the formula of the final rank [24]:

$$FinalRank = \alpha * InitialRank + (1 - \alpha) * ScientometricRank, \alpha \in [0, 1] \quad (2)$$

The initial rank is the original rank returned by the retrieval system and the scientometric rank is calculated according to scientometric score.

5   Results Visualization

In this section we focus on visualizing the textual information in different ways to facilitate the comprehension and interpretation of the returned results. Information visualization can aid the researcher in many of his/her search related tasks. First, we present some of the existing visualization approaches then we propose a multi-view visualization approach based on scientometrics.

5.1   Search Results Visualization

Different visualization techniques may be used that simplify the text, extract keywords and phrases, or exchange. Other techniques present the results as graphs or maps. Systems such as SeeSoft [25] and WebTOC [26] replace some of the lines of text with colored lines. Other researchers have investigated graphical representations of the search data such as Cugini's [27] and SQWID [28]. Colored dots are used in Dotfire [29] to represent digital library search results, Sparkler [30] uses colored dots and relevancy in a bull's-eye formation, TileBars [31] maps the position of the keywords and xFind plots relevance to y-axis and document size to the x-axis [32]. Finally, Cugini [27] compares textual and graphical interfaces.

On the other hand, HotMap [33] provides a compact visual representation of web search results at two levels of detail, and supports the interactive exploration of web search results. KARTOO[4] proposes a cartographic view of search results. Another well-known example is the WEBSOM project [34]. The map approach can take

---

[4] http://www.kartoo.com.

advantage of the cognitive aspect such as in the work of Skupin and Fabrikant [35]. However with the increase of the results and the links complexity, graphs and maps become more and more unreadable.

5.2   Proposed Multi-view Visualization Approach

List-based representation allows the evaluation of a single document, but it does not allow the manipulation of search results, comparison of documents, or finding a set of relevant documents. Certainly, the researcher is familiar with browsing and manipulating the search results through textual style interfaces, but he/her would gain additional information and better understanding of the information through different presentation methods. A researcher is not satisfied with just a classical visualization method, but seeks an analytical view of scientific information. The diversity of visualization ways allows the researcher to derive interpretations and analysis of the set of information returned by the retrieval system. On the other hand, the researcher prefers to visualize search results enriched by the different quality indicators included in his/her profile model.

Thus, rank ordered lists should be used along-side additional information and other ways of results visualization. We present a system that displays multiple views of search results. We provide three different views:

- List view: is a ranked document list enriched by scientometric indicators corresponding to the researcher's preferences.
- Cartographic view: is a graphical view consisting on the representation of search results in the form of graph enriched by scientometric data.
- Analytic view: is an evaluative way to provide to the researcher analytic information about the returned results. This information is a detailed description of the progress and stability of research activity.

5.2.1   List View

This view consists on displaying the results in a way that is clear and highlights the scientometric information. The researchers may be interested in seeing where their qualitative preferences fit in the results list and where the information is located.

Indeed, bibliographic databases such as Google Scholar and Microsoft Academic Search offer additional information when displaying results such as citations number. In our system, we present a more enriched document list with different scientometric indicators corresponding to the researcher's preferences. Figure 3 shows an example of a list view representing the returned results. In addition to the displayed scientometric information, the researcher can display more scientometric details about any scientific document in the list.

5.2.2   Cartographic View

The traditional representations are presented over multiple pages and the researchers only view a small proportion of the results in one window. They need to scroll down or move to the next page to see more results [36]. Graphical visualization of this information, coordinated with traditional text output would allow the user to more quickly choose the documents that are most interesting and useful. Such a graphical representation could display thousands of results in one view, allowing clustering operations to depict similarities of the search results and allow the researcher to find relevant information more easily. It is useful and possible to present a more data-rich presentation of scientific documents results than solely a textual representation. We enrich graphical visualization by scientometric data to provide a qualitative view of search results.

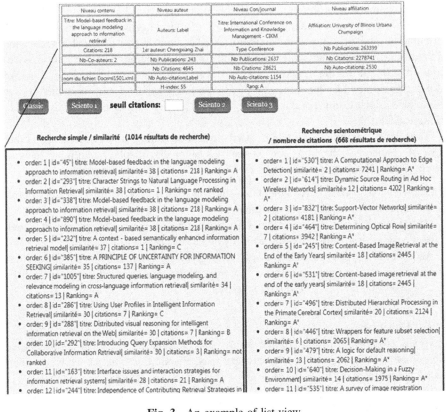

Fig. 3. An example of list view.

Our system provides to researchers different cartographic views of the returned results. We used Gephi software [37] to represent these different views. The first cartographic view consists on visualizing the returned results as a graph. Figure 4 is an example of cartographic view provided by our system. The scientific documents are presented as distinct nodes connected to the different types of quality evaluation. This view provides to the researcher a general view of the relevant documents and their quality scores. The quality scores of each returned document are presented as the weights of its connected edges. The researcher can choose documents concentrated around one or more of the quality types according to his/her preferences.

We provide a second cartographic view as the citations network. The researcher can consult the citations links existing between a set of scientific documents from our data resources. This view can help researchers in detecting the most cited and most attractive publications in a specific discipline. Figure 5 is an example of citations network provided by our system where nodes present the scientific documents and edges are the relations of citations.

The second type of cartographic view consists on visualizing the collaboration network between the different documents' authors and between their corresponding research laboratories. The study of collaboration between authors or research laboratories consists on identifying the relations of collaboration based on co-publications of articles. These data will be combined to be used in the creation of collaboration networks. The network of collaboration has the form of a related graph, where nodes represent the researchers and the arcs present the relations of collaborations between these researchers, and the thickness of these links reflects the number of collaborations between the two researchers forming the link. Figure 6 represents an example of authors' collaboration network. The nodes having the same color corresponds to authors belonging to the same research laboratory. The author being in the center is the most attractive and productive one in a particular discipline in relation of the executed query.

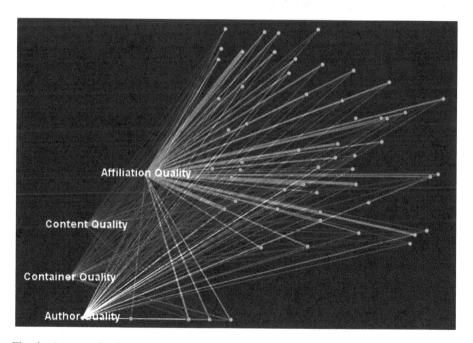

Fig. 4. An example of cartographic view corresponding to results returned by the scientometric system.

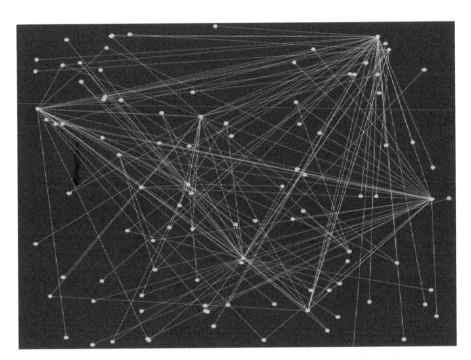

Fig. 5. An example of cartographic view corresponding to the citations network.

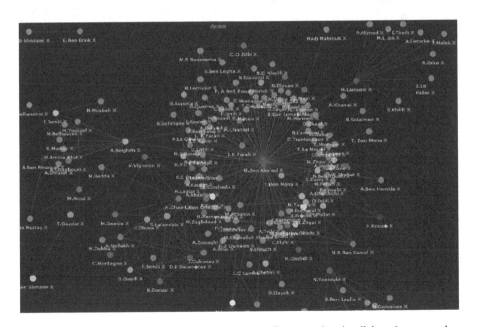

Fig. 6. An example of cartographic view corresponding to authors' collaboration network.

5.2.3 Analytic View

The analytic view of search results consists on evaluating and analyzing the scientific information returned by our scientometric retrieval system. We provide different aspects of qualitative evaluation and analysis of the returned results by the mean of the scientometric indicators. As a result of running a query, the researcher can consult the following analytic methods:

- Classification of documents' authors according to one of the scientometric indicators: this method consists on classifying a group of authors who published in a the same discipline according to one of the scientometric indicators (publications, citations, citations/year, citations/article citations/author, article/author, authors/Article, h-index, g-index, hi-index, hc-index, AWCR, AWCRpA, AW-index) [38].
- Comparison between more authors: the comparison is made between a group of researchers having the same status (PhD student, Doctor, senior researcher, etc.) by comparing the values of scientometric indicators, and their evolution over the years.
- Analysis of authors, laboratory or country's research activity: this analysis is a detailed description of the research activity of an author based on the scientometric indicators allowing research activity analysis.

Figure 7 shows an example of analytic view provided by our system. This analytic view is an example of the analysis of author's research activity.

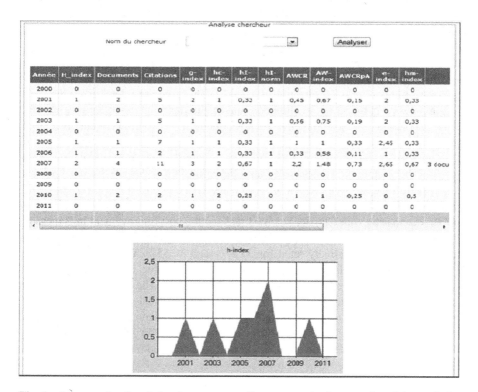

Fig. 7. An example of analytic view corresponding to an author's research activity analysis.

6 Experimentation and Evaluation

We performed different experimentations to evaluate the scientometric retrieval system.

6.1 Evaluation of the Scientometric Retrieval

To evaluate the scientometric retrieval system, we propose a multi-model retrieval system. It consists of a scientometric annotator and several retrieval models that operate this annotator. These models differ by the criteria considered when matching the document to the query:

- Classic: is a classical retrieval model based on the similarity between a document and a search query; referred to as the term frequency (tf).
- Sciento1: the first scientometric model. It is based on the similarity between document and query in addition to the container ranking.
- Sciento2: the second scientometric model. It is based on the similarity between document and query in addition to the documents citation number.
- Sciento3: the third scientometric model. It is based on the similarity between document and query in addition to both container ranking and documents citation number.

In Classic, we have not integrated scientometrics. We integrated scientometrics into the three other models (Sciento1, Sciento2 and Sciento3). We evaluated and compared the performance of the two retrieval categories based on a test collection and different evaluation measures. The test collection contains 1500 annotated research papers and 30 different queries. The annotation files are the result of the annotation of 1500 published papers extracted from MS Academic Search.

This evaluation is carried out to find out the effect of the integration of scientometrics on the performance of retrieval systems. Thus, we are interested to the comparison between classical retrieval models and scientometric retrieval ones. In order to verify the validity of scientometric retrieval models, we reinforced our evaluation presented in [2] with additional experimental results. We evaluated our retrieval system using other measures such as nDCG and P(k). Figure 8 shows a recapitulation of the results of the performed experimentations. The results show that all the scientometric models performed an improvement in performance. This improvement is proved by the different evaluation measures: F-measure, nDCG, P(k) and Mean Average Precision (MAP). Comparing with Classic, Sciento3 realized the best improvement in F-measure which is rated for 41.66%. Sciento1 and Sciento2 realized an improvement in F-measure which is respectively rated for 33.33% and 30.55%. We note a best rate of MAP improvement realized by Sciento3 which is rated for 14.03%. Sciento1 and Sciento2 realized an improvement in MAP rated for 5.26%. The best improvement rate in nDCG was provided by Sciento3 (28%). Sciento1 and Sciento2 realized an improvement in nDCG rated respectively for 14% and 8%. Same for P(k) improvement rates, the best results was realized by Sciento3 (44.73%). Sciento1 realized an improvement of P(k) rated for 26.31% and Sciento2 realized 34.21%.

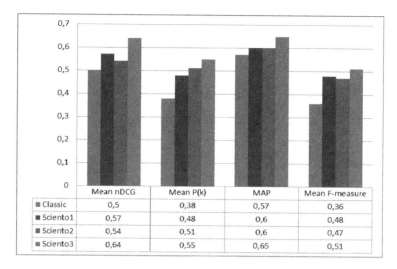

	Mean nDCG	Mean P(k)	MAP	Mean F-measure
■ Classic	0,5	0,38	0,57	0,36
■ Sciento1	0,57	0,48	0,6	0,48
■ Sciento2	0,54	0,51	0,6	0,47
■ Sciento3	0,64	0,55	0,65	0,51

Fig. 8. Experimental results of retrieval models evaluation.

It has been found that scientometrics has enhanced the relevance of results and has provided better performance to the retrieval system. The best performance is provided by Sciento3, in which both the number of document citations and container ranking were integrated.

6.2   Evaluation of the Scientometric Re-ranking

Our objective is to evaluate the proposed scientometric re-ranking algorithm among an initial ranking. We produce the personalized results and compare it to initial ones. We used the nDCGp [39] as a measure of ranking performance. We performed the evaluation based on users' database containing 171 researchers working in our research laboratory (20 known users and 151 unknown users). We collected the user's scientometric preferences by launching a survey. We opted for the bibliographic database "MS Academic Search" to extract the initial ranking and the corresponding scientometric data. Our choice is justified by the broad set of scientometric indicators covered by MS Academic Search. We used keywords based queries to perform the experimentations. All the known users executed 30 queries on the MS Academic Search.

We consider the initial rank corresponding to the top hundred results returned by MS Academic Search. Then, we re-rank top hundred initial results according to the scientometric score. Finally, we calculate the final rank (Eq. 2) for different α values ($\alpha \in \{0, 0.1, 0.2, 0.3, 0.4, 0.5, 0.6, 0.7, 0.8, 0.9, 1\}$). We evaluate the different obtained rankings by calculating nDCGp for each α value to compare the different ranking performances. In Fig. 9, we present more detailed evaluation results of our experimentations presented in [2]. We observe a variation in nDCGp values which is improving when we get closer to $\alpha = 0$, that's to say when the scientometric rank is the most considered in the final rank. By decreasing α, the mean of nDCGp increase. This shows that the integration of the scientometric rank improved ranking performance. The best improvement was rated for 14.75% compared to the MS Academic Search ranking which is obtained when $\alpha = 0.1$.

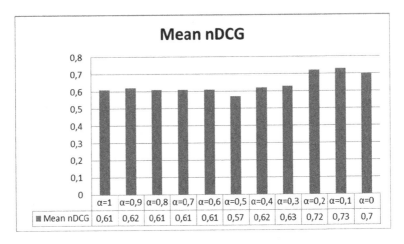

Fig. 9. Mean nDCG for the different α values.

6.3 Significance Test

A significance test allows the researcher to detect significant improvements even when the improvements are small. We want to promote retrieval models that truly are better rather than methods that by chance performed better. We opted for performing significance test to validate our experimentation on IR models. It turned out that several significance tests exist in the literature. An important question then is: what statistical significance test should IR researchers use?

Smucker et al. [40] experimented the different significance tests on IR. They discovered that Student t-test have a good ability to detect significance in IR. The t-test is only applicable for measuring the significance of the difference between means. Student t-test consists of the following essential ingredients:

- A test statistic or criterion: IR researchers commonly use the difference in MAP or the difference in another IR metric.
- A null hypothesis: is that there is no difference in the two compared systems.
- A significance level: is computed by taking the value of the test statistic for the experimental systems. Then, determining how likely a value that larger could have occurred under the null hypothesis. This probability is known as the p-value. According to the p-value we distinguish three levels of significance. Low significance when $p \leq 0.1$. High significance when $p \leq 0.05$. Very high significance when $p \leq 0.01$.

As is measured by mean average precision, scientometric retrieval models (Sciento1, Sciento2, and Sciento3) performed an improvement rated for (5.26%, 5.26% and 14.03%) compared to the classical model. However, is this statistically significant improvement? The executed experimentations produced MAPs of 0.57 for classical retrieval model, 0.6 for both Sciento1 and Sciento2 and 0.65 for Sciento3. The differences in MAP are between 0.05 and 0.08. In order to test the significance of the difference in MAP performance, we used student t-test. Table 1 shows the results of Student T-test obtained in [2].

Table 1. Student T-test on MAP [2].

	Classic vs. Sciento1	Classic vs. Sciento2	Classic vs. Sciento3
p-value	0,003338	0,000269	0,000731

We consider the high significance level ($p \leq 0.05$) to interpret our results. Table 1 summarizes the results corresponding to the student t-test performed on our different retrieval models. The p-values correspond to the difference between classical retrieval model and respectively Sciento1, Sciento2 and Sciento3. The difference in MAP performance between the three pairs is significant at $p \leq 0.05$.

Given the obtained results, we can validate our experimentations. We approved the difference in performance between the scientometric retrieval models and the classical retrieval model.

7   Conclusion and Future Work

In this paper, we focused on the retrieval of scientific documents. This field essentially interests researchers which aim to find and produce qualitative papers. Researchers are interested to the information quality. The research paper's impact is measured by the means of scientometric indicators.

The researchers are using the online bibliographic databases to perform their IR. They are facing several difficulties when searching for relevant papers. To resolve these difficulties, we proposed a personalized retrieval system dedicated to researchers. To respond to the researchers' needs, we integrated the quality into the different parts of the system. We proposed a scientometric annotator which was the base of the retrieval system. For the retrieval personalization, we proposed a profile management module and a personalized re-ranking approach of scientific documents. The user profile management module consisted on user modeling and profile ontology construction. The personalized access to information consists on re-ranking search results according to the user preferences. For a better exploitation of search results, we proposed a multi-view visualization method. This method allows to the researcher the visualization of returned results as: (1) a list of documents enriched with scientometric information, (2) a cartographic view of the different documents enriched by quality information and (3) analytic view allowing the analysis of the information contained on the returned results.

To validate the proposed approach, we performed an evaluation of the different system's modules. From the research that has been performed, it is possible to conclude that the integration of scientometrics enhanced the performance of the different modules. We approved the significance of our results by performing a student t-test. Summing up the results, it can be concluded that the application of scientometrics in the IR process was an effective way to improve search results.

In our future research we intend to concentrate on the time factor by considering the publication year of the papers. The next stage of our research will be the experimentation on other samples and the consideration of other research disciplines such as medicine and bio-medications. Then, we will study the effect of varying disciplines on the results.

References

1. Haustein, S.: Grand challenges in altmetrics: heterogeneity, data quality and dependencies. Scientometrics **108**(1), 413–423 (2016)
2. Ibrahim, N., Habacha Chaibi, A., Ben Ghézala, H.: A scientometric approach for personalizing research paper retrieval. In: The 20th International Conference on Enterprise Information Systems (ICEIS 2018), Madeira, Portugal, vol. 2, pp. 419–428 (2018)
3. Singh, A.P., Shubhankar, K., Pudi, V.: An efficient algorithm for ranking research papers based on citation network. In: The 3rd IEEE Conference on Data Mining and Optimization (DMO 2011), Putrajaya, Malaysia, pp. 88–95 (2011)
4. Plansangket, S., Gan, J.Q.: Re-ranking Google search returned web documents using document classification scores. Artif. Intell. Res. **6**(1), 59–68 (2017)
5. Tang, J., Zhang, J., Yao, L., Li, J., Zhang, L., Su, Z.: Arnetminer: extraction and mining of academic social networks. In: The 14th ACM SIGKDD International Conference on Knowledge Discovery and Data Mining (KDD 2008), Las Vegas, Nevada, USA, pp. 990–998 (2008)
6. Nascimento, C., Laender, A.H., da Silva, A.S., Gonçalves, M.A.: A source independent framework for research paper recommendation. In: The 11th Annual International ACM/IEEE Joint Conference on Digital Libraries (JCDL 2011), Ottawa, Ontario, Canada, pp. 197–306 (2011)
7. Beel, J., Gipp, B., Langer, S., Breitinger, C.: Research-paper recommender systems: a literature survey. Int. J. Digit. Libr. **17**(4), 305–338 (2016)
8. Feyer, S., Siebert, S., Gipp, B., Aizawa, A., Beel, J.: Integration of the scientific recommender system Mr. DLib into the reference manager JabRef. In: Jose, J.M., et al. (eds.) ECIR 2017. LNCS, vol. 10193, pp. 770–774. Springer, Cham (2017). https://doi.org/10.1007/978-3-319-56608-5_80
9. Knoth, P.: Linking textual resources to support information discovery. Ph.D. thesis, The Open University (2015)
10. Pohl, S., Radlinski, F., Joachims, T.: Recommending related papers based on digital library access records. In: The 7th ACM/IEEE-CS Joint Conference on Digital Libraries (JCDL 2007), Vancouver, BC, Canada, pp. 417–418 (2007)
11. Lawrence, S., Bollacker, K., Giles, C.L.: Indexing and retrieval of scientific literature. In: The Eighth ACM International Conference on Information and Knowledge Management (CIKM 1999), Kansas City, Missouri, USA, pp. 139–146 (1999)

12. Huang, W., Kataria, S., Caragea, C., Mitra, P., Giles, C.L., Rokach, L.: Recommending citations: translating papers into references. In: The 21st ACM International Conference on Information and Knowledge Management (CIKM 2012), Maui, Hawaii, USA, pp. 1910–1914 (2012)

13. Noyons, E.C., Moed, H.F., Van Raan, A.F.: Integrating research performance analysis and science mapping. Scientometrics **46**(3), 591–604 (1999)

14. Hood, W., Wilson, C.: The literature of bibliometrics, scientometrics, and informetrics. Scientometrics **52**(2), 291–314 (2004)

15. Ibrahim, N., Habacha Chaibi, A., Ben Ahmed, M.: New scientometric indicator for the qualitative evaluation of scientific production. New Libr. World J. **116**(11/12), 661–676 (2015)

16. Huggins-Hoyt, K.Y.: African American faculty in social work schools: a citation analysis of scholarship. Res. Soc. Work Pract. **28**(3), 300–308 (2018)

17. Bornmann, L., Williams, R.: Can the journal impact factor be used as a criterion for the selection of junior researchers? A large-scale empirical study based on ResearcherID data. J. Informetrics **11**(3), 788–799 (2017)

18. Alireza, N.: Google Scholar: the new generation of citation indexes. Libri Int. J. Libr. Inf. Stud. **55**(4), 170–180 (2005)

19. Lawrence, S., Lee, C.G., Bollacker, K.: Digital libraries and autonomous citation indexing. Computer **32**(6), 67–71 (1999)

20. Harzing, A.: The Publish or Perish Book: Your Guide to Effective and Responsible Citation Analysis. Tarma Software Research, Australia (2011)

21. Thelwall, M.: Microsoft academic automatic document searches: accuracy for journal articles and suitability for citation analysis. J. Informetrics **12**(1), 1–9 (2018)

22. Salimi, N.: Quality assessment of scientific outputs using the BWM. Scientometrics **112**(1), 195–213 (2017)

23. Ibrahim, N., Habacha Chaibi, A., Ben Ghézala, H.: A new scientometric dimension for user profile. In: The 9th International Conference on Advances in Computer-Human Interactions (ACHI 2016), Venice, Italy, pp. 261–267 (2016)

24. Ibrahim, N., Habacha Chaibi, A., Ben Ghézela, H.: Scientometric re-ranking approach to improve search results. In: The 21st IEEE International Conference on Knowledge-Based and Intelligent Information & Engineering Systems (KES 2017), Marseille, France, pp. 447–456 (2017)

25. Eick, S.: Graphically displaying text. J. Comput. Graph. Stat. **3**(2), 127–142 (1994)

26. Shneiderman, B., Feldman, D., Rose, A.: WebTOC: a tool to visualize and quantify web sites using a hierarchical table of contents. Technical report CS-TR-3992 (1999)

27. Sebrechts, M.M., Cugini, J.V., Laskowski, S.J., Vasilakis, J., Miller, M.S.: Visualization of search results: a comparative evaluation of text, 2D, and 3D interfaces. In: Proceedings of the 22nd Annual International ACM SIGIR Conference on Research and Development in Information Retrieval, pp. 3–10 (1999)

28. Scott McCrickard, D., Kehoe, C.M.: Visualizing search results using SQWID. In: Proceedings of the Sixth International World Wide Web Conference, pp. 51–60 (1997)

29. Shneiderman, B., Feldman, D., Rose, A., Ferré Grau, X.: Visualizing digital library search results with categorical and hierarchical axes. HCIL Technical report No. 99-03 (1993)

30. Perrine, K., Havre, S., Hetzler, E., Battelle, E.: Interactive visualization of multiple query results. In: Proceedings of the IEEE Symposium on Information Visualization (INFOVIS 2001), pp. 105–112 (2001)

31. Hearst, M.A.: TileBars: visualization of term distribution information in full text information access. In: Proceedings of the SIGCHI Conference on Human Factors in Computing Systems, pp. 59–66. ACM Press/Addison-Wesley Publishing Co. (1995)

32. Andrews, K., Gutl, C., Moser, J., Sabol, V., Lackner, W.: Search result visualisation with xFIND. In: Proceedings of the Second International Workshop on User Interfaces to Data Intensive Systems (UIDIS 2001), pp. 50–58. IEEE (2001)

33. Hoeber, O., Yang, X.D.: The visual exploration of web search results using HotMap. In: The Tenth International Conference on Information Visualization, pp. 157–165. IEEE (2006)

34. Kohonen, T., et al.: Self organization of a massive document collection. IEEE Trans. Neural Netw. **11**(3), 574–585 (2000)

35. Skupin, A., Fabrikant, S.I.: Spatialization methods: a cartographic research agenda for non-geographic information visualization. Cartography Geogr. Inf. Sci. **30**(2), 99–119 (2003)

36. Roberts, J., Boukhelifa, N., Rodgers, P.: Multiform glyph based web search result visualization. In: The Sixth International Conference on Information Visualisation, pp. 549–554. IEEE, London (2002)

37. Heymann, S.: Gephi. In: Alhajj, R., Rokne, J. (eds.) Encyclopedia of Social Network Analysis and Mining, pp. 612–625. Springer, New York (2014). https://doi.org/10.1007/978-1-4614-6170-8

38. Moed, H.F.: From journal impact factor to SJR, Eigenfactor, SNIP, CiteScore and usage factor. In: Applied Evaluative Informetrics. QQASSC, pp. 229–244. Springer, Cham (2017). https://doi.org/10.1007/978-3-319-60522-7_16

39. Jurafsky, D., Martin, J.H.: Speech and Language Processing, 2nd edn. Pearson, London (2014)

40. Smucker, M.D., Allan, J., Carterette, B.: A comparison of statistical significance tests for information retrieval evaluation. In: The Sixteenth ACM Conference on Information and Knowledge Management, pp. 623–632. ACM, Lisbon (2007)

Inferring Students' Emotions Using a Hybrid Approach that Combine Cognitive and Physical Data

Ernani Gottardo[1](✉) and Andrey Ricardo Pimentel[2]

[1] Federal Institute of Education, Science and Technology of Rio Grande do Sul, IFRS, Bento Gonçalves, Brazil
ernani.gottardo@erechim.ifrs.edu.br
[2] Federal University of Paraná, UFPR, Curitiba, Brazil
andrey@inf.ufpr.br

Abstract. There are nowadays a strong agreement in the research community that emotions directly impact learning. Then, an important feature for a software that claim to be useful for learning is to deal with students' affective reactions. These software should be able to adapt to the users' affective reactions, trying to get a more natural human-computer interaction. Some priors works achieved relative success in inferring students' emotion. However, most of them, rely on intrusive, expensive or little practical sensors that track students' physical reactions. This paper presents as its main contribution the proposal of a hybrid model for emotion inference, combining physical and cognitive elements, using cheaper and little intrusive method to collect data. First experiments with students in a traditional classroom demonstrated the feasibility of this proposal and also indicated promising results for inference of learning centered emotions. In these experiments we achieve an accuracy rate and Cohen Kappa near to 65% and 0.55, respectively, in the task of inferring five classes of learning centered emotion. Even though these results are better than some related work, we believe they can be improved in the future by incorporating new data to the model.

Keywords: Emotion inference · Learning related emotion · Affective tutoring · Affective computing

1 Introduction

Using computers as a tool to support educational process is not new and this subject has received attention from scientific community in recent years. Even so, many issues remain related to effectiveness and possible contributions of these environments to improve the learning process [1]. One of the main limitation of educational software available nowadays refers to the lack of features to customize or adapt the software according to individual needs of the learner [2].

Intelligent Tutoring Systems (ITS) try to overcome these limitations by implementing adaptive features based on learners' individual needs. However, one of the main gap presented by most of ITS available today is the absence of features to adapt to the emotional states of the students [1,3].

S. Hammoudi et al. (Eds.): ICEIS 2018, LNBIP 363, pp. 283–302, 2019.
https://doi.org/10.1007/978-3-030-26169-6_14

Ignoring students' affective reactions is an important shortcoming of an educational software considering that cognition and neuroscience researches largely agrees that emotions play a fundamental role in humans behavior [4]. Emotions directly influence simple and automatic activities, such as reaction to some threatening event, to more complex activities such as decision making and learning [3].

According to [5], good teachers are experts in observing and recognizing students' emotional states and, based on this recognition, take actions trying to positively impact learning. Furthermore, studies indicate that approximately half of the interactions between human tutors and apprentices has focused on aspects related to affective and engagement issues [6]. Thus, as observed by [4], computational environments unable to recognize emotions are severely restricted, especially in tasks such as learning or tutoring.

So, investigating the impact on learning of factors such as motivation and affective states has emerged as a promising research avenue. Previous works have shown that usability improvements obtained by computing environments that are able to infer and adapt to affective students' reactions [7].

As an example, an educational software should not interrupt learners who are progressing well, but could offer help to others who demonstrate a steady increase in frustration [8]. Another example is to implement pedagogical intervention strategies, seeking to avoid the so-called vicious cycle [3]. Vicious cycle is characterized by the repetition of affective states with negative valence that make learning difficult, such as boredom and frustration.

Of course, the computing environment can allow the user to make on-demand requests to adapt to their needs. However, it has been shown that better results regarding the usability of the system [7] or better learning experience [9] are reported with the use of systems that proactively adapt to their users. In this context, to provide any kind of adaptation to users' emotions, it's first necessary that emotions are properly recognized by the computational environment. The task of automatically inferring users' emotions by computers is a hard job and still presents several barriers and challenges to overcome [10, 11]. The challenges range from conceptual definitions related to emotions, to mapping of signals and computationally treatable patterns into emotions [4]. In order to overcome these challenges, researchers have used a wide range of techniques and methods from a relatively new research area, known as Affective Computing.

In this context, this paper presents the proposal of a hybrid model for inference of students' emotion while using a computing learning environment. This model allows us to investigate how quite distinct data modalities (eg physical reactions and contextual information) can be combined or complemented each other. The main goal of this proposal is to improve the emotion inference process, trying to fill an important gap in current research in which the proposed hybrid approach is little explored. It is also worth noting that low-cost and non-invasive strategies (logs of system events) and minimally invasive (facial expressions) strategies are used to obtain data for the model.

The results presented in this paper point to the technical feasibility of the proposed model. In addition, some promising results could be obtained in the inference process. These results illustrate how the physical and cognitive component of the model interact in the classification task for five classes of learning related emotions considered in this work.

2 Conceptual Bases and Correlated Works

The Hybrid Model of Emotions Inference - ModHEmo proposed in this work fits in a research area called 'Affective Computing'. Affective Computing is a multidisciplinary field that uses definitions related to emotions coming from the areas like psychology and neuroscience, as well as computer techniques such as artificial intelligence and machine learning [4].

Beyond the application in educational environments, which is the focus of this research, affective computing techniques have been used in areas such as entertainment, marketing, medicine, games, human-computer interaction, among others.

The proposal presented in this work relates with one of the areas of affective computing that deals with the challenge of recognizing humans' emotions by computers. However, it is important to emphasize that human emotions or affective states are not directly observable or accessed [4]. What is revealed voluntarily or involuntarily by people are patterns of expressions and behaviors. Considering these patterns, people or systems can apply computational techniques to infer or estimate the emotional state, always considering a certain level of error or uncertainty.

Building computing environments able to recognize humans emotions has proved to be a challenge. The main obstacle is the high level of ambiguity in the process of mapping between affective states and the signal data that can be used to detect them. In this sense, it should be noted that human beings also present difficulties and ambiguities in the recognition of other people's emotions [12].

Some assumptions presented in [4] were used as a base for the construction of the ModHEmo. This author advocates that an effective process of emotions inference should take into account three steps or procedures that are common when a person tries to recognize someone else's emotions. These three steps are: (I) identify low-level signals that carry information (facial expressions, voice, gestures, etc.), (II) detect signal patterns that can be combined to provide more reliable recognition (e.g., speech pattern, movements) and (III) search for environmental information that underlies high level or cognitive reasoning related to what kind of emotional reaction is common in similar situations.

Considering the three steps or procedures described above and the correlated works consulted, we observed that several studies have been based only on the step I or I and II. Much of this research makes the inference of emotions based on physiological response patterns that could be correlated with emotions. Physiological reactions are captured using sensors or devices that measure specific physical signals, such as the facial expressions (used in this work). Among these devices, it may be mentioned: sensors that measure body movements, [10], heartbeat [4, 10], gesture and facial expressions [2, 10, 13, 14], skin conductivity and temperature [4].

On the other hand, some research like [12, 15, 16] use a cognitive approach, heavily relying on step III, described above. These researches emphasize the importance of considering the cognitive or contextual aspects involved in the process of generation and control of humans' emotions. In this line, it is assumed that the emotions are activated based on individual perceptions of positive or negative aspects of an event or object.

The relevance of considering cognitive/contextual aspects together with physical reactions is illustrated by the following three examples: (I) tears can be recognized from a video of the face, however it does not necessarily correspond to sadness, and may also represent joy [4], (II) emotions with negative valence tend to increase heart rate, but heart rate alone provide little information about specific emotions, and (III) research shows that affective states such as frustration or annoyance are not clearly distinguishable from neutral affective state using only facial expressions [17, 18].

As we can be seen below in Sect. 5, the hybrid model proposed in this work stands out by simultaneously integrating physical and cognitive elements, which are naturally integrated by humans when inferring someone else's emotions.

3   Adapting the Computational Environment Based on Affective Inferences

It is important to note that recognizing emotions represents only the first step toward creating computational environments that are adaptable to the affective reactions of its users. However, as pointed out by [3], the correct identification of affective states is indispensable for the development of *affect-sensitive* computing environments.

Considering the educational domain, the work of [19] shows that approximately half of the interactions between human tutors and apprentices focus on aspects related to affective and engagement issues. For example, a good teacher, realizing that students are confused or frustrated, should revise their teaching strategies in order to meet learners' needs, which could lead to improvements in learning [2]. On the other hand, offering help that disrupts the concentration or engagement of a student may be harmful [4].

In order to simulate the behavior of a good human tutor, improvements in the process of interaction and usability of educational software could be implemented. An alternative to this is the adaptation of the environment based on tutorial intervention strategies that make use of information about the affective states of the students.

An example of the importance of adaptation is presented in [20] which note that when the affective state confusion is not properly monitored and managed the student may become bored, affective state that hampers or even impedes learning.

In this direction, [8] presents a tutorial intervention strategy that combines cognitive and affective elements. Table 1 presents some examples of this strategy, containing the cognitive and affective element that guide the choose of the most appropriate intervention strategy.

Mentoring interventions could also be used to avoid what [21] call a 'vicious cycle'. The 'vicious cycle' occurs when one or more negative cognitive-affective states recur repeatedly, indicating that interventions are necessary to assist the students in order to help them overcome potential difficulties.

4   Set of Emotion to Be Inferred

Related work [3, 20, 22, 23] has shown that some emotions have a greater impact on the learning process. However, does not exist yet a complete understanding of which emotions are the most important in the educational context and how they influence learning [22, 23].

Table 1. Adaptive strategies combining cognitive and affective elements [8].

Cognitive element	Affective element	Adequate tutorial intervention
Student makes a mistake	Student demonstrates be curious and focused	No intervention is required. Student is engaged in learning and exploration *flow*)
	Student frowns, becomes restless and look around	Intervention actions are required. Student is confused
Student is solving problems correctly	Student shows no signs of frustration or annoyance	No intervention is required. Student is in control, concentrated and focused
	Student shows boredom or disappointment (very easy problems)	Intervention is necessary, possibly increasing the difficulty of the problems

Even so, affective states such as confusion, annoyance, frustration, curiosity, interest, surprise, and joy have emerged in the scientific community as highly relevant because their direct impact in learning experiences [23].

Considering that this research focus on the application in an educational scenario, firstly it was evaluated which set of emotions should be considered in the inference process. In this context, choosing the set of emotions to be included in this work was carried out seeking to reflect relevant situations for learning. Thus, the 'circumplex model' of [24] and the 'spiral learning model' of [5] were used as reference. These theories have been consolidated and frequently referenced in related works such as [3, 12, 23, 25].

To choose the set of emotion, we also considered a mapping of learning-centered cognitive–affective states into a two integrated dimensions: valence (pleasure to displeasure) and arousal (activation to deactivation) as shown in Fig. 1. This mapping is presented in [3] and is based on Russell's Core Affect framework [26].

Taking into account the arguments presented so far in this section, it was understood that a rational, efficient and innovative approach could be making inferences based not in a specific set of emotions, but grouping correlated set of emotions into quadrants.

In this way, the Fig. 2 shows the approach used in this work to arrange the emotions related to learning. In this proposal the dimensions 'Valence' (positive or negative) and 'Activation' or intensity (agitated or calm) are used for representing emotions in quadrants named as: Q1, Q2, Q3 and Q4. It was also assigned a representative name (see Fig. 2) for each of the quadrants considering learning related states. To represent the neutral state its was create a category named QN, denoting situations in which both valence and activation dimensions are zeroed. These quadrants, plus the neutral stated, played the role of classes in the classification processes performed by the ModHEmo that will be described in the next section.

The proposal shown in Fig. 2 is aligned with the assumptions made by [5] that teachers adapt themselves to assist students based on a small set of affective reactions as opposed to a large number of complex factors. These authors suggest that it would be advisable to work with a set of simplified emotions and that this set could be refined considering the advances in the research.

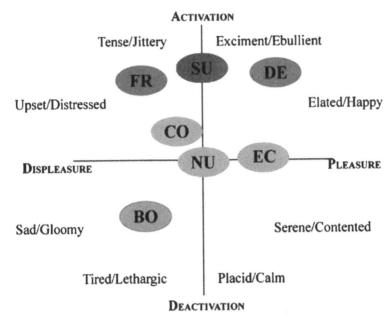

BO: Boredom, EC: Engaged Concentration, FR: Frustration, DE: Delight, SU: Surprise, NU:Neutral

Fig. 1. Learning-centered cognitive–affective states [3].

Although not considering individual emotions, it is understood that the identification of the quadrants, plus the neutral state, can be a very important aspect and enough to support many kind of adaptation actions and intervention strategies, for example.

Figure 2 also shows the main single emotions contained in each quadrant, divided into two groups: (i) physical and (ii) cognitive. These groups represent the two distinct type of data sources considered in ModHEmo. Each emotion was allocated in the quadrants considering its values of the valence and activation dimensions. The values for these two dimensions for each emotion were obtained in the work of [28] for the cognitive emotions and in [25] for the physical emotions.

The emotions in the physical group are the eight basic or primary emotions described in the classic model of [29] which are: anger, disgust, fear, happy, sadness, surprise, contempt and neutral. This set of emotions are inferred through the students' facial expressions observed during the use of an educational software.

The emotions in the cognitive group are based on the well-known cognitive model of Ortony, Clore e Collins - OCC [30]. The OCC model is based on the cognitivist theory, explaining the origins of emotions and grouping them according to the cognitive process that generates them. The OCC model consists of 22 emotions. However, based on the scope of this work, eight emotions were considered relevant: joy, distress, disappointment, relief, hope, fear, satisfaction and fears confirmed. These set of emotions were chosen because, according to the OCC model, its include all the emotions that are triggered as a reaction to events. The kind of events that occurs in the interface of an educational software are used to infer the cognitive emotions.

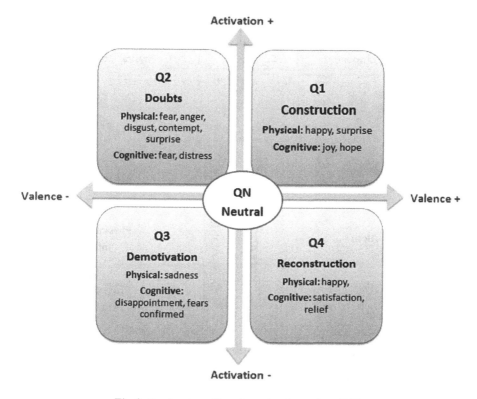

Fig. 2. Quadrants and learning related emotions [27].

It can be observed in Fig. 2 that the "happy" and "surprise" emotions in the physical component appear repeated in two quadrants, as they may have high variability in the activation and valence dimension, respectively. To deal with this ambiguity, in the implementation of the hybrid model described below, its observed the intensity of the happy emotion inferred: if happy has a score greater than 0.5 it was classified in the Q1 quadrant and, otherwise, in the Q4 quadrant. For 'surprise' emotion, which may have positive or negative valence, the solution used in the implementation of the model was to check the type of event occurring in the computational environment: if the valence of the event is positive (e.g. correct answer) 'surprise' was classified in the quadrant Q1 and, otherwise, in the Q2 quadrant.

Furthermore, the OCC model does not include a neutral state. So to infer this affective state we considered the condition when the scores of all the eight emotions of the cognitive component are equal to zero.

5 Hybrid Model of Emotion Inference

In order to evaluate the feasibility and the performance of this proposal, a hybrid model for inference of affective states - ModHEmo was proposed and implemented. This model will serve as a basis for structuring the research development and also for evaluating its results. Figure 3 schematically shows the proposed model. The main feature of

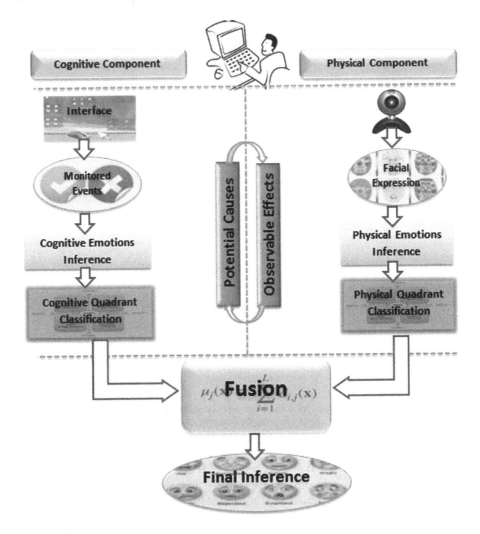

Fig. 3. Hybrid model of learning related emotions inference [27].

ModHEmo is the initial division of the inference process into two fundamentals components: physical and cognitive. This figure also shows the modules of each component and the fusion of the two components to obtain the final result.

The cognitive component, based on the OCC theory, is responsible for managing the relevant events in the computing environment. In order to implement cognitive inference, a custom version of the ALMA (A Layered Model of Affect) [28] model was used. The process of cognitive emotions inference returns *scores* normalized in the interval [0,1] for each of the eight cognitive emotions.

The physical component of ModHEmo deals with observable reactions using student's face images. Images are obtained using a standard webcam, following the occurrence of a relevant event in the interface of the computing environment. These images are used to infer the eight physical emotions included in ModHEmo by using the

EmotionAPI tool[1]. This inference process also returns *scores* normalized in the interval [0,1] for each of the eight emotions of the physical component.

Based on these initial inferences, a classification process is performed to map the emotions to the quadrants depicted in Fig. 2. At the end of this step, a normalized score in the interval [0,1] is obtained for each quadrants and also for the neutral stated in the two components.

The *Softmax* function [31] showed in Eq. 1 was the method used to normalize in interval [0,1] the ModHEmo's cognitive and physical score results. In this equation, $g_1(x), ..., g_c(x)$ are the values returned for the eight emotion for each ModHEmo's components. Then, in Eq. 1 new scores values are calculated by $g_1'(x), ..., g_c'(x), g_j'(x) \in [0,1]$, $\sum_{j=1}^{C} g_j'(x) = 1$.

$$g_j'(x) = \frac{exp\{g_j(x)\}}{\sum_{K=1}^{C} exp\{g_k(x)\}} \tag{1}$$

For the fusion of the two ModHEmo components it is assumed that some combination technique is applied. For simplicity reasons, in a first version of ModHEmo the fusion process was implemented using the *sum* function. Thus, if we denote the scores assigned to class i by the classifier j as s_i^j, then a typical combining rule is a f function whose combined final result for class i is $S_i = f(\{s_i^j j = 1, ...M\})$. The final result is expressed as $argmax_i\{S_i, ..., S_n\}$ [32]. In the context of this work, j plays the role of the physical and cognitive components while i is represented by the five classes depicted in Fig. 2.

Trying to improve the ModHEmo performance, a second version of ModHEmo was implemented. In this version, the final fusion process is performed by creating a single data set containing the scores of the quadrants of each component. After merging the two components, this dataset contains 10 attributes (5 physical + 5 cognitive) with quadrant scores for each component. The class obtained through the labeling process (to be described in the next section) is also part of the data set. Based on this data set, we trained RandomForest [33] e IBK [33] classification algorithms to perform the final inference of the model.

These algorithms were chosen because results in some initial tests with the database used in this work indicated that classification algorithms based on simple and fast techniques such as decision trees (RandomForest) and K-nearest neighbors (KNN) reached the best results.

As the main goal of this work doesn't include tuning of algorithms' parameters, we used the default Weka[2] parameters values. In addition, the 10-fold Cross-validation was used for splitting the base into test and training, considering that it's a robust and highly used technique [33].

In the next section, we will present detailed results obtained in experiments using the two versions of ModHEmo described above.

---

[1] https://azure.microsoft.com/services/cognitive-services/emotion/ developed by the University of Oxford and Microsoft.

[2] https://www.cs.waikato.ac.nz/ml/weka.

6 Experiment and Results

To verify the performance of ModHEmo inferences, experiments were performed using the two version of the model. In this experiments we used 'Tux, of Math Command' or TuxMath[3], an open source arcade game educational software. TuxMath is an educational game that allows kids to exercise their mathematical reasoning. In this game, the challenge is to answer math equation (four basic operations) to destroy meteors and protect the igloos and penguins.

The level of the game was chosen considering the age and math skill of the students. Within each level, the comets in TuxMath are released in waves with an increasing number of comets (2,4,6,8,10 ..) in each wave. A new wave begins only after all the comets of the previous wave are destroyed or reach the igloos.

Its important to notice that the experiments were approved and follows the procedures recommended by the ethics committee in research of the public federal educational institution in which the first author is professor.

Trying to reduce the interference of the research in students' behavior, the experiment was carried out in the computer lab normally used by the students and with the presence of their teacher. In addition, the students were instructed to perform the activity in a natural way without restrictions of position, movements, etc.

While students used TuxMath, some of the main events of the game were monitored. Among these events, it can be highlighted: correct and wrong math equation answers, comets that damaged penguins' igloos or killed the penguins, game over, win the game, etc.

Additionally, in order to artificially create some situations that could generate emotions, a random bug generator procedures was developed in Tuxmath. Whenever a bug was artificially inserted, it would also become a monitored event. These bugs include, among others, situations such as: (i)non-detonation of a comet even with the correct math equation response, (ii) display of comets in the middle of the screen, decreasing the time for the student to enter the correct answer until the comet hits the igloo or penguin at the bottom of the screen. The students were only informed about these random bugs after the end of the game.

These events was used as input to the cognitive component of the ModHEmo. Following the occurrence of a monitored event in TuxMath, student's face image was captured with a basic webcam and this image is used as input to the physical component of ModHEmo. With these inputs the model is then executed, resulting in the inference of the probable affective state of the student in that moment.

Before starting the game, two questions are presented to student to gather information about their goals and prospects. The first question ask students about their goals in the activity. Only data of the 15 students with 'win the game/learn math'[4] goal was considered. The second question ask students about their prospect: win or lost the game. With this information it was possible to set ALMA Tags like 'GOODEVENT', 'BADEVENT', etc.

---

[3] http://tux4kids.alioth.debian.org/tuxmath/index.php.

[4] Other goals included: have fun, participate in research and compete with colleagues.

After completing the session in the game, students were presented with a tool developed to label the data collected during the experiment. This tool allows students to review the game session through a video that synchronously shows the student's face along with the game screen. The video is automatically paused by the labeling tool at the specific time that a monitored event has happened. At this moment an image with five representative emoticons (one for each quadrant and one for neutral state) is shown and asked the student to choose the emoticon that best represents their feeling at that moment. After the student's response, the process continues.

The Fig. 4 shows a screen of the tool developed to the labeling process described above. It is highlighted in this figure four main parts: (I) the upper part shows the student's face at timestamp 2017-10-02 12:36:42.450. (II) at the bottom it is observed the screen of the game synchronized with the upper part, (III) emoticons and main emotions representative of each of the quadrants plus the neutral state and (IV) description of the event occurred in that specific timestamp (Bug - Comet Displayed in the Middle Screen).

Affective assessment using emoticons was adopted based on the fact that children perceive the classical Self-Assessment Manikin (SAM) [34] approach difficult to use and understand, according to the results presented in [35, 36]. Then, we choose to use emoticons that are familiar to kids because of its widespread use in social networks, message apps, etc.

In order to facilitate understanding about ModHEmo's operation, the results of a specific student using the first version of ModHEmo will be detailed below. The student id 6 (see Table 2) was chosen for this detailing because he was the participant with the highest number of events in the game session. Figure 5 shows the results of the inferences made by ModHEmo with student id 6. It is important to emphasize that in the initial part of the game depicted in Fig. 5 the student showed good performance, correctly answering the arithmetic operations and destroying the comets. However, in the middle part of the game, several comets destroyed the igloos and killed some penguins. But, at the end, the student recovered after capturing a power up comet[5] and won the game.

The lines in Fig. 5 depict the inferences of the physical and cognitive component and also the fusion of both. The horizontal axis of the graph shows the time and the vertical axis the quadrants plus the neutral state (see Fig. 2). The order of the quadrants in the graph was organized so that the most positive quadrant/class Q1 (positive valence and activation) is placed on the top and the most negative Q3 (negative valence and activation) on the bottom with neutral state in the center.

Aiming to provide additional details of ModHEmo's inference process, two tables with the scores of each quadrant (plus neutral state) in the physical and cognitive components were added to the Fig. 5 chart. These table show the values at the instant '10/05/2017 13:49:13' when a comet destroyed an igloo. It can be observed in the tables that in that instant, for the cognitive component, the quadrant with the highest score (0.74) was Q3 (demotivation), reflecting the bad event that has occurred (comet destroyed an igloo). In the physical component the highest score (0.98) was obtained

---

[5] Special kind of comet that enable a gun able to simultaneously destroy all the penguins in the screen.

Fig. 4. Screenshoot of labeling tool [27].

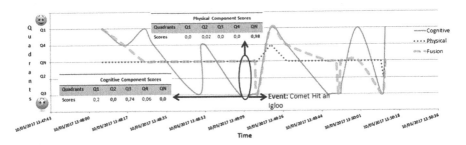

Fig. 5. ModHEmo results in one game session [27].

by QN state (neutral) indicating that student remained neutral, regardless of the bad event. Considering the scores of these tables, the fusion process is then performed. For this, initially the scores of the physical and cognitive components for each quadrant and neutral state are summed and the class that obtained greater sum of scores is chosen. As can be seen in the graph, the fusion process at these instant results in neutral state (QN), which obtained the largest sum of scores (0.98).

In the game session shown in Fig. 5 it can be seen that the physical component of the model has relatively low variation remaining most of the time in the neutral state. On the other hand, the line of the cognitive component shows a greater amplitude including points in all the quadrants of the model. The fusion line of the components remained for a long time in the neutral state, indicating a tendency of this student to not negatively react to the bad events of the game. However, in a few moments, the fusion line presented some variations accompanying the cognitive component.

6.1 Results Using *Sum* Function as a Fusion Technique

In an experiment with the first version of ModHEmo using the *Sum* function as fusion technique, eight elementary students with age ranging from ten to fourteen years old played the game.

Using the data collected with the labeling process describe above, it was possible to check the accuracy of the inferences made by ModHEmo. For example, considering the student id 6, the Fig. 6 shows the accuracy of ModHEmo inferences. This Figure shows two lines depicting the fitness between values of labels and ModHEmo inferences using the data of student id 6. For this student, the accuracy rate was 69%. So, the inferences were correct in 18 of 26 events for this students' playing session.

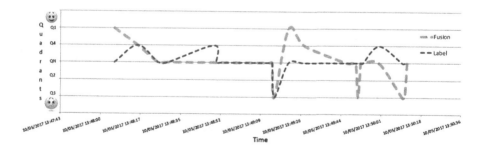

Fig. 6. Comparision between ModHEmo inferences and labels [27].

Table 2 shows the results of the eight students participating in the experiment. This table shows the number of monitored events, the number of correct inferences of the ModHEmo (Hits) and the percentage of accuracy. The number of monitored events in Table 2 is variable due to the fact that it depends, among others, on the game difficulty and student performance in the game. For confidentiality reasons, Table 2 shows only a number as students' identification. Student 6 data was used in the examples of Figs. 5 and 6 above.

6.2   Results Using Classifiers Algorithms as Fusion Technique

Trying to improve the accuracy of the ModHEmo inferences, a second version of the model was developed using classification algorithms as a fusion strategy of the physical and cognitive components.

Table 2. ModHEmo prediction accuracy [27].

Student	#Events	#Hits	% Accuracy
1	15	7	47
2	18	10	56
3	9	5	56
4	9	8	89
5	14	7	50
6	26	18	69
7	11	6	55
8	8	5	63
Total	110	66	60

To test this new version a second experiment was conducted. In this experiment participated a total of 15 students, with ages ranging from 10 to 14 years. These students were enrolled between the fifth and ninth year of elementary school in the Jaguaretê Municipal School of Education, in the rural area of Erechim-RS, Brazil.

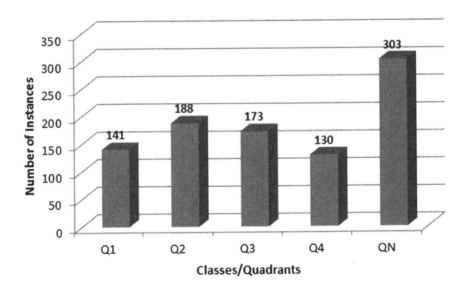

Fig. 7. Distribution of the ground truth dataset.

It is important to note that among the 15 students participating in this second experiment, it was included the data of the 8 students participating in the first experiment. This approach was used in order to achieve a larger dataset that should be more suitable for the task of training and testing the classification algorithms.

In this experiment we gather a dataset with 935 instances of monitored events in Tuxmath. Using the labeling tool described in the previous section, these 935 events were labeled by the 15 students. In this way we get a ground truth dataset that was used to train and test the classification algorithms. The Fig. 7 shows a chart with a distribution of the of the ground truth dataset created in the experiment with 935 instances.

As we can see in Fig. 7 the Class QN (neutral) was the most frequent with 303 instances (32.4%). On the other side, the class Q4 (reconstruction) was the less frequent with 130 instances (13.9%).

Table 3 shows some results achieved in the experiment using the labeled dataset with 935 instances. In this table, it's presented frequently used performance classifier metrics [33] for each algorithms.

Table 3. Global performance metrics of the two classifiers.

Algorithm	Accuracy (%)	Accuracy (instances)	Cohen's Kappa	F-Measure
RandomForest	64.81	606	0.545	0.648
IBK	63.53	594	0.532	0.635

Table 3 show that RandomForest algorithm achieved a global accuracy of 64.81% while IBK accuracy was 63.52%. The Pair-Wise T-Test [33] with significance level of 0.05 executed in Weka Experiment Environment showed that there is no statistical significant difference in accuracy between these two algorithms.

In the sequence, the Table 4 presents the confusion matrix [33] with the results of the RandomForest algorithm. The main diagonal of the confusion matrix, highlighted with gray background, represents the correct inferences for each of the five classes considered in this experiment.

Table 4. Confusion matrix for RandomForest algorithm.

Classe Correta \ Classe Prevista	Q4	Q2	Q3	QN	Q1
Q4	70	10	10	28	12
Q2	4	131	25	27	1
Q3	13	24	95	37	4
QN	13	27	37	216	10
Q1	15	12	4	16	94

The ROC (Receiver Operating Characteristic) curves [33] are a tool frequently used to check the performance of a classifier without regard to class distribution or error costs.

The Fig. 8 depict the ROC curves for the five classes obtained by the RandomForest algorithm (the curves for IBK are very similar). Inside this figure we also add a table that shows the Area Under Curve (AUC) computed in Weka. AUC report accuracy as and index ranging from zero to one (1 for a perfect and $<= 0.5$ a random classifier) [33].

6.3 Analysis of the Experiments Results

Analyzing the results of the two experiments reported above, it can be observed that in terms of global accuracy there was no significant change between the experiments. This could be considered an indication of generalization of the proposed model. However, experiments with more students are necessary to confirm the generalization of the ModHEmo results.

The task of comparing the results presented in this paper with correlated works is a sensitive and hard task because a lot of factors, like: (i) the types of sensors used in the experiments, (ii) experiment applied in a real environment or laboratory, (iii) type of interaction with the computing environment (text, voice, reading, etc.), (iv) who does the data labeling (students, external observers, etc.).

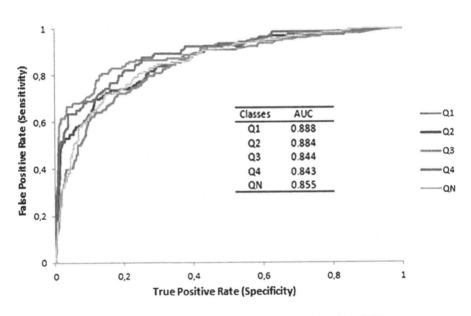

Fig. 8. ROC curves and AUC for RandomForest algorithm [37].

For example, relating to the labeling process, the work of [21] show different accuracy rates achieved when distinct actors do the labeling. These authors reported accuracy rate near to 62% when external judges or colleagues labeled the data. However, the accuracy dropped for near 52% when the student's themselves labeled the dataset.

To the best of our knowledge, there are no priors works that use exactly the same approach, kind of emotions, experimental configuration, etc. as presented in this work.

Even so, we consider important to make some comparison trying to position our results within the state of art. In this way, recent research of [8, 38–40] resemble with this work because they focus on learning related emotion and use a similar experimental design.

The works of [8] and [21] has some similarities with the present proposal because they use an identical set of emotions and experiments are made in a real learning environment. In [8], accuracy rates reported range between 80% and 89%. However, this higher accuracy is achieved by fusing a set of expensive or intrusive physical sensors, including: highly specialized camera (Kinect), chair with posture sensor, mouse with pressure sensor and skin conductivity sensor. [21] reports accuracy rates between 55% and 65% using text mining to predict emotion of students using an Intelligent Tutoring System.

Based on students' facial expression while using an ITS, [38] reported best Cohen's Kappa of 0.112. Using text mining techniques [39] showed a method to infer four emotions: bored, confused, frustrated and concentrated. For these emotions, the AUC reported was respectively 0.767, 0.777, 0.762, 0.738 and the best results for Cohen's Kappa was 0.486. The work of [40] used a deep learning approach, based on logs of students' interaction in an ITS, to predict four learning related emotion:confused, concentrating, bored, frustrated. In this work the best AUC and Cohen's Kapa was 0.78 and 0.24 respectively. Its important to note that in [40] the labeling was made by external observers.

So, the results achieved in the experiment with ModHEmo presented above show some improvements when compared with [21, 38–40]. In our experiment, Cohen's Kappa index was 0.545 and 0.532 (see Table 3) for RandomForest and IBK, respectively and AUC value was between 0.843 and 0.888 (see Fig. 8).

7   Final Consideration and Future Works

This work presented a hybrid inference model of learning related emotions that uses little or non intrusive sensors with potential for large scale and out-of-the-lab use. Inferences obtained with this model could be very useful for implementing learning environments able to appropriately recognize and adapt to learners' emotional reactions.

The model described in this paper stand out by presenting a method to combine quite distinct information (physical and cognitive) that is little explored in the research community nowadays. In this way, this proposal try to present improvements in the emotion inference process through the integration of these two important components involved in the generation and control of human emotions.

The initial results obtained can be considered promising, since, even if a direct comparison is difficult, the results obtained are similar or superior to the state of the art. However, as the hybrid approach resembles the natural process of emotions inference, it presents great opportunities for future improvements by adding new data or sensors.

Furthermore, this work is distinguished by focusing on a set of emotions relevant in teaching and learning contexts. Thus, the inferences of the proposed model, besides allowing automatic adaptations in the computational environment, could be used to depict a profile of students' affect dynamics that could drive individual pedagogical intervention.

For example, the affective states represented by the quadrants could be used to identify the so-called 'vicious-cycle' [21] which occurs when affective states related to poor learning succeed each other repeatedly. In the context of this work this 'vicious-cycle' could be detected in case of constant permanence or alternation in the quadrants Q2 and Q3. In these cases, pedagogical strategies to motivate the student should be applied.

Analyzing the results of the student id 6 presented in the previous section it can be verified that no 'vicious-cycle' could be detected nor repeated occurrences or permanence in the Q2 or Q3 quadrants. Therefore, specific actions of the educational software would not be necessary or advisable for the students used as example.

Cognitive-affective tutorial intervention strategies also could be based on the results of ModHEmo. These intervention strategies should not be applied to students who are interested or focused on the activity, even if some mistakes occurs. Furthermore, for students with constant signs of frustration or annoyance (quadrants Q2 and Q3) educational software could try strategies such as challenge or a game trying to alleviate the effects of these negative states.

As future work wed intend to expand the current dataset adding experimental data involving more students with other age groups and also other types of educational environments. It is also intended to evaluate the result of the adding new information in the physical and cognitive components. In the physical component could be aggregated information that can be obtained through the camera such as nods, blinks, etc. Information from the keyboard and mouse movements could be included in the cognitive component.

Acknowledgments. Authors would like to thank the IFRS and UFPR for financial support of this work.

References

1. Khan, F.A., Graf, S., Weippl, E.R., Tjoa, A.M.: Identifying and incorporating affective states and learning styles in web-based learning management systems. IxD&A **9**, 85–103 (2010)
2. Alexander, S.T.V.: An affect-sensitive intelligent tutoring system with an animated pedagogical agent that adapts to student emotion like a human tutor. Ph.D. thesis, Massey University, Albany, New Zealand (2008)
3. Baker, R.S., D'Mello, S., Rodrigo, M., Graesser, A.: Better to be frustrated than bored: the incidence and persistence of affect during interactions with three different computer-based learning environments. Int. J. Hum.-Comput. Stud. **68**, 223–241 (2010)
4. Picard, R.W.: Affective Computing, vol. 252. MIT Press, Cambridge (1997)
5. Kort, B., Reilly, R., Picard, R.W.: An affective model of interplay between emotions and learning: reengineering educational pedagogy-building a learning companion. In: IEEE International Conference on Advanced Learning Technologies, Proceedings, pp. 43–46. IEEE (2001)
6. Lajoie, S.P., Derry, S.J.: Motivational techniques of expert human tutors: lessons for the design of computer-based tutors. In: Computers as Cognitive Tools, pp. 83–114. Routledge (2013)
7. Becker-Asano, C., Wachsmuth, I.: Affective computing with primary and secondary emotions in a virtual human. Auton. Agent. Multi-Agent Syst. **20**, 32 (2010)

8. Woolf, B., Burleson, W., Arroyo, I., Dragon, T., Cooper, D., Picard, R.: Affect-aware tutors: recognising and responding to student affect. Int. J. Learn. Technol. **4**, 129–164 (2009)
9. Baker, R.S.J., et al.: Adapting to when students game an intelligent tutoring system. In: Ikeda, M., Ashley, K.D., Chan, T.-W. (eds.) ITS 2006. LNCS, vol. 4053, pp. 392–401. Springer, Heidelberg (2006). https://doi.org/10.1007/11774303_39
10. Grafsgaard, J.F., Wiggins, J.B., Boyer, K.E., Wiebe, E.N., Lester, J.C.: Embodied affect in tutorial dialogue: student gesture and posture. In: Lane, H.C., Yacef, K., Mostow, J., Pavlik, P. (eds.) AIED 2013. LNCS (LNAI), vol. 7926, pp. 1–10. Springer, Heidelberg (2013). https://doi.org/10.1007/978-3-642-39112-5_1
11. Baker, R.S., et al.: Sensor-free automated detection of affect in a cognitive tutor for algebra. In: Educational Data Mining 2012 (2012)
12. Conati, C.: Combining cognitive appraisal and sensors for affect detection in a framework for modeling user affect. In: Calvo, R., D'Mello, S. (eds.) New Perspectives on Affect and Learning Technologies. LSIS, vol. 3, pp. 71–84. Springer, New York (2011). https://doi.org/10.1007/978-1-4419-9625-1_6
13. Sarrafzadeh, A., Alexander, S., Dadgostar, F., Fan, C., Bigdeli, A.: "How do you know that i don't understand?" a look at the future of intelligent tutoring systems. Comput. Hum. Behav. **24**, 1342–1363 (2008)
14. D'Mello, S., Graesser, A.: Dynamics of affective states during complex learning. Learn. Instr. **22**, 145–157 (2012)
15. Jaques, P.A., Pesty, S., Vicari, R.: An animated pedagogical agent that interacts affectively with the student. In: AIED 2003, Shaping the Future of Learning Through Intelligent Technologies, pp. 428–430 (2003)
16. Paquette, L., et al.: Sensor-free or sensor-full: a comparison of data modalities in multi-channel affect detection. International Educational Data Mining Society (2016)
17. McDaniel, B., D'Mello, S., King, B., Chipman, P., Tapp, K., Graesser, A.: Facial features for affective state detection in learning environments. Proc. Cognit. Sci. Soc. **29**, 467–472 (2007)
18. Para revisão, O.: Omitido para revisão. In: Anais do XXXVI Congresso da Sociedade Brasileira de Computação, SBC, pp. 557–566 (2016)
19. Lepper, M.R., Woolverton, M., Mumme, D.L., Gurtner, J.L.: Motivational techniques of expert human tutors: lessons for the design of computer-based tutors. Comput. Cognit. Tools **1993**, 75–105 (1993)
20. Reis, H., Alvares, D., Jaques, P., Isotani, S.: Analysis of permanence time in emotional states: a case study using educational software. In: Nkambou, R., Azevedo, R., Vassileva, J. (eds.) ITS 2018. LNCS, vol. 10858, pp. 180–190. Springer, Cham (2018). https://doi.org/10.1007/978-3-319-91464-0_18
21. D'Mello, S., Picard, R.W., Graesser, A.: Toward an affect-sensitive autotutor. IEEE Intell. Syst. **22**, 53 (2007)
22. Picard, R.W., et al.: Affective learning-a manifesto. BT Technol. J. **22**, 253–269 (2004)
23. Aghaei Pour, P., Hussain, M.S., AlZoubi, O., D'Mello, S., Calvo, R.A.: The impact of system feedback on learners' affective and physiological states. In: Aleven, V., Kay, J., Mostow, J. (eds.) ITS 2010. LNCS, vol. 6094, pp. 264–273. Springer, Heidelberg (2010). https://doi.org/10.1007/978-3-642-13388-6_31
24. Russel, J.A.: A circumplex model of affect. J. Pers. Soc. Psychol. **39**, 1161–1178 (1980)
25. Posner, J., Russell, J.A., Peterson, B.S.: The circumplex model of affect: an integrative approach to affective neuroscience, cognitive development, and psychopathology. Dev. Psychopathol. **17**, 715–734 (2005)
26. Russell, J.A.: Core affect and the psychological construction of emotion. Psychol. Rev. **110**, 145 (2003)

27. Gottardo, E., Pimentel, A.R.: Hybrid model of emotions inference- an approach based on fusion of physical and cognitive informations. In: Proceedings of the 20th International Conference on Enterprise Information Systems - ICEIS 2018: vol. 2, pp. 441–450. SciTePress (2018)

28. Gebhard, P.: ALMA: a layered model of affect. In: Proceedings of the Fourth International Joint Conference on Autonomous Agents and Multiagent Systems, pp. 29–36. ACM (2005)

29. Ekman, P.: An argument for basic emotions. Cognit. Emotion **6**, 169–200 (1992)

30. Ortony, A., Clore, G.L., Collins, A.: The Cognitive Structure of Emotions. Cambridge University Press, Cambridge (1990)

31. Kuncheva, L.I.: Combining Pattern Classifiers: Methods and Algorithms. Wiley, New York (2004)

32. Tulyakov, S., Jaeger, S., Govindaraju, V., Doermann, D.: Review of classifier combination methods. In: Marinai, S., Fujisawa, H. (eds.) Machine Learning in Document Analysis and Recognition. SCI, vol. 90, pp. 361–386. Springer, Heidelberg (2008). https://doi.org/10.1007/978-3-540-76280-5_14

33. Witten, I.H., Frank, E., Hall, M.A., Pal, C.J.: Data Mining: Practical Machine Learning Tools and Techniques. Morgan Kaufmann, San Francisco (2016)

34. Bradley, M.M., Lang, P.J.: Measuring emotion: the self-assessment manikin and the semantic differential. J. Behav. Ther. Exp. Psychiatry **25**, 49–59 (1994)

35. Yusoff, Y.M., Ruthven, I., Landoni, M.: Measuring emotion: a new evaluation tool for very young chidren. In: Proceedings of the 4th International Conference on Computing and Informatics. In: ICOCI (2013)

36. Hayashi, E., Posada, J.E.G., Maike, V.R., Baranauskas, M.C.C.: Exploring new formats of the self-assessment manikin in the design with children. In: Proceedings of the 15th Brazilian Symposium on Human Factors in Computer Systems, p. 27. ACM (2016)

37. Gottardo, E., Ricardo Pimentel, A.: Improving inference of learning related emotion by combining cognitive and physical information. In: Nkambou, R., Azevedo, R., Vassileva, J. (eds.) ITS 2018. LNCS, vol. 10858, pp. 313–318. Springer, Cham (2018). https://doi.org/10.1007/978-3-319-91464-0_33

38. Bosch, N., Chen, Y., D'Mello, S.: It's written on your face: detecting affective states from facial expressions while learning computer programming. In: Trausan-Matu, S., Boyer, K.E., Crosby, M., Panourgia, K. (eds.) ITS 2014. LNCS, vol. 8474, pp. 39–44. Springer, Cham (2014). https://doi.org/10.1007/978-3-319-07221-0_5

39. Paquette, L., et al.: Sensor-free affect detection for a simulation-based science inquiry learning environment. In: Trausan-Matu, S., Boyer, K.E., Crosby, M., Panourgia, K. (eds.) ITS 2014. LNCS, vol. 8474, pp. 1–10. Springer, Cham (2014). https://doi.org/10.1007/978-3-319-07221-0_1

40. Botelho, A.F., Baker, R.S., Heffernan, N.T.: Improving sensor-free affect detection using deep learning. In: André, E., Baker, R., Hu, X., Rodrigo, M.M.T., du Boulay, B. (eds.) AIED 2017. LNCS (LNAI), vol. 10331, pp. 40–51. Springer, Cham (2017). https://doi.org/10.1007/978-3-319-61425-0_4

Visual Filtering Tools and Analysis of Case Groups for Process Discovery

Sonia Fiol González, Luiz Schirmer, Leonardo Quatrin Campagnolo,
Ariane M. B. Rodrigues, Guilherme G. Schardong, Rafael França, Mauricio Lana,
Gabriel D. J. Barbosa, Simone D. J. Barbosa, Marcus Poggi, and Hélio Lopes[✉]

Departamento de Informática,
Pontifícia Universidade Católica do Rio de Janeiro, Rio de Janeiro, RJ, Brazil
{sgonzalez,lschirmer,lcampagnolo,arodrigues,gschardong,simone,
poggi,lopes}@inf.puc-rio.br, rafael@puc-rio.br,
mauriciolana@aluno.puc-rio.br, gabrieldjb@gmail.com

Abstract. Dealing with average-sized event logs is considered a challenging task in process mining, in order to give value to event log data created by a wide variety of systems. An event log consists of a sequence of events for every case that was handled by the system. Discovery algorithms proposed in the literature work well in specific cases, but they usually fail in generic ones. Furthermore, there is no evidence that those existing strategies can handle logs with a large number of variants. We lack a generic approach to allow experts to explore event log data and decompose information into a series of smaller problems, to identify not only outliers, but also relations between the analyzed cases. In this chapter we propose a visual approach for filtering processes based on a low dimensionality representation of cases, a dissimilarity function based on both case attributes and case paths, and the use of entropy and silhouette to evaluate the uncertainty and quality, respectively, of each subset of cases. For each subset of cases, it is possible to reconstruct and evaluate each process model. Those contributions can be combined in an interactive tool to support process discovery. To demonstrate our tool, we use the event log from BPI Challenge 2017.

Keywords: Visual filtering · Process mining ·
Multidimensional projection

1 Introduction

In the world of business and services, various actors are involved in all stages of the process: designing, delivering, and offering services [1]. Companies have increasingly relied on Process Mining techniques [2] to investigate how their processes work in practice. As processes are executed, each event is recorded in a log. Process mining follows a bottom-up approach, using data mining and machine learning knowledge and techniques to extract workflow information from logs and to analyze it to generate insights about the underlying processes. From those logged events, process mining builds a structured process description [3].

Supported by Conselho Nacional de Desenvolvimento Científico e Tecnológico (CNPq) and Coordenação de Aperfeiçoamento de Pessoal de Nível Superior(CAPES).

© Springer Nature Switzerland AG 2019
S. Hammoudi et al. (Eds.): ICEIS 2018, LNBIP 363, pp. 303–323, 2019.
https://doi.org/10.1007/978-3-030-26169-6_15

The field of Business Process Management (BPM) focuses on how processes behave. Aiming to understand and to improve how processes are managed, BPM strives to support decision making and process management by analyzing, predicting, monitoring, controlling, and optimizing process activities. BPM has increasingly been supported by and inspired novel work on process mining.

The data-driven process analysis comprises Process Discovery, Conformance Checking, and Process Improvement [4]. Process discovery consists of creating a controlled structured, such as a workflow, from an event log, in a way that it represents most of the cases captured in the log. Some logs represent simple processes and allow for straightforward reconstruction of the underlying workflow. Larger and more complex workflow models, however, require more sophisticated approaches [5]. One such approach proposes to divide the event log into smaller sublogs, apply the discovery algorithm to each sublog, and then merge the results into a complete workflow structure representing the entire process. This approach significantly speeds up the discovery [6]. In our work, we also tackle the challenge of simplifying a process model so as to make it easier to understand. Conformance Checking consists in a set of techniques to compare a created process model to an actual event log that describes this model. In practice, it is used to check the execution of a business process. Process Improvement requires optimization of some kind of gain in process analysis and is beyond the scope of this work. Our work focuses on Process Discovery and Conformance Checking because they are the first steps to be overcome in process analysis. If we do not know the process, there is no way to improve it.

Several techniques have been proposed to split an event log into subsets, most of them adopting optimization strategies and resulting in a process model for each subset [7]. In our work [8], we propose a novel visual filtering approach to event logs based on multidimensional projection techniques, which create a lower dimensional representation that preserves the dissimilarity amongst cases and can be easily visualized. To calculate the dissimilarity amongst cases, we use not only the case attributes, but also the paths each case follows in the process. Using a 2D visual representation of the cases and their dissimilarity, we manually select cases that stand out or spark interest, and then generate a new event log containing only the selected ones. The filtered event log can then be analyzed using traditional process mining approaches.

To evaluate the uncertainty of each cluster, we propose to use entropy to analyze the variability of the case attributes. In addition, to evaluate the quality of each cluster, we propose to use the silhouette index to analyze the homogeneity (how cohesive) and separability. Clusters with low uncertainty and high quality are candidates to have their process models reconstructed and evaluated. Process quality measures like fitness and precision can then be calculated to assess the reconstructed process models.

The contribution of our work is therefore fourfold: (i) the visual approach for filtering processes based on a low dimensionality representation of cases; (ii) a dissimilarity function based on both case attributes and case paths; (iii) the use of entropy and silhouette to evaluate the uncertainty and quality, respectively, of each subset of cases; and (iv) the possibility to reconstruct and evaluate the corresponding process model for each subset of cases. As we will see throughout this chapter, those contributions can be combined in an interactive tool to support process discovery.

The remainder of this chapter is organized as follows. Section 2 presents related work. Section 3 introduces the main components of our approach and explains the chosen visualization techniques. Section 4 describes the filtering tool and its interaction mechanisms. Finally, Sect. 5 presents some concluding remarks and directions for future works.

2   Related Work

In the early days of BPM, process analysts had little computational support for discovering and analyzing processes [1]. More recently, several techniques, algorithms, and tools have been proposed to automate and provide intelligent support to process mining and analysis, including extracting knowledge from event logs. Visualization tools have been considered as a very useful way to explore complex data [9].

It is still challenging, however, to visualize cases captured in an event log as data points in 2D plots. At first, the human visual system is more adapted to quickly identifying visual patterns and the use of data visualizations may present some clues about the behavior of the data. However, some visualizations may suffer from occlusion and overplotting. The choice of good and adaptable visualizations is still a challenging field of research, depending on the analyzed data.

The most widely used tools for process mining are ProM, Disco, and Celonis. Van Dongen *et al.* have developed the ProM framework to support process data mining, process flow analysis, and process visualization [10]. ProM supports the following operations: data filtering (by events, by attributes, by trace attributes, etc), process discovery, conformance checking, social network mining and decision rule mining. Moreover, it is an open source, extensible environment with more than 600 plug-ins developed with several functions, such as: mining, export, import, analysis, and conversion, among others.

Disco [11] is a commercial process mining tool developed by Fluxicon with the promise of making process mining easy and fast. It has several features, such as: automated process discovery using the Fuzzy Miner algorithm [12], grouping cases by variants (different paths between activities), process animation with bottlenecks highlighting, and process statistics, among others.

Celonis[1] is another commercial process mining tool to continually monitor the analysis of process patterns and metrics. Its main features are the following: process, variant and case exploration; process discovery; data filtering; and process reporting.

Table 1 (adapted from [13]) shows a comparison between the main functionalities of these tools. As we can see, they all support process discovery and filtering the data according to some parameters. However, none of them lets the user visualize the log and group cases by attribute similarities.

Several algorithms have been proposed in the context of process mining. Closest to our area of interest we find Verbeek *et al.* [6] and Low *et al.* [14]. Verbeek *et al.* proposed an approach to group similar sequences of activities, splitting an event log file into two or more event logs with fewer variants each [6]. They implemented their approach as a plug-in in ProM6. Using six discovery algorithms, it allows the user to configure the decomposed discovery, by selecting the classifier, which maps the event log onto an activity log; the miner (or discovery algorithm).

---

[1] https://www.celonis.com/ last visited in July, 2018.

Table 1. Main features comparison between process mining tools (adapted from [13]).

Features	Prom (V. 6.4.1)	Disco (V. 1.8.2)	Celonis
Import type	mxml, xes	csv,xls, mxml, xes and fxl	csv, xls
License	open source	commercial	commercial
Output model notation	BPMN, WF, Petri nets, EPCs, transition systems, heuristics	Fuzzy model	Fuzzy model
Filtering data	X	X	X
Process discovery	X	X	X
Conformance checking	X		
Social network mining	X		
Decision rule mining	X		
Process visualization	X	X	X
Performance checking	X	X	X
Trace clustering	X		
Metrics	X		

Low *et al.* developed visualization techniques to support the analysis of resource reallocation and activity rescheduling. The visualizations help to identify resource and time-related changes which result in a cost reduction of the process. They use social network graphs to show the reallocation of resources and a timeline visualization to depict time-related information and help identify temporal patterns. Their system also allows comparing two event logs by presenting them side by side. However, it is difficult to identify issues visually when there is a large number of variants and cases, and the graph and timeline can be confusing [14].

Most process discovery tools follow the interaction scheme depicted in Fig. 1(a). First, the system receives an event log. The user can then apply concatenated filters and algorithms to analyze statistics about the log. Next, the system can generate a model and calculate various metrics to evaluate it. This type of tool usually does not allow the user to control how the model is generated.

To face the aforementioned challenges and overcome limitations of the related work, especially with respect to user control, we have developed a visual interactive filtering tool which allows users to generate smaller event logs by selecting a subset of cases. Our strategy (see Fig. 1(b)) can be considered more flexible and tractable than Verbeek *et al.*'s (Fig. 2) [6], because we allow domain experts and analysts to freely explore and analyze the data to gather insights that guide them in selecting cases and creating sublogs from their selections.

Inspired by the related work, we can state our goal of generating views from attributes filters, allowing the analyst to explore characteristics of the behavior represented in the data. In this chapter, we address the following research questions:

– RQ1: How to split the event log (data) into clusters of similar characteristics?
– RQ2: How similar are the clusters? And how different are they?
– RQ3: What are the characteristics of the clusters?

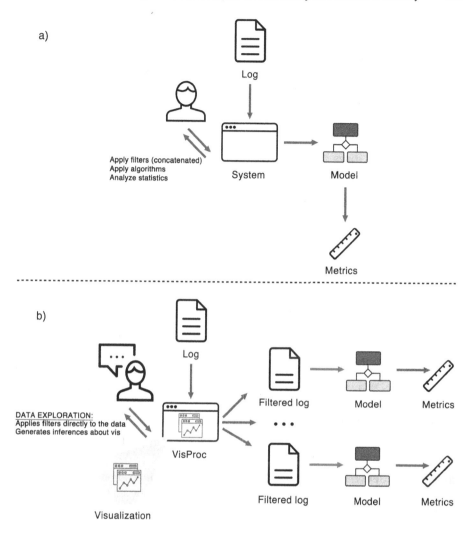

Fig. 1. Interaction scheme for the (a) usual process discovery systems (b) prototype for visually filtering event logs.

- RQ4: How to discover the process represented in each cluster sublog (*i.e.*, the log comprising the cases in a cluster)?
- RQ5: What is the quality of the process models?

3   Visual Filtering Approach

3.1   Similarity Metrics

In our approach, we allow users to evaluate the difference between cases using a set of attributes and visualizations, supported by a set of metrics.

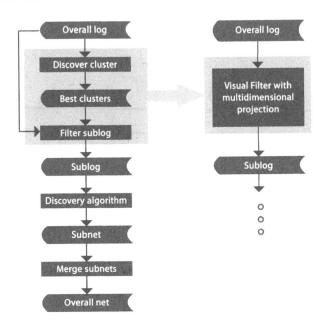

Fig. 2. Conceptual view of a decomposed discovery algorithm proposed in [6] (on the left) and our approach [8] (on the right).

Several metrics have been proposed to evaluate the differences between cases, such as metric space distance between the data, gaussian radial basis functions, among others. In previous work [8], we explain in detail the adaptations we have made to selected metrics. In this chapter, we briefly describe how we use each (adapted) metric to evaluate the difference between cases.

Dissimilarity Between Two Cases, Based on Their Attributes: For each attribute f_k we define a weight $\alpha_{f_k} \in [0, 1]$. We calculate the similarity between two different cases i, j by the weighted product of their attribute similarities:

$$sim(i, j) = \prod_{f=0}^{|F|} \left[e^{-\alpha_f (sim(f_i, f_j))} \right]$$

where $sim(f_{ki}, f_{kj})$ is calculated depending on whether f_k is numerical or categorical. The dissimilarity between the two cases is calculated as $dissim(i, j) = 1 - sim(i, j)$.

Distance Between Two Cases, Based on their Path - The Levenshtein Distance: By mapping each activity onto a letter, each path (sequence of activities) can be represented as a string. To calculate the distance (or dissimilarity) between two strings, we can use the Levenshtein distance (LD), which calculates the minimum cost of transforming one string in the other by using character insertion, removal, or substitution operations [15]. For instance, if the paths p_i and p_j of cases i and j, respectively, are $p_i = BC$ and $p_j = ABD$, we can transform p_i into p_j by inserting A at the beginning, and replacing C by D at the end. Assuming that the cost of each operation is 1, $LD(i, j) = 2$.

Distance Between Two Cases, Based on the Jaccard Index: Considering the set of activities s_i, s_j in each case i, j, we can use the Jaccard index [16] to calculate the similarity of two cases as

$$J(i, j) = \frac{s_i \cap s_j}{s_i \cup s_j}$$

The dissimilarity based on the Jaccard index is then calculated as $JD(i, j) = 1 - J(i, j)$.

3.2 Multidimensional Projection Technique

A challenge to the visualization of cases is the potentially large number of attributes used to calculate the dissimilarities between cases. Visualizing many attributes, even with the support of interaction mechanisms such as brushing and linking [17,18], can demand too much cognitive effort from users. To solve this problem, we looked for ways to represent cases and their dissimilarities in two dimensions. The Multidimensional Scaling (MDS) projection technique [19] allows us to do just that: by using an eigenvalue decomposition of the distance matrix. MDS calculates another distance matrix in a lower dimensionality space. The projected matrix preserves the relative distance between cases close to the original values, *i.e.*, the distances calculated using all available dimensions (or attributes).

Using an MDS projection, we obtain a spatial configuration in which each case is represented as a point: similar cases close to each other, and dissimilar cases further apart. To illustrate this approach, Fig. 3 shows all 31,409 cases of an event log after applying MDS.

As we saw in the previous section, the dissimilarity based on attributes may vary with the weights assigned to each attribute f_k. Therefore, the distance matrix also varies according to those weights, and consequently so do the MDS projection and its resulting spatial configuration. One may adjust those weights taking into account the variability of each attribute, so as to highlight the different groups in the data.

3.3 Cluster Quality Measures

Since clustering is an unsupervised learning method and does not have labeled data, to evaluate the quality of the resulting clusters, an internal measure like the **silhouette coefficient** is widely used [20]. Silhouette coefficient is a value between -1 and 1, and higher silhouette values correspond to more cohesive clusters while lower silhouette values to less cohesive ones.

Entropy measures the unpredictability of information content [21] and can quantify the uncertainty associated with each cluster, that is, the variability of the attributes of the cases in each cluster. The Shannon entropy [22] is the most commonly used. We used the normalized version of the Shannon entropy to have this measure of uncertainty in the unit interval [0,1] [23]. Entropy values closest to 0 mean a more homogeneous cluster, which is of most interest to us.

Mutual Information is a measure that, given any two random variables, quantifies how much information one variable shares with the other [21]. The Normalized Mutual Information (NMI) [24] is a measure between 0 and 1. NMI closer to 1 means that both variables share more information each other.

3.4 Process Metrics

To evaluate the quality of the discovered processes models, we use fitness and precision, both widely used metrics for this purpose [25].

Fitness: quantifies how well the discovered process model represents the event log.

Precision: quantifies the behavior allowed by the discovered process model, but which is not in the original event.

3.5 Case Study

We used the BPI Challenge 2017 event log as a case study to test our visual filtering approach, to find patterns and correlations between different cases based on their attributes similarities. This event log represents real-life loan applications from a financial institution. It contains all applications filed in 2016, and their subsequent handling up to February 2nd 2017. Table 2 summarizes some characteristics of this dataset.

Table 2. BPIC 2017 event log characteristics.

Applications	31, 509
Events	more than 1.2 million
Activities	26
Application attributes	4
Offer attributes	9
Possible case endings	Approved (*A_Pending*), Denied (*A_Denied*), or Cancelled (*A_Cancelled*)

We transformed the event log into a dataset with the following attributes as columns: Case ID, Activity, Resource, Timestamp, Endpoint situation (Approved, Denied or Cancelled), Variant (defined by Disco) and selected features such as Credit Score, Requested Amount, Number of Offers and Loan Goal. Each row represents a case. We also created matrices of cases × cases with the dissimilarities based on the Jaccard index and the Levenshtein distance, calculated as described in Sect. 3.

We used MDS as the projection algorithm and visually represented cases in a 2D Scatterplot chart. We experimented with different weights to calculate the dissimilarities, in order to evaluate the data and find which attributes had a good grouping factor in the dataset. The selected weights (Table 3) generated the projection shown in Fig. 3. This selection helps us to answer RQ1 (*How to split the event log (data) into clusters of similar characteristics?*). Considering only the features of Levenshtein distance and Loan Goal attribute with highest weights (1) and the other attributes with weights varying between 0 and 0.5, in the best case, the stress of the projection is 0.15.

For each group, we calculated the normalized Shannon's entropy [22] to evaluate how homogeneous the groups are; the Silhouette [20] to evaluate how cohesive the groups are; and some characteristics of the case frequencies in each group for each selected feature. More details about these calculations and our findings from the characterization of the groups can be found in [8].

Table 3. Weights defined to filter the 31409 cases.

Attribute	Value
Credit score	0.50
Requested amount	0.50
Number of offers	0.00
Loan goal	1.00
Levenshtein distance	0.00
Jaccard index	1.00

MDS

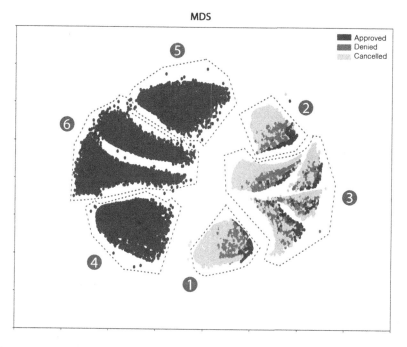

Fig. 3. Our proposed case filtering visualization using MDS projection with 6 selected clusters and the parameters specified previously.

One of the great advantages of our prototype is that we can select groups, compare the values of Silhouette, Entropy, and characteristics of the attributes and change the selection until the values of the adopted metrics are considered adequate. The final groups can be considered *clusters* of cases.

Figure 4(b) shows the result for the entropy values of the six manually selected clusters. The closer an Entropy value is to zero, the more interesting it is, as it means that the cluster is homogeneous. We use a brown-blue gradient color scale to identify the ranges, where dark blue represents clusters with entropy closer to zero, *i.e.*, more homogeneous clusters.

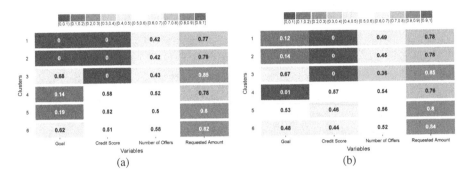

Fig. 4. Entropy value of each cluster, per variable, for clusters defined using: (a) our Visual filtering approach, and (b) K-Medoids [8]. (Color figure online)

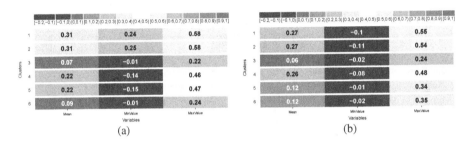

Fig. 5. Silhouette value of each cluster, per variable, for clusters defined using (a) Visual filtering approach, and (b) K-Medoids. (Color figure online)

We also use a heatmap to visually represent Silhouette values (Fig. 5(a)). Here there is a different gradient color scale to identify the ranges. Higher silhouettes (corresponding to more cohesive clusters) appear in shades of green, where the darker green is Silhouette close to 1 (most cohesive). The lower Silhouette values (less cohesive clusters) appear in shades of red, where the darker red is silhouette close to −1 (least cohesive). From the results of these two measures, we are able to answer RQ2 (*How similar are the clusters? And how different are they?*).

After grouping cases in clusters, analysts usually attempt to characterize and describe each cluster. One way to do this is to visualize the distribution of relevant attributes. Figure 6 shows the distributions of four selected attributes (Credit Score, Requested Amount, Number of Offers and Loan Goal), grouped by cluster. These distributions, together with the entropy and Silhouette heatmaps and values, allow us to answer RQ3 (*What are the characteristics of the clusters?*).

Clusters 1 and 2 have similar values of Entropy and Silhouette and presented a high percentage of *Cancelled* cases (10.8% and 7.3%, respectively – see Figs. 4(a) and 5(a), lines 1 and 2). In both clusters, the Entropy for *Goal* and *Credit Score* is 0, meaning there is no uncertainty. However, the purpose of the loans differ from one cluster to another: *Car* for cluster 1 and *Home Improvement* for cluster 2. As we can see from Fig. 3, those clusters are distant from one another, but they have similar characteristics.

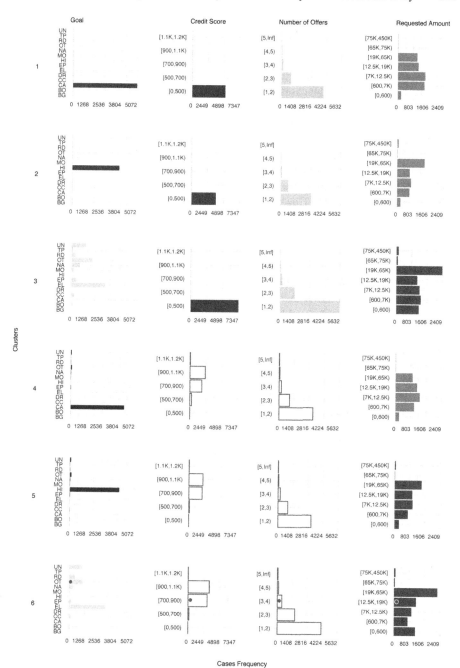

Fig. 6. Distribution of each attribute, per cluster, colored according to the entropy value. For the Loan Goal variable, the values are abbreviated as follows: UN = Unknown, TP = Tax payments, RD = Remaining debt home, OT = Other, see explanation, NA = Not specified, MO = Motorcycle, HI = Home improvement, EP = Extras pending limit, EL = Existing loan take over, DR = Debt restructuring, CC = Caravan/Camper, CA = Car, BO = Boat and BG = Business goal [8]. (Color figure online)

Clusters 4 and 5 also have similar characteristics: high entropy and low silhouette, with very similar values (Figs. 4(a) and 5(a), lines 4 and 5). As in the case of clusters 1 and 2, a striking difference between clusters 4 and 5 is the *Loan Goal*: Car for cluster 4 and Home improvement for cluster 5. These clusters are also distant visually but similarly shaped (Fig. 3). All cases in both clusters were *Approved*.

Clusters 1 and 4 have similar Entropy values for *Request Amount*, but very different values for the other attributes and for the Silhouette. They are close to each other, but very different visually. The same can be noticed in clusters 2 and 5.

Only clusters 1, 2 and 3 had cases that were cancelled: 10.81%, 7.38% and 15.00% of the total cases, respectively. Cluster 3 has mostly *Cancelled* cases, high Entropy for the selected attributes (except for *Credit Score*, which is 0) and very low Silhouette (Figs. 4(a) and 5(a), line 3). Cluster 6 has similar characteristics: high Entropy in all considered attributes and very low Silhouette (Figs. 4(a) and 5(a), line 6). However, practically all cases were *Approved*, since just one case in this group was *Denied*.

Comparing cluster 3 to cluster 6, we can see that they are visually distant from one another (Fig. 3). Their Silhouette and Entropy values are very similar, but not the *Credit Score* and *Number of Offers* attributes.

Cluster 6 has a peculiarity that called our attention: only one case in this group was *Denied*. This case is represented by the red dot in the Fig. 6. As we can see, the value of this case in each category is within limits, however the path between events differs from the paths of other cases. This leads us to conclude that, in fact, the MDS projection technique is based on the similarity of the attributes, regardless of the covered paths.

Also, some attributes have high variability for some attributes, especially *Requested Amount*. This may explain the high Entropy values for this attribute [8].

Once we had manually selected the clusters, we chose a clustering algorithm to compare the Entropy and Silhouette values. We used a version of K-Medoids [26] named Partitioning Around Medoids (PAM) to automatically group cases from the entire event log into k clusters. As we had visually identified six clusters, we also defined $k = 6$ as input to the K-medoids algorithm.

We calculated the Entropy and Silhouette for each K-medoids cluster and generated the corresponding Heatmap. As shown in Figs. 4(b) and 5(b), the Silhouette values obtained using our approach were similar to whose obtained using K-medoids. In general, the separation of data points through the visual filtering tool resulted in clusters with low uncertainty value for the Goal and Credit Score attributes, when compared to K-Medoids.

In order to compare how the datapoints are grouped using the MDS projection technique and the K-medoids algorithm, we plotted the projections of 31, 397 cases. In the case of manually selected clusters, we painted all datapoints (cases) of the same cluster with the same color (Fig. 7(a)). Next, we placed each datapoint in its respective cluster defined by K-medoids (Fig. 7(b)), ensuring to make the best correspondence based on the frequency of cases in each cluster. This way, if most of the datapoints in a K-medoids cluster C_k belong to a certain manually selected cluster C_m, C_k was assigned the same identifying number as C_m. And each datapoint was represented in the same color in both visualizations, to enable comparison. Figure 7(c) shows a concordance matrix which reveals how the data points are distributed in clusters in each approach.

Comparing both visualizations and the concordance matrix, we see that K-medoids clusters scrambles some cases, particularly those of clusters 4, 5 and 6 (*Approved* endpoint situation).

(a)   (b)   (c)

Fig. 7. Projection of the 31, 397 cases, colored according to their (a) MDS assigned cluster and (b) K-Medoids assigned cluster. (c) Concordance matrix of the distribution of data points in each cluster, per approach. Adapted from [8].

To compare both approaches numerically, we calculated the Normalized Mutual Information (NMI) to quantify the amount of information shared between the clusters across approaches. The resulting NMI of 0.84 indicates that 84% of the cases fall into the same groups in the two approaches, that is, our manual approach obtains a classification similar to the one obtained using an automatic approach.

4   Visual Filtering Prototype

We first implemented our visualizations in R and Python, as proof of concept and to conduct some empirical tests to evaluate the feasibility of the approach. We then developed a prototype to incorporate all functionalities of our filtering approach. Figure 8 shows the prototype with four highlighted regions. The basic idea is to load an event log and select some attributes or variables (region A); define weights for those attributes (C); and generate the projection (B). With the projection, it is possible to manually select groups (B) and export the selection (A) as a CSV file with the filtered cases to be used in a process mining software, such as ProM [27] or Fluxicon Disco [28].

Region C brings the filter with the selected attributes and algorithms, and their corresponding weights. In this way, the user can experiment with different weight values and generate different projections, which may in turn reveal different groupings, also taking into account the projection stress value. The stress value is a measure concerning the quality of the projection, *i.e.*, the deformation related to the data in the original space of features and the reduced dimension. Normally, the stress vary from 0 to 1.

Region D is where the descriptive analysis can be made: statistics of the entire event log (Fig. 8), cluster characterization (Fig. 9), and cluster quality metrics (Entropy and Silhouette, Figs. 10 and 11, respectively). The left-hand side of the Statistics tab shows information about variants, whereas the right-hand side shows particular information of the selected variant and for a certain attribute (in this case, Variant 1 and attribute *Loan Goal*), with respect to the total.

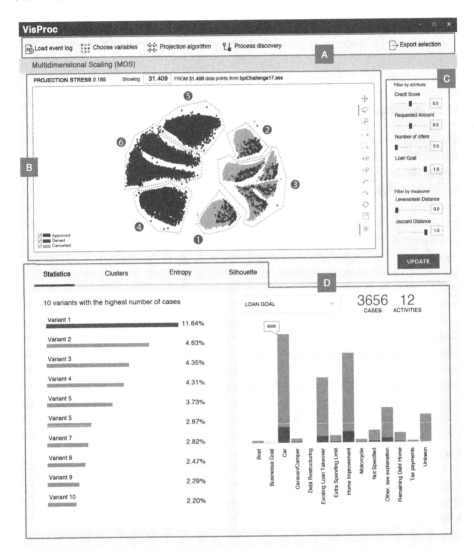

Fig. 8. Our visual filtering prototype: projection and statistics.

Figure 12 shows the resulting Petri Net (process model) when the user selects Cluster 1 in the projection and runs the process discovery functionality. This functionality calls Prom's Inductive Miner algorithm (Mine Petri Net with Inductive Miner) and calculates the Fitness (Replay a Log on Petri Net for Conformance Analysis plugin) and Precision (Check Precision based on Align-ETConformance plugin) to evaluate the process model quality.

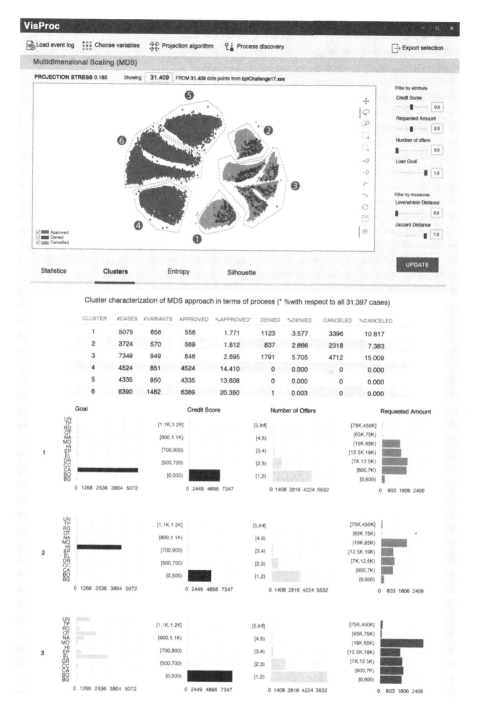

Fig. 9. Our visual filtering prototype: cluster characterization.

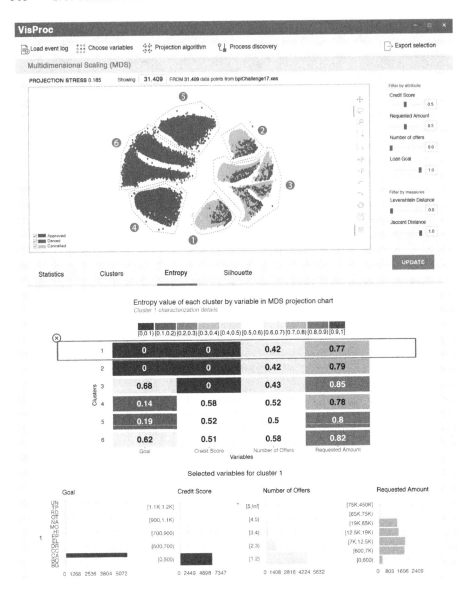

Fig. 10. Our visual filtering prototype: entropy.

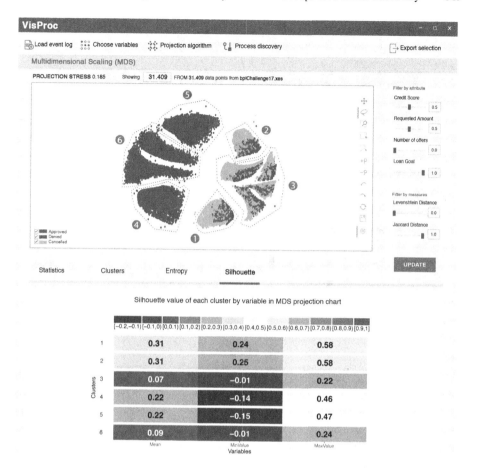

Fig. 11. Our visual filtering prototype: silhouette.

Our Cluster 1 has 62.39% for Fitness (how well the process model represents the event log) and 56.34% for Precision (how different is the generated log of the process model with respect to the original log). After generating all six Petri Nets, we are able to answer RQ4 (*How to discover the process represented in each cluster sublog?*) and RQ5 (*What is the quality of the process models?*).

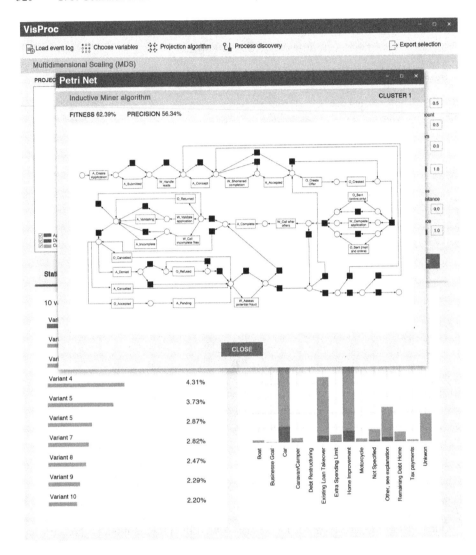

Fig. 12. Our visual filtering prototype: Petri net.

5   Conclusion

In this paper, we presented a prototype for visual filtering cases of an event log based on the approach proposed in [8]. This approach evaluates the similarity between pairs of cases using multidimensional projection techniques to plot those cases into a 2D scatterplot. Cases with similar characteristics appear close to each other in the scatterplot, so we can create smaller groups (clusters) and filter the event log to make analysis and comparisons between them.

We used the prototype to filter the BPI Challenge 2017 event log. First, we selected some attributes for analysis (Credit Score, Requested Amount, Number of Offers and Loan Goal). Then, we generated the projection using MDS and the selected weights for each attributes, so it was possible to split the log into clusters of similar characteristics and evaluate how similar or different those clusters were. It was also possible to understand specific characteristics of each cluster and to discover its corresponding process model. The prototype allowed us to evaluate the quality of the generated models, since it can calculate its fitness and precision.

In our approach, we chose to use Entropy and Silhouette as quality metrics for each cluster. The color relation used between the entropy analysis and the group characterization helped us to uncover characteristics of each cluster. Similarly, using matching colors in the visual projections generated by the MDS helped us to confirm the hypothesis that K-Medoids mixed together in a cluster data points that had different characteristics with respect to our approach.

Each visual cluster selected using our approach groups cases with similar attributes. When reconstructing the processes for each cluster, we observed that the traces (sequences of activities) were different. In other words, although the traces were different, the cases were similar in terms of attributes. This way of filtering is very interesting because we are creating clusters not only based on cases that went through exactly the same sequence of activities, but also based on attributes.

One way to investigate why these cases are grouped together despite different traces would be to execute a decision mining algorithm based on the case attributes. In this way, the decision points could be explained. Of course, it will only be possible to understand or know the decisions if the data is structured with this information.

We evaluated our analysis using only the BPI challenge log. We wish to conduct our analysis with other logs, in order to carry out a deeper validation of the chosen visualizations, methods, and prototype.

People who have used our prototype made some interesting observations with opportunities for improvement to help users better understand the process and filter cases. Regarding performance, MDS is not efficient when dealing with a large number of cases, both in terms of computational time and memory used. To solve this problem, we are including in our prototype a Local Affine Multidimensional Projection (LAMP) [29,30], which enables users to set a group of control points and dynamically project new instances. LAMP can be efficiently used with very large datasets.

We also plan to include in the prototype attribute-level linkage, similar to the analysis described in Sect. 3.5. It would allow the analyst to quickly discover which attributes contribute to the dataset variability, and thus fine-tune the attribute weights for the dissimilarity metric.

Finally, it would be useful to incorporate our tool as a ProM plug-in, so it can be more seamlessly used during the whole process mining cycle.

Acknowledgements. We thank Conselho Nacional de Desenvolvimento Científico e Tecnológico (CNPq) and Coordenação de Aperfeiçoamento de Pessoal de Nível Superior (CAPES) for partially financing this research.

References

1. Mendling, J., Baesens, B., Bernstein, A., Fellmann, M.: Challenges of smart business process management: an introduction to the special issue (2017)
2. Tiwari, A., Turner, C.J., Majeed, B.: A review of business process mining: state-of-the-art and future trends. Bus. Process Manag. J. **14**, 5–22 (2008)
3. Van der Aalst, W.M., Weijters, A.: Process mining: a research agenda. Comput. Ind. **53**, 231–244 (2004)
4. Van der Aalst, W.M.: Process Mining: Data Science in Action. Springer, Heidelberg (2016). https://doi.org/10.1007/978-3-662-49851-4
5. Van der Aalst, W., Weijters, T., Maruster, L.: Workflow mining: discovering process models from event logs. IEEE Trans. Knowl. Data Eng. **16**, 1128–1142 (2004)
6. Verbeek, H., Van der Aalst, W., Munoz-Gama, J.: Divide and conquer: a tool framework for supporting decomposed discovery in process mining. Comput. J. **60**, 1–26 (2017)
7. De Koninck, P., De Weerdt, J.: Multi-objective trace clustering: finding more balanced solutions. In: Dumas, M., Fantinato, M. (eds.) BPM 2016. LNBIP, vol. 281, pp. 49–60. Springer, Cham (2017). https://doi.org/10.1007/978-3-319-58457-7_4
8. Silva, L.J.S., et al.: Visual support to filtering cases for process discovery. In: ICEIS, no. 1, pp. 38–49 (2018)
9. Keim, D.A.: Visual exploration of large data sets. Commun. ACM **44**, 38–44 (2001)
10. van Dongen, B.F., de Medeiros, A.K.A., Verbeek, H.M.W., Weijters, A.J.M.M., van der Aalst, W.M.P.: The ProM framework: a new era in process mining tool support. In: Ciardo, G., Darondeau, P. (eds.) ICATPN 2005. LNCS, vol. 3536, pp. 444–454. Springer, Heidelberg (2005). https://doi.org/10.1007/11494744_25
11. Günther, C.W., Rozinat, A.: Disco: discover your processes. BPM (Demos) **940**, 40–44 (2012)
12. Günther, C.W., van der Aalst, W.M.P.: Fuzzy mining – adaptive process simplification based on multi-perspective metrics. In: Alonso, G., Dadam, P., Rosemann, M. (eds.) BPM 2007. LNCS, vol. 4714, pp. 328–343. Springer, Heidelberg (2007). https://doi.org/10.1007/978-3-540-75183-0_24
13. Sudhamani, Aruna Devi, T., Kumudavalli, M.: An informative and comparative study of process mining tools. Int. J. Sci. Eng. Res. **8**, 8–10 (2017)
14. Low, W.Z., Van der Aalst, W.M., ter Hofstede, A.H., Wynn, M.T., De Weerdt, J.: Change visualisation: analysing the resource and timing differences between two event logs. Inf. Syst. **65**, 106–123 (2017)
15. Levenshtein, V.I.: Binary codes capable of correcting deletions, insertions, and reversals. Soviet Physics Doklady, vol. 10, pp. 707–710 (1966)
16. Jaccard, P.: Étude comparative de la distribution florale dans une portion des alpes et des jura. Bull. Soc. Vaudoise Sci. Nat. **37**, 547–579 (1901)
17. Buja, A., McDonald, J., Michalak, J., Stuetzle, W.: Interactive data visualization using focusing and linking. In: Proceeding Visualization 1991, pp. 156–163. IEEE Computer Society Press (1991)
18. Becker, R.A., Cleveland, W.S., Hill, M.: Brushing scatterplots. Technometrics **29**, 127–142 (1987)
19. Kruskal, J.B., Wish, M.: Multidimensional Scaling, vol. 31 (1978)
20. Rousseeuw, P.J.: Silhouettes: a graphical aid to the interpretation and validation of cluster analysis. J. Comput. Appl. Math. **20**, 53–65 (1987)
21. Cover, T.M., Thomas, J.A.: Elements of Information Theory. Wiley, Hoboken (2012)
22. Shannon, C.E., Weaver, W.: A Mathematical Theory of Communication. University of Illinois Press, Champaign (1963)

23. Lopes, H., Barbosa, S.: Uncertainty measures and the concentration of probability density functions. In: Learning and Inferring: Festschrift for Alejandro Frery. College Publications (2015)
24. Strehl, A., Ghosh, J.: Cluster ensembles–a knowledge reuse framework for combining multiple partitions. J. Mach. Learn. Res. **3**, 583–617 (2002)
25. Buijs, J.C.A.M., van Dongen, B.F., van der Aalst, W.M.P.: On the role of fitness, precision, generalization and simplicity in process discovery. In: Meersman, R., et al. (eds.) OTM 2012. LNCS, vol. 7565, pp. 305–322. Springer, Heidelberg (2012). https://doi.org/10.1007/978-3-642-33606-5_19
26. Kaufman, L., Rousseeuw, P.J.: Finding Groups in Data: An Introduction to Cluster Analysis, vol. 344. Wiley, Hoboken (2009)
27. Verbeek, H., Buijs, J., Van Dongen, B., van der Aalst, W.M.: ProM 6: the process mining toolkit. Proc. BPM Demonstr. Track **615**, 34–39 (2010)
28. Rozinat, A., Günther, C.W., Niks, R.: Process Mining and Automated Process Discovery Software for Professionals-Fluxicon Disco (2017). http://fluxicon.com/disco
29. Joia, P., Coimbra, D., Cuminato, J.A., Paulovich, F.V., Nonato, L.G.: Local affine multidimensional projection. IEEE Trans. Vis. Comput. Graph. **17**, 2563–2571 (2011)
30. Pagliosa, P., Paulovich, F.V., Minghim, R., Levkowitz, H., Nonato, L.G.: Projection inspector: assessment and synthesis of multidimensional projections. Neurocomputing **150**, 599–610 (2015)

Schema-Independent Querying and Manipulation for Heterogeneous Collections in NoSQL Document Stores

Hamdi Ben Hamadou[1(✉)], Faiza Ghozzi[2], André Péninou[3], and Olivier Teste[3]

[1] IRIT, Université de Toulouse, UPS, CNRS, Toulouse, France
hbenhama@irit.fr
[2] Université de Sfax, MIRACL, Sfax, Tunisia
faiza.ghozzi@isims.usf.tn
[3] IRIT, Université de Toulouse, UT2J, CNRS, Toulouse, France
{peninou,teste}@irit.fr

Abstract. NoSQL document stores offer native support to efficiently store documents with different schema within a same collection. However, this flexibility made it difficult and complex to formulate queries or to manipulate collections with multiple schemas. Hence, the user has to build complex queries or to reformulate existing ones whenever new schemas appear in the collection. In this paper, we propose a novel approach, grounded on formal foundations, for enabling schema-independent queries for querying and maintaining multi-structured documents. We introduce a query reformulation mechanism which consults a pre-constructed dictionary. This dictionary binds each possible path in the documents to all its corresponding absolute paths in all the documents. We automate the process of query reformulation via a set of rules that reformulate most document store operators, such as select, project and aggregate. In addition, we automate the process of reformulating the classical manipulation operators (insert, delete and update queries) in order to update the dictionary according to the different structural changes made in the collection. These two processes produce queries which are compatible with the native query engine of the underlying document store. To evaluate our approach, we conduct experiments on synthetic datasets. Our results show that the induced overhead when querying or updating can be acceptable when compared to the efforts made to restructure the data and the time required to execute several queries corresponding to the different schemas inside the collection.

Keywords: Information systems · Document stores · Query reformulation

1 Introduction

Document-oriented stores are becoming very popular because of their simple and efficient abilities to manage large semi-structured data sets. Each document,

S. Hammoudi et al. (Eds.): ICEIS 2018, LNBIP 363, pp. 324–349, 2019.
https://doi.org/10.1007/978-3-030-26169-6_16

usually formatted in JSON, is stored inside a record without any control over the
its schema. Therefore, a collection groups a heterogeneous set of documents for
which no common schema is required. Although this flexibility is very efficient
at loading time, the resulting heterogeneity is a serious issue when querying
documents. Indeed, in order to obtain relevant results, users have to be aware
of all existing schemas while formulating their queries and have to combines all
the schemas in complex queries. We can consider three classes of heterogeneity
in the context of document stores [1]:

- *Structural heterogeneity* points to the different structures that exist in documents. The main issue is the existence of several paths to access the same
  attribute; e.g., the position of an attribute denoted *"name"* may not the same
  in two documents (nested or root-based for example).
- *Syntactic heterogeneity* exists when different attributes refer to the same concept; e.g., the *"name"* of a person may be denoted by *"name,"* *"names"* or
  "first_name" in different documents.
- *Semantic heterogeneity* exists when the same attribute refers to different concepts; e.g., the attribute *"name"* may designate a *"person name"*, an *"animal
  name"* or a *"disease name"* depending on documents.

In this paper, we focus on the structural heterogeneity issue in document
stores.

```
                              {  "_id":2,
                                 "name":"honore de balzac",
    {  "_id":1,                   "book":{
       "name":"victor hugo",           "title":"le pere Goriot"
       "title":"les miserables",       "year":1835
       "year":1862                 }
    }                          }

            (1)                           (2)


    {  "_id":3,                    {  "_id":4,
       "name":"charles baudelaire",    "name":"pierre de ronsard",
       "artwork":[                     "title":"les amours",
          { "title":"les fleurs du mal",  "year":1557,
            "year":1857                "details":{
          },                              "editor":{
          { "title":"le spleen de Paris",    "name":"le livre de poche"
            "year":1855                   }
          }                           }
       ]                          }
    }

            (3)                           (4)
```

Fig. 1. Illustrative example of a collection (C) with four documents describing authors.

Example. We use the example collection of Fig. 1 composed of four documents
describing authors and some of their publications. Documents are described using
JavaScript Object Notation [2].

Let us suppose we are interested in collecting information related to *"name of authors"* and their publications. The query will be formulated over the attributes *"name"* and *"title"*. Any user may expect results for the five authors of the example (except perhaps for *"paul verlaine"*) and possibly five titles. If we look at Fig. 1, the attribute *"name"* does not raise any problem since it is always in the same position in the five documents (same path in all documents). However, the attribute *"title"* may rise some issues because of its various structural positions within documents. To reach the attribute *"title"* various paths exist in the different document schemas: *"title,"* *"book.title,"* *"artwork.1.title"* and *"artwork.2.title"* (here *".1."* and *".2."* stand for the indexes in the array *"artwork"*). When using MongoDB data store system, we can formulate the query *db.C.find({}, { "name": 1, "title": 1})*. Executing such query will return the following set of documents because of the structural heterogeneity of the attribute *"title"*:

```
[ { name:"victor hugo",
    title:"les miserables"      },
  { name:"honore de balzac"     },
  { name:"charles baudelaire"   },
  { name:"pierre de ronsard",
    title:"les amours"          }
]
```

If we formulate an alternative query that matches with another path of *"title"*, *db.C.find({}, { "name": 1, "book.title": 1})*, the following set of documents is returned:

```
[ { name:"victor hugo"                    },
  { name:"honore de balzac",
    book:{title:"le pere Goriot"} }
  { name:"charles baudelaire"             },
  { name:"pierre de ronsard"         } ]
```

We can notice that each query only returns a sub-part of the expected result (author/title pairs) meanwhile returning redundant incomplete results. The incompleteness is here defined from the user point of view that can easily visually find the requires data. Moreover, without any other query, these incomplete two queries results can lead the user to interpret that *"charles baudelaire"* has no publication in the collection; and that is not true.

Our contribution offers transparent querying mechanisms able to overcome the structural heterogeneity. Therefore, the user is not asked to have full knowledge about all underlying document schemas. We develop a system that we call *EasyQ* (Easy Query for NoSQL databases), which consists of a schema-independent querying on heterogeneous documents that are supposed to describe a given entity We opt for a solution that does not affect the original documents schemas and that performs query reformulation. We introduce a data dictionary to collect and store all schemas variations. A query reformulation mechanism rewrites (reformulates) user queries according to this dictionary and thus hides the complexity of building adequate queries to overcome the schema hetero-geneity [3]. Moreover, we define how to automatically update the dictionary whenever data are updated (create, update, delete). So each query execution is reformulated using an up-to-date dictionary with regard to the collection.

This paper is organized as follows. The second section reviews the most rele-vant works that deal with querying heterogeneous documents. Section 3 explains the proposed approach and proposes its formalization. Section 4 presents our first experiments and the time/size cost of our approach regarding the size of collections and the variety of schemas.

2   Related Work

The problem of querying heterogeneous data is an active research domain studied in several contexts such as data-lake [4], federated database [5], data integration, schema matching [6]. We classify the state-of-the-art works into four main cate-gories regarding the solution given to handle the heterogeneity problems.

Schema Integration. The schema integration process is performed as an inter-mediary step to facilitate the query execution. In their survey paper, [6] presented the state-of-the-art techniques used to automate the schema integration process. Matching techniques can cover schemas or even instances. Traditionally, lexical matches are used to handle the syntactic heterogeneity. Furthermore, thesaurus and dictionary are used to perform semantic matching. The schema integra-tion techniques may lead to data duplication and possible initial underlying data structure loss, which may be impossible or unacceptable to support legacy applications. Let us notice that we built our schema-independent querying upon the ideas developed in schema level matching techniques.

Physical Re-factorization. Several works have been conducted to enable querying over semi-structured data without any prior schema validation or restriction. Generally, they propose to flatten XML or JSON data into a rela-tional form [7–9]. SQL queries are formulated based on relational views built on top of the inferred data structures. This strategy suggests performing heavy physical re-factorization. Hence, this process requires additional resources such as the need for external relational database and extra efforts to learn the uni-fied inferred relational schema. Users dealing with those systems have to learn new schemas every time they change the workload, or new data are inserted (or updated) in the collection because it is required to re-generate the relational views and the stored columns after every change.

Schema Discovery. Other works propose to infer implicit schemas from semi-structured documents. The idea is to give an overview of the different elements present in the integrated data [10,11]. In [12] the authors propose summariz-ing all document's schema under a skeleton to discover the existence of fields or sub-schema inside the collection. In [13] the authors suggest extracting collection structures to help developers while designing their applications. The heterogene-ity problem here is detected when the same attribute is differently represented (different type, different position inside documents). Schema inferring methods are useful for the user to have an overview of the data and to take the necessary measures and decisions during application design phase. The limitation with such logical view is the need to manual process while building the desired queries by including the desired attributes and their possible navigational paths. In that case, the user is aware of data structures but is required to manage heterogeneity.

Querying Techniques. Others works suggest resolving the heterogeneity problem by working on the query side. Query rewriting [14] is a strategy to rewrite an input query into several derivations to overcome the heterogeneity. The majority of works are designed in the context of the relational database where heterogeneity is usually restricted to the lexical level only. Regarding the hierarchical nature of semi-structured data (XML, JSON documents), the problem of identifying similar attributes is insufficient to resolve the problem of querying documents with structural heterogeneity. To this end, the keyword querying has been adopted in the context of XML [15]. The process of answering a keyword query on XML data starts by identifying the existence of the keywords within the documents without the need to know the underlying schemas. The problem is that the results do not consider the heterogeneity in term of attributes but assume that if the keyword is found so document is adequate and has to be returned to the user. Other alternatives to find different navigational paths leading to the same attribute is supported by [16,17]. Only the structural heterogeneity is partially addressed. There is always a need to know the underlying document structures and to learn a complex query language. In addition, these solutions are not built to run over large-scale data. In addition, we notice the same limitations considerations with JSONiq [18] the extension to XQuery designed to deal with large-scale semi-structured data.

This paper takes these ideas one step further by introducing a schema-independent querying approach that is built over the native operators supported by document stores. We believe that, in collections of heterogeneous documents describing a given entity, we are able to handle the documents heterogeneities via the use of query rewriting mechanisms introduced in this paper. Our approach is performed in a transparent way over the initial document structures. There is no need to perform heavy transformation nor to use further auxiliary systems.

3   Easy Schema-Independent Querying and Manipulation for Heterogeneous Collections in NoSQL Document Stores

In this section, we give a detailed description of the main components of our system *EasyQ* (*Easy Query*) with references to formal definitions for the document model and the querying/maintenance operators.

3.1   Rewriting Approach at a Glance and Architecture

Rewriting Approach at a Glance. Most document stores are not able to overcome the structural heterogeneity and do not offer default support for schema-independent querying. Therefore, the schemaless flexibility does not affect the loading stages. However, querying multi-structured collections becomes challenging and requires particular efforts from the users to build precise queries that cover all schemas derivation for desired results.

Let us suppose that a user chooses to execute the following projection operation (`title`) over the collection from Fig. 1. It is notable that there are three distinct locations for the attribute `title` i.e. (root based in document (1) and (4), but as a leaf-node in documents (2) and (3) with two different paths. Hence, the query can only fetch `title` information from documents (1) and (4). To bypass the heterogeneity, we introduce a transparent mechanism that reformulates the initial query (`title`) to a new query containing all corresponding locations for the attribute `title`. The attribute `title` has the following three distinct absolute paths: (`title, book.title, artwork.1.title, artwork.2.title`).

In order to facilitate the discovery of existing absolute paths, we define a dictionary mapping any partial path (sub-path included in an existing absolute path), any attribute and all absolute path in the collection to their corresponding absolute paths detected in all document structures. This process runs during the data loading stage to infer the underlying document structures and creates new dictionary entries or updates existing entries with new absolute paths are found. For instance, in the collection (C), to reformulate the projection operation, our query reformulation engine consults a dictionary, extracts the following entry (`title,[title, book.title, artwork.1.title, artwork.2.title]`). Therefore, it is possible to reformulate the query although it is b=necessary to deal with more complex cases as explained in next sections of the paper.

Moreover, the dictionary helps to reformulate queries with partial paths. This flexibility allows the user to formulate queries when absolute paths are unknown or helps him to solve attributes ambiguity, e.g. the attribute `name` in

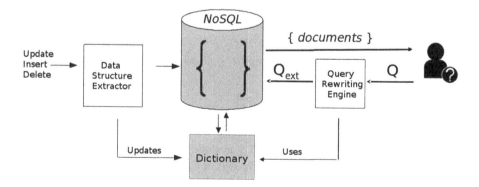

Fig. 2. EasyQ architecture: data structure extractor and query reformulation engine.

document (4) car refer to both the author name and the editor name. If the user projects out information regarding the attribute `name`, information related to the author and editor names are retrieved (since the partial path `name` is linked to `name` and `details.editor.name`. However, a query using the partial path `editor.name` helps to reduce the ambiguity and the reformulation returns only `name` information of the editors.

Architecture. We describe in Fig. 2 the architecture of our system *EasyQ* that is mainly composed of three components: the query reformulation engine, the data structure extractor and the dictionary. Moreover, Fig. 2 shows the data flow during the data loading and the query evaluation phases. We employ a data structure extractor at data loading phase to enrich the dictionary with references to all existing paths and their derivation caused by the structural heterogeneity in the collection.

Our system ensures that the dictionary is updated each time a document is updated, removed or inserted in the collection. During the query evaluation phase, *EasyQ* takes as input the query Q which is a combination of attributes (leaf nodes, partial paths or absolute paths) and the desired collection. Then, the *EasyQ* query reformulation engine consults the dictionary and generates a new query Q_{ext} that includes all existing absolute paths from the different documents structures. Finally, the document store needs only to execute a single query *Qext* to return the desired results to the user.

In the next sections, we introduce the formal definitions of a document, of a collection and the set of new definitions that we define for the purposes of this study, such as document schema, collection schema, dictionary, collection manipulation operators and the kernel of querying operators that we support in this work along with their corresponding reformulation rules.

3.2   Formal Foundations

Definition (Collection). A collection C is defined as a set of documents

$$C = \{d_1, \ldots, d_{n_c}\}$$

where $n_c = |C|$

Definition (Document). A document $d_i \in C$, $\forall i \in [1, n_c]$, is defined as a (*key, value*) pair

$$d_i = (k_{d_i}, v_{d_i})$$

- k_{d_i} is a key that identifies the document
- $v_{d_i} = \{a_{d_i,1} : v_{d_i,1}, \ldots, a_{d_i,n_i} : v_{d_i,n_i}\}$ is the document value. The document value v_{d_i} is defined as an *object* composed of a set of $(a_{d_i,j}, v_{d_i,j})$ pairs, where each $a_{d_i,j}$, is a *string* (*in Unicode* $\mathbb{A}^*$) called *attribute* and each $v_{d_i,j}$ is the *value*, which can be *atomic* or *complex* (object or array). A value $v_{d_i,j}$ is detailed below.

An atomic value $v_{d_i,j}$ $\forall j \in [1..n_i]$ can take one of following four forms:

- $v_{d_i,j} = n$ where n is a numerical value (*integer* or *float*);
- $v_{d_i,j} = $ "s" where "s" is a string formulated in *Unicode* $\mathbb{A}^*$;
- $v_{d_i,j} = \beta$ where $\beta \in B$, the set of Boolean $B = \{true, \ false\}$;
- $v_{d_i,j} = \bot$ where $\bot$ is the *null* value.

A complex value $v_{d_i,j}$ $\forall j \in [1..n_i]$ can take one of the following two forms:

- $v_{d_i,j} = \{a_{d_i,j,1} : v_{d_i,j,1}, \ \ldots, \ a_{d_i,j,m} : v_{d_i,j,m}\}$ is an object value composed of $(a_{d_i,j,k}, \ v_{d_i,j,k})$ pairs where $\forall k \in [1..m]$, $a_{d_i,j,k}$ are strings in $\mathbb{A}^*$ called *attributes* and $\forall k \in [1..m]$, $v_{d_i,j,k}$ are *values*. This is a recursive definition which is identical to the previously defined document value;
- $v_{d_i,j} = [v_{d_i,j,1}, \ \ldots, \ v_{d_i,j,l}]$ represents an array of values $v_{d_i,j,k}$, $\forall k \in [1..l]$, we note $n_l = |v_{d_i,j}|$.

Therefore, in the event of complex document values, internal values $v_{d_i,j,k}$ can also be complex and they can take the same form as document values (atomic or complex). To cope with nested documents and navigate inside documents schemas, we adopt classical navigational path notations using dots [2,19].

Definition (Document Schema). The document schema s_{d_i} inferred from the document value v_{d_i} of document d_i, is formally defined as:

$$s_{d_i} = \{p_1, \ldots, p_{n_i}\}$$

where, $\forall j \in [1..n_i]$, p_j is an absolute path leading to an attribute $a_k \in v_{d_i}$. For multiple levels of nesting, the navigational paths are extracted recursively in order to find the paths from the root to any attribute that can be found in the document hierarchy. The schema s_{d_i} of a document d_i is defined from its value $v_{d_i} = \{a_{d_i,1} : v_{d_i,1}, \ldots, a_{d_i,n} : v_{d_i,n}\}$ as follows:

- if $v_{d_i,j}$ is atomic, $s_{d_i} = s_{d_i} \cup \{a_{i,j}\}$;
- if $v_{d_i,j}$ is object, $s_{d_i} = s_{d_i} \cup \{a_{d_i,j}\} \cup \{\cup_{p \in s_{d_i,j}} a_{d_i,j}.p\}$ where $s_{d_i,j}$ is the schema of $v_{d_i,j}$;
- if $v_{d_i,j}$ is an array, $s_{d_i} = s_{d_i} \cup \{a_{d_i,j}\} \cup \{\cup_{k=1}^{n_l}$
$\left(\{a_{d_i,j}.k\} \cup \{\cup_{p \in s_{d_i,j,k}} a_{d_i,j}.k.p\}\right)\}$ where $s_{d_i,j,k}$ is the schema of the kth

value into the array $v_{d_i,j}$ (and as defined previously, $n_l = |v_{d_i,j}|$).

For example, the document schema of document (3) in Fig. 1 is: {`name`, `artwork`, `artwork.1`, `artwork.1.title`, `artwork.1.year`, `artwork.2`, `artwork.2.title`, `artwork.2.year`} and document schema of document (4) is {`name`, `title`, `year`, `details`, `details.editor`, `details.editor.name`}.

Definition (Collection Schema). The schema S_C inferred from collection C is defined by

$$S_C = \bigcup_{i=1}^{n_c} s_{d_i}$$

3.3   Dictionary

The architecture of our approach relies on the construction of a dictionary that enables the query reformulation process. We introduce the dictionary as a repository in which we store all the absolute paths from the collection schema leading to any existing path in the collection (partial/absolute paths, leaf nodes). So, we next define existing paths in documents, in the collection, and then the collection dictionary.

Definition (Document Paths). We define P_{d_i} as the set of all existing paths in a document d_i. A path is any sequence of attributes that does exist in at least one document in the collection. A path could be a sequence of attributes starting from the root of the document and leading to any attribute. In this case, the path is called an *absolute path*. In addition, it could be a *sub-path* where the sequence does not necessarily start from the root. In this case, the path is called *partial path*. It is obvious that an absolute or partial path may end with a *leaf node*. Finally, we consider leaf node attributes as paths too since they correspond to the *partial* path definition.

We give a formal and recursive definition of P_{d_i} starting from the value v_{d_i} of document d_i.

For $v_{d_i} = \{a_{d_i,1} : v_{d_i,1}, \ldots, a_{d_i,n} : v_{d_i,n}\}$

– if $v_{d_i,j}$ is atomic: $P_{d_i} = P_{d_i} \cup s_{v_{d_i,j}}$;
– if $v_{d_i,j}$ is an object: $P_{d_i} = P_{d_i} \cup s_{v_{d_i,j}} \cup P_{v_{d_i,j}}$ where $P_{v_{d_i,j}}$ is the set of existing paths for the value $v_{d_i,j}$;
– if $v_{d_i,j}$ is an array: $P_{d_i} = P_{d_i} \cup s_{v_{d_i,j}} \cup (\cup_{k=1}^{n_l} P_{v_{d_i,j,k}})$ where $P_{v_{d_i,j,k}}$ is the set of existing paths of the kth value of $v_{d_i,j}$.

For example, the document paths $P_{(3)}$ of document (3) in Fig. 1 is {_id, name, artwork, artwork.1, artwork.1.title, artwork.1.year, artwork.2, artwork.2.title, artwork.2.year, title, year}, and $P_{(4)}$ of document (4) is {_id, name, title, year, details, details.editor, details.editor.name, editor, editor.name}.

Definition (Collection Paths). The set of all existing paths in a collection is called P_c and is defined as:

$$P_C = \cup_{i=1}^{n_c} P_{d_i}$$

We notice that $S_C \subseteq P_C$ (all absolute paths to any element are included in P_C).

Definition (Dictionary). The dictionary $Dict_C$ of a collection C is defined by:

$$Dict_C = \{(p_k, \triangle_{p_k}^C)\}$$

where:

– $p_k \in P_C$ is an existing path (absolute or relative path, any attribute, leaf node) in the collection C;

- $\triangle^C_{p_k} = \{(p_{k,1}, c_{k,1}), \ldots, (p_{k,n_k}, c_{k,n_k})\}$ is the set of key-value pairs $(p_{k,j}, c_{k,j})$ where the key $p_{k,j}$ is an absolute paths leading to p_k and the value $c_{k,j} \in N$ is the number of documents having the path $p_{k,j}$. Formally, $p_{k,j} \in S_C$ and $p_{k,j}$ takes the form $p_{k,j} = p_l.p_k$ where p_l is an absolute path from the root or p_l is empty. Let us insist that $\cup_{j=1}^{n_k} p_{k,j} \subseteq S_C$. The value $c_{k,j}$ is necessary to support the documents updates (see Sect. 3.4) in order to get the dictionary coherent with the database: all existing paths are in the dictionary and only existing paths are in the dictionary.

We will adopt the following notations for the rest of the paper:

- $\forall d \in Dict_C$:
  - $path(d) \rightarrow p_k$,
  - $allPathsTo(d) \rightarrow \triangle^C_{p_k}$,
- $\forall pair \in \triangle^C_{p_k}$:
  - $absPath(pair) \rightarrow p_{k,j}$,
  - $ndoc(pair) \rightarrow c_{k,j}$ (that stands for "number of documents").

Let us depict some representative entries of the dictionary for the collection C in Fig. 1:

- `name`: {(`name`, 4), (`details.editor.name`, 1)};
- `details.editor.name`: {(`details.editor.name`, 1)};
- `details.editor`: {(`details.editor`, 1)};
- `details`: {(`details`, 1)};
- `editor.name`: {(`details.editor.name`, 1)};
- `editor`: {(`details.editor`, 1)};
- `title`: {(`title`, 2), (`artwork.1.title`, 1), (`artwork.2.title`, 1), (`book.title`, 1)}.

3.4 Data Updating: Collection Manipulation Operators

Collection manipulation operators are used to add (insert), delete, and modify (update) documents in a collection. We use classical operators of document stores. Since these operations may lead to changes in schemas of documents, we add to these operators a simultaneous operation to update the dictionary accordingly. Let us underline that manipulation operators of the collection are processed "as they are" and are not subject to any rewriting nor reformulation as for queries (see following sections on query reformulation).

Figure 3 shows the process of executing a manipulation operator on a collection. We denote Φ as the insert operator, Ψ as the delete operator and Θ as the update operator. We define any collection manipulation operator as the computation of two pseudo-collections C_{old} and C_{new} corresponding to the data changes occurring in the collection during the operator processing. Thus, we formally represent the result of any collection operator as follows:

$$operator(C) = C \backslash C_{old} \cup C_{new}$$

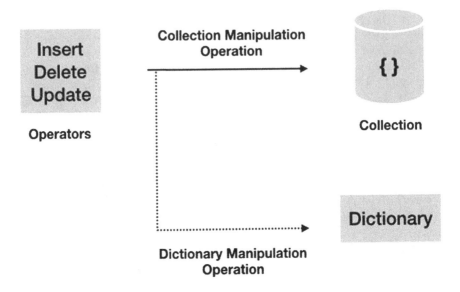

Fig. 3. Collection manipulation process.

where C is the collection to manipulate, C_{old} the set of documents to remove from C and C_{new} the set of documents to add to C.

For the different operators, we can define:

– In case of insert:
  - $C_{old} = \emptyset$,
  - C_{new} holds the set of new documents to insert in the collection.
– In case of delete:
  - C_{old} holds the documents to delete from the collection,
  - $C_{new} = \emptyset$.
– In case of update:
  - C_{old} holds the documents to be updated in their initial state,
  - C_{new} holds the set of documents to be updated after applying the update. Important note: in case of update, the documents of C_{new} and C_{old} must hold the same documents ids when necessary.

In the next three sections, we explain how to update the dictionary when processing each of the operators. The processing of the operator itself remains classical.

Definition (Dictionary Update on Documents Inserting). We define insert operation and we present how we update entries or add new entries to the dictionary. The execution of this operator is automatic whenever new data comes to the collection. We denote the insert operation as:

$$\Phi(C) \rightarrow (C_{new}, C_{old} = \emptyset)$$

The goal is to update the dictionary $Dict_C$ according to C_{new} by:

- adding new entries in the dictionary $Dict_C$ (e.g. new paths in documents);
- adding new absolute paths to initial paths existing in $Dict_C$;
- updating the number of documents for each absolute path in $Dict_C$.

The insertion of the new collection C_{new} into the collection C requires to update the dictionary $Dict_C$ as follows:

- Generate a dictionary called $Dict_{C_{new}}$ from the collection C_{new} in the same way as described in Sect. 3.3.
- Enrich the initial dictionary $Dict_C$ of the collection C as follows:
  $\forall d' = (p'_k, \triangle^{C_{new}}_{p'_k}) \in Dict_{C_{new}}$:

  - if $\nexists\ d \in Dict_c/path(d) = path(d')$, that is if no entry exists for p'_k in $Dict_C$:
    $$Dict_c = Dict_c \cup \{d'\}$$

  - if $\exists\ d \in Dict_C/path(d) = path(d')$, that is if an entry d exists for the path p'_K in $Dict_C$:
    $\forall pair' \in allPathsTo(d')$
    * if $\exists pair \in allPathsTo(d)/absPath(pair) = absPath(pair')$

    $$ndoc(pair) = ndoc(pair) + ndoc(pair')$$

    * else $allPathsTo(d) = allPathTo(d) \cup \{pair'\}$

Let us now give an example of a simple insert in the collection C of Fig. 1. The user inserts the new document (5): {"_id": 5, "description": {"name": "victor hugo", "title": "notre-dame de paris"}, "details": {"editor": {"name": "le livre de poche"}, "city": "paris"}}.
C_{new} will contain the document (5) and its dictionary $Dict_{C_{new}}$ will be:

- description: {(description, 1)};
- description.name: {(description.name, 1)};
- name: {(description.name, 1), (details.editor.name, 1)};
- description.title: {(description.title, 1)};
- details.editor.name: {(details.editor.name, 1)};
- details.editor: {(details.editor, 1)};
- details: {(details, 1)};
- editor.name: {(details.editor.name, 1)};
- editor: {(details.editor, 1)};
- details.city: {(details.city, 1)};
- city: {(details.city, 1)};

The dictionary $Dict_C$ of collection C is updated as follows (when compared to entries examples of Sect. 3.3):

- modified entries of $Dict_C$ (number of documents, italics):
  - details.editor.name: {(details.editor.name, *2*)};
  - details.editor: {(details.editor, *2*)};
  - details: {(details, *2*)};

- editor.name: {(details.editor.name, 2)};
- editor: {(details.editor, 2)};

– added entries for a path in $Dict_C$ (added path and number of documents, italics):

- name: {(name, 4), (details.editor.name, 2), (*description.name, 1*)};

– added entries in $Dict_C$:

- description: {(description, 1)};
- description.name: {(description.name, 1)};
- description.title: {(description.title, 1)};
- details.city: {(details.city, 1)};
- city: {(details.city, 1)}.

Definition (Dictionary Update on Documents Deleting). We define the dictionary delete operation to present how we update or remove entries from the dictionary. The execution of this operator is automatic whenever a delete operation is executed on the collection C. We denote the dictionary delete operation as:

$$\Psi(C) \rightarrow (C_{new} = \emptyset, C_{old})$$

The goal is to update $Dict_C$ according to C_{old} by:

– updating the number of documents for each absolute path deleted in C_{old};
– deleting unnecessary entries for absolute paths having count equals to 0;
– deleting unnecessary entries in the dictionary $Dict_C$, those having no more absolute paths in the collection to reach them.

The collection C_{old} to delete from C is treated as follows to update $Dict_C$:

– Generate a dictionary called $Dict_{C_{old}}$ from the collection C_{old} as described in Sect. 3.3.
– Update the dictionary $Dict_C$ as follows:
$\forall d' = (p'_k, \Delta^{C_{old}}_{p'_k}) \in Dict_{C_{old}}$
let $d \in Dict_C/path(d) = path(d')$
  - $\forall pair' \in allPathsTo(d')$
  let $pair \in allPathsTo(d)/absPath(pair) = absPath(pair')$
    * $ndoc(pair) = ndoc(pair) - ndoc(pair')$
    * $if\ ndoc(pair) = 0\ then\ allPathTo(d) = allPathTo(d) \setminus \{pair\}$
  - $if\ |allPathTo(d)| = \emptyset : Dict_C = Dict_C \setminus \{d\}$

Let us now give an example of a simple delete in the collection C of Fig. 1. The user deletes document _id number 2.

C_{old} will contain the document (2) and we do not detail entries of dictionary $Dict_{C_{old}}$ which will be very similar to previous example.

The dictionary $Dict_C$ of collection C is updated as follows (when compared to entries examples of Sect. 3.3):

– modified entries of $Dict_C$ (number of documents, italics):

- name: $\{$(name, *3*), (details.editor.name, 1)$\}$;
- modified entries for a path in $Dict_C$ (removed paths, italics and strike):
  - title: $\{$(title, 2), (artwork.1.title, 1), (artwork.2.title, 1), ~~(book.title, 1)~~$\}$.
  - year entry is modified similarly to title;
- removed entries from $Dict_C$:
  - ~~book: {(book, 1)}~~;
  - ~~book.title: {(book.title, 1)}~~;
  - ~~book.year: {(book.year, 1)}~~.

Definition (Dictionary Update on Documents Updating). We define the dictionary update operation to present how we update or remove entries from the dictionary. The execution of this operator is automatic whenever an update operation is executed on the collection C. We denote the dictionary remove operation as:

$$\Theta(C) \rightarrow (C_{new}, C_{old})$$

The goal is to update $Dict_C$ according to C_{old} and C_{new}. This update is processed by updating $Dict_C$ from C_{old} as explained for delete and then update the $Dict_C$ from C_{new} as explained for insert. Let us notice that the processing of update could be somehow reversed, first from C_{new} and then from C_{old}, leading to the same result.

This basic processing may be enhanced to avoid two updating steps for $Dict_C$. For instance, a simple update operation of the value of a path leads to, first, many update/delete operations in the dictionary $Dict_C$ and, then, many update/insert operations in the dictionary $Dict_C$. Furthermore, parts of documents that are not targeted by the update are processed as if they were updated (deleted then inserted). This optimisation which can be very complex is out of the scope of this paper and will be subject to future works.

3.5   Data Querying: Minimum Closed Kernel of Operators

In this section, we define a minimum closed kernel of querying operators based on the document operators defined in [20].

Definition (Kernel). The kernel K is a minimal closed set composed of the following operators:

$$k = \{\pi, \ \sigma, \ \gamma\}$$

The projection (π), the selection, also called restriction (σ) and the aggregation (γ).

In our preliminary work, this kernel was limited to the project and select operators [21]. We have extend it in recent work and we provide support for aggregation operator [22]. In this paper, we redefine the previously supported operators by adding additional features for the project and selecting operators as introduced in [20]. In our approach, we enable the reformulation of queries that have absolute paths or partial paths.

In the next sections, for each operator, we first define the operator, including the possible partial paths. Then, we define the operator reformulation that integrates the same behaviour as a classical evaluation, and we provide a reformulation example along with its evaluation.

Projection

Definition (Projection). The project operator is applied to collection C_{in} by possibly projecting existing paths from the input documents, renaming existing paths, or adding new paths as defined by the sequence of paths A. This returns an output collection C_{out}.

$$\pi_A(C_{in}) = C_{out}$$

The sequence of paths is defined as $A = a_1, \ldots, a_n$, where a_j can take the form:

- p_j is a path existing in the input collections; $p_j \in P_{C_{in}}$ which enables the projection of existing paths. As a result, the schema of the collection C_{out} contains p_j.
- $q_j : v_j$ is a key value pair composed of a path q_j and a value v_j, which can take the form:
  - v_j is an existing path in the input collection; $p_j \in P_{C_{in}}$ and its value are assigned to the new absolute path q_j in C_{out}. This form renames the path v_j to q_j in C_{out}.
  - $[p_1, \ldots, p_m]$ an array of paths where $\forall l \in [1..m]$ $p_l \in P_{C_{in}}$ produces a new absolute path q_j in C_{out} whose value is an array composed of the values obtained through the paths p_l $\forall l \in [1..m]$.
  - β is a Boolean expression which compares the values of two paths in C_{in}, i.e. $\beta = (p_a \; \omega \; p_b)$, $p_a \in P_{C_{in}}$, $p_b \in P_{C_{in}}$ and $\omega \in \{=; >; <; \neq; \geq; \leq\}$. The evaluation of the Boolean expression is assigned to the new absolute path q_j in C_{out}.

Projection Extension Process. The projection operation is extended by including additional paths which are automatically extracted from the dictionary. The original set of elements A is extended as follows:

$A_{ext} = a_{1_{ext}}, \ldots, a_{n_{ext}}$ where $a_{j_{ext}}$ is the extension of all $a_j \in A$. The extended projection operation is defined as follows:

$$\pi_{A_{ext}}(C_{in}) = C_{out}$$

In order to ensure the same results as the native document query engine, we introduce two new operators "$|''$" and "$||''$".

The operator "$|''$" may be seen as an "alternative path or remove" operator for path value pairs. Let us suppose there exists a list of paths $[p_{i,1}..p_{i,n_i}]$. An expression such as $p_i : p_{i,1}| \ldots |p_{i,n_i}$ is evaluated as follows for a document $d_i \in C_{in}$:

- if $\exists p_j \in [p_{i,1}..p_{i,n_i}]$, where $p_j \in S_{d_i}$, then the corresponding document in the output collection $d_i^{'} \in C_{out}$ contains the path p_i with the value v_{p_j} (from d_i), so $p_i \in S_{d_i^{'}}$,
- if $\nexists p_j \in [p_{i,1}..p_{i,n_i}]$, where $p_j \in S_{d_i}$, i.e. no path from list is found in the document d_i, the corresponding document in the output collection $d_i^{'} \in C_{out}$ does not contain the path p_i, so $p_i \notin S_{d_i^{'}}$.

The operator "$||$" may be seen as an "alternative path value or null value" operator. It is applied to a simple list of paths and is evaluated according to a value. Let us suppose there exists a list of paths $[p_{k,1}..p_{k,n_k}]$. The expression $p_{k,1}||\cdots||p_{k,n_k}$ is evaluated as follows for document d_i:

- if $\exists p_j \in [p_{k,1}..p_{k,n_k}]$, where $p_j \in S_{d_i}$, the operator returns the value v_{p_j} from the path p_j in d_i,
- if $\nexists p_j \in [p_{k,1}..p_{k,n_i}]$, where $p_j \in S_{d_i}$, i.e. no path of the list is found in the document d_i, the operator returns a *null* value.

We can now define the following set of rules to extend each element $a_j \in A$ based on its four possible forms:

- a_j is a path in the input collection $a_j \in P_{C_{in}}, a_{j_{ext}} = p_{j,1} \mid \cdots \mid p_{j,n_{a_j}} \forall p_{j,k} \in \triangle_{a_j}^{C_{in}}$
- a_j is a key value pair $q_j : v_j$; $a_{j_{ext}}$ is expressed as follows:
  - if v_j is a path and $v_j \in P_{C_{in}}$, then $a_{j_{ext}}$ takes the form $q_j : p_{j,1} \mid \cdots \mid p_{j,n_j}, \forall p_{j,l} \in \triangle_{v_j}^{C_{in}}$;
  - if v_j is an array of paths $v_j = [p_1, \ldots, p_m]$, then each path p_j is replaced by a "$||$" combination and $a_{j_{ext}}$ takes the form
    $$q_j : \left[p_{1,1} \mid\mid \cdots \mid\mid p_{1,n_1}, \ldots, p_{m,1}\mid\mid \cdots \mid\mid p_{m,n_m}\right]$$
    $\forall p_{j,l} \in \triangle_{p_l}^{C_{in}}$;
  - if v_j is a Boolean expression β, $a_{j_{ext}} = (p_a^{'} \ \omega \ p_b^{'})$ where $p_a^{'} = p_{a,1} \mid \cdots \mid p_{a,n_a}, \forall p_{a,l} \in \triangle_{p_a}^{C_{in}}$ and $p_b^{'} = p_{b,1} \mid \cdots \mid p_{b,n_b}, \forall p_{b,l} \in \triangle_{p_b}^{C_{in}}$.

Projection Extension Example. Let us suppose that the user asks for a projection $\pi_{tit:title}(C)$ (all titles renamed as $\texttt{tit}$), C being the collection of Fig. 1. Applying the rule previously defined, and with regards to entries examples of Sect. 3.3, the reformulation is: $\pi_{tit:title|artwork.1.title|artwork.2.title|book.title}(C)$. The query $\pi_{editor}(C)$ is reformulated as $\pi_{details.editor}(C)$.

Selection

Definition (Selection). The select operator, also called the restrict operator, filters the documents from collection C_{in} to retrieve only those that match the specified condition P, which can be a Boolean combination expressed by the logical connectors $\{\vee, \wedge, \neg\}$ of atomic conditions, also called predicates, or a path check operation. The select operator is defined by:

$$\sigma_P(C_{in}) = C_{out}$$

The condition P is defined by a Boolean combination of a set of triplets $(a_k\ \omega_k\ v_k)$ where $a_k \subseteq P_{C_{in}}$ is a *path*, $\omega_k \in \{=; >; <; \neq; \geq; \leq\}$ is a comparison operator, and v_k is a value that can be atomic or complex. In the case of an atomic value, the predicate represents an atomic condition. In the case of a complex value, v_k is defined in the same way as a document value. $v_k = \{a_{k,1} : v_{k,1}, \ldots, a_{k,n} : v_{k,n}\}$ and ω_k is always equal to " $=$". In this case the predicate represents a path check operation. We suppose that each predicate element is defined as, or normalized to, a conjunctive normal form:

$$P = \bigwedge_k \left(\bigvee_l a_{k,l}\ \omega_{k,l}\ v_{k,l} \right)$$

Selection Extension Process. The selection operation is extended by reformulating each atomic condition or path check operation as expressed in the conjunctive normal form in P with elements from the dictionary. The reformulated selection operation is defined as follows:

$$\sigma_{P_{ext}}(C_{in}) = C_{out}$$

We reformulate the normal form of predicates $P = \bigwedge_k \left(\bigvee_l a_{k,l}\ \omega_{k,l}\ v_{k,l} \right)$ by transforming each triplet $(a_{k,l}\ \omega_{k,l}\ v_{k,l})$ to a disjunction of triplets where we replace the path $a_{k,l}$ by the entries $\triangle_{a_{k,l}}^{C_{in}}$ while keeping the same operator $\omega_{k,l}$ and the same value $v_{k,l}$ as follows: $(\bigvee_{\forall a_j \in \triangle_{a_{k,l}}^{C_{in}}} a_j\ \omega_{k,l}\ v_{k,l})$. The reformulated normal form of the predicate is defined as:

$$P_{ext} = \bigwedge_k \left(\bigvee_l (\bigvee_{\forall a_j \in \triangle_{a_{k,l}}^{C_{in}}} a_j\ \omega_{k,l}\ v_{k,l}) \right)$$

Selection Extension Example. Let us suppose that the user asks for a selection $\sigma_{title='les\%' \wedge editor.name='livre\ de\ poche'}(C)$ (authors with title beginning with "les" edited by "livre de poche"), C being the collection of Fig. 1. Applying the rule previously defined, and with regards to to entries examples of Sect. 3.3, the reformulation is: $\sigma_{(title='les\%' \vee artwork.1.title='les\%' \vee artwork.2.title= 'les\%' \vee book.title='les\%')\ \wedge(details.editor.name='livre\ de\ poche')}(C)$.

Aggregation

Definition (Aggregation). The aggregate operator groups documents according to the values from the grouping conditions G and outputs computed aggregated values as defined by the aggregation function F:

$$_G\gamma_F(C_{in}) = (C_{out})$$

- G is the grouping conditions, $G = \{a_1, \ldots, a_g\}$, where $\forall k \in [1..g]$, $a_k \in P_{C_{in}}$
- F is the aggregation function, $F = q : f(a_f)$, where q represents the new path in C_{out} for the value computed by the aggregation function f for the values reached by the path a_f, where $a_f \in P_{C_{in}} \wedge a_f \notin G$, $f \in \{Sum, Max, Min, Avg, Count\}$.

Aggregation Extension Process. The aggregation operation is reformulated by first projecting out all the values reached by the paths from both G (grouping conditions) and F (aggregation function). To this end, we introduce a projection operation that renames the distinct absolute paths extracted from the dictionary for attributes in G ($G = \{a_1, \ldots, a_g\}$,) and F (attribute a_f) to the paths initially expressed in the original query. This projection "erases" the structural heterogeneity and facilitates the execution of the aggregation operation. Then we apply the classical aggregation operation to the output of the inserted projection operation.

Let Att be the set of all paths expressed in G and F, that is $Att = G \cup \{a_f\}$. The additional projection operation is defined as:

$$\pi_{A_{ext}}(C_{in})$$

where $A_{ext} = \cup_{\forall a_j \in Att}\{a_j : p_{j,1}|\ldots|p_{j,n_j}\}, \forall p_{j,k} \in \triangle_{a_j}^{C_{in}}$
The reformulated aggregation operation is formally defined as:

$$_G\gamma_F(\pi_{A_{ext}}(C_{in})) = (C_{out})$$

Aggregation Extension Example. Let us suppose that the user asks for an aggregation $_{year}\gamma_{count(title)}(C)$ (count titles group by years), C being the collection of Fig. 1. Applying the rule previously defined, and with regards to entries examples of Sect. 3.3, the reformulation is: $_{year}\gamma_{count(title)}$ $(\pi_{year:year|artwork.1.year|artwork.2.year|book.year,title:title|artwork.1.title|artwork.2.title|book.title}(C))$.

This reformulation enable: (i) to group documents on the year whatever the path to attribute `year` in documents, (ii) to count titles for each group whatever the path to attribute `title` in documents.

4 Experiments

In this section, we conduct a series of experiments to study the following points:

- Which are the effects on the execution time of the reformulated queries while varying the size of the collection and is this cost acceptable or not?
- Is the time to build the dictionary acceptable and does the size of the dictionary is affected by the number of structures in the collection?
- What is the cost of updating the dictionary during data manipulation operations?

Next, we explain the experimental protocol, then we study the queries execution cost, and finally we evaluate the dictionary generation time and its size.

4.1 Experimental Protocol

In this section, we introduce the details of the experimental setup, the process of generating synthetic datasets (available online[1]) and the evaluation queries set. Later on, we present the results of executing the evaluation set in three separate contexts. The goal is to compare: (i) the cost of executing the reformulated queries, (ii) the cost of executing the original queries on homogeneous documents, (iii) the execution time of several distinct queries that we build manually based on each schema (manual querying of the heterogeneous collection). Then, we study the effects of the heterogeneity on the dictionary in terms of size and construction time. Finally, we evaluate the impact of updating the dictionary during data manipulation operations. We conducted our experiments on MongoDB v3.4. We used an I5 3.4 GHZ machine coupled with 16 GB of RAM with 1 TB of SSD storage space that runs CentOS7.

Dataset. To study the performances of querying and manipulating schema-independent heterogeneous documents, we generate a custom synthetic datasets. First, we collected a collection of JSON documents from imdb[2] that describe movies. The original dataset has only flat documents described by 28 attributes. Then, produce new documents while injecting the structural heterogeneity. For each generated dataset, we can define several parameters e.g. the number of schemas in the collection, the percentage of the presence of each schema, and the corresponding number of grouping objects per schema. We mean by grouping object, a compound field in which we nest a subset of attributes. In other words, we cannot find the same grouping objects inside two schemas. To ensure the heterogeneity within documents, the grouping objects are unique in every schema. Only attributes from the original dataset are common to all documents. The values of those fields are randomly chosen from the original film collection to generate synthetic data (titles are randomly chosen in title list of imdb, and so on). To add more complexity, we can set the number of nesting level used for each structure. For the rest of the experiments, we built our dataset based on the characteristics that we describe in the Table 1. We generate collections of 10, 25, 50 and 100 GB of data.

We generate two collections: (i) baseline collection where all attributes are root based (flat collection) and (ii) an heterogeneous collection where attributes from baseline collection are nested in different objects at different nesting levels. The particularity of these datasets is that all attributes in the baseline collection are found in the heterogeneous collections. Furthermore, both datasets contains same values for leaf node attributes. So, for each document d in the baseline collection, it exists a corresponding document d_h in the heterogeneous collection such that: d_h has a schema different from d, each attribute of d is embedded in d_h withe the same value as in d. The baseline collection represents a proper environment to compare the execution time of the reformulated query on the

[1] https://www.irit.fr/recherches/SIG/SDD/EASY-QUERY/.
[2] imdb.com.

Table 1. Settings of the synthetic dataset.

Setting	Value
# of schema	10
# of grouping objects per schema	{5,6,1,3,4,2,7,2,1,3}
Nesting levels per schema	{4,2,6,1,5,7,2,8,3,4}
Percentage of schema presence	10%
# of attributes per schema	Random
# of attributes per grouping objects	Random

heterogeneous datasets, versus the execution time of the original query on baseline collection. Therefore, we ensure that every query returns the identical results from both heterogeneous or flat datasets. The same result implies: (i) the same number of documents, and -(ii) the same values for their attributes (leaf node attributes).

Queries. We choose to build a synthetic set of queries based on the different comparison operators supported by MongoDB. We employed the classical comparison operators, i.e $\{<, >, \leq, \geq, =, \neq\}$ for numerical values as well as classical logical operators, i.e $\{and, or\}$ between query predicates. Also, we employed a regular expression to deal with string values. We select 8 attributes of different types and under different levels inside the documents in heterogeneous datasets. The Table 2 shows that for each attribute its type and the selection operator that we used later while formulating the synthetic queries. In addition, we present for each attribute the number of possible paths as found in the synthetic heterogeneous collection, the different nesting levels and the selectivity of the predicate.

Table 2. Query predicates.

Predicate	Attribute	Type	Operator	Paths	Depths	Selectivity
p1	DirectorName	String	Regex{^A}	8	{8,2,3,9,6,5,4,7}	0,06 %
p2	Gross	Int	> 100 k	7	{7,8,2,3,9,6,4}	66 %
p3	Language	String	= "English"	7	{7,8,3,9,6,5,4}	0,018%
p4	Imdb_score	Float	<4,7	8	{8,7,2,3,4,5,6,9}	29 %
p5	Duration	Int	≤ 200	7	{7,8,2,3,6,5,4}	77%
p6	Country	String	≠ Null	6	{7,2,3,9,5,4}	100 %
p7	Year	Int	< 1950	7	{7,8,2,3,6,5,4}	23 %
p8	FB_likes	Int	≥ 500	7	{6,2,3,8,5,4,3}	83 %

4.2   Queries Execution Time Evaluation

We define three contexts on which we run the above-defined queries:

- Q_{Ext}: the initial query executed on the baseline collection (homogeneous one),
- Q_{Ext}: the reformulated query (*EasyQ* reformulation) executed on the heterogeneous collection,
- $Q_{Accumulated}$: the query is manually split in 10 queries executed on the heterogeneous collection; these 10 queries correspond to a manual querying of the heterogeneous collection where heterogeneity is managed "by the user".

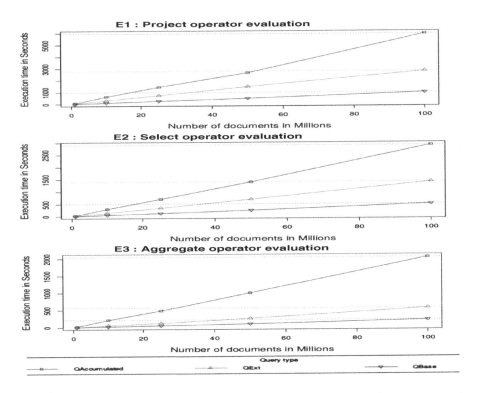

Fig. 4. Query reformulation evaluation.

For each context, we measure the average of execution time after executing each query at least five times. The order of query execution is set to be random. As shown in Fig. 4, we notice that the reformulated query, Q_{Ext}, outperforms the accumulated one, $Q_{Accumulated}$. The difference between these two queries comes from the capabilities of the reformulated query to include automatically absolute paths extracted from the collection in a single query. Hence, this query is executed only once when the accumulated query may require several read iterations for all documents inside the collection. This solution requires more

CPU loads and more intensive disk I/O operations. Let us notice that we do not evaluate the time necessary to merge the 10 queries results. The necessary time may be important for example in case of aggregation (and we do not evaluate the operation complexity).

We move now to study the efficiency of Q_{Ext} when compared to the baseline query Q_{Base}. We can notice that the overhead of our solution is up to two times (e.g., projection and selection queries) when compared to the native execution of the baseline query on the homogeneous dataset. Moreover, we score an overhead that does not exceed 2, 5 times in the case of aggregation queries. We believe that this overhead is acceptable since we bypass the needed costs for refactoring the underlying data structures. Unlike the baseline, our synthetic dataset contains different grouping objects with varying nesting levels. Then, the rewritten query includes several navigational paths which will be processed by the native query engine of MongoDB to find matches in each visited document among the collection.

4.3   Dictionary and Query Rewriting Engine at the Scale

With this series of experiments, we try to push the dictionary and the query rewriting engine to their limits. To this end, we generated a heterogeneous synthetic collection of 1 GB. We use the primary 28 attributes from the IMDB flat films collection. The custom collections are generated in a way that each schema inside a document is composed of two grouping objects with no further nesting levels. We generated collection having *10, 100, 1k, 3k and 5k* schemas.

Table 3. Scale effects on query rewriting and dictionary size.

# of schemas	Rewriting time	Dictionary size
10	0.0005 s	40 KB
100	0.0025 s	74 KB
1 K	0.139 s	2 MB
3 K	0.6 s	7.2 MB
5 K	1.52 s	12 MB

We choose a query containing a selection over 8 attributes with conditions combined by $\wedge$ and $\vee$ operators (in conjunctive normal form). We present the time needed to build the rewritten query in the Table 3. It is notable that the time to build the rewritten query is very low, less than two seconds. Also, it is possible to construct a dictionary over a heterogeneous collection of documents, here our dictionary can support up to 5 k of distinct schemas. The resulting size of the materialized dictionary is very encouraging since it does not require significant storage space. Furthermore, we also believe that the time spent to build the rewritten query is really interesting and represent another advantage of our solution. In this series of experiments, during query rewriting we try to find distinct navigational paths for eight predicates. Each rewritten query is composed of numerous disjunctive forms for each predicate. We notice 80 disjunctive forms while dealing with dataset having 10 schemas, 800 with 100 schemas, 8 k with 1 k schemas, 24 k with 3 k schemas and 40 k with 5k schemas. We believe that the dictionary and the query rewriting engine scale well while dealing with heterogeneous collection having an important number of schemas.

4.4   Dictionary Updates Evaluation

In this section, we study the dictionary constructions process. *EasyQ* can build the dictionary over existing dataset. The dictionary has the latest version of the data once all documents are inserted. So, the query reformulation engine enriches the queries based on the new dictionary, otherwise, if the process of data loading is in progress, it may do not take into account the recent changes. In the following, we study both configurations. First, we start by the evaluation of the time required to build the dictionary among pre-loaded five collections of 100 GB having 2, 4, 6, 8 and 10 schemas.

Table 4. Time to build the dictionary of pre-loaded data (100 GB collections).

# of schema	2	4	6	8	10
Required time (minutes)	96	108	127	143	156
Size of the resulting dictionary (KB)	4,154	9,458	13,587	17,478	22,997

We notice from the results in the Table 4 that the time elapsed to build the dictionary increases when we start to deal with collections having more heterogeneity. In case of the collection with 10 structures, the time does not exceed 40% when we compare it to a collection with 2 structures. Furthermore, we notice from the Table 4 the negligible size of the generated dictionaries when compared to the 100 GB of the collection.

The following tables highlight the effects of updating the dictionary during the manipulation process. We run insert, update and delete operation over a collection where we variate the number of schemas for the insert evaluation. However, for update and delete operations we variate the number of affected documents by these operations. All experiments where conducted on a collection of 1 M documents with 10 schemas expect for insert evaluation (the number of schemas is variable). We measure the time required to execute a manipulation operation without updating the dictionary, we refer to this evaluation as the baseline since we employ native mechanisms of MongoDB. Later on, we measure the time required to execute the manipulation operation while updating the dictionary. Finally, we show the overhead induced by our system (Table 5).

Table 5 shows that for 1 M of documents and for collections of up to 10 distinct schema the overhead does not exceed 47%. We find that the overhead

Table 5. Manipulation evaluation: insert operation.

#of schema	MongoDB	EasyQ	Overhead
2	201 s	269 s	33%
4	205 s	277 s	35%
6	207 s	285 s	37%
8	208 s	300 s	44%
10	210 s	309 s	47%

Table 6. Manipulation Evaluation: update operation.

#of Documents	MongoDB	EasyQ	Overhead
1k	1.3 s	2 s	53%
10k	14 s	24 s	71%
100k	149 s	285 s	91%
300k	183 s	380 s	107%
500k	239 s	527 s	120%

Table 7. Manipulation evaluation: delete operation.

#of documents	MongoDB	EasyQ	Overhead
1k	0.03 s	0.04 s	33%
10k	0.15 s	0.204 s	36%
100k	0.8 s	1.112 s	39%
300k	2.2 s	3.146 s	43%
500k	3 s	4.44 s	48%

measure does not exceed 0.5 the time required to load data on MongoDB. The evolution of the time when compared to the number of number of schemas in the collection is linear and is not exponential which is encouraging. We notice the same from Table 7 for the delete operation. However, the update operator presents important overhead that may reach 1.2 times and this is due to the fact that we do not employ optimisation for this operator in this paper.

5   Conclusion

In this paper, we developed a novel approach for querying heterogeneous documents describing a given entity over document-oriented data stores. Our objective is to allow users to perform their queries using a minimal knowledge about data schemas. Our query reformulation tool *EasyQ* is based on two main pillars. The first one is a dictionary that contains all possible paths for a given path (absolute path, sub-path or attribute). The second one is a rewriting module that modifies the user query to match all field paths existing in the dictionary. Our approach is a syntactic manipulation of queries. Therefore, it is grounded on a strong assumption: the collection describes "homogeneous entities", i.e., a field has the same meaning in all document schemas.

We also enrich *EasyQ* with an updating component able to update the dictionary when documents are updated in the collection. Each collection update query is added by a corresponding dictionary updating. We have formally defined the dictionary updating an we implemented a primary version. The dictionary updating ensures that, for a given entry path of the dictionary: (i) it always contains all paths leading to this path, (ii) it only contains existing paths. This ability of *EasyQ* ensures that the user will always query the collection using an up-to-date dictionary.

We conduct experiments to compare the execution time cost of basic MongoDB queries and rewritten queries proposed by our approach. Results show that the cost of executing rewritten queries proposed in this paper is higher when compared to the execution of basic user queries. The overhead added to the performance of our query is due to the combination of multiple access path to a queried field. Nevertheless, this time overhead is neglectful when compared to the execution of separated queries for each path. Let us notice that an interesting advantage of *EasyQ* is that each time a query is evaluated, it is first rewritten according to the dictionary and thus will take into account the latest updates in the collection (occurring between two executions of the query).

We conduct other experiments on the dictionary and we notice that the size of the dictionary is always very small when compared to the collection (e.g. 22 MB for a collection of 100 GB). Moreover, the overhead of updating the dictionary during operations on the collection (insert, delete) is acceptable (e.g. never greater than 50% for 10 schemas) and we should give particular measure to optimize the update operator to reduce the overhead.

These first results are very encouraging to continue this research way and need to be strengthened. Short-term perspectives are to continue evaluations and to identify the limitation regarding the number of paths and fields in the same query and regarding time cost. More experiments still to be performed on larger "real data" datasets. Another perspective is to study in depth the process of the dictionary building in real applications and in parallel of collection querying.

Finally, a long-term perspective is to enhance querying over a collection of documents presenting several levels of heterogeneity, i.e., structural as well as syntactic and semantic heterogeneities.

References

1. Shvaiko, P., Euzenat, J.: A survey of schema-based matching approaches. J. Data Semant. **IV**, 146–171 (2005)
2. Bourhis, P., Reutter, J.L., Suárez, F., Vrgoč, D.: JSON: data model, query languages and schema specification. In: Proceedings of the 36th ACM SIGMOD-SIGACT-SIGAI Symposium on Principles of Database Systems, pp. 123–135. ACM (2017)

3. Yang, Y., Sun, Y., Tang, J., Ma, B., Li, J.: Entity matching across heterogeneous sources. In: Proceedings of the 21th ACM SIGKDD, pp. 1395–1404. ACM (2015)
4. Hai, R., Geisler, S., Quix, C.: Constance: an intelligent data lake system. In: Proceedings of the 2016 International Conference on Management of Data, pp. 2097–2100. ACM (2016)
5. Sheth, A.P., Larson, J.A.: Federated database systems for managing distributed, heterogeneous, and autonomous databases. ACM Comput. Surv. (CSUR) **22**, 183–236 (1990)
6. Rahm, E., Bernstein, P.A.: A survey of approaches to automatic schema matching. VLDB J. **10**, 334–350 (2001)
7. Chasseur, C., Li, Y., Patel, J.M.: Enabling JSON document stores in relational systems. In: WebDB, vol. 13, pp. 14–15 (2013)
8. Tahara, D., Diamond, T., Abadi, D.J.: Sinew: a SQL system for multi-structured data. In: Proceedings of the 2014 ACM SIGMOD, pp. 815–826. ACM (2014)
9. DiScala, M., Abadi, D.J.: Automatic generation of normalized relational schemas from nested key-value data. In: Proceedings of the 2016 International Conference on Management of Data, pp. 295–310. ACM (2016)
10. Baazizi, M.A., Lahmar, H.B., Colazzo, D., Ghelli, G., Sartiani, C.: Schema inference for massive JSON datasets. In: EDBT (2017)
11. Sevilla Ruiz, D., Morales, S.F., García Molina, J.: Inferring versioned schemas from NoSQL databases and its applications. In: Johannesson, P., Lee, M.L., Liddle, S.W., Opdahl, A.L., López, Ó.P. (eds.) ER 2015. LNCS, vol. 9381, pp. 467–480. Springer, Cham (2015). https://doi.org/10.1007/978-3-319-25264-3_35
12. Wang, L., Zhang, S., Shi, J., Jiao, L., Hassanzadeh, O.: Schema management for document stores. Proc. VLDB Endow. **8**, 922–933 (2015)
13. Herrero, V., Abelló, A., Romero, O.: NOSQL design for analytical workloads: variability matters. In: Comyn-Wattiau, I., Tanaka, K., Song, I.-Y., Yamamoto, S., Saeki, M. (eds.) ER 2016. LNCS, vol. 9974, pp. 50–64. Springer, Cham (2016). https://doi.org/10.1007/978-3-319-46397-1_4
14. Papakonstantinou, Y., Vassalos, V.: Query rewriting for semistructured data. In: ACM SIGMOD Record, vol. 28, pp. 455–466. ACM (1999)
15. Lin, C., Wang, J., Rong, C.: Towards heterogeneous keyword search. In: Proceedings of the ACM Turing 50th Celebration Conference-China, p. 46. ACM (2017)
16. Clark, J., DeRose, S., et al.: XML path language (XPath) version 1.0 (1999)
17. Boag, S., et al.: XQuery 1.0: an XML query language (2002)
18. Florescu, D., Fourny, G.: JSONiq: the history of a query language. IEEE Internet Comput. **17**, 86–90 (2013)
19. Hidders, J., Paredaens, J., Van den Bussche, J.: J-logic: logical foundations for JSON querying. In: Proceedings of the 36th ACM SIGMOD-SIGACT-SIGAI Symposium on Principles of Database Systems, pp. 137–149. ACM (2017)
20. Botoeva, E., Calvanese, D., Cogrel, B., Xiao, G.: Expressivity and complexity of MongoDB queries. In: 21st International Conference on Database Theory, ICDT 2018, Vienna, Austria, 26–29 March 2018, pp. 9:1–9:23 (2018)
21. Hamadou, H.B., Ghozzi, F., Péninou, A., Teste, O.: Towards schema-independent querying on document data stores. In: Proceedings of the 20th International Workshop on Design, Optimization, Languages and Analytical Processing of Big Data (DOLAP), Vienna, Austria, 26–29 March 2018 (2018)
22. Tou, J.T.: Information systems. In: von Brauer, W. (ed.) GI 1973. LNCS, vol. 1, pp. 489–507. Springer, Heidelberg (1973). https://doi.org/10.1007/3-540-06473-7_52

Recommending Semantic Concepts
for Improving the Process of Semantic Modeling

Alexander Paulus[✉], André Pomp, Lucian Poth, Johannes Lipp, and Tobias Meisen

Institute of Information Management in Mechanical Engineering,
RWTH Aachen University, Aachen, Germany
alexander.paulus@ima.rwth-aachen.de
http://www.ima.rwth-aachen.de

Abstract. Data lakes offer enterprises an easy-to-use approach for centralizing the collection of their data sets. However, by just filling the data lake with raw data sets, the probability of creating a data swamp increases. To overcome this drawback, the annotation of data sets with additional meta information is crucial. One way to provide data with such information is to use semantic models that enable the automatic interpretation and processing of data values and their context. However, creating semantic models for data sets containing hundreds of data attributes requires a lot of effort. To support this modeling process, external knowledge bases provide the background knowledge required to create sophisticated semantic models.

In order to benefit from this existing knowledge, we propose a novel modular recommendation framework for identifying the best fitting semantic concepts for a set of data attribute labels. The framework, whose design is based on intensive review of real-world data attribute labels, queries arbitrary pluggable knowledge bases and weights/aggregates their results. We evaluate our approach with different existing knowledge bases and compare it with existing state-of-the-art approaches. In addition, we integrate it into the semantic data platform ESKAPE and discuss how it simplifies the process of creating semantic models.

Keywords: Semantic computing · Semantic model ·
Knowledge graph · Internet of Things · Data processing ·
Semantic modeling · ESKAPE

1 Introduction

Enabling semantics in data processing allow data users to understand data sets without detailed system knowledge and extensive research. It also mitigates interpretation errors or missing units of measurement and enables systems to store meta information alongside the original data set. Semantics are usually expressed using annotations to one or more data attributes of a data set containing an arbitrary but homogeneous number of data points. These annotations set each label of the data set into a semantic context to create a domain specific meaning. Without those additional information, the user (e.g., data analyst or broker) has to interpret the meaning of certain attributes only by the attribute name, the actual values of such attributes, or by using a possibly existing documentation. Unfortunately, most data sets are created by persons who assume implicit

S. Hammoudi et al. (Eds.): ICEIS 2018, LNBIP 363, pp. 350–369, 2019.
https://doi.org/10.1007/978-3-030-26169-6_17

domain knowledge or use identifiers which only they can understand, e.g., names or identifiers which have been agreed upon on company site, but which are otherwise not as easy to understand. Furthermore, if the used format does not allow any hierarchy, such as in CSV files, relations between attributes are not expressed.

In the context of the Industrial Internet of Things and Big Data approaches in todays companies, this leads to unforeseen problems when data sets from multiple sites are combined, e.g., while using a data lake. Analysts mostly do not possess sufficient detailed domain knowledge of each site and each process to fully understand implicit conventions in naming or interpreting cryptic data attribute names such as 'a24d7ff-2'. In the wake of big data technologies, data is gathered from all available sources without considering the compatibility and usability of random collected data sets from different branches, sub-companies, production sites and countries.

Using semantic annotations allow data stewards (persons who are responsible for data sets) to annotate their data sets such that other persons can understand the data without the steward's explicit knowledge. By additionally defining relations between the concepts, one can describe the data set in more detail. This process is called semantic modeling. Figure 1 shows an example data set in raw format and with its semantic model. In the annotated version, meta concepts (i.e., concepts without any data attached to them), such as 'motor vehicle' can also be added to indicate the linkage of two or more attributes. Semantic models usually also provide information about units of measurement, relations to other attributes or domain information that helps to understand the context of the acquired data. The semantic model is not limited and depends on the steward's view of the world to fully understand the information contained in the data set. However, the created semantic model must be stored in a formal way and comply with specific conventions, so that it can be interpreted not only by humans but also by machines. One established form of description may be based on an ontology describing all possible or valid relations and entities. These ontologies have a corresponding standardized form of description, e.g., by using OWL.

When a data set is about to be shared, the data steward has to create such a semantic model. Therefore, the data steward annotates each data attribute of the data set with an entity that is available in the ontology. In addition, he can define relations between the defined entities. However, defining semantic models based on existing ontologies has

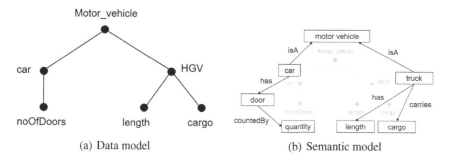

(a) Data model   (b) Semantic model

Fig. 1. Exemplary data set before and after semantic modeling. During the process, each attribute has been assigned a semantic concept which describes the attribute. In addition, relations allow to refine the meaning of the used concepts [1].

different limitations. First, an existing ontology restricts the data steward to the existing concepts and relations while he creates the semantic modeling. Therefore, he may not be able to model his point of view. Second, the manual selection and creation of concepts for each attribute can be a time consuming task. Hence, our goal is to automate this step as far as possible and to allow a data steward to describe his point of view by using a bottom-up approach rather than a top-down approach.

In this paper, which is an extended version of [1], we present our approach of a concept recommendation framework, which generates a selection of possible semantic concepts from which the user can choose. Our framework provides an abstraction layer for external sources, such as BabelNet, WordNet, specific domain ontologies or knowledge graphs. This layer enables users to also add additional knowledge bases, such as Wikipedia, to the recommendation process. Results from all sources are combined to form a single list of recommendations, relieving the user of searching for concepts and allowing an automated annotation in the best case. The framework design is based on an intensive review of the labels observed in real-world data sets that are either available on Open Data platforms or were obtained from local companies. We evaluated the framework with different existing knowledge bases, such as WordNet or BabelNet, and compared it with the existing state-of-the-art approach BabelFy. Compared to our previous work [1], we additionally show how we integrated the framework into the semantic data platform ESKAPE [2]. This enables ESKAPE to suggest more specific semantic concepts and thereby supports and simplifies the process of creating semantic models.

The rest of the paper is organized as follows: Sect. 2 motivates the necessity to develop a generic framework for gathering semantic concepts. Afterwards, Sect. 3 provides an overview of related approaches and Sect. 4 defines the problem classes which we identified when reviewing real-world data sets. Based on these classes, we present our approach in Sect. 5 consisting of querying, weighting and aggregating results from multiple knowledge bases. Section 6 gives an evaluation of our approach and Sect. 7 describes the integration of our framework into ESKAPE. Finally, we conclude the paper with a summary and a short outlook in Sect. 8.

2 Motivating Example

In this section, we provide a motivating example illustrating the necessity for annotating data with semantic models and supporting the modeling process with a framework that enables semantic concept gathering from multiple knowledge bases.

The scenario consists of a simplified production process of a large global enterprise with multiple sites in different countries. The enterprise is specializing in manufacturing products that need to be deformed and painted. Example products may be bicycles or cars. On the production sites, different versions of the good are produced in multiple steps by using different production lines and machines.

During the production process, different parts of the involved systems generate different kinds of data. As a global strategy for improving the manufacturing process based on data science, the enterprise decided to collect all these data in a centralized data lake. This lake collects all kinds of batch and streaming data produced by any production line and machine. To additionally support the process of finding exactly the data required

Table 1. Exemplary data set for which DP_1 has to create a semantic model.

Time	Pressure	E-Power	Temp	ID
1476735200	0.51	1420	276	7
1476745200	0.49	1534	302	8
1476755200	0.55	1800	342	9
. . .	. . .	. . .	. . .	. . .

by the data analysts, the management decided to set up an enterprise ontology with the help of two external experts. Based on this ontology, the employees who are responsible for a data source (e.g., the data produced by the sensors of one machine) have to create semantic models. We consider these employees to be domain experts knowing the meaning (semantics) of the data, calling them *data stewards*.

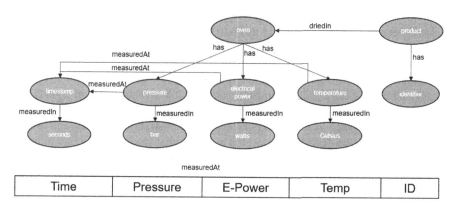

Fig. 2. Exemplary semantic model for the data set provided in Table 1. The concepts used in the semantic model are obtained from the underlying ontology of the enterprise [1].

For example, the data steward DS_1 creates the semantic model for the data set illustrated in Table 1. Please note that this is just an example data set. Industrial real-world data sets usually contain hundreds of columns. For defining the semantic model, DS_1 is forced to use all the entities and relations (vocabulary) that are available in the enterprise ontology. Figure 2 illustrates the example semantic model that was created by DS_1. Assuming that all data sets of the enterprise are annotated with semantic models, a data analyst DA_1 can now search for data sets using the vocabulary defined in the enterprise's ontology. In addition, the provided semantic model helps the data analyst to understand the meaning of each data value.

When examining this scenario, we identify different drawbacks of the common solution for the current process of data providing as well as data consuming. First, both the data steward DS_1 and the data analyst DA_1 are limited to the vocabulary provided by the underlying ontology. Terms such as synonyms, which refer to the same entity and are usually used within this context but are not present in the ontology, cannot be used for creating semantic models or searching data sources. As ontologies can become very large and unhandy, it will be challenging for both parties to get an overview about the available vocabulary. Therefore, a system that is able to maintain the ontology of the enterprise through an expanded vocabulary without the ontology having to be adjusted manually by humans would be desirable.

Another drawback of the current scenario is that data stewards have to create the semantic models manually. To support a user in creating semantic models, it will be necessary for a system to automatically identify the concepts that map best to a specific column. This is especially important if we consider large data sets containing hundreds of columns. However, comparing the data labels with the concepts available in the enterprise's ontology will also lead to different challenges. In the example illustrated above we mapped the concept *Temperature* to the column *Temp*. Here, a simple comparison of the label *Temp* with the concept *Temperature* will not yield any result. As data labels in the real-world are very heterogeneous and are rarely annotated with meaningful terms (cf. Sect. 4), a simple comparison against an enterprise ontology would fail.

Finally, when using an enterprise ontology designed by experts, the ontology would need to cover any concept and relation that will be available in data sets that are added in the future. Otherwise, the data publisher could not map any concept from the ontology to the new data attribute. While defining a comprehensive ontology may be realizable in a closed and controllable environment (e.g., inside a single department of a company), it is very unrealistic for a global company with multiple sites in different countries or in an open scenario where data sources are added over a long time period by multiple independent actors, such as local companies, city administration or private end users.

Hence, it would be desirable to develop a system that is capable of combining the variety of semantic models of an enterprise with additional external knowledge bases and pre-processing steps to identify exactly those concepts that are relevant for creating or querying semantic models.

3   Related Work

The problem of finding a correct or at least meaningful semantic concept for a given label or search term is well-known in research areas like ontology matching and alignment, schema matching, semantic tagging, semantic annotation or semantic modeling. Researchers working in these areas came up with different solutions for generating meaningful labels that help them to solve their problem.

In the areas of schema matching as well as ontology matching and alignment, the goal is to align a given ontology A to another ontology B that differ in number and kind of used relations or entity labels. To target the problem of finding the correct label in ontology B for a given entity of ontology A, approaches like structure-based, instance-based or lexical-based methods are frequently used strategies [3]. For lexical-based as well as structure-based methods, the use of upper ontologies (cf. [4]) or external sources, such as Wikipedia, DBPedia or WordNet is very common (cf. [3,5,6]).

Compared to ontology matching, the research area of semantic annotation targets the problem of finding an appropriate semantic concept for a given label of a data attribute (e.g., the label of a column in a table) [7,8]. The field of semantic modeling goes one step further by additionally generating meaningful semantic relations and more abstract concepts (e.g., combining the concepts *name*, *age* and *hair color* to the abstract concept of a *person*) [9,10]. To perform the task of semantic annotation, Goel et al. [7] use the data provided by previous data sets to train a machine learning model that learns the representation of the data enabling to suggest semantic concepts without considering the label. As opposed to this, approaches like [11] or [12] use external knowledge bases, such as WordNet, Wikipedia or Probase to suggest concepts based on the present data labels. To create full-fledged semantic models, Taheriyan et al. [9,10] additionally use specific domain ontologies and frequently occurring relations in Linked Data sources.

Beside the presented research fields, the area of semantic tagging focuses on either automatically generating or suggesting accurate tags for unstructured and binary data, such as documents, images and audio or video files [13]. Proposed solutions use tag ontologies (e.g., MOAT and SCOT) [14], search engines such as Google [15] or external knowledge bases such as WordNet, DBPedia, OpenCyc or Wikipedia [13,16,17]. Beside the already mentioned external knowledge bases WordNet, Wikipedia, OpenCyc or DBPedia, we identified additional useful sources. BabelNet [18] is a fully automatic generated multilingual semantic network combining knowledge from multiple other sources (e.g., WordNet, DBPedia or Wikipedia). However, BabelNet lacks the possibility to be extended by third-parties, which results in, e.g., missing domain knowledge. In addition, the automatic gathering of the existing knowledge bases may lead to inconsistencies. Another external knowledge base is Wolfram Alpha [19], a search engine that allows to retrieve knowledge about topics, such as physics, materials or people and history. Hence, this knowledge base covers very specific knowledge which may be missing in the other knowledge bases.

The developed approaches of the discussed research areas use different strategies to solve their problems. Here, most of the presented solutions rely on the use of one or more preset external knowledge bases to find the best matching concept. Hence, compared to the presented approaches, our work focuses on developing a single semantic search framework, which is capable of returning a set of best matching concepts. Instead of predefining a set of possible external knowledge bases, our work offers the user the possibility to add more knowledge bases and prioritize them. In comparison to BabelNet, our approach does not store the results of the connected sources. It queries, merges and sorts the results on-demand. Furthermore, it enables enterprises to connect their own external knowledge bases (e.g., a unified company-wide ontology) without leaking this internal knowledge to the public.

Compared to the discussed broader research fields, domain specific approaches like the NCBO Ontology [20] are a first attempt in recommending the best fitting ontology for a pre-defined use case. Therefore, users can enter keywords or a full-text and the recommender identifies the best fitting ontologies. However, compared to our work, the Ontology recommender aims in identifying the best fitting ontology whereas the goal of our approach is not to identify the best fitting knowledge base. Instead, our approach tries to identify the best fitting concept based on all concepts that are available in the connected knowledge bases. The underlying system can then add this concept to its ontology or knowledge graph if it is not present yet.

To identify the most fitting concept, semantic relatedness is a prominent measure to use. It helps identifying clusters of possible candidates by comparing the semantic concepts to each other and computes a measure of how likely those elements are. [21] propose the use of gloss overlaps to compute the measure. However, we extend and refine this approach by extracting keywords from the text first, thus generalizing the approach and releasing it from WordNet relations to allow general comparisons between concepts.

4   Reviewing Real-World Data Sets

Before we started to design and implement our search framework, we performed an intensive research on the way people label columns and data attributes in real-world data sets. We collected the data from multiple Open Data platforms such as San Francisco, New York, Los Angeles, Berlin, Aachen, Munich and multiple other cities as well as from OpenGov, mCloud and from multiple local partner companies. We limited our review to five common structured data formats (CSV, XML, XLSX, JSON and GJSON) and collected a total of 272 files. Afterwards, we manually reviewed each data set to identify problems that will occur when trying to identify a label for the corresponding column or data attribute. We used the gained insights to formulate problem classes for data labels as well as data sets. A label can belong to none, exactly one or multiple problem classes. However, some of the problems may occur together whereas other problems directly exclude others. Depending on the classes a label or a data set belongs to, it will be more or less difficult to identify the correct semantic concept. Altogether, we identified the following ten problem classes for labels:

- **Abbreviations:** Instead of writing the complete label, people tend to abbreviate labels. Prominent examples we found are *lat, lon, www*, etc.
- **Different Languages:** Depending on the source of the data, labels may be in different languages. Moreover, it may occur that languages are mixed within data sets.
- **Natural Language:** Instead of labeling data with a concrete concept or a single word, people tend to describe data attributes in more detail. One example is *'Number of accidents where persons got injured'*.
- **Time Labels:** Depending on the data, people tend to label columns or data attributes with points in time or time spans *(e.g., Monday, 1–2PM, etc.)*.
- **Misspelling:** The person who labeled the data made a simple mistake. Examples are *Acess Point, Telehphone Number*, etc.
- **Splitting Characters:** Beside white spaces in labels, some labels contained special characters *(e.g., '_' or '-')* to split words. One example we found is *telephone_number*.
- **Camel Case Input:** Similar to splitting characters, some persons tend to split words using the camel case syntax *(e.g., StreetNumber)*.
- **Additional Information:** In a few data sets, we identified labels that contained additional valuable semantic knowledge that can be used to specify the semantic concept in more detail *(e.g., temperature in °C)*.
- **Plural:** In multiple data sets, people labeled columns using the plural instead of the singular *(e.g., names vs. name or street vs. streets)*.

– **Random Labels:** Labels which do not follow any meaning and are just random generated strings, such as hash codes or increasing numbers. Examples are *1, 2, 8321b319b1781,* etc.

Beside the challenges that we identified for single labels, we also identified a problem class for a complete data set. We observed that identifying the correct concept for humans becomes much simpler and unambiguous if the labels within the data set belong to the same domain. Hence, we created the class domain context.

– **Domain Context:** The labels within data sets can either belong to the same domain or they may belong to different domains.

Depending on the classes a label belongs to, finding appropriate concepts that specify the information that is present in the data set can be more or less challenging. While classes like *Abbreviations, Different Languages, Misspelling, Splitting Characters, Camel Case Input* and *Plural* can be tackled by suitable pre-processing steps, classes like *Natural Language, Time Labels* and *Additional Information* or *Random Labels* require more sophisticated strategies. For instance, one will never be capable of identifying appropriate concepts for labels that belong to the *Random Label* class by just considering labels. Here, we require strategies that consider the data within the column to achieve appropriate results. On the other hand, the class of *Additional Information* requires the search framework to consider and model the additional information. Hence, the result for a label can be more than a single concept. It can also be a small graph describing the semantics of the label.

5 Semantic Concept Gathering

In this section, we describe the main concept and prototype of our recommendation framework mainly focusing on the *Domain Context* problem class. We give necessary background information on semantic networks and present the main approach afterwards.

5.1 Semantic Networks

Semantic networks help modeling information by defining concepts (e.g., *engine, boat*) and relations (e.g., *has, isA, partOf*) to represent knowledge that is available in the world, similar to an ontology. Those networks exist to help machines gain meta information to their data by modeling this knowledge in a standardized way. Semantic networks can either model domain specific or general purpose knowledge. Most of them are available online with a public API, which can have metered access in some cases.

However, when receiving a result from a semantic network, those replies may contain multiple similar concept suggestions, usually from different domains. Here, it is a challenging task to match one concept with all other concepts found for other labels in the data set. Some semantic networks offer a way of querying multiple concepts at the same time, yielding a combined result for all labels (e.g., the publicly available Babelfy).

Table 2. Example query result for 'car' from BabelNet. Linked concepts are underlined.

Field name	Field content
Label	Automobile, car, auto, machine, motorcar
Glossary	A <u>motor vehicle</u> with four <u>wheels</u>; <u>usually</u> <u>propelled</u> by a <u>combustion engine</u>
Is A	Motor vehicle
Category	Automobiles, Wheeled vehicles

For example, Table 2 shows the first resulting concept from BabelNet for the search term 'car'. In addition to the main label 'car', several synonyms are given in combination with a short glossary description of the concept. This glossary can help to distinguish between multiple similar concepts from different domains. The result also contains meta information like other related concepts (e.g., car *isA* motor vehicle). All elements obtained from a source also have a unique identifier which helps identifying equal concepts, thus allowing us to combine several search results from the same data source.

When receiving a response from a semantic network, multiple possible concepts can be included, e.g., *IP address* or *postal address* for the label *'address'*. Hence, the resulting challenge is the selection of the most fitting concepts for our queried label. By additionally considering the concepts obtained for the other labels (context) and by querying multiple semantic networks for the complete set of labels, the challenge is getting bigger. However, not all semantic networks may return a concept for a queried label. Hence, the concepts returned for other labels might originate from other semantic networks thus not allowing a comparison based on relations available in a single semantic network. In the following, we present our semantic concept recommendation framework to mitigate this problem.

5.2 Concept

Detecting suitable semantic concepts for data attributes is a multi-layered task. First, a set of possible matches has to be gathered for each label, followed by an evaluation of those candidates. From all possible candidates, the best candidates have to be selected for presentation to the user. However, those recommendations can vary heavily if we consider different domains in which our semantic model is built. A single label can have multiple meanings in different domains or in rare cases even in the same domain if combined with specific other concepts of that domain. This implies that, in order to present a matching candidate, the recommendation framework has to detect the domain and consider not only the expression but also parent or sibling elements. The framework's task is to provide as many suitable matches for semantic concepts as possible for each input label.

To achieve this goal, our framework is comprised of different parts. Before the knowledge bases are queried, the label is pre-processed in multiple steps to tackle the defined problem classes (e.g., Different Languages, Misspelling etc.) and prepare it for the connectors. Next, the communication to semantic sources is realized using connectors, which are proxy modules helping to retrieve a standardized result from the different and independent knowledge bases. All connectors provide their results to the recommendation module which computes the most likely matches from all candidates and returns the result to the user.

Querying Semantic Networks. As a first step, using connectors, a query is sent to selected semantic networks (cf. Sect. 5.1) which return a list of possible concepts for this expression. New semantic networks can be added by implementing connectors for those sources and registering them in our framework. A schematic view of a connector for a data source is given in Fig. 3. The label is prepared for each connector such that it closely matches the naming structure of the connected source. Next, each connector

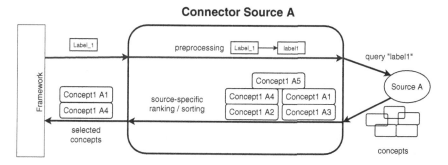

Fig. 3. Querying a semantic source by pre-processing the input, pre-selecting a fixed amount of resulting concepts and returning the result to the recommendation module.

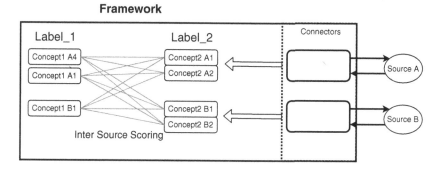

Fig. 4. Comparing all semantic concepts to candidate concepts for other labels. Each similarity boosts this concept's score.

runs the query and transforms the result to a homogeneous representation which can be handled by the framework. Based on the type of network queried, the returned set of concepts might include unique IDs, glossaries and additional linked concepts like hyper- and hyponyms. Those additional linked concepts can range from zero or a few entries to more than a thousand. Therefore, all queries are filtered by a set of considered relations (e.g., *isA* or *partOf*) to reduce the complexity of the following steps. As our framework can currently only consider a limited amount of five relations, all source-specific relation types have to be mapped to a set of preset relations or be dropped during the implementation of the connector.

Intra Source Selection. Beside the mapping of relations, a pre-selection of concepts is done inside the connector. The metric which determines the candidates selected is currently chosen by the connector's developer, but could be configurable later. Depending on the connector, results can be filtered and sorted by specified metrics (e.g., sort the concepts by the number of edges they have to others and take the first n). However, any other metric is possible. To reduce the implementation overhead for each connector, the pre-selection on the concepts is solely done for one label. The relations between the queried label and the other available labels are not considered at this point. This is currently done in the *Inter Source Scoring* step (cf. Sect. 5.2).

After all query results have been obtained and pre-selected, all candidates from different sources for a given label are combined to a single list (cf. Fig. 4). Duplicates that are obtained from the same data source are eliminated per list (e.g., BabelNet returning WordNet concepts).

Hence, formally, we have a set K of m knowledge bases and a data set with n labels. For each label l_i where $i \in \{1...n\}$, we query each knowledge base K_j where $j \in \{1...m\}$ and receive a set of concepts $C_{l_i K_j}$. Finally, we combine all results from all knowledge bases K_j and for the same label l_i into a single set C_{l_i}.

Inter Source Scoring. In this process, we compare the set of concepts C_{l_i} for each label l_i with the set of concepts C_{l_j} for each label l_j where $j \in \{1...n\}, j \neq i$ to select the most fitting concepts for each label. Therefore, all concepts are scored based on their coherence with concepts found for other labels. Assuming that multiple sources yield results from different domains, we want to identify the most prominent domain or combination of labels. As we do not have any valid relations between concepts from different semantic networks, we can only consider the concept's name and the description provided by the network as well as possible linked concepts (from the same source).

Scoring is done by comparing keywords from concept labels, glossary and related concept labels. For two concepts c_a and c_b the coherence score is computed using five partial scores s. We assume that each concept c_x consists of a set of main labels ml_x, a glossary g_x and a set of related concept labels r_x. As glossaries mostly contain natural language, a keyword extraction algorithm KE is used to extract keywords from the text.[1]

$$c_x = (ml_x, g_x, r_x)$$
$$s_1(c_a, c_b) = \frac{|KE(g_a) \cap KE(g_b)|}{min\{|KE(g_a)|, |KE(g_b)|\}}$$
$$s_2(c_a, c_b) = |ml_a \cap KE(g_b)| \tag{1}$$
$$s_3(c_a, c_b) = |ml_a \cap r_b|$$
$$s_4(c_a, c_b) = |r_a \cap r_b|$$
$$s_5(c_a, c_b) = |ml_a \cap ml_b|$$

Equation (1) shows the definition of a semantic concept c_x for the algorithm and the aforementioned five partial scores [1].

- s_1 weights the matches from glossary keywords by comparing all found keywords for both concepts and scoring matches against the total number of possible matches which is equal to the number of elements in the smaller keyword set.
- s_2 yields scores if concept labels match to keywords in the second concept's glossary.
- s_3 scores the number of concept c_a labels matching labels in c_b's related concepts (e.g., parent-child relations). From related concepts, only the labels are checked, not the glossary or even more related concepts.
- s_4 increases if matches of both concepts' related entities exist (e.g., sibling relation indicated by same parent element).
- s_5 compares the labels of both concepts and increases if there is a direct match.

With C_{l_i} being the set of concepts for each label l_i, we define $C_l = \bigcup\limits_{i=1}^{n} C_{l_i}$ as the set of concepts for all labels. Let $c_k \in C_{l_i}$ be a concept for which we want to calculate the coherence score. The total score S for the concept c_k is defined as:

$$S(c_k) = \sum_{c_o \in C_l \setminus C_{l_i}} \sum_{p \in 1,..,5} \omega_p \times s_p(c_k, c_o) \tag{2}$$

Each score is weighted by ω to allow fine tuning of the results for each comparison. The resulting comparison can be seen in Fig. 5. Here, each match on one score yields the mentioned ω value, and thus increases the score. By performing this calculation for each concept $c_k \in C_{l_i}$ and each $C_{l_i} \in C_l$ we receive a coherence score S for each concept of each label.

Sorting and Return. After weighting and comparing, the initial user preference as given in the request is applied. This user preference contains which sources shall get a higher priority when merging the results. Therefore, we multiply the retrieved scores for all concepts with a factor given for their original data source. This enables the algorithm to, e.g., prioritize domain-specific sources before common networks. The candidate list

---

[1] We use https://stanfordnlp.github.io/CoreNLP/.

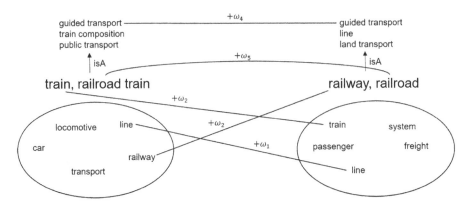

Fig. 5. Example comparison of concepts 'train' and 'railroad' obtained from BabelNet and reduced for simplicity. Each match on one of the given scores adds the assigned weighting ω to the total score [1].

of each node is then sorted in descending order and the top n elements of each list are selected and returned to the user. This way, the framework yields a number of ranked candidate concepts, including their description and possible other meta information as well as linked concepts.

5.3 Implementation

For evaluating our approach, we implemented the concept as a Java application available via REST interface. The application expects a JSON Object containing the labels of the data set that should be annotated and a weighting for each knowledge base enabling the user to easily prioritize those knowledge bases from which he expects better results (e.g., those containing domain knowledge). Connectors for WordNet, BabelNet and the internal smart city knowledge graph available via ESKAPE (cf. Sect. 7) have been implemented as proof of concepts. The Google Knowledge Graph was also connected in earlier stages but did only perform well on named entities, which are less common in data set labels. It was therefore skipped for the evaluation.

Before labels of a data set are sent to the different semantic networks, they are pre-processed to improve the result's quality and comparability. For example, to tackle the mentioned problem classes, the labels are converted to lowercase, translated to English and all special characters, such as '-' or '_', are removed. In addition, the camel case labels are split into multiple words. Further pre-processing steps, such as resolving labels for abbreviations, are not implemented yet.

After pre-processing the labels, the framework queries the semantic networks for concept suggestions for all labels. To narrow down the number of results from the semantic networks, only concepts are added to the list of suggestions. Named entities are currently not considered in the framework as they rarely appear as labels in data sets. The connectors are set to return up to $n = 5$ elements to the engine. As described in Sect. 5.2, the returned elements are filtered for duplicates and rated according to the defined steps. As the amount of comparisons between the different suggestions grows quickly with a larger data set, multi-threading is used for the rating process. Thereafter, for each label, the suggestions are sorted by their rating and the top five entries are returned.

After some evaluation with different factors, we decided to keep the initial order $\omega_1 \leq \omega_2 \leq \omega_3 \leq \omega_4 \leq \omega_5$. Compared to our previous work [1], we now initialize ω_1 with 1, ω_2 with 2.3, ω_3 with 2.7 and ω_4 and ω_5 with 2.5 and 4, respectively. We disabled all source filtering and weighted all sources equally.

6   Evaluation

We evaluated our approach by annotating different publicly available data sets using results from WordNet (WN), BabelNet (BN) and a small ESKAPE knowledge graph (KG) covering the domain of smart city and transportation. Table 3 shows the results of an annotation of the crime data set from the public domain of Vancouver[2]. For all contained labels, we measured the number of returned concepts (# column) and, if a suitable concept has been found, how high it was ranked in the returned list (c column). We observed that general concepts like 'month', 'year', 'hour', 'minute' and 'neighborhood' are easily detected as they are quite unique and can hardly be interpreted for something else. The label 'hundred_block' returned, although normalized, no results. This is mostly due to the fact that we still cannot safely handle multi word labels. In addition, our framework also lacks public semantic networks of this very specific term from the domain of rural addressing or law enforcement (which is also not covered

Table 3. Results for the crime data set for sources Wordnet (WN), WordNet and BabelNet (WN/BN), Knowledge Graph (KG) and all sources combined. The # column indicates the considered number of results from a source, c indicates the position of the (subjectively) most matching concept in the suggestion list.

	Sources	WN		WN/BN		KG		All
	Numbers	#	c	#	c	#	c	c
Label	hundred_block							
	month	2	1	4	1			1
	year	4	1	5	1			1
	heighborhood	2	1	5	1			1
	hour	4	2	5	1	1	1	1
	x	3		5		1	1	2
	y	2		5		1	1	4
	minute	5	2	5	1			1
	type	5		5		1	1	3
	day	5	3	5	1			1

---

[2] http://data.vancouver.ca/datacatalogue/crime-data.htm.

Table 4. Summary of results from WordNet (WN), WordNet and BabelNet (WN/BN) and our smart city knowledge graph (KG) on publicly available data sets (numbers in brackets indicate total number of labels). *Position* indicates the position of the (subjectively) most fitting concept in the suggestion list.

	Sources	WN			WN/BN			KG			All		
	Position	1	2	3	1	2	3	1	2	3	1	2	3
Data set	crimeData(10)	3	1	2	6	0	1	3	0	0	6	0	2
	culturalSpaces(11)	4	2	0	5	1	1	0	0	0	6	1	0
	recycling(7)	4	0	1	4	0	1	0	0	0	4	0	1
	clearance(6)	1	2	1	2	1	0	3	0	0	2	2	0
	schedules(12)	1	1	0	1	0	1	5	0	0	5	0	1

by the smart city KG). However, due to the design of ESKAPE's knowledge graph, ESKAPE is capable of learning this concept (cf. Sect. 7). The 'x' and 'y' labels, which represent coordinates in this model could not be identified, and although they were added to the KG by another source and therefore recognized, they were ranked low (rank three and four) in the process as we did not boost the KG ratings as a domain specific source. This lead to a higher ranking for more general concepts like 'X [24th letter of Roman alphabet]'. The total processing time for this request remained on average 2.18 s, including queries.

The results from all evaluation sets can be seen in Table 4. For this evaluation, we chose another data set from the public domain of Vancouver[3], two from the San Francisco transportation domain[4,5] and one from the European Data Portal[6]. The total number of labels for each data set is written in brackets, with the position columns indicating how many most fitting labels were found on that position in the returned lists. For most of the labels, we could find suitable matches, although not always in prime positions. This shows that our basic idea of presenting the top n results instead of the best ranked result will lead to better recommendations in a production system. As in the case of the crime data set, missing concepts were mostly caused by sources that did not offer any concepts at all for specific labels which we could trace back to some of our defined problem classes (cf. Sect. 4) like 'Applied Color Rule', 'Object ID', which is far too generic, or 'CULTURAL_SPACE_NAME' which could not be identified altogether. However, the effect of adding a possibly proprietary semantic source is clearly visible as multiple concepts, e.g., from the clearance data set, could be resolved by using a source containing smart city domain knowledge. Multiple of those sources could be attached to improve the results.

---

[3] http://data.vancouver.ca/datacatalogue/culturalSpaces.htm.

[4] https://data.sfgov.org/Transportation/Clearance-Heights-for-Large-Vehicle-Circulation/sccd-iwvp.

[5] https://data.sfgov.org/Transportation/Meter-Operating-Schedules/6cqg-dxku.

[6] https://www.europeandataportal.eu/data/en/dataset/east-sussex-county-council-recycling-sites.

Table 5. Comparison of Babelfy results to top concepts found by our framework. Text in brackets indicates a description to distinguish different concepts of the same name. Semantic source of both results was BabelNet only. Bold markings indicate (subjectively) better matching results.

label	Babelfy result	Framework result
computer	**computer**	**computer**
lan	**local area network**	**local area network**
network	[interconnection of things or people]	Internet
subnet	subnet [mathematic topology]	**subnetwork [IP]**
address	address [postal]	**IP address**
port	port [sea port]	**interface [computing]**

We also compared our approach to Babelfy, an online algorithm dealing with the context aware semantic annotation of sentences, keywords or labels. Those keywords can be inserted at the same time, allowing Babelfy to consider relations of the underlying BabelNet network when building the reply. We tested a general set of labels which would completely rule out the smart city knowledge graph as the labels belong to the domain *IT infrastructure*. Thus, both algorithms operate solely on the Word-Net/BabelNet networks. For labels, we chose a common combination on a list of network participants: 'computer', 'lan', 'network', 'subnet', 'address' 'port'. This combination has multiple domain specific meanings (e.g., 'address' can either be IP or MAC address or postal address) to test the detection of the right domain. The results can be seen in Table 5.

Both algorithms managed to clearly identify unambiguous labels like 'computer' or the acronym 'lan' 'network' was interpreted differently in both cases and no superior concept could be identified between both suggestions. However, considering the ambiguous labels 'subnet', 'address' and 'port', our framework performed better than Babelfy, which in all cases returned the most common concepts when querying for the label without any context and in case of 'subnet' even chose the sub par second concept for a mathematic topology. Although we cannot state that our approach will be performing well on all label combinations, it has been shown that even the baseline algorithm can improve the recommendation of semantic concepts for labels.

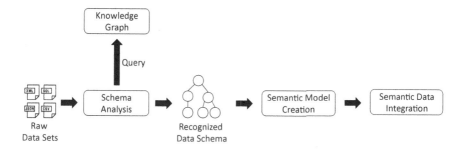

Fig. 6. Overview of the current process for adding a new data set to ESKAPE.

7   Integration into ESKAPE

To make use of our framework in a real-world application, we integrate it into the semantic data platform ESKAPE [2]. ESKAPE is a data hub that aims to shorten the time to analysis by connecting data stewards and data analysts. Therefore, data stewards add their data sets to ESKAPE. Based on the provided data, ESKAPE analyzes the schema of the data source (e.g., the data attribute labels) and provides the result to the data steward. In the next step, the data steward creates a semantic model upon the recognized schema. During this modeling process, the data steward can use all concepts and relations that are already defined in ESKAPE's knowledge graph. If he requires concepts that are not already defined in the knowledge graph, he can introduce new concepts and relations on-demand. As soon as the data steward finishes the semantic model creation, ESKAPE adds the semantic model to its knowledge graph and semantically integrates the data into a semantic data lake. As the knowledge graph serves as an index (cf. [2]), data analysts find, process and retrieve the data much faster.

Figure 6 shows the process from a raw data set to the semantic data integration again. During the conducted schema analysis step, ESKAPE queries its knowledge graph to identify possible concepts based on the labels of the data attributes. Therefore, ESKAPE compares the label of each data attribute with the name of each concept of ESKAPE's knowledge graph. If the label is a sub-string of the concept's name, the concept will be suggested to the user. This current solution has multiple drawbacks. First, it does not consider the context of the data attributes. Although some concepts are more likely to occur together, ESKAPE does not consider this. Second, matching labels against concept names may lead to wrong suggestions. For instance, the label *lat* may refer to the concepts *latitude* or *lattice*. Third, the suggestions contain only concepts that are available in ESKAPE's knowledge graph. However, by additionally querying additional knowledge bases, a broader set of suggestions for even unknown concepts would be possible.

To overcome these limitations, we modified ESKAPE's schema analysis to query our framework instead of the knowledge graph (cf. Fig. 7). Therefore, we first connected the knowledge graph to our framework so that the already existing concepts, which were already learned by ESKAPE, are also considered in the result produced by our framework. Instead of querying the knowledge graph for each data attribute separately, the schema analysis now queries our framework with all available data attributes of the data set. The framework then identifies the best fitting combination of possible concepts and returns them to the schema analysis. The schema analysis returns the result to ESKAPE's user interface where the user can now select one of these suggestions for his data attribute (cf. Fig. 8). In addition, we modified ESKAPE's user interface to be capable of dealing with suggestions for which no concept exists in the knowledge graph, yet.

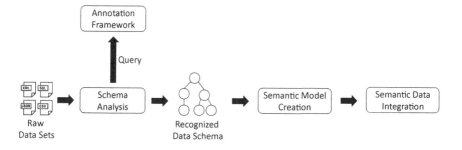

Fig. 7. Concept suggestion's in the user interface of ESKAPE.

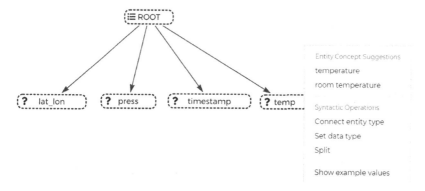

Fig. 8. Exemplary semantic model for the data set provided in Table 1. The concepts used in the semantic model are obtained from the underlying ontology of the enterprise.

8   Conclusion and Future Work

In this paper, we have shown how we use multiple semantic networks to improve the recommendation of semantic concepts during a modeling process. We built a framework to query and compare results from publicly available semantic networks as inputs and a selection of possibly matching concepts as an output. The functionality is based on the current state of a user-build semantic model with the aim to reduce the manual input for the model creator. Our framework computes the results by comparing (main) labels, glossary and labels of related concepts as no valid relations exist between concepts of separate networks. Therefore, we consider our approach suitable for future extensions to improve the modeling process even more. Currently, the recommendation framework is applied to our semantic data platform ESKAPE and serves as an integral part in all auto-detection and modeling steps.

During the evaluation period, we have achieved good results when comparing our approach to another public recommendation engine. We could show that the context awareness of the framework is working as intended and domains can be correctly identified. However not optimal, we hope to be able to increase the accuracy of the predictions with the connection of more semantic sources and the advanced integration into the ESKAPE system. Using the framework's ability to also connect to proprietary sources like company knowledge sources we are able to adapt to many use cases which initially could not be handled by ESKAPE before. We built our system to act as an interface between domain specific knowledge bases and more general public instances.

For future work, we hope to be able to build more advanced connectors to different kinds of data sources. Apart from classical semantic sources, we also aim to include available data from databases or data warehouses and convert those information to gain additional semantic concepts. Adding proprietary relations is still a concern of the overall system and will be solved in conjunction with an overhaul of the connector design. Although some work has been invested to increase the balancing between the different weights used in the comparison process, future work is still needed to allow a more fine-grained balancing of components. Preferably, this goal could be achieved using machine learning or another crowd-based approach. Similar techniques could also be used to help to improve the balancing of different sources based on the modeling context and the users previous created data sources.

References

1. Paulus, A., Pomp, A., Poth, L., Lipp, J., Meisen, T.: Gathering and combining semantic concepts from multiple knowledge bases. In: Proceedings of the 20th International Conference on Enterprise Information Systems, ICEIS, INSTICC, vol. 1, pp. 69–80. SciTePress (2018)
2. Pomp, A., Paulus, A., Jeschke, S., Meisen, T.: Enabling semantics in enterprises. In: Hammoudi, S., Śmiałek, M., Camp, O., Filipe, J. (eds.) Enterprise Information Systems, vol. 321, pp. 428–450. Springer International Publishing, Cham (2018). https://doi.org/10.1007/978-3-319-93375-7_20
3. Khan, M.H., Jan, S., Khan, I., Shah, I.A.: Evaluation of linguistic similarity measurement techniques for ontology alignment. In: 2015 International Conference on Emerging Technologies (ICET), pp. 1–6 (2015)
4. Mascardi, V., Locoro, A., Rosso, P.: Automatic ontology matching via upper ontologies: a systematic evaluation. IEEE Trans. Knowl. Data Eng. **22**, 609–623 (2010)
5. Smirnov, A., Kashevnik, A., Shilov, N., Balandin, S., Oliver, I., Boldyrev, S.: Principles of ontology matching, translation and interpretation in smart spaces. In: 2011 IEEE Consumer Communications and Networking Conference (CCNC), pp. 158–162 (2011)
6. Maedche, A., Motik, B., Silva, N., Volz, R.: MAFRA—a mapping framework for distributed ontologies. In: Gómez-Pérez, A., Benjamins, V.R. (eds.) EKAW 2002. LNCS (LNAI), vol. 2473, pp. 235–250. Springer, Heidelberg (2002). https://doi.org/10.1007/3-540-45810-7_23
7. Goel, A., Knoblock, C.A., Lerman, K.: Exploiting structure within data for accurate labeling using conditional random fields. In: Proceedings of the 14th International Conference on Artificial Intelligence (ICAI) (2012)
8. Ramnandan, S.K., Mittal, A., Knoblock, C.A., Szekely, P.: Assigning semantic labels to data sources. In: Gandon, F., Sabou, M., Sack, H., d'Amato, C., Cudré-Mauroux, P., Zimmermann, A. (eds.) ESWC 2015. LNCS, vol. 9088, pp. 403–417. Springer, Cham (2015). https://doi.org/10.1007/978-3-319-18818-8_25
9. Taheriyan, M., Knoblock, C.A., Szekely, P., Ambite, J.L.: Learning the semantics of structured data sources. Web Semant.: Sci. Serv. Agents World Wide Web **37**, 152–169 (2016)
10. Taheriyan, M., Knoblock, C., Szekely, P., Ambite, J.L., Chen, Y.: Leveraging linked data to infer semantic relations within structured sources. In: Proceedings of the 6th International Workshop on Consuming Linked Data (COLD 2015) (2015)

11. Syed, Z., Finin, T., Mulwad, V., Joshi, A.: Exploiting a web of semantic data for interpreting tables. In: Proceedings of the Second Web Science Conference, vol. 5 (2010)
12. Wang, J., Wang, H., Wang, Z., Zhu, K.Q.: Understanding tables on the web. In: Atzeni, P., Cheung, D., Ram, S. (eds.) ER 2012. LNCS, vol. 7532, pp. 141–155. Springer, Heidelberg (2012). https://doi.org/10.1007/978-3-642-34002-4_11
13. Du, W.H., Rau, J.W., Huang, J.W., Chen, Y.S.: Improving the quality of tags using state transition on progressive image search and recommendation system. In: 2012 IEEE International Conference on Systems, Man, and Cybernetics (SMC), pp. 3233–3238 (2012)
14. Kim, H.L., Passant, A., Breslin, J.G., Scerri, S., Decker, S.: Review and alignment of tag ontologies for semantically-linked data in collaborative tagging spaces. In: 2008 IEEE International Conference on Semantic Computing, pp. 315–322 (2008)
15. Singhal, A., Srivastava, J.: Leveraging the web for automating tag expansion for low-content items. In: 2014 IEEE 15th International Conference on Information Reuse and Integration (IRI), pp. 545–552 (2014)
16. Kalender, M., Dang, J., Uskudarli, S.: UNIpedia: a unified ontological knowledge platform for semantic content tagging and search. In: 2010 IEEE Fourth International Conference on Semantic Computing (ICSC), pp. 293–298 (2010)
17. Hong, H.K., Park, K.W., Lee, D.H.: A novel semantic tagging technique exploiting wikipedia-based associated words. In: 2015 IEEE 39th Annual Computer Software and Applications Conference (COMPSAC), vol. 3, pp. 648–649 (2015)
18. Navigli, R., Ponzetto, S.P.: BabelNet: the automatic construction, evaluation and application of a wide-coverage multilingual semantic network. Artif. Intell. **193**, 217–250 (2012)
19. Wolfram Alpha: Computational Knowledge Engine (2017). https://www.wolframalpha.com/
20. Jonquet, C., Musen, M.A., Shah, N.H.: Building a biomedical ontology recommender web service. J. Biomed. Semant. **1**, S1 (2010)
21. Banerjee, S., Pedersen, T.: Extended gloss overlaps as a measure of semantic relatedness. In: Ijcai, vol. 3, pp. 805–810 (2003)

Uncovering Hidden Links Between Images Through Their Textual Context

Hatem Aouadi[(✉)], Mouna Torjmen Khemakhem, and Maher Ben Jemaa

National School of Engineering of Sfax, University of Sfax,
Route de la Soukra km 4, 3038 Sfax, Tunisia
awadi.hatem@gmail.com, torjmen.mouna@gmail.com, maher.benjemaa@gmail.com
http://www.redcad.org

Abstract. Using hyperlinks to enhance page ranking has been widely studied in the literature. The main motivation is that an hyperlink underlines a page relevance. However, several hyperlinks in the web are used for navigation or marketing purposes. In addition, hyperlinks are created manually, so it is impossible to semantically link all similar pages. In our work, we propose to uncover hidden semantic links and create them automatically between all the collection's images. For this aim, we propose first to format textual context of images into topic distributions via LDA technique, and then compute semantic similarities to create links. Experiments carried out in the Wikipedia Retrieval Task of ImageClef 2011 showed that the whole textual context of images is useful for uncovering hidden links and consequently enhancing the retrieval accuracy.

Keywords: Context-based image retrieval · Implicit links · Link analysis · LDA

1 Introduction

The amount of images uploaded to the Web each day is growing exponentially. Consequently, the task of finding relevant images in response to a user request becomes increasingly difficult. As a solution, content based image retrieval (CBIR) techniques were proposed. However, despite the progress in this field, these techniques are still producing very poor results due to the lack of semantics in the visual features extracted from the image [17,65]. Alternatively, researchers are oriented to the use of textual information surrounding the images [1,17]. Thus, most current image retrieval systems are text based. However, this technique also has its limitations. First, the information may not describe the real content of the image. In addition, even if the textual information is relevant to the image, it may not contain the query keywords. Hence, different approaches has been proposed to improve the effectiveness of text-based image retrieval systems. We are interested in this paper to the use of the linkage information for ranking search results.

© Springer Nature Switzerland AG 2019
S. Hammoudi et al. (Eds.): ICEIS 2018, LNBIP 363, pp. 370–395, 2019.
https://doi.org/10.1007/978-3-030-26169-6_18

In Web link analysis domain, the main idea is that hyperlinks convey recommendations. Consequently, the quality of a Web page is generally measured according to the quality of its neighbours. Thus, the environment of a Web page provides an important indicator for its relevance. However, hyperlink may not reflect the content similarity between the interconnected web pages since the existence of spam links (arbitrary created links, navigation links, advertising links, etc.). As a solution, we propose to uncover hidden semantic links and to automatically create *implicit links* between multimedia documents using the textual context of the images.

Another problem was encountered when processing the documents that have more than one image: the relevance scores are calculated at the document level and do not reflect the individual relevance of the images in this document. To overcome this problem, we propose to segment pages into regions according to the image position. Implicit links are then created between the image regions instead of whole documents.

This paper is an extension of our previous work [4] where we propose the automatic creation of implicit links between regions of images. This proposal allows us to (1) use only semantic links in the retrieval process, and (2) cover all semantic similarities between documents (hypertext links cover only some similar documents). To create implicit links, we compute the topical similarity between the extracted regions using LDA topic model.

In this paper, we justify the choice of LDA topic model to represent textual information about images and we add more experiments about the combination of the different representations of the images. Moreover, we study the impact of using implicit links in the images re-ranking process. Our proposition are evaluated using the Wikipedia collection of ImageCLEF 2011.

This paper is organized as follows. Section 2 presents some related works. We detailed our approach for implicit link construction in Sect. 3. The experimental results are given in Sect. 4. Finally, we conclude this work and we give some perspectives in Sect. 5.

2   Related Works

2.1   Explicit Hyperlinks in Information Retrieval

There are rich dynamic structures of hyperlinks generated by humans on the Web. Links are a powerful help for people browsing the web, but they also help search engines understand the relationships between pages. These detected relationships help search engines to order web pages more efficiently. Several research works exploiting the hyperlinks were proposed notably within the framework of the Web. In what follows, we present some works of literature that exploit hyperlinks in textual and multimedia information retrieval.

Hyperlinks in Textual Information Retrieval. The link analysis algorithms have played a vital role in the ranking functions of the current generation of web search engines, including Google, Yahoo!, the search engine from Microsoft Bing and Ask. By the end of the 1990s, it was possible to produce reasonable rankings using these link analysis methods almost directly in the adopted search techniques. However, with the growth and increasing diversity of web content, link analysis algorithms have been extended and generalized considerably. PageRank was one of Google's original and central ingredients, and it has always been an essential part of its methodology. However, the importance of PageRank as a feature in Google's ranking function has been diminished over time. Over a similar period of time, the Ask search engine has rebuilt its ranking function, although its recent extensions are increasingly merged with many other features.

Link analysis alone can not provide a ranking that adapts to the user's request. Intuitively, a good ranking should take into account both the relevance of a page for the input request and the overall importance of the page. There is a clear need to integrate network structure information as well as textual content in order to produce higher quality research results. Cohn and Hofmann [16] and Richardson and Domingos [45] present probabilistic models inspired by HITS and PageRank, respectively, which integrate both the content and the structure of the links. Hashemi et al. [22] propose different ways to combine the scores obtained by the search by content (TF-IDF [44] and BM25: Best Match 25 Model [46]) with those obtained by the analysis of the links (HITS and PageRank). The combination often gives better results. Haveliwala [23] and Jeh and Widom [27] offer problem-sensitive PageRank algorithms that effectively identify authority web pages for a query at the time of the search. The idea is to compute a separate set of scores for each topic under consideration and calculate the importance of a page for a given query by combining the calculated scores with the topics relevant to the query.

A particularly effective way of combining textual content and link structure for ranking is the analysis of anchor text (clickable text that activates a hyperlink leading to another page) [13]. Anchor text is usually written by people who are not the authors of the landing page. This means that the anchor text can describe a landing page from a different perspective or focus on the most important aspect of the destination page. Bharat and Henzinger [6] and Chakrabarti et al. [13] propose modifications to HITS by weighting the links contributions according to the quality of the anchor text. Kolda and Bader [33] proposed TOPHITS, an algorithm similar to HITS but which also exploits the link text. It calculates hub scores and authorities as well as scores of terms that are used in the text links between them. The terms that have the highest scores are the most descriptive terms of a page. Najork [42] proposes an approach based on the combination of link analysis algorithms with a textual search algorithm (BM25F [61]) exploiting the text of links. This combination makes it possible to significantly improve the search results by comparing it to the pseudo use of the BM25F algorithm. In addition, HITS combined with BM25F allows a better performance than PageRank combined with BM25F.

Another form of combining text and links is the relevance propagation. Shakery and Zhai [48] use links to propagate the relevance between documents, so they indirectly leverage the contents of linked documents to increase the content of a document. The most relevant documents contribute more to the score of a document than the least relevant documents. In the same study, the authors use inbound and outbound links (forward and backward propagation) and find that both are effective and that the combination of the two is even more effective. Tsikrika et al. [53] use a random walk to propagate relevancy between documents as part of structured search. Chibane and Doan [15] also use the links to propagate relevance and then combine the score obtained by propagation with the initial relevance score calculated by BM25. The combination improves the results.

Ingongngam and Rungsawang [26] calculate scores for offline Web pages using the links to propagate similarity scores (BM25) between documents instead of the traditional popularity spread adopted by PageRank. A similar idea is proposed by Kim et al. [31] but instead of using all the textual content, the authors extract the keywords, then use the links to calculate the contribution of each term t (keyword) of a page p to the score of another page q pointed by p and containing the term t.

Hyperlinks in Multimedia Information Retrieval. Although several works exploiting links have been developed for textual information retrieval, few have been proposed for the multimedia information retrieval. In most works, classic algorithms such as HITS and PageRank are suitable for multimedia search [2].

In a hypermedia collection, Dunlop [19] proposed to use links to compute representations for multimedia (non-textual) nodes. Indeed, each multimedia node is assigned a representation composed by the textual contents of all the nodes directly linked to it. The proposed algorithm can be extended to take into account not only the immediate neighbors of a node in the hypermedia network, but also neighboring nodes obtained by following two links (a two-step link). The representations will then be used to allow the direct search of these nodes by a textual request.

Based on this model, Harmandas et al. [21] have tried to combine the textual content and the hyperlink structure for the multimedia information retrieval on the Web. The representation of an image is composed of sections and each one has been assigned a weight indicating its importance in the search. Experiments have shown that assigning a higher score to the image caption section (caption) and to the text section of documents linked by two link steps, improves the efficiency of the search.

Lempel and Soffer [36] proposed the PicASHOW system based on the application of cocitation-based approaches and methods inspired by PageRank. The assumptions behind the use of cocitation are that: (1) images that are co-contained in the same page are likely to be related to the same subject (2) images that are contained in pages co-cited by other pages are probably related to the same subject. In addition, like the PageRank spirit, the PicASHOW system assumes that images that are contained in authoritative pages are good candidates for quality images for the query.

The proposed PicASHOW system has improved web search performance of images. However, it only supports keyword queries and can not handle image content and example image queries. To solve this problem, Petrakis [43] and Voutsakis et al. [54] proposed WPicASHOW (weighted PicASHOW), allowing a weighted ranking of cocitation analysis that is based on the combination of text and visual content to regulate the influence of links between pages. WPicASHOW showed a better performance than PicASHOW.

Cai et al. [11,24] also propose a system of grouping and multimedia information retrieval on the Web, named iFind. Using a vision-based page segmentation algorithm (VIPS [12]), a Web page is partitioned into blocks, and the text and link information of an image can be accurately extracted from the block containing that image. Textual information is used for indexing images. By extracting page-to-block, block-to-image, block-to-page relationships through the link structure and layout analysis, an image graph is constructed. This method is less sensitive to noise links than previous methods such as PageRank, HITS and PicASHOW, so the image graph can better reflect the semantic relationships between images. The graph can be used to calculate an importance score for each image, which will then be combined with the relevance score to produce the final rank.

2.2   Implicit Links in Information Retrieval

The basic idea behind the use of links in information retrieval is motivated by the intuition that these links are not random and reflect a kind of resemblance between the pages. However, hyperlinks are not always indicators of content similarity. The authors of a web page can put arbitrary links to some pages that are not related to the subject of their page. Thus, hyperlinks can be created for navigation and structuring the site or for advertising purposes. These *spam* links decrease the quality of retrieval accuracy when they are used. Moreover, similar pages are not always linked to each other (generally the author of a web page creates only few links to other pages). In addition, many document collections have no links or have a very weak link structure. These problems present a major obstacle for all web search algorithms that use links in the retrieval process. As a solutions, many works proposed to automatically interlinking the documents by creating *implicit links* between them. We present in the following the use of implicit links in textual and multimedia retrieval.

Implicit Links in Textual Information Retrieval. Implicit links have been used in different areas including the ranking of search results, document classification and clustering.

Xue et al. [60] proposed to explore the user log to make implicit links between documents and then applied a modified PageRank algorithm for small web search. Despite the improved performance of the research, this method can not be applied to large collections because it is intended for a small search on the Web. Another work proposed by Kurland and Lee [34,35] used the language models to generate document cluster relationships. The application of Hits [32] and PageRank [10] algorithms in the constructed graph of relationships improved search precision. Nevertheless, these methods had not been compared with the use of explicit links. Xu and Ma [59] proposed to construct an implicit graph and combined it with the hypertext graph to improve the search performance. Experiments showed the effectiveness of the proposed approach compared to the PageRank algorithm applied in the hyperlink graph. This approach is evaluated using a collection of forums that contains several noisy hyperlinks.

For document clustering, Zhang et al. [64] defined an implicit link as co-authorship link. They also used explicit links composed of citation links and hyperlinks, and pseudo links such as content similarity links. The experimental results showed that linkage is quite effective in improving content-based document clustering.

In the document classification area, Shen et al. [49] compared the use of explicit links represented by the hyperlinks and implicit links generated from the query logs. In their study, they demonstrated that implicit links can improve the classification performance compared to the explicit links. Query logs are also used by Belmouhcine and Benkhalifa [5] to create implicit links between web pages for the purpose of web page classification. Experimental results with two subsets of the Open Directory Project (ODP) have shown that this representation based on implicit links provides better classification results.

In the biomedical domain, Lin [38] applies Hits and PageRank algorithms on implicit links (content similarity links) analysis in the context of the PubMed search engine. He demonstrated that it is possible to exploit networks of content similarity links, generated automatically, for document retrieval. Thus, the combination of scores generated by link analysis algorithms and the text-based retrieval baseline improved the precision.

Implicit Links in Multimedia Information Retrieval. In order to improve the accuracy of image retrieval, several research projects have proposed to build implicit links between images by mainly using visual content. Thanks to these visual links, a visual graph is constracted and then analyzed to calculate the relevance scores of the images. To analyse the constructed graph, random walk method (such as PageRank) has been widely adopted [28,29,56,63,66].

Xie et al. [58] proposed to construct an off-line visual graph by taking each image as a query and make a link with the k top returned images. HITS algorithm is then applied on the set of images returned at query time. In the same way, Liu et al. [40] followed the same offline step, and at query time, they merge the different graphs obtained using different descriptors. Then, they applied a local ranking algorithm on the resulted graph. Zhang et al. [62] proposed a query-specific fusion approach based on graph, where multiple lists of search results from different visual cues were merged and clustered by link analysis on a merged graph. Wang et al. [55] have incorporated several visual features in a graph-based learning algorithm for images retrieval. The creation of implicit links using the textual information is taken into account for the first time by Khasanova et al.

[30] who have built a multilayer graph where each layer represents a modality (textual, visual, etc.). The constructed graph is undirected, where each node is connected only with its k-nearest neighbours (in terms of Euclidean distance). Then, they applied a random walk on the multilayer graph by making transitions between the different layers. The proposed solution achieves good image retrieval performance compared to the state-of-the-art methods. The authors firmly believe that flexible structures like graphs offer promising solutions to capture the underlying geometry of multi-view data.

Other works have been done as part of MediaEval [7,14,20,25,39] and TRECVID [50] evaluation campaigns for video hyperlinking. Chen et al. [14] concluded that textual features work better in this task, whereas visual features by themselves can not predict reliable hyperlinks. Nevertheless, they suggest that the use of visual features to re-rank the results of text-based retrieval can improve the performance.

In conclusion, the majority of works use the visual content of the images to create implicit links between them. However, the unresolved problems associated with this modality make this type of links ineffective and unprofitable. For this reason, we propose in this paper to use textual information to automatically create links between images and to explore them in a retrieval process in order to improve the retrieval accuracy.

3   Uncovering Hidden Links Using LDA Technique: Implicit Links

Using links between similar documents is more efficient than using links between independent pages in the retrieval process. However, in the context of the Web, semantically similar pages are not always linked to each other, hence the need to automatically create implicit links between them.

3.1   Motivation

We propose in this paper to uncover hidden links and build them automatically between similar images through the calculation of the semantic similarity of the textual information surrounding these images. The similarity can be calculated using the vector representation of the texts. However, the textual information of a multimedia document may contain some details that are not related to the image. Thus, an image usually represents an illustration for the overall subject of the document. For example, a page talking about the animal *"lion"* will contain probably images of *lion*. However, words such as *"forest"*, *"meat"*, *"water"*, etc. will be present frequently. If we use the textual representation to calculate the similarity with other images, we can obtain images that are assumed to be similar but do not represent the image of a *lion*. Hence, word level document similarity can be easily spammed when the same words are used in documents with different topics. For this reason, we propose to model documents in a more generalized form.

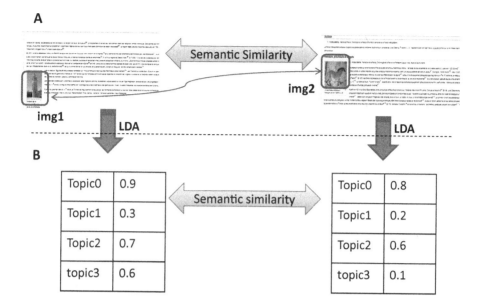

Fig. 1. Modeling documents in the form of topics using LDA topic model.

Latent Semantic Analysis (LSA) [18] was initially proposed as a topic based method for modelling words semantic. Basically, LSA finds a small representation of documents and words by applying the truncated singular value decomposition (SVD) for the document-term matrix. An improvement of this model has been proposed with Probabilistic and Latent Semantic Analysis (PLSA) [51] which uses a probabilistic method instead of using matrices. Then, the PLSA model has been generalized to Latent Dirichlet Allocation (LDA) model [8]. For this reason, we choose the LDA topic model to model documents as illustrated in Fig. 1. Indeed, this model allows to give an overview for the documents in the form of topic distributions, which allows to filter out secondary and noisy information.

We have already demonstrate in a previous work [3] the effectiveness of this model in image retrieval. Thus, we use it in this work to create implicit links between images.

In the following, we describe briefly the LDA algorithm, then we describe our method to segment a document to regions according to the image position. After that, a detailed description of our method to create implicit links is done. And finally, we present the application of link analysis algorithms on the created links.

3.2   LDA Topic Model

Blei et al. [8] have proposed LDA topic model that can reduce the representation of documents as a mixture of latent topics. The model generates automatic topical summaries in terms of discrete probability distributions on words for each topic, and infers further discrete distributions by document on topics.

LDA assumes that all documents are probabilistically generated from a shared set of K common topics, where each topic is a multinomial distribution over the vocabulary (noted by β). The generation of a document is done according to the following generative process:

(1) For each topic
    (a) draw a distribution over words $\varphi \sim Dir(\beta)$
(2) For each document
    (a) Chose $\theta_d \sim Dir(\alpha)$
    (b) For each word
        (i) generate topic $z \sim Mult(\theta)$
        (ii) generate term $w \sim Mult(\varphi)$.

We apply LDA to the textual information representing the images. The outputs of this model are then used to create implicit links between the images. More precisely, we use the topic distributions generated by LDA to compute the similarity between image representations and therefore create implicit links between them.

3.3 Textual Representations of Images

In text-based image retrieval, the basic idea consists in considering the document as an atomic unit and all its textual information is treated in a similar way. Therefore, for a given query, a relevance score is calculated for the whole document and then assigned for all its images. According to this process, all images in a document will have the same relevance score even if they have different relevance levels, or some of them are not sufficiently relevant to the query. This major weakness has led us to the idea of segmenting multimedia documents into image regions. In this way, it would be possible to differentiate images of the same document by approximating the relevance degree of each image separately.

The best textual description of the image is the associated metadata (called in our work IMD: Image Meta Data) because it is the most specific information for the image. However, metadata usually contains few terms or can be missed sometimes. For these reasons, we propose to consider other additional sources of information to describe the image. More precisely, we propose to divide the content of the document into two descriptions for each image. The first description is the container region of the image obtained after segmentation of the document. We call this description "Specific Image Description" (SID). The second description of this image is the rest of the document (without SID) called "Generic Image Description" (GID). If a document contains more than one image, the specific description of an image belongs to the generic description of other images and vice versa. Figure 2 shows the different descriptions of an image (*img2*).

In this example, the SID description of the image *img2* is the container paragraph and the GID description is all the textual content of the document except that paragraph. The segmentation of the document into paragraphs could be done easily for web documents thanks to the use of tags. In HTML documents for example, the use of title tags (<H1>, <H2>, etc.) makes it possible to segment the document into paragraphs. Wikipedia documents are also easy to be segmented thanks to their specific tags: the == tag for a first level paragraph (equivalent of the <H1> tag in HTML), the === tag for a second level paragraph, etc. We propose to define the specific description of the image as the smallest paragraph granularity containing that image.

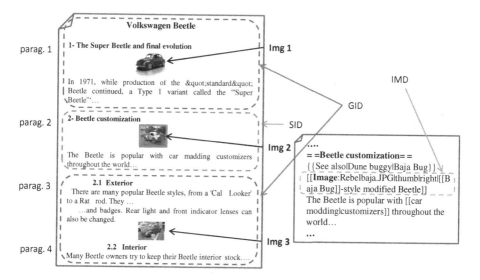

Fig. 2. Example of specific (SID) and generic (GID) representations of an image.

To conclude, each image in the collection is represented using three descriptions: (1) image metadata (IMD); (2) the paragraph containing the image as specific description (SID) and (3) the document without the paragraph containing the image as generic description (GID).

3.4 LDA Based Implicit Links: Building and Analyzing

In this section, we describe the proposed approach for creating contextual links between images based on the LDA topic model. Many steps are needed to create the links between each pair of images. The link creation process is applied separately for each image representation. Figure 3 presents an overview of the link creation process using generic image descriptions (GID).

In the following, the different steps of the link creation process are detailed.

Step 1: Topic Distributions. For the SID (resp. IMD) representation, we construct a SID (resp. IMD) collection containing the SID (resp. IMD) of all images. Then, the LDA topic model is applied to the textual content of both images to create links using the whole SID (resp. IMD) collection. More specifically, a learning phase is performed in order to estimate the topic distributions for each SID (resp. IMD) of both images.

For the GID representation, an additional inference phase is performed after the learning phase to compute the topic distributions for each GID. In this type of representation, we kept the original collection and did not create a separately GID collection. In fact, for GID representations, we propose to use the whole documents in the learning phase instead of using only GID descriptions. This decision aims at avoiding the use of redundant information: two GID representations of two images belonging to the same document will contain a lot of redundancy. To better explain this problem, we consider the example in Fig. 2. If we create a GID collection, the GID representation of the image *img1* is composed of parag. 2, parag. 3, and parag. 4, while the GID representation of the image *img2* is composed of parag. 1, parag. 3, and parag. 4. We note here that parag. 3 and parag. 4 will be used twice in the learning model and will therefore affect the quality of the topic distributions.

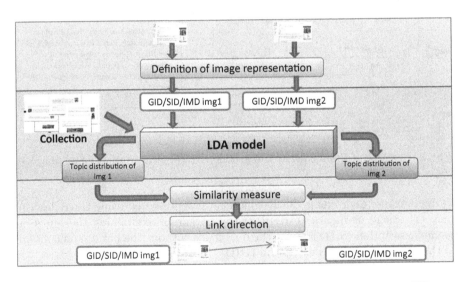

Fig. 3. Overview of LDA based link creation between two images using GID.

After applying the LDA model on each description collection, two probability distributions are generated: a document-topic distribution that represents the proportions of topics in each image representation; and a term-topic distribution that represents the weights of the terms in each topic.

Table 1 presents some topics generated using LDA model. Each line in the table presents a list of the top terms according to their weights.

Table 1. Example of some topics generated by LDA model.

id Topic	Top terms
top_1	climate global warming science carbon greenhouse temperature nature
top_2	council borough road railway county population united england
top_3	function math distribution frac probability sum random normal functions
top_4	nicolas sarkozy french france royal presidential icon pen front
top_5	audi bmw porsche mans racing quattro cars sports tdi acura volkswagen

According to this table, we note that there are some terms that are not related to the main topic described by the most of terms. For instance, the three terms "icon pen front" of topic top_4 are not related to the other terms. This event could be frequent since the LDA model is a probabilistic model. We propose thus to not use all the topics to represent the textual content, but only the topics having a strong relationship between their terms.

To fix the number of topics that will be considered for each representation, a simple way is to fix a static number (for example, each representation will be assigned the top 10 topics). However, the total number of topics varies from one representation to another (we only consider topics with positive scores). Therefore, we propose to set a percentage of the top topics to be used for each image representation (for example, each representation will be presented by 10% of the most relevant topics). Best percentage values are obtained by experiments and detailed in Fig. 7.

Figure 4 shows an example of document-topic distribution for image representations. The first table represents the topics (T_j) with their corresponding terms. The second table represents the topic distributions for each image representation (Rep_{img_i}).

The best topics for each image representation are assigned the higher scores. For example, the best topic in Rep_{img_2} is T_3 (score = 0,11).

Once the topic distributions are calculated for the representations (SID, IMD, or GID) of two images, a link weight must be calculated using a similarity measure between the topic distributions of both images.

Step 2: Similarity Measure Between Two Images. After performing the LDA process, each image representation is defined by a topic distribution vector as shown in Fig. 4. In order to create and weight the links between images, we propose to apply a similarity measure on the two by two vectors. In the information retrieval literature, the most commonly used similarity measure between two vectors is the cosine measure [37,41,47]. We therefore propose to use the cosine measure in our work as follows:

$$cos_{sim}(\overrightarrow{Rep_{img_1}}, \overrightarrow{Rep_{img_2}}) = \frac{\overrightarrow{Rep_{img_1}} . \overrightarrow{Rep_{img_2}}}{||\overrightarrow{Rep_{img_1}}|| ||\overrightarrow{Rep_{img_2}}||} \tag{1}$$

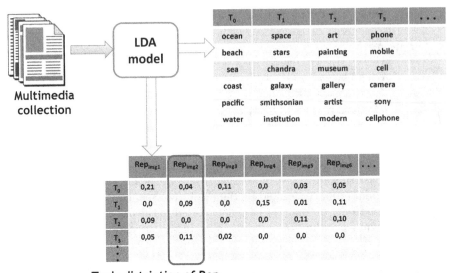

Fig. 4. An example of document-topic distribution for image representations [4].

where $\overrightarrow{Rep_{img}}$ denotes the topic distribution vector of the image representation Rep_{img} which could be GID, SID or IMD.

In our work, we propose to improve the classical cosine measure by including the number of common topics between the two image representations. The intuition of this proposition is that the more the two representations of images have common topics, the more similar they are. For example, if there are two image representations with only one common topic but with a high probability score, and two other image representations with many common topics but low probability scores, the cosine measure will favour the first two images. From another point of view, the number of common topics between two image representations could be very high with low topic distributions. In this case, the link weight will be very high, although there is no high semantic similarity between the two topic distributions. To overcome this situation, we propose to compute the number of common topics using only the most important topics for each image representation. The percentage of the most significant topics noted X% is fixed with the experiments described later. The new equation becomes:

$$sim(\overrightarrow{Rep_{img_1}}, \overrightarrow{Rep_{img_2}}) = cos_{sim}(\overrightarrow{Rep_{img_1}}, \overrightarrow{Rep_{img_2}})$$
$$\times |commonTopics(X\%\overrightarrow{Rep_{img_1}}, X\%\overrightarrow{Rep_{img_2}})| \quad (2)$$

With $\overrightarrow{Rep_{img_1}}$ (respectively $\overrightarrow{Rep_{img_2}}$) is the topic distribution of the representation Rep_{img_1} (resp. Rep_{img_2}) and $X\%\overrightarrow{Rep_{img_1}}$ (resp. $X\%\overrightarrow{Rep_{img_1}}$) is the X% of the most relevant topics according to their probability scores for Rep_{img_1} (resp. Rep_{img_2}).

Finally, after calculating the similarity scores between the images, a threshold is applied to reduce the number of implicit links between images. This similarity threshold is set to 0.1 by experiments.

Step 3: Link Direction Estimation. After constructing the implicit links between the image regions, we can use the link analysis algorithms of the literature to compute the relevance of the nodes in the constructed graph given a query. However, these algorithms that originally designed for web search assume that the links are directed, i.e. the link has a starting node and a one-way ending node. In our case the implicit links obtained by similarity calculation are bidirectional. Indeed, when we say that a node A is similar to a node B, the node B is also similar to A with the same degree of similarity. In this case, if we want to apply the HITS algorithm for example, the hub and authority scores for a given node will be the same because the number of incoming and outgoing links of these nodes will be the same. Thus, the HITS algorithm will not work properly.

To determine the direction of links, we rely on the following intuition: when two representations have some common topics, the region containing more information about these topics (high probability) is suitable to be the destination of the link. For this, we propose to calculate a direction score according to the percentage of information shared between the two representations. In other terms, we propose to determine how much the information of the representation of the image 1 (Rep_{img_1}) is presented in the representation of the image 2 (Rep_{img_2}). The following formula is used:

$$Score_{Direction}(Rep_{img1} \to Rep_{img2}) = \frac{\overrightarrow{Rep_{img_1}} \cdot \overrightarrow{Rep_{img_2}}}{||\overrightarrow{Rep_{img_1}}||} \tag{3}$$

with $Rep_{img1} \to Rep_{img2}$ means that the link is from Rep_{img_1} to Rep_{img_2}.

Note that we consider in Eq. 3 only the common topics among the X% most important topics in the Rep_{img_1} and Rep_{img_2} representations and not the whole topic distributions, as explained in the previous subsection.

Based on the intuition that the link should start from the general image representation to the more specific image representation, the direction of the implicit link between two similar representations Rep_{img_1} and Rep_{img_2} can thus be defined as follows:

- If $Score_{Direction}(Rep_{img1} \to Rep_{img2}) = Score_{Direction}(Rep_{img2} \to Rep_{img1})$, both documents have almost the same amount of information about the shared content. In this case, two links are created: one from Rep_{img_1} to Rep_{img_2} and the other in the opposite direction;
- If $Score_{Direction}(Rep_{img1} \to Rep_{img2}) < Score_{Direction}(Rep_{img2} \to Rep_{img1})$, the link should be directed from Rep_{img_1} to Rep_{img_2}. In fact, the representation Rep_{img_1} contains more information about the shared content than Rep_{img_2}. This implies that Rep_{img_1} is more general, and the representation Rep_{img_2} describes a specific part of Rep_{img_1};

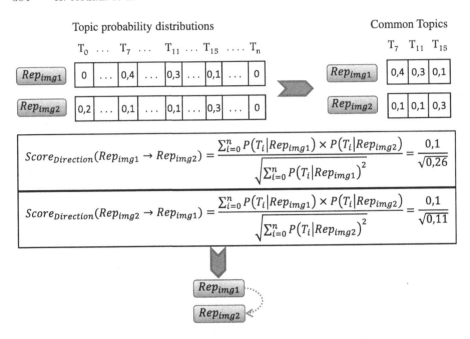

Fig. 5. Example of computing the link direction [4].

- If $Score_{Direction}(Rep_{img1} \rightarrow Rep_{img2}) > Score_{Direction}(Rep_{img2} \rightarrow Rep_{img1})$, the link should be directed from Rep_{img2} to Rep_{img1}.

Figure 5 shows an example of determining the link direction.

These two image representations share three topics: T_7, T_{11} and T_{15}. By computing the direction scores between the two representations, we obtain $Score_{Direction}(Rep_{img2} \rightarrow Rep_{img1}) > Score_{Direction}(Rep_{img1} \rightarrow Rep_{img2})$. Consequently, the link is directed from img_1 to img_2.

Implicit Link Analysis. Once the implicit links are created between the images for each type of image representation (IMD, SID, GID), a link analysis algorithm such as HITS and PageRank or a social network analysis algorithm such as Betweeness, Closeness and Degree; could be applied. Concerning the link analysis algorithms, we propose to use the HITS algorithm because it is query dependent, i.e. it is done for each new query, which allows it to be always close to the subject of this query. For the social network analysis algorithms, we propose to use the most used ones in the literature namely the Degree and Betweenness [9] centralities.

A score based on the links for each image representation is thus calculated. Therefore, each image will have three scores based on the links: the SID link score, the GID link score, and the IMD link score. Finally, to obtain a single score based on links, we propose to combine the three links based scores as follows:

$$LinkScore(img_i) = \alpha * LinkScore(IMD_{img_i})$$
$$+ \beta * LinkScore(SID_{img_i}) + \gamma LinkScore(GID_{img_i}) \tag{4}$$

where α, β and γ are parameters used to adjust the importance of each representation in the computing of the final link score for an image. Their sum equals to 1.

4 Evaluation

In this section, we begin by describing the evaluation protocol and the parameter settings of our experiments. Then we provide comparative results of different link analysis algorithms. Finally, we evaluate the efficiency of the implicit links in the re-ranking process.

4.1 Evaluation Protocol

To evaluate our propositions, we used the Wikipedia collection provided by the Wikipedia retrieval task of the ImageCLEF (The CLEF Cross Language Image Retrieval Track) 2011. The collection consists of 125 827 documents in three languages, containing 237 434 images. A set of 50 queries is also provided to perform the retrieval accuracy evaluation. We are interested in this paper only in documents written in English where the number is 42 774. However, our approach can be applied to any language and any type of document.

In order to evaluate properly our proposition, we construct a new base of assessments composed only of images belonging to the English documents. Due to computing complexity and time-space costs, we decide to run a textual search and then apply the link analysis for only the first 1000 returned results. This operation do not affect the evaluation of our approach as our main aim is to improve the image reranking and not the image retrieval. To generate the initial textual results, we have used the Lucene[1] search library.

For evaluation metrics, we have used early precisions (P@10 and P@20) since users in web serach context examine relatively the top results, and the Mean Average Precision (MAP) measure since it allows to evaluate the global effectiveness of the system.

4.2 Parameter Settings

LDA Parameters. The mallet library[2] is used to generate the LDA topical representation of documents. LDA parameters are fixed to the most common

---

[1] http://lucene.apache.org/.
[2] http://mallet.cs.umass.edu/.

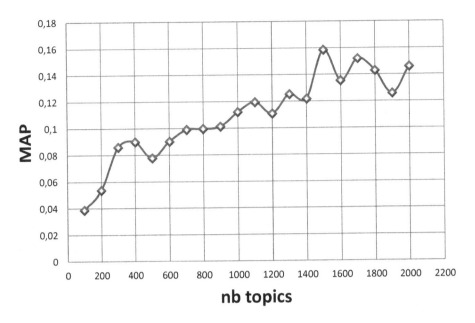

Fig. 6. Determining the best number of topics K.

values used in the literature: $\alpha = 50/K$ where K is the number of topics, and $\beta = 0.01$.

To set the best value of K, we propose to apply and evaluate the LDA model in image retrieval instead of the link creation for time and memory reasons. Thus, the documents and the queries are presented by topics and a matching function is used to retrieve the relevant images. We carried out several experiments with different K values between 100 and 2000. Figure 6 shows the variation of MAP according to K.

We note that with small K values, we obtained bad MAP values. This means that the collection covers several topics and that it is not easy to classify documents into few topics. As shown in Fig. 6, the best K value is 1500. Thus, we set $K = 1500$ topics in link building experiments.

Similarity Measure Evaluation. In this experiment, our purpose is to evaluate our proposed measure for similarity scores between images used to create links between them. More precisely, we aim to fix the best ratio of top topics according to the topic distribution of both images. Experiments of building and analysing implicit links between images are costly in terms of time and they need to fix several settings. For thus, we propose to evaluate the efficiency of the proposed measure in the image retrieval process. Indeed, we apply this similarity measure to compute relevance scores of images given a query using the Image CLEF Wikipedia collection 2011. In this experiment, the multimedia specificity is not taken into account: the relevance score is computed for the whole document, and then assigned for all

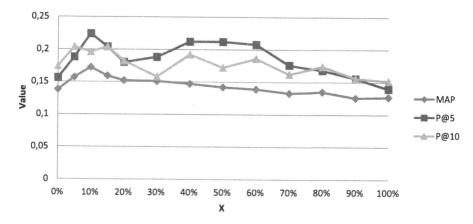

Fig. 7. Determining the best percentage X of the top topics.

its own images. In the retrieval process, the following equation is used:

$$RSV(D,Q) = cos_{sim}(Doc, Q)$$
$$\times |commonTopics(X\%\vec{D}, X\%\vec{Q})| \tag{5}$$

where $X\%$ is the X percent of the top topics representing the document or the query.

Figure 7 presents some experiments of varying the X parameter of Eq. 5.

Comparing the cosine measure ($X = 0\%$) and our proposed measure according to the MAP metric, we note that better results are obtained when X is between 5% and 60% (MAP > 0.1387). Moreover, the best MAP and P@5 values are obtained with X = 10% and the best P@10 is obtained when X = 15%. This means that the 10% of the top topic representing documents and queries are the most significant information. Thanks to our measure, the retrieval accuracy is improved by 26.31% according to MAP measure, 43.58% according to P@5 measure and 12.64% according to P@10 measure. These improvements prove that the use of the top common topics between the query and the document is a good relevance indicator.

X = 100% means that all the common topics between the query and the document will be used. We choose X = 10% for the remain of the experiments.

4.3   Experimental Comparison of Different Link Analysis Algorithms

The aims of this experiment are twofold: (1) evaluation of the separate and the combined use of the different image representations (SID, GID and IMD); (2) comparison between three link analysis algorithms applied in our work.

The combination between the three image representations is based on a simple average of the three scores without taking into account the optimal settings.

Table 2. A comparison of different link analysis algorithms according to different image representations.

	IMD	SID	GID	AverComb
Degree centrality				
P@5	0,088	0,092	0,128	**0,148**
P@10	0,104	0,072	0,108	**0,136**
MAP	0,058	0,064	**0,1**	0,094
HITS				
P@5	0,104	0,052	0,08	**0,108**
P@10	0,096	0,052	**0,106**	0,104
MAP	0,056	0,059	0,074	**0,081**
Betweeness centrality				
P@5	0,056	0,088	0,08	**0,104**
P@10	0,048	0,066	0,08	**0,084**
MAP	0,028	0,046	0,061	**0,062**

However, it is possible to run some experiments to set the optimal combination values. The combination equation is:

$$S_{lien}(img_i) = 1/3 * S_{lien}(IMD_{img_i})$$
$$+ 1/3 * S_{lien}(SID_{img_i}) + 1/3 * S_{lien}(GID_{img_i})$$

(6)

Table 2 depicts overall results, where AverComb is the run obtained by averaging the scores of the three image representations.

By comparing the MAP values of the different image representations without combination, we note that the GID run gives the best results. This means that the generic information is the best source of evidence to represent images in this work. This interpretation could be explained by the specific/generic vocabulary notion [52]: if the query vocabulary is generic, it is better to represent the image by generic information, and if the query vocabulary is specific, it is better to represent the image by specific information. We note that a query is called specific if the results represent the same object (for example, "London Bridge") and is generic if the results represent many objects (for example, "skyscraper building tall towers").

To validate this interpretation, we have computed the number of specific and generic queries in the ImageCLEF Wikipedia collection 2011 and we found that 72% of queries are generic and 28% are specific. Thus, it is not surprising that generic descriptions outperform specific descriptions.

Another interpretation could be drawn from the results: combining the three image representations by averaging their scores improves in general the results. This confirms our assumption that the use of the three sources of evidence is very useful. However, by analysing query by query, we have observed that GID representations give the best results for 40% of queries, SID and IMD gives the best results for 30% of queries for each one. So, it will be interesting to train a query classifier in order to choose the best representation to use for each query according to its class: generic or specific. We recall that the combination settings are not optimized. In our work, we decided to use a basic linear combination which is the score average in order to validate our approach without an optimal tuning of parameters. Further experiments are needed to set the best combination factors.

Finally, by comparing the use of the different link analysis algorithms, we note that the Degree Centrality gives the best performance. We could argue this result by the following reasons: Betweenness algorithm assumes that the graph should be undirected, which is not the case in our work. Moreover, the HITS algorithm idea is to select the K top ranked documents according to the query and then extend this initial set root by other documents. This basic idea is not respected in our work as we use the 1000 top documents ranked by a textual model without extension.

4.4 Combining Textual and Link Based Scores: Images Re-Ranking

The aim of this experiment is to evaluate the re-ranking process using implicit links. Table 3 reports 5 runs: the first one is the *Textual* baseline. *IMD+Text*, *SID+Text* and *GID+Text* runs are obtained by the combination of IMD, SID and GID scores with textual scores respectively. Finally, the *AverComb+Text* run is obtained by combining the AverComb scores with textual ones.

The last column of Table 3 presents the improvement percentage of the *AverComb+Text* run over the *Textual* run.

Significant differences according to Student test ($p < 0.05$) [57] of our approach over the traditional textual model are bold and starred (*).

Table 3. Results of combining textual and link based scores.

	Textual	IMD+Text	SID+Text	GID+Text	AverComb+Text	% Imp (Text)
P@5	0.384	0,416	0,388	0,368	0,400	4%
P@10	0.316	0,346	0,328	0,326	0,352	11% *
MAP	0.240	0,259	0,257	0,268	0,270	13%*

Considering the runs using implicit links of each image representation separately. The best performing run according to P@5 and P@10 is the one exploring the image metadata (*IMD+Text* run). However, the best performing run according to the MAP measure is the *GID+Text* one. This means that specific information helps to re-rank relevant images at the top rank, while generic information helps to improve the global re-ranking accuracy.

Combining the scores of the three sources of evidence with textual scores allows to improve the top ranking and the overall retrieval accuracy comparing

Table 4. Effectiveness of IMD, GID and SID representations in the reranking process.

	AverComb+text	Comb05IMD03SID02GID+text	Comb02IMD03SID05GID+text
P@5	0.400	0.404	0.400
P@10	0.352	0.348	0.338
MAP	0.270	0.2714	0.2657

to textual retrieval accuracy. Indeed, the *AverComb+Text* run outperforms significantly the baseline (Textual run) with an improvement of 4% at P@5, 11% at P@10 and 13% at MAP.

By comparing Tables 2 and 3, we note that before combining with textual run, GID run gives the best results and shows that the GID is the most interesting representation. However, after the combination, IMD gives the best results. This finding could be explained by the fact that textual scores are already computed using SID and GID representations, but it is not the case for IMD representation. In fact, when combining textual scores with SID and GID scores, the same information is used by two different ways: once the text is presented by term vectors, and once the text is presented by LDA topics. However, when using the IMD information, new specific informations for images are added to generic informations.

This interpretation confirms the effectiveness of using all textual information related to the concerned image in the reranking process.

The last experiment in this contribution is the combination of the three sources of evidences (IMD, GID and SID) with different values of combination parameters. In addition to the combination based on averaging the three scores, we propose to execute two runs. The first one gives more importance to the IMD representation (specific information), and the second one gives more importance to the GID representation (generic information) as follows:

- Comb05IMD03SID02GID run: $LinkScore(img_i) = 0.5 * LinkScore(IMD_{img_i}) + 0.3 * LinkScore(SID_{img_i}) + 0.2 * LinkScore(GID_{img_i})$
- Comb02IMD03SID05GID run: $LinkScore(img_i) = 0.2 * LinkScore(IMD_{img_i}) + 0.3 * LinkScore(SID_{img_i}) + 0.5 * LinkScore(GID_{img_i})$

Results are presented in Table 4.

In general, there is no significant difference between the three runs. Only a slight improvement is noted when giving more importance to the specific information then general one (*Comb05IMD03SID02GID* run) according to the MAP measure.

It is difficult thus to conclude about the participation degree of the three image representations in the implicit link creation process.

5   Conclusions

In this paper, we have studied the efficiency of automatically building implicit links between images and exploring them in the image retrieval process. First of all, we defined three types of textual representations for each image: (1) Specific Image

Description (SID); (2) Generic Image Description (GID) and (3) the Image MetaData (IMD).

Thereafter, we proposed a method to build LDA based links for each representation. Consequently, we obtained three types of links: SID links, GID links and IMD links. In order to decrease the number of created links, we used a threshold to select only links having a certain weight. Then, we proposed a method to define the link direction. We applied a link analysis algorithm or a social network analysis algorithm for each link type separately to compute link based scores. Finally, we combined the three link based scores to obtain a single score for each image.

For final image re-ranking, we combined implicit link based scores with textual based scores by a linear combination.

When comparing the different representations separately, the experiments showed that GID based links gives the best results which could be explained by the specific/generic vocabulary notion. Nevertheless, after the combination with the textual results, the IMD based links gives the best results which could be explained by the new information added to the existing one. combining the different representations with textual enhance the results.

As conclusion, implicit links between images are a good source of evidence that contributes in enhancing image retrieval.

In future work, we would like to more thoroughly evaluate our approach of building implicit links by comparing it with the hyperlinks based re-ranking and other implicit link creation approaches. Moreover, we aim to study the combination of explicit and implicit links in the image retrieval.

In addition, it is interesting to learn a classifier to tune automatically the best combination parameters of the image representations according to the query type: generic or specific. If the query vocabulary is generic, it is better to give more importance to the generic description than the specific one, and if the query vocabulary is specific, it is better to give more importance to the specific description than the generic one.

Finally, we plan to create implicit visual links and combine them with implicit textual ones to improve the image retrieval accuracy.

References

1. Alzu'bi, A., Amira, A., Ramzan, N.: Semantic content-based image retrieval: a comprehensive study. J. Vis. Commun. Image Represent. **32**, 20–54 (2015)
2. Aouadi, H., Khemakhem, M.T., Jemaa, M.B.: Combination of document structure and links for multimedia object retrieval. J. Inf. Sci. **38**(5), 442–458 (2012)
3. Aouadi, H., Khemakhem, M.T., Jemaa, M.B.: An LDA topic model adaptation for context-based image retrieval. In: Stuckenschmidt, H., Jannach, D. (eds.) EC-Web 2015. LNBIP, vol. 239, pp. 69–80. Springer, Cham (2015). https://doi.org/10.1007/978-3-319-27729-5_6
4. Aouadi, H., Khemakhem, M.T., Jemaa, M.B.: Building contextual implicit links for image retrieval. In: Proceedings of the 20th International Conference on Enterprise Information Systems, ICEIS 2018, Funchal, 21–24 March 2018, vol. 1, pp. 81–91 (2018)
5. Belmouhcine, A., Benkhalifa, M.: Implicit links based web page representation for web page classification. In: Proceedings of the 5th International Conference on Web Intelligence, Mining and Semantics, p. 12. ACM (2015)

6. Bharat, K., Henzinger, M.R.: Improved algorithms for topic distillation in a hyper-linked environment. In: Proceedings of the 21st Annual International ACM SIGIR Conference on Research and Development in Information Retrieval, pp. 104–111. ACM (1998)
7. Bhatt, C., Pappas, N., Habibi, M., Popescu-Belis, A.: Multimodal reranking of content-based recommendations for hyperlinking video snippets. In: Proceedings of International Conference on Multimedia Retrieval, p. 225. ACM (2014)
8. Blei, D., Ng, A., Jordan, M.: Latent Dirichlet Allocation. J. Mach. Learn. Res. **3**(Jan), 993–1022 (2003)
9. Brandes, U.: A faster algorithm for betweenness centrality. J. Math. Sociol. **25**(2), 163–177 (2001)
10. Brin, S., Page, L.: The anatomy of a large-scale hypertextual web search engine. In: Proceedings of the 7th International Conference on World Wide Web (WWW), Brisbane, pp. 107–117 (1998)
11. Cai, D., He, X., Ma, W.Y., Wen, J.R., Zhang, H.: Organizing www images based on the analysis of page layout and web link structure. In: 2004 IEEE International Conference on Multimedia and Expo 2004, ICME 2004, vol. 1, pp. 113–116. IEEE (2004)
12. Cai, D., Yu, S., Wen, J.R., Ma, W.Y.: VIPS: a vision based page segmentation algorithm. Microsoft Technical Report 79, MSR-TR (2003)
13. Chakrabarti, S., Dom, B., Raghavan, P., Rajagopalan, S., Gibson, D., Kleinberg, J.: Automatic resource compilation by analyzing hyperlink structure and associated text. Comput. Netw. ISDN Syst. **30**(1–7), 65–74 (1998)
14. Chen, S., Eskevich, M., Jones, G.J.F., O'Connor, N.E.: An investigation into feature effectiveness for multimedia hyperlinking. In: Gurrin, C., Hopfgartner, F., Hurst, W., Johansen, H., Lee, H., O'Connor, N. (eds.) MMM 2014. LNCS, vol. 8326, pp. 251–262. Springer, Cham (2014). https://doi.org/10.1007/978-3-319-04117-9_23
15. Chibane, I., Doan, B.L.: Relevance propagation model for large hypertext document collections. In: Large scale Semantic Access to Content (text, image, video, and sound), pp. 585–595. Le Centre de Hautes Etudes Internationales D'Informatique Documentaire (2007)
16. Cohn, D.A., Hofmann, T.: The missing link-a probabilistic model of document content and hypertext connectivity. In: Advances in Neural Information Processing Systems, pp. 430–436 (2001)
17. Datta, R., Joshi, D., Li, J., Wang, J.Z.: Image retrieval: ideas, influences, and trends of the new age. ACM Comput. Surv. (CSUR) **40**(2), 5 (2008)
18. Deerwester, S., Dumais, S.T., Furnas, G.W., Landauer, T.K., Harshman, R.: Indexing by latent semantic analysis. J. Am. Soc. Inf. Sci. **41**(6), 391 (1990)
19. Dunlop, M.D.: Multimedia information retrieval. Ph.D. thesis, University of Glasgow (1991)
20. Eskevich, M., et al.: Multimedia information seeking through search and hyperlinking. In: Proceedings of the 3rd ACM Conference on International Conference on Multimedia Retrieval, pp. 287–294. ACM (2013)
21. Harmandas, V., Sanderson, M., Dunlop, M.D.: Image retrieval by hypertext links. In: ACM SIGIR Forum, vol. 31, pp. 296–303. ACM (1997)
22. Hashemi, H.B., Yazdani, N., Shakery, A., Naeini, M.P.: Application of ensemble models in web ranking. In: 2010 5th International Symposium on Telecommunications (IST), pp. 726–731. IEEE (2010)
23. Haveliwala, T.H.: Topic-sensitive PageRank. In: Proceedings of the 11th international conference on World Wide Web, pp. 517–526. ACM (2002)

24. He, X., Cai, D., Wen, J.R., Ma, W.Y., Zhang, H.J.: Clustering and searching WWW images using link and page layout analysis. ACM Trans. Multimed. Comput. Commun. Appl. (TOMM) **3**(2), 10 (2007)
25. Hsu, W.H., Kennedy, L.S., Chang, S.H.: Video search reranking through random walk over document-level context graph. In: Proceedings of the 15th ACM International Conference on Multimedia, pp. 971–980. ACM (2007)
26. Ingongngam, P., Rungsawang, A.: Topic-centric algorithm: a novel approach to web link analysis. In: 2004 18th International Conference on Advanced Information Networking and Applications, AINA 2004, vol. 2, pp. 299–301. IEEE (2004)
27. Jeh, G., Widom, J.: Scaling personalized web search. In: Proceedings of the 12th International Conference on World Wide Web, pp. 271–279. ACM (2003)
28. Jing, Y., Baluja, S.: PageRank for product image search. In: Proceedings of the 17th International Conference on World Wide Web, pp. 307–316. ACM (2008)
29. Jing, Y., Baluja, S.: VisualRank: applying PageRank to large-scale image search. IEEE Trans. Pattern Anal. Mach. Intell. **30**(11), 1877–1890 (2008)
30. Khasanova, R., Dong, X., Frossard, P.: Multi-modal image retrieval with random walk on multi-layer graphs. arXiv preprint arXiv:1607.03406 (2016)
31. Kim, D.J., Lee, S.C., Son, H.Y., Kim, S.W., Lee, J.B.: C-rank and its variants: a contribution-based ranking approach exploiting links and content. J. Inf. Sci. **40**(6), 761–778 (2014)
32. Kleinberg, J.: Authoritative sources in a hyperlinked environment. In: Proceedings of 9th Annual ACM-SIAM Symposium Discrete Algorithms, pp. 668–677 (1998)
33. Kolda, T., Bader, B.: The TOPHITS model for higher-order web link analysis. In: Workshop on Link Analysis, Counterterrorism and Security (2006)
34. Kurland, O., Lee, L.: PageRank without hyperlinks: structural reranking using links induced by language models. In: Proceedings of the Annual International ACM/SIGIR Conference on Research and Development in Information Retrieval, pp. 306–313. ACM (2005)
35. Kurland, O., Lee, L.: Respect my authority!: hits without hyperlinks, utilizing cluster-based language models. In: Proceedings of the 29th Annual International ACM SIGIR Conference on Research and Development in Information Retrieval, pp. 83–90. ACM (2006)
36. Lempel, R., Soffer, A.: PicASHOW: pictorial authority search by hyperlinks on the web. In: Proceedings of the 10th International Conference on World Wide Web, pp. 438–448. ACM (2001)
37. Li, B., Han, L.: Distance weighted cosine similarity measure for text classification. In: Yin, H., et al. (eds.) IDEAL 2013. LNCS, vol. 8206, pp. 611–618. Springer, Heidelberg (2013). https://doi.org/10.1007/978-3-642-41278-3_74
38. Lin, J.: PageRank without hyperlinks: reranking with pubmed related article networks for biomedical text retrieval. BMC Bioinformatics **9**(1), 270 (2008)
39. Liu, J., Lai, W., Hua, X.S., Huang, Y., Li, S.: Video search re-ranking via multi-graph propagation. In: Proceedings of the 15th ACM International Conference on Multimedia, pp. 208–217. ACM (2007)
40. Liu, Z., Wang, S., Zheng, L., Tian, Q.: Robust imagegraph: rank-level feature fusion for image search. IEEE Trans. Image Process. **26**(7), 3128–3141 (2017)
41. Mikawa, K., Ishida, T., Goto, M.: A proposal of extended cosine measure for distance metric learning in text classification. In: 2011 IEEE International Conference on Systems, Man, and Cybernetics (SMC), pp. 1741–1746. IEEE (2011)
42. Najork, M., Zaragoza, H., Taylor, M.: Hits on the web: how does it compare? In: Proceedings of the 30th Annual International ACM SIGIR Conference on Research and Development in Information Retrieval (2007)

43. Petrakis, E.G.: Intelligent search for image information on the web through text and link structure analysis. In: Maragos, P., Potamianos, A., Gros, P. (eds.) Multimodal Processing and Interaction. Multimedia Systems and Applications, pp. 1–17. Springer, Boston (2008). https://doi.org/10.1007/978-0-387-76316-3_12

44. Ricardo, B.-Y., Berthier, R.N.: Modern Information Retrieval-the Concepts and Technology Behind Search, 2nd edn. Addison Wesley, New Jersey (2011)

45. Richardson, M., Domingos, P.: The intelligent surfer: probabilistic combination of link and content information in PageRank. In: Advances in Neural Information Processing Systems, vol. 2, pp. 1441–1448 (2002)

46. Robertson, S.E., Walker, S.: Okapi/keenbow at TREC-8. TREC **8**, 151–162 (1999)

47. Salton, G.: Automatic Text Processing: The Transformation, Analysis, and Retrieval of Information by Computer. Addison-Wesley, Reading (1989)

48. Shakery, A., Zhai, C.: A probabilistic relevance propagation model for hypertext retrieval. In: Proceedings of the 15th ACM International Conference on Information and Knowledge Management, pp. 550–558. ACM (2006)

49. Shen, D., Sun, J.T., Yang, Q., Chen, Z.: A comparison of implicit and explicit links for web page classification. In: Proceedings of the 15th International Conference on World Wide Web, pp. 643–650. ACM (2006)

50. Simon, A.R., Sicre, R., Bois, R., Gravier, G., Sébillot, P.: Irisa at trecvid2015: Leveraging multimodal LDA for video hyperlinking. In: TRECVID 2015 Workshop (2015)

51. T. Hofmann, T.: Probabilistic latent semantic indexing. In: Proceedings of the 22nd Annual International ACM SIGIR Conference on Research and Development in Information Retrieval, pp. 50–57. ACM (1999)

52. Torjmen, M., Pinel-Sauvagnat, K., Boughanem, M.: Using textual and structural context for searching multimedia elements. Int. J. Bus. Intell. Data Mining **5**(4), 323–352 (2010)

53. Tsikrika, T., et al.: Structured document retrieval, multimedia retrieval, and entity ranking using PF/Tijah. In: Fuhr, N., Kamps, J., Lalmas, M., Trotman, A. (eds.) INEX 2007. LNCS, vol. 4862, pp. 306–320. Springer, Heidelberg (2008). https://doi.org/10.1007/978-3-540-85902-4_27

54. Voutsakis, E., Petrakis, E.G., Milios, E.: Weighted link analysis for logo and trademark image retrieval on the web. In: Proceedings of the 2005 IEEE/WIC/ACM International Conference on Web Intelligence, pp. 581–585. IEEE Computer Society (2005)

55. Wang, M., Li, H., Tao, D., Lu, K., Wu, X.: Multimodal graph-based reranking for web image search. IEEE Trans. Image Process. **21**(11), 4649–4661 (2012)

56. Wang, X., Zhou, W., Tian, Q., Li, H.: Adaptively weighted graph fusion for image retrieval. In: Proceedings of the International Conference on Internet Multimedia Computing and Service, pp. 18–21. ACM (2016)

57. Wilcoxon, F.: Individual comparisons by ranking methods. Biometrics Bull. **1**(6), 80–83 (1945)

58. Xie, L., Tian, Q., Zhou, W., Zhang, B.: Fast and accurate near-duplicate image search with affinity propagation on the imageweb. Comput. Vis. Image Underst. **124**, 31–41 (2014)

59. Xu, G., Ma, W.Y.: Building implicit links from content for forum search. In: Proceedings of the 29th Annual International ACM SIGIR Conference on Research and Development in Information Retrieval, pp. 300–307. ACM (2006)

60. Xue, G.R., Zeng, H.J., Chen, Z., Ma, W.Y., Zhang, H.J., Lu, C.J.: Implicit link analysis for small web search. In: Proceedings of the 26th Annual International ACM SIGIR Conference on Research and Development in Information Retrieval, pp. 56–63. ACM (2003)
61. Zaragoza, H., Craswell, N., Taylor, M.J., Saria, S., Robertson, S.E.: Microsoft cambridge at TREC 13: web and hard tracks. TREC **4**, 1–1 (2004)
62. Zhang, S., Yang, M., Cour, T., Yu, K., Metaxas, D.N.: Query specific fusion for image retrieval. In: Fitzgibbon, A., Lazebnik, S., Perona, P., Sato, Y., Schmid, C. (eds.) ECCV 2012. LNCS, pp. 660–673. Springer, Heidelberg (2012). https://doi.org/10.1007/978-3-642-33709-3_47
63. Zhang, W., Ngo, C.W., Cao, X.: Hyperlink-aware object retrieval. IEEE Trans. Image Process. **25**(9), 4186–4198 (2016)
64. Zhang, X., Hu, X., Zhou, X.: A comparative evaluation of different link types on enhancing document clustering. In: Proceedings of the 31st Annual International ACM SIGIR Conference on Research and Development in Information Retrieval, pp. 555–562. ACM (2008)
65. Zhou, W., Li, H., Tian, Q.: Recent advance in content-based image retrieval: a literature survey. arXiv preprint arXiv:1706.06064 (2017)
66. Zhou, W., Tian, Q., Li, H.: Visual block link analysis for image re-ranking. In: Proceedings of the First International Conference on Internet Multimedia Computing and Service, pp. 10–16. ACM (2009)

Big Data Meets Process Science: Distributed Mining of MP-Declare Process Models

Christian Sturm[✉] and Stefan Schönig

University of Bayreuth, Bayreuth, Germany
{christian.sturm,stefan.schoenig}@uni-bayreuth.de

Abstract. Process mining techniques allow the user to build a process model representing the process behavior as recorded in the logs. Standard process discovery techniques produce as output a procedural process model. Recently, several approaches have been developed to extract declarative process models from logs and have been proven to be more suitable to analyze flexible processes, which frequently depend on human decisions and are less predictable. However, when analyzing declarative constraints from other perspective than the control flow, such as data and resources, existing process mining techniques turned out to be inefficient. Thus, computational performance remains a key challenge of declarative process discovery. In this paper, we present a high-performance approach for the discovery of multi-perspective declarative process models that is built upon the distributed big data processing method MapReduce. Compared to recent work we provide an in-depth analysis of an implementation approach based on Hadoop, a powerful BigData-Framework, and describe detailed information on the implemented prototype. We evaluated effectiveness and efficiency of the approach on real-life event logs.

Keywords: Multi-perspective process mining · Declarative processes · MapReduce · Hadoop

1 Introduction

Process mining is the area of research that embraces the automated discovery, conformance checking and enhancement of process models. Automated process discovery aims at generating a process model from an event log consisting of traces, such that each trace corresponds to one execution of the process. Each event in a trace consists as a minimum of an event class (i.e., the activity to which the event corresponds) and a timestamp. In some cases, other information may be available such as the performer of the activity as well as data produced by the event in the form of attribute-value pairs. Discovery is of particular value for processes that offer various options to execute them. Those processes are often referred to as flexible, unstructured or knowledge-intense. Frequently, procedural process models resulting from discovery are colloquially called Spaghetti models due to their complex structure [1]. Discovered process models can alternatively be represented as a set of declarative constraints, i.e., rules for directly representing the causality of the behaviour [18]. The advantages of declarative languages such as Declare [17] or DPIL [26] have been emphasized in the literature. It is also well

© Springer Nature Switzerland AG 2019
S. Hammoudi et al. (Eds.): ICEIS 2018, LNBIP 363, pp. 396–423, 2019.
https://doi.org/10.1007/978-3-030-26169-6_19

known that behaviour is typically intertwined with dependencies upon value ranges of data parameters and resource characteristics [9]. Therefore, Declare has been extended towards Multi-Perspective Declare (*MP-Declare*) [3]. However, state-of-the-art mining tools such as MINERful [6,7] and DeclareMiner [10] do not support MP-Declare at this moment. In [21] a first approach to enable the discovery of MP-Declare constraints has been proposed. However, it has not been investigated how this complex mining task can be performed in an efficient way.

In this paper, we address this open research problem by proposing an *efficient* mining framework for discovering MP-Declare models that leverages latest big data analysis technology and builds upon the distributed processing method *MapReduce*. We introduce parallelizable algorithms for discovering commonly used types of MP-Declare constraints. The proposed solution, however, can be applied to all other MP-Declare constraint types as well. In contrast to related solutions, the proposed framework considers traces in one direction solely which leads to a crucial benefit w.r.t. performance. Mining performance and effectiveness have been tested on several real-life event logs.

Compared to our recent work published in [23], the paper at hand extends the existing research by providing *(i)* an in-depth analysis of an implementation approach based on Hadoop as one of the leading Big Data Analysis-frameworks; *(ii)* detailed information on the implemented prototype; and *(iii)* more specific description of conceptual fundamentals. Further screenshots, the application results as well as a screencast illustrating the mining procedure are accessible on-line at http://mpdeclare.kppq.de.

The paper is structured as follows. Section 2 introduces the language and semantics of MP-Declare. Section 3 describes the distributed framework we propose to speed up multi-perspective process discovery. Section 4 describes the implementation and evaluation of the approach based on conventional, local computation hardware. Section 5 presents the implementation and evaluation of our technique based on Hadoop cluster computation. Section 6 confronts declarative process mining with the MapReduce computation model and contrasts conventional methods with the Hadoop implementation. Section 7 discusses related work before Sect. 8 that concludes the paper.

2   Fundamentals and Research Background

In this section, we first illustrate the research problem that we are addressing and summarize concepts of Declare, MP-Declare and MP-Declare mining.

2.1   Multi-perspective, Declarative Process Modelling

Declarative constraints are strong in representing the permissible behavior of business processes. Modeling languages like Declare [17] describe a set of *constraints* that must be satisfied throughout the process execution. Constraints, in turn, are instances of predefined *templates*. Templates, in turn, are patterns that define parameterized classes of properties. Their semantics can be formalized using formal logics such as Linear Temporal Logic over finite traces (LTL$_f$) [16].

A central shortcoming of languages like Declare is the fact that templates are not directly capable of expressing the connection between the behavior and other

Table 1. Semantics for MP-Declare constraints in LTL$_f$.

Template	LTL$_f$ Semantics
existence	$\top \rightarrow \mathbf{F}(e(A) \wedge \varphi_a(x)) \vee \mathbf{O}(e(A) \wedge \varphi_a(x))$
responded existence	$\mathbf{G}((A \wedge \varphi_a(x)) \rightarrow (\mathbf{O}(B \wedge \varphi_c(x,y) \wedge \varphi_t(y)) \vee \mathbf{F}(B \wedge \varphi_c(x,y) \wedge \varphi_t(y))))$
response	$\mathbf{G}((A \wedge \varphi_a(x)) \rightarrow \mathbf{F}(B \wedge \varphi_c(x,y) \wedge \varphi_t(y)))$
alternate response	$\mathbf{G}((A \wedge \varphi_a(x)) \rightarrow \mathbf{X}(\neg(A \wedge \varphi_a(x))\mathbf{U}(B \wedge \varphi_c(x,y) \wedge \varphi_t(y)))$
chain response	$\mathbf{G}((A \wedge \varphi_a(x)) \rightarrow \mathbf{X}(B \wedge \varphi_c(x,y) \wedge \varphi_t(y)))$
precedence	$\mathbf{G}((B \wedge \varphi_a(x)) \rightarrow \mathbf{O}(A \wedge \varphi_c(x,y) \wedge \varphi_t(y)))$
alternate precedence	$\mathbf{G}((B \wedge \varphi_a(x)) \rightarrow \mathbf{Y}(\neg(B \wedge \varphi_a(x))\mathbf{S}(A \wedge \varphi_c(x,y) \wedge \varphi_t(y)))$
chain precedence	$\mathbf{G}((B \wedge \varphi_a(x)) \rightarrow \mathbf{Y}(A \wedge \varphi_c(x,y) \wedge \varphi_t(y)))$
not responded existence	$\mathbf{G}((A \wedge \varphi_a(x)) \rightarrow \neg(\mathbf{O}(B \wedge \varphi_c(x,y) \wedge \varphi_t(y)) \vee \mathbf{F}(B \wedge \varphi_c(x,y) \wedge \varphi_t(y))))$
not response	$\mathbf{G}((A \wedge \varphi_a(x)) \rightarrow \neg\mathbf{F}(B \wedge \varphi_c(x,y) \wedge \varphi_t(y)))$
not precedence	$\mathbf{G}((B \wedge \varphi_a(x)) \rightarrow \neg\mathbf{O}(A \wedge \varphi_c(x,y) \wedge \varphi_t(y)))$
not chain response	$\mathbf{G}((A \wedge \varphi_a(x)) \rightarrow \neg\mathbf{X}(B \wedge \varphi_c(x,y) \wedge \varphi_t(y)))$
not chain precedence	$\mathbf{G}((B \wedge \varphi_a(x)) \rightarrow \neg\mathbf{Y}(A \wedge \varphi_c(x,y) \wedge \varphi_t(y)))$

perspectives of the process. Consider the example of a loan application process. The process modeller would like to define constraints such as the following:

1. Activation conditions: When a loan is requested and *account balance > 4,000 EUR*, the loan must subsequently be granted.
2. Correlation conditions: When a loan is requested, the loan must subsequently be granted and *amount requested = amount granted*.
3. Target conditions: When a loan is requested, the loan must subsequently be granted by a specific member of the financial board.
4. Temporal conditions: When a loan is requested, the loan must subsequently be granted *within the next 30 days*

Standard Declare only supports constraints that relates activities without considering other process perspectives. Here, the **F**, **X**, **G**, and **U** LTL$_f$ future operators have the following meanings: formula $\mathbf{F}\psi_1$ means that ψ_1 holds sometime in the future, $\mathbf{X}\psi_1$ means that ψ_1 holds in the next position, $\mathbf{G}\psi_1$ says that ψ_1 holds forever in the future, and, lastly, $\psi_1\mathbf{U}\psi_2$ means that sometime in the future ψ_2 will hold and until that moment ψ_1 holds (with ψ_1 and ψ_2 LTL$_f$ formulas). The **O**, **Y** and **S** LTL$_f$ past operators have the following meaning: $\mathbf{O}\psi_1$ means that ψ_1 holds sometime in the past, $\mathbf{Y}\psi_1$ means that ψ_1 holds in the previous position, and $\psi_1\mathbf{S}\psi_2$ means that ψ_1 has held sometime in the past and since that moment ψ_2 holds.

Consider, e.g., the *response* constraint $\mathbf{G}(A \rightarrow \mathbf{F}B)$. It indicates that if *A occurs*, *B* must eventually *follow*. Therefore, this constraint is fully satisfied in traces such as $\mathbf{t}_1 = \langle A, A, B, C\rangle$, $\mathbf{t}_2 = \langle B, B, C, D\rangle$, and $\mathbf{t}_3 = \langle A, B, C, B\rangle$, but not for $\mathbf{t}_4 = \langle A, B, A, C\rangle$ because the second occurrence of *A* is not followed by a *B*. In $\mathbf{t}_2$, it is *vacuously satisfied* [4], in a trivial way, because *A* never occurs.

An *activation activity* of a constraint in a trace is an activity whose execution imposes, because of that constraint, some obligations on the execution of other activities (target activities) in the same trace (see Table 1). For example, *A* is an activation activity for the *response* constraint $\mathbf{G}(A \rightarrow \mathbf{F}B)$ and *B* is a target, because the execution of *A* forces *B* to be executed, eventually. An activation of a constraint leads to a *fulfillment* or to a *violation*. Consider, again, $\mathbf{G}(A \rightarrow \mathbf{F}B)$. In trace $\mathbf{t}_1$, the constraint is activated and fulfilled twice, whereas, in trace $\mathbf{t}_3$, it is activated and fulfilled only once. In trace $\mathbf{t}_4$, it is activated twice and the second activation leads to a violation (B does not occur subsequently).

The importance of multi-perspective dependencies led to the definition of a multi-perspective version of Declare (MP-Declare) [3]. Its semantics build on the notion of *payload* of an event. $e(activity)$ identifies the occurrence of an event in order to distinguish it from the activity name. At the time of a certain event e, its attributes $x_1, \ldots, x_m$ have certain values. $p^e_{activity} = (val_{x1}, \ldots, val_{xn})$ represents its payload. To denote the projection of the payload $p^e_A = (x_1, \ldots, x_n)$ over attributes $x_1, \ldots, x_m$ with $m \leqslant n$, the notation $p^e_A[x_1, \ldots, x_m]$ is used. For instance, $p^e_{ApplyForTrip}[Resource] = \text{SS}$ is the projection of the attribute *Resource* in the event description. Furthermore, the n-ples of attributes x_i are represented as x. Therefore, the templates in MP-Declare extend standard Declare with additional conditions on event attributes. Specifically, given the events $e(A)$ and $e(B)$ with payloads $p^e_A = (x_1, \ldots, x_n)$ and $p^e_B = (y_1, \ldots, y_n)$, the *activation condition* φ_a, the *correlation condition* φ_c, and the *target condition* φ_t are defined. The activation condition is part of the activation ϕ_a, whilst the correlation and target conditions are part of the target ϕ_t, according to their respective time of evaluation. The *activation* condition is a statement that must be valid when the activation occurs. In the case of the *response* template, the activation condition has the form $\varphi_a(x_1, \ldots, x_n)$, meaning that the proposition φ_a over $(x_1, \ldots, x_n)$ must hold true. The *correlation* condition is a statement that must be valid when the target occurs, and it relates the values of the attributes in the payloads of the activation and the target event. It has the form $\varphi_c(x_1, \ldots, x_m, y_1, \ldots, y_m)$ with $m \leqslant n$, where φ_c is a propositional formula on the variables of both the payload of $e(A)$ and the payload of $e(B)$. *Target* conditions exert limitations on the values of the attributes that are registered at the moment wherein the target activity occurs. They have the form $\varphi_t(y_1, \ldots, y_m)$ with $m \leqslant n$, where φ_t is a propositional formula involving variables in the payload of $e(B)$.

2.2 Mining Metrics

In this subsection, we describe the metrics that we use to discriminate those constraints that are fulfilled in the majority of cases in the event log, from those that are rarely satisfied, namely support and confidence.

Querying with constraint templates provides for every possible combination of concrete values for the placeholders in the templates the number of satisfactions in the event log. Based on the number of satisfactions, two metrics, *Support* and *Confidence*, are calculated, which express the probability of an assignment constraint to hold in the process. *Support* is the number of fulfilments of a constraint divided by the number of occurrences of the condition of a constraint. The *Confidence* metric scales the support by the fraction of traces in the log wherein the activation condition is satisfied. Constraints are considered valid if their *Support* and *Confidence* measures are above an user-defined threshold. Here, we only consider the event-based support that is meant to be used for all constraints wherein both activation and target events occur. We consider two notions of support already defined in the literature, namely the event-based support [7] and the trace-based support [13]. As defined in [7], we denote the set of *events* in a *trace* **t** of an event log L that fulfil an LTL_f formula ψ as $\models^e_{\mathbf{t}} (\psi)$. The set of all the *events* in *log* L that fulfil ψ are denoted as $\models^e_L (\psi)$. Given a resource assignment constraint Ξ comprising activation ϕ_a and target ϕ_t, we define the event-based support $\mathcal{S}^e_L$ and the event-based confidence $\mathcal{C}^e_L$ as follows:

$$\mathcal{S}^e_L = \frac{\sum\limits_{i=1}^{|L|} \left| \models^e_{\mathbf{t}_i} (\Xi) \right|}{\left| \models^e_L (\phi_a) \right|} \tag{1}$$

$$\mathcal{C}^e_L = \frac{\mathcal{S}^e_L \times \left| \models^e_L (\phi_a) \right|}{|L|} \tag{2}$$

3 Map-Reduce for Declarative Process Mining

In this section, we describe an efficient framework for discovering MP-Declare constraints. After giving insights into the internal infrastructure, we explain the parallelisable discovery algorithms for commonly used MP-Declare constraints that are used to discover models under consideration of further perspectives. In contrast to former solutions, this framework can be used out of the box and the algorithm has to consider the traces in one direction solely which leads to a crucial benefit with regard to performance.

3.1 Architecture and Infrastructure

The basic idea of the algorithm builds upon the MapReduce computation model. One key advantage is the inbuilt opportunity for executing the calculations in parallel, which gives an enormous performance boost. At first, the scaffolding of the MapReduce algorithm is described briefly w.r.t. the discovery of a process model described later on. In the next section, we use an example log containing two traces defined in Eq. 3.

$$t_0 = \langle a, b, b, c \rangle \qquad t_1 = \langle a, c, d \rangle \tag{3}$$

To compute the support and confidence metrics, two MapReduce jobs are required, MR-I and MR-II (cf. Fig. 1).

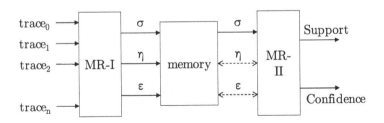

Fig. 1. Infrastructure of the calculation [23].

MR-I. In the **map**-phase of MR-I, key-value pairs are created from the locally provided event data, i.e., a single trace of a log file. Each of the key-value pairs is assigned to a number for further processing. In the case of process discovery, this number is always 1. The challenge is to generate these key-value pairs in order to address the logic for the MP-Declare constraints.

Example: Given a trace $t_0 = \langle a, b, b, c \rangle$. Consider the *response* template, i.e. whenever an event e_1 occurs, the event e_2 must follow ($response(e_1, e_2)$). The trace t_0 is therefore mapped to five different key-value pairs in the map phase: $((a,b),1), ((a,c),1), ((b,b),1), ((b,c),1), ((b,c),1)$. The keys are exactly those event pairs which fulfil the *response* template: a is followed by b and c, the first b is followed by c and the second b, which is again followed by c. Note, that a constraint can only be fulfilled once, like $response(a,b)$ is fulfilled only by the first event b. The underlying mapping algorithm containing the logic for all constraint templates is described in Sect. 3.3.

Table 2. Output mapper MR-I. [23].

Trace	σ_R		σ_{CR}	η	ϵ
a,b,c	ab,1	bc,1	ab,1	a,1	a,1
	ac,1		bb,1	b,1	b,1
	bb,1		bc,1	b,1	c,1
	bc,1			c,1	
a,c,d	ac,1		ac,1	a,1	a,1
	ad,1		cd,1	c,1	c,1
	cd,1			d,1	d,1

Table 3. Output reducer MR-I. [23].

σ_R		σ_{CR}		η	ϵ
ab,1	bc,2	ab,1	ac,1	a,2	a,2
ac,2	ad,1	bb,1	cd,1	b,2	b,1
bb,1	cd,1	bc,1		c,2	c,2
				d,1	d,1

The **reduce**-phase finally obtains the key-value pairs that have been produced. The reduce-function must be declared by the user once again. In the case of constraint checking this phase depicts a summation of values. To continue the example above, the result of the reducer with trace t_0 is: $((a,b),1), ((a,c),1), ((b,b),1), ((b,c),2)$.

σ-function. The support metric is defined as the number of fulfilments of a constraint divided by the number of occurrences of the activation. The MR-I job in the example above calculates exactly the number of fulfilments, thus the numerator of the support formula. In the following we use a function $\sigma_\gamma : E \times E \to \mathbb{N}$, where E are events, for describing this figure, e.g. in t_0: $\sigma_{response}(b, c) = 2$. γ denotes a constraint template like *response* or *chainResponse*.

η-function. To calculate the support of a constraint, the number of occurrences of the activation is necessary. For forward constraints ($\{*\}response$), this is the first event in the constraint template, e.g., b in the constraint $response(b, c)$. We define the number of occurrences of events as $\eta : E \to \mathbb{N}$, for instance in trace t_0: $\eta(b) = 2$. In order to obtain the correct values for the η-function, for each event e in the trace a key-value pair $(e, 1)$ is additionally emitted in the map phase, e.g., for t_0: $(a, 1), (b, 1), (b, 1), (c, 1)$ which is reduced to $(a, 1), (b, 2), (c, 1)$.

ϵ-*function*. A third value is necessary for determining the confidence, namely the amount of traces in which a given event occurs. We introduce the function $\epsilon : E \rightarrow \mathbb{N}$, which holds this information. Taking into account the second trace t_1 (cf. Eq. 3), MR-I outputs $\epsilon(c) = 2$ or $\epsilon(d) = 1$, as c occurs in t_0 and t_1, whereas d occurs in t_1 solely. Transferring this to MR-I, for each unique event e a key-value pair $(e, 1)$ has to be produced, neglecting multiple occurrences of events, e.g., for trace t_0: $(a, 1), (b, 1), (c, 1)$.

The Tables 2 and 3 shows the complete result of MR-I for the input log (cf. Eq. 3) considering two constraint templates: *response* and *chainResponse*. The output of all mappers serves as the input for the reducers.

MR-II. Two MapReduce jobs are performed where the event log only serves as input for the first MapReduce job. The output values of MR-I are used in MR-II to calculate support and confidence. Note that these calculations had to be extracted to a separate job because every single trace of the provided log needs to be tackled first in MR-I in order to obtain the σ-, η- and ϵ-functions. This makes MR-II mandatory; however, with a look on the performance, support and confidence can be computed in parallel again.

Using the functions introduced above, the support of a constraint $response(b, c)$ can be computed as $\mathcal{S}_R(b, c) = \frac{\sigma_R(b,c)}{\eta(b)} = \frac{2}{2} = 1$ (cf. Eq. 4), thus as the fraction between the fulfilments of the constraint and the amount of its activations. Remember that forward constraints ($FWD = \{*\}response$) are activated with e_1 (Eq. 4) and backward constraints ($BWD = \{*\}precedence$) are activated with e_2 (Eq. 5).

$$\mathcal{S}_{FWD}(e_1, e_2) = \frac{\sigma_{FWD}(e_1, e_2)}{\eta(e_1)} \tag{4}$$

$$\mathcal{S}_{BWD}(e_1, e_2) = \frac{\sigma_{BWD}(e_1, e_2)}{\eta(e_2)} \tag{5}$$

The confidence of a constraint for an event pair (e_1, e_2) is the product of the support of (e_1, e_2) with the ratio between the amount of traces in the log in which event e_1 occurs (or e_2 in case of backward constraints) and the total number of traces in the log, denoted as $|l|$ in Eq. 6 and 7.

$$\mathcal{C}_{FWD}(e_1, e_2) = \mathcal{S}_{FWD}(e_1, e_2) \cdot \frac{\epsilon(e_1)}{|l|} \tag{6}$$

$$\mathcal{C}_{BWD}(e_1, e_2) = \mathcal{S}_{BWD}(e_1, e_2) \cdot \frac{\epsilon(e_2)}{|l|} \tag{7}$$

In the running example, the confidence of the constraint $response(b, c)$ is calculated as $\mathcal{C}_R(b, c) = \mathcal{S}_R(b, c) \cdot (\frac{\epsilon(b)}{|l|}) = 1 \cdot \frac{1}{2} = 0.5$.

In terms of MapReduce, the MR-II is structured rather trivial. In the **map**-phase, the output of MR-I is conducted directly to the reducer neglecting η and ϵ, i.e., all key-value pairs of the σ-function of all constraints are emitted and obtained by the reducer. The **reduce**-function then consults the *DB* (cf. Sect. 3.2) to look up the relevant η- and ϵ-value for a given key and calculates the corresponding support and confidence values (acc. to Eqs. 4, 5, 6 and 7).

3.2   Algorithm Overview

This section provides an overview on the algorithm for declarative process model discovery (Algorithm 1). To this end, the algorithm is given in a generic way and is slightly adapted by the differing implementations in Sects. 4 and 5.

Algorithm 1. Overview [23].

```
1 for Trace t in l do
2 │   KVP = mapToKVPairs(t)
3 │   DB = accumulateKVPairs(DB, KVP)
4 end
5 for Constraint γ do
6 │   for Entry e in DB.σγ do
7 │   │   calcSupportAndConfidence(e, γ)
8 │   end
9 end
```

Given a log l with traces t, a first step is to create the key-value pairs KVP (MR-I-Mapper). These include the $KVPs$ for each constraint (σ) and for the functions η and ϵ. These values are then accumulated into a database DB (MR-I-Reducer). The DB contains information about the three functions. For the σ-function, it holds a list for each constraint separately and furthermore the entries of the lists comprising tuples ($EventTuple, fulfilments$). This DB is then used in MR-II. For each constraint γ, each tuple in the σ_γ-list is considered (MR-II-Mapper). The discovered $EventTuple$ and the corresponding amount of fulfilments is then used to calculate support and confidence by consulting the corresponding η- and ϵ-values relevant to the $EventTuple$ (MR-II-Reducer).

3.3   Mapping Relational MP-Declare Templates

We have to apply the logic of MP-Declare constraints into the MR-I mapping function to emit the necessary $KVPs$ and calculate the correct values for support and confidence. For this purpose, we developed and derived algorithms from the support functions introduced in [7]. Therefore, we defined specific σ_γ functions for each of the MP-Declare relation constraints. Note that all the algorithms are working at only one trace instead of the whole log file, which ensures the capability of parallelization.

For reasons of readability, we use an abbreviated form for representing the event data in this section. We let the set of activities be $\{a, b, c, d\}$. Further on, we restrict to one single perspective, e.g., the organizational perspective, thus the defined resources which can execute the activities are $\{x, y, z\}$. For instance, trace t_2 in Eq. 8 holds the information, that in the beginning a was executed by x, subsequently c was executed by z and so forth. In the end, the case is closed when again a was executed by x.

$$t_2 = \langle ax, cz, by, bx, dz, by, ax \rangle \tag{8}$$

The structure of the algorithm is built upon a nested for-loop, so that for each event in a given trace, every successor is considered. Henceforth i denotes the loop control variable for the outer loop and j is the counter variable for the inner loop.

In the case of t_2 (cf. Eq. 8), all successors for ax are addressed in the inner loop ($i = 0$), whereas in the next step ($i = 1$) all successors for cz are considered and so forth. While iterating over the trace, different representations of the events are requested to match the multiperspective constraint templates. We denote the events for the outer loop as ${}_ie^\Gamma$ and for the inner loop as e_j^Γ, where Γ takes either A (activation) or T (target).

For instance, for $i = 1$ and $j = 4$ and in search of activation constraints (i.e. $A = (task, resource)$ and $T = (task)$) following representations are detected: ${}_1e^A = cz$, ${}_1e^T = c$, $e_4^A = dz$ and $e_4^T = d$.

In the following, we analyse the example trace t_2 (cf. Eq. 8) and mark the pivot situations which are characteristic for each constraint template with $1_R, 2_R, ...$ for $response$, $1_{AR}, 2_{AR}, ...$ for $alternateResponse$ and so forth.

Table 4. Response (act.) [23].

	c	b	b	d	b	a
ax	✓	✓	1_R	✓	2_R	✓
cz		✓	3_R	✓	4_R	✓
by			✓	✓	5_R	✓
bx				✓	✓	✓
dz					✓	✓
by						✓

Table 5. Response (target) [23].

	cz	by	bx	dz	by	ax
a	✓	✓	✓	✓	6_R	✓
c		✓	✓	✓	7_R	✓
b			✓	✓	✓	✓
b				✓	✓	✓
d					✓	✓
b						✓

Response. The initial assignment of (i, j) is $(0, 1)$, thus the events ax and cz are considered. For **activation** constraints, only the activating event holds the additional condition; hence, $response(ax, c)$ is investigated in this first case. This constraint, activated with ${}_0e^A$ (ax) is fulfilled with e_1^T (c) and thus $\sigma_R(ax, c)$ is incremented by 1. Also for $({}_0e^A, e_2^T)$ the value for $\sigma_R(ax, b)$ is incremented. In the next step, i.e., $({}_0e^A, e_3^T)$, the σ-value must not be modified (i.e. no key-value pair is emitted), as the constraint $response(ax, b)$, activated with the event ${}_0e^A$ was already fulfilled with e_2^T (cf. 1_R in Table 4). Similar are the cases 2_R to 5_R.

For **target** constraints like $response(a, cz)$ the additional condition appears on the right-hand side. That means, the events in the outer loop must match the target template (${}_ie^T$) and in return the inner loop matches the activation template now (e_j^A). Referring to Table 5, in the cases 6_R and 7_R, $\sigma_R(a, by)$ and $\sigma_R(c, by)$ respectively must not be increased, as the constraints are also already fulfilled (with $e_2^A = by$).

AlternateResponse. The *alternateResponse* template shares the pivot constellations for (i, j) for already fulfilled constraints similar to the *response* template (cf. 1_{AR} to 5_{AR} in Table 6). For instance, the constraint $alternateResponse(ax, b)$ enforces that if the event a occurs and is executed by x than the event b follows, and there is no recurrence of x executing a in between. In the case $i = 0$, this constraint is activated by $_0e^A$ (ax) and fulfilled with the event e_2^T (b). Therefore, additional events b must be ignored (e.g. e_3^T).

Besides the already-fulfilled-errors, another class of error type is introduced: *violations*. Consider 6_{AR} in Table 6. In this case, the constraint $alternateResponse(by, a)$ is checked. Although this constellation have not been occurred so far for this activation, the value $\sigma_{AR}(by, a)$ must not be modified, because it is violated by e_5^A (by): The activating event (by) recurs before a occurs. This is forbidden within the *alternateResponse* template. Note, that the resource is also decisive, thus $alternateResponse(by, d)$, activated with $_2e^A$ is fulfilled with e_4^T, although the event b recurs. However, this is executed by x and so the constraint is not violated (marked with an asterisk in Table 6.)

Table 6. Alter.Response (act.) [23].

	c(z)	b(y)	b(x)	d(z)	b(y)	a(x)
ax	✓	✓	1_{AR}	✓	2_{AR}	✓
cz		✓	3_{AR}	✓	4_{AR}	✓
by			✓	✓ *	5_{AR}	6_{AR}
bx				✓	✓	✓
dz					✓	✓
by						✓

Table 7. Alter.Response (tar.) [23].

	cz	bx	by	dz	by	ax
a	✓	✓	✓	✓	7_{AR}	✓
c		✓	✓	✓	8_{AR}	✓
b			✓	9_{AR}	10_{AR}	11_{AR}
b				✓	✓	12_{AR}
d					✓	✓
b						✓

The analysis of the **target** constraints (cf. Table 7) shows the following anomalies: 7_{AR} and 8_{AR} are excluded because of the already-fulfilled-case and the cases 9_{AR} to 12_{AR} are excluded because of violations. For instance, 9_{AR} to 11_{AR} are activated with the event $_2e^A$ (b) and as the first event in the inner loop is also b (represented with the activation template, i.e. the activity solely (e_3^A)), all constraints with succeeding events in the inner loop are violated.

ChainResponse. The logic for the *chainResponse* template is quite trivial and is located outside the inner loop. For each event $_ie^A$, the direct successor $_{i+1}e^T$ is considered and $\sigma_{CR}(_ie^A,_{i+1} e^T)$ is incremented by one. Examples are an activation constraint like $chainResponse(ax, c)$ or a target constraint like $chainResponse(a, cz)$ (Table 8).

Precedence. Intuitively, one would iterate starting from the latest event for the backward constraints, e.g. the first (i, j)-tuple would be $(5, 6)$ going on with $(4, 6)$, i.e. the constraints $precedence(e_5^T,_6 e^A)$ and $precedence(e_4^T,_6 e^A)$ respectively. The former describes that whenever a occurs and was executed by x, then b has to precede (in the case of activation constraints $precedence(b, ax)$). Referring to the later, an example for

Table 8. ChainResponse [23].

	cz	by	bx	dz	by	ax
ax	✓					
cz		✓				
by			✓			
bx				✓		
dz					✓	
by						✓

a target constraint is if a occurs in a trace, then d has to precede and this has to be executed by z ($precedence(dz, a)$).

For the sake of a performance boost, we propose an algorithm, which handles the backward constraints also by iterating through the events in a forward direction. To do so, the events of the outer loop (i) fills the role of the target events and the events of the inner loop (j) are now the activating events.

Consider Table 9. The first constraint under investigation will be $precedence(a, cz)$, activated with e_1^A (cz) and fulfilled with $_0e^T$ (a). After than, $precedence(a, by)$ is inspected. This one now is activated with e_2^A (by) but also fulfilled with the same outer loop event $_0e^T$ (a).

Interesting is the outer loop event $_2e^T$ (b) (cf. third row in Table 9). In the case e_4^A (dz), the value for $\sigma_P(b, dz)$ must not be modified (1_P). The reason is that this constraint, activated with dz is fulfilled with the outer loop event $_3e^T$ and thus, fulfilled in future (marked with an asterisk in Table 9).

Table 9. Precedence (act.) [23].

	cz	by	bx	dz	by	ax
a(x)	✓	✓	✓	✓	✓	✓
c(z)		✓	✓	✓	✓	✓
b(y)			✓	1_P	2_P	3_P
b(x)				✓*	✓	4_P
d(z)					✓	✓
b(y)						✓

Table 10. Precedence (tar.) [23].

	c(z)	b(y)	b(x)	d(z)	b(y)	a(x)
ax	✓	✓	✓	✓	✓	✓
cz		✓	✓	✓	✓	✓
by			✓	✓	✓	5_P
bx				✓	✓	✓
dz					✓	✓
by						✓*

The **target** constraints show similar behaviour. Whenever the event $_ie^T$ occurs also in the inner loop in e_j^T, then the rest of the inner loop is neglected because the events are fulfilled later on, like $precedence(by, a)$ (5_P) is fulfilled in the asterisk-marked cell in Table 10 ($_2e^T$ (b) recurs in e_5^T (b)).

AlternatePrecedence. In addition, the *alternatePrecedence* constraints, as they are also backward constraints, are activated with the second given event in the template. The (activation) constraint $alternatePrecedence(a, by)$ at the marker 1_{AP} in Table 11 is violated because of the event e_2^A (*by*). Recurrences of the activating event are forbidden within the *alternatePrecedence* template. Similar is the case at 2_{AP}.

Consider now case 3_{AP} with the constraint $alternatePrecedence(b, dz)$. $\sigma_{AP}(b, dz)$ must not be incremented there, because this constraint activated with e_4^A (*dz*) is fulfilled with the event $_3e^T$ in the next run of the outer loop (note the asterisk in Table 11). Similar are the cases 4_{AP} to 6_{AP}.

In Table 12, the constraints at the cases 7_{AP} to 11_{AP} are violated, because of the reoccurrence of the events e_3^A (*b*) and e_5^A (*b*) in the events e_2^A and e_3^A. The constraint $alternatePrecedence(by, a)$ considered at 12_{AP} is fulfilled later in the last row of Table 12.

ChainPrecedence. The *chainPrecedence* constraint template is implemented similar to the *chainResponse* template. However, the events of the constraints are integrated in reversed order starting with $chainPrecedence(c, ax)$ (activation constraint) and in general terms $\sigma_{CR}(_{i+1}e^T, _i e^A)$ is increased.

Table 11. Alter.Precedence (act.) [23].

	cz	by	bx	dz	by	ax
a	✓	✓	✓	✓	1_{AP}	✓
c		✓	✓	✓	2_{AP}	✓
b			✓	3_{AP}	4_{AP}	5_{AP}
b				✓ *	✓	6_{AP}
d					✓	✓
b						✓

Table 12. Alter.Precedence (tar.).

	c	b	b	d	b	a
ax	✓	✓	7_{AP}	✓	8_{AP}	✓
cz		✓	9_{AP}	✓	10_{AP}	✓
by			✓		✓	11_{AP}	12_{AP}
bx				✓	✓	✓
dz					✓	✓
by						✓

3.4   Pivot Characteristics Overview and Resulting Algorithm

The anomalies detected in the previous section can be traced to three certain pivot characteristics we have to take care. They include *already fulfilled (a)*, *violation (v)* and *fulfilled later (f)*, whereby the first one corresponds to forward constraints and latter appears only on backward constraints. In this section, the four anomaly classes are identified, described and the occurrence of problems regarding the classes are resolved.

Class I ($1_R - 7_R, 1_{AR} - 5_{AR}, 7_{AR} - 8_{AR}$). These situations occur when a pair of events is considered, where the activating event was already fulfilled in this case with a previous event. For instance, in a trace $\langle ax, b?, b? \rangle$, the constraint $R(ax, b)$ is fulfilled with the first event b and must not be considered in the next step ($j = 2$). For this activation constraint, the additional perspective of the fulfilling event is not crucial (note the ?). A similar case for a target constraint is $\langle a?, bx, bx \rangle$ where $R(a, bx)$ is fulfilled when reading the second bx in the inner loop. Also the $alternateResponse$ template suffers from this anomaly: assuming a trace $\langle ax, \overline{ax}, b?, \overline{ax}, b? \rangle$, the value for $\sigma_{AR}(ax, b)$ referring to the constraint $AR(ax, b)$ would be incremented with the first b and the second b. Note that in this class it is forbidden for ax to recur as this would cause a violation (cf. Class II).

Solution. The problem is that the events in the inner loop filtered by the target template e_j^T are recurring. To prevent these Class I-failures, all events e_j^T are stored in a list L and σ is only incremented if the current e_j^T is not in L.

Class II ($6_{AR}, 9_{AR} - 12_{AR}$). Class II-errors hits the $alternateResponse$ template solely. The definition of this template forbids the activating event to recur before the second event appears. As an example serves the trace $\langle ax, ax, b? \rangle$ with the constraint $AR(ax, b)$ for an activation constraint and $\langle a?, a?, bx \rangle$ with $AR(a, bx)$ for a target constraint respectively.

Solution. If the activating event $_i e^A$ recurs in the inner loop as event e_j^A, then all succeeding constraints in the inner loop are violated by this recursion and thus the inner loop can be cancelled for this template.

Class III ($1_P - 5_P, 3_{AP} - 6_{AP}, 12_{AP}$). These anomaly is similar to Class I but for backward constraint templates. Some constraints must not be considered because they will be fulfilled later on. For instance, in a trace $\langle b?, b?, ax \rangle$ in the first outer loop run it is checked if the first $b?$ fulfils a constraint $P(b, ax)$. However, this is not true because this certain constraint is fulfilled in the second outer loop run.

Solution. The problem here is that the event of the outer loop $_i e^T$ recurs in the inner loop event e_j^T. That means that the succeeding inner loop events are fulfilled later on with succeeding outer loop events. In case of a recurrence, the consideration of succeeding events in this inner loop run can be cancelled.

Class IV ($1_{AP} - 2_{AP}, 7_{AP} - 11_{AP}$). Similar to Class II, errors corresponding to Class IV handle violations of constraints, viz. from the $alternatePrecedence$ template in this particular case. In a trace $\langle a?, bx, bx \rangle$ the activation constraint $alternatePrecedence(a, bx)$, activated with the second bx event is violated, as bx recurs, before the fulfilling event a precedes.

Solution. As a solution, we store all events e_j^A in a list. If a next event e_j^A with a greater j occurs, the consideration of $alternatePrecedence$ templates can be cancelled for a certain i.

Algorithm 2. Discovery of relational MP-Declare constraints [23].

Input: Trace trace
Output: DB

```
1  for i ← 0 to trace.events.Count do
2  |    List<Event> eR, eAR, eAP;
3  |    bool bAR, bP, bAP = false;
4  |    db.η(ᵢeᴬ);
5  |    db.η(ᵢeᵀ);
6  |    db.ε(ᵢeᴬ);
7  |    db.ε(ᵢeᵀ);
8  |    for j ← i + 1 to trace.events.Count do
        |    ;  /* Response                              */
9       |    if !eR.Contains(eⱼᵀ) then
10      |    |    db.σ.R(ᵢeᴬ, eⱼᵀ);
11      |    |    eR.Add(eⱼᵀ);
12      |    end
        |    ;  /* AlternateResponse                     */
13      |    if !bAR ∧ !eAR.Contains(eⱼᵀ) then
14      |    |    db.σ.AR(ᵢeᴬ, eⱼᵀ);
15      |    |    eAR.Add(eⱼᵀ);
16      |    |    if eⱼᴬ = ᵢeᴬ then
17      |    |    |    bAR ← true;
18      |    |    end
19      |    end
        |    ;  /* Precedence                            */
20      |    if !bP then
21      |    |    db.σ.P(ᵢeᵀ, eⱼᴬ);
22      |    end
23      |    if ᵢeᵀ = eⱼᵀ then
24      |    |    bP ← true;
25      |    end
        |    ;  /* AlternatePrecedence                   */
26      |    if !bAP ∧ !eAP.Contains(eⱼᴬ) then
27      |    |    db.σ.AP(ᵢeᵀ, eⱼᴬ);
28      |    |    eAP.Add(eⱼᴬ);
29      |    end
30      |    if ᵢeᵀ = eⱼᵀ then
31      |    |    bAP ← true;
32      |    end
33  |    end
34  |    if i < |t| − 1 then
35  |    |    db.σ.CR(ᵢeᴬ, ᵢ₊₁eᵀ);
36  |    |    db.σ.CP(ᵢ₊₁eᴬ, ᵢeᵀ);
37  |    end
38  end
```

4   Conventional Implementation

In this section, we particularly describe the implementation of MapReduce MP-Declare mining. As the algorithm is built upon the MapReduce computation paradigm, we took care to exploit this chance of parallelism by spreading the workload on multiple threads of a multicore CPU. As a first step, the XES log file has to be loaded into the applications memory. This is done by reading the file with a .NET library and parsing the information into POCOs. This step is also used to collect meta information about the event log to provide the user for instance a list of available perspectives but also some information on the expected performance of the analysis by means of the figures described in Sect. 4.2. As soon as the user has chosen the perspectives to consider, i.e. he has built the mining template (e.g. $task \land resource \rightarrow task$), a first parallel processing step builds the three characteristic functions σ, η and ϵ in MR-I. With the parallel extensions of the *Language Integrated Query*-.NET component (PLINQ: Parallel.ForEach();) we delegate the whole parallelization and task generation on to the framework itself and abstract from low level programming issues with all the upcoming advantages. We just had to take care of race hazards when joining to the global database (cf. lock-keyword). After then, when each of the traces has been considered and the characteristic functions are completed, the MR-II function can be invoked. Again, this step is executed in parallel with PLINQ.

4.1   Performance Influence Factors

Distribution of the Events. The most relevant index number for a performance analysis is the amount of loop runs the algorithm has to complete as they rise in a quadratic manner with the amount of events in a trace. For a trace with n events, the amount of loop runs $\mathcal{L}_t$ follows the formula in Eq. 9.

$$\mathcal{L}_t = (n-1) + \ldots + 1 = \frac{n \cdot (n-1)}{2} = \frac{n^2 - n}{2} \qquad (9)$$

That means, the higher the amount of traces with a huge amount of events in a log file, the higher is the computation time. For instance, first assume a log file containing 100 traces with a total amount of 1500 events, evenly distributed with 15 events per trace. Then the number of loop runs comes up to $\frac{15^2 - 15}{2} = 105$ for each trace, or summed up for the whole log $105 \cdot 100 = 10500$. Now consult a log file also with 100 traces, but now with 10 traces containing 90% of the events (945 events per trace) and the remaining 90 traces with the remaining 12 events per trace[1]. Then the total amount of loop runs is calculated as $10 \cdot \frac{945^2 - 945}{2} + 90 \cdot \frac{12^2 - 12}{2} = 4460400 + 5940 = 4466340$, which is more than 400 times higher than in the evenly distributed log. Hence, the crucial factor, i.e. the total number loop runs, can then be defined as the sum of the loop runs of each single trace (cf. Eq. 10).

$$\sum_{Trace\ t} \frac{|t|^2 \cdot (|t| - 1)}{2} \qquad (10)$$

---

[1] Round up for simplicity.

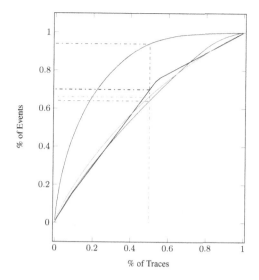

Fig. 2. Distribution of events on traces in the logs under investigation [23]. (Color figure online)

Consider Table 13. Four real-life event logs were analysed while the traces where rearranged in descending order by the amount of events. It can clearly be seen that in the Hospital Log (blue line), half of the traces contains nearly all captured events (94%). Half of the events are included in the first 130 traces (11.4% of all traces). This raises the necessary loop runs to about $33 \cdot 10^6$. In contrast, in the Municipality Log (red line), the first half of the traces contains only about 64% of the events and 50% of the events are recorded in the first 438 traces (36% of all traces), similar to the Loan Application Log and the Traffic Log (Fig. 2).

Since now, we have not seen a chance in breaking the quadratic dependency but as stated, compared to [7] we introduced an algorithm which is not in need of a two-directional investigation of the traces and thus saves half of the necessary loop runs.

Amount of Traces and Events. Apart from the dependency of the distribution of the events within the log discussed above, our implementation could handle log files with up to 150000 Traces or 1000000 captured events. Table 13 shows that the absolute amount of events and traces does not have a strong impact on the performance. For instance, the Traffic Log inherits nearly 600000 events and 150000 traces but is analysed within a mere fraction of time compared to logs either with less traces or less events.

Amount of Discovered Constraints. In order to investigate a performance restriction caused by a huge amount discovered constraints, we set the threshold of support and confidence on a minimal level, for instance 0.05 and 0.02 instead of 0.5 and 0.2. Shown with the Hospital Log, there is no noticeable change in performance when discovering about 35000 constraints instead of 2000. Therefore, this is not necessary to be further analysed.

Table 13. Real-life event logs under investigation [23].

Log name	Events	Traces	Events/Traces	Loop runs	Runtime in s
Traffic Log	561470	150370	3	$0.97 \cdot 10^6$	133
Municipality Log	52217	1199	43	$1.28 \cdot 10^6$	153
Loan Application Log	1202267	31509	38	$26.73 \cdot 10^6$	697
Hospital Log	149489	1138	131	$33.17 \cdot 10^6$	761

4.2   Performance Evaluation

We evaluated the effectiveness of our approach w.r.t. to several real-life event logs. We first evaluated our approach for the discovery of MP-Declare constraints using the **Hospital Log**[2], which records the treatment of patients diagnosed with cancer from a large Dutch hospital. In 5 of the traces at least one event does not include the additional perspective data (from *org:resource*) and thus they had to be excluded from the investigation. Furthermore, we applied our approach to the publicly available real-life event log (**Traffic Log**[3]) of an Italian local police office for managing fines for road traffic violations. This log file barely contains additional perspective data in a consistent way, so the *lifecycle:transition* attribute was considered as additional perspective, but the semantics does not affect the performance anyway. Additionally, we applied our approach to an event log pertaining to an administrative process in a Dutch municipality (**Municipality Log**[4]) as well as a log file containing **Loan Application**[5] information. All four event logs have been analysed w.r.t. all six described MP-Declare templates. The time measurements in Table 13 considers activation conditions solely, but the same tendencies could be recorded for target conditions.

The benchmark shows the expected behaviour with respect to the proposed performance influencing figures. Mapped into the coordinate system shown in Fig. 3 with the total loop runs on the abscissa and the elapsed time on the ordinate one can clearly see the dependency. Furthermore, the impact of parallelization is revealed. When working on the Traffic Log ($0.97 \cdot 10^6$ loop runs), there is almost no difference between the sequential (dashed line) and the parallel execution (solid line). The performance gain through the distributed computing is cancelled out by the additional workload for task generation and joining the MR-I mapping results. Nevertheless, with more challenging log files in terms of loop runs (e.g. the Hospital Log ($33.1 \cdot 10^6$ loop runs)), the parallelization is exploited more and more efficiently.

---

[2] https://doi.org/10.4121/uuid:d9769f3d-0ab0-4fb8-803b-0d1120ffcf54.

[3] https://doi.org/10.4121/uuid:270fd440-1057-4fb9-89a9-b699b47990f5.

[4] https://doi.org/10.4121/uuid:31a308ef-c844-48da-948c-305d167a0ec1.

[5] https://doi.org/10.4121/uuid:5f3067df-f10b-45da-b98b-86ae4c7a310b.

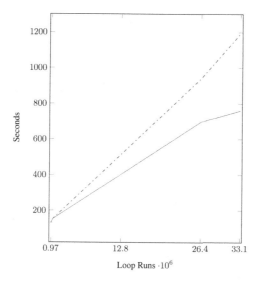

Fig. 3. Performance of sequential execution compared to parallel execution [23].

5   Hadoop-Based Implementation

In this section, we now describe the implementation of MP-Declare mining with MapReduce based on the Hadoop framework. First, we introduce the different components of the framework that are necessary.

Apache Hadoop. Hadoop is part of Apache Software Foundations active top-level projects. The concept of the framework is located in the field of big data analysis. When the size of input datasets goes beyond the technological limits of conventional processing, Hadoop can demonstrate its strength. The framework is designed to be highly scalable in horizontal direction. This is regarding the performance an extremely powerful quality, because with every extention of the cluster with a new node, more containers can be executed in parallel. The cluster is built up by one master node and a variable number of slaves. The master assumes the role of the data node, whose scope of duties consists of managing the name nodes (slaves), handle the availability of data in the case of a name node failure, replication processes etc. Name nodes stores the data in a distributed file system and execute computing duties, for MapReduce jobs for example. Last but not least, Hadoop provides a very useful web interface with helpful statistics to improve the performance of MapReduce jobs.

Yarn and MapReduce. MapReduce jobs are conventional java programms, whose classes have to implement some special interfaces provided by the org.apache.hadoop library, i.e. *.mapreduce.Mapper or *.mapreduce.Reducer. Packed as a jar archive, it is distributed to each node.

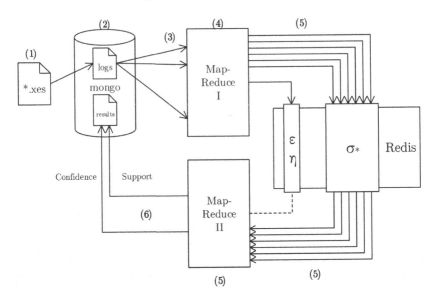

Fig. 4. Hadoop-based implementation overview.

When starting a MapReduce job, a component named Yarn is managing the whole set of resources. Yarn allocates the memory and spread the work over the whole cluster. The input data is divided into splits depending on its size and for each split one name node is assigned. The slave starts a Java Virtual Machine and in this container, the mapping algorithm (the map method from the class implementing the Mapper interface) is executed. When a slave has completed the task it can handle the next input split if necessary. The reduce tasks are handled the same way.

NoSQL Databases. In case of the Hadoop-based implementation, two databases are integrated in our application. The first one, *MongoDB*, is a document store, which helds the information in form of the JavaScript Object Notation (JSON). These information are the log data on the one hand, and the results from the mining on the other hand. The second database is the key-value store *Redis*. The simple datastructures of a key-value store fits perfectly to our needs. We simply use it as a connector of the two MapReduce jobs for piping the σ_γ, η and ϵ values. Redis holds the whole data in the RAM, whereby fast seek times are assured.

5.1   MP-Declare Mining on an Hadoop Cluster

The following paragraph shows our implementation approach for the MapReduce-Mining on Hadoop. Figure 4 provides an overview of the server-side interacting technologies and infrastructure. On a Windows Server, we built a Hadoop-Cluster in form of virtual machines with Ubuntu Server as the operating system. The user can interact via an ASP.NET application, but it is recommended to communicate directly on the Unix terminal, as there is no official supported .NET-API for Hadoop. Hereafter, the description of the dataflow shall illustrate the workflow of the application. The numbers in brackets are concerning the current progress in Fig. 4.

Preprocessing (1), (2). A special feature of our application is the use of a MongoDB-Database as the input format for the map tasks. According to our observations in the development process, this leads to a much better distribution of the splits, thus a reduction of runtime without any handmade improvements needed. In addition, the xes/xml-format cannot be used as input readily, because the usual policy of splitting each line of a text file to key-value pairs is unusable. The mapper needs at least one complete trace as input and xml formatted key-value pairs like

```
(1, <log>)
(2, <trace>)
(3, <event key="task" value="a" />)
```

are so avoided in favour of JSON notated trace descriptions:

```
(1, {_id: 1,
     events: [
         {  attributes: [
                 {  key: task, value: a },
                 {  key: group, value: u },
                 ...],
         },
         ...
     ]
})
(2, ....)
```

But of course, the database has to be build up in a preprocessing step first. As an initial step, the log file has to be load into the MongoDB. A parser builds a model of the log. Metainformational annotations (i.e. *[BsonElementAttribute("events")]*) are providing the driver the required details about how to interpret the POCO's, so that they can be converted into BSON-Documents. These documents can be inserted easily into the database.

Multidimensional Mapping (3). Hadoop transfers the whole log from the MongoDB to the MR-I-Mapper. The MR-I-Mapper gets the document as value and the key is equal to the unambiguous _id-field in the BSON-Documents. After that, the input T for Algorithm 1 has to be prepared by filtering the set of documents by the user's chosen dimensions for each side. This helps to adjust the amount of data to just right size. Every attributes object where the key is not in the userdefined dimensions lists, is filtered out with the Java 1.8-Streaming API (Fig. 5).

Two event lists are generated this way, one for the left side and one for the right side of the mining template $\bigwedge d_{k_{left}} \rightarrow \bigwedge d_{k_{right}}$.

As the communication is done via string represented events, there are unicode characters added in order to mark the output pairs with respect to the concrete constraint

Listing 1.1. Prepairing the MongoDB events.

```
1   List<List<DBObject>> events = dbEvents.stream().map(a ->
2       {
3           BasicDBObject attributesObject = (BasicDBObject) a
↪   ;
4           BasicDBList attributesList = (BasicDBList)
↪   attributesObject.get("attributes");
5           return attributesList.stream().filter(f -> {
6               BasicDBObject fObj = (BasicDBObject) f;
7               return dimensions.contains(fObj.get("key"));
8           }).map(o->{
9               BasicDBObject oO = (BasicDBObject) o;
10              DBObject ndbo = new BasicDBObject();
11              ndbo.put(oO.get("key").toString(), oO.get("
↪   value"));
12              return ndbo;
13          }).collect(Collectors.toList());
14      })
15      .collect(Collectors.toList());
```

Fig. 5. Preparing T.

they pertain. The characters are from the *private use areas* to avoid conflicts while parsing the pairs in the further application. The mapper outputs the values as follows:

```
context.write(new Text('\ue010'
    + eventsA.get(i) + '\ue002' + eventsB.get(j))
    , new IntWritable(1));
```

If a key-value output starts with *0xE010*, the reducer ascribes the information a affiliation to σ_R, the character *0xE002* separates the arguments τ_i and τ_j from each other.

Reducing (4). The reduce function is pretty simple. The only task the reducer has to fulfill, is to add the values for uniform keys. In order to make σ, η and ϵ accessible for MR-II, the reducer functions output is pipelined into a Redis-Store and serves as MR-II-Mapper input further on:

Postprocessing (5), (6). As the σ, η and ϵ functions are now available, we can compute the support and confidence indicators and visualize the result. Therby one mapper for each constraint is instantiated and the key-value pairs are passed on to the MR-II-Reducer. Here is the final calculation step when the corresponding η and ϵ values for a current combination input are queried and the support and confidence values are written to the MongoDB database.

5.2 Performance Evaluation

Hadoop is called a big data framework which means it works best with an *unusual* volume of data. This evaluation shows, if available log files are large enough and if the MapReduce computation model fits also here. In Sect. 6, we briefly sum up our research results including the suitability of Process Mining in context of MapReduce applied in conventional implementations and on a Hadoop cluster and point out the future-proofness of the later.

The performance analysis on a Hadoop cluster turned out to be much more complex compared to concerning conventional implementations. The anatomy of Hadoop's MapReduce jobs is extremely customizable with over 200 configurable parameters alone in the *mapred-site.xml*. In addition, there are also configuration files for Yarn, the Hadoop Distributed File System (HDFS) and the cluster itself, even though not every property may influences the performance (i.e. port usage for web interfaces). Consequently, a clean analysis fails due to the many interdependencies between each performance-affecting factor. Nevertheless, our measurements depicted in Table 14 show up tendencies supporting the setup of a performance-boosting configuration in future. To follow the upcoming discussion in detail, a deep understanding of Hadoops' components and their interworking is useful.

Table 14. Hospital Log: Performance measurement.

Configuration				Elapsed Time				
	M(S)	R	S	N	Map	Shuffle	Merge	Reduce	Total
1	191(1)	12	0.8	17	00:14:41	**03:13:21**	00:00:02	00:01:27	05:41:53
2	191(1)	12	0.2	17	00:15:09	05:40:42	00:00:03	00:01:23	05:56:20
3	191(1)	1	0.2	17	00:15:02	05:44:11	00:00:24	**00:11:54**	06:00:43
4	191(1)	4	0.2	17	00:15:16	05:56:12	00:00:04	00:01:43	06:03:10
5	72(3)	12	0.8	17	00:36:42	03:47:10	00:00:04	00:01:15	05:38:25
6	72(3)	4	0.8	17	00:36:24	03:43:10	00:00:02	00:03:03	05:38:21
7	43(5)	4	0.8	17	00:42:42	03:31:57	00:00:01	00:02:30	04:48:17
8	27(8)	4	0.8	17	01:19:28	03:04:25	00:00:01	00:01:41	05:29:56
9	43(5)	4	0.9	17	00:41:25	**01:18:40**	00:00:04	00:01:19	04:45:31
10	191(1)	4	0.9	8	00:07:07	02:07:50	00:00:02	00:03:10	04:47:03
11	36(6)	4	0.9	8	00:29:52	01:43:10	00:00:02	00:04:04	**04:12:29**
12	27(8)	4	0.9	8	00:44:28	01:18:23	00:00:01	00:03:29	04:30:35

Table 14 shows the results of multiple benchmarks on the **Hospital Log**. This log file includes 1143 traces with a total number of 150291 events, thus an average quotient of 131 events per one trace. The size of the log in our MongoDB comes up to 108 MB. The internal job counters from Hadoop outputs a total Mapper production of circa 16 Million key-value pairs (2.5 GB).

The configuration parameters are noted abbreviated in Table 14 and have the following meaning: the amount of **M**appers with the corresponding **S**plit size, the amount of **R**educers, the value for the reducer's **S**low start and the size of the cluster (amount of **N**odes). Interesting information can be extracted from those duration times:

The strongest impacts probably bear the amount of mappers and reducers, the input split size which defines the input split quantity, the laziness of reducers (the reducers start working after 80% of the mappers have finished for example) and so on. Additional the hardware settings of each node, like extra CPU cores or RAM, can be modified. Having levelled up the node's hardware, in turn further possibilities of cluster configurations are opened like executing more mappers on a single node and thus reducing the network load. Getting out the best of Hadoop involves adjustments to the respective use case (here: log file). Besides from complying general guiding lines, changes in performance by varying the parameters have to be observed to derive best strategies for certain kinds of log files (i.e. amount of traces, average events per trace, amount of different events, distribution of all events onto traces and so on).

The average map time rises with a simultaneous reduction of the map jobs. This can be controlled with increasing the input split size. We observe a growing average map time per mapper as each mapper has to work off a greater number of traces. There is an optimal split size between the split sizes 4 and 6. A potential explanation could be, that the latency periods for allocating new containers for the map jobs are upholding the durations for low split sizes and inefficient sorting and shuffling processes may cause increasing map times for too big split sizes.

However, this is only true within the restriction of limited nodes. Disregarding the cluster size, for a 1 MB split size, the level of parallelization is the highest and each of the 191 splits can be computed at the same time, which leads to a total map phase time of circa 15 min. The average reduce time obviously depends on the participating reducers. But there is no linear dependency as the total reduce time with 12 reducers is round about 16 min, with only one acting reducer 12 min and with 4 reducers, the elapsed time for reducing is 7 min. Those values may be contaminated by the slowstart threshold, but 4 reducers turned out to be good anyway.

The measurements for the shuffle phase are not so transparent as desired. Although there seems to be a dependency on the slowstart threshold (the bigger the value the faster is the shuffling), the idle time when waiting for the next mapper to finish has to be considered. This means with a slowstart threshold of 0.2 the first shuffle action takes place at the very beginning and thus runs longer as if the first shuffling is just right before the reducer starts. To optimize the performance, finer grained logging information has to be consulted. There are hardly any limits of possibilities for instance *(i)* analyzing which mappers work on which traces and how long; *(ii)* how evolves the mapping time? (more finished mappers causes bigger sorting and shuffling effort); *(iii)* are there valuable information hidden in a complete gantt chart of the MapReduce job? - to name only a few.

As Hadoop overpowers conventional systems more and more, the more data has to be processed, a discussion on the data volume is appropriate on top of the performance analysis as seen in Sect. 4.

Fig. 6. MP-Declare Miner control centre with available logs and executed jobs.

Due to the characteristics of the Declare constraints, the quotient of the average occurred events per trace is a crucial factor. In case of the hospital log this value is equal to 131. In the worst-case scenario for the response constraint, that is when every event in a trace is different, the mapper produces $\frac{(n-1)\times n}{2}$ key-value pairs (10153   for $n =$ 131). Multiplied with the number of traces (1143) the MR-I-Mapper output comes up to about 12×10^6 elements for the response constraint only. Assuming 250 Bytes per output pair, this leads to a total required memory space of up to 20 GB. Hence, even with current available event logs, declarative process mining may produce a quantity of data which reaches the level of available RAM in conventional systems.

5.3   System Support

The user can provide the input event log and configure the mining parameters via a web front-end shown in Fig. 6. We first load each of the event logs given as a XES file into a MongoDB. Having loaded the XES file into the MongoDB database, the event log is available in the *New Job* section shown in Fig. 7.

The tool is configured to discover the conditions under which a certain constraint is fulfilled in the log. The user can select the data attributes that should be considered for the mining. Columns refer to the activities involved in the constraint. In Fig. 7, the checked attributes specify that the activity names are taken into account for both activities. Additionally, the *org:resource* attribute is analysed for the first one, e.g., the activation of the *Response* constraint. The application sends the command to the Hadoop cluster to start the job with the given parameters. Afterwards, the distributed discovery is started and the user can check the progress in the Control Center (Fig. 6). The support and confidence values are stored in the MongoDB for further processing and the

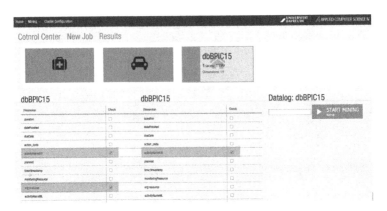

Fig. 7. User interface to start a new mining job.

graphical representation of models. Further screenshots, the application results as well as a screencast illustrating the mining procedure are accessible on-line at http://mpdeclare.kppq.de.

6 Discussion

In [23], we proposed a MapReduce approach for the discovery of a declarative process model in the form of MP-Declare constraints and have proven the feasibility in a conventional proof-of-concept implementation. As MapReduce is the inbuilt computation model of BigData frameworks like Hadoop, we here continue our work to analyse the suitability of process discovery on a Hadoop cluster using MapReduce. *Big***Data.** We stated that Hadoop needs a bunch of data to work powerful, but current available event logs are far beyond this size. Nevertheless, there are still valid arguments for this approach: Due to the nested for-loop and the characteristics of the MP-Declare constraints, a *normal-sized* event log in the megabyte range can lead to a data production of lots of gigabytes in the mapper. Thus, *our BigData* is not concerning the input size, but the output size of the mapping stage. **MapReduce.** We further misuse the idea of MapReduce a little bit. In most open examples, the mapping stage iterates over the input once and after that, the reducers combines the information in a sensible way. In contrast, we have implemented a nested for-loop in each Mapper to address the MP-Declare constraints, but as stated, this produces our *BigData*. Hence, our hardware requirements may differ from usual Hadoop clusters, as we need a powerful single-threaded CPU in the mapping nodes.

Conventional Implementation vs. Hadoop Cluster. After a comparison of both's performance, we are allowed to draw the following conclusion. For currently available event logs, the conventional implementation outperforms the too powerful Hadoop cluster which suffers from transferring data between nodes and costly management issues. On the contrary, in future due to the Internet of Things or OpenData-Initiatives much more data will be produced and incorporated into process discovery, so that conventional implementations can not handle the amount of data anymore and distributed computing on a cluster becomes much more favourable.

7   Related Work

Several approaches have been proposed for the discovery of declarative process models. In [13], the authors present an approach that allows the user to select from a set of predefined Declare templates the ones to be used for the discovery. Other approaches to improve the performances of the discovery task are presented in [8,25]. Additionally, there are post-processing approaches that aim at simplifying the resulting Declare models in terms of redundancy elimination [5,14] and disambiguation [2]. An approach similar to the SQL-based one used in this paper is presented in [19] and is based on temporal logic query checking. In [24], the authors define *Timed Declare*, an extension of Declare that relies on timed automata. In [11], an approach for analysing event logs with Timed Declare is proposed. The *DPILMiner* [20] exploits a discovery approach to incorporate the resource perspective and to mine for a set of predefined resource assignment constraints. In [15], the authors introduce for the first time a data-aware semantics for Declare and [12] first covered the data perspective in declarative process discovery, although this approach only allows for the discovery of *discriminative* activation conditions. [21] proposes an approach to enable the discovery of MP-Declare constraints by querying event logs given in relational databases with SQL. Here, a performance evaluation has not been described. In recent work [22,23], the authors presented a distributed approach for mining MP-Declare process models based on MapReduce. The paper at hand extends this work by providing an in-depth description of a Hadoop-based implementation approach as well as further information on the implemented prototype.

8   Conclusions

In this paper, we continued our work from [23], where we introduced the discovery of MP-Declare models based on the distributed processing method MapReduce. The conventional methods of the proposed proof-of-concept implementation back then is capable to handle only Event Logs having state-of-the-art size, but will fail when the amount of processed and recorded data follow latest trends and the data volume will explode in the upcoming years. For this purpose, special frameworks are available with Hadoop as the most famous representative using MapReduce as core computation method. In this paper, we propose implementation concepts of the MapReduced-based MP-Declare discovery algorithms on a running Hadoop cluster. We further provide an in-depth analysis of the implementation approach and detailed information on the implemented prototype as well as an analysis in comparison with the conventional implementation. The mining performance and effectiveness have been tested with real-life event logs. The experiments show that our technique solves this complex mining task in reasonable time. Further screenshots, the application results as well as a screencast illustrating the mining procedure are accessible on-line at http://mpdeclare.kppq.de.

The approach at hand represents a step into the direction of integrating process and data science and depicts a customisable and high performant declarative process mining technique. For future work, we plan to consider also correlation and time conditions as well as an additional integration of all MP-Declare constraints. Furthermore, we will examine how to improve performance even more, for instance with alternative MapReduce frameworks which can be set up and tested with the proposed algorithms.

References

1. van der Aalst, W.: Process Mining: Discovery, Conformance and Enhancement of Business Processes. Springer, Heidelberg (2011). https://doi.org/10.1007/978-3-642-19345-3
2. Bose, R.P.J.C., Maggi, F.M., van der Aalst, W.M.P.: Enhancing declare maps based on event correlations. In: Daniel, F., Wang, J., Weber, B. (eds.) BPM 2013. LNCS, vol. 8094, pp. 97–112. Springer, Heidelberg (2013). https://doi.org/10.1007/978-3-642-40176-3_9
3. Burattin, A., Maggi, F.M., Sperduti, A.: Conformance checking based on multi-perspective declarative process models. Expert Syst. Appl. **65**, 194–211 (2016)
4. Burattin, A., Maggi, F.M., van der Aalst, W.M., Sperduti, A.: Techniques for a posteriori analysis of declarative processes. In: EDOC, pp. 41–50. IEEE, Beijing (2012)
5. Di Ciccio, C., Maggi, F.M., Montali, M., Mendling, J.: Ensuring model consistency in declarative process discovery. In: Motahari-Nezhad, H.R., Recker, J., Weidlich, M. (eds.) BPM 2015. LNCS, vol. 9253, pp. 144–159. Springer, Cham (2015). https://doi.org/10.1007/978-3-319-23063-4_9
6. Di Ciccio, C., Mecella, M.: A two-step fast algorithm for the automated discovery of declarative workflows. In: CIDM, pp. 135–142. IEEE (2013)
7. Di Ciccio, C., Mecella, M.: On the discovery of declarative control flows for artful processes. ACM TMIS **5**(4), 1–37 (2015)
8. Di Ciccio, C., Schouten, M.H.M., de Leoni, M., Mendling, J.: Declarative process discovery with MINERful in ProM. In: BPM Demos, pp. 60–64 (2015)
9. de Leoni, M., van der Aalst, W.M.P., Dees, M.: A general process mining framework for correlating, predicting and clustering dynamic behavior based on event logs. Inf. Syst. **56**, 235–257 (2016)
10. Maggi, F.M.: Declarative process mining with the declare component of ProM. In: BPM Demo Sessions 2013, pp. 26–30 (2013)
11. Maggi, F.M.: Discovering metric temporal business constraints from event logs. In: Johansson, B., Andersson, B., Holmberg, N. (eds.) BIR 2014. LNBIP, vol. 194, pp. 261–275. Springer, Cham (2014). https://doi.org/10.1007/978-3-319-11370-8_19
12. Maggi, F.M., Dumas, M., García-Bañuelos, L., Montali, M.: Discovering data-aware declarative process models from event logs. In: Daniel, F., Wang, J., Weber, B. (eds.) BPM 2013. LNCS, vol. 8094, pp. 81–96. Springer, Heidelberg (2013). https://doi.org/10.1007/978-3-642-40176-3_8
13. Maggi, F.M., Mooij, A., van der Aalst, W.: User-guided discovery of declarative process models. In: CIDM, pp. 192–199 (2011)
14. Maggi, F.M., Bose, R.P.J.C., van der Aalst, W.M.P.: A knowledge-based integrated approach for discovering and repairing declare maps. In: Salinesi, C., Norrie, M.C., Pastor, Ó. (eds.) CAiSE 2013. LNCS, vol. 7908, pp. 433–448. Springer, Heidelberg (2013). https://doi.org/10.1007/978-3-642-38709-8_28
15. Montali, M., Chesani, F., Mello, P., Maggi, F.M.: Towards data-aware constraints in declare. In: SAC, pp. 1391–1396. ACM (2013)
16. Montali, M., Pesic, M., van der Aalst, W.M.P., Chesani, F., Mello, P., Storari, S.: Declarative specification and verification of service choreographies. ACM Trans. Web **4**(1), 3 (2010)

17. Pesic, M., Schonenberg, H., van der Aalst, W.M.P.: Declare: full support for loosely-structured processes. In: IEEE International EDOC Conference 2007, pp. 287–300 (2007)
18. Pichler, P., Weber, B., Zugal, S., Pinggera, J., Mendling, J., Reijers, H.A.: Imperative versus declarative process modeling languages: an empirical investigation. In: Daniel, F., Barkaoui, K., Dustdar, S. (eds.) BPM 2011. LNBIP, vol. 99, pp. 383–394. Springer, Heidelberg (2012). https://doi.org/10.1007/978-3-642-28108-2_37
19. Räim, M., Di Ciccio, C., Maggi, F.M., Mecella, M., Mendling, J.: Log-based understanding of business processes through temporal logic query checking. In: Meersman, R., et al. (eds.) OTM 2014. LNCS, vol. 8841, pp. 75–92. Springer, Heidelberg (2014). https://doi.org/10.1007/978-3-662-45563-0_5
20. Schönig, S., Cabanillas, C., Jablonski, S., Mendling, J.: A framework for efficiently mining the organisational perspective of business processes. Decis. Support Syst. (2016)
21. Schönig, S., Di Ciccio, C., Maggi, F.M., Mendling, J.: Discovery of multi-perspective declarative process models. In: Service-Oriented Computing, ICSOC, Banff, pp. 87–103 (2016)
22. Sturm, C., Schönig, S., Ciccio, C.D.: Distributed multi-perspective declare discovery. In: BPM Demos (2017)
23. Sturm, C., Schönig, S., Jablonski, S.: A MapReduce approach for mining multi-perspective declarative process models. In: ICEIS, no. 2, pp. 585–595 (2018)
24. Westergaard, M., Maggi, F.M.: Looking into the future. In: Meersman, R., et al. (eds.) OTM 2012. LNCS, vol. 7565, pp. 250–267. Springer, Heidelberg (2012). https://doi.org/10.1007/978-3-642-33606-5_16
25. Westergaard, M., Stahl, C., Reijers, H.: UnconstrainedMiner: efficient discovery of generalized declarative process models. In: BPM CR, No. BPM-13-28 (2013)
26. Zeising, M., Schönig, S., Jablonski, S.: Towards a common platform for the support of routine and agile business processes. In: Collaborative Computing: Networking, Applications and Worksharing (2014)

Author Index

Printed in the United States
By Bookmasters